Employment Law in Context

Third Edition

Employment Law in Context

An introduction for HR professionals

Brian Willey

With contributions from:
Adrian Murton
Enda Hannon
Susan Mison
Sanjiv Sachdev

PEARSON
Longman

Harlow, England • London • New York • Boston • San Francisco • Toronto
Sydney • Tokyo • Singapore • Hong Kong • Seoul • Taipei • New Delhi
Cape Town • Madrid • Mexico City • Amsterdam • Munich • Paris • Milan

Pearson Education Limited

Edinburgh Gate
Harlow
Essex CM20 2JE
England

and Associated Companies throughout the world

Visit us on the World Wide Web at:
www.pearsoned.co.uk

First published 2000 by Pitman Publishing, a division of Pearson Professional Ltd
Second edition published 2003 by Pearson Education Limited
Third edition published 2009

ISBN: 978-1-4058-7400-7

British Library Cataloguing-in-Publication Data
A catalogue record for this book is available from the British Library

Library of Congress Cataloging-in-Publication Data
A catalog record for this book is available from the Library of Congress

10 9 8 7 6 5 4 3 2
13 12 11 10

Typeset in 10/12.5 Minion by 35
Printed and bound in Great Britain by Ashford Colour Press Ltd, Gosport, Hants

Brief contents

Contents

mylawchamber

Visit the *Employment Law in Context, third edition* **mylawchamber** site at **www.mylawchamber.co.uk/willey** to access valuable learning material.

For students

Do you want to give yourself a head start come exam time?

Companion website support

- Use the multiple choice questions, case flashcards and exercises to test yourself on each topic throughout the course.
- Use the updates to major changes in the law to make sure you are ahead of the game by knowing the latest developments.
- Use the live weblinks to help you read more widely around the subject, and really impress your lecturers.

Preface

Particularly over the past 40 years, individual employment law has had a growing significance for managers – whether general managers or human resource practitioners. It influences and may constrain action that they want to take. One principal aim of this textbook is to help those with day-to-day responsibilities for employment relations and human resource management to manage within the law. Its purpose is to promote understanding of four aspects:

1 the essential provisions of European, statute and case law;
2 the application of the law to employment relations in respect of policy making and problem solving;
3 the social purposes behind the legislation (i.e. what the UK Parliament and the European Union are trying to achieve);
4 the contextual issues that affect the implementation of the law (e.g. particular social trends and economic considerations).

The development of corporate policies is more likely to be effective and well-informed if they are not seen, narrowly, as a series of conditions of employment to be applied mechanistically. For example, when family leave and 'work–life balance' policies are formulated, an understanding of the social trends against which they are developed is important (i.e. greater labour market participation by women; longer working hours; greater interest by fathers to be involved in childcare; the practical difficulties of reconciling work and non-work life). The social purposes underpinning the legislation should be appreciated to help ensure that the organisation's policies are compliant with the law. A manager who understands these purposes is better able to defend and argue for policy developments with colleagues.

One particular aspect of law that has grown hugely in significance since the previous editions of this textbook is the wide sweep of discrimination law across many strands. The employment relationship and the application process for employment and post employment practices are all governed by legislative provisions. From time to time, some of these provisions are being clarified and creatively interpreted by the higher courts in Britain and by the European Court of Justice. It is a commonplace to say that no HR practitioner can afford to ignore the ramifications of such bodies of law. So, an attempt has been made in the book to structure the examination of discrimination law in a way that is hopefully both illuminating and also helpful in informing problem-solving and policy formulation. There are three related chapters: one (Chapter 4) which examines the historic, social and economic context in which discrimination law is located; the second (Chapter 5) which outlines the essential framework of all strands of discrimination law; and the third (Chapter 6) which raises a number of considerations for practitioners on how their employment policies are compliant with discrimination law.

This textbook, then, aims to be integrative. It will aim principally to examine relevant law and provide a firm base knowledge for HR practitioners and other managers. It is also informed by relevant research and source material from economics and sociological studies. It is hoped that managers as students using this book will then have a full appreciation of the context of the law and will gain familiarity with and an enthusiasm for the subject of employment law; and also a confidence to analyse and handle a greater range of workplace problems.

Market for the book

This textbook is designed, principally, for those engaged in academic study. It is written for non-lawyers who wish to gain a basic understanding of the key areas of employment and discrimination law. Primarily, it is for students on postgraduate and post-experience courses. This would obviously cover those on programmes leading to graduate membership of the Chartered Institute of Personnel and Development; those on a Diploma of Management Studies course; and those studying employment law modules on, for example, Masters in Business Administration courses. It will also be useful for undergraduate students on, for example, BA Business Studies courses who are undertaking an employment law option.

Furthermore, an additional, related and important market is tutors on these courses who may be non-lawyers but wish to develop a wider understanding of the subject area.

Authorship

The first two editions of this textbook were, largely, written by myself as main author. This third edition is collaborative, drawing on the expertise of a number of colleagues who teach, undertake research and consultancy in the area of human resource management. The authorship is as follows:

Chapter 1: An introduction to employment law
Brian Willey

Chapter 2: Regulating the employment relationship
Brian Willey

Chapter 3: Managing change in the employment relationship
Brian Willey; and *Sanjiv Sachdev* on transfers of undertakings

Chapter 4: The context of discrimination at work
Brian Willey; contributions on equal pay and age discrimination from *Adrian Murton*

Chapter 5: The strands of discrimination law
Brian Willey: discrimination on grounds of sex, gender reassignment, race, sexual orientation and religion or belief
Adrian Murton: equal pay and age discrimination
Susan Mison: disability discrimination

Chapter 6: Implementing equality in the workplace
Brian Willey: contributions on equal pay and age discrimination from *Adrian Murton*

Chapter 7: Harassment and bullying at work
Brian Willey

Chapter 8: Discipline and dismissal
Enda Hannon

Approach to learning

In attempting to bridge, on the one hand, knowledge of legal provisions and, on the other, consideration of employment relations and HR issues, the textbook provides a number of opportunities for the reader to undertake exercises and activities.

Structure of each chapter

Most chapters are structured around the following sections:

- *Learning objectives*: the reader is given a list of objectives that should be attained once the chapter and the associated exercises have been completed.
- *Introduction*: this sets out the broad issues to be considered.
- *The context*: this identifies and discusses, as appropriate, social, political, economic and technological issues that form the background against which particular law is developing.
- *The legal framework*: the essential framework is outlined and discussed. As appropriate, material is drawn from European law, statute law, case law and statutory codes of practice.
- *Employment policies and practice*: this will consider the application of the law to the workplace. Drawing on research evidence, it will consider the experience of organisations and difficulties that have been encountered. It will provide some assistance for policy formulation and ways in which employment relations might be tackled.
- *Exercises*: most chapters have exercises which invite the reader to apply the concepts and legal provisions to the circumstances that are set out. The exercises are suitable for both individual and syndicate work in the classroom. Feedback on the exercises is provided in the Appendix.
- *References* of publications and research material used in each specific chapter.

Other features associated with the book

- *Glossary*: this provides definitions of terms which may not be in everyday usage, that are used on several occasions within the book. The first or any significant occurrence of a glossary term in any given chapter is **highlighted** in the text.

- *Website*: to assist both students and tutors, this will provide a periodic update and appropriate weblinks relevant to some of the key material in the chapters.
- *Further reading*: this will be indicated on the website as appropriate.

Acknowledgements

The initial idea for this book arose from a previous collaborative text, *The Corporate Environment: a guide for human resource managers* (Pearson Education), written with my colleague, Huw Morris. The discussions we held about that textbook stimulated ideas about this present one as a complementary piece of work. Also, my involvement over a number of years in teaching the Employment Law module on the accredited-CIPD human resource management Masters/Diploma course at Kingston University Business School further reinforced my view that such a textbook could be useful. Furthermore, my teaching on the University's MA/LLM course in Employment Relations and Law helped me recognise more fully the complexity of issues that non-lawyer HR practitioners often have to manage. My thanks to them for helping to germinate and sustain the idea and my admiration to many of those who wrestle with the application of the law on a day-to-day basis.

The responsibility for this text is mine as editor and principal author. However, it could not have been written without the contributions, comments, advice and support of various people. In particular, I would mention Adrian Murton who 'nudged' me into this third edition after Pearson had approached me. Thanks also to Susan Mison who agreed to contribute on the seemingly ever-changing area of disability discrimination law. Also, my two colleagues at Kingston University with whom I teach the Employment Law module on the HRM courses, Sanjiv Sachdev and Enda Hannon, have shown considerable support with this project. All co-authors have demonstrated commitment to the concept of the book as a means of helping HR practitioners evaluate the contribution they may make to the application of the law to employment relations.

Finally, such textbooks are rarely written without the support of families. In particular, I would like to thank my wife, Ann. She coped with me being welded to the computer during the summer months. Thankfully, weather was generally dreadful!

I hope that readers will find the textbook useful and, above all, that it will give them the confidence to deal with the issues that employment law will present.

Brian Willey
Visiting Fellow
Faculty of Business and Law
Kingston University

January 2009

Publisher's acknowledgements

We are grateful to the following for permission to reproduce copyright material:

Tables

Table 2.1 adapted from *Labour Force Survey*, February–April, Office for National Statistics (2008), National Statistics website: www.statistics.gov.uk. Crown Copyright material is reproduced with the permission of the Controller, Office of Public Sector Information (OPSI); Table 4.1 adapted from Office for National Statistics (2004), National Statistics website: www.statistics.gov.uk. Crown Copyright material is reproduced with the permission of the Controller, Office of Public Sector Information (OPSI); Table 4.2 from *The First Fair Treatment at Work Survey: Executive Summary – Updated*, Employment Relations Research Series No. 63, DTI, www.berr.gov.uk (Grainger, H. and Fitzner, G. 2007), Reproduced under the terms of the Click-Use Licence; Tables 4.5, 4.6, 4.8, 4.11, 4.12 from *Labour Force Survey*, Spring, Office for National Statistics (2005), National Statistics website: www.statistics.gov.uk. Crown Copyright material is reproduced with the permission of the Controller, Office of Public Sector Information (OPSI); Table 4.7 from *The State of the Modern Family, the Millennium Cohort Survey*, Equality and Human Rights Commission (Equal Opportunities Commission 2007); Table 4.9 from *Labour Force Survey*, Spring, Office for National Statistics (2001), National Statistics website: www.statistics.gov.uk. Crown Copyright material is reproduced with the permission of the Controller, Office of Public Sector Information (OPSI); Table 4.10 adapted from Office for National Statistics, National Statistics website: www.statistics.gov.uk. Crown Copyright material is reproduced with the permission of the Controller, Office of Public Sector Information (OPSI); Table 4.14 adapted from *Labour Force Survey*, Office for National Statistics (various), National Statistics website: www.statistics.gov.uk. Crown Copyright material is reproduced with the permission of the Controller, Office of Public Sector Information (OPSI); Table 4.15 from *Census 2001*, Office for National Statistics, National Statistics website: www.statistics.gov.uk. Crown copyright material is reproduced with the permission of the Controller, Office of Public Sector Information (OPSI); Table 4.16 from Employers Forum on Belief, www.efbelief.org.uk; Table 11.3 adapted from *Reassessing the 'family-friendly workplace': Trends and influences in Britain, 1998–2004*, Employment Relations Research Series No. 76, BERR, www.berr.gov.uk (Whitehouse, G. *et al.* 2007), Reproduced under the terms of the Click-Use Licence; Tables 11.4, 11.5 adapted from *The Third Work–Life Balance Employee Survey: Main Findings*, Employment Relations Series No. 58, DTI (Hooker, H. *et al.* 2007), Reproduced under the terms of the Click-Use Licence.

Text

Exhibit 2.11 from Dacas v Brook Street Bureau (UK) Ltd. [2004] *IRLR*, 358, CA, LexisNexis, Reproduced by permission of Reed Elsevier (UK) Ltd. trading as LexisNexis; Extract on page 158 from Shield v E. Coombs (Holdings) Ltd. [1978] *ICR*, 1159, CA, The Incorporated Council for Law Reporting for England & Wales; Extract on page 159 from Eaton Ltd. v Nuttall [1977] *ICR*, 272, EAT, The Incorporated Council of Law Reporting for England & Wales; Extract on page 162 from Rainey v Glasgow Health Board [1987] 1, *AC*, 224 HL, The Incorporated Council of Law Reporting for England & Wales; Exhibit 5.20 from Price v

Civil Service Commission [1978] *ICR*, 212, The Incorporated Council of Law Reporting for England & Wales; Exhibit 8.1 from *Introduction to the (draft) ACAS Code of Practice on Discipline and Grievance*, ACAS (2009) www.acas.org.uk, Reproduced under the terms of the Click-Use Licence; Extract on pages 284–85 from Browning v Crumlin Valley Collieries Ltd. [1926] 1, *KB*, 522, 528, The Incorporated Council of Law Reporting for England & Wales; Exhibit 10.7 from *Your Guide to the Working Time Regulations: sections 1–4*, BERR, www.berr.gov.uk (BERR 2008) Example 1, Section 2, Reproduced under the terms of the Click-Use Licence.

About the authors

Brian Willey is Visiting Fellow, lecturing in employment law and human resource management at the Faculty of Business and Law, Kingston University, London. He is also a member of the arbitration panel of the Advisory, Conciliation and Arbitration Service.

Adrian Murton is Subject Group Leader for Human Resource Management and Organisation Studies at the London Metropolitan Business School, London Metropolitan University.

Enda Hannon is Senior Lecturer in Employment Relations and Employment Law, in the Department of Leadership, Human Resource Management and Organisation, at the Faculty of Business and Law, Kingston University, London.

Susan Mison is Senior Employment Law Editor for a major business media publishing company.

Sanjiv Sachdev is Senior Lecturer in Employment Law, in the Department of Leadership, Human Resource Management and Organisation, at the Faculty of Business and Law, Kingston University, London.

Guided tour

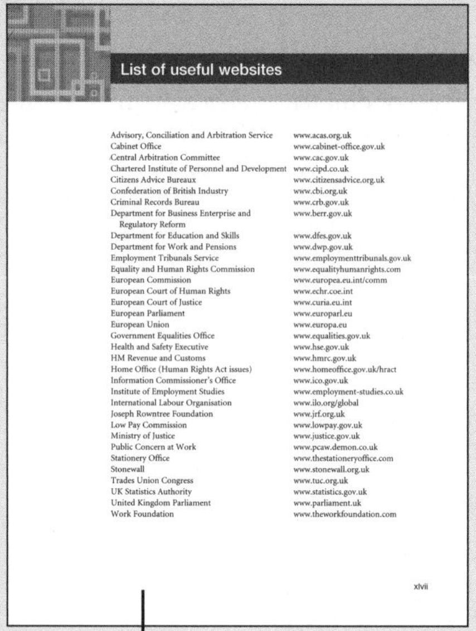
List of useful websites

Advisory, Conciliation and Arbitration Service	www.acas.org.uk
Cabinet Office	www.cabinet-office.gov.uk
Central Arbitration Committee	www.cac.gov.uk
Chartered Institute of Personnel and Development	www.cipd.co.uk
Citizens Advice Bureaux	www.citizensadvice.org.uk
Confederation of British Industry	www.cbi.org.uk
Criminal Records Bureau	www.crb.gov.uk
Department for Business Enterprise and Regulatory Reform	www.berr.gov.uk
Department for Education and Skills	www.dfes.gov.uk
Department for Work and Pensions	www.dwp.gov.uk
Employment Tribunals Service	www.employmenttribunals.gov.uk
Equality and Human Rights Commission	www.equalityhumanrights.com
European Commission	www.europa.eu.int/comm
European Court of Human Rights	www.echr.coe.int
European Court of Justice	www.curia.eu.int
European Parliament	www.europarl.eu
European Union	www.europa.eu
Government Equalities Office	www.equalities.gov.uk
Health and Safety Executive	www.hse.gov.uk
HM Revenue and Customs	www.hmrc.gov.uk
Home Office (Human Rights Act issues)	www.homeoffice.gov.uk/hract
Information Commissioner's Office	www.ico.gov.uk
Institute of Employment Studies	www.employment-studies.co.uk
International Labour Organisation	www.ilo.org/global
Joseph Rowntree Foundation	www.jrf.org.uk
Low Pay Commission	www.lowpay.gov.uk
Ministry of Justice	www.justice.gov.uk
Public Concern at Work	www.pcaw.demon.co.uk
Stationery Office	www.thestationeryoffice.com
Stonewall	www.stonewall.org.uk
Trades Union Congress	www.tuc.org.uk
UK Statistics Authority	www.statistics.gov.uk
United Kingdom Parliament	www.parliament.uk
Work Foundation	www.theworkfoundation.com

xlvii

Useful websites at the start of the book direct you to interesting further reading which is available on the Internet.

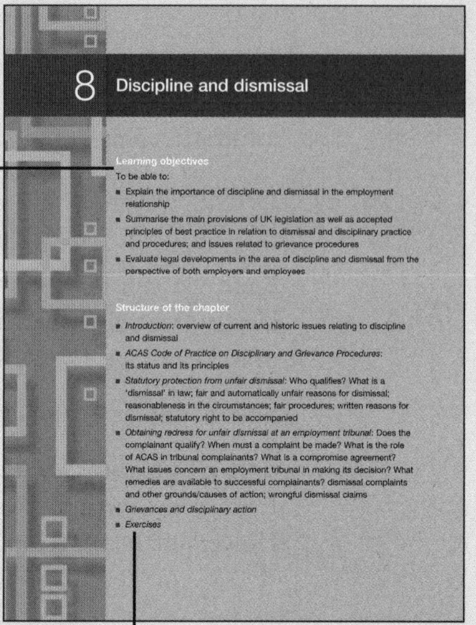
8 Discipline and dismissal

Learning objectives

To be able to:

- Explain the importance of discipline and dismissal in the employment relationship
- Summarise the main provisions of UK legislation as well as accepted principles of best practice in relation to dismissal and disciplinary practice and procedures; and issues related to grievance procedures
- Evaluate legal developments in the area of discipline and dismissal from the perspective of both employers and employees

Structure of the chapter

- *Introduction*: overview of current and historic issues relating to discipline and dismissal
- *ACAS Code of Practice on Disciplinary and Grievance Procedures*: its status and its principles
- *Statutory protection from unfair dismissal*: Who qualifies? What is a 'dismissal' in law; fair and automatically unfair reasons for dismissal; reasonableness in the circumstances; fair procedures; written reasons for dismissal; statutory right to be accompanied
- *Obtaining redress for unfair dismissal at an employment tribunal*: Does the complainant qualify? When must a complaint be made? What is the role of ACAS in tribunal complainants? What is a compromise agreement? What issues concern an employment tribunal in making its decision? What remedies are available to successful complainants? dismissal complaints and other grounds/causes of action; wrongful dismissal claims
- *Grievances and disciplinary action*
- *Exercises*

Learning objectives highlight the key points you should understand following your reading of each chapter. You can use these as a checklist of the concepts you should become familiar with during the course of your reading.

Chapter structure outlines located at the start of each chapter provide you with an instant point of reference.

Introductions to each chapter set out clearly the broad themes and issues that will be covered.

Introduction

Introduction

Work–life balance has arguably been the most high profile HR or employment related issue over recent years. It is one that HR practitioners are increasingly having to deal with, particularly in the context of the relatively tight labour market that has existed over the last number of years. Although the concept of 'work–life balance' is broad and rather nebulous, there has been notable recent legal intervention in this area with regard to rights to family leave. The goal of this chapter is to chart developments in this area and outline key rights and responsibilities of employers and employees alike.

Factors underpinning the growing interest in work–life balance

Workforce interest in striking a balance between home and work is not necessarily a new phenomenon. Indeed, it may be argued that employers and their workforces have always been in conflict over where the latter should expend their time and energy, and that both have had to show flexibility at times (Clutterbuck 2003). However, the drivers and underlying social dynamics of employment have changed dramatically in the last quarter of a century, and this has resulted in the notion of 'work–life balance' (WLB) gaining increased prominence in the contemporary employment vernacular.

Early industrialisation and the introduction of mass machinery created two distinct spheres of life – home and work (Felstead *et al.* 2005). These two spheres remained relatively distinct throughout much of the twentieth century, but the progressive development of information and communications technology (ICT) over the last two decades, whilst maximising work efficiency has extended the time and space of employment (e.g. via the use of e-mail and 'Blackberrys'). The resulting 'work intensification' has been compounded by increased global competition and the shift in many western economies from production to service-oriented industries, which increasingly operate on the basis of instant availability to customers (Suff 2002).

At the same time, major demographic and social shifts including an increasing number of women entering the workforce, declining birth rates and a rapidly ageing population, have changed the profile, attitudes and needs of the workforce (MacInnes 2002). More employees than ever have caring responsibilities, whilst simultaneously being subjected to longer working hours (TUC 2005). The result is described by Hoschild (1997) as a 'time-bind' and by Madeline Bunting (2004) as a 'crisis of human sustainability' that threatens the very fabric of family life and indeed the health and stability of society at large.

The tight nature of the UK labour market and the difficulty experienced by many organisations in recruiting and retaining staff has also been a significant recent 'push' factor, which has prompted the development and implementation of policies by employers on work–life balance and family friendly working (e.g. see CIPD 2007).

Legal and political developments have been important too. As with so many areas of employment regulation, the UK's membership of the European Union has had significant implications for the area of family rights and work–life balance. The Pregnant Workers Directive 1992 obliged the member states of the European Union to provide for a minimum 14-week maternity leave period, while also setting down standards for the protection of the health and safety of pregnant women. The Parental Leave Directive 1996 created a right to parental leave. In addition, the European Union's treaty articles and directives on gender equality have also been highly influential in this area.

335

Clear headings and subheadings keep you firmly focused and constantly aware of the context and structure of each chapter.

Glossary terms are highlighted in the text. The definitions are given in the Glossary at the back of the book.

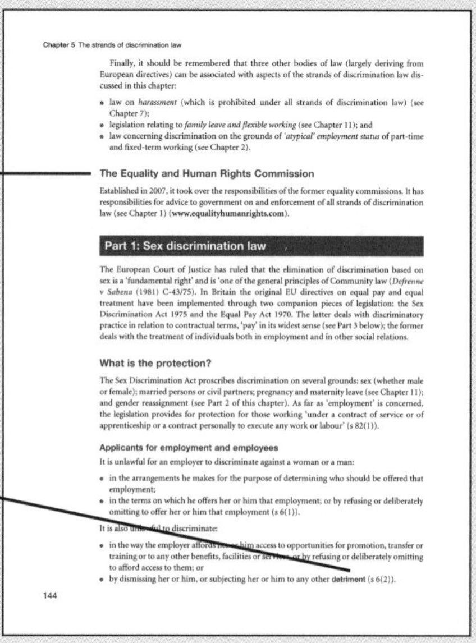
Chapter 5 The strands of discrimination law

Finally, it should be remembered that three other bodies of law (largely deriving from European directives) can be associated with aspects of the strands of discrimination law discussed in this chapter:

- law on *harassment* (which is prohibited under all strands of discrimination law) (see Chapter 7);
- legislation relating to *family leave and flexible working* (see Chapter 11); and
- law concerning discrimination on the grounds of *'atypical' employment status* of part-time and fixed-term working (see Chapter 2).

The Equality and Human Rights Commission

Established in 2007, it took over the responsibilities of the former equality commissions. It has responsibilities for advice to government on and enforcement of all strands of discrimination law (see Chapter 1) (**www.equalityhumanrights.com**).

Part 1: Sex discrimination law

The European Court of Justice has ruled that the elimination of discrimination based on sex is a 'fundamental right' and is 'one of the general principles of Community law (*Defrenne v Sabena* (1981) C-43/75). In Britain the original EU directives on equal pay and equal treatment have been implemented through two companion pieces of legislation: the Sex Discrimination Act 1975 and the Equal Pay Act 1970. The latter deals with discriminatory practice in relation to contractual terms, 'pay' in its widest sense (see Part 3 below); the former deals with the treatment of individuals both in employment and in other social relations.

What is the protection?

The Sex Discrimination Act proscribes discrimination on several grounds: sex (whether male or female); married persons or civil partners; pregnancy and maternity leave (see Chapter 11); and gender reassignment (see Part 2 of this chapter). As far as 'employment' is concerned, the legislation provides for protection for those working 'under a contract of service or of apprenticeship or a contract personally to execute any work or labour' (s 82(1)).

Applicants for employment and employees

It is unlawful for an employer to discriminate against a woman or a man:

- in the arrangements he makes for the purpose of determining who should be offered that employment;
- in the terms on which he offers her or him that employment; or by refusing or deliberately omitting to offer her or him that employment (s 6(1)).

It is also unlawful to discriminate:

- in the way the employer affords her or him access to opportunities for promotion, transfer or training or to any other benefits, facilities or services, or by refusing or deliberately omitting to afford access to them; or
- by dismissing her or him, or subjecting her or him to any other **detriment** (s 6(2)).

144

Exhibits situated throughout chapters identify the most important points, concepts and facts of key illustrative cases you should know about.

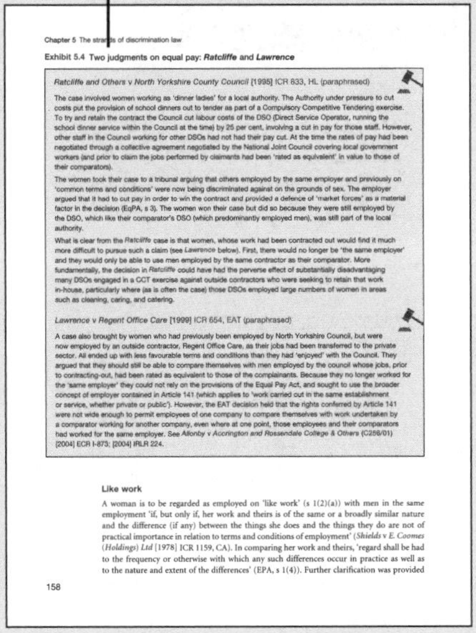
Chapter 5 The strands of discrimination law

Exhibit 5.4 Two judgments on equal pay: ***Ratcliffe* and *Lawrence***

Ratcliffe and Others v North Yorkshire County Council [1995] ICR 833, HL (paraphrased)

The case involved women working as 'dinner ladies' for a local authority. The Authority under pressure to cut costs put the provision of school dinners out to tender as part of a Compulsory Competitive Tendering exercise. To try and retain the contract the Council cut labour costs of the DSO (Direct Service Operator, running the school dinner service within the Council at the time) by 25 per cent, involving a cut in pay for those staff. However, other staff in the Council working for other DSOs had not had their pay cut. At the time the rates of pay had been negotiated through a collective agreement negotiated by the National Joint Council covering local government workers (and prior to claim the jobs performed by claimants had been 'rated as equivalent' in value to those of their comparators).

The women took their case to a tribunal arguing that others employed by the same employer and previously on 'common terms and conditions' were now being discriminated against on the grounds of sex. The employer argued that it had to cut pay in order to win the contract and provided a defence of 'market forces' as a material factor in the decision (EqPA, s 3). The women won their case but did so because they were still employed by the DSO, which like their comparator's DSO (which predominantly employed men), was still part of the local authority.

What is clear from the *Ratcliffe* case is that women, whose work had been contracted out would find it much more difficult to pursue such a claim (see *Lawrence* below). First, there would no longer be 'the same employer' and they would only be able to use men employed by the same contractor as their comparator. More fundamentally, the decision in *Ratcliffe* could have had the perverse effect of substantially disadvantaging many DSOs engaged in a CCT exercise against outside contractors who were seeking to retain that work in-house, particularly where (as is often the case) those DSOs employed large numbers of women in areas such as cleaning, caring, and catering.

Lawrence v Regent Office Care [1999] ICR 654, EAT (paraphrased)

A case also brought by women who had previously been employed by North Yorkshire Council, but were now employed by an outside contractor, Regent Office Care, as their jobs had been transferred to the private sector. All ended up with less favourable terms and conditions than they had 'enjoyed' with the Council. They argued that they should still be able to compare themselves with men employed by the council whose jobs, prior to contracting-out, had been rated as equivalent to those of the complainants. Because they no longer worked for the 'same employer' they could not rely on the provisions of the Equal Pay Act, and sought to use the broader concept of employer contained in Article 141 (which applies to 'work carried out in the same establishment or service, whether private or public'). However, the EAT decision held that the rights conferred by Article 141 were not wide enough to permit employees of one company to compare themselves with work undertaken by a comparator working for another company, even where at one point, those employees and their comparators had worked for the same employer. See *Allonby v Accrington and Rossendale College & Others* (C256/01) [2004] ECR I-873; [2004] IRLR 224.

Like work

A woman is to be regarded as employed on 'like work' (s 1(2)(a)) with men in the same employment 'if, but only if, her work and theirs is of the same or a broadly similar nature and the difference (if any) between the things she does and the things they do are not of practical importance in relation to terms and conditions of employment' (*Shields v E. Coomes (Holdings) Ltd* [1978] ICR 1159, CA). In comparing her work and theirs, 'regard shall be had to the frequency or otherwise with which any such differences occur in practice as well as to the nature and extent of the differences' (EPA, s 1(4)). Further clarification was provided

158

Activities provide practical tasks for you to complete, helping you consider carefully what you are learning by putting the law in a human resources context.

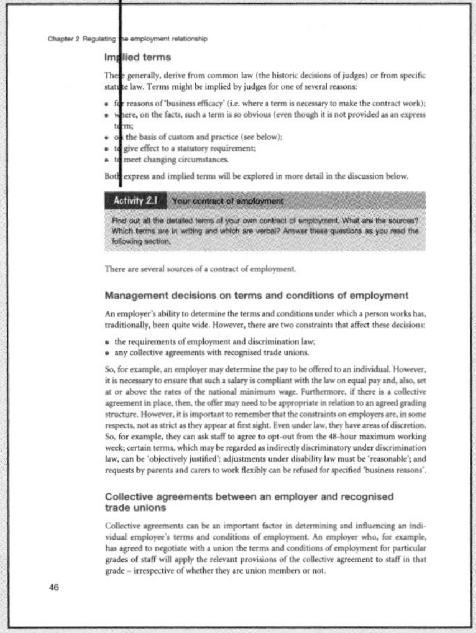
Chapter 2 Regulating the employment relationship

Implied terms

These generally, derive from common law (the historic decisions of judges) or from specific statute law. Terms might be implied by judges for one of several reasons:

- for reasons of 'business efficacy' (i.e. where a term is necessary to make the contract work);
- where, on the facts, such a term is so obvious (even though it is not provided as an express term);
- on the basis of custom and practice (see below);
- to give effect to a statutory requirement;
- to meet changing circumstances.

Both express and implied terms will be explored in more detail in the discussion below.

Activity 2.1 Your contract of employment

Find out all the detailed terms of your own contract of employment. What are the sources? Which terms are in writing and which are verbal? Answer these questions as you read the following section.

There are several sources of a contract of employment.

Management decisions on terms and conditions of employment

An employer's ability to determine the terms and conditions under which a person works has, traditionally, been quite wide. However, there are two constraints that affect these decisions:

- the requirements of employment and discrimination law;
- any collective agreements with recognised trade unions.

So, for example, an employer may determine the pay to be offered to an individual. However, it is necessary to ensure that such a salary is compliant with the law on equal pay and, also, set at or above the rates of the national minimum wage. Furthermore, if there is a collective agreement in place, then, the offer may need to be appropriate in relation to an agreed grading structure. However, it is important to remember that the constraints on employers are, in some respects, not as strict as they appear at first sight. Even under law, they have areas of discretion. So, for example, they can ask staff to agree to opt-out from the 48-hour maximum working week; certain terms, which may be regarded as indirectly discriminatory under discrimination law, can be 'objectively justified'; adjustments under disability law must be 'reasonable'; and requests by parents and carers to work flexibly can be refused for specified 'business reasons'.

Collective agreements between an employer and recognised trade unions

Collective agreements can be an important factor in determining and influencing an individual employee's terms and conditions of employment. An employer who, for example, has agreed to negotiate with a union the terms and conditions of employment for particular grades of staff will apply the relevant provisions of the collective agreement to staff in that grade – irrespective of whether they are union members or not.

46

Exercises encourage you to test your understanding of what you have read by challenging you to apply your knowledge to problem scenarios. Feedback to exercises can be found in the book's Appendix.

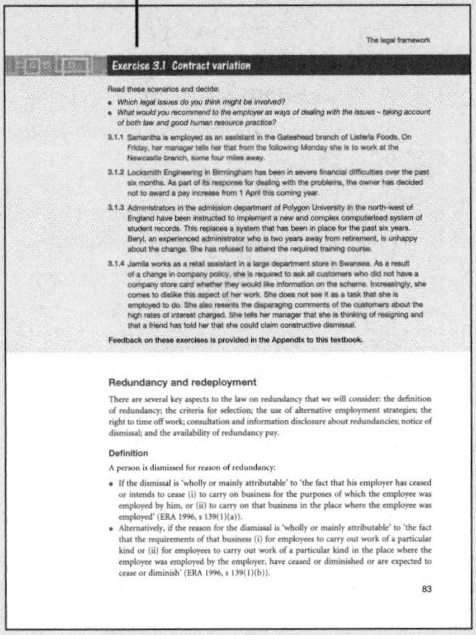
The legal framework

Exercise 3.1 Contract variation

Read these scenarios and decide:

- *Which legal issues do you think might be involved?*
- *What would you recommend to the employer as ways of dealing with the issues – taking account of both law and good human resource practice?*

3.1.1 Samantha is employed as an assistant in the Gateshead branch of Listeria Foods. On Friday, her manager tells her that from the following Monday she is to work at the Newcastle branch, some four miles away.

3.1.2 Locksmith Engineering in Birmingham has been in severe financial difficulties over the past six months. As part of its response for dealing with the problems, the owner has decided not to award a pay increase from 1 April this coming year.

3.1.3 Administrators in the admission department of Polygon University in the north-west of England have been instructed to implement a new and complex computerised system of student records. This replaces a system that has been in place for the past six years. Beryl, an experienced administrator who is two years away from retirement, is unhappy about the change. She has refused to attend the required training course.

3.1.4 Jamila works as a retail assistant in a large department store in Swansea. As a result of a change in company policy, she is required to ask all customers who did not have a company store card whether they would like information on the scheme. Increasingly, she comes to dislike this aspect of her work. She does not see it as a task that she is employed to do. She also resents the disparaging comments of the customers about the high rates of interest charged. She tells her manager that she is thinking of resigning and that a friend has told her that she could claim constructive dismissal.

Feedback on these exercises is provided in the Appendix to this textbook.

Redundancy and redeployment

There are several key aspects to the law on redundancy that we will consider: the definition of redundancy; the criteria for selection; the use of alternative employment strategies; the right to time off work; consultation and information disclosure about redundancies; notice of dismissal; and the availability of redundancy pay.

Definition

A person is dismissed for reason of redundancy:

- If the dismissal is 'wholly or mainly attributable' to 'the fact that his employer has ceased or intends to cease (i) to carry on business for the purposes of which the employee was employed by him, or (ii) to carry on that business in the place where the employee was employed' (ERA 1996, s 139(1)(a)).
- Alternatively, if the reason for the dismissal is 'wholly or mainly attributable' to 'the fact that the requirements of that business (i) for employees to carry out work of a particular kind or (ii) for employees to carry out work of a particular kind in the place where the employee was employed by the employer, have ceased or diminished or are expected to cease or diminish' (ERA 1996, s 139(1)(b)).

83

Tables throughout display informative figures and statistics to exemplify how law and policy interact in the real world.

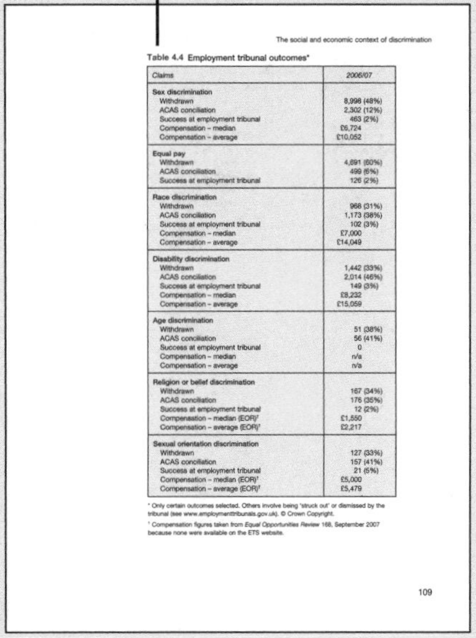
The social and economic context of discrimination

Table 4.4 Employment tribunal outcomes*

Claims	2006/07
Sex discrimination	
Withdrawn	8,998 (48%)
ACAS conciliation	2,302 (12%)
Success at employment tribunal	463 (2%)
Compensation – median	£6,724
Compensation – average	£10,052
Equal pay	
Withdrawn	4,891 (60%)
ACAS conciliation	499 (6%)
Success at employment tribunal	126 (2%)
Race discrimination	
Withdrawn	968 (31%)
ACAS conciliation	1,173 (38%)
Success at employment tribunal	102 (3%)
Compensation – median	£7,000
Compensation – average	£14,049
Disability discrimination	
Withdrawn	1,442 (33%)
ACAS conciliation	2,014 (46%)
Success at employment tribunal	149 (3%)
Compensation – median	£8,232
Compensation – average	£15,059
Age discrimination	
Withdrawn	51 (38%)
ACAS conciliation	56 (41%)
Success at employment tribunal	0
Compensation – median	n/a
Compensation – average	n/a
Religion or belief discrimination	
Withdrawn	167 (34%)
ACAS conciliation	176 (35%)
Success at employment tribunal	12 (2%)
Compensation – median (EOR)†	£1,850
Compensation – average (EOR)†	£2,217
Sexual orientation discrimination	
Withdrawn	127 (33%)
ACAS conciliation	157 (41%)
Success at employment tribunal	21 (5%)
Compensation – median (EOR)†	£5,000
Compensation – average (EOR)†	£5,479

* Only certain outcomes selected. Others involve being 'struck out' or dismissed by the tribunal (see www.employmenttribunals.gov.uk). © Crown Copyright.

† Compensation figures taken from *Equal Opportunities Review* 168, September 2007 because none were available on the ETS website.

109

End of chapter conclusions summarise the main aims, themes and ideas in a chapter.

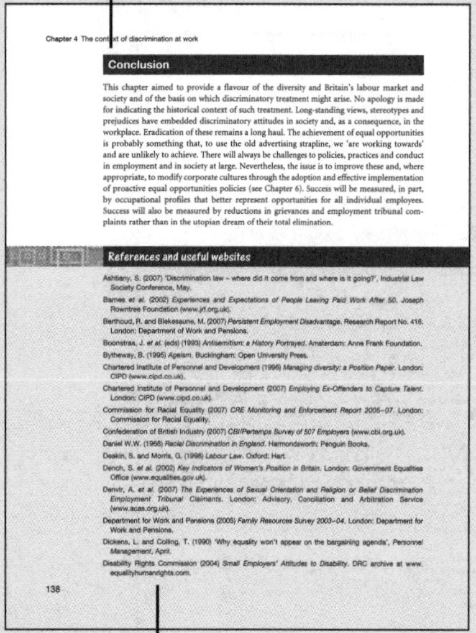

Chapter 4 The context of discrimination at work

Conclusion

This chapter aimed to provide a flavour of the diversity and Britain's labour market and society and of the basis on which discriminatory treatment might arise. No apology is made for indicating the historical context of such treatment. Long-standing views, stereotypes and prejudices have embedded discriminatory attitudes in society and, as a consequence, in the workplace. Eradication of these remains a long haul. The achievement of equal opportunities is probably something that, to use the old advertising strapline, we 'are working towards' and are unlikely to achieve. There will always be challenges to policies, practices and conduct in employment and in society at large. Nevertheless, the issue is to improve these and, where appropriate, to modify corporate cultures through the adoption and effective implementation of proactive equal opportunities policies (see Chapter 6). Success will be measured, in part, by occupational profiles that better represent opportunities for all individual employees. Success will also be measured by reductions in grievances and employment tribunal complaints rather than in the utopian dream of their total elimination.

References and useful websites

Ashtiany, S. (2007) 'Discrimination law – where did it come from and where is it going?', Industrial Law Society Conference, May.

Barnes *et al.* (2002) *Experiences and Expectations of People Leaving Paid Work After 50*. Joseph Rowntree Foundation (www.jrf.org.uk).

Berthoud, R. and Blekesaune, M. (2007) *Persistent Employment Disadvantage*. Research Report No. 416. London: Department of Work and Pensions.

Boonstras, J. *et al.* (eds) (1993) *Antisemitism: a History Portrayed*. Amsterdam: Anne Frank Foundation.

Bytheway, B. (1995) *Ageism*. Buckingham: Open University Press.

Chartered Institute of Personnel and Development (1996) *Managing diversity: a Position Paper*. London: CIPD (www.cipd.co.uk).

Chartered Institute of Personnel and Development (2007) *Employing Ex-Offenders to Capture Talent*. London: CIPD (www.cipd.co.uk).

Commission for Racial Equality (2007) *CRE Monitoring and Enforcement Report 2005–07*. London: Commission for Racial Equality.

Confederation of British Industry (2007) *CBI/Pertemps Survey of 507 Employers* (www.cbi.org.uk).

Daniel W.W. (1968) *Racial Discrimination in England*. Harmondsworth: Penguin Books.

Deakin, S. and Morris, G. (1998) *Labour Law*. Oxford: Hart.

Dench, S. *et al.* (2002) *Key Indicators of Women's Position in Britain*. London: Government Equalities Office (www.equalities.gov.uk).

Denvir, A. *et al.* (2007) *The Experiences of Sexual Orientation and Religion or Belief Discrimination Employment Tribunal Claimants*. London: Advisory, Conciliation and Arbitration Service (www.acas.org.uk).

Department for Work and Pensions (2005) *Family Resources Survey 2003–04*. London: Department for Work and Pensions.

Dickens, L. and Colling, T. (1990) 'Why equality won't appear on the bargaining agenda', *Personnel Management*, April.

Disability Rights Commission (2004) *Small Employers' Attitudes to Disability*. DRC archive at www.equalityhumanrights.com.

138

End of chapter references and useful websites direct you to relevant resources used in the chapter and to further reading that can help with assignments.

A full **Glossary**, at the end of the book, can be used throughout your reading to clarify unfamiliar terms.

Glossary

Note: (q.v.) after a word means that it is defined in this Glossary.

Act of Parliament: see **statute law** below.

Arbitration: Dispute resolution process where the arbitrator (usually a single person but may be a panel) is invited by the parties in dispute to resolve the dispute by making an award (i.e. a decision). The arbitrator is an independent person and may be appointed under the auspices of ACAS. There are two possible types of arbitration: *collective* (relating to disputes between an employer and trade unions), and *individual* (relating to an employer and an employee who has made a complaint or grievance). An example of the latter is the scheme operated by ACAS for resolving unfair dismissal and flexible working claims as an alternative to an employment tribunal claim.

Breach of contract: Circumstances in which one party to a contract does not comply with the terms of the contract (q.v.). Many breaches are minor and may be resolved by an employee lodging grievance with the employer or, alternatively, by an employer taking disciplinary action against an employee. Some breaches are serious (e.g. non-payment of wages due; or allowing persistent bullying to continue). These would be fundamental (i.e. repudiatory) breaches – the equivalent of tearing up the contract. The employee may accept the repudiation and resign and possibly claim constructive dismissal (q.v.).

Burden of proof: Sometimes this is referred to as the 'onus of proof'. It is the responsibility of a party to tribunal or court proceedings to prove an allegation by reference to certain facts and circumstances that are presented in evidence.

Case law: Law set out in judicial decisions. This can help clarify and interpret the law – particularly statute law (q.v.) – and create precedents (q.v.).

Civil law: This is a mixture of statute law (q.v.) and common law (q.v.). It concerns disputes between private individuals (including organisations). In these cases someone is sued. There are two branches of civil law: the law of contract (q.v.) and the law of tort (q.v.). The bulk of employment and discrimination law is civil and so is subsumed under the law of contract or tort. The standard of proof (q.v.) under this branch of law is 'the balance of probabilities'.

Codes of practice: There are both voluntary and statutory codes. Voluntary codes have no legal significance but they can be important in setting standards of good employment practice. Statutory codes do have legal importance. They are used by courts and tribunals in considering the extent to which an employer is liable for a breach of particular statutory employment rights. They are particularly important in respect of discrimination law and dismissal (see Chapters 5, 6 and 8).

Collective bargaining: A process where an employer and a recognised trade union (q.v..) negotiate about differences of interest. These are likely to be about terms and conditions of employment (e.g. pay and working time). They may also be about the extent of workplace

420

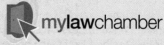

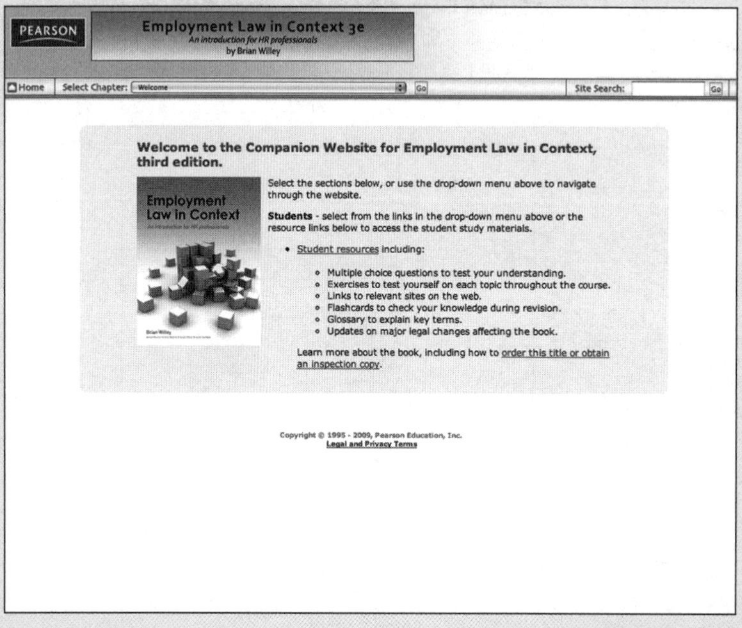

mylawchamber

Visit the *Employment Law in Context, third edition* **mylawchamber** site at **www.mylawchamber.co.uk/willey** to access:

Companion website support:
Use the multiple choice questions, case flashcards and exercises to test yourself on each topic throughout the course. The site includes updates to major changes in the law to make sure you are ahead of the game, and weblinks to help you read more widely around the subject.

List of abbreviations

ACAS	Advisory, Conciliation and Arbitration Service
AML	Additional maternity leave
BERR	Department for Business Enterprise and Regulatory Reform
BPR	Business process re-engineering
CA	Court of Appeal
CAC	Central Arbitration Committee
CBI	Confederation of British Industry
CEEP	European Centre for Enterprises with Public Participation
CIPD	Chartered Institute of Personnel and Development
CMCHA 2007	Corporate Manslaughter and Corporate Homicide Act 2007
CRB	Criminal Records Bureau
CRE	Commission for Racial Equality
DDA 1995	Disability Discrimination Act 1995
DPA 1998	Data Protection Act 1998
DfES	Department for Education and Skills
DRC	Disability Rights Commission
DSE	Display screen equipment
DTI	Department of Trade and Industry
DWP	Department for Work and Pensions
EA 2002	Employment Act 2002
EAP	Employee assistance programme
EAT	Employment Appeals Tribunal
EC	European Community
ECHR/ECtHR	European Court of Human Rights
ECJ	European Court of Justice
EEC	European Economic Community
EHRC	Equality and Human Rights Commission
EOC	Equal Opportunities Commission
EqPA 1970	Equal Pay Act 1970
ERA 1996	Employment Rights Act 1996
ERA 1999	Employment Relations Act 1999
ET	Employment Tribunal
ETO	Economic, technical and organisational
ETUC	European Trade Union Confederation
EU	European Union
EWC	European Works Council

FIFO	First in first out
GOQ	Genuine occupational qualification
GOR	Genuine Occupational Requirement
HASAWA 1974	Health and Safety at Work etc. Act 1974
HC	High Court
HL	House of Lords
HMRC	Her Majesty's Revenue and Customs
HRA 1998	Human Rights Act 1998
HRM	Human resource management
HSC	Health and Safety Commission
HSE	Health and Safety Executive
HSI	Health and Safety Inspectorate
ICT	Information and communications technology
ILO	International Labour Organisation
IRA 1971	Industrial Relations Act 1971
ISA	Independent Safeguarding Authority
IT	Industrial Tribunal
LGB	Lesbian, gay and bisexual
LIFO	Last in first out
LPC	Low Pay Commission
MHSW	Management of Health and Safety at Work [Regulations 1999]
NICA	Northern Ireland Court of Appeal
NIRC	National Industrial Relations Court
NMW	National minimum wage
NMWA 1998	National Minimum Wage Act 1998
OHS	Occupational health service
OML	Ordinary maternity leave
PPP	Public–private partnership
QMV	Qualified majority vote
RDP	Registered disabled person
RIDDOR	Reporting of Injuries, Diseases and Dangerous Occurrences Regulations 1995 SI 1995/3163
RORR	Range of reasonable responses
RRA 1976	Race Relations Act 1976
RR(A)A 2000	Race Relations (Amendment) Act 2000
SAP	Statutory adoption pay
SDA 1975	Sex Discrimination Act 1975
SI	Statutory instrument
SMEs	Small and medium sized enterprises
SMP	Statutory Maternity Pay
SOSR	Some other substantial reason
SPP	Statutory Paternity Pay

TICER 1999	Transnational Information and Consultation of Employees Regulations 1999
TQM	Total quality management
TUC	Trades Union Congress
TULRCA 1992	Trade Union and Labour Relations (Consolidation) Act 1992
TUPE 2006	Transfer of Undertakings (Protection of Employment) Regulations 2006
UNICE	Union des industries de la communanté européenne
WERS	Workplace Employee Relations Survey
WLB	Work–life balance
WTR 1998	Working Time Regulations 1998

Table of cases

Table of statutes

Table of statutory instruments

Table of statutory codes of practice

Table of European Community Law

Treaties and charters

Directives

Council of Europe: conventions

List of useful websites

Advisory, Conciliation and Arbitration Service	www.acas.org.uk
Cabinet Office	www.cabinet-office.gov.uk
Central Arbitration Committee	www.cac.gov.uk
Chartered Institute of Personnel and Development	www.cipd.co.uk
Citizens Advice Bureaux	www.citizensadvice.org.uk
Confederation of British Industry	www.cbi.org.uk
Criminal Records Bureau	www.crb.gov.uk
Department for Business Enterprise and Regulatory Reform	www.berr.gov.uk
Department for Education and Skills	www.dfes.gov.uk
Department for Work and Pensions	www.dwp.gov.uk
Employment Tribunals Service	www.employmenttribunals.gov.uk
Equality and Human Rights Commission	www.equalityhumanrights.com
European Commission	www.europea.eu.int/comm
European Court of Human Rights	www.echr.coe.int
European Court of Justice	www.curia.eu.int
European Parliament	www.europarl.eu
European Union	www.europa.eu
Government Equalities Office	www.equalities.gov.uk
Health and Safety Executive	www.hse.gov.uk
HM Revenue and Customs	www.hmrc.gov.uk
Home Office (Human Rights Act issues)	www.homeoffice.gov.uk/hract
Information Commissioner's Office	www.ico.gov.uk
Institute of Employment Studies	www.employment-studies.co.uk
International Labour Organisation	www.ilo.org/global
Joseph Rowntree Foundation	www.jrf.org.uk
Low Pay Commission	www.lowpay.gov.uk
Ministry of Justice	www.justice.gov.uk
Public Concern at Work	www.pcaw.demon.co.uk
Stationery Office	www.thestationeryoffice.com
Stonewall	www.stonewall.org.uk
Trades Union Congress	www.tuc.org.uk
UK Statistics Authority	www.statistics.gov.uk
United Kingdom Parliament	www.parliament.uk
Work Foundation	www.theworkfoundation.com

1 An introduction to employment law

Learning objectives

This chapter considers the ways in which the employment relationship is regulated by both voluntary and legal measures. Having read it, you should understand:

- The nature and purpose of both voluntary and legal regulation in general
- The principles that underpin employment and discrimination law
- The relationship that can exist between voluntary and legal regulation
- The various roles of courts, tribunals and statutory agencies

Structure of the chapter

- *Introduction*: the role of legal and voluntary regulation; economic and political perspectives
- *The nature of legal regulation and enforcement*: common law; statute law; secondary legislation; European law; the European Convention on Human Rights; tribunals and courts; the role of statutory agencies; statutory codes of practice; redress
- *Some underpinning principles*: ethics; human rights; fairness; reasonableness; equal treatment; harmonisation; natural justice; consent and freedom

Introduction

Broadly speaking, the employment relationship is regulated by both voluntary and legal measures. Voluntary measures comprise agreements and other decisions that derive from collective bargaining, arbitration, conciliation, grievance and discipline handling. They also include voluntarily accepted standards of good employment practice. Legal measures are European Union (EU) treaties and directives, British statute law, the common law of contract and of tort, case law, statutory codes of practice and some international standards. In practice, these are not isolated sets of measures. They invariably interlink and influence each other.

What are the purposes of voluntary and legal measures?

There are two broad purposes. First, at various points, they influence the function of management – i.e. the ways in which managers exercise power, control workforces and manage conflicts of interest. This influence can be illustrated in the following way. It is widely accepted that the employment relationship is characterised by an imbalance of power in favour of the employer. Both voluntary and legal regulation can restrain the unfettered exercise of this employer power. So, for example, collective bargaining with a trade union can minimise the exploitation of individuals at work by agreements on pay and conditions; and also by helping to process grievances. Furthermore, legislation can establish minimum conditions of employment (e.g. national minimum wage), and set limits on the action that an employer might take against employees (e.g. in relation to discipline and dismissal).

The second purpose of the regulation is to assert certain principles. On the one hand, there are those principles that influence the nature and quality of decisions (e.g. fairness, equal treatment, reasonableness, etc.). In addition, there are those principles which mould the regulatory process itself. Examples of this include the fundamental importance of consent in agreeing and changing contracts of employment, and of fairness and reasonableness in disciplinary procedures.

How does the law influence substantive issues?

Traditionally, it has been accepted within British employment relations that, as far as terms and conditions of employment (the substantive issues) are concerned, the law may set a general framework but the details would be determined either by employers alone or after negotiation with trade unions. Indeed, in 1954, one academic lawyer was able to make the following comment: 'There is, perhaps, no major country in the world in which the law has played a less significant role in the shaping of (industrial) relations than in Great Britain and in which the law and legal profession have less to do with labour relations' (Kahn-Freund 1954).

However, this characterisation soon began to change. Increasingly, over the following decades, statute law was enacted to establish certain principles to guide ways in which employers behave and also the terms and conditions of employment offered to staff. So, for example, fairness is now a basic criterion used to judge the reason for sacking an employee. Reasonableness is widespread as a reference point for assessing health and safety standards. The prohibition of less favourable treatment is fundamental to all strands of discrimination law.

There has also been a growing tendency towards more detailed prescription of certain terms and conditions of employment. This has arisen from some statute law and, in part, from case law. These more detailed requirements have an impact on all employers. For example, the outlawing of indirect sex discrimination – unless it can be justified – has created a body of case law which steers employers to scrutinise their employment practices. This law requires consideration about the legality and justification for such practices as seniority-based promotion, requirements that work should be full-time, age barriers in employment, etc.

Academic commentators have said that there is growing evidence in Britain (as in other European countries) of 'juridification'. This is defined as the tendency to which the behaviour of employers and unions is determined by reference to legal standards. Indeed, it is suggested that, in Britain, we have moved to a 'minimum standards' contract of employment that has been created through the continued intervention of statute law (see Chapter 2).

How does law affect procedural issues?

The procedural aspects can be subdivided into those that concern the individual employee and those which concern collective relationships.

Individual employees work under a contract of employment agreed with the employer. Consent is at the heart of contract formation and also contract variation. The courts have asserted, in numerous cases, that when an employer wishes to change terms and conditions of employment, then, procedurally, the employee must be consulted and agreement sought (see Chapter 3).

In disciplinary matters involving individuals, procedural fairness is essential. This is specified in the ACAS *Code of Practice on Disciplinary and Grievance Procedures* (2009). This has been confirmed in case law (see Chapter 8). As far as grievances are concerned, it has been established that individuals have the right, through and implied term of their contract of employment, to raise grievances through an appropriate procedure (*W.A. Goold (Pearmak) Ltd* v *McConnell and Another* [1995] IRLR 516). Also, new statutory requirements on grievance handling are explained in the ACAS code of practice. A worker also has a statutory right to be accompanied in a grievance and a disciplinary hearing (ERA 1999, s 10).

As far as collective relations are concerned, Britain, historically, has had a strong tradition of voluntarism for determining employment relations procedures. So, employers could freely decide whether or not to negotiate with trade unions and about which terms and conditions of employment. They could also determine any consultation arrangements. There is still considerable employer freedom in this area. However, European and British law have circumscribed it to some extent. The principal examples are:

- *Collective redundancies*: consultation with unions or employee representatives over specified redundancies (Trade Union and Labour Relations (Consolidation) Act 1992).
- *Transfers of undertakings*: consultation with unions or employee representatives about the transfer (Transfer of Undertakings (Protection of Employment) Regulations 2006).
- *Health and safety*: consultation with unions or employee representatives about safety standards and safety organisation in the workplace (Safety Representatives and Safety Committees Regulations 1977; Health and Safety (Consultation with Employees) Regulations 1996).
- *General workplace information disclosure and consultation*: relating to the economic circumstances of the organisation, likely changes in the labour force, and contractual changes (Information and Consultation of Employees Regulations 2004).
- *Information disclosure and consultation*: in specified multinational companies operating in the European Union (Transnational Information and Consultation of Employees Regulations 1999).

- *Recognition for collective bargaining purposes*: statutory obligations to negotiate with trade unions on certain employers who meet various statutory hurdles (Trade Union and Labour Relations (Consolidation) Act 1992).

Economic perspectives

A labour market is, arguably, defined by the limits set by law. As mentioned above, a key economic function of labour law is to determine how and when managerial authority is limited (e.g. limits to working time, minimum wages, protection against unfair dismissal). According to a leading labour law theorist, the 'main object of labour law has always been, and we venture to say will always be, to be a countervailing force to counteract the inequality of bargaining power which is inherent and must be inherent in the employment relationship' (Otto Kahn-Freund in Davies and Freedland 1983). So, labour law is seen as a potential force to counteract inequality.

The presence of labour law may provide incentives or disincentive for improving skills and productivity. The nature of labour legislation affects the efficiency of a firm in a competitive market. For some, this role of promoting economic efficiency is central. So, for example, it is argued that minimum wage laws can encourage investment in skills and technology rather than reliance on cheap labour. Labour law can also affect the movement of labour both nationally and internationally. Furthermore, such law can have, as outlined above, an important moral dimension covering such issues as slavery, child labour, unfair discrimination, privacy and bullying. Globalisation has led to a lively debate about the declining power of national labour laws and the need for labour regulation across national boundaries.

Globalisation and the changing role of labour law

One major labour law study notes that the 'study of comparative employment law has increased in importance in recent years largely because of the growing tendency towards international economic integration and the development of transnational labour standards' (Deakin and Morris 2005: 3). Globalisation has made a significant impact on the nature and profile of labour rights arguably diminishing the efficacy of national level employment law and labour market regulation with issues of labour abuses and the degradation of workers' rights being a common theme. According to Hepple (2005: 9), the 'features of the new economy mean that labour law is now inevitably global law and not just the concern of a particular nation state'. The role of international labour regulation has acquired renewed attention and pertinence. Issues of child labour, slave labour, forced labour and a variety of other forms of economic exploitation have been prominent in debates. To these debates have also been added the issue of 'social dumping' (whereby companies seek to relocate in countries with fewer or weaker employment law regimes); and the responsibilities of transnational companies in implementing and maintaining labour standards. The regulation of these transnational corporations poses many difficulties. Attempts have been made to introduce 'privatised' forms of regulation such as codes of conduct and social labelling systems. Transnational collective bargaining with international trade union confederations is barely formed. In the developed world, collective bargaining often 'takes place under the shadow of threats to relocate or to merge with foreign corporations: domestic labour laws rarely offer rights to bargain about strategic corporate-level decisions such as these' (Hepple 2005: 10).

Is there a crisis of labour law?

The consequences of 'footloose' multinational companies; of expanding globalised markets; and of migrant workers all raise serious questions about the feasibility of providing effective employment protection for working people against the exercise of employer economic power. In the United Kingdom, the cornerstone of employment protection is the contract of employment. But this is an imperfect instrument (see Chapter 2). Its defects in failing to recognise fairness and non-discriminatory treatment are gradually being rectified by statute law. However, whilst the contract of employment has some measure of effectiveness, there are many 'atypical' (as well as some 'standard') workers who remain outside its limited protection. Some of the political wrestling involved in creating the current framework of employment law and regulation is considered in the next section.

Political perspectives

It is important to remember that legislation arises within political arenas – both in Britain and also in the European Union. Shifts in approach to employment regulation reflect various political views which change over time. Politicians have views about the nature of employment law, the extent of voluntarism and the degree to which protection should be accorded to working people. It is possible to identify three different broad models of political approach which help consider the underpinning politics of employment law (Morris, Willey and Sachdev 2002: 229):

- the free collective bargaining model;
- the free labour market model;
- the employee protection or social justice model.

Each of these models, in different ways and with different emphases, considers a range of economic, social, political and human rights issues: the management of the economy, the economic consequences of collective bargaining, the concept of social justice, entitlement to job security, anti-discrimination policies, the human rights of freedom of association and freedom of expression. The models are designed to review and analyse broad trends in the development and natures of employment law. 'None of these models exists in its pure form. Contemporary employment relations in Britain are, in fact, governed by the interpenetration of the three' (Morris *et al.* 2002: 232).

The free collective bargaining model

This reflects the traditional pattern of British industrial relations which developed, particularly, from World War One onwards. Collective bargaining was seen as the central process of employee relations, usually resulting in voluntary agreements between an employer and particular trade unions. The role of consultation was comparatively marginal. This model reflected, in part, the international standards on freedom of association set in the 1940s and 1950s by the International Labour Organisation (ILO) and which British governments signed.

Philosophically, this model emphasised *voluntarism*. This was broadly subscribed to by employers, unions and governments. It was characterised by the general, though not complete, 'abstention of the law' (Kahn-Freund 1954). The limited law enacted had two principal functions. First, it created a permissive framework in which trade unions could lawfully exist, engage in collective bargaining and call for and organise industrial action. Public policy promoted collective bargaining as an acceptable method of regulating terms and conditions of employment and of 'institutionalising' the conflicts of interest endemic in employment relations.

Secondly, the law provided some very limited explicit protection for working people. One example was through Wages Councils (originally set up in 1909 and abolished in 1993). These councils set minimum pay for vulnerable groups of workers for whom collective bargaining was difficult to achieve. Another key example was health and safety legislation. A partial framework of such legislation owed its origins to social pioneers in the nineteenth century. It was only in 1974 that more comprehensive law was enacted.

Voluntarism was subject to numerous strains in the postwar years. Governments increasingly tried to balance the sectional interests and claims of unions and their members, on the one hand, and the public interest, on the other. So when, for example, the level of pay settlements achieved through free collective bargaining was perceived to be inflationary and economically damaging, governments, both Conservative and Labour, enacted statutory incomes policies and also legislative attempts to limit trade union power. After 1979, under Thatcherism, this free collective bargaining model became subject to a major political onslaught.

The free labour market model

This was gradually introduced from 1979 to support the wider economic policies of the Thatcher government. It decisively broke the prevailing consensus on industrial relations policy – which, admittedly, had been subject to considerable strains since the 1960s. The principles underlying this model were reflected in several broad policy approaches:

- Of principal importance was deregulation of the labour market. This involved the removal of certain protective measures for employees which were characterised as 'burdens on business'. Furthermore, EU employee protection polices were challenged because they were seen as obstructing overriding free market objectives.
- The promotion of economic objectives encouraging cost-effectiveness, competitiveness and flexibility in the use of labour.
- The primary importance of individualism in the employment relationship and the marginalising of collective interests and collective representation.
- The curbing of trade union power by abolishing, rather than reforming, statutory recognition rights and by constraining unions' ability to organise industrial action.

The policies pursued were principally driven by the economic interests of employers. Arguably, the countervailing interests of working people received much less consideration. The exceptions were in relation to discrimination law and health and safety. Here, the initiatives to improve protections largely derived from EU policies and from ruling of the European Court of Justice (ECJ).

The employee protection or social justice model

This reflects the broad interventionist approach adopted by the EU – at least until the late 1990s. As articulated in EU law, the principles underpinning this model are:

- protection of employees throughout the employment relationship;
- a recognition that employees have both individual and collective interests and that these have to be accommodated in a framework of employment law;

- harmonisation of conditions of employment across member states – complementing economic convergence;
- consideration of economic issues (cost effectiveness, competitiveness and labour flexibility) in the formulation of employee protection measures;
- the promotion of consensus about employment protection measures to be adopted between the social partners (i.e. employers and their organisations and employees and their trade unions);
- an acceptance of the principle of 'subsidiarity' – that is to say that some issues are more appropriately regulated at the level of the member state rather than at the level of the EU.

Consequently, the European Union has led to the enactment of, for example, the following law which has moulded terms and conditions of employment: equal treatment on the grounds of sex, race, sexuality, age, religion or belief, disability; equal pay; protections for pregnant workers; leave entitlements for parents; the establishment of wide-ranging health and safety standards; restrictions on excessive working time; protection of part-time workers and fixed-term employees. As far as employment procedures, it has been much less interventionist. However, as mentioned above it has developed, in a number of aspects of employment relations, the duty of employers to consult and disclose information to its employees to provide better understanding of corporate polices and, to some extent, influence their direction.

Contemporary British employment relations continue to be characterised by the interpenetration of all three models. The Labour government, elected in 1997, sought to maintain the Thatcherite commitment to the free market. However, it aimed to ameliorate the worst aspects of this for working people by enacting various social justice measures – some deriving from European law (e.g. the Working Time Regulations 1998), and some from home-grown initiatives (e.g. the National Minimum Wage Act 1998).

The nature of legal regulation

The legal regulation of employment will be examined by looking at the following aspects:

- ***How are legal standards set?***
  - common law;
  - primary legislation: Acts of Parliament;
  - secondary legislation: regulations;
  - European law;
  - European Convention on Human Rights 1950;
  - statutory codes of practice.

- ***How do working people enforce their rights?***
  - employment tribunals;
  - Employment Appeals Tribunal;
  - Court of Appeal;
  - Supreme Court and the House of Lords;
  - European Court of Justice;
  - European Court of Human Rights;
  - International Labour Organisation.

- ***What is the role of statutory agencies?***
  - Advisory Conciliation and Arbitration Service;
  - Commission for Equality and Human Rights;
  - Health and Safety Executive;
  - Low Pay Commission;
  - Information Commissioner;
  - Criminal Records Bureau;
  - Independent Safeguarding Authority;
  - Central Arbitration Committee.

- ***What redress is available for infringements of rights?***
  - the effectiveness of redress and remedies.

- ***What are the key underpinning principles?***
  - *substantive issues*:
    - fairness;
    - reasonableness;
    - equal treatment;
    - harmonisation.
  - *procedures*:
    - natural justice;
    - consultation;
    - consent;
    - Freedom.

How are legal standards set?

As indicated above, there are several sources of law affecting the employment relationship. We will look at each in turn.

Common law

This is formulated by judges through **case law**. They set and develop various principles (e.g. the concept of reasonableness). They can create various legal tests (e.g. to define an employee). **Common law** is used in interpreting statute law. Under the doctrine of **precedent** rulings of the judges in the higher courts are binding on the lower courts – unless they are overturned by Parliament in new legislation. There are two aspects of common law:

- *Law of contract.* A **contract** is an agreement between two or more parties which is intended to be legally enforceable. It may be oral or in writing. These parties create their own rights and duties. So, they voluntarily decide the content of the contract. Courts may be involved in discovering the intention of the parties (i.e. what they meant by a particular provision), and whether the contract was breached. Contracts may be ruled by the courts to be void if certain provisions are unlawful (e.g. contrary to discrimination law). Within employment, this branch of law has considerable significance through the contract of employment (see Chapter 2).

- *Law of* **tort**. A tort is a civil wrong other than a breach of contract. Obligations here are imposed by law. This branch of law concerns the interests of a 'person' (it can be an individual or an organisation) which may be injured by another. So, a person may be injured by another's **negligence** as a result of poor health and safety organisation, or an employer's interests may be damaged by unlawful **industrial action** organised by a trade union. A central concern for the courts in this branch of law is the issue of liability (i.e. who is liable for causing the injury). In some instances the issue of **vicarious liability** arises. This is where one person assumes liability for the actions of another. An example is where an employer is liable for all breaches of health and safety rules – even where the breach is committed by a manager or another employee. The complainant will be seeking **damages** (compensation) for the injury sustained.

Primary legislation

This is **statute law – Acts of Parliament**. These may set new legal requirements and can also overturn case-law decisions of the judges; and repeal or amend existing legislation. It is the most common way through which new general rights and duties are established. Among the most notable examples in employment and discrimination law are the Employment Rights Act 1996 and the Sex Discrimination Act 1975. In considering complaints that may arise under statute law, courts will consider the following:

- Has a provision of the legislation been infringed? (Example: the right not to be unfairly dismissed.)
- Does the complainant have a remedy? (Example: compensation and possible reinstatement or re-engagement.)
- Has the specific legislative provision been interpreted in any previous judgments (particularly by the Court of Appeal, the House of Lords or, if European law is involved, the European Court of Justice)?
- Does the legislation have to be interpreted in conformity with European law?
- Are there any implications arising from the Human Rights Act 1998? Is the legislation compatible? (See later section on the European Convention on Human Rights.)

Secondary legislation

This subordinate legislation, made by way of **statutory instruments**, is often referred to as 'regulations'. They are laid before Parliament for approval in a simpler process than passing an Act. They are made under particular statute law (e.g. the European Communities Act 1972 or the Health and Safety at Work Act 1974). As with Acts of Parliament, regulations must be compatible with the European Convention on Human Rights (see below). Increasingly, employment law is enacted through this method. The regulations include rights and entitlements which are enforceable in the courts in the same way as those under Acts of Parliament. Examples of some common secondary legislation in employment are:

- Transfer of Undertakings (Protection of Employment) Regulations 2006;
- Part-time Workers (Prevention of Less Favourable Treatment) Regulations 2000;
- Management of Health and Safety at Work Regulations 1999;
- Working Time Regulations 1998.

European Union law

In employment regulation, there are three principal aspects of European law that are relevant: the treaties of the European Union; **directives**; and rulings of the European Court of Justice.

- *Treaties.* The original Treaty of Rome 1957, founding the then European Economic Community has been amended on several occasions since – by the Single European Act 1987, the Treaty on European Union 1992 (the Maastricht Treaty), the Treaty of Amsterdam 1997, the Treaty of Nice 2000 and the Treaty of Lisbon 2008 (to be ratified). A treaty article can be enforced as a direct right in the courts of member states where it is 'sufficiently clear, precise and unconditional as to require no further interpretation'. Such a treaty article can have '**direct effect**' both 'vertically' and 'horizontally'. This means that, in the first situation, the article confers rights for the citizen against the state. In the second situation, it confers rights for the citizen to exercise against another (e.g. an employer). A clear example of such 'direct effect' is the principle of equal pay for equal work between men and women. This was in the original Treaty of Rome and has subsequently been enacted as Article 141 in the current treaty.
- *Directives.* These are the principal means for establishing employment rights within the European Union (see Table 1.1). They are proposed by the Commission. After many ministerial meetings and discussions in the European Parliament, ultimately they are agreed and adopted by the Council of the European Union (which comprises the heads of government of all member states). Traditionally, agreement had to be unanimous. However, in 1987 amendments were made to permit the adoption by '**qualified majority vote**' (QMV) of certain directives (those defined as health and safety measures).

It is also possible, under procedures adopted in the Maastricht Treaty, for the '**social partners**' to negotiate a '**framework agreement**' on a particular policy proposed by the Commission. These 'social partners' are UNICE, the European private-sector employers' confederation; CEEP, the public-sector equivalent; and the ETUC, the European Confederation of Trade Unions. Framework agreements may then be adopted by the Council of the European Union as the basis of a new directive. Three significant examples are the 1996 Directive on Parental Leave, the 1997 Directive on Part-time Workers and the 1999 Directive on Fixed-term Work.

The main advantage of such framework agreements is the ability to take into account, at the drafting stage, the practical implications (reflecting the experiences of employers and unions) of such policies proposed by the Commission. It may be that rather than provide

Table 1.1 Some key European directives on employment policy

1975	Equal pay	1996	Parental leave
1976	Equal treatment	1996	Posted workers
1980	Insolvency	1997	Part-time workers
1989	Safety and health of workers	1998	Collective redundancies
1990	Display screen equipment	1999	Fixed-term work
1991	Contract of employment information	2000	Race discrimination
1992	Collective redundancies	2000	Equal treatment in employment
1992	Pregnant workers	2001	Transfers of undertakings
1993	Working time	2002	Information and consultation
1994	European Works Councils	2003	Working time
1994	Protection of young people at work	2006	Equal treatment between men and women (consolidation directive)
1995	Data protection		

detailed provisions, general principles are agreed which can guide employment practice in individual workplaces. This is particularly so with the 1997 Part-time Workers Framework Agreement and Directive (see Chapter 2).

Generally, directives are enforceable against member states. Each country is obliged to transpose a directive into national law within a specified number of years. In Britain, this is achieved by passing an Act of Parliament or laying regulations before Parliament for approval. So, for example, the Working Time Directive 1993 was enacted through the Working Time Regulations 1998.

The enforcement of directives has a particular significance for those employed in the public sector (and in certain private-sector companies which carry out public functions under law). These employees may use a directive in a national court without it having been transposed into national law. This arises because they work for the state (the civil service) or 'an emanation of the state' (e.g. a local authority, an NHS trust or an agency created as a result of the reorganisation of central government). The directive is said to have 'direct effect'. However, a directive must be 'sufficiently precise and unconditional' to be enforced without the need for domestic legislation. In practical terms, this means that a person employed in any public-sector body can complain that a specific right has been infringed from the date of adoption of the directive by the Council of the European Union – even if there is no British legislation. Unlike a treaty article, a directive can only have '***vertical*** direct effect' – i.e. enforceability against the state or an emanation of the state.

Some employees who work in certain parts of the private sector, may be able to use this route to enforce rights. The concept of '**emanation of the state**' has been interpreted by the courts to embrace certain privatised corporations (notably British Gas and water companies). Three tests have been developed to help establish whether an organisation can be so defined:

- Is there a public service provision?
- Is there control by the state?
- Does the organisation have special powers?

It was ruled in a judgment of the European Court of Justice that 'A state body is a body, whatever its legal form, which has been made responsible, pursuant to a measure adopted by the state, for providing a public service under the control of the state, and which has, for that purpose, special powers beyond those which result from the normal rules applicable in relations between individuals' (*Foster* v *British Gas plc* [1990] IRLR 353).

- ***Rulings of the European Court of Justice*** (ECJ). The ECJ is responsible for determining the application and interpretation of European law (see Table 1.2). Together with treaty articles and directives, its rulings have been the other most significant European influence on the development of employment regulation within Britain. These rulings are binding on all member states, irrespective of the country of origin of a particular case. Among the key rulings to affect British employment relations are the following:
  - *Deciding whether an EU member state has failed to fulfil a treaty obligation.* For example, the ECJ decided that because of the failure of the Italian government to implement the 1980 insolvency directive by the due date in 1983, citizens could sue their government for the loss they had sustained, provided that there was a clear link between a government failure and the damage suffered by an individual (*Francovich and Bonifaci* v *the Republic of Italy* [1992] IRLR 84). The consequence of this case is that '*Francovich* claims' can now be made in the British courts, subject to certain conditions.

Table 1.2 The impact of European law: some key cases

Non-discriminatory retirement ages between men and women	House of Lords judgment resulted in amendments to British law in the Sex Discrimination Act 1986 (*Marshall* v *Southampton & SW Hampshire Area Health Authority* [1986] IRLR 140)
Discrimination on the grounds of pregnancy a 'direct discrimination'	This arose from an ECJ ruling which elaborated equal treatment law (*Dekker* v *Stichting Vormingscentrum* [1991] IRLR 27). The concept was also incorporated in the Pregnant Workers' Directive
Pensions being defined a 'pay'	The Court of Appeal ruled that superannuation payments were subject to European equal pay provisions (*Barber* v *Guardian Royal Exchange* [1990] IRLR 240)
Part-time workers' access to statutory rights	The House of Lords ruled that, in interpreting European equal treatment law, it was indirect discrimination against women to have an hours qualification for access to redundancy pay and unfair dismissal compensation (*R* v *Secretary of State for Employment* ex parte *Equal Opportunities Commission* [1994] IRLR 176). New regulations were introduced which provided a one-year qualification period for all employees (full-time or part-time)
Removal of ceiling on compensation in sex discrimination cases	A ceiling on compensation payments was ruled as limiting the effective implementation of the principle of equal treatment (*Marshall* v *Southampton & SW Hampshire Area Health Authority (No. 2)* [1993] IRLR 455). As a consequence, the ceilings on compensation were removed in successful sex and race discrimination cases (SI 1993/2798; SI 1994/1748). In the long term, no ceilings were imposed in other strands of discrimination law
Discrimination on the grounds of trans-sexual status ruled contrary to equal treatment law	This was determined by the ECJ in *P* v *S and Cornwall County Council* [1996] IRLR 347. In 1999 the Sex Discrimination (Gender Reassignment) Regulations amended the Sex Discrimination Act 1975
Defining 'working time' when 'on call'	The Working Time Directive 1993 was interpreted in *SIMAP* v *Conselleria de Sanidad y Consumo de la Generalidad Valenciana* [2000] IRLR 845; and *Landeshauptstadt Kiel* v *Jaeger* [2003] IRLR 804
Dismissal of woman undergoing IVF treatment can be discriminatory	*Mayr* v *Backerei und Konditorei Gerhard Flockner OHG* (2008)

- *Dealing with infraction proceedings.* For example, the failure of the United Kingdom to provide for full consultation rights in respect of redundancies and business transfers was referred by the Commission to the Court for a ruling (*EC Commission* v *United Kingdom*, C-383/92 (1994)). Ultimately, this case resulted in the adoption of new consultation regulations in Britain that were compliant with EU law.
- *Reviewing the legality of decisions of the Council of the European Union and the Commission.* For example, the court determined, following a complaint by the British Conservative government, that the Working Time Directive 1993 was properly made as a health and safety measure under the treaty procedures (*United Kingdom* v *the European Council* (1996) C-84/94).
- *Reviewing the failure to act of the Council of the European Union and the Commission where the treaty obliges them to act.*
- *To give preliminary rulings on points of European law at the request of a national court.*
- *To hear complaints on the application and interpretation of European law.*

- *To determine the wider application of European law.* For example, in 1990, the court ruled that national courts are obliged to interpret that country's domestic legislation in the light of European directives regardless of whether the domestic legislation pre-dates or post-dates the directives. This wide view of interpretation also concerns law enacted in the member states prior to that country's entry into the EU (*Marleasing SA* v *La Comercial Internacional de Alimentacion* C-106/89).

In interpreting the law, the ECJ adopts a '**purposive**' (as opposed to 'literal') approach to interpretation. So, it will consider the intention of the legislators and the 'spirit' of the legislation rather than the strict 'letter'. This is compatible with the character of much law in the original EU member states which is in the form of broad statements of overriding aims and principles. The House of Lords has accepted that such an approach might be accepted in the British courts for complying with European law (Lord Justice Templeman in *Pickstone* v *Freemans plc* [1988] IRLR 357).

European Convention on Human Rights 1950

From 2 October 2000, this Convention was incorporated into law in the United Kingdom through the Human Rights Act 1998. The Convention was drafted under the auspices of the Council of Europe – an intergovernmental body, founded in 1949, primarily to promote democracy, human rights and the rule of law throughout Europe. It is separate from the European Union, although member states of the EU are also members of the Council and the EU accepts and expects compliance with the Convention.

The Convention was ratified by the UK in 1951. Until 2000, people who alleged that their human rights had been infringed needed to embark on a lengthy process to the European Court of Human Rights in Strasbourg. Following the implementation of the Human Rights Act 1998, the Convention is gradually woven into the fabric of law in the UK and complainants have easier access to possible redress in the domestic courts. (Exhibit 1.1 sets out the key Convention rights).

The Human Rights Act 1998 has three fundamental effects which in varying ways can have an effect on law relating to employment:

- *Common law.* This must be developed compatibly with Convention rights. This means that previous judgments can be questioned. In relation to employment, this is likely, over time, to affect the common law of contract.
- *Legislation.* All legislation (Acts of Parliament, regulations and orders) must be interpreted and implemented in compliance with the Convention 'so far as it is possible to do so' (HRA 1998, s 3(1)). Where there are two possible interpretations of a statutory provision (i.e. one compatible with the Convention and one not), that which is compatible must be adopted. Previous interpretations, under case law from courts in the United Kingdom, may no longer be relied upon. Where it is not possible to interpret particular legislation compatibly, a court (in England and Wales, the High Court and above; and in Scotland, the Court of Session and the High Court of Justiciary) may:
  - Quash or disapply secondary legislation (regulations and orders).
  - Issue a 'declaration of incompatibility' (HRA 1998, s 4) for primary legislation (an Act of Parliament). This will not rescind the legislation. It will remain in force. However, the declaration will draw the issue to the government's attention and enable the appropriate minister to invoke the 'fast track' procedure to amend the legislation in Parliament by a remedial order.

Exhibit 1.1 Key rights, European Convention on Human Rights 1950

The detailed provisions of these rights are in Schedule 1 to the Human Rights Act 1998

Absolute rights

These have no restrictions or limitations:

Article 7: protection from retrospective criminal penalties
Article 3: protection from torture, inhuman and degrading treatment and punishment
Article 4: prohibition of slavery and enforced labour

Limited rights

These can be limited in specific circumstances defined in the Convention:

Article 5: The right to liberty and security

A person may be detained if the detention is lawful. It covers, for example, arrest by the police and imprisonment following conviction by a court.

Qualified rights

Many rights with a bearing on employment relations are in this category:

Article 8: right to respect for private and family life
Article 9: freedom of thought, conscience and religion
Article 10: freedom of expression
Article 11: freedom of assembly and association

It is permissible to interfere with these qualified rights in the following circumstances:

- If the interference is provided for in law.
- If the interference is necessary in a democratic society. It must fulfil a pressing social need; pursue a legitimate aim; be proportionate to the aims being pursued; and be related to a permissible aim set out in the relevant Article (e.g. the prevention of crime or the protection of public order).

Other rights

Article 6: right to a fair trial
Article 14: prohibition of discrimination (in the exercising of Convention rights)

  - Require UK courts and tribunals to take account of case law from the European Court of Human Rights in Strasbourg but not necessarily be bound by it.

- *Activities of public authorities.* It is unlawful for a public authority to act incompatibly with Convention rights. The Human Rights Act covers all activities of a public authority, for example: policy-making, rules and regulations, personnel issues, administrative procedures, decision-making. There are three broad categories of public authorities:
  - *'Obvious' or 'pure' public authorities.* This describes, for example, a government department or statutory agency, a Minister of the Crown, local authorities, NHS trusts, education authorities, fire and civil defence authorities, the armed forces, the police and the immigration service, and the prison service. Everything done by these is covered by the Human Rights Act – whether in their public functions or in their private functions (e.g. offering an employment contract).

- *Courts and tribunals.* Their responsibility for interpreting and implementing the law is outlined above. In the employment context, neither employment tribunals nor the Employment Appeals Tribunal have power to quash or disapply secondary legislation not to issue declarations of incompatibility. (If this were done in an employment case, it would be at the appeal stages in the Court of Appeal or the House of Lords.) Nevertheless, employment tribunals and the EAT must interpret the law compatibly with the Convention on Human Rights.
- *'Hybrid' or quasi-public bodies.* These are bodies which carry out some functions of a public nature. So, they are not a public authority for all their activities, but only when carrying out public functions. Examples include the privatised utilities (gas, electricity and water companies).

Remedial action. The Human Rights Act 1998 creates two effects:

1 *A direct effect.* This is where a person (i.e. a victim) can enforce Convention rights directly in court through starting legal proceedings (s 7). Such action can only be taken against a '**public authority**'. A victim may be a company or other organisation as well as a private individual. The complaint has, normally, to be made within one year of the act complained of. If a court finds that a public authority has breached a person's Convention rights, it can award whatever remedy is available to it within its existing powers and is just and equitable (s 8(1)). This may include the award of damages; quashing an unlawful decision; ordering the public authority not to take the proposed action.
2 *An indirect effect.* There is no means of enforcing Convention rights directly against private individuals (including private companies or quasi-public bodies when they are carrying out their private functions). In these cases, where a private individual or organisation is involved, there is an indirect effect. This means that the law (statute and common law and secondary legislation) in cases involving such private 'individuals' must be applied and interpreted compatibly with the Convention.

Complaints under the Human Rights Act may be initiated in a number of courts or tribunals, depending on which is appropriate. If the claim is based on a contract or in tort (e.g. a claim for personal injury), action should start in the High Court or the county court (or, in Scotland, in the Sheriff Court or Court of Session). Where the case relates to the decision of a public body, the appropriate action will usually be judicial review in the High Court. It is still possible for a complaint to be made, ultimately, to the ECHR (see Exhibit 1.2).

Statutory codes of practice

In hearing complaints, tribunals and courts may be required to take account of statutory codes of practice. These have to be approved by Parliament. The main ones currently in force which are relevant for individual employment rights are:

- *Advisory Conciliation and Arbitration Service:*
  - Disciplinary and Grievance Procedures (2009).
  - Disclosure of Information to Trade Unions for Collective Bargaining Purposes (1998).
  - Time Off for Trade Union Duties and Activities (2003).

- *Health and Safety Executive:*
  - Code of Practice on Safety Representatives and Safety Committees (1978).
  - Code of Practice on Time Off for the Training of Safety Representatives (1978).

Exhibit 1.2 Union expulsion of a British National Party member

Associated Society of Locomotive Engineers and Firemen (ASLEF) v United Kingdom [2007] IRLR 361

Facts. Lee was a train driver and a member of ASLEF, the train drivers' union. In 2002, it was reported to the union's general secretary that Lee was a well-known British National Party activist who had stood as a candidate in elections. He was said to have written and distributed racist material and harassed Anti-Nazi League protestors and been reported to the police.

The union's executive committee took the view that Lee's activities with the BNP were likely to bring the union into disrepute. A resolution to expel him was passed unanimously. Under its rules, ASLEF states that it aims to promote and enact equal treatment policies and is committed to campaigning vigorously to expose 'the obnoxious policies of political parties such as the National Front'.

Lee complained, in the first instance, that he had been unlawfully excluded from ASLEF membership (contrary to TULRCA 1992, s 174(3)). The ET upheld Lee's complaint. ASLEF appealed to the EAT which upheld the union's claim about the law. The matter was referred back to a further ET hearing; and again Lee was successful in his application. ASLEF then made an application to the European Court of Human Rights in Strasbourg. Its complaint was that it was prevented from expelling a member because of his membership of a political party that advocated views contrary to its own policies, and that this was an infringement of its right to freedom on association (under Article 11 of the ECHR).

Law. Article 11 of the Convention: freedom of assembly and association:

1 Everyone has the right to freedom of peaceful assembly and to freedom of association with others, including the right to form and join trade unions for the protection of his interests.
2 No restrictions shall be placed on the exercise of these rights other than such as are prescribed by law and are necessary in a democratic society in the interests of national security or public safety, for the prevention of disorder or crime, for the protection of health or morals or for the protection of the rights and freedoms of others. This article shall not prevent the imposition of lawful restrictions on the exercise of these rights by members of the armed forces, of the police or of the administration of the state.

The UK law which was considered as, arguably, incompatible with this Convention article was the Trade Union and Labour Relations (Consolidation) Act 1992, s 174.

ECHR judgment. The court's view was that Lee's expulsion did not impinge on his freedom of expression (Article 10). It noted that he had suffered no particular detriment apart from loss of union membership. Even in workplace employment relations, ASLEF was the bargaining agent for the terms and conditions of all train drivers, irrespective of whether they were members or not.

The court gave more weight to ASLEF's right to choose its members. It acknowledged that the union had its own clear political views. It noted that there was no suggestion that in the internal union procedures that ASLEF had erred in its finding that Lee's views and those of the union's clashed. In the absence of any identifiable hardship suffered by Lee or any abusive or unreasonable conduct by ASLEF, the court concluded that the balance between the competing Convention rights had not been properly struck. There was a violation of Article 11.

Consequences:

- TULRCA 1992 s 174 was amended in 2004 to allow a union to exclude an individual from membership on the grounds of his/her activities as member of a political party.
- Membership of a specified political party, in itself, remained as an unlawful ground for expulsion. However, the Employment Act 2008 amends the law in this respect.

- *Equal Opportunities Commission:**
  - Code of Practice on Sex Discrimination in Employment (1985).
  - Code of Practice on Equal Pay (2003).
  - Gender Equality Duty Code of Practice (2007).
- *Commission for Racial Equality:**
  - Code on the Duty to Promote Equal Opportunity (2002).
  - Code on Racial Equality in Employment (2006).
- *Disability Rights Commission:**
  - Code of Practice on Employment and Occupation (2004).
- *Department of Work and Pensions:*
  - Guidance on Matters to Be Taken into Account in Determining Questions Relating the Definition of Disability (2006).
- *Border and Immigration Agency:*
  - Avoidance of Unlawful Discrimination in Employment Practice While Seeking to Prevent Illegal Working (2008).
- *Information Commissioner:*
  - Employment Practices Data Protection Code (2005). (N.B. this code is not required to be laid before Parliament.)

* Although these codes of practices were drafted by these former equality commissions, they remain in force now that the Commission for Equality and Human Rights has taken over their responsibilities.

The status of statutory codes (as, for example, those published by ACAS) is as follows:

- Failure of a person to observe any provision of a code 'shall not of itself render him liable to any proceedings';
- However, in any proceedings before an employment tribunal, any appropriate code of practice 'shall be admissible in evidence', and 'if any provision of such a code appears to the tribunal to be relevant to any question arising in the proceedings it shall be taken into account in determining that question' (TULRCA 1992, s 207).

How do working people enforce their rights?

Normally, complaints about individual employment rights are made to an employment tribunal. It is possible for a complainant (the employee or worker) or a respondent employer to appeal, on a point of law, to the Employment Appeals Tribunal (EAT) and, then, usually with permission, to the Court of Appeal; and, then, to the House of Lords (which from October 2009, will be to the Supreme Court). If the complainant has involved the application of European law (for example, on discrimination, working time, transfers of undertakings or equal pay), an ultimate appeal, with the permission of either the Court of Appeal or House of Lords, would be to the European Court of Justice in Luxembourg. (For more detail on these bodies see below.)

In addition, various statutory agencies have responsibility for assisting in specified ways in the enforcement of employment law. They provide advice and information and most have some enforcement powers. The most notable are the Advisory Conciliation and Arbitration Service, the Health and Safety Executive, the Commission for Equality and Human Rights, the Low Pay Commission. (For more detail on these bodies see below.)

Employment tribunals

Originally set up in 1964 as industrial tribunals to deal with training levy complaints, their jurisdiction was extended to unfair dismissal in 1972. They now cover a very wide range of employment rights (e.g. all strands of discrimination law, equal pay, maternity and parental rights, rights of trade union membership, unlawful pay deductions). In 1998, they were renamed 'employment tribunals'. A full tribunal comprises three people. It is chaired by an employment judge, a legally qualified person. He or she may sit alone or may be assisted by two lay people who have experience of employment relations. The use of tribunals to deal with employment rights complaints was supposed to be beneficial in offering informality and speed. This, however, has not proved to be so. (For further discussion on the operation of employment tribunals see later section on redress.) (website: **www.employmenttribunals.gov.uk**).

Employment Appeals Tribunal

This was established in 1976 as a superior court of record to hear appeals on points of law from the (then) industrial tribunals. Each bench comprises a judge (drawn from the High Court and Court of Appeal) and two lay members from people who have experience of employment relations. In various areas of employment law, it has provided guidance for tribunals on particular issues (website: **www.employmenttribunals.gov.uk**).

Court of Appeal

Created in the late nineteenth century, it comprises two divisions: the Civil Division (presided over by the Master of Rolls) and the Criminal Division (presided over by the Lord Chief Justice). Under employment law, appeals against rulings of the EAT are heard in the Civil Division. In most cases, appeals can be made to the House of Lords – with the 'leave' (permission) of either the Court of Appeal or of the House of Lords itself (website: **www.justice.gov.uk**).

Supreme Court and the House of Lords

The House of Lords is the final court of appeal for civil and criminal cases from the Court of Appeal in England and Wales, for civil cases from the Court of Session in Scotland, and for civil and criminal cases from the Court of Appeal in Northern Ireland. Decisions of the House of Lords bind all lower courts.

If the law derives from the European Union, there can be a further appeal stage to the European Court of Justice. If there is some uncertainty about the application or meaning of a provision of European law, the House of Lords may refer this to the ECJ for authoritative guidance.

There are 12 Law Lords, who are appointed by the Queen on the advice of the Prime Minister, from senior appeal court judges from each part of the UK. The first female Law Lord (Lady Justice Hale) was appointed in 2004. Usually, the Law Lords sit as a panel of five. The number of appeals dealt with each year varies. But it tends to be between 80 and 100 – a few concerning employment related issues.

From October 2009, as a result of the Constitutional Reform Act 2005, the House of Lords in its judicial capacity is reconstituted as the United Kingdom's Supreme Court. The existing 12 Law Lords become Justices of the Supreme Court and are debarred from sitting on the House of Lords whilst holding that office. For hearing appeals, the Supreme Court consists of an uneven number of judges (website: **www.justice.gov.uk**).

European Court of Justice

Based in Luxembourg, this is the principal judicial body of the European Union. It is officially known as the Court of Justice of the European Communities. It has jurisdiction in Britain under the European Communities Act 1972 in relation to European competition and company law; and also employment and discrimination law.

The ECJ comprises 27 judges and eight Advocates-General who assist the court. The judges are nominated by member states for a six-year term. The ECJ makes final rulings on the application of European law (see Table 1.2 above). The role of Advocates-General has no equivalent in the English and Scottish legal systems. They provide a reasoned submission (an Opinion) in open court. This submission is a preliminary opinion about the points of law involved in a specific case. An Advocate-General will refer to other relevant rulings and recommend a judgment. Some months later, the court will pronounce its ruling. It is usual for the Court to accept an Advocate-General's view (website: **www.europa.eu**).

European Court of Human Rights

Based in Strasbourg, this court operates under the Council of Europe and is separate from the European Union. Its responsibility is to adjudicate on alleged violations of the 1950 European Convention for the Protection of Human Rights and Fundamental Freedoms to which Britain is a signatory. This Convention is now incorporated into law in the UK through the Human Rights Act 1998. Although it is still possible for a complainant to appeal to the ECHR, initially, s/he should apply through the domestic courts (see above) (website: **www.echr.coe.int**).

International Labour Organisation

The ILO was established in 1919. Now an agency of the United Nations, it is charged with setting universal labour standards. It is a tripartite body composed of representatives of government, employers and workers. Decolonisation has meant that its membership has grown from 52 states in 1946 to 177 in 2003. The 1944 Declaration of Philadelphia redefined the ILO's objectives and reaffirmed the key principles on which the ILO is based, in particular that:

- Labour is not a commodity.
- Freedom of expression and association are essential to sustained progress.
- Poverty anywhere constitutes a danger to prosperity everywhere.

ILO standards are set by the International Labour Conference in the form of Conventions and Recommendations. If a state ratifies a convention, it undertakes to ensure that its domestic law conforms to the convention's standards. Recommendations do not create legal obligations. Any dispute relating to ratified conventions can be referred to the International Court of Justice in the Hague.

The effectiveness of the ILO and of labour standards has been widely criticised (Hepple 2005: 66). In particular, it lacks effective sanctions against states that believe that downscaling labour standards is necessary to remain competitive and attract investment. The implementation of ratified standards is also decidedly uneven. In response to this, since 1997, the ILO has focused on 'core' standards. These include those relating to freedom of association and collective bargaining; forced labour; non-discrimination; child labour and minimum age in employment. Difficulties remain in translating these principles into practice (website: **www.ilo.org/global**).

What is the role of statutory agencies?

Advisory Conciliation and Arbitration Service

Established initially in 1974, ACAS became a statutory body in 1975. It is an independent service, charged with the general duty 'to promote the improvement of industrial relations, in particular, by exercising its functions in relation to the settlement of trade disputes' (TULRCA 1992, ss 209–14). It is governed by a Council, comprising a full-time chairperson; three members appointed after consultation with the Confederation of British Industry (CBI) and other specified employers' organisation; three after consultation with the Trades Union Congress and other specified employees' organisations; and three appointed by the Secretary of State for Business Enterprise and Regulatory Reform. It is required to publish an annual report (TULRCA, ss 247–53).

Among its functions are the following:

- *Individual conciliation*: to offer conciliation in disputes over individual statutory employment rights between individual employees and their employers or ex-employers (e.g. in unfair dismissal, discrimination claims etc.). A detailed outline of the role of ACAS in unfair dismissal cases is presented in Chapter 8.
- *Collective conciliation*: to offer and provide this in industrial disputes.
- *Arbitration*: to provide facilities for **arbitration** in industrial disputes; and to provide a scheme for arbitration in relation to individual unfair dismissal claims (as an alternative to an employment tribunal hearing).
- *Statutory codes of practice*: to draft **codes of practice** to be approved by Parliament (see earlier). (See Chapter 8 for discussion about the *Code of Practice on Disciplinary and Grievance Procedures*) (website: **www.acas.org.uk**).

Health and Safety Executive

This was established in 2008 arising from a merger of the former Health and Safety Commission and former Health and Safety Executive. It is responsible for taking appropriate steps to secure the health, safety and welfare of people at work and to protect the public generally against dangers to health and safety arising from work activities. It is headed by a governing board of up to eleven members and a chairperson. In formulating its policy it consults on all aspects of health and safety. It publishes an annual report. Its health and safety inspectors advise on health and safety legislation and have powers of enforcement (see Chapter 12) (website: **www.hse.gov.uk**).

Equality and Human Rights Commission

Established in 2007, the Commission took over the work of the Equal Opportunities Commission, the Commission for Racial Equality, and the Disability Rights Commission. Its principal functions are:

- to take legal action: this can be taken on behalf of individuals where legal requirements need to be clarified;
- to initiate formal inquiries into employing organisations;
- to make representations to government on the implementation of discrimination and human rights law;
- to provide advice and information on discrimination and human rights law; and to provide some financial support to external organisations;

- to promote good practice in relation to equal opportunities (website: **www.equalityhumanrights.com**).

Low Pay Commission

Established initially in 1997 as a non-statutory body to report on the introduction of a national minimum wage, the following year it was made a statutory body under the National Minimum Wage Act 1998. It comprises a chairman and eight other members. These generally consist of nominees from employer bodies, trade unions and academics with low pay expertise. The role of the Commission is to carry out tasks specified by the Secretary of State for Business Enterprise and Regulatory Reform. Before making recommendations it is required to consult employers' and workers' organisations. It is also obliged to have regard to 'the effect of this Act on the economy of the United Kingdom as a whole and on competitiveness' (NMWA 1998, s 7) (website: **www.lowpay.gov.uk**).

Information Commissioner

Initially known as the Data Protection Commissioner, the name was changed in 2000. The Commissioner has several principal functions:

- S/he is empowered to take enforcement action against 'data controllers' (i.e. companies and other organisations) which are in breach of the 'data protection principles' (Data Protection Act 1998, Sch 1).
- A 'data subject' (in the employment context, usually a 'worker' used in its widest sense) may complain to the Commissioner that the 'principles' are not being complied with in a particular case. The Commissioner may investigate by initiating an assessment (DPA 1998, s 42).
- S/he is under a statutory duty (DPA 1998, s 51) to promote and disseminate good practice – which includes the preparation of codes of practice.
- S/he must maintain a register of 'data controllers' who are required to notify their data processing.
- S/he may serve an *Enforcement Notice* on a 'data controller' (e.g. an employer). This requires the data controller to stop processing any personal data or any specified personal data, or processing it in a specified manner.
- S/he may serve an *Information Notice* on a 'data controller'. It specifies the information required within a given time period in order to respond to a request for an assessment, or to decide whether the data protection principles have been complied with. Appeal can be made to the Information Tribunal on both Information and Enforcement Notices (DPA 1998, s 48). Further appeal is possible to the High Court in England and Wales, the Court of Session in Scotland, and the High Court in Northern Ireland (website: **www.ico.gov.uk**).

Criminal Records Bureau

This is an executive agency of the Home Office and was established in 2002 (under the Police Act 1997). It provides a disclosure service for organisations in the private, public and voluntary service to inquire about the criminal records of specific individual applicants for employment; and those in employment. There are two checks available in England and Wales:

- *Standard disclosure*: these show current and spent convictions, cautions, reprimands and warnings held on the Police National Computer. They also show whether a person is on a government department list of those unsuitable to work with children or vulnerable adults.

- *Enhanced disclosure*: these are the highest level of check and contain the same information as standard disclosures; but also include other relevant information held by local police forces. This level of disclosure is primarily for positions that involve regularly caring for, training, supervising or being in sole charge of children or vulnerable adults.

In Scotland, there is also a *basic disclosure*. This is issued to individual applicants and provides details of convictions at national level that are not spent under the Rehabilitation of Offenders Act 1974.

Both the standard and enhanced disclosures are issued to the individual and to a registered employer. Organisations wishing to use the CRB checks must comply with its code of practice. The aim of the code is to ensure that the disclosed information is used fairly and that sensitive personal information is handled and stored appropriately and is kept for only as long as necessary. To assist employers, the CRB has also developed a sample policy statement on the recruitment of ex-offenders (website: **www.crb.gov.uk**).

Independent Safeguarding Authority

This authority began work in 2009. It will vet those who apply to work with children or vulnerable adults. It will do this by:

- working with the CRB, which will gather information on those who want to work with vulnerable groups;
- using that information to decide on a case-by-case basis who poses a risk of harm to vulnerable groups;
- storing information about an individual's ISA status for employers and voluntary organisations.

Central Arbitration Committee

Set up in the 1970s, it is an independent tribunal with statutory powers to adjudicate in various employment disputes. Its key functions are:

- to receive applications from trade unions for recognition rights with an employer;
- as appropriate, make a declaration granting recognition;
- receiving employers' applications for derecognition of a trade union;
- receiving complaints about the disclosure of information for collective bargaining purposes;
- to help resolve disputes arising under the Information and Consultation Regulations 2004;
- dealing with claims and complaints regarding the establishment and operation of European Works Councils (website: **www.cac.gov.uk**).

What redress is available for infringements of rights?

It is, of course, pointless enacting employment rights without ensuring adequate redress. In this section we will look at the effectiveness of existing processes.

The effectiveness of redress and remedies

The effectiveness of redress depends upon the effectiveness of complaints procedures and on ease of access for complainants. There are two relevant sets of procedure:

- in-house dispute resolution: i.e. internal grievance and disciplinary handling procedures;
- external complaints procedures: especially through employment tribunals.

Considerable attention by government has focused on these procedures as a way of promoting better, speedier dispute resolution; improving the quality of workplace relations; and reducing public expenditure on tribunals.

In-house procedures. Initially, statutory dispute resolution procedures were enacted in 2004. However, these were rescinded in 2008 as being overly complex and not achieving the original purpose. Currently, the situation is set out in the ACAS *Code of Practice on Disciplinary and Grievance Procedures* (2009) (see also Chapter 8).

Employment tribunals. Originally, tribunals were commended in comparison with the ordinary courts because they were said to offer 'cheapness, accessibility, freedom from technicality, expert knowledge of a particular subject' (Franks 1957). However, over the past 40 years, all these characteristics have been increasingly questioned in various academic studies (Dickens *et al.* 1985; Leonard 1987; Lewis and Clark 1993; Hepple *et al.* 2000). A contemporary evaluation of the tribunal process in providing adequate redress can be considered under the following headings:

- ***Access of complainants.*** This may be limited formally in legislation depending on employment status (i.e. is the person, in law, an 'employee'), and on length of service with the employer.
- ***Duration of procedure.*** This may be slow. However, overall, hearings before an employment tribunal are held in 26 weeks in just under 80 per cent of cases (Tribunals Service Annual Report 2006–07, www.tribunals.gov.uk).
- ***Resources.*** Those available to complainants and to respondent employers invariably differ widely. Many complainants are unrepresented; 51 per cent of applicants and 62 per cent of respondent employers used a lawyer to represent them (Hayward *et al.* 2004: 32, 117). Half of all complainants reported spending longer than 20 hours of their own time on the case. The mean time spent was 42 hours compared with the mean time of 31 hours reported by directors and senior managers. The 2003 survey (Hayward *et al.* 2004: 73) commented further on discrimination cases. These, because they were 'potentially the most complex case type', resulted in 'higher costs of advice and representation, higher personal costs for applicants (e.g. travel, communication and loss of earnings). For employers, such cases resulted in more members of staff being deployed on the case and more overall time spent.'
- ***Technicality.*** Increasingly, this has become the hallmark of the tribunal process. The presence of lawyers has encouraged tribunals to appear more like courts. Indeed, by the mid-1980s, they were described as 'quasi-courts' (Dickens *et al.* 1985). Also, some bodies of employment law together with associated **case law** (for example, equal pay and transfers of undertakings legislation) are particularly complex for lay complainants. Reliance on the expertise of lawyers is almost inevitable.
- ***Stamina.*** Complainants need stamina and resources to enter and remain in the tribunal process. Nearly one-third said that they had experienced stress as a result of their complaint; and 9 per cent reported loss of confidence/self-esteem. Complainants bringing unfair dismissal or discrimination cases were most likely to report stress and greater incidence of loss of confidence/self-esteem (Hayward *et al.* 2004: 162–3). Six per cent reported difficulty in getting re-employed. Again, this was slightly higher at 9 per cent for those in unfair **dismissal** or discrimination cases.
- ***Remedies.*** Where complainants were successful, the **remedies** can frequently be small.
  - *Discrimination law.* The remedies are unlimited compensation; an award for injury to feelings; a declaration; possible reinstatement or re-engagement if dismissal is involved.
  - *Unfair dismissal.* The remedies are limited compensation and possible reinstatement or re-engagement.

- *Employment consequences.* This relatively limited redress must also be seen in the context of the reality of employment after the tribunal complaint. Seventy-eight per cent of applicants were in employment with the overwhelming majority in full-time work; and 9 per cent were unemployed. However, 40 per cent said that their pay was less than that in their previous job (Hayward *et al.* 2004: 168–9). Sixty-nine per cent said that their status was at a higher level or about the same when compared to their previous job. Thirty-one per cent saw their new employment as 'something to do until something better comes along' (Hayward *et al.* 2004: 170). These findings show some marked changes from the 1998 data. There nearly two-thirds of complainants said that they worked for a different employer and almost a quarter were out of work. Of those who changed jobs or became self-employed 45 per cent saw their new job as a 'stop gap'. Half of these complainants reported earning lower pay and just over a third reported higher pay (DTI 2002).

What are the key principles underpinning employment law?

In the previous sections, we have referred to various principles which infuse employment law. Here, we consider them more fully and indicate their relationship to human resource management and employment relations. These underpinning principles can be divided into those that concern the substantive issues of employment relations (i.e. the outcomes – the terms and conditions of employment and other decisions); and those that affect the processes by which decisions on terms and conditions and other employment relations matters are made.

- *Substantive issues*:
  - Fairness
  - Reasonableness
  - Equal treatment
  - Harmonisation.
- *Procedural issues*:
  - **Natural justice**
  - **Consultation**
  - Consent
  - Freedom.

Substantive issues

In recent years, two overarching and interconnected policy perspectives have become increasingly influential: *ethical standards* and *human rights*. They are used as benchmarks to assess the treatment of employees and behaviour in society at large. Concern about business ethics not only covers the treatment of British employees but also extends to corporate behaviour in international supply chains which may be founded, in part, on child labour and exploitative conditions. Third World charities have expressed strong concern about this; and, indeed, Oxfam has published a code of practice to encourage employers to address the issue and take steps to establish a more ethical supply chain.

The issue of human rights is likely, over time, to become more firmly entrenched in employment practice with the incorporation of the European Convention on Human Rights 1950 into British law under the Human Rights Act 1998 (see earlier discussion; and Exhibits 1.1 and 1.2 above).

Fairness

In defining fairness, people are invariably subjective (considering the concept in relation to their own personal values). Also, they tend to define it relatively or comparatively (e.g. this is fair and that is not). When asked why they say something is fair or unfair, the tendency is quickly to move away from the abstract and explore details and practical elements of what constitutes fairness.

For example, at the heart of the debate on a statutory minimum wage is the notion of a fair wage. The idea of such a wage is long-standing. The Catholic Church has, historically, referred to a 'just' wage; and the Council of Europe defines and quantifies a 'decency threshold' – an acceptable level of pay. It is the latter that provides a clue to the practical ways in which the concept of fairness is defined. There are social expectations that pay should be sufficient, as a minimum, to enable a person to buy food and provide adequate shelter and appropriate care for both himself/herself and any dependants. Fair treatment, then, is determined against reference points. These are likely to change over time – particularly as social expectations shift.

Reasonableness

Reasonableness is, likewise, an undefined term. It is a long-established concept in law generally. For example, in criminal law there are the concepts of 'reasonable force' in relation to self-defence; and the 'reasonable chastisement' of children. In civil proceedings, the 'reasonable man' test can be used to make value judgements about a person's conduct. The fundamental difficulty with such a test and with the concept of reasonableness is that it is invariably measured against shifting criteria. As social attitudes change, even within 20 or 30 years, the socially accepted notion of reasonable behaviour changes. Also, at any one time, there will probably be differences in attitude between men and women, between older and younger people, and between people from different social and ethnic backgrounds on the standards that they have in mind when assessing reasonableness.

In the employment arena, reasonableness is of particular significance in cases involving unfair dismissal, disability discrimination and health and safety. In the former, tribunals have to satisfy themselves of the reasonableness of an employer's conduct in dismissing an employee for a particular fair reason. (See *Iceland Frozen Foods Ltd* v *Jones* [1982] IRLR 439 in Chapter 8 for more detailed discussion.) In legislation on disability discrimination, employers are required to make reasonable adjustments. Under health and safety legislation, the general duties imposed on an employer must be complied with 'so far as is reasonably practicable' (see, respectively, Chapters 5 and 12 for more details). Implied in the legislative provision of 'reasonableness' is the idea of a balance being struck between various factors: for example, cost, time and trouble involved in aiming to comply with the law.

Equal treatment

Equal treatment as a concept has developed in British employment relations as a result of a number of parallel influences: social movements originating in the United States of America and policy initiatives from the European Union. In the 1960s, in the USA, the women's movement critically questioned the role and status of women in society and the opportunities available. Simultaneously, also in the USA, the civil rights movement challenged endemic racism and asserted social, voting and employment rights. The significance of these movements was felt in Britain and energised groups who sought changes here.

Within the European Community (as the Union was then called), commitment to equal treatment has had an uneven history. The founding Treaty of Rome 1957 refers only to equal pay between men and women – and that as a result of a political compromise. No specific social provisions were included because, initially, the community was conceived primarily as a free-trade area or 'common market'. Pragmatically, a Social Action Programme in the 1970s promoted equal treatment on the grounds of sex and equal pay. By 1989, under the Community Charter of Fundamental Social Rights of Workers, a clear shift had taken place in the importance of social policy. The preamble states that 'the same importance must be attached to the social aspects as to the economic aspects and . . . therefore, they must be developed in a balanced manner'. The social policy objectives of the European Union have, as a consequence moulded much UK legislation on equal treatment (see earlier section in this chapter).

There are two aspects to equal treatment law. First, 'like must be treated alike'. In this a basis of comparison is established. The objective legal test has been defined in a House of Lords judgment on direct sex discrimination in this way: 'would the complainant have received the same treatment but for his/her sex?' (*James* v *Eastleigh Borough Council* [1990] IRLR 288). This is known in shorthand as the 'but for' test. The test is elaborated in the chapters on discrimination law. The second aspect concerns policies and practices which appear neutral in effect but should be scrutinised to see if they create some institutionalised disadvantage for a person on particular grounds (e.g. sex, race, disability, age, etc.). This is referred to, colloquially, as indirect discrimination.

Harmonisation

As an issue in British employment relations, this has developed from the early 1970s in a pragmatic and voluntary way primarily as a result of management–union negotiations. It is an aspect of equal treatment and concerns the establishment of 'single-status' terms and conditions of employment and the removal of the differential status and treatment of manual and non-manual workers (i.e. blue-collar and white-collar) workers. In particular, it resulted in common holidays and working hours and common access to sick pay and pensions. Traditionally, status distinctions had been the norm – with manual workers granted shorter holidays, working longer hours and, invariably, having no access to sick pay or pension schemes.

Under employment law, there has been no explicit differentiation between blue- and white-collar workers. The principal limitations on access have related to the number of hours worked each week and continuity of service with an employer. Although length of service remains for entitlement to some employment rights, the 'hours' threshold has been ruled to be unlawful (*R* v *Secretary of State for Employment* ex parte *Equal Opportunities Commission* [1994] IRLR 176). So, part-time workers have entitlements and, under the Part-time Workers Directive 1997, *pro rata* treatment with full-time workers.

Procedural issues

There are four key underpinning principles that are evident within the processes of employment relations.

Natural justice

This is a long-standing legal concept. There are two key rules:

- that no person may be a judge in their own case;
- that a person must be given a fair opportunity to know the allegation against them, to state their case and to answer the person making the allegation.

In employment relations, these rules have particular importance in disciplinary and dismissal cases. Procedural fairness is as important a consideration for employment tribunals as the other tests (viz. whether the dismissal is for a fair reason and whether the employer behaved reasonably in all the circumstances). The ACAS *Code on Practice on Disciplinary and Grievance Procedures* embodies the principles of natural justice (see Chapter 8).

Consultation

Within employment relations, conflicts of interest are endemic. Employers and their workforces will have different views and expectations about pay levels, job security arrangements, other terms and conditions of employment. There are two processes which can contribute to resolving workplace differences: collective bargaining and consultation. The former involves negotiations with recognised trade unions and results in 'joint regulation' (i.e. terms and conditions agreed between the employer and the recognised union).

Consultation is a weaker form of employee participation in management decision-making. Nevertheless, it is significant because it can arise in any workplace – unionised or not. Also, legislation (for example, the Information and Consultation with Employees Regulations 2004) and case law (for example, *R* v *British Coal Corporation and the Secretary of State for Trade and Industry* ex parte *Price* [1994] IRLR 72) have to some degree, over the past 30 years, enhanced its role. Its growth is, in part a result of the promotion by the European Union of 'social partnership' and the way this concept has been woven into the fabric of employment relations.

In academic literature, distinctions are drawn between 'pseudo consultation' (Pateman 1970) and 'genuine consultation'. The former is essentially information giving by management. There is little, if any, expectation that a management decision or proposal will change as a result of discussion. This form of consultation maintains the 'right to manage'. 'Genuine consultation' can be assessed by various benchmarks. Examples of these can be seen in European law on, for example, collective redundancies and transfers of undertakings. In particular, the indicators of such consultation include:

- the extent to which appropriate information for discussion is disclosed by management;
- the extent to which management representatives listen actively to the views of the workforce and its representatives;
- the depth to which managers genuinely engage in discussion;
- the extent to which managers respond to the comments, views and ideas of the workforce; and
- the willingness of management to amend a policy proposal or change a decision.

It is possible for this form of consultation to develop into what is sometimes characterised as 'integrative consultation'. This can focus on problem-solving or the implementation of substantial changes to the organisation of work and the deployment of staff. Necessarily, it involves detailed discussions about interrelated issues.

Consent

Following from the principle of 'consultation', 'consent' or agreement is an important element in employment procedures. It is central to the law on contract formulation, contract variation and to terms and conditions negotiated with trade unions or other worker representatives (see Chapter 2). It is also important to note that 'managing by consent' is good employment practice because of its contribution to minimising workplace conflict.

Freedom

Traditionally, within employment relations, employers have asserted their commitment to managerial freedom. This has often been encapsulated in the term 'the **right to manage**'. As such, this 'right' has no legal standing. It is, arguably, a moral right deriving from economic ownership. It is an assertion that management should have unfettered freedom and discretion to take whatever decisions are appropriate for the prosperity of the business. Frequently, it is strongly associated with operational issues – particularly the deployment and organisation of resources (including employees). It embraces, for example, a 'right to hire and fire', rights to determine promotion, staffing levels, disciplinary matters, production control, technological change and quality issues.

There are, however, circumstances in which managements have been, and continue to be, willing to limit their freedom to act. In determining pay and conditions, some employers have felt that their interests could be met by agreeing to negotiate with unions. Although such a concession would reduce management's freedom of action, it would be compensated for by the creation of a more orderly system of employment relations based on workforce consent.

The traditional management 'ideology' described here has been substantially challenged and changed in the past 50 years or more. The right to manage has been constrained by various frameworks of legal regulations (particularly those on discrimination and dismissal). Where **collective bargaining** continues to exist, its complete 'freedom' is open to question. Provisions of collective agreements are not isolated from the specifications of employment law. So, no collective agreement can infringe discrimination law. The terms of collective agreements (as well as the terms of contracts of employment) must not provide for terms that are inferior to those prescribed in law.

The extent to which employers have freedom and discretion is variable. It is dependent upon the combined extent to which employment law intervenes and the employer has conceded collective bargaining rights to unions. Storey (1980: 45) describes the right to manage as 'the residue of discretionary powers of decision left to management when the regulative impacts of law and collective agreements have been subtracted'.

Conclusion

The interlocking of legal and voluntary measures remains an important feature of employment regulation. The balance has decisively swung towards significant juridification over the past 30 years or more. Managers are much less likely to determine policies, employment practices and terms and conditions of employment without reference to legal standards. Nevertheless, there are still areas for management to exercise discretion and to determine some of their own standards above the statutory minima. It is unlikely that there will be a return to the high level of 'voluntarism' that existed in Britain until the 1960s. Indeed, evidence of future legislative developments suggests that voluntarism within a legal framework will continue to be the norm.

Further reading

Recent annual reports of:

- Advisory Conciliation and Arbitration Service
- Equality and Human Rights Commission
- Health and Safety Executive
- Employment Tribunals Service
- Low Pay Commission.

Key websites for developments in employment and discrimination law:

- Department for Business Enterprise and Regulatory Reform: **www.berr.gov.uk**
- Equality and Human Rights Commission: **www.equalityhumanrights.com**
- European Union: **www.europa.eu**
- Advisory Conciliation and Arbitration Service: **www.acas.org.uk**
- Chartered Institute of Personnel and Development: **www.cipd.co.uk**
- Confederation of British Industry: **www.cbi.org.uk**
- Trades Union Congress: **www.tuc.org.uk**

References

ACAS (2009) *Code of Practice on Disciplinary and Grievance Procedures*.

Davies, P. and Freedland, M. (1983) *Labour and the Law.* London: Stevens.

Deakin, S. and Morris, G. (2005) *Labour Law*. Oxford: Hart.

Department of Trade and Industry (2002) *Findings from the Survey of Employment Tribunal Applications 1998*, Employment Relations Research Series, No. 13. London: Department of Trade and Industry (see www.berr.gov.uk/publications).

Dickens, L. *et al.* (1985) *Dismissed*. Oxford: Blackwell.

Franks, Lord (1957) *Committee on Administrative Tribunals and Enquiries: Report*, Cmnd 218. London: HMSO.

Hayward, B. *et al.* (2004) *Findings from the Survey of Employment Tribunal Applications 2003*, Employment Relations Research Series, No. 33. London: Department of Trade and Industry (see www.berr.gov.uk/publications).

Hepple, B. (2005) *Labour Laws and Global Trade*. Oxford: Hart.

Hepple, B. *et al.* (2000) *Equality: a New Framework: Report of the Independent Review of the Enforcement of UK Anti-discrimination Legislation*. Oxford: Hart.

Kahn-Freund, O. (1954) 'Legal Framework', in Flanders, A. and Clegg, H. (eds) *The System of Industrial Relations in Great Britain*. Oxford: Blackwell.

Leonard, A. (1987) *Judging Equality*. London: The Cobden Trust.

Lewis, R. and Clark, J. (1993) *Employment Rights, Industrial Tribunals and Arbitration: the Case for Alternative Dispute Resolution*. London: Institute of Employment Rights.

Morris, H., Willey, B. and Sachdev, S. (2002) *Managing in a Business Context: an HR Approach*. London: Prentice Hall.

Pateman, C. (1970) *Participation and Democratic Theory*. Cambridge: Cambridge University Press.

Storey, J. (1980) *The Challenge to Management Control*. London: Business Books.

Tribunal Service Annual Report 2006–07 (www.tribunals.gov.uk)

2 Regulating the employment relationship

Learning objectives

To understand:

- Different forms of employment status
- The definition of the contract of employment
- The sources of the contract
- How contracts of employment can be varied
- The significance of breach of contract
- The remedies available for breach of contract

Structure of the chapter

- *Introduction*: the character of the employment relationship and its legal regulation
- *The context*: the concepts of 'work' and 'employment'; psychological contract; diversity of employment
- *The legal framework*: contracts for the regulation of work; employment status; the characteristics of the contract of employment; express and implied terms; references; whistleblowing; sources of the employment contract; the statement of initial employment particulars; terminating a contract of employment; subsistence of the contract; protection of 'atypical' workers

Introduction

The employment relationship

This is an exchange relationship: the exchange of work for payment. It is often known as the 'work–wage' bargain. The parties are an individual **worker** and an employing organisation. Because it is voluntarily entered into, it is different from other relationships under which work is performed – e.g. slavery, serfdom, conscription.

It is also characterised as a power relationship. The two parties – the employer and the employee – are often spoken of as if they are of equal status. However, the economic reality of employment shows that, in practice, there is, usually, no equality. In discussing the employment contract, Wedderburn (1986) described the situation this way: 'The individual employer is from the outset an aggregate of resources, already a collective power in social terms . . . In reality, save in exceptional circumstances, the individual worker brings no equality of bargaining power to the labour market and to this transaction central to his life whereby the employer buys his labour'.

Means of regulating the employment relationship

The employment relationship is not a 'free for all'. It is regulated. Four formal instruments may be used:

- the **contract** of employment with an individual;
- other contracts under which work is undertaken personally;
- **statute law** and **statutory instruments** together with **case law**;
- collective agreements with trade unions (or other workforce representatives).

All these 'instruments' produce sets of 'rules' which govern the employment relationship. The first three clearly have force of law and breaches can, as appropriate, be taken to employment tribunals and courts. The fourth set, in origin, is the result of a voluntary decision by an employer to negotiate directly with a trade union or, alternatively, to accept the provisions of a collective agreement negotiated elsewhere. Whilst collective agreements are, invariably, voluntary agreements and are presumed to be so (Trade Union and Labour Relations Consolidation Act 1992, s 179), they can and do have legal force in respect of **terms** and conditions of employment. The provisions of collective agreements, relating to pay, hours, holidays, etc. are, as appropriate, '**incorporated**' in law into an individual's contract of employment. So, in practice, all four formal instruments have legal force.

Within this chapter we will examine, in particular, the contract of employment with an individual; and other contracts under which work is undertaken personally. Throughout the textbook the various pieces of legislation will be considered; and, as appropriate, reference will be made to the ways in which collective agreements assist in the regulation of the employment relationship.

Context

In recent years, several developments have had an impact on the employment relationship and consequently on contractual issues. These are of fundamental significance because they force a reappraisal of various traditional models and practices. We will consider:

- concepts of work and employment;
- the psychological contract;
- the growing diversity of employment status.

Concepts of work and employment

In the post-war period, 'employment' has been the predominant model through which work has been carried out. Essentially, it involves a long-term arrangement between an individual and organisation with work provided on a continuing basis – day in day out, week in week out, even year in and year out. Traditionally, in employment, a 'job for life' was presumed. Contractual benefits and entitlements were often service-related – based on seniority and continuous service. For individuals, a job, in these terms, was and remains, a very valuable asset.

This model is essentially based on male employment patterns. This gender-based perspective is important in considering the issues raised in this chapter and elsewhere in the textbook. Linda Dickens (1992: 5) has commented:

> A key to women's disadvantage in the labour market . . . is that structures of employment, although apparently neutral, are in fact moulded around the life patterns and domestic obligations of men. Our systems of labour law and social security have similarly taken the male as the neutral standard of the worker to the disadvantage of women who, in not conforming to the male life and work pattern, fall outside various protections. The adoption of the male as the normal standard is revealed immediately we consider the label 'atypical' employee . . . the 'typical' employee is the male; the 'atypical' employee female.

This traditional model has been subject to considerable buffeting in the past 40 years as a result, principally, of three related factors: employers' need for both greater flexibility in resource utilisation; their drive for greater efficiency and cost-effectiveness; and the challenges, in particular, of the law on sex discrimination. The changes initiated by employers from the early 1980s have been explored by academic writers in such theoretical models as 'the flexible firm' (Atkinson 1984), and the 'shamrock organisation' (Handy 1991).

Handy argues that we should reconsider out attitude to work as a wider activity and 'stop talking and thinking about employees and employment'. His reason is that 'if work were defined as activity, some of which is paid for, then everyone is a worker, for nearly all their natural life'. He proposes a portfolio of five categories of work – the balance of which will constantly alter as people grow older:

1. *Wage or salaried work*: where individuals are paid for the time given. This represents the traditional employment model – whether a person's contract is full-time, part-time or temporary.
2. *Fee work*: where money is paid for results delivered. Its incidence increases as jobs move outside organisations.
3. *Home-work* (or '*domestic work*' to prevent confusion with the concept of 'homeworking'): this includes all tasks taking place in the home – cooking, cleaning, caring for children and

other relatives, maintaining and improving the home. This area of work is particularly susceptible to the use of other providers – depending on a person's economic circumstances.

4 *Gift work*: this is done for free outside the home for relatives, friends, neighbours, charities, local groups and as a public service. This unpaid work is particularly significant for the growing range of charitable organisations providing personal services to those who are ill or disabled.
5 *Study work*: this involves education or training designed to improve skills and increase knowledge. In an employment culture which increasingly emphasises training and development, continuous improvement and life-long learning, then, this work is of great value to both individuals and organisations.

This 'portfolio' concept of work clearly challenges the social convention that paid employment is the only appropriate definition both of people's contribution to society and of their status. So, if we were to adopt a different perspective, the domestic work, primarily undertaken by women would be recognised. The concept of 'unemployment' would be redefined. The notion of 'retirement', traditionally seen as disengagement from paid employment, would be reappraised. Furthermore, we might also acknowledge the financial contribution to society as a whole of uncosted and unpaid 'domestic' and 'gift' work.

The psychological contract

This concept was initially outlined by Schein (1988) and has since been elaborated. Essentially, it is about the expectations and assumptions that the parties bring to an employment relationship. These are likely to be moulded by previous employment experiences; by the process of socialisation in the family and the education system; by a person's values; and by economic imperatives involving the need, for example, for income and an appropriate living standard.

One author (Mant 1995: 48), summarising the nature of this contract states that:

> within that implicit contract are embedded three kinds of individual expectations and needs:
>
> - The need for equity and justice – that employees will be treated fairly and honestly and that information and explanation about changes will always be provided.
> - The desire for security and relative certainty – that employees can expect, in return for their loyalty, that they need not be fearful, uncertain or helpless (as they contemplate who might be the next to go).
> - The need for fulfilment, satisfaction and progression – that employees can trust the value that the organisation places on their current contributions and prior successes and relationships.

The achievement of 'deals' under the psychological contract is highly problematic. For the employee, it depends on several factors. First, there is the extent to which the employer is serious about what is on offer; and through employment practices and the employment contract, aims to deliver on these 'offers'. Secondly, the psychological contract can shift over time – possibly rapidly. Whether or not this is the case, there is the question of feasibly reconciling the expectations of employee and employer. Mismatches can be sources of conflict, demotivation and disaffection. Thirdly, in terms of successful delivery of the psychological contract, much will probably depend on organisational size and the grades of staff concerned. So, larger organisations with developed human resource management policies may be more successful.

Table 2.1 Labour market structure

Total in employment		*Number of employees*		*Number of self-employed*		*Other groups (unpaid family work and training programmes)*	
29.5 million		25.4 million		3.8 million		234,000	
Full-time 22.0 m	Part-time 7.5 m	FT 19.0 m	PT 6.4 m	FT 2.9 m	PT 908,000	n/a –	n/a –
Male 16.0 m	Female 13.5 m	M 13.0 m	F 12.4 m	M 2.8 m	F 1.0 m	M 111,000	F 123,000

Source: Labour Force Survey (February–April 2008) (www.statistics.gov.uk).

The growing diversity of employment status

The labour market has been characterised, historically, as comprising two broad categories of working people: 'standard' and 'non-standard' (or 'atypical' or 'marginal') workers. The first category comprises those who are, usually, employed on full-time, open-ended contracts and who may expect long continuous service. This remains the largest group in the labour market (see Table 2.1). The second group consists of a wide diversity of employment status. As a group it has been growing in the past 20 years or so. These working people can be characterised as, for example, part-time, temporary, freelance, agency, casual and zero hours workers and homeworkers (see Exhibit 2.1). Burchell *et al.* (1999: 64) have commented that although the overwhelming majority of working people (estimated at 80 per cent) are either 'employees' or 'dependent workers' and 7 per cent are clearly independently self-employed, 12 per cent 'had a status that was still unclear'. This situation is still broadly the case today as can be seen from the later discussion of case law. The social policy reasons for clarifying this area are strong.

Exhibit 2.1 'Standard' and 'atypical' forms of employment

Full-time workers. This has long been regarded as the typical or 'standard' form of employment. Most work on open-ended contracts; although some may be on fixed-term contracts. This group represents around 75 per cent of the labour force.

Part-time workers. These are usually defined as those who work less than the scheduled full-time hours in a specific organisation. In survey data, average working hours is 15 per week. There are around 7.5 million in this group – around 85 per cent of whom are female. By sector, two-thirds of part-time jobs are in 'public administration, education and health' and 'distribution, hotels and restaurants'. Some part-time employment is structured on a job-share basis. Also, the incidence of 'double jobbing' is continuing to grow with 1.1 million workers having a second job (for, on average, nine hours per week). Traditionally, many of the terms and conditions of employment under which part-time workers have worked have been inferior in comparison with full-time workers; although, in some organisations the **pro rata** principle was established.

Temporary workers. Temporary jobs can take a variety of forms. They can be for a defined time period (days, weeks or years); or they may be for the completion of a specific task. They include many of the other forms of 'atypical' employment indicated here: seasonal work, casual work, zero-hours contracts, non-permanent jobs obtained through a temporary employment agency ('agency temps'). Temporary workers comprise 7 per cent of all employees. The UK has the third lowest proportion of temporary workers in the EU. Half of temporary workers are female. By sector, 10 per cent of employees in the public sector are temporary (particularly in public administration, education and health care), compared with 6 per cent in the private sector. By occupation, the greatest concentrations of temporary employees are in professional occupations. The reasons most commonly cited by employers for recruiting temporary workers are: providing cover for absent permanent staff (e.g. on maternity leave); to cope with seasonal workload fluctuations; to staff short-term projects; and to acquire people with specialist skills which are only needed on a short-term basis or which are only available on a non-permanent basis.

Agency workers. There are two categories of 'agencies' (Employment Agencies Act 1973):

- *employment agencies* introduce working people to be employed by or to establish a business relationship with the client themselves; and
- *employment businesses* supply their staff to a client to work on a temporary basis under the control of the hirer. They are usually paid by the agency.

Overall, the total numbers of agency workers is small. However, in certain sectors and occupations, their incidence is significant (i.e. clerical and secretarial work, personal and protective services, and plant and machine operatives). There is also a growth in 'banks' of professional agency workers (e.g. nurses, further education lecturers and supply schoolteachers).

Zero-hours contract working. This has been defined as an arrangement 'where the worker was not guaranteed any work at all but in some way was required to be available as and when the employer needed that person' (Cave 1997). In such arrangements the worker has the right to refuse work. This is not a new form of working. It has, however, grown in importance as a result of variable customer demand, changing technology and managerial strategies to be more cost effective. In 1998, the government reported some 200,000 such workers (DTI 1998). In Cave's study, 22 per cent of employers used zero-hours contracts. It was also reported that women are more likely to be employed on such contracts, and that in 91 per cent of organisations, zero-hours contract workers did not have the same benefits as other employees.

Self-employed workers. There are 3.8 million self-reported self-employed persons in the UK – three-quarters of whom are male. This category has grown fitfully since the early 1980s – depending on economic circumstances. This term can and does encompass people who may be in certain other categories of 'atypical working' (e.g. temporary working, homeworking/teleworking).

Homeworking. Homeworking is a long-established feature of certain parts of manufacturing industry. It involves routine tasks carried out at home, invariably for low pay. National surveys of homeworking suggest that there are around 700,000 such workers (Social Trends 31). Over 70 per cent of homeworkers are women; and they are more likely to have dependant children than women in the workforce generally. Overwhelmingly, these workers undertake clerical and secretarial work; and craft and related work. Teleworking is a 'high tech' variant of this traditional model.

Teleworking. This is a growing 'high tech' variant of homeworking – accounting for 8 per cent of the workforce. In 2005, around 2.5 million people worked mainly from home using both a telephone and a computer to carry out their work. An important difference from the traditional model of homeworking is that home is a base and homeworking as such may constitute only part of their working life – the other parts being on the employer's premises or 'on the road'. This was the case for 1.8 million teleworkers. In fact, only, 600,000 worked mainly in their own home. Most (62 per cent) are self-employed (Ruiz and Walling 2005: 417); and two-thirds are men (Hotopp 2002).

The legal issues of employment status and the employment protection conferred upon these various categories of working people are outlined later in this chapter.

Source: unless otherwise stated, data drawn from *Labour Force Surveys* (www.statistics.gov.uk).

Recent interest in these more flexible forms of employment status derives from employers' drives for greater operational flexibility and cutting unit labour costs (Atkinson 1984). However, their use is not new. These forms have a long history in the labour market where they have, traditionally, been regarded as marginal or 'atypical' forms of working. Despite the growth of more flexible forms of working, it is, also, important to note that 'the shift away from permanent and full-time jobs to temporary, short-term or part-time work is exaggerated' (Taylor 2002).

The legal framework

In this section, we will consider three broad legal issues:

- employment status: 'employees', 'workers' and 'independent contractors' and the common law tests, mutuality of obligation, personal service, continuity of work;
- the characteristics of the contract of employment;
- employment protection for 'atypical' workers.

Employment status

In law, three broad terms are used to describe working people: employee, worker and independent contractor (i.e. self-employed). It has become increasingly important to appreciate the distinctions between these three categories. This arises because of access to statutory rights and also for determining the nature of contractual arrangements under which a person works. Statute law draws a distinction but to a very limited extent. Much of the guidance is set out in case law as will be seen below. Indeed it is admitted by government that 'the definitions of "employee" and "worker" in legislation are not sufficiently clear and "user-friendly"' (DTI 2002: 7).

The starting point for considering the distinctions between these categories must be the principal employment statute, the Employment Rights Act 1996. This states:

> In this Act 'worker' (except in the phrases 'shop worker' and 'betting worker') means an individual who has entered into or works under (or, where the employment has ceased, worked under) –
>
> (a) a contract of employment, or
>
> (b) any other contract whether express or implied and (if it is express) whether oral or in writing, whereby the individual undertakes to do or perform personally any work or services for another party to the contract whose status is not by virtue of the contract that of a client or customer of any profession or business undertaking carried on by the individual.
>
> (ERA 1996, s 230(3)).

This definition is, however, insufficient to distinguish effectively between the facts and circumstances of individual working people. Consequently, case law is necessary in order to determine whether a person is either an employee, a worker or an independent contractor. In Table 2.2 an attempt is made to distinguish the different aspects of the employment status of each category. The terminology used in the table is then discussed below.

Table 2.2 Determining employment status

Employee (i.e. a worker with a contract of employment)	*Worker (who is not an employee)*	*Independent contractor (genuinely self-employed)*
People in this category are sometimes described as having an 'employment relationship'	People in this category are sometimes described as having an 'employment relationship'	Usually described as 'in business on their own account'
Common law tests: Multiple, control, integration, economic reality Compliance with these is necessary	**Common law tests:** How many of these does the person comply with?	**Common law tests:** Usually, there is little or no evidence of compliance with these tests. However, there might be an issue about control Economic independence
Mutuality of obligation: Extent that this exists in relation to both current and the future performance of work Must be an 'irreducible minimum' of mutuality	**Mutuality of obligation:** To what extent (if any) does this exist? If no mutuality, person cannot be an 'employee' and could be a 'worker on a contract to work personally' (ERA 1996, s 230)	**Mutuality of obligation:** There will be no evidence of mutuality of obligation in respect of a particular employer. An independent contractor may 'pick and choose' the work undertaken
Personal service: Is there evidence of this? Is 'substitution' permitted – if so, on what terms? Is substitution 'unfettered'?	**Personal service:** Is there evidence of this? Is 'substitution' permitted – if so, on what terms? Is it 'unfettered'?	**Personal service:** Personal service is not necessary and work may be subcontracted
Duration of work: Is the work continuous or intermittent? If intermittent, is there a 'global contract' covering all work engagements?	**Duration of work:** Is the work continuous or intermittent? If intermittent, is there a 'global contract' covering all work engagements?	**Duration of work:** Generally, such work is for a fixed time period or until the completion of a task
Contract: A 'contract of employment' will exist if the person satisfies the common law tests and evidence of mutuality of obligation	**Contract:** A person thought to be a 'worker' (on some 'other contract' to work personally) may be an 'employee' if the common law tests and mutuality of obligation are satisfied. However, if they are only partially satisfied, then, s/he may be such a worker	**Contract:** No employment contract will exist. It will be a contract for services – a commercial contract
Remuneration: An employee will receive wages and is entitled to claim for non-payment and unauthorised deductions. Likely to be deduction of tax under PAYE and national insurance	**Remuneration:** A 'worker' (who is not an employee) is likely to receive wages and is entitled to claim for non-payment and unauthorised deductions. May be deductions of tax under PAYE and national insurance	**Remuneration:** Payment is likely to be a fee. Likely to make own arrangements for tax and national insurance
In determining a person's employment status against these tests and criteria, courts and tribunals look at the facts and circumstances of the individual case. They do not just accept the label that is given to a particular individual's employment relationship by the employer. This may be inaccurate. Determining employment status involves a mixture of law and fact.		

Common law tests

These tests have been developed by the judges over many decades. In particular, they help distinguish whether a person is an employee or self-employed – i.e. in business on his/her own account. They are as follows:

- *The control test.* This concerns the degree of control exercised by the employer. This long-standing test was at one time considered conclusive of 'employee' status. However, it is now regarded by the courts as one of the factors to be taken into account. The nature of control has, in practice changed for various reasons. For example, as a result of human resource policies of 'empowerment', and the need to recruit skilled and professional staff who can exercise discretion and can work with some degree of autonomy. Courts and tribunals recognise that control may nowadays be more a question of the employer retaining 'ultimate authority' over the employee in relation to the performance of work. The Court of Appeal has indicated that the test considers 'who lays down what is to be done, the way in which it is to be done, the means by which it is to be done and the time when it is done' (*Lane* v *Shire Roofing Co (Oxford) Ltd* [1995] IRLR 493). In respect of self-employed people, it has been argued that, according to this test, they have greater autonomy and discretion in respect of the way work is carried out. However, one writer suggests that 'the right of control fails to distinguish employment from self-employment because its presence is entirely consistent with either type of contract' (Brodie 1998: 140).
- *The integration test.* This involves considering the ways in which a person contributes to an organisation and is part of its structure: is the person 'integrated' into the organisation or 'accessory' to it? To what extent does the person contribute to service delivery or the production of goods? So, it focuses on the organisation of work and less on the issue of control or subordination. If integration is established, then a person is likely to be an 'employee'.
- *The economic reality test.* This is closely associated with the integration test and covers the issue of who bears financial risks and, as appropriate, who provides the resources for work to be done (i.e. staff, tools and equipment). It should help provide a clearer answer to the question of whether the individual is 'in business on their own account' – i.e. self-employed. Buchell *et al.* (1999: 6) say, quoting Lord Justice Nolan in *Hall* v *Lorimer* [1994] IRLR 171, that it 'implies a test of economic dependence, in the sense that employee status is the result of "the extent to which the individual is dependent or independent of a particular paymaster for the financial exploitation of his talent"'. Genuine self-employed persons are likely to provide their own tools and be responsible for their own training; and not be integrated into the structure and operation of the employer's organisation. They may hire their own staff and/or make subcontracting arrangement to carry out work. However, in practice, it may not always be possible to identify the genuine self-employed. Some self-employed may have a relationship of economic dependence on an employer. Burchell *et al.* (1999: 12) comment that this category of 'dependent self-employed', 'potentially included freelance workers, sole traders, homeworkers and casual workers of various kinds'.
- *Mutuality of obligation.* This is an essential common law test. Its use by the courts has grown in significance. It was initially laid down in *O'Kelly* v *Trusthouse Forte* [1983] IRLR 369, CA. In determining whether or not a person is an employee and whether or not a contract of employment exists, courts and tribunals will examine the obligations that the person who is working owes to the employer and vice versa. The essential requirement is to establish whether, in an employment relationship, an employer has an obligation to offer work

to an individual and whether he or she has an obligation to undertake the work offered. Normally, in a 'standard' employment relationship, an employer expects to offer work on a regular basis. The employer, also, expects the worker to undertake the work offered. If the worker refuses without good reason, then, disciplinary action may result. However, there are circumstances where this may not arise. For example, an NHS trust may phone a nurse (who is a member of a nurse 'bank') and offer a night shift at a hospital. S/he may refuse (for any reason – however trivial), but the employer will not take any disciplinary action and work may well be offered for the following night. So there are no obligations on either side to offer or perform work. However, there would, normally, be an obligation to undertake any work that has been accepted.

It has been suggested (Deakin and Morris 1998: 164–8) that there may be a second level of mutuality – mutual promises of future performance of the employment relationship. This provides the stability and continuity which is characteristic of the employment relationship of the 'standard' worker. If this second level is missing, then, there is probably no contract of employment.

One difficulty is that the contract may be silent on the issue of mutuality of obligation. The person working may have a long-established relationship with the employer; and the person may have made assumptions that he or she is an employee because of length of service, the degree of economic dependence on the employer for pay and the extent of integration into the organisation – albeit intermittently. The **landmark case**, *Carmichael and Leese* v *National Power plc* [2000] IRLR 43, HL, illustrates this (see Exhibit 2.2).

Exhibit 2.2 No mutuality of obligation

Carmichael and Leese v *National Power plc* [2000] IRLR 43, HL

Ms Leese (together with Ms Carmichael) had been employed since 1989 as a guide at a power station. She was obliged to supervise parties of visitors, explain various activities and answer questions. She also gave talks to schools. She was given training for the post. In her offer letter she was described as working on a 'casual as required' basis. The company did not have to provide work and she could refuse work. She had been unavailable for work on eight occasions.

She worked as a guide for up to 25 hours a week. She was paid, after deduction of tax and national insurance contributions at an employed person's rate. But she was only employed when she worked. There was no sick pay and no pension provision. No notice to terminate the contract was indicated. She was provided with a uniform. She was accountable to the company for the quality of her work. The grievance and disciplinary procedures for regular staff did not apply. There was no written contract of employment nor any contractual information other than that in the offer letter.

The complaint to an employment tribunal was that the company had failed to provide a written statement of initial employment particulars (under ERA 1996, s 1). The company contended that the two women were not 'employees' in law.

The case went through various appeal stages and eventually reached the House of Lords. It ruled that the objective inference from the situation as described was that when work was available the applicants were free to undertake it or not as they chose. It saw the flexibility as suiting both parties. The arrangement was based on mutual convenience and good will and had worked well in practice over the years. But it took the view that, in the circumstances of the case, there was no 'irreducible minimum of mutual obligation necessary to create' a contract of employment.

Genuine self-employed people are, in respect of mutuality of obligation, free to 'pick and choose' the work they do. Where they agree to do work, they need not provide it personally. They may delegate it to another person to undertake it. So, no mutuality exists which points to an employment contract.

- *The multiple test.* The Court of Appeal has stated that any decision on employee status does not involve a mechanical checking off of factors. An overall view must be taken of the facts and circumstances (including whether or not the individual makes his or her own arrangements for tax and social security contributions). This overall view would involve weighing the significance of particular factors; and considering, if appropriate, the intentions of the parties and their behaviour. No factor is seen as sufficient in itself. However, control, the payment of wages and mutuality of obligation are seen as essential (in *Hall (Inspector of Taxes)* v *Lorimer* [1994] IRLR 171).

Personal service and substitution

Most employers expect that both 'employees' and 'workers' will personally undertake the work offered. The implication is that if there is no personal service then certainly the person may be self-employed. However, in case law, there have been specific rulings which suggest that the issue is not clear-cut. The Court of Appeal ruled in *Express & Echo Publications* v *Tanton* [1999] ICR 693, that an 'irreducible minimum' for there being a contract of employment is personal service; and that a provision in a contract allowing the substitution of a 'suitable person' was 'fatal' to him acquiring status as an employee. This approach was also adopted by the EAT in *Staffordshire Sentinel Newspapers Ltd* v *Potter* [2004] IRLR 752. However, in *MacFarlane* v *Glasgow City Council* [2001] IRLR 7, EAT, it was held that a gym instructor whose contract provided that he could select a substitute from a list pre-approved by the gym, did not cease to be an employee because of that provision. A similar approach was adopted in *Byrne Brothers (Formwork) Ltd* v *Baird* [2002] IRLR 96, EAT where the ability to provide a substitute was limited and had to be approved.

Commenting on this situation, Daniel Barnett (web bulletin, 5 May 2004, www.danielbarnett.co.uk) stated that 'the position therefore appears to depend on the extent of the substitution clause. If the worker has an unfettered discretion to appoint a substitute, he cannot be an employee. If he has a heavily fettered discretion or requires the employer's approval, the substitution clause will not prevent him accruing employee status.'

Continuity of service

This is particularly significant in three related respects:

- considering a person's status as an employee;
- access to statutory rights which may be service-related;
- qualifying for employment benefits under a contract of employment (e.g. enhanced holiday entitlements, sick pay, access to 'flexible' benefits).

General statutory provisions

The statutory provisions on continuous employment are defined in the Employment Rights Act 1996 (ss 210–19). Generally, continuity is in relation to one employer (the exceptions are considered below). Also, continuous employment can encompass a number of contracts of employment with that one employer.

To calculate continuous employment, the legal starting point is set out as follows:

> Any week during the whole or part of which an employee's relations with his employer are governed by a contract of employment counts in computing the employee's period of employment.
>
> (ERA 1996 s 212)

The importance of establishing the existence of a contract of employment is signalled by this provision. It is also clear that the number of hours a person works each week is not relevant. There is a statutory presumption in favour of continuous employment, unless the contrary is shown by the employer.

Certain weeks count (under particular rules): where the employee is:

- 'incapable of work in consequence of sickness or injury' (ERA 1996, s 212(3)(a)); or
- 'absent from work wholly or partly because of pregnancy or childbirth' (ERA 1996, s 212(3)(d)).

Temporary cessation of work

In addition, and of significance for certain atypical workers, are those weeks which may count:

- where the employee is 'absent from work on account of a temporary cessation of work' (s 212 (3)(b)); or
- 'absent from work in circumstances such that by arrangement or custom, he is regarded as continuing in the employment of his employer from any purpose' (s 212(3)(c)).

It has been ruled in various cases that 'temporary cessation of work' need not break continuity of employment. No time period is prescribed for the cessation. The cessation is a question of fact: did it or did it not take place? The cessation can be for any reason. The 'work' referred to is the paid work of the individual employee – not the general work of the employer's business.

In the handling of cases involving the temporary cessation of work, two approaches have been used by the courts: the broad-brush approach; and the mathematical approach. Both 'tests' remain available. In the former, the focus is on the whole employment history of the individual employee. This would obviously be done in retrospect and could take account of the expectations and intentions of the parties. The second approach considers the proportions of time spent at work and the times absent because of the temporary cessation (see Exhibit 2.3).

Exhibit 2.3 A 'temporary cessation of work'

Ford v *Warwickshire County Council* [1983] IRLR 126, HL

This case involved a succession of fixed-term contracts for a further education lecturer (long before the enactment of the Fixed-term Employees Regulations 2002). Ms Ford had a series of eleven-month contracts (covering September–July inclusive) over a nine-year period. She was not required to work in August. The issue came before the courts because she wished to claim unfair dismissal and there was uncertainty about whether she had the necessary qualifying length of continuous service: was it 11 months or nine years?

Using the mathematical approach to the advantage of the complainant, Diplock LJ ruled that the interval when there was no work should be 'characterised as short relative to the combined duration of the two fixed-term contracts. Whether it can be so characterised is a question of fact and degree.' Of course, it is possible that this approach might lead to pedantic arguments about what is meant by 'short duration'. So, the broad-brush approach may have much to commend it.

Absent by arrangement or custom

This provision can cover secondments, special leave of absence, working-time scheduling such as job-share or limited hours. This arrangement must be in place when the absence begins and should not be an afterthought.

Service with more than one employer?

It was mentioned earlier that continuous employment is normally with one employer. However, there are circumstances in which the acquired service might be preserved if the employee's employer changes:

- Where there is the transfer of an undertaking (as specified in the Transfer of Undertakings (Protection of Employment) Regulations 2006).
- Where one corporate body replaced another as employer under **Act of Parliament.**
- Where the employer dies and the employee is then re-employed by the personal representatives or trustees of the deceased.
- Where there is a change in the partners, personal representatives or trustees who employ the individual.
- Where the individual is taken into the employment of an 'associated employer'.

This final circumstance can create difficulties. Control is the central issue. For the purposes of the Employment Rights Act 1996,

> any two employers shall be treated as associated if – (a) one is a company of which the other (directly or indirectly) has control, or (b) both are companies of which a third person (directly or indirectly) has control. (s 213)

A finding of 'control' can be difficult. There are technical ways of establishing it through majority shareholding. Some cases have explored the channels of influence exerted on corporate policy. The presence of these can be particularly important for employment relations issues. Although there is no authoritative guidance on this issue, there is clearly statutory authority for courts and tribunals to inquire into organisational decision-making structures.

The characteristics of the contract of employment

From the preceding discussion, it is evident that there are three types of contract in employment relations:

- contracts of employment (sometimes referred to as contacts of service);
- 'other contracts' to perform work personally;
- contracts for services (with independent contractors).

Those performing work under these different contracts is set out in Table 2.2. Our focus in this section will be on the predominant form of contract – the contract of employment.

A flawed instrument

The contract of employment is the starting point for so many issues: workplace grievances; disciplinary action and dismissal; and complaints to employment tribunals. However, although it is so fundamentally important, it is still a flawed instrument.

First, as mentioned above, it regulates an asymmetrical employment relationship which is characterised by a power imbalance under which an employee can be vulnerable to employer action. Secondly, many aspects of the contract can reinforce employer power. It provides a means of direction and control of the employee and, consequently, has been described as 'a command under the guise of an agreement' (Kahn-Freund 1983: 18). Thirdly, when it is formulated and agreed, a legal fiction is adopted that the contract is 'freely arrived at'. Technically, this is so. No employee is forced to enter a contract of employment. However, in reality, few job applicants or employees have influence over the terms of their contract. Force of economic circumstances means that most people 'take it or leave it'.

Fourthly, there are still echoes of the old 'master and servant' relationship in the way that the contract of employment is perceived. This submissive relationship which governed employment law during the nineteenth century has gradually been replaced by the, theoretically, more egalitarian contractual relationship. However, occasionally, judges in their rulings reflect this old-fashioned perspective based on status. Finally, the contract of employment has limitations as far as the adoption of universal minimum standards is concerned. Statute law is often seen as necessary to ensure universal fair treatment. For example, the Equal Pay Act 1970 (s 1) deems that 'an equality clause' shall be included in contracts of employment if one is not provided for 'directly or by reference to a collective agreement or otherwise'. Effectively, this means that no term of a contract of employment can be discriminatory on grounds of sex. It will be void if it is. The need for anti-discrimination law has been commented on by academic lawyers. 'The common law with its emphasis on freedom of contract, sees nothing inherently wrong with discrimination . . . as long as no pre-existing contract or property right is infringed' (Deakin and Morris 1998: 543). Through statute law, then, Parliament is eroding 'contractual autonomy'.

Defining the contract of employment

It is a promise or an agreement made by an employer and an individual employee following an employer's offer of work. It is freely arrived at by the parties that make it. No one compels them to agree. It is legally enforceable in the courts and is intended to be so. It is usually of indefinite duration. It involves 'consideration' – i.e. something of value – usually pay, with which the employer obtains the promise of the employee to be ready, willing and able to undertake the agreed work. It may be in writing, verbally agreed or part verbal and part in writing. It need not be signed.

Key elements in this definition are examined in more detail below:

- *Offer*. An offer to the individual employee of work to be provided by the employer. This offer may be conditional on, for example, the receipt of acceptable references; medical and/or Criminal Records Bureau checks; and work permits being provided. (See also the guidance from the Information Commissioner: Employment Practices Data Protection Code, Part 1.) An employer can withdraw an offer before the prospective employee has accepted it. There can, however, be difficulties of timing. When does the job applicant know of the withdrawal? Has s/he given notice to terminate existing employment?
- *Agreement*. It is an agreement between an employer and an employee that the employee will be ready, willing and able to undertake work that is offered. If the offer of work was conditional, then, the contract is binding once the conditions have been fulfilled. If the offer of employment has been accepted (but the prospective employee has not yet started work)

and the employer withdraws the offer, then, there can be a breach of contract. Usually, this can be dealt with by a payment in lieu of notice. If the prospective employee changes their mind about the job, it is unlikely that an employer would sue for breach of contract because it would be difficult for the employer to quantify the loss (see 'Express terms' below).

- *'Consideration'*. This legal term describes something of value with which the contract is 'sealed'. Usually, it is the pay given by the employer for the employee to be 'ready, willing and able' to undertake the work required.
- *Parties to the contract.* The term *employer* is, generally, fairly clear – although there can be occasional difficulties defining who the employer is in large conglomerate organisations where there may be associated companies. Also, as far as certain agency workers are concerned, defining their employer can pose some problems. The term *employee* is even more problematic as we have discussed above.
- *Legally enforceable.* The agreement is legally enforceable in the courts and at tribunals and is intended by the parties to be so. As a consequence, claims in the tribunals and courts can be made concerning allegations of breach of contract.
- *Freely arrived at.* Importantly, the agreement is freely arrived at – i.e. no one compels an employee to agree to enter a contract of employment on particular terms. Only exceptionally, is an employee able to influence the terms.
- *Verbal and/or in writing.* Such contracts may be verbal or in writing or part verbal or part in writing. The reality, for most employees, is that they will not receive a legally drafted document. They are more likely to receive a statement of initial employment particulars (as required under s 1, Employment Rights Act 1996) (see Exhibit 2.4). This outlines the employer's statement of the essential terms and conditions of employment. In addition to this, there will be other terms of the contract (see 'Sources of contractual terms' below) – some of which may be in writing.
- *Duration.* A contract of employment can be for any period of time. So, it may be for a fixed-term; or may be open-ended. The latter is the most common. It is sometimes described as a 'permanent' contract. Effectively, the contract exists until such time as one of the parties brings it to an end – either by resignation by the employee or dismissal by the employer.

Exhibit 2.4 Contractual information (required under Employment Rights Act 1996, s 1)

Information to be given to an employee within eight weeks of starting employment. If there is no information under any headings this should be stated. Even if the person leaves before the eight weeks, they are entitled to receive the information.

- Names of the employer and the employee.*
- Date employment began.*
- Date when continuous employment began (may include previous employment with that employer, or the consequences of a business transfer, or of transfers between companies within a group).*
- Scale or rate of remuneration; or method of calculating remuneration.*
- Intervals at which remuneration is paid (weekly, monthly or some other interval).*
- Hours of work and normal working hours.*
- Holiday entitlement, public holidays and holiday pay. (The particulars given being sufficient to enable the employee's entitlement including any entitlement to accrued holiday pay on the termination of employment to be precisely calculated.)*
- Job title or brief job description.*
- Place or places of work where the employee is required or permitted to work.*

- Terms relating to sickness, injury and sick pay.†
- Pensions and pension schemes.†
- Notice periods to terminate the contract – by both the employer and the employee.
- If employment is temporary, how long it is to last; or termination date of the fixed-term contract.
- Any collective agreement affecting terms and conditions of employment (including, where the employer is not a party to the agreement, the names of the employers and the unions by whom they were made).
- Where the employee is required to work outside the United Kingdom for a period of more than a month:
  - the period for which s/he is to work outside the UK;
  - the currency in which s/he will be paid;
  - any additional remuneration payable; and any benefits to be provided whilst outside the UK;
  - any terms and conditions relating to return to the UK.
- A note (which can refer to a reasonably accessible document) specifying:
  - any disciplinary rules applicable to the employee;
  - disciplinary procedure relating to the employee;
  - an indication of a person 'to whom the employee can apply if dissatisfied with any disciplinary decision relating to him' (s 3(1)(b)(i)) including dismissal;
  - an indication of a person 'to whom the employee can apply for the purpose of seeking redress for any grievance relating to his employment and the manner in which any such application should be made' (s 3(1)(b)(ii));
  - appeal steps should also be indicated.

* This information shall be 'included in a single document' (s 2(4)).
† For these particulars, the employee may be referred to 'some other document which is reasonably accessible' (s 2(3)).

Sources of contractual terms

There are two broad categories of terms: *express* and *implied*.

Express terms

These usually originate from management decisions and collective agreements. They set out explicitly certain terms under which an employee is to work. For example, in addition to pay and working time arrangements, an employer may want an employee to accept a mobility clause; or a restrictive covenant; or some commitment to confidentiality. Other examples, concerned with the specific circumstances of the employer's business, can include the circumstances in which an employer can physically search an employee and his/her property; dress codes; and testing for substance abuse.

Garden leave in the absence of an express term was considered by the High Court (*SG&R Valuation Service Co LLC* v *Boudrais and Others* [2008] IRLR 770). In the circumstances of the case, it was ruled that the employer was entitled to place the complainants on garden leave because of their misconduct. However, the case demonstrates the clear advantage of having an appropriate express term in contracts.

A slightly unusual example of where an express term can be valuable to an employer is a 'no show' clause. Normally, if a job applicant changes his/her mind, having accepted an offer of employment, it is unusual for an employer to take any action. However, the High Court ruled in a case involving a City of London investment firm where there was a 'no show' clause in the contract. It found that the employer was entitled to recover £293,000 from the employee (*Tullett Prebon Group Ltd* v *El-Hajjali* [2008] EWHC 1924).

Implied terms

These generally, derive from common law (the historic decisions of judges) or from specific statute law. Terms might be implied by judges for one of several reasons:

- for reasons of 'business efficacy' (i.e. where a term is necessary to make the contract work);
- where, on the facts, such a term is so obvious (even though it is not provided as an express term;
- on the basis of custom and practice (see below);
- to give effect to a statutory requirement;
- to meet changing circumstances.

Both express and implied terms will be explored in more detail in the discussion below.

Activity 2.1 **Your contract of employment**

Find out all the detailed terms of your own contract of employment. What are the sources? Which terms are in writing and which are verbal? Answer these questions as you read the following section.

There are several sources of a contract of employment.

Management decisions on terms and conditions of employment

An employer's ability to determine the terms and conditions under which a person works has, traditionally, been quite wide. However, there are two constraints that affect these decisions:

- the requirements of employment and discrimination law;
- any collective agreements with recognised trade unions.

So, for example, an employer may determine the pay to be offered to an individual. However, it is necessary to ensure that such a salary is compliant with the law on equal pay and, also, set at or above the rates of the national minimum wage. Furthermore, if there is a collective agreement in place, then, the offer may need to be appropriate in relation to an agreed grading structure. However, it is important to remember that the constraints on employers are, in some respects, not as strict as they appear at first sight. Even under law, they have areas of discretion. So, for example, they can ask staff to agree to opt-out from the 48-hour maximum working week; certain terms, which may be regarded as indirectly discriminatory under discrimination law, can be 'objectively justified'; adjustments under disability law must be 'reasonable'; and requests by parents and carers to work flexibly can be refused for specified 'business reasons'.

Collective agreements between an employer and recognised trade unions

Collective agreements can be an important factor in determining and influencing an individual employee's terms and conditions of employment. An employer who, for example, has agreed to negotiate with a union the terms and conditions of employment for particular grades of staff will apply the relevant provisions of the collective agreement to staff in that grade – irrespective of whether they are union members or not.

In law, the terms of the collective agreement that are relevant to an individual employee will then be 'incorporated' into that person's contract of employment. So, their pay, working time, holidays, shift pay, overtime rates, sick pay etc. will derive from the collective agreement.

There are three important aspects that need to be borne in mind:

- The role of the union when contractual changes are made. (This is considered in Chapter 3 under the issue of contract variation.)
- What happens when a collective agreement is rescinded by the employer? In brief, the relevant terms of a collective agreement can 'live on' in the individual employee's contract of employment. In the 1980s, British Gas unilaterally terminated an incentive bonus scheme which had been voluntarily agreed with a union. The company was entitled to give notice to terminate this collective agreement – which it did. However, the terms of the agreement had been incorporated into individual contracts. Lord Justice Kerr, in the Court of Appeal hearing, said: 'the terms (of a collective agreement) are in this case incorporated into the individual contracts of employment and it is only if and when those terms are varied collectively by agreement that the individual contract of employment will also be varied. If the collective agreement is not varied by agreement but by some unilateral abrogation or withdrawal or **unilateral variation** to which the other side does not agree, then, it seems to me that the individual contract of employment remains unaffected' (*Robertson and Jackson* v *British Gas Corporation* [1983] IRLR 202).
- The effect on a collective agreement of a business transfer. (This is considered in Chapter 3 in the discussion on the Transfer of Undertakings (Protection of Employment) Regulations 2006).

Workplace rules

The law on these is so varied that it is impossible to provide anything but broad guidelines. The rules are likely to be in an employee's contract if the employee signs them or if they are posted on notices in the workplace. But, even if they are signed, the rules may not become contractual but merely be lawful and reasonable instructions on how a job is to be carried out. The differences between a contractual rule and a lawful instruction can be described as follows:

- *Rules* can only be changed with the employee's consent. By 'working to rule' an employee is merely carrying out the contract.
- *Instructions* can be changed by the employer without consultation or agreement. By disobeying any instructions which are lawful and reasonable an employee is breaking the contract.

Custom and practice

In any workplace, there are ways of working and, in some cases, terms and conditions which are not written down and have evolved over a period of time. A critical issue can be whether or not these customary ways have become contractual. To be binding, the courts have determined that **custom and practice** must meet three conditions:

- It must be widely known and almost universally observed by the relevant employees in that workplace.
- It must be reasonable.
- It must be so certain that the individual employee can know exactly the effect that the custom has on him/her.

The implication of terms into contracts of employment can be difficult. In *Cook and Others* v *Diageo* (2005) EATS/007/04, the issue of whether an employer's policy on local holidays had achieved the status of a contractual term was considered. The EAT, drawing on the approach in previous case law (*Solectron Scotland Ltd* v *Roper* [2004] IRLR 4, EAT) ruled that a custom or established practice regularly applied may become the source of an implied contractual term only when 'the courts are able to infer . . . that the parties must be taken to have accepted that the practice has crystallised into contractual rights'.

Statute law

This affects the terms of contracts of employment in a number of particular ways:

- *Statutory imposition.* This is a direct intervention by legislation into the contract of employment. The principal example is the Equal Pay Act 1970 s 1 which deems that an equality clause shall exist in all contracts of employment.
- *General obligations.* These are designed to influence the way employers behave in the employment relationship. They cover, for example, the provisions of discrimination law and health and safety law.
- *Minimum conditions.* These must be met by employers (e.g. in respect of notice to terminate employment; paid annual leave; and maternity and paternity leave). An employer may provide, under the individual's contract, conditions better than the minimum but not lower.

Implied terms under common law

The discussion above has focused to a large extent on terms and conditions that are either formally in writing or, if not, at least generally recognised by the parties concerned. Implied terms are one source which many employees may not fully appreciate. Yet, its importance is considerable. It is drawn from case law over a long number of decades where the courts have implied into contracts of employment terms which make them work effectively and clarify the rights and duties of the parties. In some instances, as we shall see below, these implied terms have been modified by provisions of statute law. Certain key implied terms are explored below.

General duties on employers

To pay wages

Failure to pay wages that are agreed and due to the employee is regarded as a fundamental breach of the contract of employment. An employee may resign and claim constructive dismissal if a grievance does not resolve the issue. Also, under statute law (Employment Rights Act 1996, ss 13–27), the employee (irrespective of his/her length of service) may complain to an employment tribunal about the non-payment.

Not to make unauthorised deductions

An employer may only make deductions if there is legal authority to do so. This can be provided by:

- *Act of Parliament*: for example, authorised deduction of income tax, National Insurance contributions and, as appropriate, deduction through Attachment of Earnings Orders ordered by the courts.
- *Contract of employment*: this might provide for deductions to be made in certain specific circumstances. Examples include fines for disciplinary offences; deductions for cash deficiencies and stock shortages permitted, under the Employment Rights Act 1996, in the special circumstances of retail employment (see Chapter 9).
- *Individual agreement*: an employee can give agreement for the deduction of, for example, union subscriptions; or to reimburse the employer for overpayment of wages.

To take reasonable care of the employee

This wide-ranging duty encompasses not just physical care of the employee but also exposure to psychiatric harm in employment. The issues arising under this heading are explored in Chapter 12 on health, safety and welfare. It is also important to note that this implied duty on employers covers the provision of references for ex-employees (see Exhibit 2.5).

Not to breach mutual trust and confidence

This duty concerns the co-operation between the employer and the employee. Arising, over the years, from unfair dismissal cases, it has frequently been stated that an employer should

Exhibit 2.5 References

There is no general duty on an employer to provide a reference. However, it can be expressly stated in a person's contract that a reference will be provided. Where they are provided, they should comply with guidance under case law.

A duty of care is owed to the ex-employee to provide a reference that is true, accurate and fair (*Bartholomew* v *London Borough of Hackney* [1999] IRLR 246, CA). It must not give an unfair or misleading impression when considered in its totality. As a general rule, a reference does not have to provide a full and comprehensive report on all the facts relating to the person in question.

Difficulties may arise in one particular set of circumstances: when an employee resigns under threat of disciplinary action or before that action is complete. Again, case law has asserted that the principle of telling the truth is important. If the ex-employer omits any mention of the disciplinary proceedings, it could be a breach of duty owed to the recipient of the reference. It could make the referee liable for negligent mis-statement. On the other hand, a referee should not make comments about an employee on matters which have not been properly investigated. In terms of natural justice, a proper investigation involves giving the employee a chance to state his/her case. In *Cox* v *Sun Alliance* [2001] IRLR 448, the Court of Appeal found that the referee was negligent in relying on unexplored allegations of dishonest conduct attributed to the ex-employee and the communication of these views to Mr Cox' new employer.

The burden of proof is on the referee to show that the contents were true. The referee's defence might be that s/he 'honestly believed that the contents were true'.

It is also important to note that all strands of discrimination law extend to the 'post employment' situation (see Chapters 5 and 6). For example, the Sex Discrimination Act 1975 (s 20A) covers 'relationships which have come to an end'. It prohibits as unlawful any discrimination or harassment which 'arises out of and is closely connected to the relevant relationship'. Clearly, the provision of references is one of the possible issues which could be discriminatory.

Exhibit 2.6 Implementing a mobility clause

United Bank v *Akhtar* [1989] IRLR 507, EAT

Mr Akhtar worked at the Leeds branch of the bank as a junior clerk. In his contract of employment he had a mobility clause which stated: '*The bank may from time to time require an employee to be transferred temporarily or permanently to any place of business which the bank may have in the UK for which a relocation allowance or other allowance may be payable at the discretion of the bank*'.

On 5 June he was informed that as from 8 June he would be required to transfer to the Birmingham branch. He requested that the transfer be delayed for three months because of his wife's illness and the impending sale of his house. This request was refused. He then asked if he could take 24 days' leave which was due to him, to sort out his affairs. He offered to start work in Birmingham on 10 July. He received no reply to this request. His pay was stopped from 5 June. So he resigned and claimed that he had been constructively dismissed because the employer had fundamentally breached his contract of employment. His claim succeeded.

In the EAT's view, the employer, even if there is an express term in the contract, must behave reasonably in implementing it. Otherwise, the employer's behaviour may be such as to destroy or seriously damage the relationship of 'trust and confidence' between the employer and the employee.

not destroy the 'mutual trust and confidence' on which co-operation is built. This duty has been stated in this way: an employer will not, without reasonable and proper cause, act in a manner calculated or likely to destroy or seriously damage the relationship of confidence and trust between employer and employee (*Courtaulds Northern Textiles Ltd* v *Andrew* [1979] IRLR 84, EAT). Examples of breaches of mutual trust and confidence include the following:

- where an application for transfer had not been dealt with fairly;
- where there was failure to investigate a genuine safety grievance;
- where there was a false accusation of theft on the basis of flimsy evidence;
- where the right to suspend an employee was exercised unreasonably;
- where a mobility clause was not operated reasonably (see Exhibit 2.6).

The EAT has held (*Morrow* v *Safeway Stores plc* [2002] IRLR 9 EAT) that breach of mutual trust and confidence will 'inevitably' be a repudiatory breach of the contract of employment and can result in the employee's resignation and a claim for constructive dismissal (subject to a one year's qualifying length of service).

General duties on employees

To co-operate with their employer

Under case law, this has been construed to mean helping to promote the employer's business interests by working according to the terms of the contract. However, in working to contract, employees must not wilfully disrupt the employer's business.

To obey lawful and reasonable instructions

Any instruction to an employee must be both lawful and reasonable. Lawfulness means that an instruction must not, for example, breach discrimination law; or require an employee to exceed working time restrictions which are applicable to that individual. Reasonableness will be judged in the circumstances. However, factors which might be taken into account would be whether the particular employer is able (in terms of knowledge and skill) to obey the instruction and whether the instruction is consistent with the 'status' of the work s/he is employed to do. (See the discussion on contract variation in Chapter 3 and in particular the case of *Cresswell and Others* v *Board of Inland Revenue* [1984] IRLR 190, HC).

To be trustworthy

This duty is complementary to the employer's duty of mutual trust and confidence. Depending on the employer's business interests, this implied term might be elaborated into express terms setting out clear specific duties on employees as seen in some of the four aspects following:

- ***A general duty to be honest.*** Acts of deception, theft, embezzlement, forgery, etc. are breaches of trust and can lead to instant dismissal. They may also result in criminal proceedings brought by the Crown Prosecution Service in the Crown Court or in magistrates' courts.
- ***Obligation not to compete with the employer.*** This obligation can be enshrined in a restrictive covenant (as an express term in a contract of employment). Such a term restricts the work undertaken by a former employee in three possible ways:
  - *non-competition*: limiting the ex-employee from taking work with a competitor organisation;
  - *non-solicitation*: prohibiting the making of contact with clients and customers of the ex-employer;
  - *non-dealing*: not engaging in business activities with such clients and customers.

  The 'reasonableness' of restrictive covenants is an issue that can be determined by the courts. For example, the High Court ruled that the prohibition of an estate agency on a former employee from working in a specified area for two years was unreasonable and unenforceable. No other firm of estate agents in the area imposed a non-competition covenant for longer than six months. There was no evidence to suggest that the employer's business was so different to justify a longer period (*Barry Allsuch and Co* v *Harris* [2001] Industrial Relations Law Bulletin 680, HC).
- ***Obligation not to disclose confidential information.*** This can bind both current and ex-employees. It is likely that it will be an express term of the contract restricting unauthorised disclosure of information. Breach of the duty of confidentiality is likely to be regarded as gross misconduct resulting in instant dismissal. However, there may be special circumstances in which an employee might believe that unauthorised disclosure is in the public interest (see Whistleblowing below).
- ***Obligation not to benefit from work undertaken for the employer.*** This relates to work covered by legislation on patents, intellectual property right and copyright. Subject to this limitation, an employer cannot prevent a former employee from using the general knowledge and skill that has been acquired in the course of employment.

The duty of fidelity generally ends when the contract ends. However, exceptions can involve the duty not to disclose trade secrets and confidential information. Breaches of trust by an employee are invariably regarded as serious and are likely to lead to dismissal and, in certain circumstances, criminal proceedings.

Duty to take reasonable care

This is supplemented by the provisions of the Health and Safety at Work etc. Act 1974 (s 7) and its associated regulations, which requires that employees should take care of themselves and their fellow-workers and co-operate with the employer and other agencies in complying with health and safety requirements (see also Chapter 12).

Probationary periods

Employers, usually, have a probationary period for new employees. There is no legal requirement covering the length of this. It may, depending on the nature of the post, be reasonable to have a period of any time up to 12 months.

The critical problem for employers is how they deal with the termination of employment of an individual who 'fails' his/her probationary period. The following are factors that need to be taken into account:

- Does the contract of employment offered at the start of employment indicate that it is conditional on satisfactory completion of the probationary period and may be terminated at the end of this period?
- A probationary period for a specific time period does not guarantee employment to that date. The contract might be terminated earlier with due notice from the employer (*Dalgleish* v *Kew House Farm Ltd* [1982] IRLR 251, CA; *Fosca Services (UK) Ltd* v *Birkett* [1996] IRLR 325, EAT).
- Is the employee given notice to terminate at the end of the probationary period? It is uncertain, in law, whether notice needs to be given. So, best practice suggests that it is given or, alternatively, that pay in lieu of notice is provided.
- Any termination of the contract of employment from the start of employment is, potentially, affected by discrimination law. This can result in employment tribunal claims, irrespective of length of service, alleging unfair treatment. An employer, therefore, needs to be clear on the reasons for dismissing after a probationary period. These reasons should relate to those for fair dismissal among which are 'capability' and 'conduct' (Employment Rights Act 1996).
- Is the employee entitled to use a contractual disciplinary and dismissal procedure? If so, failure to allow a probationer to do so, could be a breach of contract and might lead to a wrongful dismissal claim, which can be made irrespective of length of service.
- Has the employee, during the course of the probationary period, been given appropriate support and advice relating to capability and conduct?
- An employee whose probationary period is longer than 12 months will accrue employment rights (e.g. the right to claim unfair dismissal).

Whistleblowing

There may be circumstances when an employee believes that it is 'in the public interest' to disclose information and so, potentially, breach a contractual duty of confidentiality (see Exhibit 2.7).

Exhibit 2.7 A whistleblower

ALM Medical Services Ltd v *Bladon* [2002] IRLR 807, CA

Complainant. Bryan Bladon had 20 years' experience as a nurse. In June 1999 he joined ALM at one of its private nursing homes. From mid-August to September 1999, when the matron was on sick leave, he temporarily 'acted up'.

His concerns. On 19 August he phoned Mr Sinclair, PA to the Managing Director, Dr Matta. He was concerned about some matters relating to the management of the home and the welfare and care of patients. These included poor drug records, staffing levels, patient neglect and a wound to a resident. He was asked to put his concerns in writing which he did by fax. (This was a 'protected disclosure'.) Sinclair said he would deal with the issue on his return from holiday. By 31 August, Bladon saw further deterioration in patient care. He decided to take further action and phoned the Social Services Inspectorate (SSI) (although this was not a 'prescribed person').

The inspection. On 1 September, an inspection was carried out by the SSI and an inspector from the health authority's nursing home inspectorate. On 8 September, the inspectors wrote to Dr Matta saying that four of the six concerns raised by Bladon were 'substantiated in whole or in part'. These should be investigated and addressed by the company.

Disciplinary action. On 9 September, Bladon was summoned to a disciplinary hearing without prior warning about what was to be discussed. He was given a written warning on 10 September by Matta. It was claimed in the letter that Bladon's own alleged lack of professional care was partly responsible for problems; and that they were motivated by poor relations he had with colleagues. He was denied any internal right of appeal.

Dismissal. On 16 September Bladon was summarily dismissed. It was said that in carrying out his professional duties, he fell below the standards expected of him.

ET complaint. Bladon complained that he had been subject to a **detriment** (the written disciplinary warning), and unfairly dismissed because he had made 'protected disclosures'.

Tribunal's consideration. It was appropriate for Bladon to raise his concerns with Sinclair. Bladon had a 'reasonable belief' that the information disclosed was covered by the 'qualifying disclosure' provisions. The disclosure was made in good faith because of his concern about his professional responsibilities and, in particular, about patient welfare. His disclosure to the inspectorate was reasonable since this was the appropriate body. It was reasonable for Bladon to raise the issue with the inspectors and not await Sinclair's return. Furthermore, in the absence of a whistleblowing policy and of any indication that the company would investigate his concerns, it was reasonable for him to go to the inspectorate. The tribunal accepted the employer (in particular, Dr Matta) had 'acted in a demeaning, insensitive, unprofessional, unreasonable and arrogant way' that left Bladon feeling 'belittled, professionally slurred, isolated and unable to respond in an effective way'. The employer had 'manufactured' or 'fabricated' a disciplinary situation; failed to follow its own procedures; and made no attempt to investigate Bladon's concerns. The ET only permitted evidence from the Managing Director and not from three other ALM witnesses.

Tribunal's decision. It ruled that Bladon was subject to a detriment (both the written warning and the refusal of a right of appeal); and that he was dismissed unfairly.

Financial award. Bladon was awarded £5,500 compensation for net losses to the date of the hearing; £7,500 for future losses; and £10,000 aggravated **damages** (taking account also of injury to feelings) for the detrimental treatment. Total compensation: £23,000.

Court of Appeal. This ruled that ALM was entitled to call evidence, particularly on the issue of 'protected disclosures'. This evidence was also relevant to the reasonable belief and good faith of Mr Bladon. It allowed the company's appeal and remitted the case for a tribunal rehearing.

Legislation was enacted in 1998 on public interest disclosures. This is now in Employment Rights Act 1996, Part IVA. It is designed to protect workers who make certain disclosures from both detrimental treatment and unfair dismissal by their employer. The legislation defines 'qualifying disclosures' and 'protected disclosures'.

Qualifying disclosure

This is a disclosure of information which a worker reasonably believes tends to show some malpractice – whether this is currently happening, has happened or is likely to happen in the future. Specifically, the legislation refers to:

- a criminal offence;
- the breach of a legal obligation;
- a miscarriage of justice;
- a danger to the health and safety of any individual;
- damage to the environment;
- deliberate covering up of information tending to show any of the above matters.

It does not matter that after investigation the worker's belief is found to be mistaken. However, the worker must show that, at the time of the disclosure, it was reasonable to hold the particular belief; that the information and allegation was substantially true; and that the worker acted in good faith and did not act for personal gain. (Disclosures in breach of the Official Secrets Act 1989 are excluded).

Protected disclosure

A qualifying disclosure will be a protected disclosure where it is made either directly to the employer or through internal procedures authorised by the employer; and also if it is made to a legal adviser in the course of obtaining legal advice. Furthermore, disclosure to a person prescribed by the Secretary of State may be 'protected'. 'Prescribed persons' include, as appropriate, the Health and Safety Executive, the Audit Commission for England and Wales, HM Revenue and Customs, the Serious Fraud Office, the Financial Services Agency.

Detrimental treatment

Protection from suffering detriments (in respect of a wide range of statutory rights) is covered by the Employment Rights Act 1996 Part V. Case law originally interpreted the law as covering detriments during employment. However, the Court of Appeal (*Woodward* v *Abbey National plc* [2006] EWCA Civ 822) has ruled, in a whistleblowing case, that an employer was liable for a detriment imposed after the termination of the employment contract. Following an earlier House of Lords ruling (*Rhys-Harper* v *Relaxion Group plc and other appeals* [2003] IRLR 484), Lord Justice Ward stated that 'limiting such protection against victimisation to acts committed during the existence of the employment contract and excluding acts connected with the wider "employment relationship" but committed after termination of the contract was absurd, irrational and arbitrary'. The decision in this case has much wider significance. The rights not to suffer a detriment (in ERA 1996, Part V) cover, among others, health and safety, maternity, paternity, parental and adoption leave, working time and flexible working and employee representatives. The principle established in the *Woodward* case affects all categories. An employer will be liable for post-employment retaliation – for example, refusal to provide a reference. (Similar protection is provided under discrimination law.)

If a worker resigns because of detrimental treatment by the employer and, then, claims constructive dismissal, the cut-off date for calculating compensation is the date of his/her dismissal and not the date at which the employer's conduct first amounted to a repudiation of the contract (*Melia* v *Magna Kansei Ltd* [2006] IRLR 117).

Employment tribunal applications

The public interest disclosure legislation covers a wide group of 'workers'. Complaints alleging unfair dismissal or detrimental treatment may be made to an employment tribunal irrespective of length of service or age. The tribunal will consider:

- the identity of the person to whom the disclosure was made (e.g. an appropriate professional body);
- the seriousness of the relevant failure;
- whether the relevant failure is continuing or is likely to occur again;
- whether the disclosure breaches the employer's duty of confidentiality to others (e.g. clients);
- what action has been taken (or might reasonably be expected to have been taken) if a disclosure was made previously to the employer or a prescribed person;
- whether the worker complied with any internal procedures approved by the employer if a disclosure was made previously to the employer.

Breach of contract

A contract of employment can be breached by either the employer or by the employee.

- *By employee.* If the employee breaches his/her contract, the employer will usually initiate disciplinary action (see Chapter 8). Depending on whether the breach is regarded as either minor or persistent minor misconduct or as gross misconduct, the employer will either dismiss the employee or impose a disciplinary penalty short of dismissal (some form of warning).
- *By employer.* Breach of contract by an employer may be minor or fundamental. A minor breach is likely to result in some form of grievance which may be resolved through the relevant grievance procedure. A fundamental breach is much more serious and can have a number of important consequences for the both the employee and the employer.

What is a fundamental or repudiatory breach of contract?

It is behaviour by an employer which is so serious that effectively 'tears up' the contract. Lord Denning, in the Court of Appeal, said 'if the employer is guilty of conduct which is a significant breach going to the root of the contract of employment or which shows that the employer no longer intends to be bound by one or more of the essential terms of the contract, then the employee is entitled to treat himself as discharged from any further performance . . . [T]he conduct must . . . be sufficiently serious to entitle him to leave at once' (*Western Excavating (ECC) Ltd* v *Sharp* [1978] IRLR 27). Examples can include not paying wages that are due, providing hazardous working conditions, failing to tackle harassment or other discriminatory treatment. It is likely that such conduct would be a breach of the implied mutual trust and confidence and also, possibly, a breach of the contractual duty to take reasonable care of the employee.

Usually, it is expected that an employee will initially raise a grievance (see the ACAS *Code of Practice on Disciplinary and Grievance Procedures* 2009). However, the employee must not stay too long after the unacceptable conduct by the employer because s/he might be thought by the tribunal or court to have waived the right to terminate. Of course, in some cases the behaviour may be so unacceptable that the employee might resign immediately without using the grievance procedure.

When an employee terminates the contract of employment in these circumstances, this forced resignation is regarded, in law, as equivalent to a 'dismissal'. The Employment Rights Act (s 95(1)(c)) states that an employee is dismissed by his/her employer if 'the employee terminates the contract under which he is employed (with or without notice) in circumstances in which he is entitled to terminate it without notice by reason of the employer's conduct'. In everyday speech (but not in law) this is known as 'constructive dismissal'.

Termination of a contract of employment

This issue is considered in detail in Chapter 8. Here, it is sufficient to outline briefly those circumstances in which a contract might end.

- *Notice to terminate.* Notice can be given by either the employer or the employee in accordance with the terms of the contract (which should comply with the statutory minimum periods of notice (ERA 1996, s 86)). If the contract is silent, then the employee should use them.
- **Summary dismissal.** This refers to the instant termination of the contract. It can arise where there is gross misconduct by an employee (e.g. violence or theft) and there has been appropriate investigation and a disciplinary hearing.
- *Wrongful dismissal.* This is where the contract is terminated in breach of the contractual terms (e.g. in breach of the implied term of mutual trust and confidence, or where insufficient notice is given to terminate the contract). The restrictions on making unfair dismissal claims do not apply.
- **Constructive dismissal.** This arises in circumstances where an employee resigns because of what is perceived to be a repudiatory breach of the contract of employment by the employer (see above).
- *End of a fixed-term contract.* This refers to those contracts that have a specific termination date.
- *Frustration of contract.* This is a complex area and much will depend on the specific circumstances of the case. It involves termination of the contract as a result of some unforeseen event which makes it difficult for the contract to be carried out. Frustration would cover death, long-term ill-health or imprisonment.

Subsistence of a contract

It is important to remember that there are certain circumstances when a contract of employment can subsist (i.e. it remains in existence but no work is carried out under it). An example of such circumstances arises in respect of maternity and paternity leave (see Chapter 11).

There may be other circumstances where a person is absent from work by agreement with the employer. In all these circumstances, the contract remains in existence and, even if there is no remuneration paid, certain specified terms – express and or implied – are enforceable (e.g. confidentiality, restrictive covenants, mutual trust and confidence).

Employment protection for 'atypical' workers

In Exhibit 2.1 above, various categories of 'atypical' workers were identified. In this section, we will consider the degree of employment protection they have been afforded. Some of these categories will have to establish 'employee' status before they can claim employment rights; whilst other rights are extended to the wide category of 'workers' (see Exhibit 2.8). A significant driver of employment protection for 'atypical' workers has been the European Union as can be seen from the outline and discussion below.

Exhibit 2.8 Access to certain key statutory rights

'Employee' status (i.e. workers who have contracts of employment)

- **Contractual information:** must be provided within eight weeks of employment starting (ERA 1996, s 1).
- **Minimum contractual notice:** (ERA 1996, s 86).
- **Protection against unfair dismissal:**
  - qualified by length of service (ERA 1996, ss 94, 108, 109);
  - restricted right when dismissal relates to industrial action (TULRCA 1992, ss 237–9).
- **Written reasons for dismissal:**
  - one year's continuous service (ERA 1996, s 92);
  - no qualifying service if employee pregnant or on maternity leave.
- **Maternity leave:** an unqualified right (ERA ss 71–8).
- **Shop and betting shop workers: protection in relation to Sunday working:**
  - irrespective of age or length of service (ERA ss 36–43, 45).
- **Right to parental leave:** qualified by length of service.
- **Right to request flexible working** (ERA 1996, ss 80F–80I):
  - qualified by length of service;
  - qualifying conditions re child or dependant.
- **Protection for fixed-term employees against discrimination** (Fixed-term Employees Regulations 2002):
  - irrespective of age or length of service.
- **Transfers of undertakings: dismissal/substantial detrimental change to contracts** (TUPE 2006, reg 4):
  - qualified by length of service.

'Workers' (i.e. those with contracts of employment and those on some 'other contract' to work personally)

- **Protection against sex discrimination:**
  - provisions in SDA 1975 (includes discrimination on the grounds of marital status, pregnancy, maternity, civil partnership and gender reassignment);
  - available 'in relation to employment' (SDA 1975, s 6). 'Employment' is defined as meaning 'employment under a contract of service or of apprenticeship or a contract personally to execute and work or labour and related expressions shall be construed accordingly' (s 82(1));
  - covers 'post employment' (s 20A);
  - an express provision is included in relation to 'contract workers' (s 9) (*BP Chemicals* v *Gillick* [1995] IRLR 128, EAT).

➡

Exhibit 2.8 continued

- **Protection against race discrimination:**
  - available, as sex discrimination law, in relation to 'employment' (RRA 1976, ss 4, 78(1); and
  - covers 'post employment' (s 27A);
  - in relation to contract workers (s 7) (*Harrods Ltd* v *Remik* [1977] IRLR 9, EAT).
- **Protection against disability discrimination:**
  - available in relation to 'employment' (DDA 1995, s 4);
  - covers 'post employment' (s 16A).
- **Protection against sexual orientation discrimination:**
  - available in relation to 'employment' (Employment Equality (Sexual Orientation) Regulations 2003) (reg 6);
  - covers 'post employment' (reg 21).
- **Protection against religion or belief discrimination:**
  - available in relation to 'employment' (Employment Equality (Religion or Belief) Regulations 2003) (reg 6);
  - covers 'post employment' (reg 21).
- **Protection against age discrimination:**
  - available in relation to 'employment' (reg 7);
  - covers 'post employment' (reg 24).
- **Right to equal pay:** this covers 'the ordinary basic minimum wage or salary and any other consideration whether in cash or in kind which the worker receives directly or indirectly in respect of his employment from his employer' (Article 141, Treaty of Rome).
- **Protection from deduction from wages:** available irrespective of length of service (ERA 1996).
- **Working Time Regulations 1998:**
  - provide maximum working week; paid annual leave; various rest entitlements and health requirements;
  - irrespective of length of service and hours worked.
- **Statutory national minimum wage:** various minima for workers of 16 years and above (NMWA 1998).
- **'Whistleblowing' rights:** protects from detrimental treatment and dismissal those who make a protected disclosure (ERA 1996).
- **Protection for part-time workers** against discrimination (Part-time Workers Regulations 2000).
- **Statutory right to be accompanied:**
  - applicable in relation to grievances and disciplinary action (Employment Relations Act 1999, 10);
  - explicitly covers agency workers and homeworkers.

Part-time workers

There have been three broad developments in law which have begun to improve protection and rights for part-time workers:

- *Access to statutory rights.* The European Court of Justice ruled in 1994, in respect of statutory employment rights, that it was indirect sex discrimination for Britain to have differential qualifying rights for access for full-timers and for part-timers to unfair dismissal compensation and redundancy pay.
- *Requirement to work full-time.* Under sex discrimination law, women returning from maternity leave have applied to vary the scheduling and the number of hours they work. The requirement to work full-time may be indirect sex discrimination which has to be objectively justified.
- *Comparable treatment with full-time workers.* The European Union adopted a directive in 1997 implementing a **social partners' Framework Agreement** on Part-time Work. This deals with the contractual rights of part-timers. It concerns any part-timers who have a

contract of employment or are in an employment relationship. Part-timers are workers whose normal hours of work, averaged over a period of up to a year, are less than the normal hours of comparable full-timers.

The directive outlines certain general principles which must be transposed into national law:

- Part-timers may not be treated less favourably than full-timers.
- Member states should in consultation with the social partners work to remove obstacles to part-time work.
- Employers, as far as possible, should make opportunities for part-time work at all levels; and should give consideration to requests from workers for changes from part-time to full-time work and vice versa.
- Refusal to transfer from full-time to part-time work (or vice versa) is not in itself a valid reason for dismissal.

The directive has been partially transposed into UK law through the Part-time Workers (Prevention of Less Favourable Treatment) Regulations 2000 (which were amended in 2002) (see Exhibit 2.9).

Exhibit 2.9 Part-time Workers (Prevention of Less Favourable Treatment) Regulations 2000

Who is a part-time worker? This is defined by exemption – as a person who is not a full-time worker in a particular workplace. Also, the regulations cover 'workers' and not just 'employees'.

Who is the comparator? The part-time worker and the full-time worker comparator are to be employed at the same time, by the same employer, at the same establishment, under the same type of contract, and be engaged in the same or broadly similar work (taking into account, as appropriate, whether they have a similar level of qualification, skills and experience) (reg 2(4)). A comparison can be made with either a full-time worker on a permanent contract; or one on a fixed-term contract.

If there is no comparator at the same establishment, a person who works at a different establishment of that employer can be chosen. It is *not* possible to have a hypothetical comparator.

The principle of equal treatment. In respect of the terms of the contract, a part-timer has the right not to be treated by the employer less favourably than a full-time worker is treated. This right applies only if the less favourable treatment 'is on the ground that the worker is a part-time worker' and that the discriminatory treatment is 'not justified on objective grounds'. To test whether there has been less favourable treatment, the *pro rata* principle shall apply unless it is 'inappropriate' (reg 5(3)).

The regulations also prohibit a part-timer being subject to any '**detriment** by any act, or deliberate failure to act, of the employer' (e.g. denial of promotion opportunities) (reg 5(1)).

Objective justification. Discriminatory treatment can only be justified if it can be shown that the less favourable treatment is necessary to achieve a legitimate objective (e.g. a genuine business objective) and is an appropriate way of achieving that objective.

Rate of pay. A part-time worker must not receive a lower basic rate of pay than a comparable full-time worker. This protection also covers special rates of pay (e.g. bonuses, shift allowances and unsocial hours and weekend payments).

Overtime. Under current case law, part-timers do not have an automatic right to overtime payments when they work beyond their normal hours. However, once a part-timer exceeds the normal hours of a full-timer, the part-timer has a legal right to the applicable overtime payments (*Stadt Lengerich* v *Helmig* [1995] IRLR 216, ECJ).

➡

Exhibit 2.9 continued

Contractual sick and maternity pay. There must be no less favourable treatment in calculating the rates of pay; the qualifying length of service for the pay; and the length of time for which the payment is received. The benefits must be provided *pro rata* unless the differential treatment is objectively justified.

Other contractual benefits. A part-timer must not be treated less favourably in terms of benefits such as health insurance, company cars, subsidised mortgages and staff discounts.

Conditions of access. There should be no discrimination over access to an occupational health scheme, a profit-sharing scheme or a share option scheme unless it is objectively justified.

Leave entitlements. Part-timers are entitled to statutory leave entitlements. Where an employer provides enhanced arrangements under contractual terms, then, part-timers should have the same entitlements as full-timers – on a *pro rata* basis.

Access to training. Part-time workers should not be excluded from training. Training provision should be at convenient times for the majority of staff including part-timers.

Redundancy. Selection criteria and different treatment of part-timers must be justified on objective grounds.

Conversion to part-time status. This is not a right. It is a matter for the employer to consider requests. A full-time worker who converts by reducing working hours is entitled not to be treated less favourably than they were treated as regards terms and conditions of employment; or being subject to a detriment (reg 3).

Statement of reasons for treatment. A worker who believes s/he has been discriminated against may ask the employer in writing for 'a written statement giving particulars of the reasons for the treatment' (reg 6). If there is a case for objective justification, this should be stated. This statement is admissible at employment tribunal. A tribunal may draw 'any inference that it considers just and equitable, including an inference that the employer has infringed the right in question' if the employer has 'deliberately and without written excuse' not provided such a statement; or considers the statement 'evasive or equivocal' (reg 6(3)).

Unfair dismissal and victimisation. Dismissal or selection for redundancy is automatically unfair if the reason or principal reason concerns the exercise of rights under the regulations. A worker may complain to an employment tribunal; and also in relation to victimisation.

Employment tribunal application. A worker may complain within three months of either the date of the alleged discriminatory action; or the last in a series of discriminatory actions. It is for the employer to identify the ground for the less favourable treatment or detriment (reg 8(6)).

Liability. Reflecting the provisions of other discrimination law, an employer is vicariously liable for the behaviour of managers, supervisors and other workers 'in the course of employment' whether or not the behaviour was with the employer's knowledge and approval (reg 11(1)). An employer's defence is that it 'took such steps as were reasonably practicable' to prevent the discrimination (reg 11(3)).

Remedies. If an employment tribunal finds a complaint to be well-founded, it is required, as it considers 'just and equitable' (reg 8):

- to make a declaration of the rights of the complainant and the employer;
- to order the employer to pay compensation to the worker. A two-year limitation on remedies in relation to an occupational pension was ruled by the House of Lords to be incompatible with European law and was removed in 2002 (*Preston* v *Wolverhampton Healthcare Trust (No. 2)* [2001] ICR 217).
- to recommend that, within a specified period, the employer takes action to deal with the discrimination against the complainant which appears to the tribunal to be reasonable in the circumstances of the case. Failure to comply with the recommendation may result in increased compensation.

Fixed-term contract workers

There are three legal issues involving these workers:

- *Continuity of service*. This is a basic and, in many cases, a vitally important issue for those workers on successive fixed-term contracts. It may be possible to 'stitch together' such contracts to establish continuity of service. In this context, it is also important to consider the significance of temporary cessations of work and the significance of breaks between contracts (see earlier discussion and also *Ford* v *Warwickshire County Council* [1983] IRLR 126, HL).
- *Statutory employment rights*. These accrue to fixed-term contract workers depending on whether they can, under the legal tests discussed earlier, be defined as an 'employee' or as a 'worker' on some other contract to work personally.
- *Comparable treatment with permanent workers*. The European Union adopted the Fixed-term Workers Directive 1999 implementing a social partners' framework agreement. This is to be transposed into the law of member states. The purposes of the framework agreement were stated as follows:
  - to improve the quality of fixed-term work by ensuring the application of the principle of non-discrimination;
  - to establish a framework to prevent abuse arising from the use of successive fixed-term employment contracts or relationships.

  The directive has been partially transposed into UK law through the Fixed-term Employees (Prevention of Less Favourable Treatment) Regulations 2002 (see Exhibit 2.10).

Exhibit 2.10 Fixed-term Employees (Prevention of Less Favourable Treatment) Regulations 2002

Who is covered? The regulations apply to 'employees' (whose status will have to be determined under the common law tests). The directive, however, applies to 'workers'.

The principle of equal treatment. A fixed-term employee should not be treated less favourably, in respect of terms and conditions, than a 'permanent' employee on the grounds of being fixed-term (reg 3). Also, the regulations prohibit the fixed-term employee, because they are fixed-term, being subject to any 'detriment by any act or deliberate failure to act of the employer' (reg 3(1)(b)).

Objective justification. Less favourable treatment may be objectively justified. Justification depends on the circumstances of the case. The regulations provide that discrimination in relation to a particular contractual term will be justified where the fixed-term employee's overall package of terms and conditions is not less favourable than the comparable permanent employee's (reg 4).

Which contracts are covered? A fixed-term contract means a contract of employment which is one of the following (reg 1(2)):

- one which is made for a specific term which is fixed in advance (e.g. three months, a year); or
- one which ends automatically on the completion of a particular task or upon the occurrence or non-occurrence of any specific event. Examples include those contracts covering maternity leave breaks; peak demands for a service or production; or tasks covering defined projects like setting up a database.

Who is the comparator? This is a 'permanent' employee – i.e. someone on an open-ended contract of employment (reg 2). S/he should be employed by the same employer at the same establishment doing the same or broadly similar work. Where relevant the comparator should have similar skills and qualifications to the fixed-term employee. Where there is no comparator in the same establishment, then a comparison can be made with a similar permanent employee working for the same employer in a different establishment.

Exhibit 2.10 continued

Successive fixed-term contracts. The use of successive fixed-term contracts is limited to four years, unless further fixed-term contracts can be justified on objective grounds. It is possible for employers and employees to increase or decrease this period through a collective agreement or, in non-union organisations, through a workforce agreement (reg 8 and Sch 1).

There is no limit on the duration of the *first* fixed-term contract. However, if this contract is of four years or more and is renewed, it will be treated from then as 'permanent' unless the use of a fixed-term contract is objectively justified.

Furthermore, if a fixed-term contract is renewed after the four-year period, it will be treated as a contract for an indefinite period unless the use of a fixed-term contract is objectively justified. A fixed-term employee has the right to ask the employer for a written statement confirming that their contract is permanent or setting out objective reasons for the use of a fixed-term contract beyond the four-year period. The employer must provide this statement within 21 days (reg 8).

Written statement of reasons. A fixed-term employee has a right to ask their employer for a written statement setting out the reasons for the discriminatory treatment that they believe has occurred. The employer must provide this within 21 days of the request (reg 5). The statement is admissible in employment tribunal proceedings. A tribunal may draw 'any inference that it considers just and equitable, including an inference that the employer has infringed the right in question' (reg 5(3)) if the employer has 'deliberately and without written excuse' not provided such a statement or considers that 'the written statement is evasive or equivocal'.

Redundancy waiver. If included in a fixed-term contract agreed, extended or renewed after 1 October 2002 it will be invalid.

Protection against unfair dismissal and victimisation. Dismissal or selection for redundancy is automatically unfair if the reason or principal reason concerns the exercise of rights under the regulations. An employee may complain to an employment tribunal irrespective of age or length of service. Similar protection is provided against victimisation (reg 6).

Termination of a fixed-term contract. From 1 October 2002, the end of a 'task' contract that expires when a specific task has been completed or a specific event does or does not happen will be a dismissal in law. Likewise, the non-renewal of a fixed-term contract concluded for a specific period of time will be a dismissal. Employees of one year or more have the right to a written statement of reasons for dismissal and the right not to be unfairly dismissed. If the contract lasts for two years or more and it is not renewed because of redundancy, the employee has the right to statutory redundancy pay.

Application to employment tribunal. A worker may complain to an employment tribunal about less favourable treatment or victimisation (reg 7). The complaint should be made within three months of either the date of the action or of the last in a series of discriminatory actions. Where an employee complains, it is for the employer to identify the ground for the less favourable treatment or detriment (reg 7(6)).

Liability. An employer is vicariously liable for the behaviour of managers, supervisors and other workers 'in the course of employment' whether or not the employer knew or approved the behaviour (reg 12(1)). The defence is that he 'took such steps as were reasonably practicable' to prevent discrimination (reg 12(3)).

Remedies. If an employment tribunal finds a complaint to be well-founded, it is required, as it considers 'just and equitable' (reg 7):

- to make a declaration of the rights of the complainant and the employer;
- to order the employer to pay compensation to the worker which the tribunal considers to be just and equitable;
- to recommend that, within a specified period, the employer takes action to deal with the discrimination against the complainant which appears to the tribunal to be reasonable in the circumstances of the case. Failure to comply with the recommendation may result in increased compensation.

Statutory sick pay. Employees on contract of less than three months are entitled to statutory sick pay from October 2008.

Casual and zero-hours contract workers

The role of casual workers is of growing importance in particular sectors (e.g. as nurses, supply teachers or in hotels and catering). Clearly, they have an employment relationship. However, the question is what kind of relationship? What is the employment status? Is it one that confers statutory rights?

There is no specific statutory framework governing the position of casual workers. Various legal issues have arisen in case law over the past 20 years or so:

- Whether there is explicit 'mutuality of obligation'?
- Whether the person can be defined, under common law tests as an 'employee' in law?
- Whether there is a 'global contract' covering all assignments of work?
- What counts as 'working time'?

'Regular casuals' in catering The case of *O'Kelly* v *Trust House Forte plc* [1983] IRLR 369, CA concerned waiters whose names were on a list to be called first for banqueting functions. They worked only for THF and did so virtually every week for varying hours (from three to 57). They were paid weekly, deductions were made for tax and national insurance and they also received holiday pay. They worked under the control of the head waiter and were provided with uniforms. However, they did not have to agree to work if they did not wish to. Likewise the company was not required to provide work. Refusal could, however, result in removal from the list. The Court of Appeal ruled that there was no mutuality of obligation and so they were not 'employees'.

'Bank' nurses It was ruled by the Court of Appeal in *Clark* v *Oxfordshire Health Authority* [1998] IRLR 125, CA that no contract of employment existed, even if there was a 'global contract' in existence, if there was no mutuality of obligation 'subsisting over the entire duration of the relevant period'.

Long-serving tour guides In the landmark ruling in *Carmichael and Leese* v *National Power plc* [2000] IRLR 43, HL the House of Lords determined that there needed to be an 'irreducible minimum' of mutuality of obligation for a person to be an employee (see Exhibit 2.2 above).

Working Time Regulations 1998 The paramount importance of 'mutuality of obligation' deprives many long-serving working people of statutory employment rights (viz. on unfair dismissal, redundancy pay, parental rights, the provision of contractual information). However, such workers are likely to have some rights and entitlements in respect of the Working Time Regulations 1998. These regulations provide an entitlement to a maximum working week and to paid annual leave (on, if appropriate, a *pro rata* basis). Furthermore, case law from the European Court of Justice has defined 'working time' for working people who are 'on call' (*SIMAP* v *Consellaria de Sanidad y Consumo de la Generalidad Valenciana* [2000] IRLR 845; *Landeshauptstadt Kiel* v *Jaegar* [2003] IRLR 804) (see Chapter 10).

National Minimum Wage Act 1998 This legislation can also provide entitlements for certain casual and zero hours contract workers. Again, the issue tested in the courts was what constituted the eligible 'working time' of a nightwatchman who was allowed, during his shift, to sleep on duty. The EAT ruled that where a worker was required to be on the employer's premises to carry out his duties over a specific number of hours, then, all the hours were eligible for the national minimum wage (*Wright* v *Scottbridge Construction* [2001] IRLR 589) (see Chapter 9).

Homeworking

The status of homeworkers can be problematic. Each case has to be considered on its own facts and circumstances to determine whether or not there is compliance with the common law tests and, therefore, 'employee' status. The issues that can arise in cases are:

- the fact that the work is undertaken in premises not under the control of the employing organisation;
- the provision, probably by the employer, of equipment and materials to be used;
- whether there is mutuality of obligation;
- whether the work is continuous or intermittent;
- whether there is a global contract in existence governing the employment relationship.

Two notable cases have arisen in this area:

- *Airfix Footwear* v *Cope* [1978] IRLR 396, EAT. This concerned Mrs Cope who worked at home making shoe heels. The company provided her with tools and issued instructions and, over a seven-year period, she generally worked a five-day week. There was close supervision of her work. She was paid on a piecework basis without deductions for tax and national insurance. She was held by the EAT to be an employee.
- *Nethermere (St Neots) Ltd* v *Gardiner & Taverna* [1984] IRLR 240, CA. In this, homeworkers worked for a company for three years for between five and seven hours a day sewing children's clothes. In some weeks, there was no work, and Ms Taverna usually took off 12 weeks each year. Subject to a minimum set by the company, the workers could specify the amount of work they wanted to be supplied with. The Court of Appeal found that contracts of employment existed. It stated that well-founded expectations of continuing homework consisting of the regular giving and taking of work for periods of a year or more could crystallise into an enforceable contract of employment spanning weeks in which no work was done and preserving continuity. So, the length of the relationship and the regularity of dealings between the homeworker and the employer were sufficient to establish an 'irreducible minimum of obligation'.

Agency workers

There are a number of uncertainties about the position of agency workers in employment law. Their degree of employment protection is, in a number of cases, not clearly established. This situation is complicated by the existence of a triangular relationship between the agency, the worker and the 'end user' or client organisation. The legal issues that have arisen in the past 10 years have concerned case law in Britain, the EU proposals for a new directive, the British government's policy initiatives for 'vulnerable' workers and in political concerns about the behaviour of gangmasters in their treatment of migrant agency workers. The key legal issues are considered as follows:

- the employment relationship of an agency worker;
- determining the status of an agency worker;
- the employment obligations to the worker;
- the employment relationship with the 'end user';
- the EU principles of equal treatment for agency workers;
- the specific employment protection for migrant agency workers.

The employment relationship of an agency worker

Agencies must comply with the Employment Agencies Act 1973 and the Conduct of Employment Agencies and Employment Businesses Regulations 2003. There are two categories of organisation: the employment agency and the employment business. (Although, it is fair to say that the term agency is used to encompass all organisations which provide staff.) The 'agency' provides introductions to a hiring organisation for whom the worker will work on either an open-ended or fixed-term contract. In such a case the hirer will be the employer. The 'employment business', however, will place staff on a temporary basis with a client. The contractual relationship is with the employment business (or 'temp agency' as these are commonly known).

Determining the status of an agency worker

This issue is left to the courts to consider on the facts of each individual case using the common law tests. In *McMeechan* v *Secretary of State for Employment* [1997] IRLR 353, the Court of Appeal considered whether, following the insolvency of the agency, the worker was entitled to a payment from the National Insurance Fund as an 'employee'. The Court of Appeal weighed the various facts in the case which point to or away from an employment relationship. Among the evidence was a document signed by McMeechan which stated that he would provide his services as a 'self-employed worker and not under a contract of service'. However, there was also evidence that the agency had power of dismissal for misconduct and the right to end assignments. It had the right to make deductions from an hourly rate of pay for poor performance or bad time-keeping. His pay was subject to deduction of tax and National Insurance contributions. Furthermore, the agency provided a grievance procedure and McMeechan owed a duty of fidelity and confidentiality. The Court of Appeal found that there was an employment relationship with the agency but only for the purposes of the specific engagement.

The employment obligations to the worker

Where a worker has an employment relationship with the agency, it must provide a written statement of employment particulars and an indication of whether the person is employed on a contract of employment or a contract for services (i.e. as an independent contractor). Subject to whatever qualifications exist in law, agency workers are eligible for the national minimum wage, entitlements under the Working Time Regulations and statutory sick pay. Apart from in the entertainment and modelling sectors, the agency worker should not be charged by the agency for finding work.

Whilst the employment contract might be with the agency, the 'end user' has a number of legal obligations to the worker – particularly under discrimination law and health and safety legislation.

The employment relationship with the 'end user'

In the past 10 years, there have been instances of some agency workers being placed with a client organisation and, for various reasons, remaining with that 'end user' for a prolonged period of time. As a consequence, the courts have dealt with a number of cases to consider how the nature of the contractual relationship has evolved over time between the agency worker and the 'end user'.

Initially, in the triangular relationship, the contractual relationships are likely to be as follows:

- *Agency worker and agency* – a contract of employment (i.e. the worker is an 'employee'), or a contract for services (i.e. the worker is self-employed).
- *Agency and client organisation or 'end user'* – a commercial contract to provide staff as specified.
- *Agency worker and client organisation or 'end user'* – whilst there are legal obligations governing the conduct of both and the performance of the worker, there is no contract of employment between these two parties. The agency is the employer.

In recent years, several complaints to employment tribunals by agency workers who had worked for long periods of time with 'end users' resulted in rulings by the Court of Appeal to determine the issue of employment status and contractual obligation in these triangular relationships (*Dacas* v *Brook Street Bureau (UK) Ltd* [2004] IRLR 358, CA; *Cable & Wireless plc* v *Muscat* [2006] IRLR 354, CA; *James* v *London Borough of Greenwich* [2008] IRLR 302, CA). In the first of these cases, the possibility of an implied contract of employment evolving over time with the 'end user' was raised (see Exhibit 2.11). This ruling was subsequently elaborated

Exhibit 2.11 The *Dacas* case

Dacas v *Brook Street Bureau (UK) Ltd* [2004] IRLR 358, CA

Facts. Mrs Dacas was a cleaner working for the London Borough of Wandsworth. She was not employed directly by the Council. She was engaged through Brook Street Bureau as a'temp'. She worked for Wandsworth for four years when the Council finished with her services.

Complaint. Unfair dismissal. Two potential employers were involved: Brook Street Bureau and the London Borough of Wandsworth. However, on appeal, the complaint was only made in relation to the Bureau.

Court of Appeal's ruling. It held that Brook Street Bureau was not her employer within the meaning of the Employment Rights Act 1996. Lord Justice Mummery giving the leading judgment stated that the mere fact that the contract recorded that Mrs Dacas was not the employee of either Brook Street or Wandsworth could not be determinative. Tribunals should always investigate whether an implied contract of employment has arisen between the worker and the 'end user'. He stated:

> . . . the fact and degree of control over the work done by Mrs Dacas at West Drive is crucial. The Council in fact exercised the relevant control over her work and over her. As for mutuality of obligation, (a) the Council was under an obligation to pay for the work that she did for it and she received payment in respect of such work from Brook Street; and (b) Mrs Dacas, whilst at West Drive, was under an obligation to do what she was told and to attend punctually at stated times. As for dismissal, it was the Council which was entitled to take and in fact took the initiative in bringing to an end work done by her at West Drive. But for the Council's action, she would have continued to work there as previously. It is true that the obligations and the power to dismiss were not contained in an express contract between her and the Council. The fact that the obligations were contained in express contracts made between Mrs Dacas and Brook Street Bureau and between the agency and the Council does not prevent them from being read across the triangular arrangements into an implied contract and taking effect as implied obligations as between Mrs Dacas and the Council.

in *James* v *London Borough of Greenwich* [2008] IRLR 302. In this case, it was stated that the implication of a contract should only be done on the grounds of 'necessity'.

The key issues arising from the *James* case are:

- *'Necessity' and 'business reality'*. Where there is no express contract between an agency worker and the 'end user', the first question for the purposes of determining employment status is whether or not it is necessary, according to established common law principles, to imply a contract between these parties to give the situation business reality.
- *The implication of a contract with the 'end user'*. On the facts, the relationship between the agency worker and the end user was fully explained by express contracts between the agency and the worker and between the agency and the 'end user'; and the arrangements were not a sham. In these circumstances, it was not necessary to imply a third contract between the worker and the 'end user'. 'The mere passage of time did not justify the implication of a contract between the worker and the end user as a matter of necessity'.
- *The contractual situation*. As there was no express or implied contract between the worker and the 'end user', it followed that she could not be an employee of the 'end user'.

The view of many commentators is that the emphasis on 'necessity' in the *James* case will now make it more difficult for agency workers on long-term placements to establish an employment relationship with the 'end user'.

EU principles of equal treatment for agency workers

Discussions within the institutions of the European Union have been taking place since the late 1990s to agree the Temporary (Agency) Workers Directive. This would be a companion piece of legislation to the directives governing part-time workers and fixed-term contract workers (see above). In May 2008, the British government announced that an agreement had been reached between the Confederation of British Industry and the Trades Union Congress on the treatment of temporary agency workers after 12 weeks' employment. This agreement might overcome an obstacle to European-wide agreement and implementation of the draft directive.

The directive has the following key provisions:

- *Coverage*. It applies to 'workers with a contract of employment or employment relationship with a temporary agency who are posted to undertakings to work temporarily under their supervision'. (Article 1)
- *The purpose of the directive* is:
  - 'to ensure the protection of temporary workers and to improve the quality of temporary work by ensuring that the principle of non-discrimination is applied to temporary workers and recognising temporary agencies as employers';
  - 'to establish a suitable framework for the use of temporary work to contribute to creating jobs and the smooth functioning of the labour market'. (Article 2)
- *The principle of non-discrimination*. 'The basic working and employment conditions of temporary workers shall be, for the duration of their posting at a user undertaking, at least those that would apply if they had been recruited directly by that enterprise to occupy the same job'. (Article 5)
- *Access to permanent quality employment*. 'Temporary workers shall be informed of any vacant posts in the user undertaking to give them the same opportunity as other workers in that undertaking to find employment'. (Article 6)

The specific employment protection for migrant agency workers

Many, but certainly not all, legal migrant workers are likely to be covered by British employment legislation. However, at the margins of the labour market there are certain vulnerable groups. One such group are those who work for gangmasters in, for example, agriculture, horticulture, dairy farming, gathering shellfish and related fish processing and packaging. The Gangmasters (Licensing) Act 2004 was enacted to deal with what were described in Parliament as 'unscrupulous rogue gangmasters who are exploiting and intimidating workers, often breaching human rights and engaging in a range of criminal activities such as illegal deductions from wages, failure to pay the minimum wage or sickness pay, tax fraud, human trafficking, smuggling and the supply of drugs' (7.01.2004).

Labour providers in these sectors require a licence and details are available on a public register maintained by the Gangmasters Licensing Authority. The legislation creates two new criminal offences: supplying labour without a licence and using an unlicensed labour provider. Offenders can face up to 10 years in prison. Workers provided by the labour provider (agency) have various employment rights and also protection under discrimination and health and safety legislation (see **www.gla.gov.uk**).

Activity 2.2 'Atypical' workers in your organisation

Check whether or not your organisation employs people who may be defined a 'atypical' workers. Which of the categories outlined above are used? Undertake an audit of a particular small group. It may be helpful to select from the following questions:

- What is the gender and ethnic profile of the staff you have selected?
- What description (from the categories of 'atypical' workers discussed above) would you use for these people?
- Using the common law tests, is the description of their employment status by the employer accurate?
- Is there evidence of mutuality of obligation?
- Is there evidence of a global contract?
- Are any of them provided by an employment agency?
- If so, have any problems arisen from the triangular relationship with the agency? How have they been resolved?
- How do their terms and conditions compare with employees on open-ended contracts of employment?
- Is there any evidence of breaches of discrimination law?
- Would you be recommending any reforms to your employer? What would these be?

Complaints relating to employment contracts

Complaints relating to contracts are likely to fall into one of the following categories:

- *Grievances that certain contractual terms and/or statutory rights have not been complied with.* If the grievance is not satisfactorily dealt with through the internal grievance procedure, most of these issues can be raised as complaints at an employment tribunal (subject, of course, to the complainant's employment status and length of service with the employer). The remedies will be those outlined under the appropriate legislation (see the other chapters in this textbook). It is possible for certain contractual grievances to be raised in the High Court where they do not relate to specific employment rights or discrimination law but rather to specific terms of the contract. Examples can be found in respect of claims concerning restrictive covenants or allegations about unlawful contract variation (*Burdett-Coutts and Others* v *Hertfordshire County Council* [1984] IRLR 91, HC; *Cresswell and Others* v *Board of Inland Revenue* [1984] IRLR 190, HC).

- *Unfair dismissal claims* (including those relating to redundancy) which can be made at an employment tribunal – depending on qualifying service (see Chapter 8).
- *Wrongful dismissal claims* which concern the termination of the contract which breaches the terms of that contract including the providing of insufficient notice (see Chapter 8).

Conclusions

The regulation of the employment relationship is being subjected to two parallel developments in law. First, statute law is progressively determining a framework of minimum rights which mould the terms of the contract of employment. Other 'contracts to carry out work personally' are also being influenced by statutory requirements. Although these are more limited in scope, they do cover two of the essential bases of an employment relationship: pay (through the national minimum wage and equal pay legislation); and working time regulation. The general political thrust of British and European employment law acknowledges that those in the 'flexible labour market' are entitled to minimum rights and that the general restriction of access to statutory rights to full-time permanent employees has ceased to be defensible. Consequently, legislation is gradually recognising the circumstances of part-time workers, those on temporary contracts, agency workers and homeworkers. Where there are gaps in employment protection, case law is taking some tentative steps towards improvement. However, a principal obstacle is the combined effect of restricting so many employment rights to those with 'employee' status; and the impact of 'mutuality of obligation' in excluding so many 'atypical' workers – particularly, casual workers – from employment protection.

References and useful websites

Advisory, Conciliation and Arbitration Service (2009) *Code of Practice on Disciplinary and Grievance Procedures*. London: ACAS.

Atkinson, J. (1984) 'Manpower Strategies for Flexible Organisations', *Personnel Management*, August 28–31.

Brodie, D. (1998) 'The Contract for Work', *Scottish Law and Practice Quarterly*, 2.

Burchell, B. *et al.* (1999) *The Employment Status of Individuals in Non-standard Employment*, Employment Relations Research Series 6. London: Department of Trade and Industry.

Cave, K. (1997) *Zero Hours Contracts*. Huddersfield: University of Huddersfield.

Deakin, S. and Morris, G. (1998) *Labour Law*. London: Butterworth.

Dickens, L. (1992) *Whose Flexibility? – Discrimination and Equality Issues in Atypical Work*. London: Institute of Employment Rights.

Department of Trade and Industry (1998) *Fairness at Work*, Cm 3968. London: Stationery Office.

Department of Trade and Industry (2002) *Discussion Document on Employment Status in Relation to Statutory Employment Rights*. London: Department of Trade and Industry.

Handy, C. (1991) *The Age of Unreason*. London: Arrow Business Books.

Hotopp, U. (2002) 'Teleworking in the UK', *Labour Market Trends*, Vol. 110, No. 6.

Kahn-Freund, Sir Otto (1983) *Kahn-Freund's Labour and the Law* (P. Davies and M. Freedland, eds). London: Stevens.

Mant, A. (1995) 'Changing Work Roles' in Tyson, S. (ed.). *Strategic Prospects for HRM*. London: Chartered Institute of Personnel and Development.

Ruiz, Y. and Walling, A. (2005) 'Home-based Working Using Communication Technologies', *Labour Market Trends*, Vol. 113, No. 10.

Schein, G. (1988) *Organisational Psychology*, London: Prentice Hall.

Social Trends 31, *Homeworking by occupation and gender, 1996 and 2000*. (www.statistics.gov.uk).

Taylor, R. (2002) *Britain's World of Work – Myths and Realities*. London: Economic and Social Research Council.

Wedderburn, Lord (1986) *The Worker and the Law*. Harmondsworth: Penguin Books.

Useful websites

Gangmasters Licensing Authority **www.gla.gov.uk**

Information Commissioner's Office **www.ico.gov.uk**

UK Statistics Authority **www.statistics.gov.uk**

Visit **www.mylawchamber.co.uk/willey** to access multiple choice questions, case flashcards and exercises to test yourself on this chapter.

mylawchamber

3 Managing change in the employment relationship

Learning objectives

This chapter considers the legal consequences for the employment relationship of changing managerial and employment policies. Having read it you should understand:

- The ways in which terms in contracts of employment might need to be varied to accommodate changing business conditions
- The ways in which an employer might build 'flexibility' into contractual terms
- The circumstances under which an employer might lawfully make staff redundant
- The employment protection conferred on employees in redundancies
- The socio-economic context in which the Transfer of Undertakings (Protection of Employment) Regulations operate
- The employment protection conferred on employees in business transfers

Structure of the chapter

This chapter comprises the following sections:

- *Introduction*
- *The context*: organisational culture; strategic considerations; operational factors; incidence of redundancies; socio-economic context of business transfers; tensions between 'business needs' and legal standards
- *The legal framework*: variation of contracts of employment, flexibility in existing contractual terms, redundancy and redeployment, transfers of undertakings
- *Exercises*: N.B. these are located after each of the key sections on the law

Introduction

Changes within organisations, to organisational structures and to employment practices arise for various economic, technological and, occasionally, political reasons. The ways in which employers respond to change-drivers can be affected by four broad frameworks of employment law relating to:

- variation of contracts of employment;
- 'flexible terms' within contracts of employment;
- redundancy and redeployment of **employees**;
- the transfers of undertakings (i.e. business transfers).

It is important to note that, in some circumstances, all four aspects of law can and do interweave in the day-to-day operation of employment relations.

Having briefly considered the nature of the changing business context, we will look at each of these areas of law in turn.

Context

It is a commonplace to say that management is increasingly the management of change, and that business is always in a state of flux. The principal drivers of change are pressures to compete more effectively in product markets; trends in the global economy; the need to respond to technological changes in product manufacture, service delivery, information storage and communication; and the need to achieve satisfactory standards of quality. Additionally, changes may be a consequence of political decisions. Examples include the operation of public–private partnerships; the shifting of government funding and subsidies; the reorganisation and privatisation of public organisations; or policy initiatives on, for example, climate change.

Whatever the source of the change, there are several aspects that should be taken into account. These, to a greater or lesser extent, have implications in law. They are: the organisation's **culture**; strategic considerations; operational factors; aspects of the economic context; and the tensions between business needs and legal requirements. We will look at each of these in turn.

Organisational culture

The culture of a particular organisation may be difficult to define. Indeed it might be argued that, in some organisations, no *single* culture exists. Culture has been described as 'the characteristic spirit and belief of an organisation, demonstrated, for example, in the norms and values that are generally held about how people should behave and treat each other, the nature of the working relationships that should be developed and attitudes to change. These norms are deep, taken-for-granted, assumptions, which are not always expressed, and are often known without being understood' (Torrington and Hall 1998: 100). Clearly, there is a strong connection with the 'psychological contract' (see Chapter 2).

Cultural norms develop over a long period of time. They can and do, for example, mould recruitment and selection policies, day-to-day working practices and attitudes to reward systems. They can pose significant barriers to change – particularly in rooting out discriminatory treatment and patterns of harassment; and also where there are business transfers. Large organisations have reputations for promoting 'cultural change'. This is seen by chief executives and senior management as a means of eradicating what are perceived to be inefficient practices and failures to achieve corporate business objectives. Given the entrenched nature of cultures, change programmes can encounter considerable difficulties. Indeed, there is likely to be a cultural clash between what is believed by senior managers to be the new formal culture and the traditional cultural norms that staff aim to preserve. It may be that a 'counter-culture' emerges.

The extent to which an organisation's culture can facilitate change is particularly dependent upon the effectiveness of the techniques of communication, persuasion and consultation within that organisation.

Strategic considerations

'Strategy' is a term frequently used in management texts in an approving way. It is an *integrative* process that involves *planning*. Strategic decisions have a medium to long-term perspective and are likely to have major resource implications. They bring together data and assessments from a wide range of organisational activities (production or service delivery, marketing, finance, employment relations, etc.). As a result of the fluidity of the business context, strategies are implemented in a context of on-going uncertainty and risk. Finally, the outcome of strategic decision-making tends to involve significant change in the size, equipment, staffing arrangements or other aspects of the organisation's physical and human resources. So, to have any prospect of success, a change in management strategy has to take account of various relevant factors: organisational culture; internal 'politics' (i.e. power structures – both formal and informal); the nature and degree of resistance to change; ways of achieving economic and operational outcomes; and whether changes are legally compliant.

Operational factors

In dealing with the management of change, the repercussions of particular changes need to be anticipated and considered. This is particularly so when operational changes are initiated. One example will illustrate the wide range of possible consequences. If an organisation is considering the installation of new, more technologically advanced, equipment there are various implications:

- *Economic factors*: e.g. the cost of purchase; the effect on unit costs and unit labour costs; the impact on product market competitiveness.
- *Operational*: e.g. the organisation of work, the working practices to be adopted; the redefinition of jobs; staffing levels; the scheduling of working time.
- *Health and safety*: compliance with the employer's general duties in law and with any appropriate specific regulations.
- *Employment relations*: i.e. requirements to consult about changes; whether redundancy or redeployment is proposed; consequences for terms in contracts of employment; impact on payment systems; consequences for working practices and for the scheduling of working time.

So, a coherent implementation plan should enable likely difficulties to be anticipated and appropriate action to be taken.

Finally, one particular aspect of operational factors, relevant to contractual change, is the nature and extent of 'flexibility' in the way work is undertaken. The flexibilities that are likely to arise are mobility and working from and at home (*geographic flexibility*); the schedule of working time or *temporal flexibility* (e.g. annualised hours contracts, overtime working, shift working, part-time working, job share, weekend working and flexitime); payments by results and performance-related pay (*reward flexibility*); and *functional flexibility* (i.e. requirements to undertake a variety of tasks) (Atkinson 1984) (see Chapter 2).

The economic context

For the purposes of this chapter, there are two broad aspects: the extent to which staff are made redundant; and the socio-economic and political context of business transfers.

Incidence of redundancies

During the period 1997–2007, a period of labour market growth, the quarterly statistics recorded between 111,000 and 196,000 redundancies – relatively low numbers. Even in the quarter February–April 2008, during the early stage of the economic downturn, the figure was 110,000 (**www.statistics.gov.uk**). It is, however, unlikely that this level will be sustained in the medium term. In its most recent survey on the topic the Chartered Institute of Personnel and Development (2002) recorded that 'organisational restructuring' was the most common reason given for redundancies (at 66 per cent). Forty-two per cent reported the need to 'reduce costs'; and 34 per cent 'falling sales'. (More than one reason was given by respondents.)

Socio-economic and political context of business transfers

There are several aspects to this:

Mergers and acquisitions

These now play a significant part in the UK economy. In the second quarter of 2007, a record £49 billion was spent on acquisitions in the UK by foreign companies; and £7.1 billion was spent by UK firms acquiring other UK firms. The totals for the whole of 2006 were £77.7 billion and £28.5 billion respectively (see **www.statistics.gov.uk**). Clearly, substantial numbers of employees are affected by such transactions.

Outsourcing

Outsourcing has been defined as circumstances 'where an organisation passes the provision of a service or execution of a task, previously undertaken in-house, to a third party to perform on its behalf' (Reilly *et al.* 1996). It is far from being a new economic activity. In the sixteenth century, Machiavelli, the Italian political philosopher, in *The Prince*, criticised a form of military outsourcing – the employment of mercenaries – on the ground that 'there is no loyalty or inducement to keep them on the field apart from the little they are paid and this is not enough to make them die for you'.

Since the late 1970s, the scale of outsourcing, subcontracting or contracting has grown significantly. These practices now play an important part in the organisation of most firms. Within public services, some commentators argue that we are witnessing the emergence of a 'contract state'. This is where public services are organised around market relations and commercial contracts between purchasers and providers. So, the state has a lesser role in providing services but a greater role in co-ordinating and monitoring service delivery through contracts (Collings 1999; Timmins 2005). Areas such as health care, criminal justice and the military now see the private sector playing an increasingly prominent role in the delivery of public services (Sachdev 2006).

Disquiet at some of the implications of outsourcing – especially loss of knowledge and control – has led one commentator to argue that 'there are signs everywhere that the outsourcing fashion has gone too far' (Shapinker 2003, 2005). Controversy has dogged certain forms of outsourcing including the school meals service, gangmaster labour, hospital cleaning and the organisation of the railways.

As far as the Transfer of Undertakings (Protection of Employment) Regulations (TUPE) are concerned, these may have prevented (or at least played a key role in preventing) a more extensive or even wholesale privatisation of the Prison Service. Private sector involvement was eventually more modest and piecemeal (see Exhibit 3.1). TUPE acted as an effective countervailing force to the deregulatory labour market ideology of the Conservative government and (in significantly modified form) the New Labour government.

Exhibit 3.1 TUPE and the prison service

According to Derek Lewis, the former Director General of the Prison Service, Sir Peter Levene (the efficiency adviser of Prime Minister John Major) 'believed that the *whole* service could be contracted out to the private sector'. It was only the re-interpretation of TUPE by the European Court of Justice that prevented the (then) Home Secretary, Kenneth Clarke, from 'privatising up to twenty prisons at a stroke. It is, also, obviously, another reason why only the private sector is being allowed to bid for newly built prisons' (Ryan 1994).

When it was discovered that TUPE applied to the prison service, Lewis says that 'disaster struck'. In a leaked letter the Home Secretary said: 'In relation to prison education services, my view is that the consequences of the [TUPE] case are very damaging because we stand to lose almost all the efficiency and cost savings achieved if all existing staff have to be taken on by new contractors on their present terms and conditions' (cited in Foley 1994).

Sir Richard Tilt, Director General (1995–2000) highlighted the impact of TUPE in limiting the scope of privatisation: 'At the time I was involved in it we on the whole were not enthusiastic about [private sector providers running existing prisons] mainly because, well I think TUPE was one problem, we couldn't really see how the private sector people were necessarily going to make huge inroads into the way in which the prison was run if they had to take on existing staff and their existing conditions'.

Incidence of outsourcing

Evidence is reported in the Workplace Employment Relations Survey (WERS) 2004 (Kersley *et al.* 2006). Managers in organisations employing 10 or more staff were asked whether independent contracts provided any of 11 services. In 86 per cent of private-sector workplaces and 87 per cent of those in the public sector 'at least one' of these services was contracted out. The key findings were:

- *The incidence of contracting out*: building maintenance (in 59 per cent of workplaces); cleaning (52 per cent); training (34 per cent); transport of documents or goods (29 per cent); security (29 per cent); payroll (28 per cent).

- *Reasons for contracting out*: cost savings (47 per cent); improved service (43 per cent); focus on core activities (30 per cent).
- Within human resource activities, the scale of outsourcing is significant although the extent of it appears to have levelled out (1998 figures in brackets):
  - 34 per cent of workplace outsourced training (34 per cent);
  - 28 per cent outsourced payroll (19 per cent);
  - 16 per cent outsourced temporary filling of vacant posts (22 per cent);
  - 12 per cent outsourced recruitment (12 per cent).

Tensions between 'business need' and legal standards

The legal framework which is discussed in this chapter is, then, set in the context of often rapid and substantial organisational and operational change. Given the speed of response demanded by employers, it is not surprising that attempts may be made to short-circuit or, perhaps, deliberately ignore legal obligations. Also, in some instances, with the growing complexity of legal requirements, employers may not fully understand the 'juridification' of employment relations that has been taking place since the 1970s. So, at the heart of the management of change, there is likely to be a tension between, on the one hand, the economic imperatives of business and, on the other hand, employees' interests (for example, in respect of job and income security and fair treatment).

Activity 3.1 The employment consequences of organisational change

Draw up a list of the changes that your organisation has experienced in the past 12 months (and may be still experiencing). Are these a consequence of technological, economic or political factors? What impact have they had on the organisation's structure and way of working?

Using the sections below on the legal framework as your guide, as appropriate, think about:

- the impact of changes on employees' terms and conditions of employment and whether they were changed;
- whether any employment changes could be accommodated under existing terms of contracts of employment;
- whether any redundancies occurred and how they were handled;
- whether the changes experienced occurred within a 'transfer situation' and how this was managed.

How would you assess the effectiveness of your organisation's employee relations / human resources functions in dealing with the changes? What lessons could be learned?

The legal framework

Four aspects of the law relating to business change are examined:

- *Flexibility available with existing contracts of employment.* This covers situations where the existing terms of a contract of employment have sufficient flexibility to help an employer achieve operational objectives (e.g. relating to the mobility of staff; or the range of tasks an employee carries out).

- *Variation of contractual terms.* This concerns those circumstances where an employer wishes to change an existing term or terms of a contract of employment.
- *Redundancy and redeployment.* This concerns employers' policies to reduce and reorganise workforces because of changing business circumstances.
- *Transfers of undertakings.* This relates to the protection of an employee's existing terms and conditions of employment when the undertaking they work for is transferred to another organisation.

Flexibility within the contract of employment

Changes to contracts of employment are extremely common because a contract is agreed at a particular point in time. However, an organisation is likely to experience, sometimes considerable, changes over time: in the technology used; in its product market; in terms of the skills and competences needed; to respond to competition and so on. Consequently, a contract of employment cannot remain static. It will need to be adapted to new circumstances. Some changes are beneficial to the employee (e.g. pay increases, increased holidays and shorter working hours). Other changes, of course, can be adverse (e.g. relocation and redeployment, pay cuts, increased working time).

However, rather than changing contractual terms, some employers may be able to respond to operational changes by using terms of existing contracts of employment to implement changes to working practices. There is evidence from case law of the use of both *implied* terms (e.g. the **duty** to obey lawful and reasonable instructions) and *express* terms (e.g. a mobility clause, a flexible working hours clause, or a general variation clause).

Implied terms

An important illustration is seen in a case from the early 1980s which, in terms of law, is still applicable today (*Cresswell and Others* v *Board of Inland Revenue* [1984] IRLR 190). It involved the computerisation of certain clerical and administrative tasks which hitherto had been performed manually. In this case, the trade union concerned claimed that the employer had breached the employees' contracts of employment by requiring them to use the new computerised technology. However, it was ruled in the High Court that the employer's instruction was lawful and reasonable and so was consistent with the contracts of employment.

Mr Justice Walton stated that employees could not conceivably have the right to preserve their working obligations completely unchanged during their employment. They could reasonably be expected, after proper training, to adapt to new techniques. All that would happen with the computerisation was that jobs would remain 'recognisably the same but done in a different way'. However, this ruling does not give the employer free rein. Each case would be considered by the tribunal or court on its merits and decide whether or not the employer was 'reasonable'. It is also likely, that the implied duty to obey lawful and reasonable instructions would apply only to work practices and related *operational* issues.

It is also accepted that each contract of employment has an implied duty on the employee to co-operate with the employer. This irreducible minimum of co-operation includes an obligation not to obstruct technological change or changes to work organisation. However, with contractual terms relating to pay, employee benefits and hours cannot be overridden by invoking the duty to co-operate. Essentially, these can only be changed by engaging in the process of variation.

Express terms

There are several examples of these.

Mobility clauses and place of work

At the heart of mobility clauses in contracts of employment is the implied term of mutual trust and confidence. Effectively, courts and tribunals consider the nature of the provisions of a mobility clause; its application to the circumstances of an employee's employment; and the consequences for the employee. The employer, in implementing the mobility clause should be reasonable. If the employer's conduct is not reasonable, then, mutual trust and confidence may be breached and there can be a consequential repudiation of the contract of employment. The employee may, then, resign and claim **constructive dismissal** (see Exhibit 3.2).

Exhibit 3.2 Mobility clauses

An express mobility clause

Home Office v *Evans and another* [2008] IRLR 59, CA

Facts. Mr Evans and Mr Laidlaw were employed as immigration officers at Waterloo International Terminal. It was announced that this was to close on 13 May 2004. The employer proposed to transfer staff who had an express mobility clause in their contracts of employment (to work anywhere in the UK or abroad) to positions that met its operational needs. Evans and Laidlaw refused to engage in consultation and in August 2004 they were told that they would be transferred to Heathrow airport. They resigned claiming constructive dismissal.

Court of Appeal ruling. It agreed that the Home Office had a choice about whether to invoke the contractual mobility clause to avoid redundancy dismissals or to implement the agreed redundancy procedure. The employer did not propose dismissals; was able to transfer staff under the terms of their contracts; and, in fact, chose this course of action. The instruction to the staff to relocate was not a breach of the contract of employment.

An implied mobility clause

Courtaulds Northern Spinning Ltd v *Sibson and the Transport and General Workers' Union* [1988] IRLR 305, CA

A heavy goods vehicle driver was transferred from one depot to another a mile away. There was no express term within his contract of employment. The Court of Appeal ruled that this transfer did not breach his contract because there was an implied term that the employee could be transferred anywhere within reasonable commuting distance of his home. His constructive dismissal claim failed. Having ruled on the facts and circumstances of this particular case, the Court emphasised that each case will depend on its own facts.

Moving departments

BPCC Purnell Ltd v *Webb* EAT 129/1990

The employee was transferred from one pre-press department of a printing company to another. Because of the different nature of shift working in the new department, he was likely to lose £80 per week in earnings. His employment contract contained a clause requiring 'total flexibility between all pre-press departments'. The EAT, finding unfair constructive dismissal, stated that this term must not be used in such a way to destroy mutual trust and confidence. The £80 reduction in weekly wages out of a total of £305 was unacceptable and was a clear breach of the term.

Transfers between posts

The Court of Appeal has held that when an employer acts within the contract, the fact that loss is thereby caused to the employee does not render that action a **breach of contract** (*Spafax Ltd* v *Harrison* [1980] IRLR 442). However, a malicious or grossly unfair transfer could amount to a breach of mutual trust and confidence. Various other cases, relating to express terms, illustrate the potential for flexibility. For example, in *Bex* v *Securicor Transport Ltd* [1972] IRLR 68, the nature of the employee's work was changed. Although he regarded this as a demotion, it was found that the company was expressly entitled to require him to carry out these duties. There was no repudiation of contract. In other cases, the transfer might be subject to a proviso. So, in *White* v *Reflecting Roadstones* [1991] ICR 733, EAT, redeployment to a less well-paid job was permissible provided operational efficiency made it necessary. In *Risk Management Services (Chiltern) Ltd* v *Shrimpton* (1977) EAT 803/77, short notices of changes in shift and duties had to be 'in an emergency'.

General variation clauses

There may be a general variation clause within contracts of employment. However, a wide-ranging clause, enabling the employer to change all contractual terms is unlikely to be enforceable. It is doubtful whether an agreement including such a term could be a contract at all. There would be, in effect, no agreement on the terms of the contract. In one case where there was a general express term, the EAT ruled that it would not permit substantial changes but only those of a minor and non-fundamental nature (*United Association for the Protection of Trade Ltd* v *Kilburn* EAT 787/84). To use such a clause, the employer must give notice of the proposed change and be prepared to consult.

Variation of contract

The critical question for an employer is: *how is a contract of employment varied lawfully?* In answering this question, it is important to remember that a contract of employment is an agreement and, therefore, it cannot be changed arbitrarily by the employer. Broadly, there are two alternative courses of action available to employers who wish to make contractual changes:

- They may attempt to make the changes by discussion and agreement with the employees concerned, either individually or through trade union or other employee representatives. This is referred to as 'consensual variation'.
- They may terminate the existing contract, after consultation and with due notice (i.e. whatever a particular individual is entitled to) and offer a new contract embodying the changed terms and conditions of employment (see also Chapter 8).

It is important to remember that there are particular provisions in law where the variation takes place in a 'transfer situation' (Transfer of Undertakings (Protection of Employment) Regulations 2006, regs 4 and 9) (see later section in this chapter).

Consensual variation

This refers to agreed changes to contractual terms (see Exhibit 3.3). This agreement can be by the individual employee or through a collective agreement with a trade union. This may be express agreement – clear and unequivocal in writing; or it may be implied by the behaviour of the employee. The courts, on occasion, have been reluctant to find implied consent particularly where the effect of the contractual change has no immediate effect.

Exhibit 3.3 Consensual variation: guidance

In order to achieve **consensual variation**, good practice suggests that a number of steps should be considered by the employer:

- Consider whether the changes relate to specific contractual terms or may concern lawful and reasonable instructions.
- Provide information about the proposed contractual changes to each affected employee.
- Be prepared to discuss, consult and/or – if unionised – negotiate.
- Try to obtain the employee's consent. This might involve making some concessions or offering 'consideration'.
- Be prepared to justify contractual changes against the organisation's operational requirements and business needs.
- Anticipate the arguments that might be put at a court or tribunal – for example, in terms of the scale of the change and the issue of reasonableness.
- Check to ensure that none of the proposed changes infringe statutory employment rights or discrimination law (see Chapters 5 and 6).
- Check whether the affected employees are not protected by the Transfer of Undertaking (Protection of Employment) Regulations 2006 (see later section in this chapter).

So, for example, if an employer imposes a pay cut and the employee continues working without objection, then, because the change has 'immediate practical application', the employee could be taken to have impliedly agreed (*Jones* v *Associated Tunnelling Co Ltd* [1981] IRLR 477, EAT). In contrast, in a case involving the implementation of a mobility clause some five years after it had been introduced (*Anglia Regional Cooperative Society* v *O'Donnell* EAT 655/1991), the EAT ruled that the fact that the employee had continued to work after 1987 did not necessarily mean that she had agreed to the mobility clause which was not applied to her until 1992.

Variations can be agreed through a recognised trade union which has authority to negotiate collective agreements covering particular groups of staff. Usually, appropriate terms of collective agreements are expressly incorporated into contracts of employment (see Chapter 2 in relation to '**incorporation**'). An employer may include a phrase in contractual information saying that an individual's terms and conditions are 'as negotiated from time to time by XYZ Union'. The employee (whether or not s/he is a union member) is bound by an agreement reached with the union, regardless of whether s/he agrees to it. If there is no express incorporation, then, it might be implied by **custom and practice**. If a collective agreement is rescinded by the employer, then, any relevant terms of a collective agreement can 'live on' in the individual employee's contract of employment. (See the Court of Appeal's ruling in *Robertson and Jackson* v *British Gas Corporation* [1983] IRLR 202 outlined in Chapter 2.)

It is important to remember that the contractual terms that may be incorporated are most likely to be those relating to an individual's terms and conditions of employment. Other provisions of collective agreements may be more problematic. The Court of Appeal has ruled on the status of a 'no compulsory redundancy' agreement (*Kaur* v *MG Rover Group Ltd* [2005] IRLR 40). It stated that the job security provision of a collective agreement which included the words, 'There will be no compulsory redundancy', when construed in the context of the agreement as a whole was no more than 'a statement of collective aspiration' and was not appropriate to be incorporated into individual contracts of employment.

Dealing with resistance to contractual change

Several issues have been considered in **case law**: the use by the employer of unilateral variation; employees continuing to work 'under protest'; whether there was implied consent by the employee; the possibility of a constructive dismissal claim; and the circumstances under which a contract of employment might be terminated.

Unilateral variation

Consent to proposed contractual changes is not always forthcoming. Unilateral variation arises where an employer imposes a contractual change (either because agreement cannot be reached on the variation or because there has been no attempt at discussion to try and reach agreement). In most cases, this is unlawful. So, where an employer imposes a pay cut without consultation and agreement, he is in breach of contract. Even if the employer has good economic reasons for reducing labour costs, the courts will hold the employer to the existing contracts; and (as in *Burdett-Coutts and Others* v *Hertfordshire County Council* [1984] IRLR 91, HC) award **damages** in the form of back-pay to the employees concerned.

Employees faced with unlawful unilateral variation have four possible courses of action:

- to work under protest;
- to accept the new contractual terms;
- as appropriate, make a claim for unlawful deduction of wages (Employment Rights Act 1996, Part II) (see also Chapter 9);
- to resign, alleging a repudiatory breach of contract, and claim constructive dismissal (if they qualify in terms of employment status and length of service).

Working under protest

For an employee, this is one response to unilateral variation. The employee continues to work – but 'under protest'; and s/he holds the employer to the original contract. In *Rigby* v *Ferodo* [1988] IRLR 517 (a case involving the imposition of a pay cut), the House of Lords outlined the essential elements of 'working under protest':

- The employer's action amounted to a repudiatory breach of contract but not to termination of the contract.
- The employees had not accepted the employer's proposed changes in terms and conditions of employment.
- The employees were entitled to sue for the difference between the amount of wages they should have received and that which they had in fact received.
- As long as there is a continuing contract, not terminated by either side, the employer will remain liable for any shortfall in contractual wages.
- If the employer wants to limit liability, he must bring the contract to an end, although in doing so, he will run the risk of unfair dismissal claims.

Acceptance of the new terms by the employee

An employer might impose a unilateral variation and the employee(s) might impliedly consent – in that they do not protest and continue to work under the new terms and conditions. As indicated earlier, there can be uncertainty about how reliable an employee's agreement is in these circumstances.

A constructive dismissal claim

This might arise if the employee takes the view that the employer's conduct (e.g. imposing a pay cut) is such that it fundamentally breaches the contract of employment. In these circumstances, the employee may resign and, subject to having 12 months' continuous service, may claim unfair constructive dismissal at an employment tribunal. In the leading case, Lord Denning described the circumstances in which repudiation of a contract can arise in the following terms: 'If the employer is guilty of conduct which is a significant breach going to the root of the contract of employment, or which shows that the employer no longer intends to be bound by one or more of the essential terms of the contract, then the employee is entitled to treat himself as discharged from any further performance . . . The conduct must . . . be sufficiently serious to entitle him to leave at once . . .' (*Western Excavating (ECC) Ltd* v *Sharp* [1978] IRLR 27, CA). Clearly, pay is an essential term of the contract. The imposition of a pay cut without consent would go 'to the root of the contract'.

Fair dismissal

If an employer wishes to change existing contracts and, in particular, encounters difficulties in reaching an agreed variation, it is possible to terminate the existing contract and offer a new one including the changed terms. Such a termination will be a dismissal in law. So, to avoid the possibility of an allegation of unfair dismissal and an employment tribunal complaint, the employer must ensure that various steps are complied with:

- *Reason for the dismissal.* This is likely to be 'business need' and would be 'some other substantial reason for dismissal' (Employment Rights Act 1996 s 98) (see Exhibit 3.4) (see also Chapter 8).
- *Consultation.* The employer should have discussed the issues as advised under the ACAS *Code of Practice on Disciplinary and Grievance Procedures* (2009).
- *Due notice.* The employer must give the amount of notice to terminate the contract that the individual employee is entitled to under the contract of employment and bearing in mind the statutory minima (Employment Rights Act 1996, s 86).

Exhibit 3.4 Hollister and the National Farmers' Union

Hollister v *National Farmers' Union* [1979] IRLR 238, CA

Facts. Mr Hollister was employed by the National Farmers' Union as a group secretary in Cornwall. To rectify anomalies between group secretaries throughout the country, the employer terminated the contracts of employment of the Cornish group secretaries and offered them new contracts on the same terms as those employed elsewhere. In most respects, Mr Hollister would have been better off. However, his pension rights would have been reduced. He refused the new contract and complained of unfair dismissal.

Judgment. The case, on appeal, eventually reached the Court of Appeal and became a 'leading' case in this area of law. The Court rejected his claim of unfair dismissal. It accepted that the reorganisation of the business was 'some other substantial reason' for dismissal. Since this case, employment tribunals have usually accepted 'business need' as some other substantial reason for dismissal – provided the employer adduced evidence to show why the changes were required. 'Reasonableness' in handling the whole process is also expected with the employer showing that the employee's interests have been considered and that reasonable procedures have been followed before the employer insisted on the adoption of the changes.

Exercise 3.1 Contract variation

Read these scenarios and decide:

- *Which legal issues do you think might be involved?*
- *What would you recommend to the employer as ways of dealing with the issues – taking account of both law and good human resource practice?*

3.1.1 Samantha is employed as an assistant in the Gateshead branch of Listeria Foods. On Friday, her manager tells her that from the following Monday she is to work at the Newcastle branch, some four miles away.

3.1.2 Locksmith Engineering in Birmingham has been in severe financial difficulties over the past six months. As part of its response for dealing with the problems, the owner has decided not to award a pay increase from 1 April this coming year.

3.1.3 Administrators in the admission department of Polygon University in the north-west of England have been instructed to implement a new and complex computerised system of student records. This replaces a system that has been in place for the past six years. Beryl, an experienced administrator who is two years away from retirement, is unhappy about the change. She has refused to attend the required training course.

3.1.4 Jamila works as a retail assistant in a large department store in Swansea. As a result of a change in company policy, she is required to ask all customers who did not have a company store card whether they would like information on the scheme. Increasingly, she comes to dislike this aspect of her work. She does not see it as a task that she is employed to do. She also resents the disparaging comments of the customers about the high rates of interest charged. She tells her manager that she is thinking of resigning and that a friend has told her that she could claim constructive dismissal.

Feedback on these exercises is provided in the Appendix to this textbook.

Redundancy and redeployment

There are several key aspects to the law on redundancy that we will consider: the definition of redundancy; the criteria for selection; the use of alternative employment strategies; the right to time off work; consultation and information disclosure about redundancies; notice of dismissal; and the availability of redundancy pay.

Definition

A person is dismissed for reason of redundancy:

- If the dismissal is 'wholly or mainly attributable' to 'the fact that his employer has ceased or intends to cease (i) to carry on business for the purposes of which the employee was employed by him, or (ii) to carry on that business in the place where the employee was employed' (ERA 1996, s 139(1)(a)).
- Alternatively, if the reason for the dismissal is 'wholly or mainly attributable' to 'the fact that the requirements of that business (i) for employees to carry out work of a particular kind or (ii) for employees to carry out work of a particular kind in the place where the employee was employed by the employer, have ceased or diminished or are expected to cease or diminish' (ERA 1996, s 139(1)(b)).

Selection criteria

In selecting employees for redundancy, an employer must have fair and objective criteria against which an individual's selection can be defended. Traditionally, **LIFO** ('last in first out') has been a customary way of selecting staff for compulsory redundancies. Millward *et al.* (1992) reported its incidence in 47 per cent of workplaces as against other criteria: employee's level of skills or qualifications at 29 per cent; employee's performance record at 23 per cent; and disciplinary record or attendance at 19 per cent. The CIPD (2002) survey of HR professionals records the nature of the shift in criteria that has been taking place (see Table 3.1).

The selection criteria must be disclosed in writing to employee representatives for the purpose of consultation (TULRCA 1992, s 188(4)(d)). The EAT has ruled that reasonable employers should use criteria 'which as far as possible do not depend solely upon the opinion of the person making the selection but can be objectively checked against such things as attendance record, efficiency at the job, experience or length of service' (*Williams* v *Compair Maxam Ltd* [1982] IRLR 83). There is no statutory obligation to follow customary arrangements such as LIFO.

There are three factors an employer should be aware of:

- the likelihood of detrimental treatment against a specific employee;
- direct discrimination; and
- the possibility of indirect discrimination.

Selection for redundancy may be ***detrimental treatment*** on various grounds: e.g. where an individual is being victimised for involvement in an employment tribunal complaint; asserting trade union membership rights; participating in elections as a workplace representative; carrying out functions as a workplace representative; or asserting certain statutory employment rights (ERA 1996, s 104).

The issue of ***direct discrimination*** is relatively clear-cut. It is unlawful to select employees for redundancy on grounds prohibited under the various strands of discrimination law. ***Indirect discrimination*** relates to a 'provision, criterion or practice' which, although apparently neutral, can be discriminatory in effect. It must be justified as a 'proportionate means of achieving a legitimate aim' (i.e. some clear business objective). One notable example from case law concerns a decision to select part-time workers first in a redundancy programme. All part-timers in the company were female. The EAT stated that this criterion had a disproportionate and adverse impact on women in the workforce and could not be justified objectively (*Clarke* v *Eley (IMI) Kynoch Ltd* [1982] IRLR 482). The Court of Appeal has held that selection of fixed-term employees first in a redundancy situation was indirect sex discrimination (*Whiffen* v *Milham Ford Girls School and Another* [2001] IRLR 468). In this case it was also said that LIFO might

Table 3.1 Selection criteria for compulsory redundancy (%)*

Main selection criteria	*Manufacturing industry*	*Services*	*Public services*	*All*
Role within the organisation	64.4	70.2	80.6	68.1
Job performance/efficiency	61.1	63.9	36.1	61.7
Employee ability/flexibility	51.8	52.9	41.7	51.6
Length of service	30.8	23.9	13.9	26.5
Absence/disciplinary record	29.6	19.3	8.3	23.4

* Survey of 536 organisations: respondents asked to indicate the three most important criteria used (CIPD 2002).

Source: Based on CIPD (2002) *Survey of Redundancies*, www.cipd.co.uk.

be discriminatory because 'by reason of childbearing and other domestic commitments, fewer women than men might have long service'. It would be a matter for each tribunal to determine, on the facts, whether or not the use of LIFO is justifiable and non-discriminatory under discrimination law (see *Rolls Royce* v *Unite* [2008] EWHC 2420, HC; and also Chapter 5).

The EAT has ruled on the application of selection criteria (*McCormack* v *Sanmina* SCI (UK) Ltd [2006] All ERD (D) 138). In this case, it accepted that the selection criteria were reasonable and sufficiently precise. However, there were defects in the way that they were applied. There was an inconsistent approach by the employer in the assessment of an employee's willingness to work overtime and in the assessment of employees' skills.

Alternatives to redundancy

There are various alternatives:

- Restrictions on recruitment of permanent staff.
- Leaving vacancies unfilled allowing for a gradual decrease in numbers through 'natural wastage'.
- Where practical (and taking account of discrimination law), terminating the employment of temporary or contract staff.
- Using short-time working to cover temporary fluctuations in labour requirements.
- Retraining and redeployment, where appropriate, of existing staff into internal vacancies which arise or are expected to arise.
- Retirement of staff beyond normal retirement age (taking account of age discrimination legislation).
- Seeking applicants for early retirement or voluntary redundancy amongst existing staff before declaring compulsory redundancy.

The CIPD (2002) survey reported that the principal measures used to minimise redundancies were offering alternative employment to employees in affected posts (in 74 per cent of cases); placing a freeze on recruitment (in 56 per cent); achieving workforce reduction through natural wastage (in 55 per cent).

Suitable alternative employment

Where an employee is offered and accepts re-engagement on the same terms as previous employment, that person is *not* regarded as dismissed and there is no entitlement to redundancy pay. If the terms offered by the employer (or an associated employer) are different from those in the previous contract, then, when the old contract has ended, a trial period of four consecutive weeks can be invoked (ERA 1996, s 138(3)). It is possible to extend a trial period for the purposes of retraining. This must be in the form of a written agreement between the employer and the employee (or their representative) (s 138(6)). This offer must be made before the previous employment ends and the take-up of the new offer must be within four weeks of the end of the previous employment. During the trial period, the employee may resign and be treated as dismissed (by the employer under the old contract by reason of redundancy).

If an employee unreasonably refuses an offer of suitable alternative employment or unreasonably terminates the contract during the trail period, the entitlement to statutory redundancy pay is lost. Employment that could be considered as unsuitable would be that involving adverse changes in pay, changes in skill requirements, loss of status and requirements for travelling time (see Exhibit 3.5).

Exhibit 3.5 Unsuitable alternative employment

Commission for Healthcare Audit and Inspection v *Ward* EAT/0579/07

Facts. Ms Ward's job was identified as redundant in a restructuring exercise. She was offered an alternative post that the employer considered suitable. Ms Ward felt that the job was unsuitable on the grounds of the reduced status of the job; differences in job content; inferior job prospects; and weaker job security. She also alleged that the employer had not properly discussed the alternative job with her.

Tribunal ruling. The EAT, agreeing with the employment tribunal, stated that whether or not an employee's refusal of alternative work is unreasonable must be judged on the basis of *the facts as they appear to him or her at the time*. The *degree of suitability* of the post can also be relevant. Where the new job offered is overwhelmingly 'suitable' it may be a little easier for the employer to show that an employee's refusal was unreasonable. In this case, Ms Ward was successful. Her refusal was reasonable and she was awarded a statutory redundancy payment of £2,175.

Time off work

An employee who is under notice of dismissal because of redundancy and who has two years' continuous service on the date on which the notice is due to expire, 'is entitled to be permitted by his employer to take reasonable time off during the employee's working hours before the end of his notice in order to (a) look for new employment or (b) make arrangement for training for future employment' (ERA 1996, s 52(1)). The employee is entitled to remuneration for the time off (s 53). If an employer unreasonably refuses and the employee is successful at employment tribunal, the maximum award payable is two-fifths of a week's pay for that employee.

Consultation and information disclosure

Much of the legislation in this area is founded on European Union law (the Collective Redundancies **Directive** 1998). There are three aspects to this topic:

- *Information disclosure*: that which is essential to effective consultation.
- *Collective consultation*: the duty on an employer to consult with either a recognised independent trade union or, in non-union workplaces, with employee representatives.
- *Individual consultation*: the obligation on an employer to discuss the employee's **dismissal** in accordance with ACAS guidance and the requirements of the ACAS *Code of Practice on Disciplinary and Grievance Procedures* (2009).

Information disclosure

For the purposes of consultation the employer should disclose in writing the following information to the 'appropriate representatives' (TULRCA 1992, s 188(4)):

- the reasons for the redundancy proposals;
- the numbers and descriptions of the employees whom it is proposed to dismiss;
- the total number of employees of any such description employed by the employer at the establishment in question;
- the proposed method of selecting the employees who may be dismissed;
- the proposed method of carrying out the dismissals 'with due regard to any agreed procedure including the period over which the dismissals are to take effect' (s 188(4)(e));

- the proposed method of calculating any redundancy pay which is in excess of statutory redundancy pay.

Collective consultation

Under statute law it is stated that 'where an employer is proposing to dismiss as redundant twenty or more employees at one establishment within a period of ninety days or less, the employer shall consult about the dismissals all the persons who are appropriate representatives of any of the employees who may be affected by the proposed dismissals or may be affected by measures taken in connection with those dismissals' (TULRCA 1992, s 188(1)). Where the employer is proposing to dismiss 100 or more, there should be 'at least' 90 days' **consultation**; and where between 20 and 99 employees are involved, the period should be 'at least' 30 days.

The nature of this consultation is not explicitly detailed in legislation. However, from case law and the principles set out in the directive, it is possible to discern standards that might be adopted. In one case involving redundancies in the coal-mining industry, Lord Justice Glidewell stated that 'fair consultation involves giving the body consulted a fair and proper opportunity to understand fully the matters about which it is being consulted and to express its view on those subjects, with the consulter thereafter considering those views properly and genuinely' (*R* v *British Coal Corporation and Secretary of State for Trade and Industry* ex parte *Price* [1994] IRLR 72, CA). This guidance is relevant for consultation on both collective redundancies and individual cases.

The legislation on collective consultation, reflecting the Directive, states that it shall begin 'in good time' (TULRCA 1992, s 188(1A)). It 'shall be undertaken by the employer with a view to reaching agreement with the appropriate representatives' (s 188(2)). The purpose of the consultation should be to include discussion on avoiding the dismissals, reducing the numbers of employees to be dismissed and mitigating the consequences of the dismissals. The European Court of Justice (*Junk* v *Kuhnel* [2005] IRLR 310) elaborated the last point by ruling that, under the originating 1998 directive, consultation 'shall, at least, cover ways and means of . . . mitigating the consequences by recourse to accompanying social measures aimed, *inter alia*, at aid for redeploying or retraining workers made redundant'.

The Employment Appeals Tribunal (in *UK Coal Mining Ltd* v *NUM (Northumberland Area) and Another* [2008] IRLR 4) has clarified, in an authoritative judgment, the extent of consultation under TULRCA 1992 (s 188) following legislative amendments arising from the 1998 directive. In this case consultation should have included the 'reasons for the redundancies'. Employers are required to consult, among other things about ways of 'avoiding dismissals'. The EAT agreed with the union's claim that if there was no obligation to discuss the decision to close a workplace, then, this made a mockery of the obligation to consult about avoiding dismissals. It noted that, given the broad duties to consult about economic decisions under the Information and Consultation of Employees Regulations 2004 (see below), it would be strange if this obligation to consult applied up to the point of redundancies being proposed and then ceased as the 1992 Act took effect.

If the employer fails to consult according to the statutory requirements, the employees are entitled to a protective award. This will be an award of pay for the protected period which the employment tribunal considers just and equitable having regard to the seriousness of the employer's default (TULRCA 1992, s 189). The Court of Appeal has provided detailed guidance to employment tribunals on this matter (*Susie Radin Ltd* v *GMB and Others* [2004] IRLR 400). 'Special circumstances' for not consulting are permitted. This term is not defined.

Nevertheless, the employer must 'take all such steps towards compliance . . . as are reasonably practicable in those circumstances' (s 188(7)).

As indicated above, it is important to remember that consultation with 'appropriate representatives' (under TULRCA 1998, s 188) might well be affected by duties under the Information and Consultation of Employees Regulations 2004. These impose a duty on an employer to inform and consult on matters that have a considerable bearing on the economic context in which redundancy is taking place; and in relation to the measures affecting individual employees. The following provisions are key (reg 20):

- *Disclosure of information* on 'the recent and probable development of the undertaking's activities and economic situation'.
- *Information and consultation* on 'the situation, structure and probable development of employment within the undertaking and on any anticipatory measures envisaged, in particular, where there is a threat to employment within the undertaking'.
- *Information and consultation* on 'decisions likely to lead to substantial changes in work organisation or in contractual relations'. The duty on this last point will cease once the employer is consulting about redundancies under TULRCA 1992 (s 188).

Individual consultation

This arises under the law on unfair dismissal (see Chapter 8). A person who has been made redundant might complain to an employment tribunal of unfair dismissal. Redundancy is a fair reason (ERA 1996, s 98(2)). However, the tribunal would need to consider whether there was a genuine redundancy; whether the complainant had been fairly selected; and whether it was reasonable to dismiss the person for that reason. Evidence of individual consultation would go a long way to establishing procedural fairness. Such consultation is particularly important where there is no statutory duty to consult (i.e. where there are fewer than 20 people being made redundant). Even in the context of collective redundancies (i.e. involving 20 or more staff) individual consultation is good practice and certainly expected under the ACAS *Code of Practice on Disciplinary and Grievance Procedures.*

Notice of dismissal

An employee being made redundant is entitled to due notice (bearing in mind the statutory minima and any enhanced notice under the contract of employment). The trigger date for this notice has been clarified by the European Court of Justice (*Junk* v *Kuhnel* [2005] IRLR 310). It ruled that giving notice of redundancy is not the same as notice of dismissal. So, an employer must consult and notify employees of the redundancies *before* issuing notice of dismissal.

Redundancy pay

Potentially, there are two kinds of redundancy pay: that provided under statute (ERA 1996, ss 135 and 162); and enhancements to the statutory minimum provided at the discretion of the employer under the individual's contract of employment. In the CIPD survey (2002), it was reported that 73 per cent of employers paid redundancy compensation above the statutory minimum.

The right to statutory redundancy pay is set out as follows: 'An employer shall pay a redundancy payment to any employee of his if the employee (a) is dismissed by the employer by reason of redundancy or (b) is eligible for a redundancy payment by reason of being laid off or kept on short-time' (ERA 1996, s 135(1)).

Under European equal treatment law, it has been ruled by the European Court of Justice that 'pay' includes redundancy pay (Article 141, Treaty of Rome, as amended and consolidated). Consequently, redundancy benefits must be provided to men and women on the same terms.

Exclusions to the right to statutory redundancy payment arise in various circumstances:

- where the employee is dismissed for gross misconduct during the obligatory notice period;
- where an employee unreasonably refuses an offer of suitable alternative employment;
- when the employee is taking part in a strike (but not other forms of industrial action) before the employee is under the redundancy notice to terminate employment.

Statutory redundancy pay is calculated as follows (ERA 1996, s 162):

- one and a half weeks' pay: for a year of employment in which the employee was not below the age of 41;
- one week's pay: for a year of employment between 40 and 22 years;
- half a week's pay: for each year of employment between the ages of 18 and 21 years.

This structure was amended in 2006 to take account of age discrimination law. Nevertheless, employment before the age of 18 is not included. The maximum number of years that can be taken into account is 20. A 'week's pay' is revised annually and in February 2009 was set at £350 (see **www.berr.gov.uk/employment** for updates). Redundancy pay (both statutory and contractual) is tax free up to a specified limit which varies from time to time (see **www.hmrc.gov.uk**).

Exercise 3.2 Managing redundancies

Read the scenarios and decide on the following:

- *What legal issues do you think might be involved?*
- *Taking account of law and good employment practice, what would you recommend to the employer?*

3.2.1 The owner of a small print shop, because of technological change, has decided to make two print operators redundant. He is planning to give them a written notice of dismissal with their pay cheque.

3.2.2 Because of a fall in sales, a medium-sized regional grocery chain is proposing redundancies. The managing director suggests that staff employed on temporary contracts should be dismissed. The HR manager asks to discuss the proposal with him.

3.2.3 Because of technological change and a reorganisation to 'promote greater administrative efficiency', Trisha has been told that her post as a course administrator in a further education college's administration department will no longer exist. She is one of two such staff to be made redundant. To date, Trisha has worked for a course leader and has had a reasonable amount of autonomy in the day-to-day organisation of her work. Now, she has been offered a new position as a member of the 'course support team'. This will involve carrying out a wider range of administrative and secretarial functions together with two other members of staff. It means greater functional flexibility. She, along with the other administrators will have contact with course leaders – but it will be a pool of five rather than one. Her monthly pay and hours will remain the same. But she will be expected to schedule her working hours differently to provide greater cover. This will involve occasional work until 7 p.m.

Feedback on these exercises is provided in the Appendix to this textbook.

Transfers of undertakings

Evolution of the regulations

The Transfer of Undertaking (Protection of Employment) Regulations have had a convoluted evolution. They are an aspect of law that is sometimes seen as lacking clarity, stability, and has been viewed by most practitioners as being unduly complex. Case law has been particularly prominent in the law's development – and, arguably, its confusion. The original 1981 Regulations supposedly transposed the EU Acquired Rights Directive 1977 into British law. One particularly significant flaw was the 'unjustified restriction' (Cavalier 1997: 6) of these regulations to 'commercial ventures'– so excluding public sector bodies. This was rectified in 1993, ahead of a ruling in the European Court of Justice (*European Commission* v *UK* [1994] IRLR 392). A consequence of this early partial implementation of the Directive was that, in the 1980s, competitive tendering exercises in local government and the National Health Service, which resulted in changed and adverse terms and conditions for staff, were not challenged.

In 2001, the European Directive was amended and eventually transposed into British law as the Transfer of Undertaking (Protection of Employment) Regulations 2006 – rescinding the 1981 Regulations. Crucially, the new Regulations go beyond the Directive's requirements bringing within the scope of TUPE's employment protection the vast majority of service provision changes (i.e. those arising from outsourcing, in-sourcing and re-tendering exercises).

Purpose of the regulations

Initially, arising from concerns about the effects on employees of increased competition and, in particular, greater worker insecurity, arising from mergers and from the EU's 'single market', this European legislation sought to protect employees when the business they work for changes hands through a takeover, a merger or a form of subcontracting. The main effect of the regulations is to enable the contract of employment of an employee to be transferred over to the buyer of a business in the event of a business sale. They also apply where work is contracted out from a central organisation to subcontractors; or where one subcontractor succeeds another.

The pre-existing contractual terms and conditions of the relevant employees are to be preserved. A transfer should not affect their security of employment. Their continuity of employment is not broken. Also, both the seller and the purchaser (i.e. the '**transferor**' and the '**transferee**') are under an obligation to inform and consult representatives of those employees who may be affected by the transfer. This consultation should be with a view to seeking agreement on any proposed measures affecting these employees. Whilst, TUPE, potentially, benefits employees, it can also be advantageous to employers: it 'may have indirect benefit for management by reducing the probability that experienced staff will seek to leave once a potential transfer is mooted' (Rubery and Earnshaw 2005: 169).

Conceptually, TUPE constitutes a significant legal innovation. The regulations are '. . . a major limitation on both the principle of freedom of contract and the power of employers to arrange their commercial and corporate affairs in such a way as to minimise or fragment their employment law liabilities' (Deakin and Morris 2005: 216).

Coverage

The regulations apply to 'public and private undertakings engaged in economic activities whether or not they are operating for gain' (reg 3(4)). They clearly cover the public and voluntary sectors. In Britain, a non-statutory *Statement of practice on staff transfers in the public sector* was issued by the Cabinet Office in 2000 (and revised in 2007). As a supplementary document, it sets out guiding principles and guidance on transfers resulting from public–private partnerships; second and subsequent transfers; transfers back into the public sector; and transfers and reorganisations in the civil service.

Effectively, then, there are two employing organisations described in the Regulations as the:

- *transferor*: the employer who is transferring the staff;
- *transferee*: the new employer who is taking on the staff.

The working people to be protected under the 2006 regulations are 'employees'. They define (reg 2) an 'employee' as 'any individual who works for another person whether under a contract of service or apprenticeship or otherwise but does not include anyone who provides services under a contract for services'. Clearly, workers who have a contract of employment are covered; and the self-employed who are under contracts for services are excluded. It is not explicit, however, what 'otherwise' means and whether workers 'on some other contract to work personally' might be protected (see Chapter 2).

Although the regulations are silent on this matter, the Business Transfers Directive 2001 (Article 2(2)) states that member states shall not exclude from the scope of this directive contracts of employment or employment relationships solely because:

- of the number of hours performed;
- there is a fixed-duration contact of employment;
- there is a temporary employment relationship.

What is a 'relevant transfer'?

To determine this, three other questions must be answered:

- Was there a transfer to another person?
- Did an 'economic entity' transfer?
- Did the 'economic entity' retain its 'identity' after the transfer?

Was there a transfer to another person?

This is relatively straightforward. The regulations cover transfers as a result of a legal transfer or merger – generally a sale of a business between a vendor and a purchaser. Generally, share sales are not covered. The regulations also cover service provision changes:

- outsourcing and contracting out: i.e. where a service previously undertaken by an organisation is contacted out;
- where a contract is assigned to a new contractor on subsequent re-tendering;
- in-sourcing: i.e. where a contract ends with the service being performed 'in house'.

Did an 'economic entity' transfer?

An 'economic entity' is defined as 'an organised grouping of resources which has the objective of pursuing an economic activity, whether or not this activity is central or ancillary' (reg 3(2)). This is a question of fact for a tribunal or court to determine. The Employment Appeals Tribunal outlined guidance to determine whether an economic entity exists (*Cheeseman and Others* v *R. Brewer Contracts Ltd* [2001] IRLR 144):

- It must be a stable economic entity.
- It must be sufficiently structured and autonomous.
- It need not have significant tangible or intangible assets. (So, for example, in cleaning or surveillance, the assets are often reduced to their most basic and the activity is essentially based on manpower).
- A group of wage earners who are specifically and permanently assigned to a common task may (in the absence of other factors of production) amount to an economic entity.
- An activity is not an entity – other elements are needed.

Did the 'economic entity' retain its 'identity' after the transfer?

Identity must be retained for the regulations to apply. This is the decisive criterion. The EAT (in *Cheeseman and Others* v *R. Brewer Contracts Ltd* [2001] IRLR 144), drawing on the ECJ in the *Spijkers* case (1986), indicated a multifactoral test identifying the factors which were important. As the ECJ commented in a later case: 'It should be noted, however, that all those circumstances are merely single factors in the overall assessment which must be made and cannot therefore be considered in isolation' (*Sophie Redmond Stichtung* v *Bartol* [1992] IRLR 366, ECJ).

- Did the operation of the activity resume or continue?
- Are most of the employees taken over by the new employer?
- Are tangible assets transferred?
- What is the degree of similarity of the activities carried on before and after the transfer?
- Are the customers transferred?
- A transfer may exist without the existence of a formal contract.

The first case involving a service provision change involving the transfer of staff to two new service providers, resulted in some guidance from the Employment Appeals Tribunal (*Kimberley Group Housing Ltd* v *Hambley and Others*; *Angel Services (UK) Ltd* v *Hambley and Others* [2008] IRLR 682). The EAT stated that the apportionment of liabilities in a service provision change should be treated in the same way as a traditional transfer (i.e. the transfer of an economic entity which retains its identity). It ruled that Kimberley Group had taken the vast majority of the activities to which the employees were assigned. Therefore, it was responsible for all liabilities under their contracts of employment. 'The EAT has confirmed that the approach in the case of a service provision change should be no different to the approach already established for traditional transfers. This means that tribunals must determine as a matter of fact whether the employee is assigned to activities involved in the service provision change. If so, the employee will transfer to the new service provider taking on those particular activities' (Helen Hall, Partner, DLA Piper, *Personnel Today*, 8 July 2008).

Cross-border transfers

As long as the economic entity being transferred retains its identity, the Regulations are theoretically capable of applying to cross-border transfers. McMullan (2008) comments that 'case law . . . is thin on the ground, perhaps, because the issue does not often arise as a matter of contention: if there is a transfer of a business across borders, the employees rarely wish to move, especially when the transfer is to a geographically distant jurisdiction. The employees and trade unions tend to focus on negotiating the best redundancy package from the UK-based transferor'.

The European Union has published a case for cross-border applications within the European Union (CMS Employment Practice Area Group study at **ec.europa.eu**). Neither the 2001 directive (nor the 2006 regulations which transpose this into British law) applies itself to this issue. Theoretically, the directive could do so. It could potentially extend its scope across the EU and so significantly increase its significance.

The Employment Appeal Tribunal, under the 2006 regulations, has considered the issue in a case that involved the transfer to Israel of an undertaking which made curtain poles and tracks in *Tamworth* (*Holis Metal Industries Ltd* v *GMB and Another* (2008) EAT/0171/07). McMullan (2008) comments that, 'from the starting point that TUPE expressly applies to transfers of undertakings situated immediately before the transfer in the UK (as was the case here), the EAT held that set against the purpose of protecting the rights of workers in the event of a change in employer, a purposive approach to workers' rights requires that they should be protected even if the transfer is transnational. Enforcement might present a problem, but not an insuperable one.'

Contractual issues

There are several of these: continuity; rights, duties and liability; collective agreements; right to refuse transfer; occupational pensions; variation of contract.

Continuity

An employee's service under their contact of employment will continue and not be regarded as broken by the transfer. So accrued service with a previous employer or employers will count towards entitlements to statutory and contractual rights.

Rights and duties

The transferee takes over all the transferor's rights, powers and duties in respect of contracts of employment in force immediately before the transfer (reg 4). Apart from usual contractual terms such express terms as mobility clauses and restrictive covenants will also be transferred. The only exception, as far as terms and conditions are concerned relates to occupational pensions (see below).

Liabilities

These are also transferred. The transferee inherits the transferor's liability in, for example, employment tribunal claims and other civil proceedings. The following are some examples of the transfer of claims:

- *Sex discrimination*: *DJM International* v *Nicolas* [1986] IRLR 76
- *Accident at work*: *Bernadone* v *Pall Mall Services Group and Another* [1999] IRLR 617
- *Transferor's right of indemnity* under an employer's liability insurance policy is a right which transfers: *Martin* v *Lancashire County Council* [2000] Court of Appeal.

Employee liability information

The regulations impose a requirement on the transferor to disclose this information to the transferee (reg 11) (see Exhibit 3.6). It must be in writing or made available in reasonably accessible form or provided by a third party at least two weeks before the completion of the transfer. The transferee may complain to an employment tribunal, within three months of the date of the relevant transfer, that the transferor has failed to provide specific information (reg 12). If the complaint is well-founded, the tribunal shall make a declaration and may award compensation to the transferee that it considers 'just and equitable'.

Exhibit 3.6 Employee liability information

The information to be provided by the transferor to the transferee:

- Identity of employees who will transfer.
- The ages of those employees.
- Information in the 'statements of employment particulars' of each employee (ERA 1996, s 1).
- Information relating to any collective agreements which apply to those employees.
- Instances of any disciplinary action within the preceding two years taken by the transferor in respect of those employees.*
- Instances of any grievances raised by those employees within the preceding two years.*
- Instances of any legal actions taken by transferring employees against the transferor in the previous two years. (This would cover employment tribunal complaints and other civil proceedings in the courts.)
- Circumstances where transferor reasonably believes legal action may be brought.

* Although rescinded in 2009, the statutory dispute resolution procedures may still be relevant in these cases.

Collective agreements

Collective agreements and union recognition agreements are transferred to the new owner (regs 5 and 6) until they are terminated or are replaced. It appears that transferred employees are able to benefit from pay increases negotiated through collective bargaining following a transfer – even though the relevant union has been derecognised. This arises if the individual contracts of employment have not been varied by agreement; or the employee had been dismissed and re-engaged on terms that did not include the adherence to the agreement (*Whent* v *T. Cartledge*, 1997, EAT). Two particular issues should be noted in respect of the application of collective agreements. First, their terms will be incorporated into individual contracts and can 'live on' after a collective agreement has been rescinded (see Chapter 2). Secondly, the normal principles of contract variation are applicable; but are in the case of relevant transfers supplemented by special provisions (see below).

Right to object to the transfer

The enforced transfer of an employee to a new employer is not permissible (reg 4 (7 and 8)). The employee's objection terminates the contract of employment and he or she shall not be regarded as being dismissed by the employer. S/he is not obliged to give notice of resignation, other than to make an objection (which does not have to be done in writing). This provision arises from an earlier case in the European Court of Justice (*Katsikas* v *Konstantinidis* [1993] IRLR 179). The employee, in these circumstances is not entitled to any statutory or contractual rights (for example, relating to dismissal or redundancy pay).

Occupational pensions

These remain excluded from the terms and conditions of employment transferred; and were specifically excluded in the original Acquired Rights Directive 1977. There are certain caveats that can be made about the current situation.

- *The general private sector position.* Occupational pension rights earned up to the time of the transfer are protected by social security legislation and pension trust arrangements. The transferee is not required to continue identical occupational pension arrangements for the transferred employees. Where these employees were entitled to participate in the transferor's occupational pension scheme, the new employer must establish a minimum level of pension provision for the transferred employees. Under the Pensions Act 2004 and the Transfer of Employment (Pension Protection) Regulations 2005, the minimum 'safety net' requires the transferee to match employee contributions up to 6 per cent of salary into a stakeholder pension or offer an equivalent alternative.

- *Public sector employees.* The government continues to follow the policy set out in HM Treasury note, *A Fair Deal for Staff Pensions* (2004). A private sector transferee, receiving public sector workers, must offer 'a good quality pension scheme' that is 'broadly comparable' to that previously enjoyed by these employees.

The transfer period

Determining this period of time is often difficult for HR practitioners. There is no certainty about its duration. The DTI guidance states the following: 'There is likely to come a time when the link with the transfer can be treated as no longer effective. However, this must be assessed in the light of all the circumstances of the individual case and will vary from case to case. There is no "rule of thumb" used by the courts or specified in the regulations to define a period of time after which it is safe to assume that the transfer did not impact directly or indirectly on the employer's actions' (see Exhibit 3.7).

Exhibit 3.7 TUPE and harmonisation

Taylor v *Connex South Eastern Ltd* EAT/1243/99

Facts. Mr Taylor, in 1995, started work as a company administrator with British Rail. With privatisation, his contract of employment was transferred in 1996, under TUPE 1981, to Connex South Eastern Ltd. In 1997, he was offered a new contract by Connex but the terms and conditions were never agreed between the parties. He continued employment on his transferred British Rail terms. In 1998, Connex began a rationalisation involving SE Ltd and another part of the group, South Central Ltd. As a result, Taylor was presented with another new contract which was to his detriment in relation to contractual redundancy and holiday entitlements. All but a couple of the 250 staff agreed the new terms. As a result of his refusal to agree the new contract, Taylor was dismissed. He complained of unfair dismissal to an employment tribunal; and then went on appeal to the EAT.

EAT judgment. The crucial issue for the EAT to consider was whether his dismissal was *connected with the transfer*. When there was an elapse of time since the date of the transfer there was an issue of whether there was a weakening of 'the chain of causation' which maintained the connection. However, the EAT ruled, that the mere passage of time without anything happening does not *in itself* constitute a weakening to the point of dissolution of the chain of causation. It also ruled that the fact that the overwhelming majority had accepted the changes was not relevant. The rights under the Regulations were individual not collective rights; and were capable of being asserted by the individual.

Comment. '. . . once the Regulations are found to apply to a transfer (which is a matter of law that cannot be excluded by the agreement of the parties) its effects are far-reaching and can continue for a considerable time after the point of transfer. This can cause severe practical problems for transferees seeking to harmonise terms and conditions. This case emphasises that if an employee is dismissed for refusing to accept a variation of terms and conditions, something more than the mere passing of time is needed to sever the connection between the reason for dismissal and the transfer' (Industrial Relations Services, *Industrial Relations Law Bulletin*, 662).

TUPE Regulations 2006. These now permit contract variation for **ETO** reasons (see below). If that is not achievable by an employer, then, the principles established in the *Taylor* case still apply.

Variation of contract

- *General law on contract variation.* The basic principle applies that an employer can only change a contract of employment with the agreement of the employee (see above). However, there are some important qualifications to be made under the Transfer of Undertakings Regulations which are considered below.

- *No inferior terms and conditions.* Other than in the special circumstances of insolvency, it is unlawful to make 'a substantial change in working conditions to the detriment' of an employee who is transferred. In these circumstances, the employee can regard the contract as terminated and s/he as being dismissed (reg 4(9)). The employee may then claim at an employment tribunal. This statutory right to complain does not prevent the employee resigning and claiming constructive dismissal for a repudiatory breach of contract (reg 4(11)).

- *No variation in transfer period.* As indicated above, the purpose of the regulations is to protect employees during business transfers; and so to ensure that the terms of their contracts of employment remain unchanged in the transfer period. A question that often arises from human resource managers is whether it is possible to change contracts after the transfer has taken place. Until 2006, the short answer was 'no' if the proposed variation related to the transfer. Indeed, the situation is still that 'any' variation of a contract related to the transfer is 'void' (reg 4(4)). The restrictions on changing terms and conditions of employment also apply to anticipatory changes – i.e. where the transferor is contemplating changed terms and conditions for those employees who are likely to transfer. However, under the latest iteration of the regulations, there are specific circumstances when variation might take place: where the change is for an 'economic, technical or organisational reason entailing changes in the workforce', and in insolvency situations.

- **ETO** *reasons.* Changes to contracts of employment are permitted if the sole or principal reason for the variation is either:
  - a reason connected with the transfer that is an 'economic, technical or organisational reason entailing changes in the workforce';
  - a reason entirely unconnected with the transfer (for example a sudden loss of an order or an upturn in demand for a service).

  There is no statutory definition of these ETO reasons. However, the following have been suggested in guidance from the former Department of Trade and Industry:
  - *Economic*: a reason relating to the profitability or market performance of the transferee's business.
  - *Technical*: a reason relating to the nature of the equipment or production processes which the transferee operates.
  - *Organisational*: a reason relating to the management or organisation structure of the transferee's business.

  The phrase 'entailing changes in the workforce' also has no statutory definition. The DTI described it this way: 'interpretation by the courts has restricted it to changes in the numbers employed or to changes in the functions performed by employees'. If any changes of terms and conditions are proposed by the employer, they should be agreed with the recognised trade union or with the individual employees.

- *Beneficial contractual changes.* A case, under the 1981 regulations, involving a beneficial contractual change (concerning contractual retirement age and prior to the enactment of age discrimination legislation) which a transferee had initially proposed and then reneged on, was ruled on by the Court of Appeal (*Regent Security Services Ltd* v *Power* [2008] IRLR 66). The Court of Appeal took the view that nothing in public policy, reflected in European or British legislation nor in case law, prevents an employee from obtaining an additional right (i.e. an improved contractual term). The employee is able to agree with the transferee to obtain an additional right by reason of the transfer. The employee would be treated as obtaining an additional right, not as waiving a transferred acquired right. So, Mr Power's reliance on the retirement age of 65 agreed with the transferee, even for a reason connected with the transfer of the undertaking, was ***not*** contrary to the prohibition on employees contracting out of the protection and safeguards of the TUPE.

This case was brought under the 1981 regulations. The 2006 regulations, as indicated above, preclude 'any' variation (unless it is for an ETO reason) and rule that it would be 'void' (reg 4(4)). This obviously raises some uncertainty in the application of the law. John McMullen (2008) comments that 'it is perhaps more likely that the tribunals and courts will interpret reg 4(4) in line with the Court of Appeal decision in *Power* given the strong message that the purpose of the Acquired Rights Directive is to protect employees' and not employers' rights'.

- *Insolvency situations.* In these circumstances, where an insolvent business is being transferred, the restrictions on the variation of contracts would be waived subject to certain conditions (reg 9):
  - *Permitted variation.* These must be agreed with appropriate representatives of the affected workforce. The purpose of such variations must be 'to safeguard employment opportunities by ensuring the survival of the undertaking' (reg 9(7)(b)). Such variations may include, in the exceptional circumstances of insolvency, pay reductions and other inferior terms and conditions. No variations should breach any statutory entitlements.
  - *Agreements.* These may be with representatives of recognised **independent trade unions** and will be in the form of a collective agreement. Non-union representatives are empowered to agree permitted variations subject to the following requirements: the agreement must be in writing and signed by the representatives; and before signature, the employer must provide all affected employees with a copy of the agreement and any necessary guidance.

Dismissal

A dismissal is automatically unfair if the reason or principal reason for the dismissal is the transfer or a reason connected with it. The only exception to this is where the dismissal is for an 'economic, technical or organisational reason entailing changes in the workforce' of either the transferor or the transferee before of after the relevant transfer (reg 7). The responsibility rests with the employer who is dismissing the employee to show that the dismissal is for an ETO reason. The test of reasonableness will apply (see Chapter 8). If the reason for the dismissal is redundancy, then, the usual arrangements for handling redundancies apply and the dismissed employee may be entitled to statutory redundancy pay (see above in this chapter).

The European Court of Justice has ruled that if an employee is dismissed in breach of the, then, 1977 Acquired Rights Directive (Article 4(1)), s/he must be considered still to be employed by the undertaking at the date of the transfer (*Bork (P) International A/S* v *Foreningen af Arbejdsledere i Danmark* [1989] IRLR 41). This was implied into the 1981 regulations by the House of Lords.

Consultation and information disclosure

The requirement for employers to share information and to consult with 'affected employees' collectively both before and after a transfer has taken place is a key feature of the regulations (reg 13). Obligations are placed on both the transferor and the transferee. The workforces which may be affected include:

- those employees who are to be transferred;
- staff of the transferor who will not transfer but whose jobs might be affected;
- employees of the transferee whose jobs might be affected.

Since 1999, where there is a recognised independent trade union, it must be consulted. In non-union workplaces, appropriate employee representatives must be consulted (reg 13). Sargeant (2002) found that 'where trade unions were present then effective consultation seemed to take place at an early stage and at quite a detailed level. It is in other situations that there must be a real concern.'

Duty to inform

This requires the disclosure of the following information:

- the date or proposed date of the transfer;
- why the transfer is taking place;
- the legal, economic, organisational and social implications of the transfer;
- measures envisaged arising from the transfer.

Duty to consult

This duty is to consult with employee representatives and not with individual employees (although, good practice suggests that, on occasion, that might be sensible). The consultation must be with a view to seeking their agreement to the measures to be taken. It must take place long enough before the transfer. The employer must respond to any representations made by workforce representatives; and if the representations are rejected, reasons must be given.

Rights of representatives

They are entitled to facilities to enable them to carry out their function; and to protection against dismissal or any detrimental treatment (ERA 1996, s 103).

Exercise 3.3 Managing transfers

Read the scenarios and decide on the following:

- *What legal issues do you think might be involved?*
- *Taking account of both law and good employment practice, what would you recommend to the employer?*

3.3.1 A facilities management company has acquired a contract cleaning company. The managing director tells the HR manager that he wants there to be a common pay structure for existing and recently acquired cleaning staff. In addition, work rotas and holiday arrangements must be harmonised.

3.3.2 A non-union catering company has successfully bid for the contract to provide facilities at Somerset University. The existing terms and conditions of the staff to be transferred have been negotiated with the recognised union, UNISON. Relevant provisions of collective agreements have been incorporated into the individual contracts of employment. The managing director of the transferee tells the HR manager that he wants to preserve a union-free company.

3.3.3 Some weeks after the transfer of a security company the transferee receives correspondence from an employment tribunal citing it as respondent employer in a race discrimination complaint involving harassment. The single incident of harassment is said to have occurred several weeks before the transfer date when the complainant and the perpetrator were employed by the transferor.

3.3.4 A company which manages parks and gardens is to acquire staff who work at a large privately owned country house. Some of the staff to be transferred are permanent employees, some are on seasonal contracts (working between March and October) and some are called self-employed (although they work most of the year in the park). The HR manager of the transferee questions whether these 'self-employed' staff should be transferred; and also how the contract staff should be dealt with.

Feedback on these exercises is provided in the Appendix to this textbook.

Conclusion

The consequences of business change can be fraught with complexities – not just for operational reasons but also, as indicated above, as far as the law is concerned. This is particularly so where the various bodies of law interpenetrate. Clear business objectives, careful planning, understanding of the employer's duties and their liabilities in law, genuine consultation and appropriate information disclosure and attention to the good employment practice will all contribute to a satisfactory outcome.

References and useful websites

Advisory, Conciliation and Arbitration Service (2009) *Code of Practice on Disciplinary and Grievance Procedures*. London: ACAS.

Atkinson, J. (1984) 'Manpower strategies for flexible organisations', *Personnel Management*, August.

Cavalier, S. (1997) *Transfer Rights: TUPE in Perspective*. London: Institute of Employment Rights.

Chartered Institute of Personnel and Development (2002) *Survey of Redundancies* (www.cipd.co.uk).

Collings, H. (1999) *Employment Law*. Oxford: Oxford University Press.

Deakin, S. and Morris, G. (2005) *Labour Law in Britain*. Oxford: Hart.

Foley, K. (1994) 'The lessons of market testing: the experience of prison education', in *Privatisation and Market Testing in the Prison Service*. London: Prison Reform Trust.

Kersley, B. *et al.* (2006) *Inside the Workplace: Findings from the 2004 Workplace Employment Relations Survey*. London: Routledge.

McMullen, J. (2008) 'TUPE Case Law Update', Industrial Relations Services, *Employment Review* 892, February.

Millward, N. *et al.* (1992) *Workplace Industrial Relations in Transition*. Aldershot: Dartmouth.

Reilly, P. *et al.* (1996) *Outsourcing: a Flexible Option for the Future?* London: Gower.

Rubery, J. and Earnshaw, J. (2005) 'Employment policy and practice: crossing borders and disordering hierarchies', in Marchington, M., Grimshaw, D., Rubery, J. and Wilmott, H. *Fragmenting World*. Oxford: Oxford University Press.

Ryan, M. (1994) 'Privatisation and corporate interest and the future shape and ethos of the prison service', in *Privatisation and Market Testing in the Prison Service*. London: Prison Reform Trust.

Sachdev, S. (2006) *The Impact of Contracting Out on Employment Relations in Public Services*. London: Institute of Employment Rights.

Sargeant, M. (2002) 'New transfer regulations', *Industrial Law Journal*, Vol. 31, March.

Shapinker, M. (2003) 'A cost-effective way to lose control of your business', *Financial Times*, 15 October.

Shapinker, M. (2005) 'Outsourcing the essentials is bad for your health', *Financial Times*, 26 January.

Timmins, N. (2005) 'Revolution in the way public services are delivered heads towards fruition', *Financial Times*, 26 October.

Torrington, D. and Hall, L. (1998) *Human Resource Management* (4th edn). Hemel Hempstead: Prentice Hall Europe.

Useful websites

Department for Business Enterprise and Regulatory Reform **www.berr.gov.uk**

Chartered Institute of Personnel and Development **www.cipd.co.uk**

European Commission **ec.europa.eu**

HM Revenue and Customs **www.hmrc.gov.uk**

UK Statistics Authority **www.statistics.gov.uk**

Visit **www.mylawchamber.co.uk/willey** to access multiple choice questions, case flashcards and exercises to test yourself on this chapter.

mylawchamber

4 The context of discrimination at work

Learning objectives

- To understand the key concepts used in equal opportunities
- To appreciate the importance of historic and contemporary patterns of discrimination
- To understand the population and labour market profiles of various groups within society
- To understand the social and economic factors affecting discrimination
- To examine the degree of overall success of the statutory framework of discrimination law

Structure of the chapter

- *General concepts*: discrimination; equal opportunities and equal treatment; managing diversity; institutional discrimination; positive action; positive discrimination; 'political correctness'
- *The social and economic context of discrimination*: the population profile; the incidence of discrimination at work; the context of discrimination on the grounds of sex, race, disability, age, sexual orientation, and religion and belief
- *The state of the law and the proposed single Equality Act*: summary of proposals; what problems is it designed to tackle; grounds of discrimination; complexity and 'bureaucratisation' of equal opportunities; extending limits of law; covert discrimination; the 'tie-break' and positive action; multiple discrimination; sectoral problems; monitoring; weak enforcement

Introduction

The extensive framework of discrimination law covering employment and the wider society has been enacted to deal with a wide range of policies and practices founded on stereotyping, prejudice and in some instances, hatred. The genesis of such discriminatory behaviour, for many different reasons, is, generally, in the past. This historical origin means that many of the attitudes are deeply embedded in our culture, have often formed part of socialisation and so can be difficult to challenge and eradicate. This chapter is designed to consider the key concepts that arise in discrimination law; and set out the social and economic context of discrimination. The law relating to the various strands of discrimination is examined in Chapter 5, and employment policies and practices are outlined in Chapter 6.

General concepts in equal opportunities

These are central to any examination of discrimination across all strands.

Discrimination

As a phenomenon, this occurs widely both within employment and within society at large. Clearly, it is about the exercise of choice – for example, in recruitment or in promotions. Implicit in this exercise of choice is the fact that action can be taken *in favour* of one person and *against* another. The critical issue is the grounds on which that discrimination or choice is made. So, for example, when a manager appoints a person to a post, the key question is: 'what were the grounds for making that choice and rejecting other applicants?' Were the applicants considered against ***objective criteria*** for the position – e.g. experience, skills and qualifications? Was there evidence that ***unlawful criteria*** were used – e.g. avoiding the recruitment of a pregnant woman or a disabled person?

The concept of discrimination, of course, encompasses wider patterns of social, economic and political behaviour whereby particular groups of people are stereotyped, victimised and discriminated against on the presumption that they possess certain characteristics. Various social and employment barriers can reinforce unfair discrimination and prevent a person achieving equal treatment. For example, the social role of caring for children which is, traditionally, ascribed to women has been found to be a considerable obstacle in the attainment of promotion, career progression and equal pay.

Equal opportunities and equal treatment

Anti-discrimination measures are invariably discussed in the context of equal opportunities and equal treatment policies. 'Equal opportunities', as a concept, derives from the United States of America and was imported into British civil rights and employment law in the 1970s. Less common in usage is the term 'equal treatment' originating from European Union discrimination law. Differentiating between these two terms is difficult and, probably, pointless. In practice – in the thinking of managers, in the experience of working people and, usually, in the interpretation of the law – they have become synonymous. Superficially, 'equal opportunities' is an attractive term because it is aspirational. It seems to go beyond the present situation to consider access to improved conditions and circumstances, the provision of better standards and the encouragement of those who are disadvantaged. Nevertheless, it is important to note that it is EU equal treatment law that has facilitated a considerable range of opportunities for women. So, in terms of outcomes, there may be little to suggest that either term is preferable.

Managing diversity

In some literature in the early 1990s (Kandola *et al.* 1994), this was seen as a concept opposed to 'equal opportunities'. The latter was seen as restrictive and relying on piecemeal compliance. Managing diversity was seen as more inclusive and business-related. However, 'managing diversity' has been a controversial concept. As originally conceived, it individualises equal opportunities, so distracting attention from the group basis of discrimination. However, when promoting the concept in Britain, from the mid-1990s, the Chartered Institute of Personnel and Development saw it as an evolutionary step in the development of equal opportunities. The Institute saw equal opportunities and managing diversity as 'complementary', 'interdependent' and 'not alternatives'. In its view managing diversity is related to strategic management issues and it encompasses the entire employment relationship. Managing diversity was seen as helpful in making 'the business case' for equal opportunities.

Diversity management can now be characterised as follows:

- It provides *a coherent approach* which integrates both business and personal needs with ethical standards and equal treatment law. The CIPD (1996) said that it is 'based on the concept that people should be valued as individuals for reasons related to business interests, as well as for moral and social reasons'.
- It provides *a strategic approach* to equal opportunities. So, it is associated with such strategic business and human resource issues as quality management, productivity and cost effectiveness, empowerment, performance management and continuous development. It has an explicit economic focus in respect of labour cost-effectiveness.
- It is *inclusive*. It embraces all corporate policies and working practices and expects that they are tested against the criteria of diversity management. Such policies and practices should be assessed when they are being formulated, when they are implemented and when audit and review takes place.
- The essential focus is on *the individual employee*. It is concerned with his/her characteristics, needs, aspirations and differences. The success of the policy is, then, determined by the extent to which the interests of individuals are accommodated by corporate policies. (Having said that, there must be acknowledgement that discriminatory treatment has a group base. Stereotyping of individuals arises because they are presumed to have the same characteristics as similar people. Unlawful discrimination can only be tackled effectively by addressing both the individual and the group dimensions.)
- It is *management driven*. It is line managers, team leaders and human resource managers who are responsible for establishing the ways in which both legislative requirements and individual needs result in corporate action. The human resource department or individual equality officers should not be left as the isolated 'guardians' of equal opportunities. There is a clearer and wider management responsibility.

Institutional discrimination

In the report of the Stephen Lawrence Inquiry (1999), institutional racism was reported as a characteristic of the Metropolitan Police Service. It was defined as: 'the collective failure of an organisation to provide an appropriate and professional service to people because of their colour, culture or ethnic origin. It can be seen or detected in processes, attitudes and behaviour which amount to discrimination through unwitting prejudice, ignorance, thoughtlessness and racist stereotyping which disadvantage minority ethnic people.'

This useful definition of one type of discrimination can in fact be generalised. It is possible for organisations to be institutionally discriminatory across many, if not all, strands of discrimination law, in their employment practices, their service delivery and the way they deal with suppliers and contractors. Recognition that this may be a characteristic of organisations has resulted in two related initiatives: the mainstreaming of equal treatment; and the enactment of statutory duties on public authorities to promote equal opportunities and eradicate discrimination (see Chapter 5).

Positive action and positive discrimination

These two concepts are, theoretically, defined quite separately. However, in practice, they can be blurred. *Positive action* is provided for in all strands of discrimination law. Largely, it is conceived as encouragement for under-represented groups to apply for posts and promotion opportunities and to participate in training opportunities. However, decisions to appoint or promote must be made against objective criteria. *Positive discrimination*, by contrast is sometimes referred to as 'reverse discrimination'. Essentially, it is preferential treatment on the grounds of a particular characteristic, for example, sex or race. Apart from a House of Lords ruling on disability discrimination (see Exhibit 4.1), it is unlawful under British discrimination law. However, in practice, there may be no clear-cut theoretical distinction. For example, preferential access to training and development opportunities may be both positive action and positive discrimination – particularly if the course is 'rigidly confined' to the disadvantaged group (Pitt 1992: 283).

As a general comment, Deakin and Morris (1998: 592) state that 'as part of an equal opportunities policy it is arguable that an employer may legitimately decide to employ or promote, for example, a woman, who is found to be *equally well-qualified* with a male applicant or colleague with the aim of improving the balance of women and men in particular parts of its workforce'. This practice reflects the 'tie-break' situation which has been ruled upon by the European Court of Justice (see Exhibit 4.2); and also has been proposed as an aspect of a Single Equality Act in the UK (see Exhibit 4.4 later).

The arguments for and against positive discrimination are various. In favour are the following:

- ***Eradication of historic patterns of disadvantage.*** This argument is founded on the view that historic patterns are still influential today in framing social attitudes and expectations towards women, members of various ethnic groups and religions, disabled people, and homosexual and transgender people. The various historic obstacles to equal opportunities have included male social dominance; the legacy of colonialism, slavery and racism; the social marginalisation and low expectations held of disabled people; and the legacy of criminality and 'perversion' affecting opinions of sexual orientation. So, 'the point of positive discrimination is to give them [disadvantaged people] the capacity and the confidence to

Exhibit 4.1 Positive discrimination and disability discrimination: the extent of the 'reasonable adjustment' duty

Archibald v *Fife Council* [2004] UKHL 32, HL

Facts. Ms Archibald was a road sweeper employed by Fife Council between May 1997 and March 2001. In April 1999, she underwent a minor surgical procedure that led to a rare complication resulting in severe pain over her heels, rendering her unable to walk. Initially, she had to use a wheelchair and later was able to walk only with the aid of sticks. The Council obtained medical advice in July 2000 that she remained unfit for work as a road sweeper but that she was fit for a sedentary job.

In the meantime, the employer had explored whether suitable alternative work could be offered to her. She applied, unsuccessfully, for over 100 posts in various departments. Some were office-based and on marginally more pay than she received as a road sweeper. Despite representations from her union, she had to undertake competitive interviews in line with the Council's redeployment policy.

In March 2001, the Council took the view that the deployment procedure had been exhausted and that she should be dismissed, given the length of her absence and the report that she would be unable to return to work as a road sweeper in the foreseeable future.

Her complaint:

- that she had been discriminated against on grounds of disability;
- that she should not have had to compete for alternative employment if she could show that she could perform the duties and responsibilities of the post applied for;
- that the council had failed to comply with the duty to make reasonable adjustment.

House of Lords ruling:

- The duty to make reasonable adjustments (DDA 1995) *may* require an employer to treat a disabled person more favourably than a non-disabled person in order to remove the disadvantage caused by the disability. This may include transferring an employee to a suitable vacant position.
- Lady Justice Hale said that under the Sex Discrimination Act 1975 and the Race Relations Act 1976, everyone is treated equally. 'Men and women, black or white as the case may be, are opposite sides of the same coin . . . Treating men more favourably than women discriminates against women. Treating women more favourably than men discriminates against men'. The DDA does not expect disabled and non-disabled people to be treated in the same way. It makes provision for reasonable adjustments to be made to meet the special needs of disabled people. It is clear that the DDA 'entails *a measure of positive discrimination*, in the sense that employers are required to take steps to help disabled people which they are not required to take for others'. However, it is also the case that employers are required to take only those steps 'which in all the circumstances it is reasonable for them to take'. The steps that are reasonable include the extent to which it is practicable for the employer and the financial costs incurred.

decide their goals for themselves, to empower them, to remove their existential marginality and to assure them that no area of life is necessarily and inherently inaccessible to them' (Parekh 1992: 270).

- ***Compensatory action.*** 'Social justice' implies compensatory action for past systematic breaches of fair treatment. Such action can take various forms (public training courses for women or different ethnic groups; assistance with childcare; appointing people from disadvantaged groups to public office as both representatives of particular interests and as role models; and, in employment, setting quotas for the recruitment or promotion of particular under-represented groups). This action helps avoid social exclusion, promote social cohesion and the moral obligations and rights of a liberal democracy.

Exhibit 4.2 Equal treatment, positive discrimination and the 'tie-break'

Marschall v *Land Nordrhein-Westfalen* [1998] IRLR 39

Facts. A German secondary school teacher, Helmutt Marschall, applied for promotion to a higher-grade teaching post. The civil service law of the Federal State of North Rhine-Westphalia provides that where 'there are fewer women than men in the particular higher-grade post in the career bracket, women are to be given priority for promotion in the event of equal suitability, competence and professional performance unless reasons specific to an individual (male) candidate tilt the balance in his favour'. He was informed that an equally qualified woman was to be appointed. He initiated legal proceedings in Germany.

ECJ ruling. This practice was not incompatible with the Equal Treatment Directive. The provision in civil service law was compatible provided that:

- in each individual case there is a guarantee that the candidates will be subject to an objective assessment which takes account of all criteria;
- where one or more of those criteria tilts the balance in favour of a male candidate, the priority accorded to female candidates will be overridden; and
- such criteria are not discriminatory against female candidates.

Although approving the possible legality of the 'tie-break' in the *Marschall* case, the ECJ has asserted that 'positive discrimination is incompatible with equal treatment law. In an earlier German case it stated that rules which guarantee women absolute and unconditional priority for public sector appointments (where women are under-represented) go beyond promoting equal opportunities and overstep the limits of the Equal Treatment Directive (*Kalenke* v *Freie Hansestadt Bremen* [1995] IRLR 660). Disapproval of positive discrimination was confirmed in a later case (*Abrahamsson and Anderson* v *Fogelqvist* (2000) C-407/98).

Positive action in the form of targets, for recruitment, selection and promotion, has been considered and ruled to be compatible with equal treatment law. The proviso was that women should not be offered automatically and unconditionally preferential treatment over men (*Badeck* v *Land Hessen* (2000) C-158/97, IRLR 432).

Against positive discrimination are arguments that it is inappropriate to compensate for the past wrongs experienced by previous generations; and that it is, potentially, socially divisive. On the one hand, any compensatory action may only benefit some members of the disadvantaged group. Furthermore, in employment in particular, it may result in a 'backlash' because the discrimination cannot be defended on objective grounds; and it may result in further discrimination if better qualified applicants for jobs and for promotion are rejected.

Language and 'political correctness'

One of the more controversial aspects of discrimination law and the promotion of equal opportunities is the acceptability of language (or what is called 'political correctness' by certain commentators and some politicians who appear hostile to attempts to examine the connotations of particular language). Words are powerful instruments for identifying, categorising, stereotyping and demeaning people. They carry with them connotations and coded messages.

Over time there can be shifts in the use of acceptable language. For example, the word 'negro' has ceased to be used because it was associated with racism and slavery in the southern states of the USA and in particular with its corrupted form 'nigger'. It was replaced, in the late 1960s by the term 'black' – reflecting the growth of 'black consciousness' and 'black power' political movements. In recent years, the term African-Caribbean (or, if appropriate, African-American) has become more acceptable, and has closer associations with ethnicity in the way that colour does not. This process of evolving language indicates ways of attempting to arrive at descriptions that are acceptable and without pejorative connotations. Above all, this language is aiming to demonstrate respect. Whether the recipients of the language are women, young people, older people, people of various sexual orientations, disabled persons or those with specific religious beliefs, the connotations of the words used should be considered. If not, they may be found to be discriminatory or evidence of harassment (see Chapter 7). It is particularly important when advertising jobs that employers are careful about the language used because this may infringe provisions of the relevant legislation (see Chapter 5).

The social and economic context of discrimination

An overall view

The incidence of discrimination at work is considered and then the historic and contemporary context of each strand of discrimination law is examined.

The population profile

The total population of Britain is just over 58 million people (Census 2001) comprising:

- *disabled people*: 10 million;
- *ethnic minority people*: 4.6 million;
- *gay, lesbian and bisexual people*: estimated between 2.3 million and 3.2 million;
- *belonging to non-Christian religions*: 3.2 million;
- *gender and age profile*: see Table 4.1.

Table 4.1 Population profile on basis of gender and age

Age bands	*Women*	*%*	*Men*	*%*
Under 16 years	5,489,000	18	5,773,000	20
16–64 years	18,847,000	63	18,668,000	66
65 and above	5,353,000	18	3,994,000	14
Total	**29,690,000**	**100**	**28,435,000**	**100**

Source: Adapted from Office for National Statistics (2004).

The incidence of discrimination at work

It is difficult to be precise about the scale of employees' experience of discrimination at work. This is because of various factors: for example, determining whether particular conduct is discriminatory in the view of the victim; the possibility that the victim may deny that they are being discriminated against; whether objectively others would regard the behaviour as discrimination.

In the 2003 British Social Attitudes Survey (Kaur 2004: 8), 'very few employees said that they were aware of their employer discriminating unfairly against an employee on the grounds of sex, age, disability, race or ethnicity, sexual orientation or religion or belief when getting a job. Employees were mostly aware of their employer treating an employee unfairly in the last five years when getting promotion. This was across sex, age and race discrimination.' More detailed data is in *The First Fair Treatment at Work Survey* (Grainger and Fitzner 2007) (Table 4.2).

Table 4.2 Personal experience of discrimination at work in the last two years by equality strands (%)

	Male	*Female*	*White*	*Non-white*	*Total*
Disability discrimination (including long-term illness)	1.4	0.9	1.3	0.4	1.2
Sex discrimination (including marital status and pregnancy)	0.5	1.4	1.0	0.7	0.9
Race discrimination	1.0	0.6	0.4	4.0	0.8
Age discrimination	0.9	0.8	0.9	0.7	0.8
Religious discrimination	0.3	0.2	0.2	1.1	0.2
Sexual orientation discrimination	*	*	*	*	*
All types of discrimination at work	**3.6**	**3.5**	**3.3**	**5.6**	**3.5**

Survey population: 3,936 employees. Interviewed between November 2005 and January 2006.

* Less than 10 cases.

Source: Heidi Grainger and Grant Fitzner (2007) *The First Fair Treatment at Work Survey: Executive Summary – Updated*, Department of Trade and Industry (www.berr.gov.uk).

In this survey (Grainger and Fitzner 2007: 10), employees who said that they had been treated unfairly at work in the last two years were asked if they would consider it discrimination: 70 per cent said they did; and significantly more respondents said that they had witnessed others being treated unfairly than had experienced unfair treatment personally. Employment tribunal complaints and their outcomes also provide some indication of the extent of discrimination and harassment. However, these data and official statistics need to be considered with some caution. Nevertheless, they provide a reasonable snapshot of the situation at a particular point in time (Tables 4.2, 4.3 and 4.4).

Other research for ACAS (Denvir *et al.* 2007) suggests from an analysis of employment tribunal claims (made between January 2004 and September 2006) that there is clear evidence of discrimination and particularly harassment (sometimes over a number of years) on the grounds of sexual orientation in the private sector. As far as discrimination on the grounds of religion or belief, bullying and harassment was significant. Some applicants also cited problems around working hours, time off or leave (in relation to religious observance).

Table 4.3 Employment tribunal discrimination complaints

Claims	*2004/05*	*2005/06*	*2006/07*
Sex discrimination	11,726	14,250	28,153
Pregnancy	1,345	1,504	1,465
Equal pay	8,229	17,268	44,013
Race discrimination	3,317	4,103	3,780
Disability discrimination	4,942	4,585	5,533
Age discrimination	n/a	n/a	972
Religion or belief discrimination	307	486	648
Sexual orientation discrimination	349	395	470

Source: Selected statistics (www.employmenttribunals.gov.uk). © Crown Copyright.

Table 4.4 Employment tribunal outcomes*

Claims	*2006/07*
Sex discrimination	
Withdrawn	8,998 (48%)
ACAS conciliation	2,302 (12%)
Success at employment tribunal	463 (2%)
Compensation – median	£6,724
Compensation – average	£10,052
Equal pay	
Withdrawn	4,691 (60%)
ACAS conciliation	499 (6%)
Success at employment tribunal	126 (2%)
Race discrimination	
Withdrawn	968 (31%)
ACAS conciliation	1,173 (38%)
Success at employment tribunal	102 (3%)
Compensation – median	£7,000
Compensation – average	£14,049
Disability discrimination	
Withdrawn	1,442 (33%)
ACAS conciliation	2,014 (46%)
Success at employment tribunal	149 (3%)
Compensation – median	£8,232
Compensation – average	£15,059
Age discrimination	
Withdrawn	51 (38%)
ACAS conciliation	56 (41%)
Success at employment tribunal	0
Compensation – median	n/a
Compensation – average	n/a
Religion or belief discrimination	
Withdrawn	167 (34%)
ACAS conciliation	176 (35%)
Success at employment tribunal	12 (2%)
Compensation – median (EOR)†	£1,550
Compensation – average (EOR)†	£2,217
Sexual orientation discrimination	
Withdrawn	127 (33%)
ACAS conciliation	157 (41%)
Success at employment tribunal	21 (5%)
Compensation – median (EOR)†	£5,000
Compensation – average (EOR)†	£5,479

* Only certain outcomes selected. Others involve being 'struck out' or dismissed by the tribunal (see www.employmenttribunals.gov.uk). © Crown Copyright.

† Compensation figures taken from *Equal Opportunities Review* 168, September 2007 because none were available on the ETS website.

Sex discrimination: the context

There are several important contextual issues in this section: the historic situation of women; changing perspectives; women's participation in the labour market; and women's pay.

The historic situation of women

Historically, predominant social attitudes have seen women's contribution to society outside the home as largely peripheral. Women were generally regarded as inferior and dependent upon men, having no separate legal identity. Blackstone, the eighteenth-century jurist, put the situation as follows: 'by marriage, the very being or legal existence of woman is suspended, or at least incorporated and consolidated into that of the husband, under whose wing, protection and cover she performs everything'. In the middle of the nineteenth century, a fictional lawyer in George Eliot's novel, *The Mill on the Floss*, commented, 'We don't ask what a woman does, we ask to whom she belongs'.

The overwhelming emphasis was on the importance of male roles in society. It was not until the late nineteenth century that slow legislative progress started which began piecemeal improvements in both status and rights. This gradual process of legislative change continues to the present day. Some of these key changes are outlined below.

First of all, on marriage, ***a woman's property and income*** became her husband's by law. In 1882, the Married Woman's Property Act enacted the principle, revolutionary at the time, that married women should have the same rights over their property as unmarried women and that husbands and wives should have separate interests in their property. Wives were also enabled to carry on trade and business using their property.

Secondly, ***government and political activity*** were regarded as male preserves (in fact, largely the preserve of property-owning males). It was not until 1918 (following campaigning by the Women's Suffrage Movement) that certain women (those over the age of 30 years) were granted the vote in Parliamentary elections; and 1928 before they acquired it on equal terms with men in respect of age. The first woman to be elected to Parliament, who took up her seat, did so in 1919. Women have, however, continued to remain a small minority of elected MPs – with women constituting only 19.5 per cent of MPs in 2005.

Thirdly, ***education*** was seen as essential for boys but not for girls. Various views – often eccentric by present-day standards – were used to justify this discriminatory attitude. In the mid-nineteenth century 'educating girls was thought to damage their health as adolescence was the time their reproductive organs were growing and so . . . rest was essential. Schooling might damage this process by being too taxing. Experts predicted infertility or, at the very least, an inability to breastfeed' (Holdsworth 1988: 41). Biologically, 'Women were thought to have smaller brains and, it followed, less intellectual potential. It was also a common belief that women were behind men in evolution as their prime function, motherhood, kept them closer to nature. In short they were inferior' (ibid.: 42).

In 1870, compulsory education, up to the age of 14 years in elementary schools, was introduced. 'Such official thought as went into the education of working-class girls (and that does not appear to have been a great deal) concentrated on preparing them to be wives and mothers or taking work as domestic servants' (ibid.: 47). Cookery, hygiene, laundry work and housewifery were all on the curriculum of elementary school girls, sometimes supplemented by infant-care lessons. At university level, access was gradually available from the latter part of the nineteenth century. For example, in 1878, the University of London admitted women for the first time. Oxford permitted women to take degrees from 1920; Cambridge not until 1947 although Girton College had been opened there in 1870 but was not recognised by the university.

Finally, ***full-time work and the 'breadwinner role'*** were ascribed to men. Women, on marriage, were generally expected to give up work and ultimately care full-time for their husband and children. 'Men lost face if they could not support their wives' (Holdsworth 1988: 62). The two World Wars (1914–18 and 1939–45) did disturb the conventional views about men's and women's roles – both in society and in employment. Women took up employment in jobs which were previously thought unsuitable for them such as ambulance drivers, stokers, tool setters, welders, carpenters and bus conductors. However, they did not establish any rights to equal pay. It is generally agreed that any changes in the world of work were short-lived and the general expectation by employers, politicians, men and many women was that, after both wars, women would return to their 'proper' roles of being wives and mothers. After World War Two, however, one factor was different from the situation after World War One: immediately the economy began to grow and there were labour shortages. This was a primary influence in the subsequent growing labour market participation of women.

Changing perspectives

It would be a mistake to see the emergence of changing perspectives of women's role in society, politics, the economy and employment as a recent phenomenon. Questioning and challenging the inferior and dependent status ascribed to women has been evident in Britain for the past two centuries. One early writer who articulated the problems of women's status and advocated alternative views was Mary Wollstonecraft in *A Vindication of the Rights of Women* (1792). Her ideas influenced other women in the nineteenth century and the gradual action taken through legislation.

It was not, however, until the 1960s that a feminist critique of gender roles in society received more serious consideration among a wider audience. One of the fundamental objectives of the feminist movement was 'consciousness raising'. Essentially, this involved women appraising and understanding their social, economic and political roles and status together with the expectations that usually underpinned these. Invariably this diagnostic approach was restricted to women only. This deliberately fostered segregation and focus on 'women's issues' was controversial. On the one hand, it was argued that it gave women confidence and facilitated more in-depth discussion of women's concerns. On the other hand, it was contended that it would perpetuate the segregation and marginalisation of 'women's issues'. Added to this was the view that, given that power structures necessary for effecting change (e.g. the political system, the judicial system, employing organisations, and the trade union movement) were male-dominated, attention should be focused on changing these and creating alliances with sympathetic men. The feminist movement was not a single entity. It was characterised by diversity. It was cross-cut by class differences, ethnic differences, different political perspectives, different employment experiences and different attitudes about tactical alliances.

From the experience of the past 40 years, it is possible to draw the following tentative conclusions. Structurally, male dominance persists in many aspects of society: for example, in the political system, the judicial system, corporate and public service management, health care and education. Nevertheless, there is some evidence of slow, piecemeal change and there have existed since the mid-1970s legal mechanisms to challenge discriminatory practice. Despite the evidence of poor compliance, there is also some evidence of some achievements. The reality is that the progress made is evidence of small steps on a very long road to full equal treatment.

In summary, since World War Two the following key expectations have changed:

- initially, that married women should be able to return to work;
- increasingly, that women with childcare responsibilities should be encouraged to return to work;
- increasingly that women returners should be able to fulfil career aspirations;
- that employers should facilitate parenting as a joint female and male responsibility;
- increasingly that employers should accommodate to some extent the dependency responsibilities of their staff.

Participation in the labour market

There are four important aspects to female participation:

- greater tendency for women to have peripheral or flexible employment (see Tables 4.5 and 4.6);
- increasing economic activity in child-bearing/rearing years (see Tables 4.5 and 4.6);
- women with dependency responsibilities (Table 4.7);
- a tendency for women to be segregated often into lower skilled, lower paid and lower status employment – and in particular sectors.

Dependency

The provision of care is a complex issue. However, it is still largely a female role and can inhibit a women's participation in the labour market or, if she is in employment, can limit career opportunities and affect the number of hours worked. In general terms, there are two particular phases of care: for children, and for adult dependants. Reporting on the Millennium

Table 4.5 Employment by age and gender

	In employment full-time (%)	*In employment part-time (%)*	*Employment rate (%)*	*Unemployment rate (%)*
Women				
16–24 years	56	44	57	10.0
25–44 years	60	40	74	3.6
45–64 years	55	45	63	2.3
65 and above	18	82	4	–
All aged 16–64 years	58	42	67	4.1
Men				
16–24 years	72	28	60	13.4
25–44 years	96	4	88	3.9
45–64 years	91	9	77	3.3
65 and above	37	63	9	est 2.1
All aged 16–64 years	91	9	79	5.1

Source: ONS (2005) *Labour Force Survey Spring 2005*.

Table 4.6 Part-time and flexible working: employees 16–64 years

	Women		*Men*	
	(000s)	*%*	*(000s)*	*%*
Part-time	4,845	42	1,093	9
Flexitime	1,387	12	1,055	9
Annualised hours	514	4	524	4
Term-time working	888	8	162	1
Job share	150	1	16	–
Homeworking	195	2	124	1
Any flexible arrangement	**6,538**	**57**	**2,766**	**23**

Source: ONS (2005) *Labour Force Survey Spring 2005.*

Cohort Survey (of some 30,000 parents), the former Equal Opportunities Commission (2007) stated that the 'breadwinner dad, homemaker mum' family model represented less than three in 10 millennium families). From a sample of mothers interviewed, the following profile was recorded of family arrangements when their child is three years old (Table 4.7):

Table 4.7 Millennium families when their child is 3, partnership and economic status

Status	*Percentage*
Lone parent not employed	11
Lone parent employed	6
Father employed, mother not employed	29
Both parents employed full-time	11
Father employed full-time/mother part-time	35
Mother employed/father part-time or not employed	4
Both not employed	4

Source: Equal Opportunities Commission (2007) *The State of the Modern Family, the Millennium Cohort Survey*, Equality and Human Rights Commission.

Having dependent children has a substantial impact on a women's participation in the labour market. The former Equal Opportunities Commission (2006) reviewing Labour Force Survey data showed that as far as fathers with children up to the age of 18 years were concerned, there was no shift to part-time employment. Over 90 per cent worked full-time whatever the age of their youngest child. The response rates for women were significantly different (see Table 4.8).

Underlying these data is evidence of divisions of social class in respect of childcare and family support. The Millennium Cohort Survey (EOC 2007) showed that there is a substantial difference in the experience of semiskilled/unskilled mothers in comparison to managerial/professional mothers. For example, 7 per cent of the former used formal childcare when the child was 9–10 months in contrast to 65 per cent of the managerial/professional group. Access to family friendly provisions for mothers at three years was mentioned by 59 per cent of semiskilled/unskilled mothers as opposed to 79 per cent of managerial/professional ones.

As far as caring for adults is concerned, there is a gender divide here. The Department for Work and Pensions (2005) found that for women adult carers, 54 per cent were in full-time employment (in contrast to 89 per cent of male adult carers); and 46 per cent of women were in part-time employment (as opposed to 11 per cent of men). The ageing of the population

Table 4.8 Women's employment and dependent children

	In employment full-time (%)	*In employment part-time (%)*	*Employment rate*	*Unemployment rate*
All women parents	**42**	**58**	**67**	**4.4**
Youngest child				
0–4 years	36	64	55	5.5
5–10 years	39	61	71	4.8
11–15 years	50	50	77	3.1
16–18 years	56	44	79	3.2
No dependent children	67	33	67	4.0

Source: ONS (2005) *Labour Force Survey Spring 2005*.

will produce more demands on adult carers. The 2001 Census recorded that of employees in full-time work, some 1.6 million are providing at least some unpaid care.

Occupational segregation

There are two forms: horizontal and vertical. *Horizontal* describes the situation where, for example, men and women in an organisation may work in different types of jobs – men's work and women's work. Workforce surveys indicate heavy concentrations of women workers in relatively few occupations. These are frequently those with a large demand for part-time labour (e.g. clerical and related work, catering, cleaning, hairdressing, personal services, professional and related in education, welfare and health, retail selling; and, in manufacturing, repetitive assembly and product packaging). This occupational segregation reflects, in large part, stereotypical female responsibilities: caring, cleaning and cooking. Such occupational segregation is a factor in the difficulties of achieving equal pay (see later section in this chapter).

Vertical segregation describes the situation where men predominate in the higher graded post in an organisation and women in the lower grades. Its existence has been described as evidence for many women of 'a glass ceiling blocking their aspirations, allowing them to see where they might go, but stopping them from arriving there' (Hansard Society 1990). The Labour Force Survey (Spring 2001) highlighted a 'glass ceiling' that was more or less penetrable depending on the sector concerned (see Table 4.9).

According to research published by the Equality and Human Rights Commission (2008), women's progress into top positions of power and influence across public and private sectors has stalled or reversed.

Table 4.9 Proportion of female managers in selected managerial occupations

Occupation	*Female managers as a proportion of all managers (%)*
Production managers	6
Financial institution managers	37
Advertising and PR managers	45
Personnel, training and IR managers	57
Office managers	66
Health and social services managers	73
All managers and senior officials	**30**

Source: ONS (2001) *Labour Force Survey, Spring 2001*.

Segregation and education

The discrimination, attitudes and behaviour underpinning this segregation can be difficult to eradicate because most is a result of socialisation. This is the process through which attitudes, values and standards of behaviour are inculcated and developed particularly within the family, within education, within religious organisations, within the workplace and within society at large. Examples of this can be seen in a number of the early life-time choices made by girls and young women which often determine ultimate employment and career opportunities.

For example, the EOC (2006) (data for England from the Learning and Skills Council, 2005) has reported on the educational choices of young women and men. These show marked gender segregation which will be reflected in employment and careers. Overwhelming numbers of women (at least 85 per cent of those enrolled) chose apprenticeships in 'early years care and education'; hairdressing; health and social care. The overwhelming male choices (at least 97 per cent) were engineering; automotive industry; construction; plumbing; and electro-technical.

Subject segregation in further education and higher education is almost as extreme. The choice of 'hairdressing and beauty therapy' courses was overwhelmingly female (93 per cent of those enrolled); with 'health and social care' at 66 per cent. By contrast 'engineering, technology and manufacturing' and 'construction' courses had predominantly male students (at 87 per cent and 95 per cent respectively). In other subject areas there was a closer balance between the sexes: 'science and mathematics' and ICT. First degree segregation in higher education was also evident (data for Great Britain from the Higher Education Statistics Agency, 2005). 'Education' was predominantly female (at 82 per cent). There were smaller majorities of women in 'law' and 'medicine and dentistry'. 'Computer science' and 'engineering and technology' were predominantly male (at 81 per cent and 86 per cent respectively). There were smaller majorities of men in 'physical sciences' and 'mathematical sciences'.

Women's pay

Pay discrimination against women is outlawed by the Equal Pay Act 1970. This is a companion piece of legislation with the Sex Discrimination Act 1975. It covers contractual terms (EqPA 1970, s 1). Progress at addressing the underlying causes of unequal pay has been slow and uneven. Some professions (e.g. teaching and the civil service) established the principle and practice of equal pay – at least for 'like work' – in the 1950s. However, research evidence shows flawed progress overall (see Table 4.10). Most of the decline in the full-time 'pay gap' took place in the 1970s. It remains a third higher than the average for the European Union as whole. It has been commented, pointing to the inadequacy of the legislation, that 'in the twenty-two years from 1974 to 1996, the gap narrowed by a mere 5.9 per cent' (Fredman 1997: 225).

The aggregate figures disguise important variations in the pay gap. The gap increases with age. At present it is largest for those women in their forties: 22.8 per cent for full-time workers; and 41.2 per cent for part-timers. It also varies by region – being the highest in London and the South-east. In the City of London it is estimated to be as high as 40 per cent (TUC 2008a: 17).

Recent reductions in the gap for both full- and part-time employees are largely attributable to the impact of the national minimum wage. The former Equal Opportunities Commission stated to the Low Pay Commission that 'the NMW's contribution to the narrowing of the pay

Table 4.10 Male/female mean hourly pay differential

Year	*Full-time pay gap (%)*	*Mean part-time pay gap (%)*
1970	56.3	n/a
1976	35.0	n/a
1987	26.6	n/a
1993	23.5	n/a
1998	22.0	41.9
2002	22.0	42.6
2005	19.0	38.5
2007	17.0	35.6

Source: ONS, National Statistics website: www.statistics.gov.uk

gap at the bottom end of the pay distribution represented a substantial achievement both for the LPC and for the government'. One discrimination lawyer has argued further that the NMW also has had an important indirect impact on pay above the rates it sets by incentivising employers to up-skill low paid jobs – jobs that are again undertaken disproportionately by women (Ashtiany 2007: 6) (see also Chapter 9).

Explaining the gender pay gap

It is estimated that around 36 per cent of the gender pay gap could be explained by gender differences in lifetime working patterns – including periods of part-time work and interruptions to careers. A further 18 per cent is the result of labour market rigidities including gender segregation; the fact that women are more likely to work in small firms; and are less likely to be unionised; 38 per cent is explained by direct discrimination and women's and men's career preferences and motives; and 8 per cent the result of educational attainments (Olsen and Walby 2004). In earlier work, these authors estimated that these factors contributed to a major productivity gap because skills and deficits and labour market failures are particularly pronounced for women (Walby and Olsen 2002).

Social and economic factors

Three have been identified as underlying the gender pay gap (Grimshaw and Rubery 2007):

Undervaluing of women's work

Two factors are critical: women tend to be paid less than men for the same performance in the same job; and the jobs women are likely to perform tend to attract lower wages than do men's jobs. The authors identify five 'V's that they claim work to create lower pay:

- *Visibility*. Women's skills are often not recognised by 'large undifferentiated' pay and grading bands.
- *Valuation*. Even where skills are recognised there is a long tradition of not giving a high value to such skills (for example, caring, nurturing skills).
- *Vocation*. It is assumed that women's skills are natural, which underlines their low valuation.
- *Valued added*. Men's jobs are more likely to involve high 'value-added' processes or service delivery. This can lead them to be more highly rated even where there is little difference in the skills involved.

- *Variance*. The existence of women's caring responsibilities underscores the view that women's work is in a separate sphere; and, indeed, less central or necessary for women. Part-time work, in particular, is frequently seen as synonymous with unskilled work both by employers and by women themselves.

Gender segregation and pay

This characteristic of labour markets is considered above. As far as the 'pay gap', research data points to a number of complexities and entrenched problems. Sixty per cent of women work in 10 occupations (out of a total of 77); and 60 per cent of women part-timers work in industries where 70 per cent or more of the employees are women (*Kingsmill Report* 2001). A related aspect of this is that women are 'vastly over-represented in low paid, part-time unskilled work' (Ashtiany 2007: 6). The Women and Work Commission (2006) linked gender segregation to broad features in our society: gender-stereotyped early environments; limited choices for girls in education; attitudes of teachers, parents and carers; and the images of women in the media and in popular culture.

Employment penalty for mothers

The Equalities Review (**www.equalities.gov.uk**) confirmed this – identifying that 'becoming mothers' is the biggest cause of women's labour market inequality. Specific evidence relied on by the Review indicated that women with children under 11 years, irrespective of whether they were on their own or with a partner, face significant problems in getting jobs; and are over 40 per cent more disadvantaged than men with partners (Berthoud and Blekesaune 2007) (see Chapter 11).

Race discrimination: the context

Britain's ethnic diversity

Britain is a diverse society in terms of the ethnic and national origins of its citizens. It has become particularly so since the middle of the nineteenth century. This ethnic diversity derives from a number of principal causes of migration:

- Britain's position adjacent to continental Europe which has been characterised by religious and political persecution, ethnic cleansing and genocide. Examples are the migration of Jews fleeing pogroms in Russia and eastern Europe in the late nineteenth century; and from the Nazi genocide after 1933.
- Britain's former role as an imperial power with colonies in all other continents and the perception of Britain as 'the mother country'.
- Occasional severe labour shortages, particularly after World War Two which encouraged recruitment campaigns by employers (for example, in the Caribbean in the 1950s and 1960s for employment in public transport and the National Health Service).
- A loose, imperfectly implemented, moral commitment to protect people whose human rights have been abused in other countries. Examples are East African Asians who were expelled from Kenya (1968) and Uganda (1972) as a result of 'Africanisation' policies.

Additionally, Britain, like most industrialised societies has experienced other *ad hoc* migration: internally, between England, Scotland, Wales and Northern Ireland (and from the Republic of Ireland); and, as a consequence of the 'free movement of labour' policy, within the EU.

Concepts

To explore the issue of racial discrimination we need to consider the meaning of two key concepts: race and ethnicity; and in addition, the issue of 'colour'. All are used in everyday language and also indicated in race relations legislation as characteristics of 'racial groups'.

Race

This, as a concept originally emerged in the late eighteenth century and led to the development of a 'race science' based on *biological* differences. It established a hierarchy of inferiority and superiority between races and was used to reinforce existing power structures (primarily, the domination of white people over other races). This 'science' enabled certain races to be defined as 'non human' and, therefore, they could be enslaved, treated as a commodity and denied any basic human rights. These 'non human' 'out groups' were often equated with animals. Dilip Hiro (1973: xii) records the historic comment that Africans were regarded as 'an equivocal race between man and monkey'. 'Race science' underpins Nazi ideology. Under this, the Aryan people are seen as supreme. The north-European Aryans and the Jews were 'as far apart as humans and animals' (Boonstras *et al.* 1993: 76). By the end of World War Two, this 'science' had become generally discredited.

'Race' has also been defined as a *sociological* concept. Again, it is seen as a form of categorisation, but as such it is imperfect. Among the categories identified are: European, African, Semitic, Chinese. The implication is that people organise themselves and behave in certain ways according to racial origin. But, given that these are extremely broad categories, which themselves cover a wide degree of diversity, the sociological definition of 'race' is comparatively unhelpful.

Ethnicity

This, on the other hand, is a more useful term for helping to structure discussions on discrimination. Most academic commentators would 'stress some sort of cultural distinction as the mark of an ethnic grouping' (Mason 1995: 12). Evidence of this distinctiveness can be seen in common descent (e.g. Jews originating in what is today the state of Israel); common cultural heritage or traditions; common traditions relating to marriage and family life (e.g. the arrangement of marriages); possibly, a common religion (which may be linked to the two previous characteristics); probably, a common language; and such factors as dress (for example, the hijab worn by some Islamic women). At the heart of ethnicity is a sense of belongingness to a group and to certain 'roots' – with distinctions drawn, especially by first generation immigrants, between 'natural' and 'adopted' home countries. The significance of these indicators of ethnicity will vary, often substantially, between different ethnic groups. In part, this will be dependent on the extent to which such groups are integrated into the 'host' society.

In Britain, ethnicity has also been defined, conventionally, by skin colour. As a consequence, various European groups, for example, are not generally perceived as ethnic groups (e.g. Italians, Poles, Ukrainians) – but as white people. Indeed, 'white British people are apt to see ethnicity as an attribute only of others – something that distinguishes "them" from "us" ' (Mason 1995: 14). This is a distortion of the concept and, in this text, ethnicity will be used to reflect any cultural distinctiveness.

In part, then, ethnicity is rooted in 'the self-definitions of members' (Mason 1995: 12). Rather than being an entirely ascribed category, like race, ethnicity enables individuals to determine their belonging to an ethnic group. So a person can have a range of different ethnic identities depending on the situation. A person might be a Hindu ***and*** an Indian ***and*** a Kenyan *and* British – depending upon the circumstances they are in and the treatment they receive at the hands of other people. As subsequent generations become established in the host society, individuals will probably manifest these multi-ethnic characteristics.

Colour

This term features in the legislation and, historically, it has been used to differentiate between people. Indeed, in most ethnic monitoring schemes, there can be, even today, an unsatisfactory confusion of racial, ethnic and colour categories. Mason (1995: 6) comments that characterising people by colour is 'of considerable importance because of the way in which the colours black and white were emotionally loaded concepts in the English language'. These colours are 'polar opposites'. Also, 'white' represents 'good, purity and virginity' whilst 'black' is 'the colour of death, evil and debasement'. Such contrasts can be seen as long-standing features of our language, literature and philosophy as well as being elements in racist political rhetoric. Colour can be useful as *one* characteristic of an ethnic group (or 'racial group' under the legislation) but that is all. Otherwise, it provides a crude and unhelpful categorisation.

Historic labour market experience

Within the labour market since World War Two, there is considerable evidence of racist practices. These reflected the attitudes in the wider society. In one substantial research project, where employers' representatives and trade union officials were interviewed (Daniel 1968: 89), three general conclusions were drawn about attitudes to the, then, recent African-Caribbean migrants to the UK:

> The first is that there was a high degree of generalisation and stereotyping and little attempt to distinguish between different types of coloured people in terms of level of ability, personality or character, although some distinctions were drawn in terms of race or country of origin. The second is that . . . whether or not they themselves saw coloured immigrants in all the ways described, informants said or assumed that other people (their clients in the case of employment exchanges and bureaux; their members in the case of trade unions; their other employees, customers or clients in the case of employers) objected to coloured people for these reasons.

Indeed, in this context, the retail and distributive trade sector were 'the most resistant to the employment of coloured people . . . [and] most of them displaced responsibility on to customers or the public'. The third and most important point, and this is partly a consequence of the first two, is that 'coloured immigrants had been and were being considered by employers, if at all, only where no suitable white English personnel were available'.

In terms of promotion, there were even more difficulties. Non-white ethnic workers 'become less acceptable or unacceptable in jobs that imply authority over white subordinates, reciprocal relationships with white colleagues in other departments and other functions and contact with clients and the general public' (ibid.: 107). Daniel (1968: 83) commented that it was not surprising that 'many of the coloured immigrants who were interviewed had been very disappointed and even bitter about their experience of life in Britain and of the white British people with whom they had come into contact'.

Legislative action

In the 1960s, two legislative steps were taken by the Labour government. In 1965 it enacted legislation to prohibit racism in 'certain places of public resort' (e.g. hotels, restaurants, public houses, theatres, dance halls, swimming pools, public transport, etc.). In 1968, further legislation extended protection by outlawing direct (but not indirect) discrimination in employment. In 1976, the Race Relations Act was passed and implemented.

Comparing Britain with other EU member states, Justice, the human rights group commented some years later that it was 'unique' in having had legislation against discrimination on racial grounds on the statute book for some 30 years. Although all EU states 'have written Constitutions that prohibit race discrimination in some way, detailed implementing legislation is often lacking. Where it does exist, it may be limited to acts committed by organs of the State' (1996: 28). The situation within the EU gradually moved on with the enactment in 2000 of the directive requiring equal treatment on the grounds of racial and ethnic origin.

Labour market participation today

Although there continues to be evidence of racism in employment, there has been some incremental change for the better over the past 30 years. Whilst, on the one hand, there is evidence of some segregation in employment (which may be exacerbated by both gender issues and social class), there is also evidence of a more positive approach being taken to equal opportunities, particularly in the public sector. Of particular importance is the commitment of public policy (through equality duties) and legislation to the eradication of racism and the promotion of equal opportunities.

An overview of employment by ethnic group is given in Table 4.11, and some more detailed outline of concentrations of ethnic minority employment is set out in the following data. (Annual Population Survey 2004, **www.statistics.gov.uk**):

- ***Self-employment***: this status was more evident among Pakistanis (21 per cent); Chinese (16 per cent) and white Irish (15 per cent) than among the white British population (12 per cent).
- ***Industry concentrations***: certain ethnic groups are concentrated in particular industries:
  - *distribution, hotel and restaurant industry*: three-fifths of Bangladeshi men and just under half of Chinese men in employment worked in this sector compared with one-sixth of white British counterparts. Forty per cent of Chinese women and one-third of Bangladeshi women worked here compared with 20 per cent of all women in employment;
  - *transport and communications*: Pakistani men were the group most likely to work in this industry – 23 per cent of them compared with 10 per cent of all men employed;
  - *construction*: white Irish men were more likely than other men to work in this industry – 20 per cent compared with 13 per cent overall;
  - *public administration, education or health sector*: 54 per cent of Black Caribbean and 52 per cent of Black African women worked in this sector.
- ***Occupations***:
  - *managerial or professional occupations*: those most likely to be employed in managerial or professional occupations were Chinese, Indian, white Irish and other non-British white groups (between 32 and 38 per cent). White British people were at 27 per cent. The lowest proportions in this occupational group (between 19 and 22 per cent) were Black Caribbean, Black African and Bangladeshi;
  - *driving*: one in seven Pakistani men in employment was a taxi driver, cab driver or chauffeur compared with one per cent of white British men;
  - *catering*: over a quarter of Bangladeshi men were chefs, cooks or waiters;

Table 4.11 Employment by ethnic group (Great Britain: people aged 16–64 years)

	In full-time employment (%)	*In part-time employment (%)*	*Employment rate*	*Unemployment rate*
Women				
White	57	43	69	3.7
Mixed	66	34	64	10.3
Indian	68	32	61	5.8
Pakistani	55	45	23	21.7
Bangladeshi	52*	48*	18	–
Black Caribbean	73	27	64	7.6
Black African	73	27	48	9.4
Chinese	74	26	55	–
All ethnic groups[†]	**68**	**32**	**50**	**9.1**
All aged 16–64 years	**58**	**42**	**67**	**4.1**
Men				
White	91	9	80	4.6
Mixed	85	15	63	9.9*
Indian	91	9	75	6.4
Pakistani	80	20	63	10.1
Bangladeshi	61	39	54	19.1
Black Caribbean	87	13	71	14.6
Black African	78	22	63	15.4
Chinese	82	18*	49	14.4*
All ethnic groups[†]	**84**	**16**	**66**	**10.7**
All aged 16–64 years	**91**	**9**	**79**	**5.1**

* Estimate may be unreliable

[†] All non-white groups including those not listed separately

Source: ONS (2005) *Labour Force Survey, Spring 2005*.

- *healthcare*: 4 per cent of Indian men worked as medical practitioners – 10 times higher than the rate for white British men. Around one in 10 Black African women and one in seven women from the Other Asian group were working as nurses compared with one in 30 white British women;
- *packers, bottlers, canners and fillers*: Indian, Pakistani and Black African women were around four times more likely than white British women to be working at these jobs;
- *sewing machinists*: Pakistani and Indian women were, respectively, six times and four times more likely than white British women to be working at this job.

Disability discrimination: the context

Defining disability

The most common problems affecting people with a disability (Twomey 2001) are:

- musculoskeletal (relating to arms, legs, back, hands and feet): 36 per cent;
- chest or breathing problems: 13 per cent;
- heart, blood pressure and circulatory conditions: 11 per cent;
- mental illness: 8 per cent.

Models of disability

There are two distinct approaches to defining disability: The 'medical model' and the 'social model'. The traditional definition (the 'medical model') is that used by the World Health Organisation (Wood 1991). This categorised the following:

- *Impairment*: any loss or abnormality of psychological, physiological or anatomical structure or function.
- *Disability*: any restriction or lack of ability (resulting from an impairment) to perform an activity in the manner or within the range considered normal for a human being.
- *Handicap*: a disadvantage for a given individual, resulting from an impairment or a disability that limits or prevents the fulfilment of a role (depending on age, sex and social and cultural factors) for that individual.

This 'medical model' concentrates on dysfunction and on how to make the person well or on the aids necessary for the person to function 'normally'. So, the amputee is fitted with an artificial limb. The implication is that people with functional limitations need to adapt to fit into society. The TUC (2008b), in a critique, has commented that 'the medical model underlying the DDA has a long history. For a long period, disability was thought by almost everyone to signify an inability to live a "normal life". Disabled people were seen as either the pathetic and helpless objects of charity or else, if they managed despite everything to succeed in their careers and lives, as heroic figures overcoming their "defects" (not, note, the barriers) by superhuman effort.'

The 'social model' sees disability as 'resting in society rather than in any factor inherent in disabled people' (Massie 1994). This is not to deny the medical aspects of disability which may be considerable. It acknowledges that the impact of disability frequently depends on the 'context in which someone lives' (ibid.). Against this background, Disabled People's International has adopted the following definitions:

- *Impairment*: the functional limitation within the individual caused by physical, mental or sensory impairment.
- *Disability*: the loss or limitation of opportunities to take part in the normal life of the community on an equal level with others due to physical or social barriers.

This 'social model' enables people to have an impairment without having a disability. It is social factors that translate the 'impairment' into a 'disability'. So, if the physical and attitudinal barriers that exist within society are reduced, then, so is the disability. Individuals will still have the physical or mental impairment and the consequent pain and emotions but their ability to participate in society will be enhanced. The importance of this second model is that it focuses attention on the individual's interface with the environment and not on the individual's impairment. Thus, people are seen as individuals – and not as 'the disabled' – with effort being put into addressing any social and physical barriers that exist. It helps move away from the notion that 'disability' equates with 'inability'.

The statutory disability duty on public authorities (DDA 1995, s 49A) is based on the social model of disability. Godwin (2008a: 10) in a survey of 132 employers found that 44 per cent of organisations said that they used the 'social model'; 21 per cent said that they had not; and 35 per cent did not know. The research officer commented that this suggests that 'a substantial number of organisations have adopted policies without first establishing the fundamental principles underlying such a policy'.

Social context

There are two relevant dimensions which affect the day-to-day living and employment opportunities of disabled people: prevailing social attitudes; and social infrastructure.

Attitudes

Disabled people are frequently subject to stereotyping and preconceptions about the nature and consequences of their disability. First, there is the ever-present tendency to regard 'the disabled' as an undifferentiated group. In reality, the spectrum of impairment is extremely wide. Consequently, the impact of an impairment on a person's ability to carry out day-to-day activities, to live independently, to travel and so on varies very significantly from person to person. This may seem an obvious statement but it is surprising how it is still forgotten in the whole range of social activities and in the employment arena.

Secondly, disabled people can be treated with suspicion, apprehension, ridicule and pity. They may also experience well-meaning patronising attitudes from people who think that they 'know best' about any assistance required. Thirdly, social attitudes frequently fail to consider the situation of a disabled person from that person's perspective. For example, expressions are used such as 'confined to a wheelchair' when, in fact, the wheelchair may liberate the user by providing mobility. Someone may be described as suffering from a particular condition when that person does not regard the condition as a disability but as a normal part of life. There can be a failure to allow the disabled person to take the initiative in deciding the adjustments and assistance that they want or do not want. One survey (Honey *et al.* 1993) found that employers tended to hold inaccurate or exaggerated beliefs about the restrictions that impairments place on employment. Many of the prevailing social attitudes reflect the traditional medical model of disability where the focus is on the individual's condition and care and welfare.

A final comment on attitudes (and evident in all areas of discrimination) is the pernicious and deterrent effect that stereotyping, prejudice and insulting behaviour has on the self-esteem of disabled people. This creates a further psychological obstacle that needs to be overcome in order that they may become active participants in society and employment. This has been described as the 'discouraged worker' syndrome – whereby people withdraw from the labour market after repeated rejection and lack of opportunities. They tend to devalue their own potential. Recent research confirms the persistence of many negative attitudes (Fevre *et al.* 2008).

Social infrastructure

People with impairments face difficulties associated with public transport and building design. These, inevitably, can cause access problems in relation to training, employment, the purchase of goods and services, entertainment. Access problems in one area can exacerbate access in others. For example, difficulties in acquiring education and training, which may be caused in part by transport problems, can obstruct entry into the labour market and employment. The ability to lead a constructive and rewarding life is inhibited.

Attitudes and social infrastructure issues are linked in providing five obstacles to the entry of disabled people into employment (Weiss 1974: 457):

- physical and vocational problems during rehabilitation and training;
- barriers created by architectural design and transport systems;
- resistance by employers to hiring disabled persons;
- self-doubt as a result of previous prejudice;
- overcoming ill-focused and often unnecessary medical tests.

Historical perspective

Until the enactment of the Disability Discrimination Act 1995, there had been little progress in protecting disabled people from discrimination and facilitating full social and economic participation. Aside from legislation relating to the provision of information to disabled people and a requirement (in 1980) on companies employing 250 or more staff to include a general statement in their annual report about their treatment of disabled people, the principal legislation was the Disabled Persons (Employment) Act 1944. This was seen as a major piece of legislation when enacted towards the end of World War Two. It was expected to go some way to assisting demobilised and injured members of the armed forces. It introduced a registration scheme for disabled people; a quota scheme in employment; and reserve occupations. The quota scheme required employers with 20 or more employees to have at least 3 per cent of their workforce as registered disabled persons (RDPs). It was unlawful to engage an able-bodied person or to dismiss an RDP without reasonable cause if the quota was, or would fall below, 3 per cent. In fact, the number of people registering gradually fell to approximately one per cent of the working population. Employers universally were unlikely to achieve the quota and many applied for exemption certificates. Prosecutions for non-compliance were few and the last was in 1975. The maximum fine was £100. As far as reserve occupations, only the positions of passenger electric lift attendant and car park attendant were ever designated as occupations to be carried out by RDPs.

Clearly, a political shift was necessary to provide a more coherent and effective framework of law for all disabled people in employment and in the provision of goods and services. Initiatives were being developed within the EU. In 1986 there was a non-binding Recommendation of the European Council on the Employment of Disabled Persons in the European Community. From the early 1980s, campaigning was taking place in Britain by pressure groups of disabled people, trade unions and the solicitors' organisation, the Law Society. There were 15 unsuccessful attempts by backbench Members of Parliament to gain consent for private member's Bills. The Conservative government remained opposed until 1994 when, eventually, it proposed legislation and Parliament enacted the Disability Discrimination Act 1995 (with an exemption for small employers). This Act has subsequently been amended and improved as a result of the European Employment Equality Directive 2000 and, in 2005, domestic legislation (see Chapter 5).

Employment context of the 1995 Act

Surveys (Honey *et al.* 1993; Pidduck 1995) undertaken in the mid-1990s show that the employment context in which the new legislation was enacted would not be generally propitious.

Honey *et al.* (1993) found that overall, it was the larger employers who were more likely to employ people with disabilities; to have a written policy which included disabled people; to have realistic perceptions of the costs and problems involved; to use the disability '*Two Ticks*' symbol; to seek to recruit and accommodate disabled persons; and to look for external help and advice. Employers who adopted one of these initiatives were more likely to have adopted others. On the whole, smaller organisations did not appear to have taken on board the legal, moral and good practice reasons for employing people with disabilities. Those employers who did not employ anyone with a disability were more likely to perceive physical and safety problems and to anticipate costly accommodations. They tended to hold stereotyped and exaggerated views of 'wheelchair bound' applicants bringing a range of difficulties relating to the type or level of work and to safety and to the premises.

Pidduck (1995), surveying mostly 'good practice' employers just prior to the implementation of the Disability Discrimination Act, suggested that employers' perceptions and their associated behaviours could be categorised into one of five groups. The incidence of the first three was reported to be generally found among small to medium-sized employers. The other two categories tended to be medium to large organisations.

- Those who were ignorant of the legislation and deliberately disregard it.
- Those who adopt an approach of minimal compliance. They generally have sufficient knowledge of the law to avoid being seen as directly discriminatory but they have little understanding of indirect discrimination.
- Those whose position is one of neutral reactivity. They have the potential to comply with not just the letter but also the spirit of the law. However, they need direction and encouragement.
- Those who, in both the public and private sector, have started to review their policies and to implement changes. They have seen the wider business reasons for accommodating those with disabilities.
- Those (many in the public sector) who constitute a positive and proactive group. Often they are members of the Employers' Forum on Disability. They are well-informed and have and continue to take a wide range of initiatives to facilitate the recruitment and retention of people with disabilities. The impetus for their initiatives has both a moral and business foundation dating back prior to the 1995 Act. The Act provided an added stimulus to their activities. They have developed a clear strategy.

More recent data (Disability Rights Commission 2004) in a survey of 1,000 small organisations employing up to 50 staff (some of whom came under the requirements of the Act for the first time that year) found a variety of responses – some optimistic and some stereotypical:

- 64 per cent of small business owners don't think that disabled people will take more sick leave than other people;
- 80 per cent do not think that disabled people will be 'less productive' than other workers;
- 45 per cent believe it would be 'very/quite difficult' to employ a disabled person;
- 87 per cent think that disabled people 'would fit into their team';
- 41 per cent said that when they hear the word 'disability' they immediately think of people in a wheelchair or someone with a physical impairment. (In fact, only around 7.5 per cent of disabled people are wheelchair users.)

Since the enactment of the 1995 Act and its subsequent amendments there has been progress – some fitful – in employment policies (see Chapter 6).

Labour market participation

Despite an increase of 8 per cent since 1999, the participation of disabled people in the labour market is markedly lower than for the non-disabled (see Table 4.12).

Employment rates vary greatly according to a person's type of impairment. Those with mental health issues have the lowest employment rates (at 21 per cent). People with diabetes have the highest at 68 per cent. The rate for people with learning difficulties was 23.2 per cent (down marginally from 1999).

Table 4.12 Employment by disability (Great Britain: people of working age)

	In full-time employment (%)	*In part-time employment (%)*	*Employment rate*	*Unemployment rate*
Women				
Disabled*	54	46	49	6.2
Not disabled	59	41	75	3.9
All of working age (16–59 years)	58	42	70	4.3
Men				
Disabled*	87	13	52	8.8
Not disabled	91	9	85	4.5
All working age (16–64 years)	91	9	79	5.1

* People with a current disability, including DDA disabled and work-limiting disabled.

Source: ONS (2005) *Labour Force Survey, Spring 2005*.

Age discrimination: the context

The concept of 'ageism'

According to Age Concern, the term 'ageism' was first coined in the 1960s by Robert Butler to denote a process of stereotyping and discrimination against people just because of their age. It is concerned with prejudice and discrimination based on age and more formally as 'a set of attitudes that generate fear and denigration of the ageing process and stereotyping presumptions regarding competence' (Bytheway 1995). More recently, MacNicol (2006: 11) has defined ageism in terms of attitudes and social relations as age-based group characteristics applied to individuals which are seen as embedded in patterns of thinking and which are 'rampant' in modern western societies. These in turn give rise to discrimination based on age – 'the most complex and difficult of discriminations that affect modern societies in that it is very difficult to identify, detect and prove' (ibid.: 6).

Other writers have also noted that age discrimination is unusual in that unlike other discrimination grounds where we can usually identify a distinct category of persons, we all have an age and could be potentially affected at some point in out lives. The life cycle also involves members of an 'in group' (prime age workers) eventually becoming members of an 'out group' (older workers). So, young people experience ageism as do older people. The definition of 'older people' can also be problematic. For some commentators it is an undifferentiated group over 50 years (the so-called 'Saga' generation); whilst others distinguish between 'young' old age (60–75 years) and 'old' old age (75 years and above).

The incidence of ageism

There is overwhelming evidence that ageist attitudes and prejudice are widespread in Britain and that age discrimination is strongly embedded in many parts of social and economic life (Bytheway 1995; MacNicol 2006). The Discrimination Law Review estimated that around 28 per cent of people have suffered discrimination on the grounds of age. A further survey reported that one in five employers indicated that they felt some jobs were more suitable for some age groups than others (Metcalf and Meadows 2006). In evidence to the House of Lords

Select Committee on the Economics of an Ageing Population (2003), the Trades Union Congress and a number of individual representations suggested that many line managers were simply unaware that the processes and procedures they used might be age discriminatory. The Report stated: 'we conclude from the evidence that there is significant age discrimination in employment and that this discrimination . . . is frequently the unconscious outcome of an employer's more general human resource management policy and procedure'.

Indeed, it is reasonable to comment that 'almost any HR policy or practice, term or condition is likely to have a disproportionate impact on some age group or another' (Rubenstein 2006) and as a result could be 'potentially indirectly discriminatory' (Fredman 2003: 58). So, as O'Cinneide (2005) comments, 'experience, "know-how", educational qualifications, decision-making capabilities, emotional maturity and almost any other neutral criterion that might be applicable in the employment context could put persons of a particular age at a disadvantage'. The experience of the past 25 years, then, suggests that the issue of age discrimination in the labour market is complex with particular groups disproportionately affected.

The 'drivers' of legislation

Despite evidence of ageism and age discrimination, proposals to legislate against it have, until recently been rare. In Britain, some age-related discrimination was tackled through sex discrimination law (see Chapter 5). In some countries (Canada, the Netherlands and, to some extent, Ireland) measures to tackle age discrimination have emerged from a 'human rights' perspective. In the United States and the European Union the approach has been more pragmatic, reflecting a more utilitarian orientation (O'Cinneide 2005) aimed at addressing public policy issues. These policy concerns have centred on older workers and have sought to deal with their economic activity rates (see Tables 4.13 and 4.14). The underlying issues are possible social exclusion; the wider concerns surrounding an impending pensions crisis in many European economies; and concerns about a 'rising dependency ratio' (Exhibit 4.3).

Table 4.13 Economic activity rates by age (%)

	1975	*1981*	*1985*	*1990*	*1995*	*2000*	*2006*
Men aged							
55–59	93.0	89.4	82.5	81.4	73.7	74.8	76.1
60–64	82.3	69.3	55.4	54.6	50.1	50.3	53.9
Women aged							
55–59	52.4	53.4	52.0	54.8	55.7	57.6	62.0
60–64	28.6	23.3	18.8	22.7	25.0	25.9	31.9

Sources: *Labour Force Survey* 2006; OECD (2001) 1985–2000 data; Taylor and Walter (1994) (1975–81 data).

Table 4.14 Economic activity rates: above state pension age (%)

	1992	*1994*	*1998*	*2002*	*2006*
Men (65+)	7.5	8.1	7.1	8.1	9.8
Women (60+)	7.6	7.7	8.1	8.9	11.7

The fourth quarters in the years indicated.

Source: *Labour Force Survey* (various).

Exhibit 4.3 Drivers of age discrimination legislation

Population, life expectancy and dependency ratios. In Europe, the median age of people is projected to rise from 29.2 years in 1950 to 49.5 years in 2050. At this date the average man in Britain will live to 83 years and the average woman to 90 years. To ensure that rising numbers drawing state pension do not impose a huge financial burden on those in work requires two possible policy approaches:

- that people save more through pensions whilst in work; and
- the rate at which people retire is raised to maintain the level of the pensions.

The old-age dependency ratio (the number of people of pensionable age as a proportion of the working age population) was around 24 per cent in the OECD states in 2005 – approximately a fifth higher than in 1980. In Germany, Greece, Italy and Japan it was between 30 and 35 per cent; in the UK around 30 per cent; whilst in Turkey it was only 10 per cent. By 2050, it is estimated that with no change in retirement ages, this ratio will rise to 52 per cent in the OECD area; with rises to over 70 per cent in Italy, Spain and Japan (OECD 2006). The UK estimate is of a rise to 49 per cent (ONS 2008).

Raising economic activity rates of those over 50 years. This rate fell off sharply in the 1980s and 1990s. Official statistics show it has started to recover. Most of the reduction in older people's employment rates was involuntary. Evidence of activities undertaken by this cohort suggests that capability is not an issue.

Promoting the 'knowledge economy'. A key element of the EU Lisbon summit was a commitment to develop Europe as 'the most dynamic, knowledge based economy in the world'. The shift to this kind of service economy places far less premium on physical attributes. Knowledge may continue to be gained throughout working life and decays slower than physical ability. This underlines the continuing utility of older workers.

Social inclusion and exclusion. A major EU concern is that those leaving the labour market risk being isolated, unable to participate economically, socially and politically and may experience serious problems. 'Far from retirement being a time of passive dependency, most of those interviewed were making a real contribution to society. They were taking part in a huge range of activities, including various forms of unpaid work, learning activities, domestic work and caring for family, helping out friends and neighbours, and leisure and educational pursuits' (Barnes *et al.* 2002).

Equality principles. The principles of social justice, fairness and dignity have informed legislation in a number of jurisdictions.

So, European policy initiatives have emphasised a 'supply side' agenda – removing barriers to the greater participation of older workers in the labour market. By the 1990s in Europe there was a greater willingness to consider age discrimination legislation. In 2000, the EU Employment Equality Directive included provisions for equal treatment on the grounds of age.

Older workers in the labour market

The labour market position of older workers has become a major policy concern throughout industrial and post-industrial economies. This has been prompted by a steady flow of these workers leaving the labour market in the 1980s and 1990s (see Tables 4.13 and 4.14). Those exiting were principally men: in manual occupations where there was a lack of demand for their skills; and those in financially secure higher occupations who chose economic inactivity. In contrast, the growing service economy created significant employment opportunities that have benefited women generally and older and younger women in particular.

The Discrimination Law Review (**www.equalities.gov.uk**) has helpfully refocused attention on the labour market disadvantages faced by certain groups. It remains the case that some are significantly more disadvantaged with respect to age than others. Furthermore, as with other forms of discrimination, age combines with other factors to reinforce disadvantage. The labour market vulnerability of some groups of older men is evidenced by the fact that a fifth has no formal qualifications. They have a significantly greater chance of becoming unemployed than their younger counterparts; and once unemployed are more likely to remain so for longer. Such data are potentially self-reinforcing and shape stereotypes of older workers as 'slow', 'resistant to change' and 'unwilling to embrace new ideas'. These are particular concerns when employers are increasingly looking for flexibility, dynamism and new ideas. This situation will change over time because of greater access to tertiary education. It is estimated that the share of older workers with University or equivalent qualifications will rise from 22 per cent (2000) to 31 per cent (2025) in OECD countries. The proportion with less than an upper-secondary level of education will fall over the same period from 40 per cent to 21 per cent (OECD 2006).

Sexual orientation discrimination: the context

The Employment Equality (Sexual Orientation) Regulations 2003 are concerned with discrimination on the grounds of *all* sexual orientation. However, the social wrongs committed historically have largely been on the grounds of homosexuality and, in particular, male homosexuality.

Historical situation

Negative social attitudes and punitive legislative action in relation to homosexuality have a very long history. Stonewall (**www.stonewall.org.uk**) records evidence of the first mention in English common law of a punishment for homosexuality as 1290, with sodomites being burned alive in 1300. Under the first statute law, the Buggery Act 1533, hanging was the penalty. Whilst capital punishment for buggery was abolished in 1861, the nineteenth century saw the continued possibility of criminal liability. Legislation was passed in 1885 which created the offence of 'gross indecency' for a homosexual act. This criminal activity could result in blackmail. It was for an allegation of 'indecency' that Oscar Wilde the writer unsuccessfully sued the Marquis of Queensbury for criminal libel and was himself subsequently arrested and sentenced, in 1895, to two years' imprisonment with hard labour. The criminal law was slowly dismantled in the United Kingdom between 1967 and 2001 (see below).

Social attitudes

Homosexuals, both historically and at the present, have been the subject of abuse, harassment, assault and murder on the grounds of sexual orientation. Furthermore, views about the cause of their sexual orientation have often fuelled unacceptable conduct. Some historic attitudes, drawing on false science, have characterised homosexuality as a disease that can be 'cured'. Grotesque 'medical treatments' were perpetrated in Britain until the 1960s. This view continued to be propagated despite arguments from the late nineteenth century onwards that it was neither a disease nor a crime. It was asserted that homosexuality was innate. In recent years, ongoing scientific research has established satisfactorily that this is the case.

Acceptance of differences in sexual orientation and more positive social attitudes have been more in evidence in recent years. Stonewall, the campaigning gay rights group, commissioned a *YouGov* survey of some 2,000 adults (2006) which reported the following among its findings:

- Only a quarter of people surveyed said they have a low opinion of lesbians and gay men.
- However, 55 per cent think that there is general public prejudice against gay people in Britain today. 'Women, people from ethnic minorities and younger people are most likely to acknowledge that anti-gay prejudice exists and to want it addressed' (para 2.3).
- 'In general, older white British men are least likely to support legal equality for lesbian and gay people. They are more likely to believe that anti-gay prejudice is not an important issue and should not be tackled' (para 2.3).
- 59 per cent of those surveyed 'think that public prejudice is caused by religious attitudes, despite the fact that this research demonstrates that "people of faith" are no more likely to be prejudiced than anyone else' (para 2.4). In fact, 84 per cent of religious people *disagreed* with the statement that 'homosexuality is morally unacceptable in all circumstances'. Also, 64 per cent of religious people would be 'comfortable if their local religious representative was gay' (para 3.6).
- 'Anti-gay bullying at work is also widespread. 13 per cent have witnessed verbal anti-gay bullying at work . . . Physical bullying also occurs at work and has been seen by 4 per cent of workers' (para 2.5) (see Chapter 7).

Developments in legislation

Over the past 50 years, there have been a number of important incremental steps to achieve civil and employment rights for homosexuals.

Criminal law

After considerable campaigning, the report of the Wolfenden Committee (1957), and press publicity relating to homosexual acts by high profile individuals (including journalists, actors and politicians), in 1967, Parliament started the process of decriminalisation and moves towards positive human rights. The legislative action was as follows:

- *Decriminalisation.* The Sexual Offences Act 1967 decriminalised, in England and Wales, homosexual acts 'in private' between two consenting men over 21 years of age. Eventually, homosexuality was decriminalised in Scotland in 1980. Age of consent reduced to 18 in 1994; and to 16 (the same as for heterosexuals) in 2001. In 1981, the British government was ruled to be breaching Article 8 of the ECHR by refusing to legalise consenting homosexual behaviour in Northern Ireland. It was eventually decriminalised in the province in 1982. It was not decriminalised, under its special constitutional circumstances of the Isle of Man, until in 1992.
- *Civil Partnerships Act 2004.* This legislation enabled a couple of the same sex to register their partnership. It confers on them the same rights as a married couple in respect of tax, social security, inheritance and workplace benefits. The first registrations took place in December 2005. The Sex Discrimination Act 1975 was amended to provide protection against direct and indirect discrimination on the grounds of civil partnership (s 3).
- *Equality Act (Sexual Orientation) Regulations 2007.* These make discrimination in the provision of goods and services unlawful from 2007.
- *Criminal Justice and Immigration Act 2008.* This provides protection against incitement to homophobic hatred and violence. There is a controversial 'religious defence' in the legislation.

Employment

Conferring employment rights and protection against discrimination has been a long, tortuous process. The Conservative government (1979–97) did not provide a facilitating political environment, with legislative opposition to 'the promotion of homosexuality'. The European Union took its first significant step to legislation in the Employment Directive 2000. It was transposed into British law as the Employment Equality (Sexual Orientation) Regulations 2003. In employment, it is also important to note that the Civil Partnership Act 2004 has a bearing on an employee's entitlements under their contract; and eligibility for non-contractual benefits (for example, the travel concessions in dispute in the Grant case). Such claims are likely to be brought under the Sex Discrimination Act 1975 (s 3) (see Chapter 5).

Views on legislation

The Stonewall survey reported the following findings:

- 93 per cent supported the Employment Equality (Sexual Orientation) Regulations 2003 concerning discrimination and harassment at work;
- 68 per cent supported the Civil Partnership Act 2004 concerning the legal status and rights of homosexual partners;
- 85 per cent supported the Equality Act (Sexual Orientation) Regulations 2007 concerning the provision of goods and services.

The quality of employment relations

Stonewall has constructed a Workplace Equality Index to measure progress in the achievement of equal treatment on the grounds of sexual orientation (**www.stonewall.org.uk/workplace**). Employers are ranked according to various criteria including implementation of an effective equal opportunities policy; granting equal benefits for same-sex partners; and regularly consulting lesbian, gay and bisexual staff (LGB) networks. In 2008, 241 organisations entered the index to have their work recognised – an increase of 201 from the previous year. The top 100 were differentiated by the following: monitoring sexual orientation; broaching diversity issues with suppliers; involvement in or support of the LGB community; and the presence of openly gay staff on the board or senior management team. The top organisations were: NACRO, the Greater London Authority and the Hampshire and Staffordshire Constabularies.

Discrimination on the grounds of religion and belief: the context

Incidence of religion/belief

Historically and formally, Britain is a Christian country. The Census 2001 for England and Wales reported that 37.3 million people stated that their religion was Christian (see Table 4.15). Much of this stated religious adherence may be nominal because it contrasts with the small percentage who attends Sunday worship. Indeed, it is argued that Britain is a more secular society than its formal commitment to Christianity suggests. Christianity reflects a wide spectrum of belief and religious practice: ranging from the puritanical Plymouth Brethren through various non-conformist religions to the 'established' Church of England

Table 4.15 Recorded membership of religions

	England	*Wales*	*Scotland*
Christian	35.3 m	2.1 m	3.3 m
Muslim	1.5 m	21,700	43,000
Jewish	257,600	2,200	6,400
Hindu	546,900	5,400	5,600
Sikh	327,343	2,000	6,600
Buddhist	139,000	5,400	6,800
No religion	7.17 m	538,000	1.4 m
Religion not stated	3.77 m	234,000	278,000

The question was voluntary.

Source: Census 2001 statistics. National Statistics website: www.statistics.gov.uk

(of which the monarch is the 'Defender of the Faith') and to the Catholic Church. A similar spectrum of orthodoxy and belief is reflected also in the two other major and historically important religions in European societies: Judaism and Islam. Neither has a high degree of uniformity of either belief or practice.

Social tensions and religion

Religious belief can, of course, be the source of good works. However, there are circumstances in which tensions, sometimes serious, with religious organisations can arise:

- ***Fundamentalism***: debates about the extent to which a relevant holy text (the Bible, the Torah or the Qur'an) is to be interpreted literally have been and remain consistent aspects of religions. This can give rise to 'fundamentalist' views and, as a consequence a religion may become embedded in a political ideology. 'Fundamentalist' forms of such religious ideology can lead to the justification of intolerance, violence and murder. There is evidence of this 'fundamentalist' form of all three major religions.
- ***Conflicting values***: this can arise from the relationship between an individual's personal religious belief and prevailing social values and legislation (see Exhibit 5.17).
- ***Political activity***: the involvement of religion in politics by campaigning for specific objectives and trying to influence public policy and legislation, whilst legitimate, may not reflect the prevailing social views (on for example, abortion or gay rights).
- ***Religious observance***: efforts to influence employers and society at large to facilitate particular religious observance. For employers this can arise in respect of observance of days of worship, religious festivals, religious dress and not being required to undertake work that conflicts with religious belief (see Chapters 5 and 6).

Other beliefs

Alongside religious belief, it is important to remember that there are also the values and views of secularism. Within British society there is a long-standing strand of opinion that supports and promotes atheism, agnostic views, rationalism and humanism. Many adherents of these opinions and values seek to minimise the social and political role of religion and restrict it to

Table 4.16 What clothes or accessories should people *not* be allowed to wear for work?

Clothes/accessories	*Percentage*
Burkha/niqab/covering the whole body and face	65
Veil/hijab/covering the face	56
Religious knife or kirpan	19
Turban/kiffayeh/similar male headwear	8
Crucifix	5
Jewish skull cap/yamulke	3
Silver ring of abstinence	2
Orthodox Jewish hair and hat	2
Bindi/red Hindu dot on the face	2
Sari	2
Dreadlocks	2
Beard	1
Star of David/Mogon Davod	1

1,000 face-to-face interviews (December 2007). Based on statistically representative sample of religious and non-religious populations in Great Britain.

Source: Employers Forum on Belief (www.efbelief.org.uk).

a person's private life. In addition, as a consequence of amendments enacted by the Equality Act 2006, political beliefs can also potentially be protected (see Chapter 5).

Incidence of discrimination/attitudes to religion or belief

A survey commissioned by the Employers' Forum on Belief (2008, **www.efbelief.org.uk**) indicated a fairly consistent general view (across religions and non-religious people) that people should not be allowed to wear whatever they wanted according to their religious views. Almost half (48 per cent) agreed with this statement. Attitudes to specific religious clothes or accessories were tested (see Table 4.16). Views about the acceptability of wearing clothes that express their religion varied: 64 per cent thought teachers should not be allowed to wear such clothes; 51 per cent for police officers; and 44 per cent for doctors and nurses.

The state of the law and the proposed single Equality Act

What progress and what problems?

Since the enactment of the first legislation in the 1970s, various commentators have drawn attention to problems with discrimination law – particularly as it has developed across six strands. Aside from technical-legal issues, the key areas of concern are:

Grounds of discrimination

These have expanded considerably but an inevitable question is whether or not they are sufficiently comprehensive. Some commentators point to the absence of discrimination on the grounds of ***social origin*** (which is included explicitly in the European Convention on Human Rights (Article 14)). The Chair of the Equality and Human Rights Commission commented in a speech (21 July 2008): 'While we are used to talking about inequality between different groups based on race, gender, disability and age, we need to think much bigger than that. We need to regain the habit of talking about vertical inequality – or, in other words, that taboo subject, economic class . . . The divide between rich and poor has widened to its highest level for 40 years according to recent research by the Joseph Rowntree Foundation'. In the British Social Attitudes Survey, 76 per cent of people considered the gap between rich and poor to be too large.

Other commentators draw attention to discrimination in respect of ***genetic information.*** 'As biotechnology progresses, it is becoming increasingly feasible to test for genetic traits that indicate a susceptibility to developing specific illnesses or disorders' (Rubenstein 2007b: 31). Federal legislation was enacted on this issue in the United States in 2008 (to be implemented in 2009) covering employers and health insurers (*Equal Opportunities Review*, 177, June 2008). The British government has stated it has decided 'not to extend protection against discrimination on the ground of genetic predisposition. We have recently agreed to the insurance industry's proposal to extend until 2014 the existing arrangements for a voluntary moratorium on insurers' use of predictive genetic test results and consider that this, along with continued monitoring [by the Human Genetics Commission] of the use of genetic testing in the UK should provide sufficient reassurance' (*The Equality Bill – Government Response to the Consultation*, 2008, para 15.1). The UK is behind many other EU member states who have legislated. Action in the UK to extend protection against discriminatory treatment will only arise from both social and political pressure.

Other writers and lobby groups point to the failure to cover effectively those with ***criminal convictions.*** Given that it is recorded that a third of men have a criminal record, the potential for discrimination is considerable. The legislation, the Rehabilitation of Offenders Act 1974, was described in a Home Office report (2002) as being 'confusing' and 'not achieving the right balance between resettlement and protection'. No immediate action looks likely to clarify this area. Nevertheless, the circumstances may be propitious for greater clarification of the law and a public policy commitment in favour of rehabilitation – particularly given the excessively high (mostly male) prison population. The CIPD research (2007) has found that three-quarters of employers would consider recruiting ex-offenders if they had relevant skills but only if government improves support for employers (in respect of rehabilitation and training; and guidance on risk assessments). But relatively few employers offer work to people just released from prison.

Implementing public-sector equality duties

Criticism has arisen in part as a result of the ways in which the initial statutory duties on public authorities (particularly in relation to race) have been implemented. Surveys in *Equal Opportunities Review* show that 'organisations can become too focused on process rather than outcomes'. They 'can view the publishing of their equality scheme as the completion of the legal requirement rather than the starting point' (Godwin 2007). The Commission for Racial Equality (2007) (in a final report before it was wound up) listed its main areas of concern: a failure to collect data for all required areas; a failure to collect data using appropriate ethnic monitoring categories; the very high numbers of staff whose ethnicity was not known; a failure to analyse data; a failure to publish employment data; no action plan in the organisation's race equality schemes; and schemes that just reiterated the wording of the race equality duty.

Other research suggests a slightly more positive aspect. Research among 113 public-sector organisations (mostly in the health service and local government) reported that 44 per cent of the respondents had chosen to produce a single equality scheme or adopt a combined approach across all strands of discrimination law. The reasons being: to avoid duplication, reduce costs in communication and in staff training. However, two-thirds of organisations had separate equality schemes as well as an overall single scheme (Schneider-Ross 2007).

The complexity and 'bureaucratisation' of equal opportunities inherent in having parallel duties may start to be tackled with the proposed single duty in the new legislation.

Covert discrimination

Secrecy bedevils the identification of discriminatory treatment; and in particular the achievement of equal pay. The limitations on obtaining reliable evidence and data make it difficult to formulate a persuasive and convincing complaint. The explicit use of contract law to compound the secrecy is a serious problem because of the likely consequence of breach of contract by the employee that might arise. Equal Opportunities Commission research (2004, **www.equalityhumanrights.com**) recorded that 22 per cent of employers did not permit employees to share pay information with colleagues. The proposal to outlaw secrecy clauses will be one step towards at least diagnosing more accurately the nature of the problem.

Positive action

As indicated earlier in this chapter, this action can be particularly contentious and confusing. A survey by the Confederation of British Industry (2007) reported that just over a quarter of companies said that they had not adopted it because they were unsure of what was allowable positive action and unlawful positive discrimination. The extension of positive action through the use of the 'tie break' has been evident in some other European countries and is compatible with European law (see Exhibit 4.2). It has obvious merits in dealing with under-representation. However, clarity on its objectives and operation will be particularly important.

Compound discrimination

Currently, people can only bring a claim that someone has treated them unfairly because of *one* particular characteristic. But there are situations where people are discriminated against because of a particular combination of characteristics. This means that 'there is little information about the number of people that are prevented from bringing claims as a result of this limitation' (Moon 2008). Drawing on evidence from Ontario which includes Toronto, one of the most diverse cities in Canada, it has been noted that 'the Ontario Human Rights Commission, which can support claims of multiple discrimination, found that 48 per cent of its cases between 1997 and 2000 involved multiple discrimination . . . it seems likely that a similar pattern could be found in some parts of Britain too' (Moon). Other evidence points to potential multiple discrimination, such as:

- Bangladeshi and Pakistani women experiencing racism, sexism and anti-Muslim prejudice;
- African people with HIV experiencing racism and homophobia (and sexism if they are female).

This is a complex issue but one which is being considered in the proposed new legislation.

Monitoring

This remains a perennial problem for the achievement of effective equal opportunities. The Discrimination Law Review (**www.equalities.gov.uk**) stated that 'a reporting regime which could guarantee the necessary degree of accuracy would be bureaucratic, burdensome on employers and costly to run and enforce'. Behind these, perhaps dispiriting, words are the essential problems of monitoring: time, trouble and cost. Evidence on the limited compliance with statutory equality duties (see above) shows the difficulties. Although a statutory duty on employers (with more than ten employees) to monitor and report does exist under religious discrimination law in Northern Ireland, it is not part of discrimination law in the rest of the UK. Monitoring is only recommended in the statutory codes of practice published by the former equality commissions. The proposed Equality Bill White Paper is silent on the issue.

Weak enforcement

There are several issues that have been commented upon:

- *Recommendations by employment tribunals.* As around 70 per cent of employees involved in discrimination complaints leave the organisation. This 'ties the hands of tribunals' who may only make recommendations for that complainant (Rubenstein 2007a).
- *Individual complaints.* Current legislation is founded upon individual complaints. One proposal for overcoming this limitation to the enforcement process would be to permit 'representative actions' (where a common problem affected a group of employees). The Discrimination Law Review was 'not persuaded' there should be a move to these. However, they are proposed by the government (see Exhibit 4.4).

Exhibit 4.4 'Framework for a fairer future – the Equality Bill'

In June 2008, the government published *Framework for a fairer future – the Equality Bill*. This is effectively a 'declaration of intent' on proposed measures to 'de-clutter and strengthen the law' on equality. It is founded largely on the Discrimination Law Review (2005–07); and is a step towards a new Equality Bill which should consolidate the existing strands of discrimination law into a single statute.

Equality duty on public authorities. This new duty will bring together the three existing statutory duties and extend coverage to gender reassignment, age, sexual orientation and religion or belief. This streamlining 'will help public authorities to focus their efforts on outcomes, rather than on producing plans and documents'. As under the three existing duties, public authorities will be required to tackle discrimination and promote equality through their procurement activity.

Age discrimination. Unjustifiable age discrimination by those providing goods, facilities and services will be outlawed. Particular attention is drawn to health and social care; and to restricted access to some financial services such as insurance.

Greater transparency. This is needed to deal with inequalities in gender pay, ethnic minority employment and disability employment. Several measures are proposed:

- Ban on secrecy clauses in contracts of employment which prevent disclosure of pay information. Otherwise, 'it is difficult to see where unequal pay exists' and it is 'more difficult to challenge employers who unfairly and unlawfully pay less'.

- Particular attention is given to 'delivering transparency in the public sector' whereby public authorities will be required to publish data on gender pay; ethnic minority employment; and disability employment. This will enable progress year by year to be seen.
- 'Delivering transparency in the private sector' will be tackled, in part, by the promotion of equality through purchasing functions of public authorities (when purchasing from the private sector) and 'working with business to improve practice on equality issues'.

Equality and Human Rights Commission inquiries. 'The level of inequality varies between different sectors'. These will be initiated in particular sectors, including the financial services and the construction industry.

Kite mark. This will relate to an organisation's effectiveness in closing the gender pay gap, and being 'transparent about reporting their progress on equality'.

Positive action. Extending this provision to permit arrangements for dealing with two equally qualified candidates in the context of under-representation of, *for example*, women or people from an ethnic minority group. This is 'not about employment quotas and will not allow people to promote one candidate above another if that person is less suitable' (see Exhibit 4.2 on compatibility with European equal treatment law).

Strengthening enforcement. Several proposals are indicated:

- 'At present the individual who has experienced discrimination shoulders the considerable financial and emotional burdens of bringing a claim'. So, the possibility of 'representative actions' in discrimination law is considered. These could be brought by trade unions, the ECHR and other bodies to take cases on behalf of groups of people who have been discriminated against.
- 'We know that much discrimination arises as a result of institutional policies and practices, many of which have been in place for years and are part of an organisation's culture. Tackling this behaviour requires a systemic approach.' So, tribunals will be allowed to make wider recommendations which go beyond those specifically benefiting the individual.
- The possibility of discrimination claims being brought on multiple grounds.

Trade union equality representatives. Training supported through the Union Modernisation Fund.

Presented to Parliament by the Lord Privy Seal, Leader of the House of Commons and Minister for Women and Equality, Cm 7431 (www.equalities.gov.uk).

A Bill based on this White Paper was announced in the Queen's Speech (December 2008).

- *Workplace enforcement*. There are two aspects of this: collective bargaining and workplace trade union representation. Both have limitations because of the relatively low density of trade union membership and recognition. Twenty years ago, in one survey of research studies, Dickens and Colling (1990) pointed to the weakness of collective bargaining as an instrument for promoting and reinforcing equal opportunities policies. Largely the negotiating focus was on a traditional pay and conditions agenda. Recent steps to help overcome these problems include unions appointing equality workplace representatives. A report to the Wales TUC (May 2008) concluded that unions had made considerable progress mainstreaming equal pay and incorporating flexible working into their bargaining priorities. Large unions like Unite have adopted a Model Agreement for such representatives; and the government-funded Union Modernisation Fund is promoting training (Godwin 2008b).

Conclusion

This chapter aimed to provide a flavour of the diversity and Britain's labour market and society and of the basis on which discriminatory treatment might arise. No apology is made for indicating the historical context of such treatment. Long-standing views, stereotypes and prejudices have embedded discriminatory attitudes in society and, as a consequence, in the workplace. Eradication of these remains a long haul. The achievement of equal opportunities is probably something that, to use the old advertising strapline, we 'are working towards' and are unlikely to achieve. There will always be challenges to policies, practices and conduct in employment and in society at large. Nevertheless, the issue is to improve these and, where appropriate, to modify corporate cultures through the adoption and effective implementation of proactive equal opportunities policies (see Chapter 6). Success will be measured, in part, by occupational profiles that better represent opportunities for all individual employees. Success will also be measured by reductions in grievances and employment tribunal complaints rather than in the utopian dream of their total elimination.

References and useful websites

Ashtiany, S. (2007) 'Discrimination law – where did it come from and where is it going?', Industrial Law Society Conference, May.

Barnes *et al.* (2002) *Experiences and Expectations of People Leaving Paid Work After 50*. Joseph Rowntree Foundation (www.jrf.org.uk).

Berthoud, R. and Blekesaune, M. (2007) *Persistent Employment Disadvantage*. Research Report No. 416. London: Department of Work and Pensions.

Boonstras, J. *et al.* (eds) (1993) *Antisemitism: a History Portrayed*. Amsterdam: Anne Frank Foundation.

Bytheway, B. (1995) *Ageism*. Buckingham: Open University Press.

Chartered Institute of Personnel and Development (1996) *Managing diversity: a Position Paper*. London: CIPD (www.cipd.co.uk).

Chartered Institute of Personnel and Development (2007) *Employing Ex-Offenders to Capture Talent*. London: CIPD (www.cipd.co.uk).

Commission for Racial Equality (2007) *CRE Monitoring and Enforcement Report 2005–07*. London: Commission for Racial Equality.

Confederation of British Industry (2007) *CBI/Pertemps Survey of 507 Employers* (www.cbi.org.uk).

Daniel W.W. (1968) *Racial Discrimination in England*. Harmondsworth: Penguin Books.

Deakin, S. and Morris, G. (1998) *Labour Law*. Oxford: Hart.

Dench, S. *et al.* (2002) *Key Indicators of Women's Position in Britain*. London: Government Equalities Office (www.equalities.gov.uk).

Denvir, A. *et al.* (2007) *The Experiences of Sexual Orientation and Religion or Belief Discrimination Employment Tribunal Claimants*. London: Advisory, Conciliation and Arbitration Service (www.acas.org.uk).

Department for Work and Pensions (2005) *Family Resources Survey 2003–04*. London: Department for Work and Pensions.

Dickens, L. and Colling, T. (1990) 'Why equality won't appear on the bargaining agenda', *Personnel Management*, April.

Disability Rights Commission (2004) *Small Employers' Attitudes to Disability*. DRC archive at www.equalityhumanrights.com.

Equal Opportunities Commission (2006) *Facts about Women and Men in Great Britain*. Manchester: Equal Opportunities Commission (www.equalityhumanrights.com).

Equal Opportunities Commission (2007) *The State of the Modern Family*, the Millennium Cohort Survey. Manchester: Equal Opportunities Commission (www.equalityhumanrights.com).

Equality and Human Rights Commission (2008) *Sex and Power 2008*. London: Equality and Human Rights Commission (www.equalityhumanrights.com).

Fevre, R. *et al*. (2008) Work Fit for All: Disability, Health and the Experience of Negative Treatment in the British Workplace. London: Equality and Human Rights Commission.

Fredman, S. (1997) *Women and the Law*. Oxford: Oxford University Press.

Fredman, S. (2003) 'The age of equality', in Fredman, S. and Spencer, S. (eds) *Age as an Equality Issue*. Oxford: Hart.

Godwin, K. (2007) 'Positive action: possibilities and limits', *Equal Opportunities Review*, 170, November.

Godwin, K. (2008a) 'Disability policies: EOR survey 2008', *Equal Opportunities Review*, 177, June.

Godwin, K. (2008b) 'The missing link: union equality representatives at work', *Equal Opportunities Review*, 173, February.

Grainger, H. and Fitzner, G. (2007) *The First Fair Treatment at Work Survey: Executive Summary – Updated*, Employment Relations Research Series, No. 63. London: Department of Trade and Industry (www.berr.gov.uk).

Grimshaw, D. and Rubery, J. (2007) *Understanding Women's Work*. Manchester: Equal Opportunities Commission.

Hansard Society (1990) *Women at the Top: the Report of the Commission on Women at the Top*. London: The Hansard Society.

Hiro, D. (1973) *Black British, White British*. Harmondworth: Penguin Books.

Holdsworth, A. (1988) *Out of the Doll's House*. London: BBC Books.

Home Office (2002) *Breaking the Circle: a Report of the Review of the Rehabilitation of Offenders Act*. London: The Home Office.

Honey, S. *et al*. (1993) *Employers' Attitudes Towards People with Disabilities*. Brighton: Institute of Manpower Studies.

House of Lords (2003) *Select Committee Report on the Economics of an Ageing Population*. London: Stationery Office.

Justice (1996) *The Union Divided: Race Discrimination and Third Country Nationals in the European Union*. London: Justice.

Kandola *et al*. (1994) *Diversity in Action: Managing the Mosaic*. London: Chartered Institute of Personnel and Development.

Kaur, H. (2004) *Employment Attitudes: Main Finding from British Social Attitudes Survey 2003*, Employment Relations Research Series, No. 36. London: Department of Trade and Industry (www.berr.gov.uk).

MacNicol, J. (2006) *Age Discrimination: an Historical and Contemporary Analysis*. Cambridge: Cambridge University Press.

Mason, D. (1995) *Race and Ethnicity in Modern Britain*. Oxford: Oxford University Press.

Massie, B. (1994) *Disabled People and Social Justice*. London: Institute for Public Policy Research.

Metcalf, H. and Meadows, P. (2006) *Survey of Employers' Policies, Practices and Preferences Relating to Age*, Employment Relations Research Series, No. 49. London: Department of Trade and Industry (www.berr.gov.uk/employment).

Moon, G. (2008) 'Multi-dimensional discrimination: justice for the whole person', *Equal Opportunities Review*, 173, February.

O'Cinneide, C. (2005) *Age Discrimination and European Law*. Brussels: European Commission.

Olsen, L. and Walby, S. (2004) *Modelling Gender Pay Gaps*. Manchester: Equal Opportunities Commission.

Organisation for Economic Cooperation and Development (2006) *Live Longer, Work Longer*. Ageing and Employment Series. Paris: Organisation for Economic Cooperation and Development.

Parekh, B. (1992) 'A case of positive discrimination', in Hepple, B. and Szyszczak, E.M. (eds) *Discrimination: the Limits of the Law*. London: Mansell.

Pidduck, J. (1995) (unpublished) 'The Implications of the Disability Discrimination Act for People with Disabilities'. Kingston-upon-Thames: Kingston University Business School.

Pitt, G. (1992) 'Can reverse discrimination be justified?', in Hepple, B. and Szyszczak, E.M. (eds) *Discrimination: the Limits of the Law*. London: Mansell.

Rubenstein, M. (2006) 'Age regulations 2006 – part 1: key general principles', *Equal Opportunities Review*, May, No. 152.

Rubenstein, M. (2007a) 'Discrimination law review: EOR guide', *Equal Opportunities Review*, No. 167: 30.

Rubenstein, M. (2007b) What is the next frontier for discrimination law? *Equal Opportunities Review*, July, No. 166.

Schneider-Ross, diversity consultants (2007) *The Public Sector Equality Duties – Making an Impact*. (www.schneider-ross.com).

Stephen Lawrence Inquiry Report (1999) Cm 4262-1. London: Stationery Office.

Stonewall (2007) *Living together: British attitudes to Lesbian and Gay People* (www.stonewall.org.uk).

Taylor, P. and Walter, A. (1994) 'The ageing workforce: employers' attitudes towards employing older people', *Employment and Society*, Vol. 8, No. 4.

Trades Union Congress (2008a) *Closing the Gender Pay Gap: an Update Report for TUC Women's Conference 2008*. London: Trades Union Congress (www.tuc.org.uk).

Trades Union Congress (2008b) *Trade Unions, Disabled Members and the Social Model*. London: Trades Union Congress (www.tuc.org.uk).

Twomey, B. (2001) *Disability and the Labour Market: Results from Summer Labour Force Survey*. London: Labour Market Trends.

Walby, S. and Olson, L. (2002) *The Impact of Women's Position in the Labour Market on Pay and Implications for UK Productivity.* London: Women and Equality Unit.

Weiss, S. (1974) 'Equal treatment and the disabled: a proposal', *Columbia Journal of Social Problems*, 10.

Wood, P. (1991) *International Classification of Impairments, Disabilities and Handicaps*. Geneva: World Health Organisation.

Useful websites

Advisory, Conciliation and Arbitration Service **www.acas.org.uk**

Chartered Institute of Personnel and Development **www.cipd.co.uk**

Confederation of British Industry **www.cbi.org.uk**

Department for Business Enterprise and Regulatory Reform **www.berr.gov.uk**

Employment Tribunals Service **www.employmenttribunals.gov.uk**

Equality and Human Rights Commission **www.equalityhumanrights.com**

Government Equalities Office **www.equalities.gov.uk**

Joseph Rowntree Foundation **www.jrf.org.uk**

UK Statistics Authority **www.statistics.gov.uk**

Schneider-Ross **www.schneider-ross.com**

Stonewall **www.stonewall.org.uk**

Trades Union Congress **www.tuc.org.uk**

Visit **www.mylawchamber.co.uk/willey** to access multiple choice questions, case flashcards and exercises to test yourself on this chapter.

mylawchamber

5 The strands of discrimination law

Learning objectives

To understand:

- The wide scope of the 'grounds' on which discrimination is prohibited
- The underpinning by European Union directives of much discrimination law
- The terminology used in the various pieces of legislation
- Differences and common elements in the provisions of the law
- Aspects of discrimination law that still need clarity
- The enforcement process for individuals to obtain remedies

Structure of the chapter

This chapter is organised as follows:

- Part 1: sex discrimination
- Part 2: gender reassignment
- Part 3: equal pay
- Part 4: race discrimination
- Part 5: disability discrimination
- Part 6: sexual orientation discrimination
- Part 7: religion or belief discrimination
- Part 8: age discrimination
- *Exercises*

Introduction

This chapter provides an outline of the various strands of discrimination law. The social, economic and political context in which this law was formulated and enacted was discussed in Chapter 4. The key employment policy implications for human resource practitioners are outlined in Chapter 6.

The bulk of UK discrimination legislation is underpinned by European law. In most cases it is compliant with the principles and provisions of EU **directives**. However, there are aspects of some British legislation, as outlined below, which are 'home grown'; and there are some cases where compliance is challenged. The relevant EU directives are:

- *Equal treatment of men and women (2006)*: this directive consolidates and updates four major directives, namely on equal pay (1975); on equal treatment (1976); on occupational social security schemes (1986); and on the **burden of proof** (1997). These earlier directives are repealed.
- *Directive for establishing a general framework for equal treatment in employment (2000)*: this is often referred to as the Employment Equality Directive. It provides for anti-discrimination measures in respect of age, disability, sexual orientation and religion or belief.
- *Equal treatment irrespective of racial or ethnic origin (2000)*: this is often referred to as the Race Directive.

The principal implementation of these directives in Britain has, as appropriate, been through the following legislation:

- Sex Discrimination Act 1975 (as amended);
- Equal Pay Act 1970 (as amended);
- Race Relations Act 1976 (as amended);
- Disability Discrimination Act 1995 (as amended);
- Employment Equality (Sexual Orientation) **Regulations** 2003;
- Employment Equality (Religion or Belief) Regulations 2003;
- Employment Equality (Age) Regulations 2006.

One significant consequence of the European base of much discrimination law is that issues of interpretation of **statutory** provisions and of non-compliance can be taken to the European Court of Justice. In the following Parts of the chapter there will be references to various important ECJ rulings.

The fact that there are various strands of discrimination law can create confusion and uncertainty for employment law and human resource practitioners about interpretation. It can also create difficulties where a complaint might cover the provisions in more than one strand. It is proposed by government that there should be a 'single equality Act' encompassing these discrete pieces of legislation (see Chapter 4 and Exhibit 4.4).

In the present fragmented framework of law there are a number of concepts in common. However, it is important to remember that there may be some important differences in the way they are framed in particular statutes. Among the key ones are:

- *direct discrimination* or 'less favourable treatment' than a particular comparator;
- *indirect discrimination* whereby an apparently neutral employment practice may be discriminatory in effect. It is important to note that it is possible for claims of direct and indirect discrimination to arise from the same facts;

- ***the issue of 'justification'*** whereby in specific circumstances an employer might defend discriminatory treatment – effectively for reasons of business necessity. Depending on the legislation, justification can arise in relation to direct discrimination as well as indirect discrimination;
- ***genuine occupation qualification or requirement***: this is where an employer in a person specification requires an individual with a particular characteristic that appears to infringe discrimination law. Such a requirement has to be justified against the appropriate legislation;
- ***positive action***: the encouragement in recruitment and training of under-represented groups (see Chapter 4);
- ***post employment***: there are common provisions in all strands governing discrimination directly connected with the former employment relationship;
- **liability *and* vicarious liability** for discriminatory treatment. This is generally expressed in the same terms under the various statutes. There is the strict liability of the employer; the employer's vicarious liability; and the personal liability of perpetrators of discrimination and harassment;
- ***defence against liability***: similar provisions in all strands involving the taking of 'such steps as are reasonably practicable';
- ***time limits*** for complaints to employment tribunal. There are similar provisions in each piece of legislation;
- ***burden of proof*** in discrimination claims to an employment tribunal. There are two broad aspects: the employee needs to make a ***prima facie*** case, and then the burden shifts to the respondent employer;
- ***questionnaire***: the facility for a complainant to complete such a questionnaire is provided for in each statute;
- ***employment tribunal complaints***: these can be made under any strand of discrimination law by a person with an employment relationship, irrespective of length of service;
- **victimisation**: designed to protect those involved in employment tribunal complaints;
- **remedies**: the same structure of remedies is available under all discrimination law. Information on outcomes at employment tribunal is provided in Chapter 4 (Tables 4.3 and 4.4);
- ***statutory equality duties on public authorities***: these arise under sex, race and disability discrimination law. A single equality **duty** is proposed under changes to legislation (see Chapter 4, Exhibit 4.4);
- ***contracts and collective agreements***: under all strands of law, discriminatory **terms** in these are void (i.e. unenforceable).

Codes of practice

There are several of these (see Chapter 6 and Exhibit 6.1). They were drafted by the former equality commissions and laid before Parliament. They are still in force. Breach of any provisions may be used in proceedings before an employment tribunal.

Other related legislation

It is important to note that *most* discrimination law encompasses provisions relating to the treatment of individuals in a wider range of social relationships (i.e. in the provision of goods, facilities and services). In this chapter, however, the focus is, obviously, on the employment relationship. Nevertheless, interpretations of the law in non-employment cases may be relevant.

Finally, it should be remembered that three other bodies of law (largely deriving from European directives) can be associated with aspects of the strands of discrimination law discussed in this chapter:

- law on *harassment* (which is prohibited under all strands of discrimination law) (see Chapter 7);
- legislation relating to *family leave and flexible working* (see Chapter 11); and
- law concerning discrimination on the grounds of *'atypical' employment status* of part-time and fixed-term working (see Chapter 2).

The Equality and Human Rights Commission

Established in 2007, it took over the responsibilities of the former equality commissions. It has responsibilities for advice to government on and enforcement of all strands of discrimination law (see Chapter 1) (**www.equalityhumanrights.com**).

Part 1: Sex discrimination law

The European Court of Justice has ruled that the elimination of discrimination based on sex is a 'fundamental right' and is 'one of the general principles of Community law (*Defrenne* v *Sabena* (1981) C-43/75). In Britain the original EU directives on equal pay and equal treatment have been implemented through two companion pieces of legislation: the Sex Discrimination Act 1975 and the Equal Pay Act 1970. The latter deals with discriminatory practice in relation to contractual terms, 'pay' in its widest sense (see Part 3 below); the former deals with the treatment of individuals both in employment and in other social relations.

What is the protection?

The Sex Discrimination Act proscribes discrimination on several grounds: sex (whether male or female); married persons or civil partners; pregnancy and maternity leave (see Chapter 11); and gender reassignment (see Part 2 of this chapter). As far as 'employment' is concerned, the legislation provides for protection for those working 'under a contract of service or of apprenticeship or a contract personally to execute any work or labour' (s 82(1)).

Applicants for employment and employees

It is unlawful for an employer to discriminate against a woman or a man:

- in the arrangements he makes for the purpose of determining who should be offered that employment;
- in the terms on which he offers her or him that employment; or by refusing or deliberately omitting to offer her or him that employment (s 6(1)).

It is also unlawful to discriminate:

- in the way the employer affords her or him access to opportunities for promotion, transfer or training or to any other benefits, facilities or services, or by refusing or deliberately omitting to afford access to them; or
- by dismissing her or him, or subjecting her or him to any other **detriment** (s 6(2)).

An exception to these rights is in relation to work done 'wholly or mainly' outside Great Britain (s 10).

Contract workers

Contract **workers** are also covered (s 9). The 'principal' (the person for whom the work is undertaken) must not discriminate against a contract worker:

- in the terms on which he allows her or him to do that work; or
- by not allowing her or him to do it or continue to do it; or
- in the way he affords her or him access to any benefits, facilities or services or by refusing or deliberately omitting to afford her or him access to them; or
- by subjecting her or him to any other detriment.

Self-employed persons

The self-employed may also be protected by the Sex Discrimination Act. The issue is whether they are employed under contract 'personally to execute any work or labour' (s 82(1)). In one case (*Quinnen* v *Hovels* [1984] IRLR 227, EAT) a self-employed salesman of 'fancy goods' who had 'pitches' in various department stores recruited some temporary assistants to work for him on a commission basis. Although they were self-employed, the EAT ruled that they were protected by the Act.

Direct discrimination

The Sex Discrimination Act states that 'a person discriminates against a woman in any circumstances relevant for the purposes of any provisions of this Act if on the ground of her sex he treats her less favourably than he treats or would treat a man' (s 1(1)(a)). This legislation applies equally to men (s 2). There are parallel 'less favourable treatment' provisions in respect of married persons or civil partners (s 3); and in respect of pregnant women and those exercising rights to statutory maternity leave (s 3A)(see Chapter 11 on Family leave and work–life balance).

Comparator: the 'but for' test

This is the key test for determining direct discrimination (*James* v *Eastleigh Borough Council* [1990] IRLR 288). Lord Goff in the House of Lords judgment in this case stated that 'cases of direct discrimination under s 1(1)(a) can be considered by asking the simple question: would the complainant have received the same treatment from the defendant but for his or her sex?'. It is important, in this context, that the court or tribunal has to arrive at a view, *on the facts*, that the less favourable treatment was on the grounds of sex (even in part) and on no other grounds. Motive and intention are not relevant in cases of direct sex discrimination. No justification or defence is allowable. Lord Goff (in *R* v *Birmingham City Council* ex parte *EOC* [1989] IRLR 173) stated that 'the intention or motive of the defendant to discriminate . . . is not a necessary condition to liability; it is perfectly possible to envisage cases where the defendant had no such motive and yet did in fact discriminate on the grounds of sex'.

Indirect discrimination

Whilst the direct discrimination provisions cover clear and blatant unfair discrimination, those relating to indirect discrimination in employment (SDA 1975, s 1(2)(b)) are designed to tackle the less obvious and unintentional discriminatory treatment that might arise in the course of employment. Welcoming the original incorporation of the concept into the legal framework, Mary Redmond (1986: 476) said that 'the proscription of indirect discrimination represents a landmark in British anti-discrimination legislation. The continuing absence of women and of minority groups from important areas of employment is due, in large measure, to indirect discrimination.' However, she adds an important word of warning that 'the road to be travelled by a person alleging indirect discrimination is strewn with complexities'.

The provisions in the Sex Discrimination Act relating to employment are that:

> a person discriminates against a woman if he applies to her a provision, criterion or practice which he applies or would apply equally to a man but
>
> - which puts or would put women at a particular disadvantage when compared with men,
> - which puts her at that disadvantage and
> - which he cannot show to be a proportionate means of achieving a legitimate aim. (s 1(2)(b))

The phrase 'provision, criterion or practice' is wider than the original formulation of 'requirement or condition'. To this extent it should strengthen the scope of anti-discrimination protection in dealing with a wider range of employment practices.

Prior to the 2001 amendment of the Sex Discrimination Act, a number of employment arrangements were challenged as discriminatory on the grounds of sex (and would still be relevant under current law):

- *Age barriers in recruitment.* These may be discriminatory against women who have taken time out of employment to care for children (*Price* v *Civil Service Commission* [1978] IRLR 3, EAT).
- *Requirements on length of service.* These can disadvantage women who have had breaks in employment to bring up children.
- *Mobility conditions.* These may cause disadvantage to women in contrast to a man because of childcare responsibilities.
- *Unsocial hours requirements.* These can disproportionately affect women because of family responsibilities (see Exhibit 5.1).
- *Requirement to work full-time.* This may be indirectly discriminatory against women returners from maternity leave if the work can be undertaken on a part-time or more formal **job share** basis (see Chapter 11).
- *Redundancy selection.* A decision to select **part-time workers** first for redundancy could be indirectly discriminatory because of the predominance of women in part-time employment (*Clarke* v *Eley (IMI) Kynoch Ltd* [1982] IRLR 482).

The 'justification' of indirect discrimination

Unlike direct sex discrimination, indirect sex discrimination can potentially be justified. As indicated above, the employer would need to show the discrimination to be 'a proportionate means of achieving a legitimate aim'. The 'legitimate aim' would be some relevant business objective. The means of achieving that aim should be 'proportionate'. In the Equal Treatment Directive 2006 (Article 2) it refers to 'means' as being 'appropriate and necessary'.

The reference to 'necessity' reflects earlier **case law** relating to the objective justification of a 'requirement or condition'. The European Court of Justice ruled that the objective

Exhibit 5.1 Unsocial work requirements

London Underground Ltd v *Edwards (No. 2)* [1998] IRLR 364, CA

Facts. A female train operator, who was a single parent, was required to work a new roster or face dismissal. Prior to this, for five years, she had been able to organise a shift pattern which enabled her to work and care for her child. The roster would have required her to work longer hours than previously. She complained of unfair dismissal.

EAT ruling. The tribunal ruled that London Underground had not established justification. It stated that it could have easily accommodated Ms Edwards without losing the objective of its business plan and reorganisation. It had been well aware of her misgivings and difficulties and had not addressed itself to them. She had been working for this employer for nearly 10 years and there had been no complaints about her work performance. Her family demands were of a temporary nature. London Underground could have accommodated her reasonable demands.

Court of Appeal ruling. The court upheld the EAT ruling that the rostering system requiring an early morning start had an adverse impact on women even though only one out of 21 women drivers positively complained about the arrangement.

standards of 'justification' require that the employer has a real need and that the discriminatory action is necessary and appropriate to achieve that end (*Bilka-Kaufhaus Gmbh* v *Weber von Hartz* [1986] IRLR 317, ECJ). This view was adopted by the Court of Appeal where it was acknowledged that a balance had to be struck between, on the one hand, the discriminatory effect of the condition or requirement and, on the other hand, 'the reasonable needs of the person who applies the condition' (*Hampson* v *Department of Education and Science* [1989] IRLR 69, CA).

Genuine occupation qualifications

There are several circumstances where a person's sex can be a genuine qualification for a job (s 7):

- 'The essential nature of the job' requires either a man or woman 'for reasons of ***physiology*** (excluding physical strength or stamina)'; or 'for reasons of ***authenticity***' in drama and other entertainment.
- 'The job needs to be held' by a man or a woman 'to preserve ***decency or privacy***'. This is because the job requires 'physical contact' or because the holder of the job might work in circumstances where members of the opposite sex 'are in a state of undress or are using sanitary facilities'.
- The job is likely to involve the job holder doing work, or living, in ***a private home*** and needs to be held by, for example, a man because objection might reasonably be taken to allowing a woman the degree of physical or social contact with the person living in the home; or the knowledge of intimate details of such a person's life.
- ***Single-sex accommodation*** where it is 'impractical' for the job holder to live elsewhere than in the employer's premises; 'the only such premises which are available' are for one sex and these 'are not equipped with separate sleeping accommodation . . . and sanitary facilities'; and 'it is not reasonable to expect the employer either to equip those premises with such accommodation and facilities or to provide other premises'.

- ***Single-sex establishments*** which are 'a hospital, prison or other establishment for persons requiring special care, supervision and attention'; and that 'it is reasonable, having regard to the essential character of the establishment or that part' that the job should be held by a person of a specified sex.
- The job holder 'provides individuals with ***personal services*** promoting their welfare or education, or similar personal services and those services can most effectively be provided' by a person of a specified sex.
- The job involves ***work outside the United Kingdom*** 'in a country whose law and customs are such that the duties could not, or could not effectively' be carried out by a person of a specified sex.
- The job is one of two to be held by a married couple or by civil partners.

If an employer is challenged about his reliance on a particular GOQ, then, he would have to show that it related to the provisions of this Act.

Discriminatory advertisements

It is unlawful to publish an advertisement which 'indicates or might reasonably be understood as indicating an intention' to discriminate unlawfully. The publisher of an advertisement is liable unless he can prove that it was not unlawful (s 38). An example would be reliance on the GOQ provisions in the legislation.

Instructions and pressure to discriminate

It is unlawful for a person in authority over another person to pressurise him or her to discriminate; and to threaten detrimental action or offer benefit (ss 39 and 40). Legal action against such pressure can only be taken by the Equality and Human Rights Commission (see Equality Act 2006, s 25) either in an employment tribunal; or in the county court (England and Wales) or to the sheriff (in Scotland). The Commission may apply for an injunction (an interdict in Scotland) to stop the discriminatory pressure.

Aiding unlawful acts

A person who knowingly aids another person to do an unlawful act under sex discrimination law will be treated as doing an unlawful act 'of the like description' (s 42). For example, a manager was jointly and severally liable to pay compensation for acts of sex discrimination against the claimant even though some of the acts were carried out by other managers in circumstances on which the manager could be regarded as having unlawfully aided and consciously encouraged the discrimination (*Gilbank* v *Miles* [2006] IRLR 583, CA).

Positive action

In the legislation (SDA 1975, ss 47 and 48) this covers access to various forms of training and encouraging women (or, as appropriate, men) to take opportunities for doing particular work (see also Chapter 4).

Post employment

It is unlawful for an employer, when an employment relationship has come to an end, to 'discriminate against the woman by subjecting her to a detriment where the discrimination arises out of or is closely connected to the relevant [i.e. the employment] relationship' (s 20A). There is a similar prohibition on harassment (see Chapter 7). This provision also applies to men. The European Court of Justice determined in 1997 that protection against action by an employer extended to circumstances after the employment relationship ended. The case involved a refusal to provide a reference to an employment agency for a woman who had alleged that she had been dismissed because of pregnancy. Any retaliatory measures by an employer (whether in cases of dismissal or not) were unlawful. They could deter workers from pursuing claims and might seriously jeopardise the Equal Treatment Directive's aim (*Coote* v *Granada Hospitality Ltd* C-185/97, [1998] ECR I-5199; [1998] IRLR 656 ECJ 171, 207).

A change in UK discrimination law arose from the House of Lords decision in *Rhys-Harper* v *Relaxion Group plc*; *DeSouza* v *London Borough of Lambeth*; and *Jones* v *3M Healthcare Ltd* [2003] IRLR 848. It ruled in these joint appeals that employees should be protected against certain acts of post-termination discrimination by their employer. It was stated that it is the employment relationship that triggers the employer's obligation not to discriminate; and it makes no sense to draw an arbitrary line at the point when the contract ends.

Liability and vicarious liability

Liability rests with the employer and with the perpetrator of the discrimination. The employer is vicariously liable for the discriminatory behaviour of a manager, a supervisor or another employee. The Sex Discrimination Act states: 'anything done by a person in the course of his employment shall be treated for the purpose of this Act as done by his employer as well as by him, whether or not it was done with employer's knowledge or approval' (s 41(1)). Furthermore, 'anything done by a person as agent for another person with the authority (whether express or implied and whether precedent or subsequent) of that other person shall be treated for the purposes of this Act as done by that person as well as by him' (s 41(2)). This would cover managers.

In one of the important commonalities between case law on the Sex Discrimination Act 1975 and the Race Relations Act 1976, the Court of Appeal ruled on the meaning of the phrase 'in the course of employment' (*Jones* v *Tower Boot Co Ltd* [1997] IRLR 68). It stated that these words should be interpreted broadly, in line with 'the natural meaning of those everyday words'. It added that:

> [T]his is not to say that when it comes to applying them to the infinite variety of circumstances which is liable to occur in particular instances – within or without the workplace, in or out of uniform, in or out of rest breaks – all laymen would necessarily agree as to the result . . . The application of the phrase will be a question of fact for each [employment tribunal] to resolve in the light of the circumstances presented to it, with a mind unclouded by any parallels sought to be drawn from the law of vicarious liability in **tort**.

This wide construction of the phrase 'in the course of employment' would cover not just presence on the employer's premises, but possibly travelling to work, travelling during working hours, work-related training events and conferences. The EAT has also ruled that an employer can be liable for discrimination in a social gathering where people are having drinks after work (*Chief Constable of Lincolnshire Police* v *Stubbs and Others* [1999] IRLR 81). This would, of course, cover Christmas parties.

Defence against liability

The law provides a defence for an employer against liability in tribunal or court proceedings. 'It shall be a defence . . . to prove that he took such steps as were reasonably practicable to prevent the employee from doing that [discriminatory] act, or from doing in the course of his employment acts of that description' (s 41(3)). The nature of such 'reasonable steps' to prevent discriminatory treatment are employment policies and practices and are considered in Chapter 6.

Time limits

A complaint to an employment tribunal should be made within three months of the discriminatory act complained of. However, 'a court or tribunal may nevertheless consider any such complaint, claim or application which is out of time if, in all the circumstances of the case, it considered that it is just and equitable to do so' (s 76(5)). The Sex Discrimination Act envisages two types of situation: a single act of discrimination; and a pattern of discrimination that might extend over a period of time (s 67(6)(b)). Greater difficulties in establishing the appropriate time limit can arise with the latter. There is information and advice on the Tribunal Service website (**www.employmenttribunals.gov.uk**) on the process: describing the making of the complaint (on an ET1 form) and the response from the employer (on the ET3 form).

Burden of proof

The burden of proof has shifted in discrimination cases in the past 10 years by tilting the balance more in favour of the complainant. Essentially, as described in the Sex Discrimination Act (s 63A), the complainant must make a *prima facie* case of discriminatory treatment. This is an outline of the key facts known to him or her which in the view of the complainant point to discrimination. It has been stated that there does not have to be *positive evidence* that the difference in treatment is on grounds of race or sex in order to establish a *prima facie* case (*Network Rail Infrastructure Ltd* v *Griffiths-Henry* [2006] IRLR 865, EAT). It is then for the respondent employer to demonstrate that there was no unlawful discrimination in the treatment of the worker. The Court of Appeal has approved 13-point guidance on how the burden of proof rules in discrimination cases should be applied (*Igen Ltd* v *Wong* [2005] ICR 931) (see Exhibit 5.2).

The question of inferences has been ruled on by the EAT (*D'Silva* v *NATFHE* [2008] IRLR 412, EAT). Mr Justice Underhill stated that it was not a 'correct approach' for complainants to 'rely' on a respondent's failure to answer a questionnaire or otherwise provide documents. 'It is necessary in each case to consider whether in the particular circumstances of that case the failure in question is capable of constituting evidence supporting the inference that the respondent acted discriminatorily in the manner alleged . . .'. Effectively, inadequate replies and information can be taken into account. But there must be a link between the failure to provide information and the act of alleged discrimination.

Questionnaire

A complainant to an employment tribunal, under the Sex Discrimination Act is entitled to serve on the employer a questionnaire (Sex Discrimination (Questions and Replies) Order

Exhibit 5.2 Guidance on the burden of proof

Igen Ltd v *Wong* [2005] ICR 931 (paraphrased)

1 ***The complainant***. S/he must prove, on the balance of probabilities, facts from which the tribunal could conclude (in the absence of an adequate explanation) that the respondent employer has committed an act of unlawful discrimination against the claimant.

2 If the claimant does not prove such facts s/he will fail.

3 ***Direct evidence***. It is important to bear in mind, in deciding whether the claimant has proved such facts, that it is unusual to find direct evidence of sex discrimination. Few employers would be prepared to admit such discrimination even to themselves.

4 ***Inferences***. In deciding whether the complainant has proved such facts, it is important to remember that the outcome, at this stage of the analysis by the tribunal, will usually depend on what inferences it is proper to draw from the primary facts it finds.

5 ***Could there be discrimination***? At this stage, the tribunal is not reaching a definitive determination that such facts ***would*** lead to a conclusion that there was an act of unlawful discrimination. It is looking at the primary facts before it in order to see what inferences of secondary fact could be drawn from them.

6 In considering what inferences or conclusions can be drawn from the primary facts, the tribunal must assume that there is no adequate explanation for those facts.

7 ***Evasive and equivocal replies***. These inferences can include (in appropriate cases) those that it is just and equitable to draw from an evasive or equivocal reply to a questionnaire or any other questions that fall within discrimination legislation.

8 ***Relevant code of practice***. The tribunal must decide whether any provision of an applicable code is relevant and has been taken into account in determining such facts. Inferences may be drawn from failure to comply with any relevant code.

9 ***The burden of proof***. This moves to the respondent employer where the claimant has provided facts from which conclusions could be drawn that s/he has been treated less favourably on the ground of sex (or other unlawful grounds of discrimination).

10 It is, then, for the respondent to prove that he did not commit, or as the case may be, is not treated as having committed that act.

11 ***Discharging the burden of proof***. It is necessary for the respondent to prove, on the balance of probabilities, that the treatment was in no sense whatsoever on the grounds of sex (or, as appropriate, other unlawful grounds).

12 ***Tribunal assessment***. That requires the tribunal to assess whether the respondent has proved an explanation for the facts from which such inferences can be drawn; but further that it is adequate to discharge the burden of proof on the balance of probabilities that unlawful discrimination was not a ground for the treatment alleged.

13 ***Cogent evidence from respondent***. Since the facts necessary to prove an explanation would normally be in the respondent's possession, the tribunal would normally expect cogent evidence to discharge the burden of proof. In particular, the tribunal will need to examine carefully explanations for failure to deal with the questionnaire procedure and/or code of practice.

1975). Its purpose is to obtain information and documents in order to decide whether to start proceedings, to establish as far as possible the facts and to establish the reasons for the treatment (e.g. what criteria have been applied and to find out how others have been treated in similar circumstances). The replies are admissible in evidence; and a refusal to reply without reasonable excuse may allow the tribunal to draw adverse conclusions. An equivocal reply might also lead a tribunal to infer that there has been discrimination. With the permission of the tribunal, a supplementary questionnaire may be served on the employer to seek, for example, data on workforce profile where documents are not readily available.

Victimisation

The Sex Discrimination Act (s 4) protects people involved in employment tribunal complaints in the following ways:

- The victim must have taken a sex discrimination action; given evidence in a sex discrimination case; or alleged that sex discrimination has taken place.
- It must be demonstrated that the treatment of the victim has been less favourable than that of someone who has not been involved in a sex discrimination case (*Chief Constable of West Yorkshire* v *Khan* [2001] IRLR 830). In a more recent equal pay case (*St Helens Borough Council* v *Derbyshire and Others* [2007] IRLR 540), the House of Lords drew a distinction between what might be an employer's attempt to 'settle or compromise a claim' and a letter which 'contained what was effectively a threat'. It was asserted by Lady Justice Hale that an employer must avoid doing anything that might 'make a reasonable employee feel she is being unduly pressurised to concede her claim'.
- It must also be demonstrated that the less favourable treatment is a direct result of the involvement in the sex discrimination case (*Aziz* v *Trinity Street Taxis Ltd* [1988] ICR 534, CA).

This protection relates to both sex discrimination and equal pay claims.

Remedies

Where an employment tribunal upholds a complaint, it must grant one or more of the following three available remedies:

1 ***A declaration.*** This is 'an order declaring the rights of the complainant and the [employer] in relation to the act to which the complaint relates (s 65(1)(a)). A tribunal has a **duty** to make one. In itself, it can have little deterrent effect, unless the employer is concerned about adverse publicity. In practice, a declaration is usually accompanied by compensation and/or a recommendation.

2 ***Compensation.*** In practice, this is the remedy that complainants most frequently seek and, if successful, are awarded. Since 1993, the upper limit has been removed as a result of a ruling in the European Court of Justice (*Marshall* v *Southampton and South West Hampshire Area Health Authority* (No. 2) [1993] IRLR 445). The court reasoned that 'where financial compensation is the measure adopted in order to achieve the [1976 Equal Treatment Directive's] objective, it must be adequate, in that it must enable the loss and damage actually sustained as a result of the discriminatory dismissal (or other circumstances) to be made good in full in accordance with applicable national rules'. In this case it was also ruled that interest is 'an essential component of compensation'. Compensation is awarded for ***financial loss***, if any, and for ***injury to feelings***.
   - *Financial loss.* This can comprise loss of earnings, past and projected; loss of fringe benefits (e.g. pension rights, subsidised travel or company car; and expenses associated with the discrimination claim). The assessment of compensation is based on the principle that the complainant must be put into the position they would have been in had the unlawful discrimination not happened. The Court of Appeal (*Coleman* v *Skyrail Oceanic Ltd* [1981] IRLR 398) has indicated that the objective of restitution was subject to four qualifications:

  - *Foreseeable damage*: compensation for damage arising directly from the unlawful discrimination;
  - *Mitigation of loss*: the complainant is obliged to take all reasonable steps to minimise his/her loss (e.g. by seeking alternative employment);
  - *Behaviour*: compensation may be reduced because of the conduct, character and circumstances of the complainant;
  - *Non-financial loss*: this is difficult to establish and tribunals have fairly wide discretion.
- *Injury to feelings*. This refers to emotional harm; and it is almost inevitable that compensation under this heading will arise in discrimination cases. The issues which can influence this level of award are:
  - the complainant proving most or all of his/her claim;
  - evidence of a long-term campaign of discrimination;
  - the consequences of the discrimination (e.g. stress, depression);
  - a power relationship between the perpetrator and the victim;
  - management's approach in dealing with the matter through the organisation's grievance procedure.

  It has been stated that an award for injury to feelings should include an element of *aggravated damages* where the employer has 'behaved in a high-handed, malicious, insulting or oppressive manner' in discriminating against the complainant (*Alexander* v *Home Office* [1988] IRLR 190, CA). The Court of Appeal has set out three bands for awards for injury to feelings (*Vento* v *Chief Constable of West Yorkshire Police* [2003] IRLR 102) (see Table 5.1).

  It has been commented that harbouring a legitimate and principled sense of grievance is not to be confused with suffering an injury to feelings (*Moyhing* v *Barts and London NHS Trust* [2006] IRLR 860, EAT).
- *Personal injury*. Claimants can also claim for personal injury (including psychiatric injury) arising out of discriminatory treatment without having to satisfy an additional test that the losses were reasonably foreseeable (*Essa* v *Laing* [2004] IRLR 313, CA).

3 ***Recommendations***. A tribunal's powers to make recommendations are limited to recommendations for action that will affect the individual complainant (see Chapter 4, Exhibit 4.4). If a respondent employer fails 'without reasonable justification' to comply with a recommendation, a tribunal may, if it thinks that it is just and equitable, increase the amount of compensation to be paid or, if no order for compensation has been made, it may make one.

Table 5.1 ***Vento*** **guidelines**

Top band £15,000–£25,000	Designed to cover the most serious cases (e.g. lengthy campaign of discrimination). Awards over £25,000 should be exceptional
Middle band £5,000–£15,000	For serious cases that do not merit a top band award
Lowest band £500–£5,000	For less serious cases – e.g. where the discriminatory act is an isolated incident

Gender duty on public authorities

This duty (s 76A) involves the elimination of unlawful discrimination and harassment and the promotion of equal opportunities between men and women. It was implemented in 2007 and parallels the duty in respect of race discrimination which was enacted earlier (see Part 4).

Part 2: Gender reassignment discrimination law

The European Court of Justice ruled that discrimination on the grounds of gender reassignment was contrary to the principle of equal treatment in the 1975 Equal Treatment Directive (*P* v *S and Cornwall County Council* [1996] IRLR 347). In 1999, regulations were approved by Parliament amending the Sex Discrimination Act 1975 to incorporate protections.

What is the protection?

The protection against discrimination is for a person who 'intends to undergo, is undergoing or has undergone gender reassignment' (SDA 1975, s 2A). Gender re-assignment is defined as 'a process which is undertaken under medical supervision for the purpose of reassigning a person's sex by changing physiological or other characteristics of sex and includes any part of such process' (s 82(1)).

Direct discrimination

This is defined as less favourable treatment than others on the grounds of intending to undergo, undergoing or having undergone the process of gender reassignment. The proscribed 'less favourable treatment' can involve a comparison of arrangements for sick absence (for employees who are not reassigning their gender) and the absence necessary for gender reassignment medical treatment. The issue of indirect discrimination is not included in the legislation.

The need to clarify the application of the 'less favourable treatment' provisions to the gender reassignment *process* arose in one case involving the use of toilet facilities (*Croft* v *Royal Mail Group plc* [2003] IRLR 592). There are, effectively, three stages in the gender reassignment process: intention to reassign; undergoing the reassignment under medical supervision; and the completion of the reassignment (i.e. the post-operative stage). It is possible that a person at any of these three stages may experience different treatment. However, it is a matter for the courts to determine whether this is 'less favourable treatment' within the terms of the legislation.

In the case of Ms Croft, a *pre-operative* 'male to female' transsexual undergoing medical treatment, there were concerns from the existing workforce about her use of toilet facilities. The employer, as a pragmatic response, provided access to a gender-neutral disabled toilet rather than the women's toilet (the gender to which she was reassigning).

The Court of Appeal ruled that in considering what amounts to less favourable treatment on grounds of gender reassignment, it does not follow that all such persons are entitled *immediately* to be treated as members of the sex to which they aspire. It added that the moment at which a person at the 'real life test' stage is entitled to use female toilets depends on all the circumstances. The employer must take into account the stage reached in treatment, including the employee's own assessment and the way that they present themselves – although the employer is not bound by the employee's self-definition when making a judgement as to when the changes occurred. The employer is also entitled to take into account, though not to be governed by, the susceptibilities of other members of the workforce. In the circumstances of this case, the Court of Appeal ruled that the measures taken by the employers were appropriate in the circumstances. Therefore, they were entitled, for a period of time, to rely on the unisex disabled toilet as being a sufficient facility for Ms Croft to use. The time had not come when they were obliged to permit her to use the female toilets.

The House of Lords, subsequently, has held that for the purposes of employment law a *post-operative* transsexual should be treated as having their reassigned sex (*A* v *Chief Constable of West Yorkshire Police* [2004] IRLR 573).

Genuine occupation qualification

The provisions under the Sex Discrimination Act (ss 7A and 7B) are:

- It is a defence to a claim of less favourable treatment if an employer can show that being a man or a woman is a genuine occupational qualification for a particular job and that the treatment (which could include **dismissal** or redeployment) is reasonable in the circumstances.
- GOQs apply where a postholder is required to undertake 'intimate physical searches pursuant to statutory powers' (s 7B(2)(a)).
- GOQs cover circumstances where a postholder is working or living in a private home and 'objection might reasonably be taken' to allowing that person physical or social contact or allowing 'knowledge of intimate details of such a person's life' (s 7B(2)(b)).
- In relation to those intending to undergo or undergoing gender reassignment, GOQs allow an employer to take discriminatory action where issues of 'decency and privacy' arise in relation to accommodation and facilities shared with either sex; and it is not reasonable to expect the employer to make adaptations or alternative arrangements (s 7B(2)(c)).
- Furthermore, discrimination is possible where a postholder 'provides individuals with personal services promoting their welfare or similar personal services; and in the reasonable view of the employer those services cannot be effectively provided by a person whilst that person is undergoing gender reassignment' (s 7B(2)(d)).

Post employment

The same protection as described in Part 1 applies.

Enforcement

The provisions in respect of employer liability, defence against liability, burden of proof, the questionnaire, time limits and victimisation are those described in respect of the Sex Discrimination Act (Part 1 above). The remedies are those outlined in Part 1.

Gender Recognition Act 2004

This additional legislation provides rights relevant to employment and in the wider society for people who are reassigning their gender and have obtained a Gender Recognition Certificate. It arose from a ruling in 2002 by the European Court of Human Rights following an application from Christine Goodwin (*Goodwin* v *United Kingdom* [2002] IRLR 664, ECHR). The key provisions are:

- A person undergoing gender reassignment can apply for a Gender Recognition Certificate. Those born in the UK can obtain a new birth certificate.
- This new birth certificate is likely to have a bearing on any evidence provided to human resource departments for entry to, for example, occupational pension schemes.
- Any disclosure that a person has such a Gender Recognition Certificate is a criminal offence with a fine of up to £5,000. This obviously applies to employers, prospective employers and any of their employees.

Part 3: Equal pay law

Who is covered?

The law on equal pay covers the potential disparate treatment between women and men in employment, irrespective of length of service. It does *not* encompass pay inequality on other grounds (for example, ethnic origin or disability).

The Equal Pay Act 1970 and European law

Legal measures to address questions of unequal pay – and by implication the gender pay gap – have largely rested upon the provisions of the Equal Pay Act 1970, the EU Equal Treatment Directive 2006 (which consolidates previous Directives) and Article 141 of the Treaty of Rome. In the UK, equal pay legislation marked the beginning in what has now become a comprehensive patchwork of legislation regulating discriminatory practices in the employment field. This Act is a companion to the Sex Discrimination Act 1975 (see Part 1).

The Equal Pay Act regulates gender discrimination on the grounds of pay and other benefits. Although it is primarily intended to address pay equality issues for women it is available to any man or woman who believes they have been discriminated against in pay or other benefits. The claimant does not have to prove discrimination, but has to show that they have been less favourably treated in some contractual terms than a suitable comparator (actual but not hypothetical; and it may be a predecessor in the job) of the opposite sex. The Act effectively operates through the insertion of an equality clause into contracts of employment (s 1(2), EqPA). In practice, the clause addresses any provision relating to terms. Case law, particularly the findings of the European Court of Justice, has given a wide construction to the concept of what is meant by pay (see Exhibit 5.3). Indeed, Article 141 (which asserts the broad principle in EU law that men and women should receive equal pay for equal work) states that 'pay means the ordinary basic or minimum wage or salary and any other consideration, whether in cash or in kind, which the worker receives, directly or indirectly, in respect of his employment from his employer'.

The effect of the equality clause is to secure equality in pay and other benefits for men and women employed on:

- like work (s 1(2)(a));
- work rated as equivalent (s 1(2)(b));
- work of equal value (s 1.2(c)).

Exhibit 5.3 What is 'pay'? Examples from equal pay case law

- ***Sick pay*** (*Rinner-Kunn* v *FWW Special-Gebaudereinigang GmbH and Co* [1989] IRLR 493, ECJ).
- ***Bonuses*** and other one-off *ad hoc* payments.
- Payments for retrospective performance or future loyalty (*Lewen* v *Denda* [2000] IRLR 67, ECJ).
- ***Paid leave*** (*Arbeiterwohlfahrt der Stadt Berlin* v *Botel* [1992] IRLR 423, ECJ).
- ***Occupational pensions*** (*Bilka-Kaufhaus GmbH* v *Weber von Hartz* [1986] IRLR 317, ECJ; *Barber* v *Guardian Royal Exchange Assurance Group* [1990] IRLR 240, CA).
- ***Contributions*** to pension schemes (*Lewen* v *Denda* [2000] IRLR 67, ECJ).
- ***Severance pay*** (*Kowalska* v *Freie and Hansestadt Hamburg* (1992) C-33/89, ECJ).
- ***Travel concessions*** (*Garland* v *British Rail Engineering Ltd* [1982] IRLR 111, ECJ).
- ***Statutory and non-statutory redundancy pay*** (*R* v *Secretary of State for Employment* ex parte *Seymour-Smith and Perez* [1999] IRLR 253, ECJ; *Rutherford and Another* v *Secretary of State for Trade and Industry* [2006] IRLR 551, HL; *Hammersmith and Queen Charlotte's Special Health Authority* v *Cato* [1987] IRLR 483, EAT).
- ***Statutory unfair dismissal compensation*** (*Seymour-Smith and Perez*; and *R* v *Secretary of State for Employment* ex parte *Equal Opportunities Commission* [1994] IRLR 176, HL).

The Equal Pay Act requires an actual comparator, so a woman has to compare herself with a man 'in the same employment'. This is defined as employment by the same employer or an associated employer; under a contract of service, apprenticeship or contract personally to carry out work or labour; at the same establishment, or at establishments in Great Britain (including the one at which the complainant works) and 'at which common terms and conditions of employment are observed either generally or for employees of the relevant classes' (s 1(6)).

Potential difficulties

Before proceeding further it is important to reflect on these criteria within the Act in terms of how they affect the issue of equal pay in practice. It is clear that the Act creates a number of potential areas of difficulty. As well as what is meant by 'like work', 'work rated as equivalent' and 'work of equal value', dealt with below, there are the restrictions imposed by a reliance on individual claimants, and the requirement for a claimant to provide an *actual* rather than a *hypothetical* comparator (although Article 141 does provide for the latter in cases of indirect 'pay' discrimination). Furthermore, the legislation requires that such comparisons must be made with someone in the same employment and where 'common terms and conditions . . . are observed' for the employees concerned. These requirements substantially restrict the scope and impact of the EqPA, and do little to address the underlying causes of the gender pay gap, for as we have seen one of the major causes of this is women's concentration in predominantly female workplaces (McColgan 2005: 435). One illustration of the limitations of the Act can be seen in the contrast of two decisions in Exhibit 5.4.

The decisions in the *Ratcliffe* and *Lawrence* cases are important in light of the increasing role of contracting out of work in many organisations. To these should also be added the declining importance both of collective bargaining in the UK, and of individuals working under 'common terms and conditions'. They also raise the potential of employers creating separate independent employing organisations as a way of avoiding compliance with the law, something that arguably arose most clearly in the case of *Allonby* v *Accrington and Rossendale College and Others* (C-256/01) [2004] ECR I-873; [2004] IRLR 224 (see Exhibit 5.5).

Exhibit 5.4 Two judgments on equal pay: *Ratcliffe* and *Lawrence*

Ratcliffe and Others v *North Yorkshire County Council* [1995] ICR 833, HL (paraphrased)

The case involved women working as 'dinner ladies' for a local authority. The Authority under pressure to cut costs put the provision of school dinners out to tender as part of a Compulsory Competitive Tendering exercise. To try and retain the contract the Council cut labour costs of the DSO (Direct Service Operator, running the school dinner service within the Council at the time) by 25 per cent, involving a cut in pay for those staff. However, other staff in the Council working for other DSOs had not had their pay cut. At the time the rates of pay had been negotiated through a collective agreement negotiated by the National Joint Council covering local government workers (and prior to claim the jobs performed by claimants had been 'rated as equivalent' in value to those of their comparators).

The women took their case to a tribunal arguing that others employed by the same employer and previously on 'common terms and conditions' were now being discriminated against on the grounds of sex. The employer argued that it had to cut pay in order to win the contract and provided a defence of 'market forces' as a material factor in the decision (EqPA, s 3). The women won their case but did so because they were still employed by the DSO, which like their comparator's DSO (which predominantly employed men), was still part of the local authority.

What is clear from the *Ratcliffe* case is that women, whose work had been contracted out would find it much more difficult to pursue such a claim (see *Lawrence* below). First, there would no longer be 'the same employer' and they would only be able to use men employed by the same contractor as their comparator. More fundamentally, the decision in *Ratcliffe* could have had the perverse effect of substantially disadvantaging many DSOs engaged in a CCT exercise against outside contractors who were seeking to retain that work in-house, particularly where (as is often the case) those DSOs employed large numbers of women in areas such as cleaning, caring, and catering.

Lawrence v *Regent Office Care* [1999] ICR 654, EAT (paraphrased)

A case also brought by women who had previously been employed by North Yorkshire Council, but were now employed by an outside contractor, Regent Office Care, as their jobs had been transferred to the private sector. All ended up with less favourable terms and conditions than they had 'enjoyed' with the Council. They argued that they should still be able to compare themselves with men employed by the council whose jobs, prior to contracting-out, had been rated as equivalent to those of the complainants. Because they no longer worked for the 'same employer' they could not rely on the provisions of the Equal Pay Act, and sought to use the broader concept of employer contained in Article 141 (which applies to 'work carried out in the same establishment or service, whether private or public'). However, the EAT decision held that the rights conferred by Article 141 were not wide enough to permit employees of one company to compare themselves with work undertaken by a comparator working for another company, even where at one point, those employees and their comparators had worked for the same employer. See *Allonby* v *Accrington and Rossendale College & Others* (C256/01) [2004] ECR I-873; [2004] IRLR 224.

Like work

A woman is to be regarded as employed on 'like work' (s 1(2)(a)) with men in the same employment 'if, but only if, her work and theirs is of the same or a broadly similar nature and the difference (if any) between the things she does and the things they do are not of practical importance in relation to terms and conditions of employment' (*Shields* v *E. Coomes (Holdings) Ltd* [1978] ICR 1159, CA). In comparing her work and theirs, 'regard shall be had to the frequency or otherwise with which any such differences occur in practice as well as to the nature and extent of the differences' (EPA, s 1(4)). Further clarification was provided

Exhibit 5.5 The *Allonby* case

Allonby v *Accrington and Rossendale College and Others* (C256/01) [2004] ECR I-873; [2004] IRLR 224

The claimant was working as a part-time teacher for Accrington and Rossendale College and with a number of colleagues was dismissed and then offered a contract to carry out the same work on a self-employed basis through an outside agency. She was now working on terms and conditions that were 'less favourable' than those she had enjoyed when working directly for the college, and lodged a number of claims under the Equal Pay and Sex Discrimination Acts. Her equal pay claim relied on a male comparator still employed full-time as a lecturer in the college.

The Equal Pay case suffered in similar ways to that brought in *Lawrence*. She was now employed by a separate employing organisation, so although Allonby worked alongside her male comparator, they were not working for the same employer, nor were they associated employees. Furthermore, their terms and conditions, were not common and did not come from a single source. The case went to the ECJ, which found against Allonby.

Although Allonby was successful in other aspects of her claims, notably that her exclusion from the pension scheme constituted indirect sex discrimination, as Fredman (2004) has argued, the judgment in *Allonby* concerning equal pay raises important questions about the effectiveness of equal pay laws in the face of employers 'who deliberately fragment the supervisory and remunerative dimensions of the managerial function'.

by the EAT decision in *Capper Pass Ltd* v *Lawton* [1977] QB 852, EAT where the judgment indicated that 'like work' should involve a general consideration of similarities and differences and that this should mean no account is taken of 'trivial differences not likely in the real world to be reflected in terms and conditions of employment' (McColgan 2005: 427).

Work rated as equivalent

This relates to circumstances where a woman is employed on work rated as equivalent with that of a man in the same employment. This could mean that the jobs undertaken by a woman and her comparator are very different in nature but that her job and his job have been given an equal value, in terms of the demands made on them under various headings (e.g. effort, skill, discretion) by a job evaluation study. Such a study must have covered the jobs done by all or any of the employees in an undertaking or group of undertakings. Although there is a range of job evaluation techniques available to organisations (e.g. ranking, points method), non-analytical methods that provide greater scope for subjective judgments have been considered invalid by the courts (*Bromley* v *H & J Quick Ltd* [1988] ICR 623, CA). Job evaluation needs to be 'analytical', 'thorough in analysis and capable of impartial application' (*Eaton Ltd* v *Nuttall* [1977] ICR 272, EAT). In effect, job demands must, as far as possible, be subject to objective assessment; broken down by category (skill, effort, training), analysed and then evaluated. (Exhibit 5.6 details the variety of schemes in more depth).

There is no legal requirement for an employer to have a job evaluation scheme, and many, particularly smaller organisations, do not. A question arises as to what happens in cases where an individual is claiming unequal pay but no satisfactory basis for comparison exists. The third of the grounds for claiming pay discrimination is the mechanism the law provides to address such claims, that of 'work of equal value'.

Exhibit 5.6 Job evaluation: analytical and non-analytical

Job evaluation is a set of processes designed to establish pay structures within an organisation and is a systematic process designed to establish the relative worth of jobs within a single work organisation. What job evaluation attempts to do is to provide some internal equity, by organising jobs into a hierarchy based on an evaluation of those jobs in terms of their skill, levels of responsibility, experience required and contribution to the organisation. This raises important questions of:

1 How the jobs are evaluated, in terms of the criteria used;
2 The choice of relevant factors in evaluating jobs;
3 Who is doing the evaluation;
4 The broader issue of objectivity of the process and its overall validity.

In general, four methods are normally used in job evaluation.

Non-Analytical:
(a) Ranking method – ranking of jobs based on a subjective evaluation of value.
(b) Job-grading method – jobs are classified and then placed in grades or hierarchy.

Analytical:
(c) Factor-comparison – evaluates jobs on the basis of a range of factors, these factors are weighted and benchmark jobs created from the factors that are then assigned a monetary value.
(d) Points method – works in a similar way to (c) but uses points to assign to each factor. The points are added up and a hierarchy of jobs produced which then equate to pay. The most commonly used job evaluation method.

In effect, job evaluation assigns pay to the job and, in theory, provides a pay structure that is objective and defensible from the employer's perspective. In practice, no scheme is entirely free from subjective bias, but (c) and (d) are more robust than (a) and (b). It should also be remembered that, despite the advantages of job evaluation, many organisations (particularly small, private-sector companies) do not operate such schemes.

A 2002 e-reward report of 236 organisations revealed that less than half operated a job evaluation scheme, and of these, 68 per cent of public and voluntary sector organisations operated one, in contrast to less than 40 per cent of private-sector employers. However, Workplace Employment Relations Survey 2004, covering a broader sample of workplaces found that only one in five operated such schemes, although this rose to two in five in the public sector, and where trade unions were recognised. Of the schemes that were in operation, 70 per cent of those in the public sector and just over half in the private sector were points-based schemes. While the e-reward report implied that just over a third of their sample of employers was operating a job evaluation scheme that could be defended on equal pay grounds (**www.e-reward.co.uk** 2003), WERS 2004 suggests that this may be true of only one in seven workplaces (Kersley *et al.* 2006).

Work of equal value

This amendment was enacted in 1983. A claimant who is not employed on 'like work' or 'work rated as equivalent' can claim equal pay with a comparator in the same employment provided their work is of 'equal value' to that of the person they have specified as their comparator. In the absence of an existing evaluation system covering both jobs, 'equal value' is assessed either by an *independent expert* appointed by the employment tribunal or by the tribunal itself. The assessment of jobs involves an examination and comparison of the jobs in question in isolation, using whatever factors the expert or tribunal consider to be most relevant in the jobs. If the jobs are assessed as being of equal value in this context then, assuming the man is being paid more than the woman, discrimination on the grounds of sex, is defined as having taken place. An early and most significant equal value case was that of *Hayward* v *Cammell Laird Shipbuilders Ltd* (*No. 2*) [1988] AC 894 (Exhibit 5.7).

Exhibit 5.7 Equal value

Hayward v *Cammell Laird Shipbuilders Ltd* (*No. 2*) [1988] AC 894

The ***Hayward*** case turned on the question of whether pay should be 'equal' in overall terms (taking into account benefits such as free meals, etc.) or at the level of each element of the pay package (McColgan 1997: 148). Hayward was a canteen worker who presented an equal pay claim naming a painter, a joiner and an insulation engineer as her comparators. Her employer argued that equal pay in 'overall terms' was what mattered and that Hayward's basic pay and overtime rates were lower than her comparators, her sickness benefits and meal breaks were more favourable than theirs and that taken as a whole 'her contractual terms were no less favourable to her than their's were to them' (McColgan 2005: 425). The case went to the employment tribunal, the EAT and ultimately to the House of Lords. The earlier decisions of the tribunal and EAT rejected her claim reflecting a concern that a woman who succeeds in claiming equal value with a man might trigger claims by men in different jobs, 'thereby ratcheting up the whole payment structure' (Fredman 1997: 245). Indeed, the EAT argued that agreeing to the Hayward claim 'would necessarily involve leap-frogging, [and] would . . . result in widespread chaos in industry and inflict grave damage on commerce' (transcript of EAT judgment [1986] IRLR 287, 291).

However, the House of Lords unanimously decided that s 1(2) of the EqPA meant what it said. That is, in the words of Lord Goff if 'one looks at the man's contract and at the woman's contract, and if one finds in the man's contract a term benefiting him that is not included in the woman's contract, *then that term is included in hers*' (italics added, quoted in McColgan 2005: 425). In other words, each contractual term must be treated separately, so that 'the employer is not entitled to argue that inequality with regard to one term is outweighed by an advantage elsewhere in the terms and conditions of the complainant and his or her comparator' (Deakin and Morris 2005: 689). It follows that differences in rates of pay cannot be offset by differences in working hours or in fringe benefits.

The equal value provision has provided opportunities for some groups to make a serious challenge to entrenched pay discrimination. The case of *British Coal Corporation* v *Smith and Others* [1996] ICR 515 HL is notable; as is the case brought in 1990 by the trade union USDAW against Sainsburys which sought to secure equal value for check-out operators with their mainly male warehouse comparators. The case was settled out of court and resulted in the introduction of a job evaluation exercise that led to a 20 per cent increase in rates of pay to the check-out operators. A number of schemes followed in other major retail outlets. More recently, the job evaluation scheme in the NHS *Agenda for Change* has resulted in major changes to pay for many staff. Also, the restructuring of pay schemes in local authorities following a national agreement in 2002, has forced a major restructuring of pay that has benefited large numbers of staff as well as generating a spate of equal value claims (see Exhibit 5.8).

Despite very considerable advances resulting from the equal value route (s 1(2)(c)), it has not been without its problems. Prior to changes in 1996, the procedure for dealing with claims on equal value grounds provided for potentially long delays in resolving such cases both before and once they had reached a tribunal. It has not been unusual for equal pay cases to take over five years. The expense of such a complaint often is a sufficient deterrent to individuals, particularly in the absence of unions willing to support them.

Some acknowledgement of the problems experienced by those trying to pursue equal value claims has come with the Employment Tribunals (Constitution and Rules of Procedure) (Amendment) Regulations 2004, which has provided for the appointment of tribunal panels with specialist equal value expertise. It has attempted to make processes more 'user-friendly' and has imposed time limits at various stages (McColgan 2005: 432). In the annex to the regulations, it states that equal value claims using independent experts should take no longer than 37 weeks to determine, those not involving these, no more than 25 weeks.

Indirect pay discrimination

It should be noted that unequal pay can arise as a result of either direct or indirect discrimination. As outlined above, unlawful pay discrimination occurs largely because women and men tend to do different jobs or to have different work patterns. That is, it is the nature of women's work, which has traditionally been undervalued, and how that work is undertaken, frequently on a part-time basis rather than through a male pattern of full-time permanent employment, that is critical to the discussion of unequal pay and the gender pay gap. These are factors that the Equal Pay Act remains ill-equipped to tackle, and where claimants look to Article 141 to combat such deficiencies.

Employer defences

Where a woman compares herself with a man (s 1(2)), and is found to be discriminated against by being paid less for 'like work', 'work rated as equivalent' or 'work of equal value' it may still be possible for the employer under s 1(3) to show that any variation between the woman's contract and that of the man's contract is genuinely the result of a *material factor* which is not the difference of sex. That is, the equality clause will not operate if there are good reasons – encouraging loyalty, and other sound business reasons which are 'not the difference of sex' – why a comparator man was paid more than a woman.

Under EqPA (s 2(a) or (b)), i.e. 'like work' or 'work rated as equivalent', the non-operation of the equality clause *must* be the result of a *material difference* between the women's case and the man's. However, equal value provisions introduced in 1983 a broader genuine material factor defence so that in the case of an equality clause falling under ('work of equal value', s 2(c)), it is only necessary to show that the variation is genuinely due to a material factor which *may* be a *material difference*. Furthermore, where the genuine material difference is indirectly discriminatory, the employer must provide an objective justification.

To qualify as a material factor (s 1(3)) that which is relied upon may be a 'material difference', and in any event the onus is upon the employer to show the material factor defence applies. In the early years of the EqPA the 'material difference' defence had been assumed to be narrowly confined to factors 'personal' to the workers concerned (Ewing *et al.* 2006). In *Rainey* v *Glasgow Health Board* [1987] 1 AC 224 HL, it was held that such personal factors related to 'much longer length of service . . . superior skill or qualifications . . . bigger output or productivity . . . or owing to downgrading, in a protected pay category ('red circling') or to other factors personal to the worker in doing his job'. Subsequent cases have continued to permit a market forces defence as well as the use of 'separate collective bargaining structures', and 'administrative reasons', all of which encompass 'extrinsic factors' beyond the 'personal equation.

However, the ECJ in particular has sought to limit the breadth of such defences. For example, in the *Enderby* case, the EAT accepted that collective bargaining arrangements could be a defence to an equal value claim, but when the case went to the ECJ it was held that:

> It is not sufficient for an employer, faced with an equal pay claim, to explain the difference by reference to some factor, such as market forces, different pay structures or collective agreements . . . He or she must go further and establish . . . that the factor is neutral as regards sex, or, to the extent that it serves to disadvantage either sex, that reliance upon it is nevertheless justified, consistent with European law. (*Enderby* v *Frenchay Health Authority* [1993] IRLR 591, ECJ)

Cases of indirect discrimination in respect of equal pay have required further justification from employers. The House of Lords decision (*Rainey* v *Glasgow Health Board* [1987] 1 AC 224) that in cases of indirect discrimination an employer must show 'objectively justified grounds' for the difference in pay has been further extended by the decision in *Allonby* that in cases of indirect discrimination it has not been necessary to identify an actual comparator, merely to show that 'a much higher percentage of women than men' would be 'disadvantaged by the practice at issue' (Monaghan 2007: 431). More recently, the ECJ decision in *Cadman* v *HSE* [2006] IRLR 969 indicated that where length of service is used to determine pay, and this has a disparate impact between men and women, the employer should be required to show (1) that the use of the criterion takes into account business needs, and (2) that its use is proportionate, so as not to minimise its disadvantageous impact on women.

In summary, a factor which is 'not the difference of sex' (s 1(3)) must be one which is neither directly discriminatory nor, in the absence of adequate justification, indirectly discriminatory. Significantly, the ECJ added in *Danfoss* that where an undertaking operates a pay system 'wholly lacking in transparency, it is for the employer to establish that the pay system is not discriminatory, if a female worker establishes, in relation to a relatively large number of employees, that the average pay of women is less than that of men'. This decision has had a major impact on litigation in the equal pay area and one that has potentially significant implications for a number of private sector employers where pay systems are often less transparent than in the public sector.

Employment tribunal claims

Such claims must be made by individuals – although, very frequently, the unequal pay complained of covers the remuneration of, sometimes quite sizeable, workgroups. As part of the complaint process, a complainant may use a questionnaire provided for under Equal Pay (Questions and Replies) Order 2003. Furthermore, the employment tribunal will take into account the provisions of the Code of Practice on Equal Pay (2003).

Remedies in equal pay cases

The general position in equal pay cases is that where a tribunal finds in favour of a claimant, it makes an order requiring that the employer observes the equality clause in the contract of employment. The immediate effect is that a woman's pay is equalised with that of her male comparator (or vice versa). Where unequal pay has persisted for some time it is also usual for the tribunal to order that back-pay or payments in arrears are made to compensate for the period in which the pay was unequal. The sums of money involved can be considerable, and a recent case where a woman successfully compared herself with her male successor (*Bodman* v *API* (2006) ET/2403504/05) received £25,000 in compensation.

Where multiple claims are pursued, the costs to the employer could potentially run into millions of pounds (see Exhibit 5.8).

In the case of back pay and payment in arrears it is for the claimant to show how long they 'have unlawfully been paid at a lower rate than (their) comparator', and since 1996 these payments have included interest. Furthermore, following the ECJ decision in *Levez* v *TH Jennings (Harlow Pools) Ltd* [1999] IRLR 36, up to six years' payments in arrears may be claimed. In general, claims tend to be relatively straightforward when they concern pay, but compensation is more complex when claims concern other benefits such as holiday entitlements or staff

Exhibit 5.8 Equal value in local authorities

The 1997 Single Status Agreement required local authorities to review pay structures 'using a job evaluation process and then develop their own local pay grades fixed to points on a national pay spine' (Equal Opportunities Review (2006): 16), with a view to ensuring equality proofing of pay structures. As a result of the 2004/06 pay deal, under the National Joint Council, it was agreed that all local authorities would enter into negotiations 'with a view to reaching agreement on new local pay structures by April 2006, and complete and implement local pay reviews by 31 March 2007' (ibid.: 16).

Achieving agreements locally has proved difficult in many authorities and has generated a considerable amount of litigation. UNISON has been particularly active in supporting claims, often multiple claims on behalf of members in equal pay cases; as have 'no-win, no-fee' lawyers. However, by the end of 2006, despite the 2004 NJC agreement requiring all local authorities to have completed and implemented equal pay reviews (Local Government Employers 2006), around two-thirds of councils still had not implemented a new pay structure prior to the 31 March 2007 deadline.

Where agreement and implementation has taken place, the costs of this re-alignment of pay structures has been considerable because of back pay and pay protection issues. Some local authorities have had to find as much as six years' back pay for women who have experienced pay discrimination (*Bainbridge* v *Redcar and Cleveland Borough Council* [2007]) IRLR 494 (UNISON 2007; LGE 2008). The Local Government Employers estimated that local authorities might require £5 billion to cover back-pay liability; and some authorities have found that the implementation of new pay structures has led to a substantial worsening of their employment relations (Birmingham City Council issued redundancy notices to 40,000 staff in September 2007; and acknowledged that new pay structures could mean lower pay for up to 7,000 staff).

Furthermore, the influence of 'no-win, no-fee' lawyers has severely constrained unions in their role in assisting the moves to single status and has made them reluctant to negotiate local agreements (see *GMB* v *Allen* [2007] IRLR 752, EAT). According to the Local Government Employers, the overall impact of introducing equality based pay structures could mean as much as a permanent 5 per cent increase in costs for local authorities (LGE 2006).

discounts, and in such cases tribunals must make a judgment about the level of compensation deemed appropriate although few clear guidelines exist on this point.

Part 4: Race discrimination

What is the protection?

The Race Relations Act 1976, in its employment provisions, covers anyone with an employment relationship and this has been construed in a wide way similar to that described under sex discrimination legislation. This protection from unlawful discrimination is irrespective of a person's length of service, the number of hours s/he works or age.

It is unlawful for an employer to discriminate against a person on 'racial grounds' (s 4) at both the application stage and in employment. 'Employment' for these purposes means 'employment under a contract of service or of apprenticeship or a contract personally to execute any work or labour and related expressions shall be construed accordingly' (s 78(1)). Much of the case law relating to the interpretation of employment is found under sex discrimination law (see Part 1 of this chapter). Such case law is accepted by the courts as applicable also to the interpretation of a person's status under race discrimination law.

Applicants

Discrimination on racial grounds is prohibited (s 4(1)):

- in arrangements made for deciding who shall be offered employment;
- in the terms on which employment is offered;
- by refusing or deliberately omitting to offer the person employment.

Employed people

The areas of prohibited discrimination are (s 4(2)):

- in the terms of employment provided;
- in the ways in which access is provided or refused to opportunities for promotion, transfer and training or any other benefits or services;
- by dismissing the person or subjecting him/her to any other detriment.

Those employed in private households are exempted (s 4(3)).

Agency and contract workers

It is unlawful (s 7(2)) for 'the principal' (i.e. the agency or other supplier of work) to discriminate on the following grounds:

- in the terms on which an organisation allows an individual to work for it; or
- by not allowing the individual to do the work or not do the work; or
- in the way the organisation affords access to any benefits, facilities or services or by refusing or deliberately omitting to afford access to them; or
- by subjecting the individual to any other detriment.

The Act (s 14) explicitly forbids discrimination by an employment agency (defined in s 7.78(1)) against a person:

- in the terms on which the agency offers to provide any of its services; or
- by refusing or deliberately omitting to provide any of its services; or
- in the way it provides its services.

'Racial grounds'

This is defined as meaning 'any of the following grounds, namely colour, race, nationality or ethnic or national origin' (s 3(1)). The term 'racial grounds' has been interpreted to extend beyond the characteristics of a complainant. In 1984, Mr Justice Browne-Wilkinson said that this phrase was capable of covering any reason for an action based on race:

> We find it impossible to believe that Parliament intended that a person dismissed for refusing to obey an unlawful discriminatory instruction should be without a remedy . . . We therefore conclude that s 1(1)(a) covers all cases of discrimination on racial grounds whether the racial characteristics in question are those of the person treated less favourably or of some other person. The only question in each case is whether the unfavourable treatment afforded to the claimant was caused by racial considerations.
>
> (*Showboat Entertainment Centre Ltd* v *Owens* [1984] IRLR 7, EAT)

A 'racial group'

This is defined by 'colour, race, nationality or ethnic or national origin' (s 3(1)). A person may be a member of several 'racial groups' simultaneously and these can be indicated in any complaint alleging discrimination.

In a **leading case** which tested whether Sikhs qualified as a racial group, the House of Lords (*Mandla* v *Dowell Lee* [1983] IRLR 209) ruled that 'ethnic origin' was a wider concept than 'race' to be construed in a 'broad, cultural historic sense' (Bourn and Whitmore 1993: 57). To be an 'ethnic group' under the Act, a group must have certain essential characteristics:

- a long shared history, of which the group is conscious as distinguishing it from other groups and the memory of which keeps it alive;
- a cultural tradition, including family and social customs and manners (which may be associated with religious observance).

Also, some of the following factors may be relevant in distinguishing the group:

- common geographical origin or descent from common ancestors;
- a common language (not necessarily restricted to the group);
- a common literature particular to that group;
- a common religion (different from that of neighbouring groups or from the general community);
- being a minority or being an oppressed or a dominant group within a large community.

In addition to these objective factors, self-designation is also a consideration: 'provided a person who joins the group feels himself or herself to be a member of it and is accepted by other members, then, he is for the purposes of the Act a member' (Lord Justice Fraser).

This test has been applied to define gypsies as an ethnic group (*Commission for Racial Equality* v *Dutton* [1989] IRLR 8, CA). Although the Race Relations Act does not expressly cover religious discrimination, because of the application of this test, Jews and Sikhs have been protected; although Rastafarians (*Dawkins* v *Department of Environment* [1993] IRLR 284) and Muslims have not. The legal situation in respect of religious groups changed in 2003 with the implementation of the Employment Equality (Religion or Belief) Regulations (see Part 7).

Direct discrimination

This is defined as follows: 'A person discriminates against another in any circumstances relevant for the purposes of any provision of this Act if . . . on racial grounds he treats that other less favourably than he treats or would treat other persons' (RRA, s (1)(1)(a)). It is also stated that 'for the purposes of this Act, segregating a person from other persons on racial grounds is treating him less favourably than they are treated' (s 1(2)).

Comparator

The 'but for' test (see Part 1) can be used. The comparison must be between the treatment received by the complainant and the actual or hypothetical treatment of another person, who had all the characteristics of the complainant apart from his/her racial group or attitude to race. By looking at the facts and then excluding racial issues, it is possible to decide whether the differential treatment is on racial grounds. The Court of Appeal has ruled that if there is no actual comparator, then, an employment tribunal must construct a hypothetical one. Failure to do so is an error in law (*Balamoody* v *UK Central Council for Nursing, Midwifery and Health Visiting* [2002] IRLR 288).

More than one cause

The racial grounds underlying the less favourable treatment need not be the *sole* grounds for the less favourable treatment. There can be other non-racial grounds. Mr Justice Knox stated that where an employment tribunal 'finds that there are mixed motives for the doing of an act, one or some but not all of which constitute unlawful discrimination, it is highly desirable for there to be an assessment of the importance, from the causative point of view, of the unlawful motive or motives. If the tribunal finds that the unlawful motive or motives were of sufficient weight in the decision-making process to be treated as a cause, not the sole cause but as cause, of the act thus motivated, there will be unlawful discrimination' (*Nagarajan* v *Agnew* [1994] IRLR 61, EAT).

Indirect discrimination

In relation to employment, the Race Relations Act defines indirect discrimination as circumstances where an employer applies to a person 'a provision, criterion or practice which he applies or would apply equally to persons not of the same race or ethnic or national origins as that other' (s 1(1A)). The application of such a provision criterion or practice does or would put an individual at a disadvantage in comparison with other people.

This provision on indirect discrimination was enacted in 2003. Prior to then, the provision related to the potentially narrower phrase of 'requirement or condition'. An example of indirect discrimination under the former provisions is seen in Exhibit 5.9.

The issue of 'justification'

This is in similar terms to that under sex discrimination law. The employer would have to show that the indirect discrimination was a 'proportionate means of achieving a legitimate aim' (s 1(1A)(c)) (see earlier discussion in Part 1).

Genuine occupation qualification or requirement

Being a member of a racial group can be a genuine occupational qualification for a post (s 5). Essentially, there are two broad reasons:

1 *Authenticity*. Examples are acting and entertainment; modelling for clothes and in the production of works of art; the provision of food and drink in a particular setting like a Chinese restaurant.

Exhibti 5.9 Postcode lottery?

Hussein v *Saints Complete House Furnishers* [1979] IRLR 337

A job applicant was not considered because he lived in one of a group of Liverpool postal districts with a high proportion of non-white residents. It was found by the tribunal that 50 per cent of the population in the specified postal districts were non-white; compared with 2 per cent for the rest of Merseyside. The tribunal found the particular racial group was disproportionately affected.

Exhibit 5.10 GOQ and personal services

Tottenham Green Under Fives' Centre v *Marshall* [1989] IRLR 147

In a notable case, the EAT set out guidance on the application of the GOQ on personal services:

- The particular racial group must be clearly, even narrowly, defined because it must be the same for the postholder and the recipient of the personal services.
- The postholder must be directly involved in the provision of the services. It is insufficient if they are merely directing others.
- If the postholder provides several personal services to the recipient, then provided one of these genuinely falls within the subsection, the defence is established.
- 'Promoting the welfare' is a very wide expression and the meaning should be interpreted widely in the light of the facts of each case.
- The Act assumes that the personal services could be provided by others, but the question is whether they can be 'most effectively provided' by a person of that racial group.

2 *Personal services promoting welfare.* Examples cover counselling and other social welfare posts where specific knowledge of an ethnic group and its cultural practices is required; and these can be most effectively provided by a person of that racial group (see Exhibit 5.10).

GOQs do not apply when filling vacancies where an employer already has a sufficient number of employees of the racial group in question whom it is reasonable to employ on those duties. An employer's use of GOQs can be challenged and must be defended. This requirement to defend a GOQ can bring to light trivial or false work duties that are claimed to be covered by the Act. However, these may be devices to introduce positive discrimination.

In 2003, implementing the Race Directive 2000, an additional genuine occupational requirement was enacted (s 4A). This applies where the 'nature of the employment or the context in which it is carried out' makes being of a particular race or ethnic origin or national origin 'a genuine and determining occupational requirement'; and that it is 'proportionate to apply that requirement in the particular case'.

Discriminatory advertisements

These are outlawed (s 29). The European Court of Justice has ruled that, under the Race Directive 2000, it is not necessary to have an identifiable victim of discriminatory job advertisements (*Centrum voor gelijkheid van kansen en voor racismebestrijding* v *Firma Feryn NV* [2008] IRLR 732, ECJ). This ruling may have implications for other strands of EU equal treatment law (Rubenstein 2008b: 23).

Instructions and pressure to discriminate

It is unlawful for a person in authority over another person to pressurise him or her to discriminate; and threatening detrimental action or offering benefits (ss 30 and 31). Action against such pressure can only be taken by the Equality and Human Rights Commission (see Equality Act 2006, s 25) either in an employment tribunal; or in the county court (England and Wales) or to the sheriff (in Scotland). The Commission may apply for an injunction (an interdict in Scotland) to stop the discriminatory pressure).

Positive action

This is permitted (ss 37 and 38) in the following situations: access to facilities for training which help fit members of a particular racial group for particular work; and encouraging people from a particular racial group 'to take advantage of opportunities' for doing that work. This is subject to the following qualification: that it 'reasonably appears' to the employer that, within the preceding 12 months, 'there were no persons of that group among those doing that work' in an area of Great Britain. Furthermore, the Act (s 35) allows the provision of facilities or services, in training, education or welfare to meet the special needs of people from particular racial groups (e.g. classes in the English language) (see also Chapter 4).

Post employment

This provision (s 27A) reflects that under sex discrimination law (Part 1, above); and is in common with all strands of discrimination law.

Liability and vicarious liability

The provision in the Race Relations Act (s 32(1) are similar to those under the Sex Discrimination Act (see Part 1 above). Individual employees are also liable for unlawful discriminatory acts for which their employer is liable (s 32(2)). This is so, whether or not the employer has a defence. In *Yeboah* v *Crofton* [2002] IRLR 634, CA, the Court of Appeal, in a case where a senior council employee 'knowingly' aided unlawful discrimination, confirmed that employees can be personally liable for acts of unlawful discrimination against colleagues and can be so liable even where the employer itself is not found to have acted unlawfully.

Defence against liability

The possibility of a defence is provided for (s 32(3)). It would be expected that the 'reasonable steps' that the employer took would involve, as appropriate, various procedural steps and the enforcement of non-discriminatory workplace policies and practices.

Enforcement

The elements outlined in Part 1 also constitute the enforcement process under race discrimination law. The ***time limit*** for an employment tribunal complaint is within three months of the alleged incident, with the tribunal having discretion to hear 'out of time' complaints where it is 'just and equitable' to do so (s 68). The complainant should make out a *prima facie* case. To assist in this s/he may use the ***questionnaire process*** under the Race Relations (Questions and Replies) Order 1977. The ***burden of proof*** is that approved by the Court of Appeal (in *Igen Ltd* v *Wong* [2005] ICR 931) (see Exhibit 5.2).

Victimisation

The Race Relations Act (s 2) provides parallel provisions on victimisation to those in sex discrimination law (see Part 1).

Remedies

These are a declaration; an award of compensation and possibly for injury to feelings; and a recommendation (see Part 1).

Race equality duty

The Race Relations Act 1976 was amended in 2000 to include a statutory duty on public authorities (specified in RRA, schedule 1A)(e.g. government departments, local authorities, the police, NHS trusts, public-sector schools, further and higher-education institutions). Any public services provided under contract by private or voluntary organisations are also covered and subject to the duty. The public authority has the responsibility to ensure compliance with the statutory duty by the contracted service providers. Also, agencies that inspect or audit public authorities (e.g. Ofsted) are bound by the duty to promote race equality.

This duty (s 71) has two elements:

1 to eliminate unlawful racial discrimination;
2 to promote equality of opportunity and good relations between persons of different racial groups.

This requirement covers both service delivery and employment. It imposes specific duties concerning monitoring on grounds of ethnic origin and producing a race equality scheme. The statutory duty is supported by a code of practice (2002) on the duty to promote racial equality.

The duties on public authorities in respect of employment are enforced in a different way from individual complaints. The *general duty* to promote race equality and eliminate unlawful racial discrimination is enforceable through judicial review in the High Court or, in Scotland, the Court of Sessions. The enforcement of the specific duties is with the Equality and Human Rights Commission. It can use powers to investigate and issue a compliance notice if it is satisfied that a person has failed or is failing to meet a specific duty. This is enforceable through the county court or, in Scotland, the sheriff court. Where the public authority fails to obey the order of the court it will be in contempt of court.

Part 5: Disability discrimination law

The Disability Discrimination Act 1995 has been substantially amended by the Disability Discrimination Act 2005 and, in the context of employment law, by the Disability Discrimination Act 1995 (Amendment) Regulations 2003. These Regulations implement the EU Employment Equality Framework Directive 2000. This refers to the need to accommodate the workplace to the individual's disability by such measures as adapting premises and providing equipment or adjusting patterns of working. These practical measures promote the fundamental principle of equal treatment by making it possible for an individual with a disability to compete on equal terms in the workplace.

Once measures have been taken to adapt the workplace to accommodate the disabled person's disability, that individual still has to demonstrate competence, capability and availability to perform the essential functions of the post concerned. The directive, therefore, aims to integrate disabled persons by removing from the workplace the difficulties caused by the disability and enabling the person to compete on equal terms. It lays down minimum standards and member states still have the option of introducing or maintaining more favourable provisions that might include positive action to promote the employment and training of people with disabilities.

There are important exceptions to the principle of equal treatment. The directive does not, for example, require the armed forces and the police, prison or emergency services to employ individuals with disabilities if it could adversely affect operational capacity.

Who is protected?

The Act protects applicants for employment; those with an employment relationship; and contract workers (who typically is a person employed by an employment agency to perform work for a 'principal'). The Act also prohibits discrimination against some office holders. This is subject to such conditions as, for example the office holder discharging his/her function personally and being entitled to remuneration. A further category included in the employment provisions are trustee and managers of occupational pension schemes. (The Act provides that it is unlawful for such trustees and mangers in carrying out their functions to discriminate against disabled persons.)

The meaning of 'disability' under the Act

This is the starting point for all claims for disability discrimination. The burden of proving that a claimant is disabled rests with that person. The Disability Discrimination Act 1995 states that 'a person has a disability for the purposes of this Act if he has a physical or mental impairment which has a substantial and long-term adverse effect on his ability to carry out normal day-to-day activities' (s 1). Each element of the definition has to be met. It is therefore possible for a person to appear to be disabled but not to meet the definition relevant under the Act. The definition is considered in more detail drawing on the *Guidance on Matters to Be Taken into Account in Determining Questions Relating to the Definition of Disability* (2006). (This *Guidance* is used by employment tribunals and courts to determine whether or not a person meets the definition in section 1.)

Physical or mental impairment

In general, the term 'physical or mental impairment' should be given its ordinary meaning. The *Guidance* emphasises that the important question is the *effect* of the impairment and *not its cause*. So, whilst alcoholism is specifically excluded as a disability, cirrhosis of the liver that may be caused by alcoholism is not excluded. So, an alcoholic may be able to establish that s/he has a disability because of the effects of liver disease. Similarly, an alcoholic suffering from depression, albeit caused by the alcoholism, may be able to establish that he or she has a mental impairment (i.e. depression) within the meaning of the Act. It is no longer necessary for a person suffering from a mental impairment to show that it is a 'clinically well-recognised' condition in order for it to be recognised as impairment under the Act.

It may be apparent in many cases that the person has a 'disability'. However, not all disabilities will be apparent and the issue for judicial consideration will be whether the effects of the impairment are sufficient to fall within the definition (s 1).

In addition to specific regulations rendering certain conditions as automatically within or outside the definition of disability, the legislation provides that certain persons will be deemed to be disabled. Thus, a person who has cancer, HIV infection or multiple sclerosis (MS), or a person who is registered blind will not have to show that they have an impairment that has a 'substantial and adverse long-term effect on their ability to carry out normal day-to-day activities'.

Conversely, certain other conditions are specifically excluded e.g. seasonal allergic rhinitis – hay fever; tendency to light fires, voyeurism, severe disfigurement caused by tattoos or body piercing. Other severe disfigurement, however, is treated as having a substantial adverse effect on the ability to carry out normal day-to-day activities (Sch 1, para 3). This issue arose in *Cosgrove* v *Northern Ireland Service* [2007] IRLR 397. The claimant was turned down for an ambulance post on grounds that he had severe psoriasis. The evidence was that he was not rejected for the post because of the condition but because it was considered that his skin condition would put him at increased risk of infection from patients and there was a risk he could infect patients. The Northern Ireland Court of Appeal ruled that his differential treatment was not due to disfigurement but the risk of infection. So he could not rely on the deeming provision.

Substantial adverse effect

The claimant has to show substantial adverse effect on his/her ability to carry out day-to-day activities. A 'substantial' effect is more than 'minor' or 'trivial'. It is explained in the *Guidance* by reference to factors that assist in making a qualitative judgement. One such factor is the time taken to carry out an activity. An individual may have the ability to carry out a normal day-to-day activity such as washing and dressing. But it may take that individual considerably longer than it would take a person who did not have the impairment in which case the effect of the impairment would be considered 'substantial'. Similarly, a comparison might be made of the way in which a person with an impairment carries out a particular activity – perhaps, in comparison with a non-disabled person, introducing a considerable degree of complexity to execute a simple task.

The cumulative effects of the impairment should also be considered so that even if the individual effects may not be substantial when all effects are considered together the effect will be 'substantial'. The *Guidance* gives the example of a man suffering from depression whose symptoms include loss of energy and motivation so that he neglects simple household tasks such as shopping. This eventually results in him having no food to eat. The cumulative effect would therefore be substantial.

It may be possible for a person to modify his/her behaviour and so reduce the effects of an impairment on day-to-day activities. So, it might be reasonable to expect a person with back pain to avoid extreme activities such as parachuting. But it would not be reasonable for example, for a person with a stammer to place severe restrictions on social interaction as a coping mechanism. As a result of this particular coping mechanism, such a person might not appear to have a disability, but the effect of the coping mechanism may well be substantial on his/her ability to cope with everyday activities such as social interaction. The fact that a person is able to mitigate the effects of his/her impairment does not mean that the effect is not 'substantial'. In addition to the effect of behaviour, it is also necessary, in assessing whether adverse effects are 'substantial', to consider the extent to which environmental conditions may exacerbate the effect of an impairment.

Long-term effect

> The effect of an impairment is a long-term effect if
>
> (a) it has lasted at least twelve months;
>
> (b) the period for which it lasts is likely to be at least twelve months; or
>
> (c) it is likely to last for the rest of the life of the person affected. (DDA 1995, Sch 2, para 2)

The *Guidance* states that an event is 'likely' to happen 'if it is more probable than not that it will happen'. In calculating the period of 12 months, the total period that the impairment has lasted or is likely to last should be taken into consideration including any period before the alleged act of discrimination. Factors such as age or the general health of the individual are relevant in deciding whether an impairment is likely to last for 12 months. If the effects of an impairment are likely to recur or fluctuate, the impairment will be treated as continuing even if it ceases to have a substantial adverse effect on a person's ability to carry out normal day-to-day activities.

Progressive conditions

Examples of progressive conditions that will change over time include cancer, multiple sclerosis, muscular dystrophy and HIV infection. A person with any of these conditions will be deemed to be a disabled person under the Act from the initial diagnosis. A special characteristic of a progressive condition is that the person will be treated as having an impairment with substantial adverse effects on the ability to carry out day-to-day activities before the effects are fully manifested. So, as soon as some degree of impairment is apparent the effect will be treated as a substantial adverse effect provided that it is more likely than not to become substantial. It is important in such cases to obtain a medical prognosis of the likelihood of the effect of the condition becoming more substantial. It is important to note that the effect of an impairment on an individual's ability to carry out normal day-to-day activities must be considered without taking into consideration any treatment or correction.

Past disabilities

The employment provisions of the Act apply to past disabilities in the same way as to a person who has the disability now (DDA s 2(1); Sch 2). Furthermore, the question as to whether the person had a disability at a particular time is to be considered as though the relevant provisions of the Act were in force at the time. A person who was registered under the Disabled Person (Employment) Act 1944 will be treated as having a disability in the past. A past disability will be considered as a disability if its effects lasted for 12 months or more after the first occurrence; or if a recurrence happened or continued until more than 12 months after the first occurrence.

Normal day-to-day activities

The *Guidance* (section D) sets out a list of capacities that apply to both physical and mental impairments. An impairment affects the ability of a person to carry out normal day-to-day activities only if it affects that person in respect of one or more of the following:

- mobility;
- manual dexterity;
- physical co-ordination;
- continence;
- ability to lift, carry or otherwise move everyday objects;
- speech, hearing or eyesight;
- memory or ability to concentrate, learn or understand;
- perception of the risk of physical danger.

This list of capacities should be distinguished from day-to-day activities; but an impairment will only be treated as affecting a normal day-to-day activity if it involves at least one of the capacities on the list. A day-to-day activity is one that most people carry out on a regular basis. It would include, for example, shopping, reading and writing, having a conversation, getting washed and dressed, preparing and eating food, travelling by various forms of transport and taking part in social activities. However, it would not include the sort of activities that might be normal for a particular type of work. So, for example, the dexterity required of a watch repairer would not be a normal day-to-day activity for most people.

There is, therefore, a distinction to be drawn between work related activities and other activities (see Exhibit 5.11). The high level of skills required of a musician or professional footballer do not involve activities to a level that would be considered normal for most people. But, there will be a certain amount of overlap. So, a pianist who is no longer able to play to concert standard because of carpal tunnel syndrome may experience difficulty in using a computer keyboard which may be considered as a normal day-to-day activity. Such a person may, therefore be considered to have an impairment that affects manual dexterity.

Discrimination

There are three aspects to discrimination under the Act: direct discrimination; disability-related discrimination; and failure to comply with the duty to make reasonable adjustments. Table 5.2 provides an overview and comparison of these provisions, which are then discussed in more detail subsequently.

Table 5.2 Discrimination under the Disability Discrimination Act 1995

	Direct discrimination	*Disability-related discrimination*	*Failure to comply with duty to make reasonable adjustments*
	s 3A(5)	s 3A(1)	s 3A(2); s 4
Circumstances	Less favourable treatment on grounds of disability	Less favourable treatment for a disability-related reason	Where a provision, criterion or practice, or a physical feature, causes substantial adverse effect
The complainant	The person is disabled and the discrimination is because of his/her disability. It does not have to be the sole cause of the complaint	A disabled person	An applicant for employment or an employee about whose disability the employer ought reasonably to know
Comparator	A person (whether real or hypothetical) not having that disability – and whose circumstances are the same or not materially different	A person to whom the disability-related discrimination does ***not*** apply	Persons who are not disabled
Justification	Cannot be justified	Justification is possible if the 'reason is material to the circumstances of the particular case and substantial'	No justification. The employer is to take such steps as are reasonable in all the circumstances of the case to prevent the 'substantial adverse effect'

Exhibit 5.11 Normal day-to-day activities or job-related activities?

Kenny v *Hampshire Constabulary* [1999] IRLR 76

Facts. Mr Kenny who suffered from cerebral palsy applied for a position as a computer analyst/programmer. He was regarded as the best applicant and was offered the job on condition that appropriate arrangements were made for his needs. He told his prospective employer that he needed assistance when going to the toilet. That assistance consisted of holding a bottle for him to urinate into, emptying it and then lifting him back into his wheelchair. The prospective employer thought that a rota of employee volunteers might be arranged. This did not materialise because of the full extent of the assistance expected. Mr Kenny's suggestion that he work from home with a computer modem link was not considered feasible. The possibility of a support worker being obtained under the Access to Work Scheme was explored. His problem was considered as 'novel' and a decision about funding would take about 60 days. Ultimately, because of the urgent need to finalise the position regarding his recruitment, the offer of employment was withdrawn.

EAT ruling. He was found to be disabled within the meaning of the Disability Discrimination Act 1995. Withdrawing the offer of employment was potentially a discriminatory act. The prospective employer's treatment of Mr Kenny was found to be justified. Not every failure to make an arrangement which deprives an employee of a chance to be employed is unlawful. It was going too far to suggest that employers are under a statutory duty to provide carers to attend to their employee's personal needs. The duty to make adjustments only applies to 'job-related' matters. It does not extend to each and every arrangement that could facilitate employment.

Paterson v *Commissioner of Police of the Metropolis* [2007] IRLR 763, EAT

Facts. Mr Paterson joined the police force in 1983. After taking various professional examinations he achieved the rank of Chief Inspector. In 2004, he discovered that he had dyslexia. He claimed he had a disability and that his employer had failed to make reasonable adjustments when he applied for promotion to the rank of Superintendent. He claimed disability discrimination.

Employment tribunal. It found that he was not disabled within the meaning of the Act. In its view any adverse effects he suffered as a result of his impairment were minor. The reason for this was that although Mr Paterson was substantially disadvantaged with respect to taking part in the promotion examinations, this was not a day-to-day activity. In its assessment, the tribunal compared him with the ordinary average norm of the population as a whole for whom taking professional examinations was not a regular occurrence. He appealed to the EAT.

EAT ruling. The tribunal was wrong to compare his performance with the average person in the population at large. The correct comparison was between what the individual could do and would be able to do without the impairment. It was not disputed that Mr Paterson was suffering from a substantial disadvantage because of the effects of his disability in the examination process. Indeed, the employer had allowed him 25 per cent additional time at each stage of the assessment process.

The proper inference to be drawn was that those effects must involve a more than trivial effect on the employee's ability to undertake normal day-to-day activities. A day-to-day activity was not defined by asking whether the majority of the population did it. On the contrary, 'normal' was best defined as anything which is not abnormal or unusual. Carrying out an assessment or examination was an activity relevant to participation in professional life; and accordingly, it could properly be described as a normal day-to-day activity.

Comment. The definition of day-to-day activity seems to have been widened by this EAT decision. The effect of Mr Paterson's impairment meant he experienced difficulty reading and comprehending which are clearly day-to-day activities. From the list of capacities it was his 'memory or ability to concentrate, learn or understand' that were affected. The EAT went on to find that his disability could not be selectively interpreted. The way he carried out the examination was different to how he would have carried it out if he were not impaired. His participation in professional life which included taking part in professional examinations was therefore substantially adversely affected.

Direct discrimination

This occurs when, 'on the ground of the disabled person's disability, (a person) treats the disabled person less favourably than he treats or would treat a person not having that particular disability whose relevant circumstances, including his abilities, are the same as or not materially different from those of the disabled person' (s 3A(5)). To be direct discrimination the less favourable treatment must therefore be caused by the disability of the particular individual. This means that the disabled person would not have been treated as he or she was but for the disability. This disability, then, was an effective cause of the treatment complained of (see Code of Practice, paras 4.5–4.23).

One example given in the code of practice is of a blind woman who is not shortlisted for a job working on computers because of the employer's stereotypical view of blind people. The woman has been less favourably treated because she is not shortlisted. This treatment is on the ground of her disability and so constitutes direct discrimination which cannot be justified. The correct comparator in a case of direct discrimination is a person who does not have the same disability as the claimant (or indeed any disability). It is important that the comparator's relevant circumstances, including in particular the respective abilities of the comparator, are as close to those of the claimant as possible.

Disability-related discrimination

A person discriminates against a disabled person if 'for a reason which relates to the disabled person's disability, he treats him less favourably than he treats or would treat others to whom that reason does not or would not apply' (s 3A(1)). Examples of what constitutes disability-related discrimination are provided in the Code of Practice (paras 4.27–4.32). It describes disability-related discrimination as occurring when the reason for the discrimination relates to the disability but is not the disability itself.

An employer does not discriminate against the disabled person if it can be shown that the treatment in question was justified. Justification is only relevant in defence of disability-related discrimination. Such justification can be established if it is 'both material to the circumstances of the particular case and substantial' (s 3A(3)).

Chapter 6 of the Code of Practice provides examples of what constitutes justification and when the defence may be relevant. One such example is of a carpet fitter who suffers from severe back pain and cannot fit carpets. His application is rejected because he cannot undertake the basic requirements of the job. This rejection would be justified because the reason is substantial and material to the job. However, the threshold for establishing that an employer's action is justified was stated by the Employment Appeals Tribunal (*WJ Heinz Co Ltd* v *Kenrick* [2000] IRLR 144) to be 'very low'. The EAT considered that the condition of material and substantial had to be no more than 'necessary and sufficient'.

Two cases illustrate the nature of disability-related discrimination:

- *Pay reduction.* The Court of Appeal ruled that a reduction in the pay of a disabled employee, in accordance with the employer's sick pay rules, was disability-related discrimination, but that the discrimination was justified (*O'Hanlon* v *Commissioners for HM Revenue and Customs* [2007] IRLR 404, CA).
- *Absences.* The EAT ruled that the Disability Discrimination Act does not impose an absolute obligation on an employer to refrain from dismissing an employee who is absent wholly or in part on grounds of ill health due to disability. He may take into account disability-related absences in operating a sickness absence procedure. It is rare for such absences to be

disregarded. Whether or not the employer acts unlawfully by taking disability-related absences into account will generally depend on whether or not the employer is justified (*Royal Liverpool Children's NHS Trust* v *Dunsby* [2006] IRLR 351, EAT).

At the time of writing, the previous law on this issue was overturned in a significant ruling by the House of Lords (*Mayor and Burgesses of the London Borough of Lewisham* v *Malcolm* [2008] UKHL 43) (see also Exhibit 5.12).

Knowledge of disability

The House of Lords has considered the extent to which knowledge of a person's disability is relevant (*Mayor and Burgesses of the London Borough of Lewisham* v *Malcolm* [2008] UKHL 43) (see Exhibit 5.12).

Reasonable adjustments

The Act (s 4A) places a duty on employers to make reasonable adjustments to physical and non-physical features within the workplace that could lead to a disabled person being severely disadvantaged. The relevant section refers to 'a provision, criterion or practice' carried on by the employer; or to a 'physical feature' of the employer's premises which would have the

Exhibit 5.12 Knowledge of disability

Mayor and Burgesses of the London Borough of Lewisham v *Malcolm* [2008] UKHL 43

Facts. The conduct of Mr Malcolm in subletting and ceasing to live in a flat let to him by the London Borough of Lewisham had the effect of destroying the security of tenure he had previously enjoyed; and breaching the terms of his tenancy. This gave Lewisham what was, in terms of housing law, an unanswerable claim to possession.

To defeat that claim, Mr Malcolm relied on Part III of the Disability Discrimination Act 1995 relating to the provision of goods, facilities and services. He claimed that his schizophrenia had caused him to breach the terms of his tenancy and that the Borough, therefore, had discriminated against him of the grounds of disability.

House of Lords ruling:

- *Knowledge of disability*. Knowledge, or at least imputed knowledge, of Mr Malcolm's disability was necessary. The Borough, which had no knowledge of his disability had not discriminated against him on the grounds of disability.
- *Disability-related discrimination*. Mr Malcolm argued that had he not been suffering from schizophrenia he would never have breached his tenancy agreement. In considering whether he had been discriminated against of the grounds of disability, the House of Lords considered the correct comparator to be 'others' with whose treatment that of Mr Malcolm was to be compared. Such others were persons without a mental disability who had sublet a Lewisham flat and gone to live elsewhere. Mr Malcolm has not therefore been treated less favourably on the grounds of disability.

Comment. 'This judgment completely undermines the DDA's concept of disability-related discrimination in an employment context' (Rubenstein 2008a). If that is the case, then, the remaining provision of direct discrimination will be the sole basis for complaints – apart from those related to the duty to make reasonable adjustments. Indeed, 'the main consequence of Malcolm is to shift the focus of attention in a DDA employment claim almost entirely to the issue of reasonable adjustments' (ibid.).

effect of putting a 'disabled person at a substantial disadvantage in comparison with persons who are not disabled' (s 4(1)). A comparator is not therefore necessary in establishing the employer's duty to make a reasonable adjustment as it is the employer's duty to that particular individual that is relevant. The duty only arises if the employer knew that the individual is disabled. But it is incumbent of the employer to find out about the employee's disability. So, warning signs such as extensive absence from work should therefore always be investigated. There is no duty to consult about making reasonable adjustments but clearly it would be good practice.

The duty is to make 'reasonable' adjustments and so the resources available to an employer will be a factor in considering whether the employer has complied with the duty. Clearly, a large employer is more likely to be better placed to make adjustments than a small employer. (There is now no threshold which excludes small organisations from the Disability Discrimination Act). It should be noted by employers that there are publicly funded schemes, like *Access to Work*, which provide financial and practical assistance to employers – as in, for example, the cost of purchasing specialist computer equipment. There is no defence of justification to a failure to comply with the requirement to make reasonable adjustments.

Specific examples of the steps an employer might need to take in order to comply with the duty to make reasonable adjustments include allocating some of the disabled person's duties to another person, altering hours of working or the time of training, modifying procedures for testing or assessment or providing a reader or interpreter (s 18B). Two notable related points from case law:

- The Act, as a matter of law, does not preclude the creation of a new post in substitution for an existing post being a reasonable adjustment. It must depend on the facts of the case (*Southampton City College* v *Randall* [2006] IRLR 18, EAT).
- However, there is no obligation on an employer to create a post specifically, which is not otherwise necessary, merely to create a job for a disabled person (*Tarbuck* v *Sainsbury's Supermarkets Ltd* [2006] IRLR 664, EAT).

Further guidance on compliance with the duty to make reasonable adjustments is in the Code of Practice (Chapter 8).

It should also be noted that in respect of the duty to make reasonable adjustments, the House of Lords has ruled (*Archibald* v *Fife Council* [2004] UKHL 32) that the Disability Discrimination Act 1995 may entail a measure of positive discrimination (see Chapter 4, Exhibit 4.1).

Association with a disabled person

A ruling by the European Court of Justice, interpreting the scope of the Employment Equality Directive 2000 has significantly extended protections arising under that Directive (see Exhibit 5.13).

Instructions and pressure to discriminate

It is unlawful for anyone who has authority over another person to instruct that person to do anything unlawful under the Act (s 16C). Furthermore, it is unlawful to induce another to behave unlawfully by offering inducements, making threats or subjecting him/her to a detriment. Proceedings can be brought by the Equality and Human Rights Commission.

Exhibit 5.13 'Associative' discrimination

Coleman v *Attridge Law and Another* [2008] IRLR 722

Facts. Ms Coleman worked for a firm of solicitors as a legal secretary. Her son was born in 2002 with a severe breathing condition requiring specialised and particular care which she provided for him. She alleged that she was subjected to direct discrimination and harassment by her employer whom she claimed refused her requests for flexible working and subjected her and her child to abusive and insulting comments. In August 2005, she made a complaint at an employment tribunal alleging unfair constructive dismissal and that she had been treated less favourably because she had to care for her disabled son. The novel point in this case was that Ms Coleman was claiming that she had been treated less favourably on the grounds of her son's disability rather than her own.

Employment tribunal. The first question for it was whether Ms Coleman could plead discrimination against her former employer on the ground that she was subjected to less favourable treatment connected with her son's disability. This claim could not be raised under the Disability Discrimination Act 1995 (as amended). However, such 'associative' discrimination on the grounds of disability may have been unlawful under European law (the Employment Equality Directive 2000). The tribunal stayed (adjourned) the case whilst the matter was referred to the European Court of Justice for a ruling.

The reference. The employment tribunal asked the ECJ to consider whether the directive prohibited direct discrimination and/or harassment in a case of associative discrimination where the employee was not disabled but alleged less favourable treatment on the grounds of her son's disability. (The EAT dismissed an objection to this reference to the ECJ being made.)

ECJ ruling. It noted that the purpose of the Employment Equality Framework Directive was to lay down a general framework for combating discrimination on various grounds including disability. The principle of equal treatment meant that there was to be no direct or indirect discrimination 'whatsoever' on any of these grounds. The ECJ concluded that the directive which was designed to safeguard the principle of equal treatment could not be limited to people who were themselves disabled. Its purpose 'as regards employment and occupation, is to combat all forms of discrimination on grounds of disability'. In the present case, although Ms Coleman was not herself disabled, it was disability that caused the less favourable treatment that she complained of.

The directive was intended to combat all forms of discrimination on the grounds of disability in employment and occupation. The directive's application was not limited to a particular category of person but by reference, as appropriate, to religion or belief, disability, age or sexual orientation. This was the situation with regard to both direct discrimination and harassment.

Comment. By confirming that 'associative' discrimination on the grounds of disability is unlawful under European law, the ECJ has emphasised the importance of the directive and of national legislation implementing that directive in combating disability discrimination. In ruling that the protection applies to discrimination on grounds of disability and not to a particular category of person, the ECJ has reinforced the protection.

'This judgment has important implications for the rights of those who care for disabled people and elderly people'. (*Equal Opportunities Review*, 179, August 2008)

Employment tribunal. In December 2008, an employment tribunal accepted that it had jurisdiction to hear the case.

Advertisements

In common with other strands of discrimination law, it is unlawful to publish an advertisement which discriminates on the grounds of disability (s 16B). Only the EHRC may initiate legal proceedings.

Post employment

Where an employment relationship has come to an end, it is unlawful for further acts of discrimination to be committed by the employer or 'relevant person' (s 16A).

Liability and defence against liability

The provisions of the Act (s 58), concerning an employer's liability and vicarious liability, are written in the same terms as those in other strands of discrimination law (see Part 1 of this chapter). The defence is, likewise, that the employer shows that he took such steps as were reasonably practicable to deal with the discrimination.

Enforcement

In relation to a 'provision, criterion or practice' applied for determining who should be offered employment or promotion, a claim may be brought by an applicant. In any other case, a claim may be brought by an employee or applicant on the grounds that a physical feature of the employer's premises has placed him or her at a substantial disadvantage when compared to persons who are not disabled. The duty to make reasonable adjustments does not apply where the employer 'does not know and could not be reasonably expected to know' that a disabled person may be an applicant or potential applicant for employment or that a person, who is an employee, has a disability.

The ***time limit*** for employment tribunal claims is three months from the act complained of. The period may be extended by the tribunal where it is just and equitable to do so. A complainant can serve a ***questionnaire*** on the employer requiring a detailed response about the allegation of discrimination (Disability Discrimination (Questions and Replies) Order 2004). This must be served within three months of the alleged act of discrimination (or six months if an extension has been agreed). The employer has eight weeks in which to respond.

Initially, the **burden of proof** is with the claimant (DDA 1995, s 17). S/he has to prove facts from which the employment tribunal could uphold the complaint in the absence of an adequate explanation by the respondent employer that it acted lawfully. The burden of proof then shifts to the respondent which must prove that it did not discriminate against the complainant on the grounds of disability. As far as establishing that the claimant has a disability, the burden rests with the claimant and never shifts to the respondent employer.

The **remedies** available when a complainant is successful are similar to those under other stands of discrimination law. The employment tribunal may order the employer to pay compensation. It can also make a declaration of rights and make a recommendation that the employer should take action to obviate or reduce the adverse effect of any matter to which the claim relates. An award for compensation is not capped and in addition to loss of earnings will be subject to an amount for injury to feelings. If the employer fails to comply with the recommendation, then, the tribunal may increase the amount of compensation by any amount it considers 'just and equitable'.

Victimisation

The Act (s 55), in common with other discrimination law, protects from discrimination individuals who are involved in an employment tribunal claim. A claim may be brought by a non-disabled person who perhaps gave evidence it assisted or supported the claimant (see Code of Practice 2004).

Part 6: Sexual orientation discrimination law

Protection against discrimination on the grounds of sexual orientation in employment is now provided under the Employment Equality (Sexual Orientation) Regulations 2003. There are also ancillary legislative provisions for people who are homosexual. The Sex Discrimination Act 1975 has been amended to include anti-discrimination measures on the grounds of civil partnership (to equate with the original protection for married persons).

The achievement of such statutory protection took some time and various cases tested the scope of both the EU Equal Treatment Directive 1975 and also the European Convention on Human Rights 1950. In respect of the first challenge, the European Court of Justice ruled that sexual orientation was not covered by the Equal Treatment Directive 1975. It stated, in a case involving the eligibility of the partner of a lesbian member of staff for travel concessions, that 'an employer is not required by Community law to treat the situation of a person who has a stable relationship with a partner of the same sex as equivalent to that of a person who is married to or has a stable relationship outside marriage with a partner of the opposite sex' (*Grant* v *South West Trains Ltd* [1998] IRLR 188).

The judgment in a European Court of Human Rights (ECtHR) case (*Smith and Grady* v *United Kingdom* (*No. 1*) [1999] IRLR 734) exposed the gaps in protection on the grounds of sexual orientation. The complainants contended that investigations by the armed forces into their homosexuality constituted violations of the Convention Articles 8 (the right of privacy) and 14 (non-discrimination). The ECtHR found that the investigations, interviews and the discharges of Ms Smith and Mr Grady were an 'exceptional intrusion'. It was also found that there was not an effective remedy available to the complainants (as required under Article 13).

In 2000, the Employment Framework Directive was adopted by the European Union. Its transposition into British law through the Employment Equality (Sexual Orientation) Regulations 2003, has gone some way to deal with the previous limitations of the law. In 2007, this was supplemented by further legislation to tackle discrimination in the provision of goods, facilities and services (Equality Act (Sexual Orientation) Regulations 2007).

What is the protection?

The Employment Equality (Sexual Orientation) Regulations 2003 cover any person with an employment relationship in the same terms as other discrimination law; those applying for employment; and the circumstances when that relationship has ended.

Applicants and employees

It is unlawful (reg 6(1)) for an employer to discriminate against a *job applicant*:

- in the arrangements he makes for determining to whom he should offer employment;
- in the terms on which he offers that person employment;
- by refusing to offer, or deliberately not offering, him employment.

It is unlawful (reg 6(2)) for an employer to discriminate against *a person in employment*:

- in the terms of employment which he affords that person;
- in the opportunities which he affords him for promotion, a transfer, training or receiving any other benefit; by refusing to afford him, or deliberately not affording him, any such opportunity; or
- by dismissing him, or subjecting him to any other detriment.

What is 'sexual orientation'?

The regulations state (reg 2(1)) that it means sexual orientation towards:

- persons of the same sex (homosexuals);
- persons of the opposite sex (heterosexuals);
- persons of the same sex and of the opposite sex (bisexuals).

The Explanatory Memorandum accompanying the regulations stated that they can cover 'perception' of sexual orientation. 'This means that people will be able to bring a claim even if the discrimination was based on (incorrect) assumptions'. The issue of the scope of the protection was ruled on by the Court of Appeal in a harassment allegation (see Exhibit 5.14).

Direct discrimination

Under the Regulations (reg 3(1)), 'a person (A) discriminates against another person (B) if on the grounds of sexual orientation A treats B less favourably than he treats or would treat other persons'.

Exhibit 5.14 The English case

English v *Thomas Sanderson Blinds Ltd* [2008] EWCA Civ 1421, CA

Facts. Mr English complained to an employment tribunal that he had suffered unlawful harassment on the grounds of sexual orientation. He alleged that he had been subjected to homophobic taunts from colleagues because he had been educated at a boarding school and lived in Brighton. These facts were perceived by colleagues as characteristics associated with a homosexual person. Mr English is heterosexual and, despite their alleged behaviour, he accepted that his workmates did not genuinely believe him to be gay.

Employment tribunal. This dismissed the complaint because someone who was not gay, and was not mistakenly or genuinely thought to be gay, and was not harassed because of any gay associations or friendships, could not fall within the provisions of harassment on the grounds of sexual orientation.

EAT. This dismissed the appeal. It said that the problem was that Mr English's alleged harassers did not perceive him to be gay, and he fully accepted that they did not. The homophobic behaviour was a vehicle for teasing him, but it could not be said to be 'on grounds of sexual orientation' as required under reg 5.

Court of Appeal. This held by a majority that the Sexual Orientation Regulations 2003 do cover homophobic abuse even where the victim is not gay and not perceived to be gay.

Exhibit 5.15 Civil partner's rights

Maruko v *Versorgungsanstalt der deutschen Buhnen* [2008] IRLR 450, ECJ

Facts. Tadao Maruko entered into the German equivalent of a civil partnership. His partner was a member of a pension scheme, and when he died, the scheme refused to recognise Maruko's entitlement to a widower's pension. He claimed discrimination on the grounds of sexual orientation contrary to the Employment Equality Framework Directive 2000.

ECJ ruling. It asserted that member states must comply with EU law and with the principle of non-discrimination. It is direct discrimination on grounds of sexual orientation not to provide a surviving partner with a survivor's benefit equivalent to that granted to a surviving spouse.

Comment. 'The *Maruko* judgment appears to mean that reg 25 does not comply with EU law . . . It would seem that occupational pension schemes in the UK will now have to fully harmonise their provisions on survivor benefits as between civil partners and married partners' (*Equal Opportunities Review*, 176, May 2008).

The issue of comparison inevitably arises. It is stated that, in looking at the circumstances of A's situation and B's, these should be 'the same or not materially different' (reg 3(2)). If the comparison is between a person who is married and one who is a civil partner, then, that is not to be regarded as a material difference (reg 3(3)) (see Exhibit 5.15).

Indirect discrimination

The regulations (reg 3(1)(b)) proscribe indirect discrimination on the grounds of sexual orientation in the same terms as other discrimination law – i.e. where there is a provision, criterion or practice which creates a disadvantage to a person (compared to other persons). It has to be objectively justified.

The issue of 'justification'

This is presented in the same terms as other strands of discrimination law. The indirect discrimination must be a 'proportionate means of achieving a legitimate aim' (reg 3(1)(b)) (see Part 1).

Genuine occupational requirement

It is possible for an employer to have a GOR in a person specification. This occurs where being of a particular sexual orientation is 'a genuine and determining occupational requirement' and 'it is proportionate to apply that requirement in the particular case' (reg 7(2)).

This regulation has particular provisions in respect of 'an organised religion'. It is possible to specify sexual orientation 'so as to comply with the doctrines of the religion, or because of the nature of the employment and the context in which it is carried out, so as to avoid conflicting with the strongly held religious convictions of a significant number of the religion's followers' (reg 7(3)).

Harassment

The issues (reg 5) are examined in Chapter 7 (see also Exhibits 5.14 and 7.4).

Aiding unlawful acts

A person who knowingly aids another to do an act which is unlawful in the Regulations shall be treated as doing that unlawful act (reg 23).

Positive action

This is permissible where it constitutes access to training and encouraging particular people to take advantage of opportunities for doing particular work (reg 26).

Post employment

Where an employment relationship has come to an end, it is unlawful for a person to be subjected to a 'detriment' or 'harassment' where that treatment on the grounds of sexual orientation 'arises out of and is closely connected to' that relationship (reg 21).

Liability and defence against liability

These provisions (reg 22) are in the same terms as other strands of discrimination law (see Part 1 of this chapter).

Enforcement

The enforcement process for employment complaints comprises the usual elements. The ***time limit*** for an employment tribunal complaint is within three months of the alleged incident, with the tribunal having discretion to hear 'out of time' complaints where it is 'just and equitable' to do so (reg 34). The complainant should make out a ***prima facie*** case (reg 29). To assist in this, s/he may use the ***questionnaire process*** (Sch 2). The ***burden of proof*** (reg 29) is that approved by the Court of Appeal (in *Igen Ltd* v *Wong* [2005] ICR 931) (see Exhibit 5.2). The remedies are a declaration; compensation and a recommendation.

Victimisation

The regulations (reg 4) provide parallel provisions on victimisation to those in sex discrimination law (see Part 1). The protection against victimisation does not apply if 'the allegation, evidence or information was false and not made [or given] in good faith' (reg 4(2)).

Part 7: Religion or belief discrimination law

The Race Relations Act 1976 does not expressly cover discrimination on the grounds of religion. However, in certain specific circumstances, some religious groups were ruled as 'racial groups' under that legislation following a House of Lords ruling (*Mandla* v *Dowell Lee* [1983] IRLR 209) (see Part 3 of this chapter). It was not until 2003 that specific employment legislation was enacted to protect against discrimination on the grounds of religion or belief (religious or secular). The Employment Equality (Religion or Belief) Regulations 2003 transposed into British law the relevant provisions of the EU Employment Directive 2000. In 2007, supplementary regulations were implemented in respect of discrimination in the provision of goods, facilities and services.

There is a critical problem at the heart of this strand of discrimination law. It is the extent to which it can be equivalent to the other strands. The principal 'grounds' for discriminatory treatment (sex, race, disability, age, gender reassignment and sexual orientation) are concerned with individual '*innate*' characteristics. The 'grounds' of 'religion' or 'belief' are concerned with '*acquired*' characteristics – what a person chooses to believe; whether to accept the tenets of a particular religion; whether to adopt a literal translation of a holy book; whether to have a commitment to extremist political views; or whether to reject theism as irrational. As a consequence, the issue of 'trumping' arises. There can be, and are, conflicts between one person's belief and another's right to be protected on other discrimination grounds. So, courts and tribunals have to determine in particular cases whose rights are paramount (see Exhibit 5.17).

What is the protection?

The regulations cover any person with an employment relationship in the same terms as other discrimination law, those applying for employment, and the circumstances when that relationship has ended.

Applicants and employees

It is unlawful (reg 6(1)) for an employer to discriminate against a *job applicant*:

- in the arrangements he makes for determining to whom he should offer employment;
- in the terms on which he offers that person employment;
- by refusing to offer, or deliberately not offering, him employment.

It is unlawful (reg 6(2)) for an employer to discriminate against *a person in employment*:

- in the terms of employment which he affords that person;
- in the opportunities which he affords him for promotion, a transfer, training or receiving any other benefit; by refusing to afford him, or deliberately not affording him, any such opportunity; or
- by dismissing him, or subjecting him to any other detriment.

What is 'religion' and 'belief'?

The regulations prohibit discrimination on grounds of 'religion' or 'belief'. These terms are not defined in any detail; although there is some help coming from case law. We will examine each in turn. Under the interpretation regulation the following are stated:

- 'Religion' means 'any religion' (reg 2(1)(a)).
- 'Belief' means 'any religious or philosophical belief' (reg 2(1)(b)).
- A reference to religion includes a reference to lack of religion (reg 2(1)(c)).
- A reference to belief includes a reference to lack of belief (reg 2(1)(d)).

'Religion'

There is probably a wide consensus in society about whether certain organisations constitute religions. If the tests are that there is belief in an external deity, collective worship, an authoritative holy book, some kind of leadership or priesthood, the use of prayer and the observance of certain holy days, then, adherents of the three major religions in western society (Judaism, Christianity and Islam) would be covered. However, within these broad religious groups there are spectrums of opinion – some of a particularly fundamentalist nature. There are also 'beliefs' which claim that they are 'religious' but may, arguably, be cults and are often regarded as anathema to the main religions. Clearly, the extent to which non-orthodox views are protected is to be tested on a case-by-case basis.

'Belief'

This is a potentially far-reaching category. It covers not just 'religious belief' but 'philosophical belief'. So, this category can encompass humanism, various secular views and atheism; and, arguably, political philosophies. Furthermore, an individual who is not part of a collective religious organisation might claim to have his/her own personal religious belief (see Exhibit 5.16).

The Explanatory Memorandum accompanying the regulations stated that they can cover 'perception' of religion or belief. 'This means that people will be able to bring a claim even if the discrimination was based on (incorrect) assumptions.'

Exhibit 5.16 What is a 'religion' and a 'belief'?

Opinion. The EAT considered a discrimination claim from a Justice of the Peace who, as a practising Christian, objected to hearing family court cases where a child was to be placed with a same-sex couple. He claimed that such placements had not been sufficiently researched and were 'an experiment in social science'.

The EAT ruled that 'to constitute a belief there must be a religious or philosophical viewpoint in which one actually believes. It is not enough "to have an opinion based on some real or perceived logic or based on information or lack of information available".' The test for considering whether views can properly be considered to fall into the category of a philosophical belief is 'whether they have sufficient cogency, seriousness, cohesion and importance and are worthy of respect in a democratic society'. Mr McClintock was found to have an opinion and not a religious or philosophical belief (*McClintock* v *Department for Constitutional Affairs* [2007] IRLR 29).

Comment. This test for a philosophical belief is drawn from the European Court of Human Rights case, *Campbell & Cosans* v *United Kingdom* [1982] 4 EHRR 293. The concept of the belief being 'worthy of respect in a democratic society' is particularly interesting. This might form the basis for rejecting a claim for protection under the religion or belief regulations from someone such as a British National Party member who is claiming that 'fascism' or 'British nationalism' amounts to a 'philosophical belief' (*Equal Opportunities Review*, 175 April 2008).

Rastafarianism. This was held by the EAT to be a philosophical belief under the regulations (*Harris* v *NJL Automotive Ltd and Matrix Consultancy UK Ltd* (2007) EAT 0134/07).

Anti-hypnotism. This was ruled *not* to be a 'religion' (although it is one of the tenets of the Hindu faith) and so the complainant was not protected. However, it has been commented that since 2007 (under the Equality Act 2006) the grounds for protection from discrimination have been extended to cover 'religious belief' and this claimant may have been covered (*Sethi* v *Accord Operations Ltd* Case 3201823/06) (*Equal Opportunities Review*, 175 April 2008).

Direct discrimination

The regulations (reg 3) prohibit 'less favourable treatment' by one person (A) against another (B) where that treatment is 'on the grounds of religion or belief'. A will be treating B less favourably than s/he would treat others. It is immaterial whether or not the religion or belief in question is also A's.

As far as the issue of comparison is concerned, the regulations state: a comparison of B's case with that of another person 'must be such that the relevant circumstances in the one case are the same, or not materially different, in the other' (reg 3(3)) (see Exhibit 5.17).

Indirect discrimination

The regulations (reg 3(1)(b)) proscribe indirect discrimination on the grounds of religion or belief in the same terms as other discrimination law – i.e. where there is a provision, criterion or practice which creates a disadvantage to a person of a particular religion or belief (compared to other persons). It has to be objectively justified (see Exhibit 5.18).

Exhibit 5.17 The registrar and civil partnerships

Facts. Ms Lillian Ladele is employed by the London Borough of Islington as a registrar. Until December 2007, registrars effectively worked on a freelance basis and could swap with each other to avoid civil partnership ceremonies. Since that date they came under the direct control of the local authority and there was said to be less flexibility in the arrangements. She objected to officiating at civil partnership ceremonies because of her evangelical Christian beliefs. She claimed that she was picked on, shunned and accused of being homophobic for refusing to carry out civil partnership ceremonies, and that she was discriminated against on grounds of her religious beliefs.

Employment tribunal. It found that she had been harassed and discriminated against directly and indirectly on the grounds of religious belief. The Council had assumed that protection against discrimination on the grounds of sexual orientation should be paramount, and it had disregarded and displayed no respect for her genuinely held religious belief. The tribunal took the view that the starting point was that all rights are to be valued equally. The Council was able to provide facilities for civil partnership services without Ms Ladele by using staff who did not share her views.

See Johnstone, S. (2008) 'Round-up of recent decisions', *Equal Opportunities Review*, No. 181: 31.

Reactions to ET ruling:

> Public servants like Registrars have a duty to serve all members of the public without fear or favour. Once society lets some people opt out of upholding the law, where will it end?
>
> (Peter Tatchell, campaigner for gay rights, *BBC News* website, 10 July 2008)
>
> This important ruling confirms that gay rights should not be treated as trumping religious rights.
>
> (Mike Judge, The Christian Institute, which financially supported the complainant)
>
> [The decision] appears to place religious 'conscience of registrars' above their legal duty to carry out Parliament's legislation [. . .] Will registrars with similar religious convictions now be allowed to opt out of conducting civil marriages for divorcees, or for couples they believe have had sex before marriage or even couples from other faiths? [. . .] Would a racist council employee be allowed to excuse themselves in cases involving ethnic minorities on the basis of their 'deeply held beliefs' or 'religious consciences'?
>
> (Terry Sanderson, President of the National Secular Society, press release, 10 July 2008 www.secularism.org.uk/registrarjudgementpotentiallycat.html)

Employment appeal tribunal. It ruled that the employment tribunal had erred in law. There was no unlawful religious discrimination by the Council (*London Borough of Islington* v *Ladele* [2008] UKEAT/0453/08).

Exhibit 5.18 Islamic dress code

Azmi v *Kirklees Metropolitan Borough Council* [2007] IRLR 484, EAT

Facts. Mrs Azmi was a schoolteacher who was suspended for refusing an instruction not to wear when in class with pupils, a niqab (a veil covering her face with only her eyes visible). She was employed as a bilingual support worker which required her to work as part of a team to support the learning and welfare of pupils, particularly ethnic minority pupils who were at risk of underachieving. Consequently, the employer stated that 'making verbal and non verbal-communication/facial expression/eye contact [is] vital'.

The headteacher had not previously received a request from someone to wear a veil at all times in the presence of male colleagues. Other Muslim women wore the headscarf and not the veil. The advice of the education service was that 'the desire to express religious identity does not overcome the primary requirement for optimal communications between adults and children'.

Prior to receiving this advice the headteacher had allowed Mrs Azmi to wear the niqab and her work was observed. It was concluded that she did not carry out her role as effectively when wearing the veil as when she was unveiled.

She was then instructed by the headteacher that she should not wear the veil when teaching children.

EAT ruling. This upheld the employment tribunal view that there had been *no direct discrimination* because a non-Muslim person (the correct comparator) would have been treated in the same way. It found that there was *indirect discrimination* but it could be *justified*. The employer's requirement not to wear clothing that covers a considerable part of the face and/or mouth was a 'proportionate means of achieving a legitimate aim'. This measure was to ensure effective teaching.

It was noted at the employment tribunal that, on the employer's part, the instruction was not given immediately; time was taken to consider the position; the instruction not to wear the veil was confined to times when she was teaching the children; and there had been observations on the effectiveness of her teaching.

The issue of 'justification'

This is presented in the same terms as other strands of discrimination law. The indirect discrimination must be a 'proportionate means of achieving a legitimate aim' (reg 3(1)(b)).

Genuine occupational requirement

'Having regard to the nature of the employment or the context in which it is carried out', then there are two possible circumstances in which GORs (reg 7) apply:

- Where 'being of a particular religion or belief is a genuine and determining occupational requirement'; and it is 'proportionate to apply that requirement in the particular case' (reg 7(2)). An obvious example would be where a religious organisation was to employ a person to promote its particular religious faith as part of their employment. They may not necessarily hold religious office but, under the person specification, may be expected to speak with authority about the faith and to engage with members of the public (see Exhibit 5.19).
- Where 'an employer has an ethos based on religion or belief and [having regard to that ethos and the nature of the employment or the context in which it is carried out] being of a particular religion or belief is a genuine and determining occupation requirement; and it is 'proportionate to apply that requirement in the particular case'. The concept of 'ethos' is problematic and, potentially, contentious. There will be differing views about whether,

Exhibit 5.19 An atheist teacher in a Catholic school

Glasgow City Council v *McNab* [2007] IRLR 476, EAT

Facts. Mr McNab worked as a teacher of mathematics and computing in a Catholic school maintained by Glasgow City Council. He was an atheist. He applied for the post of acting principal teacher of pastoral care. He was not shortlisted. The school argued that there was a non-statutory agreement between the Church and the local authority that certain posts would be reserved for Catholics only.

Employment tribunal. This found no statutory basis for the agreement; and stated that just because the agreement specified that a teacher had to be a Catholic for certain posts did not mean that the requirement had to be regarded as a genuine occupational requirement. The respondent had not established the GOR (reg 7(2)). Furthermore, the respondent could not rely on the claim that it had an 'ethos' (reg 7(3)). 'An education authority does not, in any event, have a religious ethos'.

EAT ruling. It upheld the employment tribunal's ruling that Mr McNab had been discriminated against because none of the exceptions under reg 7(2) and (3) applied.

for example, a person's faith is relevant to certain posts within a religious organisation. It might be asked why, for example, a maintenance worker, a cleaner or an administrator need to be believers of a particular faith.

Note that there are provisions under the Employment Equality (Sexual Orientation) Regulations 2003 (reg 7) in respect of the GOR for 'organised religions' (see Part 6).

Harassment

The issues (reg 6(3)) are examined in Chapter 7.

Aiding unlawful acts

A person who knowingly aids another to do an act which is unlawful in the regulations shall be treated as doing that unlawful act (reg 23).

Positive action

This is permissible where it constitutes access to training and encouraging particular people to take advantage of opportunities for doing particular work (reg 25).

Post employment

Where an employment relationship has come to an end, it is unlawful for a person to be subjected to a 'detriment' or 'harassment' where that treatment on the grounds of religion or belief 'arises out of and is closely connected to' that relationship (reg 21).

Liability and defence against liability

These provisions (reg 22) are in the same terms as other strands of discrimination law (see Part 1 of this chapter).

Enforcement

The enforcement process for employment complaints comprises the usual elements. The ***time limit*** for an employment tribunal complaint is within three months of the alleged incident, with the tribunal having discretion to hear 'out of time' complaints where it is 'just and equitable' to do so (reg 34). The complainant should make out a *prima facie* case (reg 29). To assist in this, s/he may use the ***questionnaire process*** (Sch 2). The ***burden of proof*** (reg 29) is that approved by the Court of Appeal (in *Igen Ltd* v *Wong* [2005] ICR 931) (see Exhibit 5.2). The remedies are a declaration, compensation and a recommendation.

Victimisation

The regulations (reg 4) provide parallel provisions on victimisation to those in sex discrimination law (see Part 1). The protection against victimisation does not apply if 'the allegation, evidence or information was false and not made [or given] in good faith' (reg 4(2)).

Part 8: Age discrimination law

Legal framework

Introduction

Aspects of age discrimination have been covered under the indirect discrimination provisions of the Sex Discrimination Act 1975. Examples include the use of age bars for recruitment and promotion decisions which have been held to constitute indirect sex discrimination (see Exhibit 5.20). In addition, unequal retirement and pension ages for men and women have been seen as constituting direct sex discrimination, ultimately resolved through the harmonising of compulsory retirement ages (*Marshall* v *Southampton and SW Hampshire Area Health Authority* [1986] IRLR 140, ECJ; *Barber* v *Guardian Royal Exchange Assurance Group plc* [1990] IRLR 240, ECJ). However, despite the significance of this area of law, it is protection afforded on the grounds of sex, not of age; and as such steers clear of the controversies surrounding specific legislation outlawing age discrimination itself. The effectiveness of age in sex discrimination cases has also depended 'in any given case on how the relevant total population is determined and whether the tribunal considers the resulting difference in the proportionate treatment of men and women to be sufficiently large to trigger the Act' (Deakin and Morris 2005: 627). Furthermore, indirect discrimination creates the possibility of justification and this 'makes a successful outcome for the complainant far from certain even where a *prima facie* finding of adverse impact is made' (Deakin and Morris 2005: 628).

The Employment Equality Framework Directive 2000

This marked a significant advance in discrimination law by extending the scope of discrimination law to areas such as religion, sexual orientation and age. The protection it affords those claiming age discrimination is however limited to the areas of employment and occupations. However, employment and occupations are defined broadly including access to employment, recruitment, promotion, all types and levels of vocational training, working conditions, pay, dismissal and membership of or involvement in employer bodies, trade unions and professional organisations.

Exhibit 5.20 Age and the Sex Discrimination Act 1975

Price v *Civil Service Commission* [1978] IRLR 3

Facts. Price, a 35-year-old woman wanting to work for the Civil Service after maternity leave, challenged an age limit of 28 for a particular post. She argued that the age limit constituted indirect sex discrimination on the grounds that proportionately fewer women could apply for the post than men, because many women were engaged in child bearing and rearing in their late twenties.

Judgments. The original tribunal found in favour of the employer on the grounds that it was possible for any woman aged 17 and a half and 28 to apply and that in practice the proportion who were able to do so was not considerably smaller than the proportion of men who were able. However, the EAT found in favour of Price arguing that 'it is safe to say that the condition (of an age limit of 28) is one which it is in practice harder for women to comply with than it is for men'. Adding that there are clearly women who 'cannot comply with the condition, because they are women, that is to say, because of their involvement with their children' (Phillips J).

Jones v *University of Manchester* [1993] IRLR 218

Facts. This case was brought by a 44 year-old woman and concerned a situation where her employer had imposed a maximum age bar in order to achieve a better age balance in the relevant department (age band of 27–35). The employer argued further that a careers officer post should be occupied by a younger person, on the grounds that they would be able to relate more closely to the students that they would be giving advice to. Ms Jones had studied for a degree as a mature student and claimed that the age limit discriminated against women who obtained their degree as mature students.

Judgments. Although the tribunal found in her favour, both the EAT and the Court of Appeal found in favour of the employer on the grounds that the tribunal had erred in law in using a 'pool' which consisted of mature graduates with relevant experience only when it should have used the numbers of men and women who can comply with the requirement as a proportion of those in the whole of the relevant population, rather than using a subdivision of the larger pool (mature graduates with relevant experience).

Comment. It should be noted that today in light of the Employment Equality (Age) Regulations, Jones would now be able to bring a claim for direct age discrimination; and although the employer could argue for 'justification' it is unlikely that a court would accept the argument that an age band would be justified in light of the target audience.

The directive provides for protection against direct discrimination, indirect discrimination, harassment and victimisation (Article 2). Articles 4 and 6 provide for exceptions to the principle of equal treatment as they apply to age. Article 4 covers occupational requirements and is consistent with other areas of discrimination law. Article 6 is more controversial, providing for specific exemptions from the principle of equal treatment, so that differences of treatment are to be allowed where they can be 'objectively and reasonably justified by a legitimate aim, including legitimate employment policy, labour market and vocational training objectives' and the means of achieving the aim must be 'appropriate and necessary'.

The directive (Article 6) provides for a defence of justification for both direct *and* indirect discrimination, which alongside disability discrimination, sets it apart from other areas of discrimination law that confine justification to indirect discrimination only. In Article 6(1) the directive provides some examples of what may constitute justifiable differences of treatment, although the list is not exhaustive. These include:

- setting special conditions on access to employment and vocational training;
- fixing minimum conditions of age, professional experience or seniority in service for access to employment;

- fixing maximum ages for recruitment, based on training requirements for the post, although the list is not exhaustive.

A Spanish case (*Palacios de la villa* v *Cortefiel Servicios SA* [2006] IRLR 989, ECJ) provides an illustration of how the objective justification defence can operate in practice. The case concerned the legitimacy of national laws relating to mandatory retirement ages and whether these were inconsistent with the directive. The European Court of Justice held that mandatory retirement ages were indeed discriminatory but that these could be justified in the context of employment policy and labour market objectives. So, these are legitimate aims and mandatory retirement ages are a proportionate response to achieving the legitimate aims of promoting employment and labour market opportunities across different age groups.

More generally it has been argued that because of policy concerns to raise labour market participation and the wish not to alienate employers, the directive, and to a greater extent the Employment Equality (Age) Regulations 2006 have effectively become a means of legitimising age discrimination in employment. The absence of an aim to 'protect and promote individuals' rights not to be discriminated against on the grounds of age' (Sargeant 2006a, 2006b) means that what is embodied in government statements and in the legislation is a diversity approach that seeks to balance the effectiveness of legislation against a concern not to impose an unacceptable burden on employers in terms of costs or 'bureaucracy'.

Employment Equality (Age) Regulations 2006

These were introduced under the European Communities Act (s 2). As such, the regulations follow the directive closely, prohibiting direct and indirect discrimination, harassment, as well as victimisation. There are, however, some significant differences in comparison with other strands of discrimination law.

Regulation 7 defines the scope of the legislation, identifying the areas that are deemed unlawful for an employer to discriminate on age grounds, these cover:

- arrangements for offering employment (reg 7(1)(a));
- the terms in which employment is offered or by refusing or deliberately omitting to offer employment (reg 7(1)(b));
- subjecting someone to harassment on the grounds of age (reg 7(1)(c));
- opportunities offered for promotion, transfer, training or receipt of other benefits (reg 7(2));
- refusing or deliberately not affording a person an opportunity covered in reg 7(2) (reg 7(2)(b)).
- dismissing or harassing a person seeking an opportunity covered in reg 7(2) (reg 7(2)(c)).

Direct discrimination

Under reg 3(1)(a) direct discrimination occurs where 'on grounds of B's age, A treats B less favourably than he treats or would treat other persons . . . and A cannot show the treatment . . . to be a proportionate means of achieving a legitimate aim'.

Although this extends to 'B's apparent age' (reg 3(3)(b)), it is not necessary for age to be the *sole reason* for a dismissal. (On the question of 'sole reason' see the judgment in *Owen and Briggs* v *James* [1982] ICR 618, CA.) The scope of reg 3(1) is narrow and substantially weak, given that the justification defence, is extended here to direct discrimination.

Comparator

In keeping with other discrimination grounds 'less favourable treatment' requires a comparator, which as has been noted earlier is a particular difficulty in the case of age given its fluid nature, but hypothetical comparators are permitted under reg 3(1)(a). This raises the question of what ages might constitute relevant comparators. Although a different jurisdiction, but within the EU, recent case law in the Irish Republic has indicated that comparative age differences may not need to be large for a claim to succeed (McEwen 2004, in Duncan *et al.* 2007, suggests more than three years but fewer than eight!).

Indirect discrimination

Defined in reg 3(1)(b), it is broadly consistent with the definitions in other fields of discrimination law. It provides that such discrimination occurs 'where A applies to B a provision, criterion or practice which A applies or would apply equally to persons not of the same age group as B but which puts persons of same age group as B at a particular disadvantage when compared with other persons, and which also puts B at that disadvantage and which A cannot show to be a proportionate means of achieving a legitimate aim'.

'Age group' is defined as 'a group of persons defined by reference to age or a range of ages' and would seem to provide the claimant with scope to define the disadvantaged group as he or she wishes.

Following the Employment Equality Directive 2000, the definition of indirect discrimination as the application of a 'provision, criterion or practice' has considerably broadened its scope; and extends beyond strict 'requirements or conditions'. As well as covering formal selection criteria for recruitment, redundancy, training promotion and retirement it seems sufficiently broad to include informal workplace practices. This has important implications for human resource management as it forces practitioners to go beyond the issue of 'age proofing' policies and consider how these may become embedded in workplaces to ensure they are reflected in practice. Amongst other things it draws attention to training and re-training and heightening awareness of initiatives and good practice at the workplace. The regulations provide a considerable potential reach to challenge informal workplace practices.

Objective justification

Much attention has focused on the 'objective justification' test under reg 3. To meet the justification defence for ***both*** direct and indirect discrimination, the employer must show by way of a defence that:

(a) in a claim for direct age discrimination, the less favourable treatment was 'a proportionate means of achieving a legitimate aim'; and that
(b) in a claim for indirect age discrimination, the provision, criterion or practice which placed persons of the claimant's age group at a disadvantage was a proportionate means of achieving a legitimate aim – reg 3(1)(a) and (b).

Regulation 3 has attracted considerable attention and criticism, with arguments that it is too flexible to allow what is and what is not permitted to be predicted. Furthermore, 'almost any criterion or practice can be potentially indirectly discriminatory' on grounds of age (Fredman 2003: 58).

How the objective justification test will be applied in practice will depend much on the view of the courts and tribunals as to the importance and status of age discrimination as an equality ground and the uncertainty surrounding this explains the pressure placed on organisations by

Exhibit 5.21 The principle of proportionality

Mangold v *Helm* [2006] IRLR 143

Facts. This concerns German laws that set limits on the length of fixed-term contracts and the number of times they could be renewed. In an effort to combat unemployment, the laws were relaxed for those workers over a certain age giving them less job protection. In 2001 this age had been reduced from 60 to 52. The German government argued that the laws operated to assist with 'the vocational integration of unemployed older workers in so far as they encounter difficulties in finding work' and that this constituted a legitimate aim of policy, and therefore justified age discrimination. The case was referred to the European Court of Justice.

ECJ ruling. It accepted the German government's argument that this constituted *a legitimate aim* **but** did not accept that the limits were 'appropriate and necessary' as required by the directive. The key issue for the ECJ was the argument that the limit applied to all workers over 52, 'whether or not they were unemployed before the contract was concluded and whatever the duration of any period of unemployment', which they argued infringed the principle of proportionality.

The ECJ therefore held that because the legislation being challenged took the age of the worker as the only criterion for the application of the legislation 'regardless of any other consideration linked to the structure of the labour market in question or the personal situation of the person concerned' it went 'beyond what is appropriate and necessary in order to attain the objective pursued'. As the judgment said: 'Observance of the principle of proportionality requires every **derogation** from an individual right to reconcile, so far as is possible, the requirements of the principle of equal treatment with those of the aim pursued'.

the CIPD, ACAS and the Employer's Forum on Age to review all their policies for evidence of potential age bias (Rubenstein 2006a; ACAS 2006). The government's position in *Coming of Age* (DTI 2005) was that 'the test of objective justification would not be an easy one to satisfy', a view that seems to have been confirmed by the ECJ decision in *Mangold* v *Helm* [2006] IRLR 143 (see Exhibit 5.21).

However, the recent decision in *Bloxham* v *Freshfields Bruckhaus Deringer* [2007] ET 2205086/06, one of the first significant employment tribunal cases arising under the regulations, suggests a broader interpretation might prevail than many had envisaged (see Exhibit 5.22). The interpretation of this defence is likely to be critical to the future effectiveness and impact of the regulations. To explore this further we examine the two elements of the defence: the concept of legitimate aims, and that of proportionality.

Legitimate aims

The Department of Trade and Industry consultation on the regulations stated that to be considered legitimate 'the aim must correspond with a real need on the part of the employer', and, therefore, is intended to correspond to the 'real need' test in EU sex equality law (see Part 1). As noted earlier, Article 6 of the directive produced a non-exhaustive list of factors that might qualify under the objective justification defence. It left open potentially difficult areas of employment practice. It remains unclear whether legitimate aims can themselves have an age-discriminatory aspect; whether positive discrimination might constitute a legitimate aim; and whether cost-saving might also be considered legitimate. The general view appears to be that whilst these may in some circumstances constitute a legitimate aim, they are unlikely to be viewed by the courts as proportionate responses by employers.

For example, where a high street clothes store is trying to target a particular age group as customers, it may also wish to target people of that age group as employees to support its

Exhibit 5.22 Objective justification

Bloxham v *Freshfields Bruckhaus Deringer* (2007) ET/2205086/06

Facts. It concerned a law firm (Freshfields Bruckhaus Deringer) that wished to reform its pension arrangements. Freshfields consulted with staff affected and introduced a scheme in May 2006 that was generally accepted as less generous to staff than the scheme it replaced. As part of the move to the new pension scheme the firm introduced a set of transitional arrangements. These provided that partners in the firm who were over 50 could retire under the old scheme so long as they did so before 31 October 2006. However, under the old scheme partners who retired before 55 received a reduced level of pension of approximately 20 per cent.

Bloxham was a partner in the firm and had planned to retire when he reached the age of 55, which would have been in March 2007. In light of the changes to the scheme he decided to retire on 31 October 2006. The pension he received was reduced in line with the terms of the old scheme and he claimed that this change amounted to direct age discrimination.

Employment tribunal ruling. It agreed that Bloxham had been discriminated against on the grounds of age by Freshfields, as this amounted to 'less favourable treatment'. However, it held that the firm had provided objective justification for the decision. It had introduced a new pension scheme that 'reduced the intergenerational unfairness on younger partners' and that this constituted a legitimate aim. The claim that this was legitimate was based on this fairness issue, not one of cost. Justifying their actions on the basis of the latter would almost certainly not have been seen as legitimate. Moreover, the tribunal held that the response had also been proportionate, arguing that the changes were necessary, took into account balancing the conflicting interests between different generations and that 'there was no less discriminatory means available to the company'. The fact that Freshfields had undertaken a wide and thorough consultation process and took expert advice prior to the introduction of the changes clearly helped its case (*Personnel Today*, 29 October 2007).

Seldon v *Clarkson Wright and Jakes* (2008) ET 1100275/07

This concerned a partner in a law firm who was dismissed upon reaching the age of 65. The firm claimed that the compulsory retirement provisions were introduced to meet legitimate business needs to facilitate long-term workforce planning. He claimed discrimination under the legislation. The tribunal held that the use of a compulsory retirement age was a proportionate means of achieving legitimate aims and therefore did not discriminate in forcing him to retire at 65 (*Equal Opportunities Review*, 173:26). Seldon has appealed to the EAT.

Hampton v *Lord Chancellor and Another* [2008] IRLR 258, ET

This concerned a south London recorder (part-time judicial office) where a retirement age of 65 applied, rather than 70 for other judicial posts. The Ministry of Justice argued that the 65 age was necessary to ensure room for new appointments. However, the tribunal held that the Ministry of Justice had failed to show that the age requirement of 65 was a proportionate means of meeting that aim.

business objectives. This may well constitute a legitimate business aim but the difficulty would be in arguing that the 'age discriminatory aspect' was a proportionate response.

Cost considerations. One particularly troublesome issue is whether employers can cite cost considerations as a legitimate aim particularly as 'economic factors such as business needs and considerations of efficiency may be legitimate aims' (Davies 2005: 11). As Rubenstein (2006a: 16) has argued: 'cost is an especially important consideration in the age discrimination context and the approach taken by the courts is likely to be an important determinant of the ultimate reach of the new legislation'. This has particular relevance for older workers' pay and benefits, and the sensitivity with which older workers are viewed in terms of their relative cost to organisations, especially where length of service and seniority-based rewards are well established. Case law suggests that costs should be considered but cannot be determinate, and it is unclear what weight should be placed on them. In *Cross* v *British Airways plc* [2005] IRLR 423 it was argued that costs alone cannot constitute a legitimate aim but that it is appropriate to take cost into account in deciding whether or not an employer's discriminatory treatment is a proportionate means of achieving the employer's aim. As the Employment Appeals Tribunal judgment concluded, economic justification may not often be highly valued, for example where discrimination is substantial, obvious and deliberate, (but) it must be considered.

Proportionality

This requires that the legitimate aim be weighed against the discriminatory effect of the requirement. In effect this is saying that 'one should not discriminate more than is necessary'. It suggests that because there is almost always going to be a less discriminatory way of achieving a legitimate aim than imposing a blanket age requirement that direct age discrimination will only be justified in extremely rare circumstances (Rubenstein 2006a: 13). The proportionality requirement is the key to how the regulations will operate in practice. The fact that age frequently operates as a 'cheap screen' for employers means that 'a key battleground for interpreting the age regulations, will be the extent to which tribunals find that an employer fails to satisfy the requirement of proportionality where it directly discriminates on grounds of age' (Rubenstein 2006a: 18). Some insight into the way in which the Courts are likely to move on this has been seen (*Bloxham* case; and the ECJ decision in *Mangold*).

Genuine occupational requirements

Regulation 8(2) relates to employment or its context where:

- possessing a characteristic related to age is a genuine and determining occupational requirement; and where
- it is proportionate to apply that requirement; and where
- a person does not meet the requirement or an employer is not satisfied that he meets it.

The obvious example is a requirement for child actors in particular stage productions where this would be seen as a 'genuine and determining occupational requirement' and it would not be discriminatory to refuse employment to those who clearly did not meet such requirements.

Harassment

The issues (reg 6) are examined in Chapter 7.

Aiding unlawful acts

A person who knowingly aids another to do an act which is unlawful in the regulations shall be treated as doing that unlawful act (reg 26).

Post employment

Regulation 24(2) provides protection to individuals from discrimination arising out of an employment relationship but taking place after the ending of that relationship. That is, where employment has come to an end it will be unlawful for one party to the employment relationship to subject another to detriment or harassment in respect of age where such discrimination or harassment arises out of or is closely connected to that relationship.

Positive action

Regulation 29(1) provides justifications for certain forms of positive action. These justifications apply in situations where 'it reasonably appears to the person doing the act that it prevents or compensates for disadvantages linked to age suffered by persons of that age or age group doing that work or likely to take up that work' (reg 29(1)). The two instances identified by the regulations that meet these criteria are providing access to training facilities which would assist people in undertaking certain work, and to encourage people of a particular age or age group to take advantage of opportunities for undertaking certain types of work.

National minimum wage

Regulation 31(1) and (2) expressly gives exemption to the National Minimum Wage (NMW) in respect of its age bands. It remains lawful to continue to operate an adult rate, youth development rate and a separate rate for 16–17-year-olds. Although the Employers Forum on Age has raised concerns about the continuation of age discriminatory pay bands in respect of the NMW, the government's view is that differential rates are needed to ensure continuing employment opportunities for younger workers (see Chapter 9).

Retirement ages

The government consulted widely on this issue prior to the introduction of the regulations. Although its decision to opt for a mandatory retirement age of 65 has been heavily criticised in some areas, it seems to have been persuaded by employer arguments that a set retirement age makes it easier to engage in workforce planning. A more subtle interpretation is that, as with other aspects of the regulations, the government is trying to nudge firms towards a greater proceduralisation and formalisation of 'good practice' in how it deals with age-related matters. If one accepts the extent of ageist attitudes and their embedded nature, a staged process of change (the mandatory retirement age is to be reviewed in 2011) can be seen as an attempt at a gradual move towards a more significant culture change among employers, and in society generally.

The use of mandatory retirement ages is generally accepted as an example of direct age discrimination, but these can be objectively justified (*Palacios* v *Cortefiel Servicios SA* [2007] IRLR 989, ECJ). The government is facing a similar challenge at the European Court of Justice from the campaigning organisation, *Heyday* on this issue. However, acknowledging the symbolic nature of retirement and 'retirement age' in the UK, it is trying to move employers towards an acceptance of 'transitions out of work' and a more considered approach to retaining staff who are performing and wish to remain in work.

The legal position on retirement ages (through the introduction of a mandatory retirement age of 65) is that it is unlawful for organisations to operate retirement ages below 65 unless these can be objectively justified (reg 30).

'Fair' retirement

This requires employers to notify employees in writing of their intention to retire an employee no more than a year but more than six months before the intended date of retirement. They must also have told employees of their right to request to continue working. This element is in keeping with the concept of good practice: the statutory right to request not to retire must be in writing; and the employer is under a duty to consider (Sch 6). (For a detailed diagrammatic representation of 'fair retirement' see ACAS 2006: Annex 5 (**www.acas.org.uk**).) The employer is then required to hold a meeting with the employee although is under no obligation to agree to any request not to retire; nor to provide a reason although it would clearly be good practice to do so (see Chapter 8 for a more detailed outline).

Seniority and length of service

Direct discrimination by an employer using age-related pay or benefits has to be objectively justified, but employers are permitted to continue to award pay and benefits, such as enhanced holiday entitlement, to employees using the criterion of length of service. Because of the argument that employers may want to 'encourage loyalty', 'encourage motivation' and 'reward experience', benefits based on length of service of up to five years are permitted (reg 32).

Benefits based on service beyond five years will ***not*** constitute unlawful service-based discrimination as long as it 'reasonably appears' to the employer that the way the criterion of length of service is used 'fulfils a business need of his undertaking (for example, either prospectively by encouraging loyalty or motivation, or retrospectively by rewarding experience, of some or all of his workers)' and that they have given consideration to whether or not they have that business need.

In effect this would seem to be saying that an employer does not have to show objective justification for the use of length of service criteria. The use of service-related benefits is then a proportionate means of achieving the aim in question. 'The legitimate aim justifying the retention of service-related benefits is employment planning, in the sense of being able to attract, retain, and reward experienced staff. They help maintain workforce stability by rewarding loyalty, as distinct from performance, and by responding to employees' reasonable expectations that their salary should not remain static. The exact formulation of the exempting provisions ensures that the actual reward remains proportionate' (The government's outline of 'proportionality').

This raises a number of issues. First, seniority is arguably more embedded within organisations than the regulations acknowledge (MacNicol 2006) and separating out the wider and pervasive influence of seniority within many established workplace cultures from 'legitimate' rewards for loyalty, motivation and experience may be less easy than is often presumed. Second, the issue of rewarding 'loyalty' could be interpreted as potentially giving rise to indirect sex discrimination claims if this is equated with long service and used as a justification for higher remuneration. The decision in *Cadman* v *HSE* [2006] IRLR 969 (an equal pay case), is relevant here. In *Cadman* the Advocate General stated: 'I see no basis for a general and unconditional endorsement of a seniority criterion'. However, the European Court of Justice did not adopt this Opinion and held that since recourse to the criterion of length of service is generally appropriate to attain the legitimate objective of rewarding experience that enables a worker to perform his or her duties better, an employer need not specifically justify its use. This would apply unless serious doubts are raised about its appropriateness.

This suggests that the use of a length of service justification should not be accepted unquestioningly by the courts, and that it needs to be subject to closer scrutiny in future. Experience in other European jurisdictions (Ireland and the Netherlands) 'clearly demonstrate that seniority-based distinctions may be more vulnerable to challenge than is usually presumed, especially if they reflect an unquestioned assumption that longer service should be matched by greater rewards' (O'Cinneide 2007: 11–12).

Despite these important qualifications, the consensus among lawyers appears to be that length of service criteria would be relatively easy to satisfy. However, employers will need to convince an employment tribunal why they believe that the service-related benefit is effective in fulfilling that need, and some evidence will be required to show that the belief was reasonable.

'Provided an employer complies with statutory requirements, the burden placed on them of justifying the length of service criterion appears to be extremely low' (Rubenstein 2006b: 26). Furthermore, length of service need not mean length of continuous service, it is about how long a person has been 'working for him in total', and pay and benefits can be based on service in a particular grade. Crucially it is for the employer to decide which definition to use to calculate length of service – total time in employment or length of time working for him doing work he reasonably considers to be at or above a particular level.

Liability and defence against liability

These provisions (reg 25) are in the same terms as other strands of discrimination law (see Part 1 of this chapter).

Enforcement

The enforcement process for employment complaints comprises the normal elements. The ***time limit*** for an employment tribunal complaint is within three months of the alleged incident, with the tribunal having discretion to hear 'out of time' complaints where it is 'just and equitable' to do so (reg 42). The complainant should make out a *prima facie* case (reg 37). To assist in this, s/he may use the ***questionnaire process*** (Sch 3). The ***burden of proof*** (reg 37) is that approved by the Court of Appeal (in *Igen Ltd* v *Wong* [2005] ICR 931) (see Exhibit 5.2). The ***remedies*** as with other areas of discrimination law are a declaration: an award of compensation payable to the complainant; and a recommendation.

Victimisation

The regulations (reg 4) provide parallel provisions on victimisation to those in sex discrimination law (see Part 1). The protection against victimisation does not apply if 'the allegation, evidence or information was false and not made [or given] in good faith' (reg 4(2)).

Conclusion

Whether, the nature of age discrimination will mean increased litigation as compared with other areas remains to be seen. One view is that the legislation has the potential to bring about major changes in workplace culture (Equal Opportunities Review 2006: 17) This is an argument based on the absence of an upper limit on compensation in these cases, so that employers have an incentive to effect substantial changes in employment policies and practices. However, this would apply equally to other discrimination grounds; and despite this, the gap between formal policy and practice remains wide in many organisations (Hoque and Noon 2004). Also, other than in a few well-publicised instances, the majority of race and sex discrimination cases rarely provide large compensations for those affected and arguably most employers are aware of this (see Chapter 4). Evidence from the USA also suggests that the main beneficiaries of such legislation have been men in professional and management positions. Early indications from employment tribunal cases following the introduction of the age regulations suggests professional workers have been particularly quick to see the opportunities presented by the legislation (Hornstein 2001; Sargeant 2006b).

Exercises

5.1 **Whose rights are paramount?** Bearing in mind the issues raised in the Ladele case (Exhibit 5.17) and the reactions of various groups to the employment tribunals' decision, think of a situation in your own organisation where there may be a clash of rights.

What approach would you advise your employer to adopt, in the light of the EAT's decision, to ensure that you are compliant with the law and also able to deal with the relevant management and employment relations issues?

5.2 Three young cable-layers from Bradford who were friends were sent to Warwick, a predominantly white town, to lay TV cables for a Manchester-based company. Ninja, Toffo and Parksy were white, Asian and African-Caribbean respectively. On arrival they were told they were 'too scruffy for our customers' by a senior manager. When they returned to their van to load up their gear, Ninja was taken aside by the manager. He was offered work and told that there was no problem with him – 'it's the other two'. He added, 'you know what I mean'. Ninja refused and returned to Bradford with his colleagues. Toffo commented that 'the guys who sacked me and Parksy were sly. They thought they'd not be found out because Ninja would have the same racist views as them.'

What infringement of discrimination has occurred and what remedies are available?

5.3 Mrs Hill was an accounts assistant / secretary for an agricultural contractor. All employees at the depot – apart from her and the female cleaner – were invited to a 'gentlemen's evening'. When a customer asked the depot manager, Mr Parker, why they were not taking Mrs Hill out, he said that the event was 'gentlemen only' to thank the lads for their hard work. He suggested that the customer took Mrs Hill out if he wanted to.

Mrs Hill felt dispirited and no longer part of the team. She told her line manager that she was thinking of resigning. When Mr Parker heard of this, he told her she was overreacting. He falsely told her that Mr Webster (who had started work the day before the event) had not been invited. Mr Parker said that had she been his wife he would not have wanted her to go. He told her that she ought to go home as it was time to make her husband's tea. Mrs Hill resigned shortly afterwards.

What are the relevant legal issues? What do you think the outcome of an employment tribunal complaint would be? What are your reasons?

5.4 You are an HR officer and your organisation is expanding and is advertising supervisory posts. The section manager says that the person specification must include 'commitment' to the organisation. He says that this means having worked for the company on a full-time basis for a number of years; and being prepared to work long hours as required and sometimes at short notice.

You have been asked to advise on this specification. Do you anticipate that there will be any implications under discrimination law?

5.5 Sarah, a young woman, was verbally offered employment at a small packaging company. When she mentioned, in passing, that she occasionally experienced panic attacks, the company did not formally write to her confirming the offer of employment. When she queried the situation on the phone she was told that she was 'not suitable' and was not being offered the job.

Does she have any rights under discrimination law to complain? What would be her remedies?

5.6 Lou, one of the marketing executives of a pharmaceutical company, was recently diagnosed as having multiple sclerosis. There are no obvious symptoms at the present time. He is working full-time and is able to drive and carry out his normal day-to-day work responsibilities. He told his manager in confidence about his medical situation and said that he would notify him if any problems arise as regard his fitness to carry out particular duties. An opportunity for promotion has just arisen. Lou decided that he would like to apply for the post. It would involve more opportunities to work in the office and possibly, on an occasional basis at home. He was not shortlisted for interview. He was told by his manager 'we didn't think it was worth interviewing you in the circumstances. We are looking for a long-term appointment'.

Does he have any rights under discrimination law to complain? What would be his remedies?

5.7 A budget airline, in a highly pressured and competitive market was advertising for a senior manager to be in charge of airline regulation. The rather buccaneering chief executive said that he wanted someone that was young and dynamic and to be available to undertake considerable travel to ensure that the best interests of the company were attended to. 'I know the sort of person I don't want!' he told his HR manager. 'For a start, I don't want someone who will be wanting flexible working hours and time off. They must show considerable commitment.'

What pitfalls in terms of discrimination law might arise? What advice should the HR manager give as far as the advertisement, the person specification and the selection process is concerned?

5.8 Fatima, who has permission to work in Britain, spent the first eighteen years of her life in Iraq. She is now 30 years old. She has applied for a position as a receptionist in a large medical practice in a multi-ethnic city. The advertisement stated that applicants must have GCSE in English and Maths as a minimum qualification. You are the practice manager and, in the sifting process, a doctor who is the senior partner tells you that she should not be considered for an interview because she has no GCSE qualifications.

What advice would you give him/her?

5.9 You work as the HR adviser to a small charity that promotes cultural and artistic activities among the Chinese community in a large northern city. You are to appoint a fund-raiser and administrator who is to liaise with community groups and individual artists and promote its objectives. You have been told by the chair of the management board that you must appoint someone of Chinese ethnic origin and preferably who was born in Britain.

What advice would you give about the law?

5.10 Afzal is qualified as an electrician; and has reasonable skills as a general handyman. Responding to an advertisement in a local paper, he calls into the offices of a Christian local charity which is looking for such a person to work in their various social welfare centres (for single parents, for drug users and for elderly people). The office manager says that they were specific in the advertisement that the postholder must be a Christian to fit in with the ethos of the various centres. Afzal replies that he is Muslim.

What advice would you give him about his rights under discrimination law?

Feedback on these exercises is provided in the Appendix to this textbook.

References and useful websites

ACAS (2006) *Age and the Workplace: Putting the Employment Equality (Age) Regulations 2006 into Practice*. London: ACAS.

Bourn, C. and Whitmore, J. (1993) *Race and Sex Discrimination* (2nd ed). London: Sweet and Maxwell.

Davies, J. (2005) 'The Employment Equality (Age) Regulations: Sweeping Reform or Stop-Gap Measure'. Paper presented at Industrial Law Society Conference, Oxford, 9–11 September.

Deakin, S. and Morris, G. (2005) *Labour Law*. Oxford: Hart.

Department of Trade and Industry (2005) *Coming of Age: a Consultation Paper*. London: DTI (www.berr.gov.uk).

Duncan, C., Loretto, W. and White, P. (2007) 'Ageism in the workplace: implications of UK anti-discrimination law', *Personnel Review.*

Equal Opportunities Review (2006) 'Equal value update 2006', *Equal Opportunities Review*, No. 153.

Ewing, K., Collins, H. and McColgan, A. (2006) *Labour Law: Texts and Materials*. Oxford: Hart.

Fredman, S. (1997) *Women and the Law*. Oxford: Oxford University Press.

Fredman, S. (2003) 'The Age of Equality', in Fredman, S. and Spencer, S. (eds) *Age as an Equality Issue*. Oxford, Hart.

Fredman, S. (2004) 'European developments – marginalising equal pay laws', *Industrial Law Journal*, Vol. 33: 3.

Hornstein, Z. (ed.) (2001) *Outlawing Age Discrimination: Foreign Lessons, UK Choices*. York: Joseph Rowntree Foundation.

Hoque, K. and Noon, M. (2004) 'Equal opportunities policy and practice in Britain: evaluating the "empty shell" hypothesis', *Work, Employment & Society*, Vol. 18(3): 481–506.

Johnstone, S. (2008) 'Round-up of recent decisions', *Equal Opportunities Review*, No. 181: 31.

Kersley, B., Alpin, C., Forth, J. *et al.* (2006) *Inside the Workplace: Findings of the 2004 Workplace Employment Relations Survey*. London: Routledge.

Local Government Employers (2006) *Unblocking the Route to Equal Pay in Local Government*. London: Local Government Employers.

Local Government Employers (2008) *Equal Pay: Case Law Developments*. London: Local Government Employers.

MacNicol, J. (2006) *Age Discrimination: An Historical and Contemporary Analysis*. Cambridge: Cambridge University Press.

McColgan, A. (1997) *Just Wages for Women*. Oxford: Oxford University Press.

McColgan, A. (2005) *Discrimination Law*. Oxford: Hart.

Monaghan, K. (2007) *Equality Law*. Oxford: Oxford University Press.

O'Cinneide, C. (2007) Industrial Law Society Lecture, paper downloaded from (www.industriallawsociety.org.uk/papers).

Redmond, M. (1986) 'Women and minorities', in Lewis, R. (ed.) *Labour Law in Britain*. Oxford: Blackwell.

Rubenstein, M. (2006a) 'Age Regulations 2006, Part 1: key general principles', *Equal Opportunities Review*, No. 152, May: 15–21.

Rubenstein, M. (2006b) 'Age Regulations 2006, Part 2: discrimination in employment', *Equal Opportunities Review*, No. 153 June: 20–27.

Rubenstein, M. (2008a) 'Highlights of key cases', *Equal Opportunities Review*, 179, August.

Rubenstein, M. (2008b) 'In the courts: highlights of key cases', *Equal Opportunities Review*, No. 181.

Sargeant, M. (2006a) 'The Employment Equality (Age) Regulations 2006: a legitimisation of age discrimination in employment', *Industrial Law Journal*, Vol. 35(3): 209–27.

Sargeant, M. (2006b) *Age Discrimination in Employment*. Aldershot, Gower.

Useful websites

Advisory, Conciliation and Arbitration Service **www.acas.org.uk**

Department for Business Enterprise and Regulatory Reform **www.berr.gov.uk**

e-reward **www.e-reward.co.uk**

Industrial Law Society **www.industriallawsociety.org.uk**

Employment Tribunals Service **www.employmenttribunals.gov.uk**

Visit **www.mylawchamber.co.uk/willey** to access multiple choice questions, case flashcards and exercises to test yourself on this chapter.

mylawchamber

6 Implementing equality in the workplace

Learning objectives

- To understand the strategic business perspective necessary for implementing equal opportunities
- To consider the implications of specific ***key*** provisions of legislation and of case law for human resource management policy and practice
- Have sufficient understanding of the relevant issues to provide initial advice on steps to be taken

Structure of the chapter

- *Introduction*: employer liability; the business case; social justice; statutory codes of practice
- *Human resource strategy*: establishing a strategic approach; evidence of strategy; and the incidence of equal opportunities policies
- *Specific aspects of the employment relationship*: recruitment and selection; contract of employment; pay and other terms and conditions; working time issues; training and development; promotion; dress and appearance; dismissal; post-employment issues

Introduction

There are three fundamental reasons for employers to consider effective implementation of equal opportunities policies: legal standards and duties; the 'business case'; and social justice (i.e. a moral commitment to fair treatment).

Legal standards

- *Employer liability*. This issue has been outlined previously (Chapter 5). All strands of discrimination law make clear the employer's strict and vicarious liability for discrimination 'in the course of employment'. This phrase is widely construed within its everyday meaning. Liability covers applications for employment, employment and certain post-employment circumstances.
- *Defence against liability*. The employer's potential defence is that he took 'such steps as are reasonably practicable' to deal with discrimination. These 'steps' are essentially policies, procedures and practices that can be adopted by the employer. The implementation of these is the main focus of this chapter. Guidance is provided by various statutory **codes of practice** (see Exhibit 6.1).

Business case

In human resource management, 'managing diversity' is about effective resourcing – accessing staff with the best kills and competences whatever their personal characteristics. It also concerns using the skills and capabilities of ***all*** staff; and so ensuring effective and, as appropriate, profitable links with other parts of a business. In product design and provision, knowledge of the diverse spectrum of customer needs can help businesses meet demands. In marketing, a diverse workforce can help establish effective sales relationships with customers. In public relations, a diverse organisation can achieve a positive reputation and credibility within the wider society. So, it is argued, diversity management and equal opportunities make 'business sense'.

Social justice

The CIPD (2008) comments that 'arguably, the social justice and business case arguments for diversity are complementary because unless people are treated fairly at work they will feel less than fully committed and will therefore under-perform'. The Institute defines the social justice argument in these terms: it is 'based on the belief that everyone should have a right to equal access to employment and when employed should have equal pay and equal access to training and development, as well as being free of any direct or indirect discrimination and harassment or bullying'. This view of the social purpose of discrimination law is clearly reflected in the social policies of the European Union; and in the provisions of the European Convention on Human Rights and Fundamental Freedoms 1950.

Exhibit 6.1 Statutory codes of practice

- Code of practice (1985): *sex discrimination in employment* (Equal Opportunities Commission);
- Code of practice (2002): *the duty to promote racial equality* (Commission for Racial Equality);
- Code of practice (2003): *equal pay* (Equal Opportunities Commission);
- Code of practice (2004): *employment and occupation* (Disability Rights Commission);
- Code of practice (2005): *racial equality in employment* (Commission for Racial Equality);
- Code of practice (2007): *gender equality duty* (Equal Opportunities Commission);
- Guidance (2006) *on matters to be taken into account in determining questions in relation to the definition of disability* (Secretary of State for Work and Pensions).

Status in law. These codes and the guidance are laid before Parliament. They do not impose any legal obligations in themselves. However, they can be used in legal proceedings (e.g. an employment tribunal complaint) where a court or tribunal must take account of any part of the appropriate code that might be relevant to a question arising in those proceedings.

Since 2007, the **Equalities and Human Rights Commission** has taken over the work of the three original equality commissions. These statutory codes and the guidance, however, remain extant and continue to be used in legal proceedings.

Human resource strategy

The view that employers should have a more strategic approach to managing diversity has gained hold in management circles, particularly since the mid-1990s. Unfortunately, as research evidence suggests (see below), 'strategy' still tends to be more part of management rhetoric rather than reality. In fact, effective diversity management should be integral to both an organisation's human resource strategy and its corporate strategy. There are two principal 'drivers' of this 'joined up' approach: the 'business case' mentioned above which is applicable for private, public and voluntary organisations; and the statutory duty on public sector organisations to promote equal opportunities in all their functions.

Establishing a strategic approach

To be effective in promoting equal opportunities all organisations need to undertake a circular process involving:

- diagnosis of the existing situation;
- the setting of objectives, planning of action to be taken, and the implementation of policies;
- monitoring and review, and so returning to further diagnosis.

Diagnosis

This requires, for example, collection of data of the existing workforce profile; the identification of any barriers to equal opportunities (e.g. in promotion to higher grades); evidence of complaints of unfair treatment and lessons that may be learned from them. Fundamental to diagnosis is critical examination of organisational culture and whether there is evidence of institutional discrimination in any functions.

Objective, planning and implementation

The debate about the concepts 'equal opportunities' and 'managing diversity' (see Chapter 4) drew attention to a view that equal opportunities policies are frequently marginal to wider organisational objectives and that diversity management, at least theoretically, has a more integrative approach. Consequently, objective setting and planning requires answers to several questions:

- Is the scope of the equal opportunities policy to be restricted to areas of unfair discrimination prohibited by law or is it to be extended?
- Which barriers to equal opportunities, both internal and external, are to be given priority for eradication?
- Are targets for 'positive action' to be set? Would these be compliant with legislation? (See Chapters 4 and 5.)
- How can the commitment of managers be ensured? (Research evidence indicates potential and real tension between the 'hard' day-to-day operational business needs of managers and what is perceived to be the 'soft' HRM issue of equal opportunities.)
- How can the workforce be engaged in policy formulation, implementation and review? This may require **consultation** arrangements and, as appropriate, engagement with union equality representatives.
- What resource allocation is necessary to make the policy effective?

Monitoring and review

This is an essential step in this circular process. Data acquired can inform further diagnosis about the degree to which equal opportunities objectives have been achieved. Evidence of systematic monitoring shows that it is patchy. When asked, in the Workplace Employment Relations Survey 2004, about the monitoring of gender, ethnicity, disability and age issues, less than a quarter of respondents said that they undertook it. 'Larger workplaces, public sector workplaces and workplaces with a recognised union were more likely to carry out monitoring and reviewing activities' (Kersley *et al.* 2006). The Industrial Relations Services study also found that only a quarter of their sample had conducted audits into employment (IRS 2006).

Looking at specific HR practices, it has been reported that a fifth of workplaces monitored and reviewed procedures relating to recruitment and selection in respect of gender and ethnicity but only 10 per cent did so in relation to promotions, and even fewer did so in respect of relative pay (5 per cent for ethnicity and 7 per cent for gender). Findings that cast 'some doubt on the effectiveness of organisational equality policies given that promotion and pay-setting processes can be infused with discriminatory bias' (Walsh 2007: 307).

It appears that effective monitoring will remain a matter for employers rather than for further statutory intervention given the views of the *Discrimination Law Review* and the silence of government in the White Paper, *Framework for a Fairer Future – the Equality Bill* (see Chapter 4).

Equal opportunities policies

One important formal way of co-ordinating these practical steps is to formulate an equal opportunities policy. The 2004 Workplace Employment Relations Survey (WERS) (Kersley *et al.* 2006) recorded that 73 per cent of workplaces (having 10 or more **employees**) had such a formal policy – in contrast to 64 per cent in the 1998 survey. They were much more common in larger workplaces (with over 100 employees) where the incidence was 96 per cent. The question inevitably asked is whether such policies remain 'on the shelf' or are practical documents guiding and informing practice in the organisation. Research does suggest that many equality initiatives can be superficial gestures containing little of any substance, little more than 'an empty shell' (Hoque and Noon 2004).

A related issue is the scope of equal opportunities policies. They should be revised to cover all grounds of discrimination. However, there can sometimes be quite significant gaps – even where the 'grounds' for discriminatory treatment are set out in **statute law**. For example, the CIPD (2008) has recorded that 'although the vast majority of employers surveyed have a formal diversity policy, only one in three employers has an explicit policy on managing religious beliefs in the workplace. The proportion of employers surveyed with an explicit policy is far higher in the public sector (55 per cent) than in the voluntary sector (31 per cent), private sector services (30 per cent) and, especially, manufacturing and production, where fewer than one in five employers (17 per cent) have a policy'. Given that there may be contentious employment relations issues about religious observance, time off and dress codes, this incidence is surprisingly low.

Evidence of a strategic approach

Research evidence suggests that a strategic approach to managing diversity is still ill-formed. A survey, commissioned by the Chartered Institute for Personnel and Development (2007a: 19), of staff responsible for diversity issues in private, public and voluntary sector organisations found that 'the state of the nation in managing diversity reflects a more cosmetic than deep-rooted success'. Two principal factors contributed to this situation: the limitations of corporate strategy, and the focus on legal compliance.

Limitations of corporate strategy

The researchers identified the concept of 'sophistication' of management approaches to diversity management. 'To be sophisticated in managing diversity, organisations need to meet their legal duties in addition to integrating diversity into all their operational activities' (ibid.: 19). They reported on variations between sectors: only 7 per cent of private sector organisations achieve the highest levels of sophistication compared to 34 per cent of public sector organisations and 18 per cent of voluntary organisations. Larger organisations are more likely to be 'sophisticated' (ibid.: 5).

Other findings indicated the weakness of a strategic and integrative approach and only limited achievement of diversity objectives at operational level:

- *Strategic objectives.* Seventy per cent of the diversity professionals admitted they do not set objectives to progress diversity. This 'suggests that it's not a strategic issue in their organisations . . . diversity management activities in the majority of UK organisations remain at a very superficial level' (ibid.: 10).
- *Senior management.* Only 16 per cent 'strongly agreed' that senior management encouraged diversity. As far as 'ownership of diversity', this decreased by job level from senior to middle management to junior management (ibid.: 13–14).
- *Operational management.* Whilst 54 per cent had undertaken manager diversity training, only 16 per cent of respondents included diversity objectives as part of managers' performance assessment (ibid.: 11).

- *Centrality of diversity.* Eighty-two per cent of respondents said that diversity is 'central to HR'. This contrasted with, among other findings, its stated centrality to customers and consumers (at 51 per cent); to marketing and sales (35 per cent); to manufacturing and production (18 per cent); and suppliers (23 per cent). On this last point, the researchers comment that this is 'despite the duty in the public sector to promote the importance of equality regarding race' (ibid.: 18).

Legal compliance

Law is the major influence on organisations in progressing diversity – indicated by 32 per cent of respondents as being the most important of the top five 'drivers of equality'. Only 16 per cent indicated the 'business case', and 13 per cent said 'because it is morally right' (ibid.: 7). When asked which skills were needed most in diversity management jobs, 'understanding the law' was the highest – cited by 79 per cent of respondents. It was closely followed, at 71 per cent, by 'understanding HR procedures', and 'understanding the business environment' was reported by 54 per cent. The researchers comment that 'this is because most activities focus on compliance with legislation and people management and development issues rather than operational activities and the production of goods and services' (ibid.: 16).

A long way to go?

The research evidence presented above indicates that steps are being taken towards more strategic approaches – particularly in large organisations. But these are quite fitful requiring stronger business links and greater management commitment.

Recruitment and selection

There are likely to be particular concerns in all strands of discrimination law about employers' actions in this area. Discrimination (in the meaning of making choices) is at the heart of this HR process. These choices must be made against objective criteria and not reflecting stereotyping and assumptions about particular categories of people. In considering recruitment policy, employers should, first of all, identify the existing profile of their workforce. This can reveal historic patterns of discrimination and evidence of occupational segregation. An employer may need to decide whether any positive action is necessary. Part of this process could involve establishing targets for the recruitment of particular groups under-represented in the workforce. Furthermore, consideration may need to be given to the appropriateness of 'genuine occupational qualifications/requirements'.

The practices and policies in recruitment and selection include: advertising, recruitment targets, criteria for person specifications, job descriptions, and the interview process.

Advertising and recruitment targets

- ***The language of advertisements.*** This must be non-discriminatory. This involves careful phrasing of language to avoid discriminatory connotations. For example, the Sex Discrimination Act states that it is unlawful to 'publish or cause to be published' a discriminatory advertisement – either internally or externally (SDA, s 38(1)). The advert must not 'indicate or be reasonably understood as indicating an intention by a person to do any act which is or might be unlawful' (s 38(1)). Job descriptions with 'a sexual connotation' (e.g. stewardess, salesgirl, postman or fireman) 'shall be taken to indicate an intention to discriminate, unless the advertisement contains an indication to the contrary' (s 38(3)).

- ***GOQs/GORs.*** If either *genuine occupation qualifications* or *requirements* are relevant to the post then this should be stated on the advertisement indicating the specific legislation. The employer should be prepared to defend this requirement.
- ***Location of advertising.*** This may be important as part of a positive action policy to encourage under-represented groups, or to assist with recruiting on the basis of a GOQ/GOR. Particular publications (e.g. those whose readership is predominantly female or of a particular age or ethnic group) and geographic locations may be chosen. Location and media used may be potentially discriminatory. Some media may lead to certain age groups being under-represented (e.g. e-recruitment). The issue of graduate recruitment has also attracted particular attention, in that a focus on recent *young* graduates may well discourage recent *older* graduates.
- ***Information on jobs.*** For disabled applicants, it is likely to be a reasonable adjustment for an employer to provide, on request, information in a format that is accessible to them – taking account of the use of IT and their requirements.
- ***'Word of mouth' recruitment.*** Given the cost of the recruitment process, this can, for certain jobs, be an attractive informal and cost-effective option for employers. Furthermore, managers may feel more certain of the reliability and acceptability of potential employees recommended through this process. However, it could be indirect discrimination which covers 'practices' – whether formal or informal. It can reinforce the existing profile of a work group – particularly on the grounds of gender or ethnicity and possibly age. For example, it is suggested that, probably because of the nature of informal social networks, men are more likely to mention job vacancies to other men; women to other women; members of ethnic groups to people of their group.
- ***Targets.*** If these are indicated, they should be part of a clearly articulated positive action policy. It is important that the distinction between 'targets' and 'quotas' is understood. Use of the latter would be evidence of unlawful positive discrimination.

Criteria of person specifications and job descriptions

- ***Relevant criteria for the post.*** There are a number of criteria that traditionally have arisen in person specifications: qualifications; skills and competences; experience in relevant work; health; age; suitability; and GOQ/GOR. Discrimination law requires scrutiny of the relevance of these specifications to determine whether they can be objectively justified under the appropriate legislation.
- ***Relevant or marginal?*** In relation to disabled people the inclusion of unnecessary or marginal requirements in a job description or person specification can be discriminatory. Also, stating that a certain personal, medical or health-related characteristic is essential or desirable can lead to discrimination if the characteristic is not necessary for the performance of the job.
- ***Suitability.*** This can be a complicating factor. It concerns the extent to which 'acceptability criteria' are used as opposed to 'suitability criteria'. The latter should more readily be objectively defensible (e.g. by reference to relevant experience, skills, and appropriate qualifications). 'Acceptability criteria' may be more difficult to defend as non-discriminatory. They are associated with 'fit' – and this involves, among other factors, an applicant's compatibility with the organisation's culture (which itself may be discriminatory).

- *Qualifications.* In terms of race discrimination, criteria like English language qualifications or degrees of proficiency should be justified by the nature of the job. Recognition of overseas qualifications should be accepted after appropriate investigations to establish equivalence.
- *Skills and competences.* There is research evidence to show that two particular groups experience discrimination in relation to this criterion: older **workers** and disabled workers. Part of the discriminatory practice is the unwillingness to invest in training and development of these workers. Also, there can be stereotyping in regard to perceived capability – as opposed to actual capability.
- *Experience.* This is linked with skills and competences and the issue is the extent to which it is relevant and can be justified; and where the experience was gained: was it, for example, overseas; or in the voluntary sector; or in caring for dependant children or adults? An imaginative approach to examining experience gained – both in a formal workplace environment or otherwise – might avoid unfair discrimination.
- *Age.* Under the age discrimination regulations, employers are encouraged to move away from an emphasis on the more potentially litigious factors such as length of service and age. In research it has been found that almost half of establishments surveyed had a maximum recruitment age; and 60 per cent used some form of selection criteria that were likely to be problematic in light of the regulations but could be acceptable if they were objectively justified (Metcalf and Meadows 2006). The CIPD (2001) found that 10 per cent of those between the ages of 45 and 54 years claimed they had been rejected from a job in the previous 12 months because they had been too old (despite *little hard evidence* of discrimination). However, recent work has shown employers have responded to the Regulations with considerable evidence of changed recruitment practices particularly with respect to job/person specifications (McNair and Flynn 2007).
- *Genuine occupational qualifications/requirements.* These are in all strands of discrimination law and must be defended. In most strands the specifications are reasonably specific. However, in relation to religion or belief, for example, there may be the potential for discrimination in relation to the rather vague provision relating the maintenance of a religious 'ethos'. It has been noted, particularly in faith-based schools and also in some religious charities that virtually all posts can be reserved for those of a particular religion – even if the post does not require promoting a particular religious view (Stinson 2008).

Application forms

Two principal issues arise here: the format of the application form, and the information requested.

Format

The standard formats usually require completion in writing or on-line. Standard on-line forms may be discriminatory by excluding people with no access to or facility to use computers. The Disability Code of Practice (2004) provides guidance on accessible formats that an applicant might request from an employer. This would be a reasonable adjustment.

Information

There are likely to be three categories of information that an organisation will request:

1 Information providing an indication of an applicant's competence and likely suitability for a particular job. Primarily, this will cover experience, skills and qualification (if

appropriate). This information will be used in selection for interview and as an aid in the interview process.

2 Information for monitoring purposes: to identify applicants and prospective employees in terms of age, gender, ethnicity, etc. to help assess the effectiveness of an equal opportunities policy.
3 Information about successful applicants in relation to, for example, health, criminal convictions, etc.

Good practice and legal compliance suggests that the first two categories of information can be requested of applicants – but separated before sifting – and the monitoring information not available to interviewers. The third category would be requested with a conditional offer of employment.

Selection process

This process involves several stages: the short-listing of job applications; the interview process; possible administration of tests; and decisions to offer employment or to reject applicants. It is a process where various assumptions and stereotyping might arise on, for example, the abilities of a disabled person; the capabilities of an older worker; the experience of a younger worker; the likelihood of a young woman becoming pregnant. Decisions to accept or reject in this process need to be capable of justification.

Interview process

The CIPD commented (in a voluntary code on equal opportunities) that the interview 'as a predictive device is an extremely fallible instrument, highly susceptible to interviewer bias and stereotyped perceptions'. So, care must be taken to avoid questions which could be construed as discriminatory; to make offers of employment that can have been determined by structured decision-making; and to record the interview process. This implies proper training for managers who interview.

For particular groups of applicants there can be special issues which may arise in the interview process. For example, it has been commented by disability campaigners that there are four main barriers to the employment of disabled people:

- *Lack of credibility*. Potential employees have to convince recruiters of their skills and abilities to complete the tasks required. This can be difficult for a disabled person if s/he is rejected prior to interview, or if the focus of the selection process is on what they cannot do rather than on identifying potential.
- *Anxiety over taking risks*. The risk perceived by employers often relates to the cost of adaptations; the belief that the disabled person will have greater sick absence; the likelihood that s/he is accident prone; the perceived attitudes, including possible hostility, of existing staff.
- *Lack of imagination*. Many employers may not know the ways in which technology can be used to enable full and active participation in work. Furthermore, there may be a lack of creative thinking about the way work can be organised, its location and its working hours.
- *Lack of appropriate access*. The majority of disabled people have no additional access requirements and need no additional equipment. Generally, the individual's impairment will have little or no bearing upon the capacity to realise their employment potential.

Another example concerns certain ethnic minority applicants. Two interpersonal factors can enter the selection process, particularly at the interview stage: body language and cross-cultural communication. Clearly, there can be difficulties in both verbal and non-verbal communication between people of different ethnic origin. First, an applicant might have limited proficiency in the English language and may not fully understand the subtleties of expression, technical language, jargon and idioms. Secondly, 'ethnocentrism' on the part of the interviewer can involve the interpretation of another person's behaviour/communications in terms of the interviewer's own cultural framework. Frequently, this is done unconsciously. Thirdly, an applicant may have pronunciation difficulties.

Testing

Discrimination law does not prohibit the use of tests. However, the primary consideration is that they should be relevant to the requirements of the specific job. Recruiters need to be alert to the facts that selection tests could be discriminatory on racial grounds if they contain irrelevant questions or exercises which may be less familiar to ethnic minority applicants than to indigenous applicants. They may also be discriminatory on the grounds of disability if reasonable adjustments are not made to assist an applicant to complete the test (Disability Code, 2004, para 7.25).

Training of recruiters

Staff responsible for short-listing, interviewing and selecting candidates should be:

- clearly informed of the selection criteria and the need for their consistent application;
- given guidance or training on the effects which generalised assumptions and prejudices about all grounds for discrimination can have on selection decisions;
- made aware of the possible misunderstandings that can occur in interviews between persons of different cultural backgrounds.

Contract of employment

Statute law moulds the terms of **contracts** in various ways (see Chapter 2): by setting minimum standards; by imposing certain entitlements; and be requiring compliance with discrimination law. *Both* contracts and the terms of collective agreements (which are incorporated into contracts of employment) are subject to discrimination law. The detailed terms of contracts are considered below. As a preliminary, it is important to remember three important legal issues:

- The Equal Pay Act 1970 (s 1(1)) expressively imposes an 'equality clause' into all contracts of employment in relation to discrimination between men and women.
- Discriminatory terms are unlawful and, in contracts and collective agreements they are 'void' (SDA 1986, s 6; RRA 1976, s 72; DDA, Schedule 3A; Religion or Belief Regulations 2003, Sch 4; Sexual Orientation Regulations, Sch 4; Age Discrimination Regulations 2006, Sch 5).
- Contractual terms which are indirectly discriminatory need to be objectively justified.

Pay and other terms and conditions

Discrimination law affects pay and contractual terms in two principal ways: in respect of indirect discrimination under the various strands; and by explicit prohibitions against discriminatory pay and conditions. Indirect discrimination provisions mean that, for example, remuneration may be challenged on racial grounds if the factual circumstances support such a complaint. The direct discrimination provisions arise in respect of gender and age. Both issues are separate in the legislation (SDA 1975; Age Regulations 2006). However, in practice, given entrenched patterns of discrimination they are frequently interlinked.

Gender

The Equal Pay Act 1970 (s 1) statutorily imposes an equality clause affecting all terms of a contract of employment. Compliance with this is required in comparing the terms of women and men – unless a genuine material factor or difference is relevant.

Furthermore, employers need to be alert to other gender issues. First, is the possibility of structural discrimination if the workforce is segregated on the basis of gender. Secondly, the possibility of indirect sex discrimination in respect of, for example, full-time employment requirement, working time requirements, work location and mobility requirements.

Age and length of service

A key issue is the use of this as a basis in systems of remuneration. Research (in a national sample of over 2,000 establishments) shows that around a third of establishments had incremental pay scales; a third had some form of merit based pay; and over 40 per cent used length of service as a basis for reward; with a further 41 per cent using years of relevant experience (Metcalf and Meadows 2006: 9).

Although this criterion is generally ruled to be unlawful after its use for five years, it is possible in certain specified circumstances in the legislation to use it, with justification, for rewarding experience, loyalty and motivation. Work on reward systems undertaken six months after the introduction of the Regulations suggests that significant changes have been made to pay and holiday entitlements in many larger employers, notably the Civil Service and some larger private sector firms.

Disability

Particular issues arise in respect of pay and disability discrimination. The Disability Code of Practice states: 'terms and conditions of service should not discriminate against a disabled person. The employer should consider whether any reasonable adjustments need to be made to the terms and conditions which would otherwise apply' (para 8.4). It continues: 'Where the terms and conditions of employment include an element of performance-related pay, the employer must ensure that the way such pay arrangements operate does not discriminate against a disabled employee. If, on the ground of disability, an employee is denied the opportunity to receive performance-related pay, this is likely to be direct discrimination. Even if less favourable treatment of an employee in relation to performance-related pay is not directly discriminatory, it will amount to disability-related discrimination unless the employer can show that it is justified' (para 8.5). Additionally, 'if an employee has a disability which adversely affects his rate of output, the effect may be that he receives less under a performance-related scheme than other employees. The employer must consider whether there are reasonable adjustments which would overcome this substantial disadvantage' (para 8.6).

Working time issues

The issue of working time features significantly in most strands of discrimination law for various specific reasons. Whatever the impact of discrimination law, the provisions of the Working Time Regulations 1998 also apply.

Sex discrimination

The law relating to indirect sex discrimination enables a worker to claim that a 'provision, criterion or practice' causes them a disadvantage. The employer can justify objectively the particular employment practice. Applications to work some form of 'non-standard' employment is one of the issues that has been considered in case law and is likely to be a continuing issue for employers. Dependency is the principal reason for such requests – whether it is to care for dependant children of whatever age or dependant adults. It is clear from the evidence that this issue will have a growing impact on employment relations in the foreseeable future (see Chapters 4 and 11).

The ability to make a request under sex discrimination law is additional to the right to request flexible working (Flexible Working (Eligibility, Complaints and Remedies) Regulations 2002). Under discrimination law, for example, a woman returning from maternity leave, having previously worked on a full-time 'standard' contract, may request any of various forms of flexible working (e.g. part-time work; compressed working week; term-time working; job share). The employer faced with such an application will need to consider very carefully the operational and employment relations implications of agreeing. Objective justification would involve showing that rejection of the application and the need to maintain the requirement to work standard hours was 'a proportionate means to achieve a legitimate aim' (see Chapter 5).

This sex discrimination route has a number of advantages for employees:

- *Qualification.* None is required under sex discrimination law in respect of employment status or length of service. The Flexible Working Regulations require that the complainant is an 'employee' and must have a minimum of 26 weeks' continuous service. There are various other relevant conditions relating to the application process (see Chapter 11).
- *Reason for refusal.* Under sex discrimination law, this needs to be set out in some detail as an objective justification. Under the Flexible Working Regulations refusal can be from a specified list of 'business reasons'.
- *Repeated requests.* Sex discrimination law does not limit the possibility of a repeated application. There is a restriction under the Flexible Working Regulations.
- *Remedies.* Under the Flexible Working Regulations, there is no penalty for refusal for rejection of the application, merely compensation for the employer's failing in his duty to consider the application. Under discrimination law, a complainant subject to unjustified indirect sex discrimination can receive compensation which is uncapped; an award for injury to feelings; a declaration of his/her rights; and a recommendation to the employer.

Disability discrimination

An employer is under a duty to make a reasonable adjustment requested by a disabled person. **Flexibility** of working time might be an appropriate arrangement. The issue as to its 'reasonableness' is likely to depend on operational factors. The employer needs to be confident that any refusal is based on a sound business case.

Religion or belief discrimination

This area of discrimination law raises a number of potentially contentious issues for the management of those with religious belief. Essentially, there are two sets of issues: the accommodation of religious observance during the working week; and arrangements for special leave of absence (see also Chapter 5) (see Table 6.1).

- *Religious observance.* There are two aspects to this: observance during the working day; and time off for a religion's Sabbath or holy days. There is no obligation for employers to provide time for religious observance. The critical issue under discrimination law is whether or not there is indirect discrimination against people of a particular religious view and whether or not the employer can justify their policy objectively. ACAS (2008) (**www.acas.org.uk**) provides detailed advice as to how employers might deal with requests. In essence, there is a need to balance the operational needs of the organisation, the interests of the religious adherents and the interests of other employees. Consultation and planning of the steps to be taken are particularly important. It may be that the use of rest breaks and the adoption of flexible working arrangements during the working week could accommodate some of the religious observance (for example, prayers for Muslims; observance of the Jewish Sabbath).
- *Special leave of absence.* If this is requested for religious reasons, it might be accommodated under the annual holiday scheme or under standard policies for special unpaid leave of absence.

There is, clearly, a need to balance the operational needs of the organisation, the interests of the religious adherents and the interests of other employees. It is essential for good employment relations that there is perceived consistency and fair treatment in respect of rest breaks, time off and special leave of absence. This can be achieved by the adoption of a policy which would cover all these issues for all staff whether or not they are adherents of particular religions or have no religious belief. Workplace tensions can arise if it is perceived that religious groups are privileged. CIPD research (2007b) found that although the vast majority of employers

Table 6.1 Religious belief and working time

	Manufacturing (%)	*Voluntary sector* (%)	*Private services* (%)	*Public services sector* (%)	*All* (%)
All special time off	69	82	74	81	76
Time off in addition to annual leave	21	20	20	13	14
Provide time/facilities in workplace for religious observance	38	69	56	78	61

Source: Based on CIPD (2007b) *Labour Market Outlook*, Winter. Survey of 1369 employers (www.cipd.co.uk).

surveyed had a formal diversity policy, only one in three had an explicit policy on managing religious beliefs. This varied between sectors: public sector (55 per cent); voluntary sector (31 per cent); private sector services (30 per cent); and manufacturing (17 per cent).

Age discrimination

This legislation is, in part, designed to encourage older workers to be economically active after retirement. However, there are very weak tools in the legislation to promote such participation in work. The retiree can make a request to continue work and procedural arrangements must be complied with. However, no reason for refusal needs to be provided by the employer.

In managing the retirement process in a proactive way, employers should not only consider the procedural steps they need to undertake (see Chapter 5). They should, also, consider each application against an audit as to whether particular individuals meet their continuing skill needs. Additionally, serious consideration needs to be given to working time issues. The whole gamut of flexible working should be open to consideration: e.g. part-time work; compressed working week; job share; short fixed-term contracts.

Training and development

Employees

Training and development is a significant issue in terms of entry into employment; the achievement of performance standards in work; equipping people to gain promotion and enhance career progression; and being transferred to new responsibilities. Restricted access to training opportunities can be evidence of either direct or indirect discrimination. For example, women may have limited access where they are either in part-time employment or some other form of flexible working; or where they have been on maternity leave. Workers from certain ethnic groups may have limited opportunities to develop proficiency in the English language and in communication skills.

Under age discrimination law, training is identified as one where the justification defence could be relied upon by employers. This would probably apply to training of older workers where the employer might argue that the costs of so doing will be unable to be recouped over the remainder of an individual's working life. Otherwise, in general, a refusal to train workers of a certain age is unlikely to be justified. It is significant that in their study of employers McNair and Flynn (2007) found that most claimed they did not discriminate on age grounds when selecting for training but did not actively encourage it among older workers.

Management development

To support the promotion of equal opportunities and to avoid potentially expensive litigation, managers and supervisors may benefit from various types of training:

- Familiarisation with the purposes of equal opportunities and with associated organisational policies.
- Appropriate training in interview skills, human resource management and grievance and disciplinary procedures handling.
- Awareness training (e.g. relating to women, ethnic and religious groups, disabled workers).

Possible policy measures

- As part of positive action, it is permissible to encourage under-represented groups into training schemes to develop particular skills for development and promotional opportunities.
- Provide mentoring schemes (particularly for women, ethnic groups and disabled workers). These schemes can assist in acclimatisation into work; the provision of advice and a 'sounding board' on career progression; and suitable training underpinning promotional opportunities. Recent evidence (Silcox 2007) of women in the medical profession shows that a lack of role models and mentoring is, among other factors, one of the barriers to promotion – particularly to surgery where participation rates are low.
- 'Keeping in touch days': these became available in 2007 under maternity leave provisions. They enable return-to-work training and support to be undertaken (see Chapter 11).
- As far as disabled workers are concerned, there may need to be reasonable adjustments to ensure access to and participation in appropriate training is facilitated (Code of Practice 2004, paras 8.7 and 8.8). Special mention is made of the importance of induction training as being clearly structured and supportive.

Promotion

The issue of promotion raises similar issues to those discussed above in relation to selection. Employers need to identify competencies and promotion criteria need to be transparent and defensible. Training and development is integral to this issue. Testing whether or not there is indirect discrimination in any of the promotion criteria or availability of training opportunities is a critical part of any defence.

Harassment

This important dimension of discrimination law is considered in detail in Chapter 7.

Dress and appearance

This potentially contentious issue can arise under most strands of discrimination law. Issues of human rights may also be invoked by complainants in relation to freedom of expression. Employers in most organisations have views and policies about standards of dress, uniforms and safety protection measures. Sometimes there is a clear rationale for these policies; sometimes they are introduced on a whim to enhance corporate image. Dress and appearance requirements are governed generally by the implied contractual term of mutual trust and confidence. So, a requirement to wear clothing that was demeaning to an employee may be argued to be a **repudiatory breach of contract**.

A more likely legal **remedy** would be under discrimination law. The test in any particular instance will be whether the proposed dress code is directly or indirectly discriminatory under any strand of discrimination law; and whether, if it is indirectly discriminatory, it may be justifiable.

Particular issues (some of which are still not decisively resolved) are:

- ***Gender.*** An early case in this area involved a complaint that a woman shopworker was, unlike a male shopworker, not allowed to wear trousers (*Schmidt* v *Austicks Bookshops Ltd* [1977] IRLR 360, EAT). In a later case about hair length (*Smith* v *Safeway plc* [1996] IRLR 457) the Court of Appeal approved the earlier approach. It found no sex discrimination. Codes, it stated, were not discriminatory provided they merely imposed general rules that enforced a conventional or smart appearance (with relevant changes to account for the difference in sex). The question to be asked, taken overall, was whether there was less favourable treatment in a particular case.
- ***Gender reassignment.*** This is a process and different arrangements are likely to be adopted at different stages. Guidance suggests that when the person is undergoing gender reassignment, dress code is one of the issues that the employer should consult about. At some point s/he will wish to attend work in the clothes appropriate for the gender to which he/she is reassigning. When the process of reassignment is completed, then, the appropriate clothes for employees of that gender will be worn.
- ***Disability.*** This can, in some cases, be a problematic issue. Certain appearances (like tattoos) are explicitly excluded from the Disability Discrimination Act. However, facial disfigurements caused by a medical condition are expressly protected from discrimination.
- ***Race.*** Issues of dress code *may* also relate to those on religious grounds. Essentially, it is likely to be an issue of indirect discrimination on racial grounds. The employer would need to justify the provision, criterion or practice as a proportionate means to a legitimate aim.
- ***Religious grounds.*** Two issues arise under discrimination law: religious dress requirements; and the wearing of religious accessories (see Table 6.2). Direct and indirect discrimination might be alleged. The intricacy of the problems that may face employers is seen in the *Azmi* case (see Exhibit 5.18 in Chapter 5). The issues that need to be considered will vary in importance from workplace to workplace. However, those issues that may be considered in drafting a dress code are: communication standards in the course of employment; potential health and safety hazards. In respect to the latter issue it is important to note that, under the Employment Act 1989 (s 11), Sikhs are exempt from any statutory requirement to wear safety helmets on construction sites.

Although not an employment case, the High Court, in ruling on whether a school could prohibit a Sikh female pupil from wearing a Kara, set out a view which ***may*** be adopted elsewhere (*R* (*On Application of Watkins-Singh*) v *Governing Body of Aberdare Girls High School* (2008), HC). The underlying principle set out by Mr Justice Silber is that: 'The need for equality of respect for those with different ethnic or religious beliefs . . . may mean taking reasonable steps to alter the "usual" rules so as to enable different situations to be dealt with differently'. Rubenstein (2008: 24) comments that 'this is akin to setting a standard of "reasonable accommodation" for manifestations of religious belief'.

As far as religious accessories are concerned, health and safety is a possible concern. The views of other staff, if they are prominent, are a consideration. The symbolism of an accessory is also a factor. Employers need also to remember that accessories do not have to be about religious belief but about political and non-religious belief. So, badges and other insignia would be covered (including those of campaigning groups, mainstream political parties and extremist groups). Any policy would need to set standards of acceptability so as not potentially to inflame workplace relations.

Table 6.2 Religious belief and dress

	Manufacturing (%)	*Voluntary sector* (%)	*Private services* (%)	*Public services sector* (%)	*All* (%)
Allow staff to meet religious dress code	51	64	61	74	65
Impose restrictions on religious dress	26	9	14	13	13

Source: Based on CIPD (2007b) *Labour Market Outlook*, Winter. Survey of 1369 employers (www.cipd.co.uk).

Dismissal

There are standard issues of fair treatment in relation to dismissal (see Chapter 8). The ACAS Code of Practice (2009) is an essential starting point for establishing the framework of **natural justice** and reasonable conduct by the employer. There are however, three other specific issues to mention explicitly: dismissal on the grounds of pregnancy, redundancy, and retirement.

Pregnancy

Dismissal on these grounds continues to be a clear example of unlawful and unfair treatment – contrary to the provisions of sex discrimination law. Employers should consider their policies in this area in a co-ordinated way taking account of the wider framework of law relating to parenting and dependency care. Dismissal of a pregnant worker must be unconnected with her pregnancy.

Redundancy

The main practical concern in this area has focused on the criteria used for redundancy. The need is to ensure that the criteria used are based on some kind of clear objectively defensible rationale. In the past it was common for firms to use some form of 'last in first out' (**LIFO**) or 'first in first out' (FIFO) policy that would be difficult to defend on objective grounds, and has the potential to disadvantage some age groups at the expense of others. The legislation points to a need for employers to consider redundancy selection very carefully – as well as the use of clear criteria and selection methods use would also be expected to be made of appraisal records where these are deemed appropriate (see Chapter 3).

Retirement

Under the regulations, retirement now becomes a sixth potentially unfair reason for dismissal. Retirement requires not only the avoidance of discrimination but also the need for employers to introduce new practices. This is crucially about procedure and formalisation and the research undertaken since the introduction of the regulations indicates significant variation in this area (McNair and Flynn 2007).

Employers have expressed some concern over how to refuse requests to continue working beyond retirement age, something that has often looked like an evasion of managerial responsibility. Furthermore, although appraisal appears well established in many organisations, there has been a reluctance to use this as an aid to retirement decisions. Overall, research suggests employers are anxious about the implementation of new provisions on retirement, and the management challenges this might present. Significantly, recent tribunal evidence suggests that one common problem area is the failure to follow the process regarding retirement and issues over how organisations treat people in relation to selection and promotion.

Post employment

All strands of discrimination law extend protection to issues arising after the employment relationship has ended. The complaint about discriminatory treatment must arise out of the former employment relationship and be closely connected with it. The principal issue is likely to be the provision of references which may show evidence of discriminatory behaviour (see Chapter 2). It is, of course, possible that there could be discriminatory treatment in respect of contractual terms at the end of the relationship and, for example, in the enforcement of a restrictive covenant.

References

Advisory, Conciliation and Arbitration Service (2008) *Religion or Belief in the Workplace: a Guide for Employers and Employees*. London: ACAS (www.acas.org.uk).

Advisory, Conciliation and Arbitration Service (2009) *Code of Practice on Disciplinary and Grievance Procedures*. London: ACAS (www.acas.org.uk).

Chartered Institute for Personnel and Development (2001) *Age Discrimination at Work*. London: Chartered Institute for Personnel and Development (www.cipd.co.uk).

Chartered Institute for Personnel and Development (2007a) *Diversity in Business: a Focus for Progress*. London: Chartered Institute for Personnel and Development (www.cipd.co.uk).

Chartered Institute for Personnel and Development (2007b) *Labour Market Outlook*, Winter 2007. London: Chartered Institute for Personnel and Development (www.cipd.co.uk).

Chartered Institute for Personnel and Development (2008) *Diversity: an Overview*. London: Chartered Institute for Personnel and Development (www.cipd.co.uk).

Hoque, K. and Noon, M., (2004) 'Equal opportunities policy and practice in Britain: evaluating the "empty shell" hypothesis', *Work, Employment & Society*, Vol. 18(3): 481–506.

Industrial Relations Services (2006) 'From recruitment to retirement', *IRS Employment Review*, 857: 49–56.

Kersley, B. *et al*. (2006) *Inside the Workplace: Findings from the 2004 Workplace Employment Relations Survey*. London: Routledge.

McNair, S. and Flynn, M. (2005) *The Age Dimension of Employment Practices: Employer Case Studies*, Employment Relations Research Series, No. 42. London: Department of Trade and Industry (www.berr.gov.uk/employment).

McNair, S. and Flynn, M. (2007) *Employer Responses to an Ageing Workforce: A Qualitative Study*, Research Report, No. 455. London: Department of Work and Pensions.

Metcalf, H. and Meadows, P. (2006) *Survey of Employers' Policies, Practices and Preferences Relating to Age*, Employment Relations Research Series, No. 49. London: Department of Trade and Industry (www.berr.gov.uk/employment).

Rubenstein, M. (2008) 'In the courts: highlights of key cases', *Equal Opportunities Review*, No. 181.

Silcox, S. (2007) 'Women in medicine: barriers to progression in professional roles', *Equal Opportunities Review*, December.

Stinson, H. (2008) 'Discrimination against the non-religious', *Equal Opportunities Review*, April.

Walsh, J., (2007) 'Equality and diversity in British workplaces: the 2004 Workplace Employment Relations Survey', *Industrial Relations Journal*, Vol. 38(4), 303–19.

7 Harassment and bullying at work

Learning objectives

To understand:

- The definitions of 'harassment' and 'bullying'
- The ways in which harassment and bullying can be tackled through the law of contract and through discrimination law
- The liability of employers and their possible defence against liability
- The range of policy measures and practices that employers might initiate
- The remedies available to working people
- The relevance of the Protection from Harassment Act 1997

Structure of the chapter

- *Introduction*: Why the growing concern about harassment?; How are 'harassment' and 'bullying' defined?; contextual issues; the incidence of harassment and bullying; the characteristics of workplaces; the recipient's response
- *Legal framework*: contract of employment – employer's duties; employee's duties; discrimination law – background, two-step test, harassment provisions under strands of discrimination law, direct discrimination, particular terminology, combined claims, post employment, employer vicarious liability and defence, burden of proof, victimisation; redress and remedies; Protection from Harassment Act 1997
- *Conclusion*
- *Exercises*

Introduction

Workplace bullying and harassment historically, have been a feature of working life. Examples can be seen in, for example, initiation ceremonies for young new workers, in insulting nicknames, in the 'casting couch' in the film industry, and in the intimidation of 'out groups'. Only since the mid-1980s have harassment and bullying in the workplace gradually become high-profile issues of public concern. Generally, they are considered in the context of equal opportunities and anti-discrimination strategies like the management of diversity. The range of behaviour that constitutes harassment covers a very wide spectrum and, in its extreme form, can be a crime.

Why the growing concern about harassment?

This has arisen for several reasons:

- The standards of acceptable behaviour in society at large are changing and being articulated more clearly.
- Some employers are beginning to recognise the disruptive and economically damaging consequences of tensions, conflict and victimisation within the workplace. Additionally, corporate image can be adversely affected; and the management costs of dealing with complaints can be considerable.
- Coherent workplace responses to harassment (through the adoption of policies and procedures) have been encouraged by the original equality commissions and their successor, the Equality and Human Rights Commission.
- More effective legal standards and remedies have become available since the original harassment case in 1986 which proscribed sexual harassment as 'direct sex discrimination' (*Porcelli* v *Strathclyde Regional Council* [1986] IRLR 134).
- The removal of the ceiling on compensation in discrimination cases has concentrated the minds of many employers.
- Finally, there are wider social concerns, expressed through **criminal law**, about the manifestations of sexual, racial and religious harassment and violence – what are described as 'hate crimes'.

How 'harassment' and 'bullying' are defined

These terms are interrelated and, in practice, it can be difficult to distinguish between them. However, some distinction can be attempted. Harassment ***may*** be initiated for purely interpersonal reasons. However, it is normally for 'social' reasons – relating to the victim's membership or association with a social group. So, it concerns gender, sexuality, ethnic origin, disability, age, etc. The intention of the perpetrator is to demean and/or intimidate the victim because of a particular characteristic. It is in this context that 'harassment' arises as a provision in discrimination law.

Bullying, on the other hand, is more likely to be interpersonal and can often be related to the exercise of power. It may not necessarily relate to, for example, sex or race. Where it exists, it is likely, but not exclusively, to be part of a management style that is aggressive, overbearing, heavily critical, demeaning and intimidatory. It is invariably an abuse of power.

When the details of the law are discussed below, the characteristics of harassment and bullying are outlined. Essentially, it concerns behaviour; this is unwanted by the recipient because it is unreasonable or offensive; and the unacceptable conduct may be a single act or a pattern of behaviour.

Contextual issues

There are two principal issues which are interrelated:

- ***Power relations.*** 'Power' is a key element in social relationships. Historically, in many organisations, it has been exercised by men and, in Britain, by white men. Consequently, there is likely to be both a sex and race bias in organisations and the way that they function (see Chapter 4). In a society that is increasingly redefining the role and contribution of women and also acknowledging its multi-ethnic character, tensions will inevitably exist. It is said by many commentators that all harassment is about power. Collier (1995: 27) argues from her experience as a counsellor and from a study of the literature that the common assumption that sexual harassment is about flirtation or about sex is incorrect. It too is about power.
- ***Cultural factors.*** '**Culture**' refers to the values, norms or standards and the traditions that exist in society at large or within particular groups in society. There are two issues that arise under this heading: tensions between groups; and the discriminatory character of an organisation's culture (see Exercise 7.1).
  - *Tensions.* These will exist when one group in society has different expectations and values from another. One example is the conflict of views about homosexuality with some Christian and Muslim religious organisations strongly critical about statutory rights relating to sexuality. The issue that inevitably arises in debate is whether one view can 'trump' another. Current debate suggests that a distinction can be drawn between those characteristics which are 'innate' (i.e. which an individual is unable to alter like sex, sexuality, race, age or disability) and those which are 'acquired' like religious belief or other philosophical belief. So, one argument is that discrimination / harassment against individuals on the grounds of sexuality 'trumps' religious views.
  - *Discriminatory culture.* The pervasiveness of the cultural values of a particular group within an organisation can be illustrated best by the following comment from a police officer: 'Sexual harassment has always been an acceptable part of the police environment and any worthwhile female officer can deal with it herself and give as good as she gets' (Home Office 1993). This statement reflects a number of things:
    - that the standards of 'acceptable' behaviour are determined by male police officers;
    - that this behaviour is in-built – it has 'always' been so;
    - that the appropriate response is not to challenge the norms (the standards of behaviour) but to accept and 'give as good as you get';
    - there is no acknowledgement that the recipient might be upset and need support.

This use of harassment is 'political'. It is designed to preserve male 'power' and 'male reality'. Collier (1995: 36) goes further by characterising it is as heterosexual male reality, adding that this 'compulsory heterosexuality' is the foundation for much homophobia and hostility to transsexuals.

The police service is not alone in having these characteristics. There is evidence in many, if not most organisations. The issue is how to tackle them. If the cultural fabric of an organisation is not free from discrimination, then, attempts to deal with individual allegations of harassment will be very difficult.

To help tackle these two contextual issues, there are two sets of suggested measures. First, there needs to be a diagnosis within employing organisations of institutional discrimination – whether on the grounds of sex or race or otherwise. This, necessarily, should result in effective policies on equal opportunities and managing diversity. This should, in theory, create a more conducive context within which harassment and bullying can be minimised. Secondly, for public authorities, there are the statutory duties to promote equal opportunities (see Chapters 4, 5 and 6).

The incidence of harassment and bullying

This is difficult to quantify with any accuracy because of an individual's perceptions, his/her interpretation of behaviour, the issue of subjectivity, and the occasional denial by the recipient that they are being treated in such a way.

A systematic analysis of fair treatment at work was undertaken, among 3,936 **employees**, by researchers for the former Department of Trade and Industry (Grainger and Fitzner 2007) (see **www.berr.gov.uk**). Bullying and harassment was defined to respondents as 'any unwelcome behaviour that creates a hostile working environment'. These employees were then asked whether in the past two years they had experienced such treatment. The incidence of bullying in British workplaces 'appears to be quite high – almost one million employees (3.8 per cent of all employees)' (ibid.: 13). Having said that, the authors acknowledge that their results show 'a lower incidence of unfair treatment at work than most other British or UK employee surveys have found' (ibid.: 16).

Disaggregating the overall statistic, the following results were reported:

- ***Women*** (4.9 per cent) were 'significantly more likely to have been bullied than men' (2.8 per cent).
- ***Foreign-born employees*** were more 'at risk of being bullied' than UK-born (5 per cent compared with 3.6 per cent).
- Among ***disabled employees or those with long-term illness***, the incidence was 10.6 per cent, and for disabled women, it was even higher at 14.4 per cent ('almost four times the national average').
- *Sectors*: the incidence was twice as high in the public sector as in the private sector (5.8 per cent compared with 2.7 per cent). It was noted that 'this is in part a compositional effect. The public sector hires a higher proportion of women and disabled employees than the private sector.'

The following results were also reported:

- *Perpetrators*: 'An employee's supervisor or manager was involved in two-thirds of bullying cases; and a work colleague in one-third'.
- *Duration*: 54 per cent of those who had been bullied said that it was still ongoing. Ongoing bullying was 'much more common for men' (74 per cent) than for women (45 per cent).
- *Advice*: 64 per cent of employees who had been bullied sought advice. ('However, one-quarter of black employees who had been bullied or harassed at work said that they had sought advice.')
- *Witnessing bullying*: 10.6 per cent of employees who worked with others said that they were aware of another person at their place of work being bullied or harassed in the last two years.
- *Reporting bullying of others*: those most likely to do this were employees with a disability or long-term illness; public sector employees; those employed in larger organisations; and trade union members.

Sexual harassment

The researchers specifically inquired about this issue (ibid.: 15). They defined sexual harassment to the respondents as 'any unwelcome sex or gender-related behaviour that creates a hostile working environment'; and asked whether in the last two years with your current employer the respondent had 'experienced sexual harassment at work'.

The results showed that 'relatively few' employees (0.9 per cent) had experienced it. Women (at 1.1 per cent) had a higher incidence than men (at 0.7 per cent). 'Nonetheless, 41 per cent of British employees who said that they had been sexually harassed were men'. Of employees who worked with others, 3.7 per cent said that they were aware of another person at their place of work who had experienced sexual harassment in the last two years (ibid.: 15).

The characteristics of workplaces

The social factors outlined earlier are reflected in any workplace. There will be a range of power relations. The culture of the organisation will reveal particular values, attitudes, norms and traditional practices. Groups and individuals can be marginalised and regarded as (part of) an 'out group' – i.e. those who do not 'fit' into the existing situation.

Essentially, there are three likely categories of perpetrators of harassment: managers/supervisors, individual fellow workers, and workgroups. These perpetrators, in their various ways, wish to preserve the existing situation. So, harassment may be used as a tool – as a means of preventing disruption to the status quo; or to discourage applications for promotion and breaking through 'the glass ceiling', and so, to make working life sufficiently uncomfortable for individuals to leave.

Evidence from various employment tribunal cases and from research indicates that harassment can be particularly fierce where a 'different' person breaks through into a workgroup. Some of the worst examples of sexual and racial harassment have occurred in traditionally white male-dominated employment: City of London financial institutions, the construction industry, the railways, the police service and the armed forces. In these circumstances, the few women or members of minority ethnic groups who are 'pioneers' have frequently been targeted. The nature of the harassment can and does cover the entire spectrum of unacceptable conduct (see Exercise 7.1 and Exhibit 7.3 for examples).

The recipient's response

For recipients, there are four possible consequences deriving from incidents of harassment and bullying:

1 *Action to tackle it.* In this situation the employee may obtain advice under a dignity at work procedure from a harassment adviser, from a union representative, or from the human resources department; and then possibly raise the issue formally with the employer as grievance.
2 *Deliberate submission by the individual.* This may occur when the individual decides rather than face the difficulties of making a complaint. The victim may isolate himself/herself from the harassment and bullying as far as practicable; or behave in ways that the perpetrator(s) wants. So, a person might be sufficiently discouraged from applying for training courses or may keep out of the way of the work group at lunch breaks or tolerate or even engage in sexist, racist or homophobic banter.
3 *Denial of its occurrence.* This is where (particularly in the early stages of a pattern of unacceptable conduct) the recipient does not explicitly accept that it is occurring and tries to ignore it.
4 *Escape.* This is the most likely outcome. The recipient is moved by the employer away from the perpetrator; or resigns. As an outcome this does not tackle the fundamental source of the problem.

Any of these consequences may be accompanied, variously, by symptoms of physical or mental illness and behaviour changes. Examples can include migraine, raised blood pressure, loss of appetite, inability to sleep, panic attacks, becoming withdrawn, depression and increased consumption of tobacco or alcohol.

Exercise 7.1 Harassment in the City

The workplace

Money brokers act as independent intermediaries between two financial institutions, usually banks, assisting them in buying or selling money products on the wholesale money market. This market is not located in any one place as participants communicate through a global network of telecommunications and computer links. A money broker acts like an auctioneer between the client and other market participants, communicating bid and offer prices at high speeds. Millions of pounds can be transacted in a matter of seconds.

The money brokers

The brokers in broking houses and banks, as in the money market generally, are predominantly white men. There are few female brokers (mostly in junior grades), and about one per cent is of non-white ethnic origin. (Overall, women are concentrated in non-management grades.) Brokers work in teams in extremely pressurised and cramped conditions with up to 50 people in one small area. When the market is busy, it is a frenzied, noisy environment with brokers shouting prices at each other and at clients. They work long hours (nine per day plus evening entertainment). They rarely sustain their career beyond 45 years of age. Where they do, they usually move into management but retire at 55 years.

The issue

This close team environment breeds familiarity, friendships and, because there are few women, a 'laddish' culture. Brokers both talk openly and joke about their latest sexual conquests and physical attributes. Cartoons and pornographic pictures are adapted to depict fellow staff and are circulated. Everyone has a nickname which can usually be related to their physique, religion, race or personality. Pin-ups of women, some nude, are displayed in the dealing rooms. Women, who work in the back-office area, commonly hear sexual remarks and innuendoes. The motivation for this behaviour is varied. It can be to have 'fun'. So, 'bad' language, playing pranks and jokes on colleagues are seen as part of everyday life.

Sometimes the pressure of the job leads to loss of tempers, to the use of foul and abusive language and to what could be perceived as crude behaviour among brokers – particularly when a deal goes wrong. (This is not intentionally offensive. If it is so, it is only meant to be short-lived and is soon forgiven.) On other occasions, the purpose is to vent anger at a subordinate or to teach them not to repeat mistakes and to 'toughen' junior staff to make them better brokers. Sometimes unruly behaviour can be triggered by a broker after a 'boozy' client lunch.

The situation is compounded by the fact that departmental managers are brokers promoted because of their broking expertise. They have had no management or discrimination awareness training. The overwhelming majority have not read the company's equal opportunities policy. So, if someone reacts badly, the usual view is that they cannot handle the pressure. Indeed, over 80 per cent of managers do not consider foul language, verbal abuse when tempers fray or exclusion from the group on the grounds of sex or race as forms of harassment. They are seen as typical of the working environment. Nevertheless, just over 40 per cent of managers have received complaints about harassment. The HR department has recorded seven complaints in the past five years. In only one case did the dismissal of a broker result. The company is concerned that someone may claim racial or sexual discrimination at an employment tribunal.

What steps would you recommend for working towards effective culture change?

The legal framework

The framework of law governing harassment and bullying encompasses both the law of contract and also discrimination law. In addition, the hybrid criminal and civil legislation, the Protection from Harassment Act 1997 can also be involved in tackling such issues.

The contract of employment

Employer's duties

Two implied contractual terms are important in respect of harassment and bullying: the **duty** of the employer to take reasonable care of the employee; and the mutual trust and confidence that the employer should ensure underpins the employment relationship. A breach of mutual trust and confidence will invariably be regarded as a **repudiatory breach of contract** and may result in the employee's resignation and possible claim of **constructive dismissal**. Breach of the duty of care may, depending on the circumstances, be regarded as such a breach. So, an employer receiving a grievance complaint relating to harassment or bullying must deal with the issue promptly and properly in accordance with the organisation's grievance and/or harassment procedures. There may also be concerns about the employee's health, safety and welfare.

Employee's duties

Employees are under an implied contractual duty to obey lawful and reasonable instructions; and to comply with the disciplinary rules set by their employer. In most organisations, it is likely that any form of bullying or harassment would be regarded as gross misconduct and could make the employee liable to instant dismissal. That dismissal must, of course comply with the requirements of the organisation's disciplinary and dismissal procedure and the guidance set out in the ACAS *Code of Practice on Disciplinary and Grievance Procedures* (2009).

Harassment and bullying outside of discrimination law

Under discrimination law, as outlined below, there are explicit free-standing rights protecting working people from harassment on various grounds. However, some harassment and bullying, as suggested earlier, may ***not*** be linked to grounds under discrimination law. It may be purely interpersonal and concerned with the exercise of power. In these circumstances, if the employer fails to deal effectively with the complaint about the unacceptable behaviour, the redress and remedies available to such a victim would only be those for a repudiatory breach of contract and not for breach of discrimination law.

If the victim of the unacceptable behaviour was to resign because of the employer's repudiation of the contract, then, s/he could only claim constructive dismissal if he or she had 12 months' continuous service with the employer and was also able to prove that s/he was an 'employee' in law. So, clearly, outside of the provisions of discrimination law, working people are vulnerable with limited redress. The remedies available to them would be those for unfair dismissal: a capped award of compensation. (The maximum set in February 2009 is £66,200. This amount is updated annually – see **www.berr.gov.uk**.) An order for re-instatement or re-engagement may be made if requested. These remedies contrast poorly with those available under discrimination law (see below).

Discrimination law

Background

Discrimination law has only tackled harassment in a piecemeal way. Indeed, it is only since 2005 that there has been a wide framework of free-standing prohibitions against harassment. A long campaign to have the issue treated seriously and effectively began, in the courts, with the case of *Porcelli* v *Strathclyde Regional Council* [1986] IRLR 134. The Sex Discrimination Act 1975 (at that time) contained no express prohibition against harassment. Ms Porcelli invoked the direct sex discrimination provisions (s 1) arguing that the harassment she experienced from her two male lab technician colleagues would not have been used against another man. She said that she, as a woman, was suffering 'less favourable treatment'. The Scottish Court of Session (the equivalent to the Court of Appeal in England and Wales) accepted this argument and, consequently, sexual harassment as an issue was encompassed by the direct sex discrimination provisions. Because of the way the courts implemented the common legal provisions of the Race Relations Act 1976, it was also accepted that racial harassment was 'less favourable treatment' and covered by its direct race discrimination provisions (s 1).

It was European Union policy and legislation which helped accelerate greater protections in the area. In 1991, a European Recommendation and a Code of Practice was published on the 'protection of the dignity of men and women at work'. Although this was not law it was to be taken into account by courts and tribunals in member states. National courts 'are bound to take Recommendations into consideration in order to decide disputes submitted to them, in particular where they clarify the interpretation of national provisions adopted in order to implement them or where they are designed to supplement community measures' (*Grimaldi* v *Fonds des Maladies Professionelles* [1990] IRLR 400 ECJ).

From 2000, new EU **directives** were enacted and gradually transposed into legislation in Britain. Consequently, there are now free-standing harassment prohibitions in the following Acts:

- Sex Discrimination Act 1975: this was amended by **regulations** in 1999 providing for protection relating to gender reassignment, and in 2008 to define sexual harassment and harassment related to sex;
- Race Relations Act 1976 (as amended);
- Disability Discrimination Act 1995 (as amended);
- Employment Equality (Sexual Orientation) Regulations 2003 (as amended);
- Employment Equality (Religion or Belief) Regulations 2003 (as amended);
- Employment Equality (Age) Regulations 2006.

The statutory provisions relating to harassment, across all these pieces of legislation, have broadly the same details. That in age discrimination legislation is used here as an illustration. This states that:

> (1) For the purposes of these Regulations, a person (A) subjects another person (B) to harassment where, on grounds of age, A engages in unwanted conduct which has the purpose or effect of –
> (a) violating B's dignity; or
> (b) creating an intimidating, hostile, degrading, humiliating or offensive environment for B.

(2) Conduct shall be regarded as having the effect specified in paragraph (1)(a) or (b) only if, having regard to all the circumstances, including in particular the perception of B, it should reasonably be considered as having that effect. (Employment Equality (Age) Regulations 2006, reg 6)

A two-step test

Essentially, there is a two-step test for determining whether or not an act or acts amount to harassment:

- An employment tribunal will consider the facts and make an *objective assessment* about whether the conduct experienced by the complainant is unreasonable and disadvantageous to him or her.
- The *subjective test* considers how the recipient felt about the conduct.

Harassment provisions under specific discrimination legislation

The specific grounds under each piece of legislation, prohibiting harassment, are summarised in Exhibits 7.1 and 7.2:

Exhibit 7.1 Harassment on grounds of sex and gender reassignment

Sex discrimination law outlaws harassment on three grounds:

1 where the perpetrator engages in unwanted conduct and creates a harassing environment that is ***'related to' the sex of the recipient*** (Sex Discrimination Act 1975 s 4A(1)(a));

2 where the perpetrator engages in 'unwanted verbal, non-verbal or physical conduct of ***a sexual nature***' (s 4A(1)(b));

3 where, on the grounds that a person intends to undergo, is undergoing or has undergone ***gender reassignment***, the perpetrator engages in unwanted conduct and creates a harassing environment (SDA 1975, s 4A(3)).

This legislation also defines as harassment the circumstances where the person, who is experiencing the unwanted conduct, is treated less favourably because either they rejected the unwanted conduct or submitted to it (SDA, s 4A(1)(c) and (3)(b)).

In all three cases, conduct shall be regarded as violating dignity or creating a harassing environment 'only if, having regard to all the circumstances', including in particular the perception of the victim, 'it should reasonably be considered as having that effect' (s 4A(2) and (4)).

The distinction between harassment 'related to sex' and harassment 'of a sexual nature'. This was enacted in 2008 (Sex Discrimination Act 1975 (Amendment) Regulations 2008). The distinction between these concepts has been described as follows:

- *'Related to sex'*. This would cover conduct that is associated with a woman's sex and it would be no defence to argue that men also were subject to similar comments relating to their sex. An example of such sex-related conduct, given by the government, is where male workers dislike a female colleague and decide to put equipment on a high shelf making it harder for her to reach. This could be sex-related harassment because women are, on average, shorter than men. Furthermore, a claim under this heading can relate to the treatment of a person other than the victim. So, a woman or a man may be offended by the constant humiliation of another colleague, arguing that this creates a degrading work environment. The 'observer' 'will have an independent cause of action regardless of whether (the) colleague brings a claim' (Rubenstein 2008).
- *Conduct of a 'sexual nature'*. This conduct concerns conduct such as obscene images, innuendoes and foul language as well as patterns of insulting and demeaning comments.

The other legislation on discrimination law has a similar provision to that in SDA, s 4A(2) and (4) on whether or not the behaviour should 'reasonably' be considered as being harassing. However, there is no provision relating to the 'less favourable treatment' of the victim because of his/her rejection or submission to harassment. The law is summarised in Exhibit 7.2.

Exhibit 7.2 Harassment under other strands of discrimination law

Race discrimination:

- Where 'on grounds of race or ethnic or national origins' a person's dignity is violated or a prohibited environment is created (Race Relations Act 1976, s 3A).

Disability discrimination:

- Where a person subjects a disabled person to harassment (as described in the earlier examples) 'for a reason which relates to the disabled person's disability' (Disability Discrimination Act 1995, s 3B).

There is an additional 'employment' provision. 'It is also unlawful for an employer, in relation to employment by him, to subject to harassment – (a) a disabled person whom he employs; or a disabled person who has applied to him for employment' (DDA, s 4(3)).

In relation to disability discrimination, it is important to note that the legislation defines a 'disabled person' in specific terms (DDA, s 1) (see Chapter 5).

Religion or belief:

- Where there is harassment (as defined above) 'on grounds of religion or belief' (Employment Equality (Religion or Belief) Regulations 2003, reg 5).

The initial legislation did not define a 'religion' or a 'belief'. The Equality Act 2006 amended the 2003 Regulations to protect people with a lack of religion or belief (see Chapter 5).

Sexual orientation:

- Where there is harassment (as defined earlier) 'on grounds of sexual orientation' (Employment Equality (Sexual Orientation) Regulations 2003, reg 5).

These regulations define 'sexual orientation' as 'sexual orientation towards persons of the same sex; persons of the opposite sex; or persons of the same sex and of the opposite sex' (reg 2 (1)).

Age: see above.

Direct discrimination

The discrimination law mentioned in this discussion has a provision on direct discrimination (i.e. 'less favourable treatment'). As mentioned earlier, this was the early legal route to providing some protection against harassment under sex discrimination law. This statutory provision can still be used to deal with harassment at work.

Perception

Discriminatory treatment may occur because a person is 'perceived' to have particular characteristics. This arises under the law on sexual orientation and religion or belief. The regulations do not explicitly prohibit this. However, the explanatory memorandum published with the legislation stated that people will be able to bring a claim even if the discrimination or harassment was based on, possibly incorrect, assumptions about a person's religion, belief or sexual orientation. They will not be required to disclose their religion, belief or sexual orientation. 'It will be sufficient that they have suffered a disadvantage because of the assumption made . . .' So, this would be evidence of less favourable treatment.

Particular terminology

There are several aspects of the language in the legislation that deserve further comment.

Unwanted conduct

This phrase introduces an element of subjectivity into the area. Harassing behaviour covers a very wide spectrum of conduct – ranging from an arm around a woman's shoulder to physical assault. So, for example, at the lower end of the spectrum, the behaviour might be judged acceptable by one woman but not by another. The issue of seriousness, then, arises. Clearly, there are many other forms of conduct which would be socially unacceptable and are likely to be crimes. Other forms of conduct may be 'shrugged off' with a riposte.

In this context, then, it is worth noting the provisions in all the legislation which draws attention to the issue of 'reasonableness'. For example, in the Sex Discrimination Act, it is stated that conduct shall be regarded as violating dignity or creating an unacceptable environment 'only if, having regard to all the circumstances', including 'in particular' the perception of the victim, 'it should reasonably be considered as having that effect' (s 4A(2) and (4)). Clearly, the facts and circumstances of each incident or pattern of incidents need to be examined and judgements made, in the end, by the employer as to 'reasonableness'.

Violating dignity and creating a harassing environment

These two aspects of the statutory provisions are likely to be intimately linked (see Exhibit 7.3). The 'violation of dignity' is, effectively, the 'personal' aspect of harassment law – in the sense that the conduct demeans the victim. It could be a single incident that is demeaning or it could be a pattern of behaviour that is directed at a particular individual. The 'environment' refers to patterns of behaviour that may well reflect an organisation's culture. If this is the case, then, more fundamental action needs to taken by the employer. Whatever the diagnosis, employers are liable for harassment in the course of employment and can only defend themselves if they can show that they took such steps as are reasonably practical to deal with it (see later section on defence against **liability**). These reasonable steps are likely to comprise dealing with grievances seriously and promptly, appropriate disciplinary action and, in the more entrenched cases, promoting equal opportunities programmes and effecting cultural change.

Combined claims

So far the discussion has outlined the two principal bodies of law involved in legal proceedings relating to harassment and bullying: contract law and discrimination law. It is important to remember that claims under the law of contract (for example, for repudiatory breach and constructive dismissal) and under both the direct discrimination and harassment provisions of discrimination law can and do co-exist in any single employment tribunal case. For an illustration of this see Exhibit 7.4.

Exhibit 7.3 Harassment at work

Raymondo Jones

Jones v *Tower Boot Co Ltd* [1997] IRLR 68

Raymondo Jones, whose mother was white and father was African-Caribbean, worked as a machine operative for one month until he resigned. During that time he was subjected to a number of incidents of racial harassment from work colleagues. One employee burnt his arm with a hot screwdriver; metal bolts were thrown at his head; his legs were whipped with a piece of welt; someone stuck a notice on his back bearing the words 'Chipmonks are go'. He was called names such as 'chimp', 'monkey' and 'baboon'.

Bernard Manning

Burton and Rhule v *de Vere Hotels* [1996] IRLR 596

Freda Burton and Sonia Rhule were employed as waitresses at a private Greater Manchester police social function. Both were Afro-Caribbean. They were subject to racial harassment during and after Manning's act. He made a number of very offensive racist and sexist remarks to the woman as they were clearing tables. They were very upset by the remarks, the consequential banter from the predominantly male gathering and sexual harassment by some guests. They brought claims of racial discrimination against their employer because of the racial harassment they had experienced.

On the question of liability, the EAT held that the employer was liable for the harassment committed by the third party (Manning). It could have protected the women. It failed to instruct managers to watch the situation and withdraw the waitresses when it became unpleasant. It was established that the employer had control over the circumstances in which the harassment happened. The women were successful in their complaint.

Mrs Fowles

Summarised from case no. 1701754/01

Mrs Fowles worked for a transport company for three years. During that time she was subject to sexual harassment and general bullying from the company directors. Both directors made offensive comments, sexual innuendo and sexual contact. The managing director was the main instigator of the behaviour. When she was attempting to contact her union representative about the harassment, she was dismissed.

The employment tribunal made awards against the two directors personally and no additional award against the company. The tribunal observed that, in reality, the directors were in control. She received loss of earnings and awards for injury to feelings of £5,000 and £2,500 from each of the directors.

Post employment

Discrimination law now provides an important additional protection. Under the heading of 'relationships which have come to an end' it prohibits post-employment discrimination. For example, the Employment Equality (Sexual Orientation) Regulations 2003 state that 'where a relevant relationship has come to an end . . . it is unlawful for A (a) to discriminate against B by subjecting him to a **detriment**; or (b) to subject B to harassment, where the discrimination or harassment arises out of and is closely connected to that relationship' (reg 21). The provision covers an act of discrimination or harassment which relates to a relationship which came to an end before these regulations came into force. There are similar provisions in the Employment Equality (Religion or Belief) Regulations 2003, reg 21; Sex Discrimination Act 1975 s 35C; Race Relations Act 1976 s 27A; Disability Discrimination Act 1995, s 16A; Employment Equality (Age) Regulations 2006, reg 24.

Exhibit 7.4 Offensive graffiti

Martin v *Parkham Foods Ltd* ET case 1800241/06

Chris Martin, an openly gay man, worked for Parkham Foods as a Quality Assurance Assistant. In May 2005, offensive graffiti appeared in the men's toilets with his name by it.

His verbal complaint was ignored. He wrote to the employer (11 May 2005) complaining about the graffiti and also about offensive homophobic remarks made to him the previous day in the presence of supervisors who had laughed. He indicated that he was reluctant to attend work because of this treatment.

At a meeting (24 May) he explained that he felt humiliated and undermined in his managerial role. Although his name had been painted over, the drawing remained (as it did for several months). The employer reacted by displaying the company's equal opportunities policy prominently and instructing managers to be vigilant about vandalism and graffiti.

In October 2005, Chris Martin wished to change his name because of his imminent civil partnership. His new name appeared by the graffiti. He sent the employer several letters setting out his grievances. His name – but not the graffiti – was removed. Notices were placed in the toilets warning against graffiti. At a meeting (7 November) the employer reported that it was not possible to identify the culprit.

On 11 November, Chris Martin wrote to request a copy of the employer's equal opportunities policy and also to ask what was happening to his grievance. According to the grievance policy this should have been investigated within five days.

Mrs Smith (who received the letter) regarded his conduct as aggressive and told him to stop harassing her. She recorded in a memo her belief that his complaints were not related to sexual orientation but were a 'transparent attempt to exploit his sexual orientation' as evidence by his repeated (but factually incorrect) assertion that he was 'the only gay in the company'.

On 15 November, Chris Martin raised a further grievance about an incident with a colleague. That day the company suspended him on full pay in accordance with its stress policy. On 17 November he submitted a sick note for two weeks' absence. The next day he was removed from full pay and told he would receive only statutory sick pay.

He resigned in early December regarding his suspension as 'the last straw'. He complained to an employment tribunal in Leeds.

Tribunal findings:

- That pornographic, offensive and homophobic graffiti remained on the toilet wall for months even after Chris Martin had complained about it.
- The employer failed to investigate his grievances properly.
- Action that the employer took did not address the underlying issue of homophobia but focused instead on the issue of graffiti.
- The employer could have taken firmer action to show how seriously they regarded homophobia and that perpetrators would be at risk of dismissal.
- There was evidence that the employer 'viewed the problem as being that of Mr Martin who needed personal counselling to cope with the "situation" he was in'.
- The employer wrongly treated his 'distress and despair' as aggressive behaviour and wrongly suspended him under the stress policy.

The tribunal upheld claims of direct discrimination and harassment on the grounds of sexual orientation. It also upheld the claim for unfair constructive dismissal.

A claim for victimisation on grounds of sexual orientation was dismissed.

Employer liability

Employer liability under discrimination law is outlined in Chapter 5. Essentially, the same provisions are reflected in all the pieces of legislation which provide for protection against harassment. For example under the Race Relations Act 1976 (s 32(1)), the employer is liable in the following terms:

> Anything done by a person in the course of his employment shall be treated for the purposes of this Act . . . as done by his employer as well as him, whether or not it was done with his employer's knowledge or approval.

Effectively, the employer is liable for his behaviour towards staff in the course of employment. He is also liable for the conduct of all staff, supervisors and managers if their behaviour is harassing. This is known as employers' 'vicarious liability'. The Court of Appeal has ruled in *Jones* v *Tower Boot Co Ltd* [1997] IRLR 68 (see Exhibit 7.3) that the phrase 'in the course of employment' should be interpreted broadly in line with 'the natural meaning of these everyday words'. In another case, involving sexual harassment, the concept of 'employment' was extended to cover conduct that took place off the employer's premises after work (*Chief Constable of Lincolnshire Police* v *Stubbs* [1999] IRLR 81, EAT). Clearly, employers need to consider that their liability extends to cover a wide range of work-related circumstances both formal and informal: training courses and conferences, travel to work, travelling in the course of work, parties, etc.

A problem relating to employer liability arose in a case concerning employment tribunal jurisdiction to hear a complaint. Sexual harassment was alleged to have taken place when the complainant was working in both London and in Paris. The EAT ruled that an employment tribunal had no jurisdiction to consider the complaints relating to Paris. However, evidence relating to alleged discrimination and harassment in Paris may be allowed by the tribunal as background material tending to support or weaken either party's case as to what occurred in London (*Tradition Securities and Futures SA* v *X and Another* [2008] EAT/0202/08).

Third party harassment

In the course of employment, employees may have dealings with contractors, suppliers and customers. An employer is liable for the treatment of employees during these contacts. Management are responsible for raising the issue with the 'third party' (see Manning case in Exhibit 7.3).

It is important to note that in 2008, under amendments to sex discrimination law on harassment, there was a change in relation to employer liability for harassment by third parties but only in relation to harassment 'related to' sex or 'sexual harassment' (and not in relation to other strands of discrimination law). It is unlawful for an employer to subject a woman to harassment in the following circumstances:

- where a third party subjects the woman to harassment in the course of her employment; and
- the employer has failed to take such steps as would have been reasonably practicable to prevent the third party from doing so (SDA 1975, as amended, s 6(2B)).

'Third party' means a person other than the employer or a person employed by the employer (for whom, of course, vicarious liability remains). The legislation also states that 'it is immaterial whether the third party is the same or a different person on each occasion' (s 6(2D)).

This provision does not apply 'unless the employer knows that the woman has been subject to harassment in the course of her employment on at least two other occasions by a third party' (s 6(2C)). It is possible that a woman might be placed in a situation where it is known that a particular individual (client or customer) subjects women to harassment. The particular employee will have to comply with the legal requirements set out above and it is argued that the employer 'can escape liability on the technicality that (she) herself has not been subject to harassment by a third party on two other occasions' (Rubenstein 2008).

This 'third party' harassment is also subject to the test of reasonableness. So, as indicated earlier, conduct shall be regarded as violating dignity or creating a harassing environment 'only if, having regard to all the circumstances', including in particular the perception of the victim, 'it should reasonably be considered as having that effect' (s 4A(2) and (4)).

Employer's defence against liability

This is stated this way (as an illustration of the provisions under all discrimination law): 'in proceedings brought under this Act against any person in respect of an act alleged to have been done by an employee of his it shall be a defence for that person to prove that he took such steps as were reasonably practicable to prevent the employee from doing that act, or from doing in the course of his employment acts of that description' (RRA 1976, s 32(3)).

The defence argument can cover a range of employment relations practices and policies. The existence of an equal opportunities policy and a 'dignity at work' policy could be evidence that the employer views harassment as unacceptable. Training of managers and briefing staff about acceptable standards of conduct would be further supportive evidence. Finally, the existence and prompt and effective use of grievance and harassment procedures and of the disciplinary procedures in particular cases could assist the defence. It could show the employer's commitment to taking appropriate action to deal with complaints and allegations

It is also important to note that individuals can be personally liable for harassment (see Mrs Fowles in Exhibit 7.3).

Burden of proof

As in discrimination law generally, the **burden of proof**, at employment tribunal, in harassment cases requires the complainant to make a ***prima facie*** case. The respondent employer, then, has to explain the behaviour and show whether or not there was discrimination / harassment. In *Igen Ltd* v *Wong* [2005] ICR 931, the Court of Appeal set out a 13-point guidance note on how the burden of proof rules in discrimination cases should be applied (see Chapter 5).

In disability discrimination law, the burden of proof, first of all, requires the employee to show that they are disabled within the meaning of the Disability Discrimination Act 1995 – unless the employer has conceded the point. Then, before the burden of proof shifts to the employer, the complainant must show that they have been disadvantaged or suffered a detriment.

Victimisation

Under all discrimination law, there is protection against the **victimisation** of complainants. Victimisation is a form of direct discrimination. The protection extends to those alleging harassment under discrimination law at an employment tribunal; or those providing evidence or information in relation to a harassment allegation. There are three elements to be satisfied:

- The victim must have made a complaint or given evidence in such a case or alleged that discrimination/harassment has taken place.
- It must be demonstrated that the treatment of the victim is less favourable than that of someone who has not been involved in such a complaint. This comparator was determined by the House of Lords (*Chief Constable of West Yorkshire Police* v *Khan* [2001] IRLR 830).
- It must be demonstrated that the less favourable treatment is a direct result of the involvement in the complaint.

Redress and remedies

There are two possible sets of circumstances here: claims ***not*** covered by discrimination law; and those that are.

Claims for bullying and harassment *not* covered by discrimination law

- Grievance should be raised with the employer under the appropriate workplace grievance procedure and in accordance with the ACAS *Code on Disciplinary and Grievance Procedures* (2009).
- Prior to this, the complainant may have used the employer's confidential harassment or 'dignity at work' procedure or employee assistance programme. This would be optional and voluntary.
- Failure by the employer to resolve the grievance promptly and effectively could result in the employee resigning.
- S/he would need to show that there was a fundamental breach of the **contract** of employment by the employer. This is likely to be a breach of 'mutual trust and confidence' or, possibly, a breach of the duty to take reasonable care of the employee.
- If a repudiatory breach was established and the employee resigned, s/he could claim constructive dismissal at an employment tribunal. The tribunal would only hear the claim if the person was an employee with twelve months' continuous service with the employer.
- If the employment tribunal claim was successful, the claimant would receive compensation (as limited in unfair dismissal cases); and possibly reinstatement or re-engagement or, alternatively, further compensation where that was refused by the employer. There is no award for injury to feelings in unfair dismissal cases.
- Failure to use the internal grievance procedure may result, depending on the circumstances, in either an increase in compensation if the fault was the employer's, or a reduction if the fault was the employee's (see ACAS *Code of Practice on Disciplinary and Grievance Procedures*).

Claims for bullying and harassment under discrimination law

- The first four of the steps outlined above would still apply.
- However, the employee need not resign to bring a claim under discrimination law. Although it may be unlikely, s/he can remain in employment and seek redress at employment tribunal. There is no qualifying length of service for a claim under discrimination law. Furthermore, there is no need to establish status as an 'employee'.
- If the employment tribunal claim was successful, the following remedies are available:
  - *Compensation* which is unlimited in discrimination cases.
  - *Award for injury to feelings*: this refers to emotional harm and is almost inevitable in successful harassment claims. It may also be the only form of compensation if financial loss is not experienced. The EAT outlined two categories – higher and lower awards (*ICTS (UK) Ltd* v *Tchoula* [2000] IRLR 643). A higher level award is based on the following factors:

- the complainant proving most of the complaint;
- evidence of a long-term campaign of discrimination;
- the consequences of the discrimination/harassment (e.g. stress, depression);
- a power relationship between the perpetrator and the victim;
- management's approach in dealing with a complaint through the grievance procedure.

In 2003, the Court of Appeal outlined guidance determining three broad bands (*Vento* v *West Yorkshire Police* (No. 2) [2003] IRLR 102, CA):

- *Top band*: between £15,000 and £25,000. This is for the most serious cases such as a lengthy campaign of harassment. Only exceptionally should the ceiling be exceeded.
- *Middle band*: between £5,000 and £15,000. Used for serious cases that do not merit an award in the highest band.
- *Lowest band*: between £500 and £5,000. Appropriate for less serious cases where, for example, the act of discrimination is an isolated or one-off occurrence. Awards of less than £500 should be avoided altogether.

An award for injury to feelings should include an element of aggravated **damages** where the employer has 'behaved in a high-handed, malicious, insulting or oppressive manner' in discriminating against the complainant (*Alexander* v *Home Office* [1988] IRLR 190, CA).

- A *declaration* of the rights of the complainant and of the employer.
- An order for *re-instatement or re-engagement* (if dismissal is an element of the harassment).

- Failure to use the internal grievance procedure may result, depending on the circumstances, in either an increase in compensation if the fault was the employer's, or a reduction if the fault was the employee's (see ACAS *Code of Practice on Disciplinary and Grievance Procedures*).

The Protection from Harassment Act 1997

Introduction

This legislation was enacted to deal with the issue of 'stalking'. It is not specifically an employment law measure. It relates to a 'course of conduct' causing harassment (s 2) and to a 'course of conduct causing fear of violence' (s 4). Magistrates' courts and the Crown Court have the power to impose a fine, a community penalty or custody. The courts can also impose a restraining order on the offender. It is possible for the victim to bring a claim in the county court for damages for the conduct outlined in s 2.

Under the legislation, harassment is not defined in detail. It covers situations where a person causes another 'alarm' or 'distress' (s 7). Obviously, it can cover sending text or e-mail messages, phoning, sending messages through the post, making threats, loitering outside a person's home or workplace, sending unwanted gifts, and unsolicited contact at work, etc. It is not limited to incidents based on sex, race or the other areas covered by discrimination law. A 'course of conduct' involves conduct on at least two occasions. 'Conduct' involves speech.

Parliament in enacting this legislation expected that the two principal parties would be the victim and another individual as perpetrator. There are no specific provisions in the Act making the employer vicariously liable for the acts of employees who may be engaging in a 'course of conduct' whilst in the course of their employment. However, in a recent case (*Majrowski* v *Guy's and St Thomas' NHS Trust* [2006] IRLR 695), the House of Lords ruled on this issue of employer vicarious liability in the circumstances of this legislation (see Exhibit 7.5).

Exhibit 7.5 The *Majrowski* case

Majrowski v *Guy's and St Thomas' NHS Trust* [2006] UKHL 34, HL

The facts. Mr Majrowski was employed by the Guy's and St Thomas' Hospital NHS Trust as a clinical audit co-ordinator. He alleged (from April 1998) that during his employment he was bullied, intimidated and harassed by his departmental manager, Ms Freeman, who was acting in the course of her employment. He claimed that she was excessively critical of and strict about his time-keeping and his work; that she isolated him by refusing to talk to him and treated him differently and unfavourably compared to other staff; that she was rude and abusive to him in front of other staff; and that she imposed unrealistic targets for his performance, threatening him with disciplinary action if he did not achieve them. In June 1999, he was dismissed by the Trust for reasons unrelated to his complaint.

In February 2003, he brought proceedings, initially in the county court, claiming damages from his employer because of his manager's behaviour. In a preliminary hearing, the judge struck out his claim, ruling that the employer was not vicariously liable. The legislation was intended to protect individuals from harassment by other individuals and did not include the concept of employer's vicarious liability.

He appealed on the question of liability to the Court of Appeal (where broadly he was successful in his argument about liability). The case then went to the House of Lords because the NHS Trust appealed. The Law Lords dismissed the Trust's appeal.

The judgment

- Lord Nicholls observed that vicarious liability is a **common law** *principle* of strict, no-fault liability. A blameless employer is liable for a wrong committed by an employee while acting in the course of his/her employment.
- Their Lordships took the view that it is difficult to see a coherent basis for confining the common law principle of vicarious liability to common law wrongs.
- The Protection from Harassment Act 1997 does *not* expressly or impliedly *exclude* vicarious liability.
- An employer will be vicariously liable for breach of the statutory duty under this Act.
- For the principle to apply, the course of conduct must be *so closely connected* with the acts that the employee is authorised to do that his or her conduct may fairly and properly be regarded as being done in the course of employment.
- The conduct complained of must be 'oppressive and unacceptable' not merely unreasonable.

The case returned to the county court for a full hearing.

The implications

- Although the ruling was unanimous, four of the law Lords 'thought there was considerable force in the Trust's argument that parliament's intention may have been that liability in damages should be personal to the perpetrator of the harassment'. However, their ruling arose from their construction of the language of the Act (*Industrial Relations Law Bulletin* 792, September 2006).
- 'Common law vicarious liability is strict: if the harassment took place in the course of employment, the employer will be liable' (ibid.).
- Unlike the vicarious liability provisions in discrimination law, the employer has no defence that he took such steps as were reasonably practicable to deal with the harassment.
- It was argued by the Trust that the ruling could lead to a greatly increased volume of employee claims based on stress, anxiety or other emotional problems at work.
- This ruling provides an alternative potential **remedy** for employees subjected to bullying without them having to resign and claim constructive dismissal.
- The time limit for bringing claims under this Act is six years.
- However, bringing claims in the county court is more expensive than an employment tribunal. There are cost implications for complainants where their claims fail.

It is important to remember that this legislation is unlikely to be a principal route under which harassment claims will be made for the reasons set out in Exhibit 7.5. Claims are much more likely to continue to arise under the various strands of discrimination law. Nevertheless, in those circumstances where discrimination law does not apply, and a person has either no redress or, if they qualify, their redress is to claim constructive dismissal, then, use of the Protection from Harassment Act 1997 may be a tempting – albeit financially risky – route. Even the remote possibility of such claims should prompt employers to make serious attempts to tackle that bullying behaviour which falls outside discrimination law.

Conclusion

The liability of employers for harassment and bullying in the workplace requires them to think strategically and develop policies, procedures and practices which will create a reasonably acceptable work environment and also enable an arguable defence to be made (see Chapter 6, Implementing equality in the workplace).

In brief, among the steps to be taken are the following:

- Ensuring that the issue of harassment and bullying is integral to an equal opportunities policy.
- If a public authority, ensure that 'dignity at work' policies are compliant with statutory duties to promote equal opportunities.
- Publicising and enforcing a code of conduct of acceptable behaviour for employees, customers and suppliers.
- Providing appropriate induction and 'awareness' training for managers and staff.
- Ensuring that managers understand the concept of the employer's vicarious liability.
- Ensuring that appropriate disciplinary rules are in force and, where disciplinary action is taken, that it is in accordance with the ACAS code of practice.
- Providing a dignity at work policy which encompasses access to confidential counselling for complainants.
- Ensuring that the formal grievance procedure is used and is compliant with the ACAS code of practice.
- Providing the facility, if necessary, for an independent external person to undertake a fact-finding investigation (particularly where a pattern of persistent harassing behaviour is alleged).
- Provide for mediation as an opportunity to resolve any interpersonal disputes.
- Ensuring that, alongside equal opportunities policies, the incidence and handling of harassment and bullying complaints is monitored.

Exercises 7.2–7.4

Exercise 7.1 is earlier in the chapter.

7.2 **Indira.** One morning, when Indira logged onto her computer at work in a large insurance brokers, she found an offensive e-mail message. It contained some sexist comments and a picture attachment. It appeared that it had been sent to everyone in the department by Jez who had a reputation for being a 'lad'. She was upset by the message and commented on it to her supervisor. He said that she should laugh it off and forget about it. When Indira mentioned the matter to other female staff, they told her to ignore it and said that Jez was 'just an idiot'. The following day, Indira accidentally met Jez in the lift and he made an offensive personal comment to her and told her that she was 'soft' for moaning about his jokey e-mail. No one else was in the lift, so this conversation was not witnessed. She went to see Angela in the HR department and told her that she felt very uncomfortable working in the organisation and was thinking of leaving. The company had recently adopted a harassment policy as a result of a recent employment tribunal case which had attracted a great deal of adverse publicity.

What advice should Angela give Indira about the courses of action open to her? What reasonable steps would you expect the employer to take if Indira lodges a grievance?

7.3 **Ronke.** Ronke, a Nigerian woman, has worked for twelve years as a senior administrator for a company that ran a number of residential care homes. She had always been regarded by her managers as a good performer with good interpersonal skills who is interested in her own professional development. (She, in fact, successfully undertook a management studies diploma course in the past three years.) Her new manager, Joan Philips, was very demanding. She was attempting to introduce new computerised administrative systems. She refused to listen to Ronke's advice which was based on her knowledge and experience of working within the company. The manager required long working hours and quick turnarounds for the tasks that she gave Ronke. When Ronke complained to her about her unreasonable behaviour, Joan said, 'that's the trouble with people like you, you don't know what hard work is'. Very upset by the slur, Ronke chatted to a friend who worked in a human resources department of another organisation.

What advice would you expect her friend to give Ronke about what the issues are and how she might tackle the situation?

7.4 **Winston and Harry.** Harry works in the warehouse of a department store. His eldest son is homosexual and had recently been seen on a television news broadcast about a Gay Pride march in London. Harry's supervisor, Winston, started making offensive comments to Harry about this. Winston belongs to an evangelical Christian church which believes that homosexuality is a sin. He has repeatedly told Harry that his son will 'go to hell' and that he should 'get him treated'. At first Harry thought that Winston was joking and told him to 'shut up'. The comments continued and, after a while, Harry became very irritated by what he found to be offensive behaviour. He mentioned the situation to the warehouse manager who had just overheard one of the comments. He told Harry to ignore the comments saying that 'you know that Winston's a bit of a religious maniac'. A few days later a fight broke out between Harry and Winston. Winston had repeated his comments about homosexuality being a sin and had wondered if Harry, himself, wasn't 'a bit queer'. At this point Harry had punched Winston in the face. The warehouse manager asked them to come to his office and explain themselves because he was thinking of disciplinary action. Harry has asked for his union representative to be present. He has advised Harry to lodge a grievance with the warehouse manager for not dealing with the harassment he had experienced from Winston.

What advice would you give to the various parties on the legal situation?

Feedback on these exercises is provided in the Appendix to this textbook.

References and useful websites

ACAS (2009) *Code of Practice on Disciplinary and Grievance Procedures*. London: ACAS.

ACAS website: guidance on harassment and bullying (www.acas.org.uk).

Collier, R. (1995) *Combating Sexual Harassment in the Workplace*. Buckingham: Open University Press.

Grainger, H. and Fitzner, G. (2007) *The First Fair Treatment at Work Survey: Executive Summary (Updated)*, Employment Relations Research Series, No. 63. London: Department of Trade and Industry (see www.berr.gov.uk/employment).

Home Office (1993) *Aspects of Sex Discrimination within the Police Service*. London: Home Office.

Rubenstein, M. (2008) 'Sex Discrimination Act (Amendment) Regulations 2008: an EOR Guide', *Equal Opportunities Review*, No. 176, May.

Useful websites Advisory, Conciliation and Arbitration Service **www.acas.org.uk**

Department for Business Enterprise and Regulatory Reform **www.berr.gov.uk**

Visit **www.mylawchamber.co.uk/willey** to access multiple choice questions, case flashcards and exercises to test yourself on this chapter.

mylawchamber

8 Discipline and dismissal

Learning objectives

To be able to:

- Explain the importance of discipline and dismissal in the employment relationship
- Summarise the main provisions of UK legislation as well as accepted principles of best practice in relation to dismissal and disciplinary practice and procedures; and issues related to grievance procedures
- Evaluate legal developments in the area of discipline and dismissal from the perspective of both employers and employees

Structure of the chapter

- *Introduction*: overview of current and historic issues relating to discipline and dismissal
- *ACAS Code of Practice on Disciplinary and Grievance Procedures*: its status and its principles
- *Statutory protection from unfair dismissal*: Who qualifies? What is a 'dismissal' in law; fair and automatically unfair reasons for dismissal; reasonableness in the circumstances; fair procedures; written reasons for dismissal; statutory right to be accompanied
- *Obtaining redress for unfair dismissal at an employment tribunal*: Does the complainant qualify? When must a complaint be made? What is the role of ACAS in tribunal complainants? What is a compromise agreement? What issues concern an employment tribunal in making its decision? What remedies are available to successful complainants? dismissal complaints and other grounds/causes of action; wrongful dismissal claims
- *Grievances and disciplinary action*
- *Exercises*

Introduction

Historic situation

Legislation outlining required procedures and standards in relation to discipline and dismissal of **employees** is comparatively recent. Historically, relationships at work in the UK were predominantly regulated by the **common law contract** of employment, with no role for **statute law**. The nature and conduct of relationships at work was largely left to employers and employees to resolve among themselves, with the only recourse for a dismissed **worker** being a claim for 'wrongful dismissal' under the common law contract of employment, for which the remedies available were limited. As a consequence, there was effectively very little control over employers in relation to discipline and dismissal of their employees.

However, during the 1960s, the UK government came under increasing pressure from a number of different sources to introduce greater protection for employees against dismissal. The adoption by the International Labour Organisation in 1963 of a Recommendation on Termination of Employment (No. 119), to which Britain as a member of the ILO subscribed, was important. In addition, a number of reports on industrial relations in the late 1960s highlighted the dissatisfaction of trade unions and employers with the lack of legal regulation in the area. Allied to wider support for change among politicians and the general public, these pressures culminated in the enactment of unfair dismissal provisions in 1971. These introduced mandatory standards and rules for employers to follow when dismissing employees which have been amended in subsequent legislation. Although there have been notable developments, the central components of the law on unfair dismissal have remained largely stable since then.

Historic redress

Historically, there were only two possible and difficult routes to redress under common law: claims for wrongful dismissal; and proceedings concerning frustration of contract.

Wrongful dismissal

This, however, would only be successful if the employer had breached the contract of employment. Describing the situation extant under common law and prior to 1971, Anderman (1986: 416) stated that 'as long as proper contractual notice of termination was given, an employer was legally entitled to dismiss an employee for whatever reason he wished. There was no obligation on the employer to reveal his reason for dismissal to the employee, much less to justify it.'

An employee dismissed in circumstances where his honesty was questioned and who, as a consequence, found it difficult to obtain other employment, might only have available an action for defamation – which would be costly, complex and uncertain. An employee dismissed on grounds that could be construed as **victimisation** or discriminatory would have had no special protection. Certainly, the common law, emphasising freedom of contract, did not proscribe discriminatory treatment.

If upheld, the **remedy** for a wrongful dismissal claim is **damages** equal to the amount of pay the employee would have received in their notice period (i.e. effectively pay in lieu of notice) or the amount of pay he or she would have received in both the period of notice and the period during which the procedural requirements in the contract would have been completed. However, as notice periods tend to be relatively short, a claim for wrongful dismissal is not particularly attractive for the majority of employees.

Nowadays, actions alleging wrongful dismissal can still be made and, sometimes, are made alongside unfair dismissal claims (see later section on obtaining redress, Table 8.2).

Common law doctrine of frustration

This doctrine is applicable where because of an event outside the control of the employer or employee, it becomes impossible to perform the contract. Examples of the kinds of circumstances that can give rise to a finding of frustration of contract include death, imprisonment or long-term sickness or incapability on the part of an employee. Where there is frustration the employment contract is terminated automatically and there is no dismissal in law.

In general terms, the doctrine of frustration has been superseded by the legislation on unfair dismissal and employers need to be very cautious in cases of incapability of an employee in claiming frustration of contract, as the tribunals and courts are reluctant to accept such a claim where to do so would allow the employer to get around their obligations under unfair dismissal law.

That said, in certain situations tribunals may still find that a contract has been frustrated and it is therefore important for employers and human resource management practitioners to be aware of the concept. It has emerged from a number of decisions that factors such as the length of service of the employee; the duration of the contract; the nature and likely duration of incapability; whether the contract makes provision for sick pay; and the nature and importance of the role undertaken, are important in establishing whether a contract has been frustrated or not (*Marshall* v *Harland and Wolff Ltd* [1972] 2 All ER 715, NIRC; *Egg Stores* v *Leibovici* [1976] IRLR 376, EAT). There is some historical precedence that the courts and tribunals may be more willing to establish a case of frustration where the employee in question is in a key post or where the contract is of relatively short duration, however more recent cases have challenged these positions and highlight the extent to which employers' claims for frustration will be examined very carefully, irrespective of such features or characteristics.

Current overview

For HR practitioners, rules and **regulations** in the area of discipline and dismissal are of central importance. The primary objective of most organisations, whether public or private, is to undertake particular activities in a profitable, efficient or cost-effective manner. The ability to set standards and control the performance of staff is therefore key, as is the possibility to deal with circumstances arising which impact on organisational performance such as staff absence or sickness. Workers and employees, on the other hand, have an equally legitimate interest in the existence of limits on the exercise of managerial discretion, and in particular on management's ability to terminate the employment relationship.

Unfair dismissal has for many years been the most common reason for applications to employment tribunals. There were 33,352 unfair dismissal claims registered at tribunals in 2007–08. These accounted for 22 per cent of all claims (ACAS Annual Report 2007–08 (**www.acas.org.uk**)). The fact that it is estimated that only around one in seven dismissals lead to a tribunal claim (Knight and Latreille 2000: 541) provides a good indication of how high profile and important dismissal is across the labour market more broadly. Indeed the Department of Trade and Industry (1999) estimated that over a million workers in the UK are dismissed each year, although this figure includes those who have been made redundant or retired or whose fixed term contracts have expired.

Further information on the use of disciplinary and dismissal processes is provided by the results of the 2004 Workplace Employee Relations Survey (Kersley *et al.* 2006). This survey, which was sponsored by the Department of Trade and Industry, ACAS and a number of other organisations, comprised a nationally representative survey of workplaces with five or more employees located in Great Britain, and is widely regarded as the most authoritative source of evidence on employment relations in Britain.

The survey included questions on the use of disciplinary sanctions. It found that 55 per cent of managers surveyed had used at least one of a range of disciplinary sanctions in the year prior to the survey, namely formal verbal or written warnings, suspension with or without pay, deduction from pay, internal transfer or dismissal. Forty-five per cent of workplaces had issued a verbal warning; 37 per cent a written warning; while one-fifth had suspended an employee without pay. Only 5 per cent of workplaces had made deductions from pay and 6 per cent internal transfers. Perhaps most notably for our purposes here, 28 per cent of workplaces had made at least one dismissal in the year preceding the survey (Kersley *et al.* 2006: 224–30). Common reasons for taking disciplinary action were poor performance, unauthorised absence, poor timekeeping and theft or dishonesty, with other reasons including **negligence**, abusive or violent behaviour, disobedience, health and safety breaches and alcohol or drug use.

The survey findings made it possible to calculate a disciplinary sanction rate for the workplaces surveyed, i.e. the average number of disciplinary sanctions applied per 100 employees. In this regard, the overall average was 5.7 sanctions per 100 employees. Average rates were somewhat higher in smaller firms (8.0 in workplaces of 10 to 24 employees), and in the private sector, 6.9, compared to the public sector at 1.9. The rate of disciplinary sanctions was highest in the 'other business services' sector, with hotels and restaurants and wholesale and retail also having relatively high rates. In contrast, sanction rates were comparatively low in the education, public administration and health and social work sectors (ibid.).

The WERS figures again serve to emphasise the importance of discipline and dismissal in the contemporary employment relationship and highlight the strong need for legislation in this area.

Table 8.1 provides a summary of the overall situation relating to complaints about dismissal depending on a worker's employment.

Table 8.1 Protection against unfair dismissal by employment status

Employment status	*Protection*
Employee (i.e. with a contract of employment) with minimum of one year's continuous service with an employer	Full/comprehensive protection against unfair dismissal and also claims in relation to wrongful dismissal
Employee with less than one year's continuous service	Only able to claim unfair dismissal where dismissal for an 'automatically unfair' reason (but may, depending on the circumstances, be able to bring claim for 'wrongful dismissal')
Worker without 'employee' status (i.e. not having a contract of employment, but having some other contract to work personally)	Not entitled to claim unfair dismissal, but may have alternative claim (e.g. under discrimination law or for unlawful deduction of wages)

Legislation on unfair dismissal

The legislation on unfair dismissal is contained in the Employment Rights Act 1996 (Parts X and XI). The provisions are supplemented by the ACAS *Code of Practice on Disciplinary and Grievance Procedures* (2009). This statutory code sets out detailed guidance and recommendations for employers to follow in relation to discipline and dismissal. Failure to comply with the code does not 'of itself render (a person) liable to any proceedings'. However it will be 'admissible in evidence' before an employment tribunal in deciding whether a dismissal is fair or unfair (TULRCA 1992, s 207).

The ACAS code of practice has recently been given greater force by the Employment Act 2008. This provides that where an employer or employee has unreasonably failed to comply with the code, an employment tribunal may, if it considers it just and equitable, increase or decrease any award it makes by up to 25 per cent.

The Employment Rights Act 1996 and the ACAS code are further supplemented by the Employment Relations Act 1999 and additional provisions of the Employment Act 2008. The former outlines the statutory right for workers to be accompanied by a fellow worker or trade union official at disciplinary or dismissal meetings (ERA 1999, s 10). The latter introduced a number of important changes in dismissal law, most notably abolishing the statutory dispute resolution procedures which had been introduced by the Employment Act 2002 and were in force from 2004 to 2009. These are discussed further below, but essentially they made it mandatory for employers to follow a particular three step procedure in dismissing or disciplining an employee. Where this procedure (which involved informing the employee of the relevant issue in writing, holding a meeting to discuss it and allowing the employee to appeal any decision made) was not followed a dismissal would be ruled by a tribunal to be automatically unfair. (The Employment Act 2002 also made it compulsory for employees to follow a similar procedure when raising a grievance with their employer.)

The requirements of the statutory dispute resolution procedures caused a lot of confusion and were very unpopular with employers, employees and employment law practitioners alike. As a consequence they were abolished by the Employment Act 2008. However, as outlined above, the same legislation also attempted to strengthen procedural requirements in relation to dismissal and discipline situations, by providing for a 25 per cent increase or decrease in awards made by tribunals where provisions of the ACAS code of practice are not followed. In addition, it should also be noted that the Employment Act 2002 is likely to continue to have a significant influence on the area of discipline/dismissal, in that it is likely that employment tribunals will continue to draw on judicial decisions interpreting that legislation (e.g. in cases concerning what constitutes a grievance).

The ACAS code of practice

The ACAS code of practice outlines a number of key principles and also numerous specific pieces of guidance and advice to employers in relation to discipline and dismissal and also grievance-handling in the workplace (see Exhibit 8.1). It is supplemented by a detailed handbook of good employment practice (see **www.acas.org.uk**).

Exhibit 8.1 ***ACAS Code of Practice on Disciplinary and Grievance Procedures* (2009)**

This code is designed to help employers, employees and their representatives deal with disciplinary and grievance situations in the workplace.

- ***Informality***. Many potential disciplinary or grievance issues can be resolved informally. A quiet word is often all that is required to resolve a problem. However, where informality does not work the matter may be pursued formally.
- ***Rules and procedures***. Fairness and transparency are promoted by developing and using rules and procedures for handling disciplinary and grievance situations. These should be set down in writing, be specific and clear and be agreed wherever applicable with trade unions or employee representatives. It is also important to ensure that employees and managers understand how they are to be used.
- ***'Reasonable' formal action***. Where some form of formal action is needed, what action is reasonable or justified will depend on all the circumstances of the particular case. The size and resources of the employer should always be taken into account. In small organisations it may sometimes not be practicable to take all of the steps set out in this Code. However, the key elements of good practice that employers and employees should work to are set out in the paragraphs that follow.
- ***Workplace resolution***. Employers and employees should do all that they can to resolve disciplinary and grievance issues in the workplace. The use of an independent third party as a mediator should be considered. Recourse to an employment tribunal should only be a last resort.
- ***The formal process***. Whenever a formal process is being followed, it is important to deal with issues fairly. There are a number of elements to this:
  - Issues should be dealt with ***promptly***. Meetings and decisions should not be unduly delayed.
  - Employers and employees should act ***consistently***.
  - Appropriate ***investigations*** should be made by employers to establish the facts of the case.
  - Any grievance or disciplinary meeting should, so far as possible, be conducted by a manager who was ***not involved*** in the matter giving rise to the dispute.
  - Where the employer is raising a ***performance problem*** the immediate manager would be involved.
  - An employee should be ***informed*** of the basis of the problem and have an opportunity to ***put their case*** in response before any decisions are made.
  - An employee has the right to be ***accompanied*** at any disciplinary or grievance meeting.
  - An employee should be allowed to ***appeal*** against any formal decision made.
- ***Records***: it is good practice to keep written records during disciplinary and grievance cases. A written record should be kept of the outcome.

Summary of key provisions. For the full code of practice see: **www.acas.org.uk**.

Several issues which arise in the extract contained in Exhibit 8.1 require some further elaboration:

- approach and aim of disciplinary action;
- disciplinary rules;
- acting reasonably;
- disciplinary penalties.

Approach and aim of disciplinary action

The 2004 version of the ACAS code of practice set out explicitly that disciplinary procedures are seen primarily 'as a means of encouraging improved performance or conduct' from employees, as opposed to merely consisting of sanctions for wrongdoings. This objective is now implicit in the 2009 code. Nevertheless, the encouragement of improvement is an important principle for employers to have in mind.

Disciplinary rules

Organisations' policies should clearly set out disciplinary rules and the likely consequence of breach of these, including examples of gross misconduct that may warrant **summary dismissal.**

Workplace rules will reflect the operational and business circumstances of each particular employer. Rules are likely to cover the following areas:

- attendance at work;
- compliance with safety standards;
- theft of company property;
- confidentiality when dealing with customers/clients;
- harassment and bullying of fellow workers, suppliers, clients and customers;
- alcohol and drug abuse;
- standards of behaviour outside work;
- misuse of company internet and e-mail facilities;
- behaviour which is likely to bring the organisation into disrepute.

Acting reasonably

A key reference point in the code is that employers should act reasonably in dealing with employees. It is recommended that instances of minor misconduct or unsatisfactory performance be dealt with informally, for example by a manager having a quiet word with the employee in question. Where the issue is rather more serious, the code recommends that employers consider taking formal action. In this case the employee should be adequately informed of the issue or problem in question and invited to a meeting to discuss it, at which they should have the right to be accompanied by a fellow worker or a trade union representative.

At the meeting the employer should explain the complaint against the employee, going through relevant evidence, and the employee should be allowed to ask questions, set out their case and answer any allegations made. Following the meeting the employer should decide whether disciplinary action is necessary or not. The code outlines that if disciplinary action is seen to be necessary this will usually take the form of a written warning which highlights the performance or conduct problem, the improvement or change in conduct required within a specified period and information about any support the employer will provide to assist the employee. This warning should explain that failure to make the necessary changes could lead to a final written warning and subsequently dismissal and also that the employee is entitled to appeal the decision.

Where the conduct or performance problem is sufficiently serious it may be appropriate to issue a final warning as the first stage of disciplinary action. In addition, where the conduct or performance problem is sufficiently serious – where there is what is known as a situation of 'gross misconduct' (for example, involving theft, fraud or violence) – dismissal may be the appropriate disciplinary action to be taken. However even here, ACAS advise that reasonable behaviour from employers requires there to be an investigation and an opportunity for the employee to defend him or herself and put their case across.

Disciplinary penalties

The ACAS code of practice refers to several forms of disciplinary penalty. It is worth summarising them here and commenting briefly on some of the implications of imposing them (see Exhibit 8.2).

Exhibit 8.2 Disciplinary penalties

- *Informal verbal warning*. Recommended first step for minor poor performance and minor misconduct.
- *Formal written warning*. Normally, the penalty imposed after a disciplinary hearing for continuing poor performance and persistent minor misconduct.
- *Final written warning*. May be imposed as a result of the failure to comply with previous warnings, or may be a first penalty (short of dismissal) for an act of gross misconduct or serious unsatisfactory performance.
- *Dismissal with notice or pay in lieu of notice*. This would follow a disciplinary hearing. The notice due to the employee – bearing in mind the statutory minima (ERA 1996, s 86) and entitlements under the contract of employment.
- *Summary (or instant) dismissal*. This is likely to arise where there has been gross misconduct. The decision to dismiss must, however, have been reached after compliance with the workplace disciplinary procedure.
- *Suspension without pay; fines; demotion; and disciplinary transfer*. If an employer proposes to use these disciplinary penalties, then it is essential that the authority for doing so is provided through an express term of the contract of employment. The imposition of these penalties without contractual authority is likely to be regarded as a repudiatory breach of the contract and may result in resignation and a constructive dismissal claim by the employee.

Warnings should set out the nature of the improvement in performance or the change in conduct required, and should specify an appropriate time period for this improvement.

In some cases (those likely to lead to final written warnings or dismissal), the employee might be suspended on full pay pending the disciplinary hearing. Suspension without pay in these circumstances is likely to be a breach of contract.

It is recommended by ACAS that warnings should, after a period specified by the employer be disregarded.

See the ACAS code of practice and the relevant handbook for more detail: **www.acas.org.uk**.

Statutory protection from unfair dismissal

In order to deal with an application for unfair dismissal, an employment tribunal addresses a number of questions in turn (ERA 1996):

- *Who qualifies*? Is the individual complainant an 'employee' with one year's continuous service?
- *A dismissal*? Has there been a dismissal in law?
- *Reasons for dismissal*? What was this reason? Was the reason, or if there is more than one reason, the principal reason, potentially fair or automatically unfair?
- *Reasonableness*? Was the dismissal reasonable in the circumstances of the case?

If the answer to the first question is 'no', then a claim for unfair dismissal cannot be heard. If the answer to this question is 'yes', then the tribunal goes on to examine the second question. It will then consider, under the Employment Rights Act 1996, a number of categories of 'fair reasons' for dismissal as well as a list of 'automatically unfair' reasons. These are outlined in some detail below. If the reason for the dismissal was a fair one then the tribunal goes on to consider the fourth question, which is whether the decision to dismiss was reasonable in the circumstances. If, on the other hand, the reason for dismissal was not a fair one or was an automatically unfair reason then the process will stop at that stage, with the dismissal being found to be unfair. In addressing the issue of reasonableness, in addition to considerations such as whether the disciplinary punishment was proportionate to the act or situation in question, of central importance is an examination of procedural fairness, i.e. whether or not the employer has followed a fair procedure in dismissing the employee.

These elements of the law on unfair dismissal will now be discussed in turn.

Who qualifies?

As a general rule, protection against unfair dismissal applies only to those with a contract of employment with one year's continuous service with an employer. This means that employees with less than one year's service are not covered. In addition, casual or other 'atypical' workers who do not have employee status are also not able to claim unfair dismissal if dismissed by the organisation or person they are working for (see Chapter 2).

However, in certain specified circumstances the requirement for employees to have one year's continuous service does not apply. There are a number of reasons for dismissal that are 'automatically unfair' (for example dismissal on grounds of pregnancy or for claiming entitlement to the national minimum wage), and in these situations employees do not need to have one year's service in order to claim unfair dismissal at an employment tribunal (see further below).

In relation to workers who do not have a contract of employment, although they are unable to claim unfair dismissal, this does not necessarily mean that they will have no employment law claim or remedy at all. For example, if an agency worker is dismissed by the client organisation (or 'principal') because she is pregnant, although she may not be able to claim unfair dismissal, she would have a claim for sex discrimination. (It should be noted that employees, whether with or without one year's service, may also be entitled to bring such claims in addition to or instead of a claim for unfair dismissal.)

Historically, employees aged 65 or over or who had reached the normal retiring age in their organisations were not eligible to claim unfair dismissal. These restrictions have now been removed under the Employment Equality (Age) Regulations 2006.

Is there a dismissal in law?

The Employment Rights Act (s 95) defines the circumstances that come within the meaning of a dismissal for the purpose of the unfair dismissal legislation. A 'dismissal' includes the following:

- termination of an employment contract by an employer either with or without notice;
- expiry of a fixed term contract;
- circumstances where an employee is entitled to terminate his or her contract without notice by reason of the employer's conduct which has fundamentally breached the contract. (This is known as a 'constructive dismissal'.)

These are considered in more detail as follows:

Termination of contract by the employer

That this is classed as a 'dismissal' is arguably self-evident – the termination of an employee's contract by his or her employer is what immediately comes to mind when thinking of the area of dismissal. However, it is important to note that the decision to dismiss should be clear and unambiguous. In some cases, when an argument has arisen in the workplace, an employee who is told to 'fuck off' may interpret this as dismissal when, in fact, it is not but merely telling him to 'clock off' for the day (*Futty* v *D & D Brekkes Ltd* [1974] IRLR 130). An employment tribunal in determining whether or not there was a dismissal would consider how this language might be interpreted in the circumstances of a particular industry.

Fixed-term contracts

It is notable and arguably rather curious that the fact that a fixed term contract coming to an end also comes within the definition of a dismissal under the legislation – even though the contract merely comes to an end and there is no positive dismissal by the employer (for example relating to an employee's conduct or performance), this situation still constitutes a dismissal under the legislation.

Constructive dismissal

The third category is also arguably rather unusual, but on a closer consideration makes a lot of sense. Essentially, this provision means that where an employer does not dismiss the employee but acts in such a way as to fundamentally breach the contract of employment, the employee is not obliged to stay in employment but can resign because of the employer's fundamental breach of the contract and claim unfair dismissal. The key point is that there has been a breach which goes 'to the root of the contract' or which involves the employer demonstrating that they no longer intend to be bound by an essential term of the contract (*Western Excavating Ltd (ECC)* v *Sharp* [1978] IRLR 27, CA).

Examples of this would include a situation where an employer breaches an express term of the contract, for example by non-payment or late payment of wages or by cutting pay without an employee's consent. In addition, making changes to duties that are not provided for in the contract, changing working hours or the reallocation of job responsibilities could also be covered. In addition, breach of the implied terms of the contract of employment will also typically provide grounds for a constructive dismissal, for example breach of the **duty** to take reasonable care of the employee (which may occur when an employer fails to protect an employee from a serious case of bullying or harassment), or the implied duty of trust and confidence between employer and employee.

Notably, in addition to one-off, fundamental breaches of contract, an accumulation of minor infringements or unjustified actions has also been held to give rise to a situation of constructive dismissal (*Lewis* v *Motorworld Garages* [1985] IRLR 465, CA). Importantly, as with other unfair dismissal claims, in order to claim constructive dismissal employees are required to have one year's service.

The circumstances surrounding the ending of employment

Finally, in relation to the issue of establishing the existence of a dismissal, the tribunals and courts will carefully examine the circumstances surrounding the ending of employment in order to ascertain whether a dismissal has in fact taken place. It may be that an employee has not been dismissed but has instead voluntarily resigned his or her position, but tribunals will examine any supposed resignation very closely to determine whether or not the situation is more accurately interpreted as one of dismissal. There have been instances where an employee will resign instead of being dismissed, which the courts have held to constitute cases of dismissal (e.g. *Sheffield* v *Oxford Controls Co Ltd* [1979] IRLR 133, EAT).

Reasons for dismissal

Having established the eligibility of the complainant and that there has been a dismissal in law, the next step an employment tribunal takes is to establish the reason for the dismissal. The Employment Rights Act 1996 outlines both a list of potentially fair and what are conventionally called 'automatically unfair' reasons for dismissal. This latter term does not feature in the legislation.

Fair reasons

The six categories of potentially fair reasons are:

1 capability and qualifications;
2 conduct;
3 redundancy;
4 contravening a statutory duty or restriction;
5 'some other substantial reason' (SOSR);
6 retirement.

If an employer can show that the dismissal came within one of these reasons, the dismissal is potentially fair, and the tribunal will go on to consider the issue of reasonableness. So, just because an employer can demonstrate that the reason for dismissal came within those specified does not mean that the dismissal will be found to have been fair.

Capability and qualifications

The ERA (s 98(3)(a)) outlines that capability refers to 'skill, aptitude, health or any other physical or mental quality'. Understandably, this includes a person's competence or ability to do the job they have been employed to do. Such a reason can be related to either a disciplinary or non-disciplinary matter. For example, poor performance or substandard work is likely (but not necessarily) to be a relevant disciplinary matter, while dismissal on the grounds of ill-health is not. In relation to this latter issue, care also needs to be taken to ensure that related statutory rights are not infringed (for example, under the Disability Discrimination Act 1995).

'Qualifications' encompass the possession of educational and vocational qualifications (for example, A levels, an apprenticeship or university degree) (s 98(3)(a)). In addition, qualifications include the requirement to posses a valid driving licence as well as to pass an aptitude test (*Blackman* v *Post Office* [1974] ICR 151, NIRC). Misrepresentation of qualifications would probably be construed as gross misconduct.

Conduct

As with capability and qualifications, an employee's conduct at work may constitute grounds for a fair dismissal (ERA, s 98(2)(b)). The expectations in any workplace are likely to be set out in the disciplinary rules. As indicated above in the discussion of the ACAS code, a common distinction made in this regard is that between 'minor' or 'ordinary' misconduct and cases of 'gross' misconduct. The former includes lateness and excessive personal use of e-mail, while the latter would include violence or bullying, theft, fraud, a serious breach of health and safety or insubordination (i.e. a refusal to follow management instructions).

Redundancy

Where an employer's business has ceased or the specific work activity that an employee was undertaking has ceased or diminished, it is potentially fair for an employer to dismiss the employee or employees in question on grounds of redundancy (ERA, s 98(2)(c)) (see also Chapter 3).

Contravening a statutory duty or restriction

The Employment Rights Act provides for fair dismissal where 'the employee could not continue to work in the position which he held without contravention (either on his part or on that of his employer) of a duty or restriction imposed by or under an enactment' (s 98(2)(d)). This provision enables employers to dismiss an employee fairly where their employment or continued employment would be in breach of a statute. Examples here include dismissing an employee who has been disqualified from driving and, therefore, is unable to take a job where having a valid driving licence is a requirement; or dismissing an employee whose work permit has expired. Such dismissals will be fair, provided that they are carried out in a reasonable manner.

'Some other substantial reason' (SOSR)

This has been described as a 'residual' category which is used by employers to justify a dismissal which does not easily come within the other categories of potentially fair reason. The relevant provision of the ERA (s 98(2)(b)) defines this category of fair reason for dismissal as follows: 'some other substantial reason of a kind such as to justify the dismissal of an employee holding the position which the employee held'.

The Court of Appeal has emphasised that there is a burden on the employer to show that the reason in question is 'substantial' and not trivial (*Kent County Council* v *Gilham (No.2)* [1985] IRLR 18).

Examples of SOSR from **case law** are outlined below:

- *Dismissing employees who do not agree to organisational restructuring or change in working patterns.* This may be a dismissal for a fair reason under the SOSR heading if the employer can demonstrate that the change in question was necessary. For example, in *Scott & Co* v *Richardson* [2005] All ER (D) 87, EAT the dismissal of a debt collector who would not agree to work a new shift system was found by the EAT to come within the definition of SOSR. It repeated an earlier **landmark case** on this subject (*Hollister* v *National Farmers' Union* [1979] IRLR 238, CA) which established that having a 'sound good business reason' for the change in question is sufficient to establish SOSR for dismissing an employee who refuses to accept the change to terms and conditions – provided that the employer adduced evidence to show why the change was necessary. In the case of *Scott & Co* v *Richardson* [2005] an increased requirement for debt collection work to be undertaken in the evenings, which made the employer adjust working patterns such that evenings became part of the normal rota, was held by the EAT to constitute a sound business reason that potentially justified dismissal of Mr Richardson for SOSR.
- *Transfers of undertakings.* Where an employer wishes to dismiss an employee for an '**ETO** reason' (economic, technical or organisational reason) connected with a transfer of undertaking, this is also potentially fair under the SOSR category (Transfer of Undertakings (Protection of Employment) Regulations 2006, reg 7) (see Chapter 3).
- *Pressure from customers or clients of the employer.* This may also provide valid grounds for a dismissal on the basis of SOSR. For example, in the case of *Edwards* v *Curtis t/a Arkive Computing* [1996] EAT 845/95, the EAT held that the dismissal of an employee following a complaint by the company's only customer regarding the quality of his work was fair, coming within the category of SOSR. Here the customer insisted that the employee in question be dismissed, but provided that there is clear evidence of customer pressure to dismiss, there does not need to be an express instruction to dismiss or an ultimatum from a customer. It is important to note, however, that customer pressure must not infringe discrimination law.
- *Employee charged or convicted of a criminal offence outside of work.* The (draft) ACAS code of practice states that the fact that an employee is charged with or convicted of a criminal offence is not normally in itself a reason for disciplinary action. Consideration needs to be given to the effect of the charge or conviction on the employee's ability to do their job and their relationship with their employer, work colleagues and customers. The employer

should establish the facts and determine whether the matter is serious enough to warrant disciplinary action. It should be noted that the former ACAS code (2004) notes that the primary determinant of an employer's response should be whether the offence in question is one that makes the employee 'unsuitable' for the type of work they are undertaking. An employee should not be dismissed solely because they are absent from work as a result of being remanded in custody. This approach may continue to be adopted by employers as good employment practice.

- ***An employee's difficult personality.*** This may be a possible 'substantial reason'. An example is the case of *Perkin* v *St. George's Healthcare Trust* [2005] IRLR 934, CA. The employer, an NHS trust, instigated disciplinary proceedings against a finance director, Mr Perkin, on the basis that his aloof manner and intimidating management style were causing difficulties at work. At the disciplinary meeting Mr Perkin made a number of unfounded allegations against senior management at the trust. He was subsequently dismissed on the basis of a breakdown of the relationship between him and the executive team and the fact that he was unable to establish good working relationships more generally. Mr Perkin brought a case for unfair dismissal which subsequently came to the Court of Appeal, which held that personality, of itself, could not be a ground for dismissal, but that an employee's personality must manifest itself in such a way as to bring the actions of the employee within one of the headings of fair reason for dismissal. In this regard it noted that an employee with a difficult personality could possibly be dismissed on grounds of conduct or SOSR. The Court of Appeal outlined that where there was a breakdown in confidence between an employer and a senior executive for which the executive was responsible and that was damaging to the operations of the organisation or meant that senior executives were unable to work as a team, such circumstances could amount to SOSR for a dismissal.

Dismissal on grounds of retirement

Historically employees aged 65 or over or who had reached the normal retiring age in their organisations have not been eligible to claim unfair dismissal. These restrictions have now been removed as a consequence of the implementation of the Equal Treatment in Employment **Directive** 2000. However, the possibility for older employees to bring successful unfair **dismissal** claims remains very limited because the Employment Equality (Age) Regulations 2006 (as well as amendments to the Employment Rights Act 1996, ss 98ZA–ZH) make it lawful for employers to dismiss employees on grounds of 'retirement' provided particular procedural requirements are complied with.

The Employment Equality (Age) Regulations 2006 provide that employers can legally adopt a default retirement age of 65, or a lower age if this is objectively justified. Related to this, the regulations and new provisions inserted into the Employment Rights Act 1996 outline that employers may fairly dismiss employees on the grounds of retirement where they reach the age of 65, or the lower age if relevant. However, the relevant provisions also provide employees with the right to request to continue working and, therefore, in order for retirement dismissals to be fair, they must comply with this and other procedural requirements, as follows:

- Six to 12 months before the retirement date the employer must inform the employee in writing of the intended retirement date and also their right to request to continue working (ERA 1996, s 98ZG; Employment Equality (Age) Regulations 2006, Sch 6).
- If an employee requests to continue working, the employer must consider the request and hold a meeting for that purpose and subsequently inform the employee of its decision.
- The employee must be allowed to appeal the decision made.

Where an employer dismisses an employee for retirement without having notified the employee of his or her intended retirement date and right to request to continue working, or without having considered their request to continue working or provided an opportunity to appeal a decision made in this regard, then the dismissal will be unfair (ERA 1996, s 98ZG). However, the duty to consider an employee's request to continue working is procedural only – employers are not required to give a reason for refusing a request and an employee is not entitled to challenge the validity of the employer's reasons; the primary requirement is that the employer follow the procedure.

Requests to continue working must be made between three and six months before the intended date of retirement and must specify whether the employee wants the employment to continue indefinitely or for a certain, stated period. Employees have a right to be accompanied by a fellow employee at the meeting and appeal. If a request to continue working is granted, the same duty to consider procedure must be followed in relation to the new retirement date unless this is six months or less from the original date. In addition to a possible claim for unfair dismissal, employees whose employer has not notified them of their right to request to continue working may be awarded up to eight weeks' pay as a remedy by an employment tribunal.

Retirement dismissals that are undertaken according to these rules and procedures will not constitute age discrimination. However, if the latter are not followed they will constitute age discrimination (in addition to unfair dismissal) unless the dismissal can be justified by the employer. Dismissal solely on the grounds of age (other than in relation to retirement) will constitute an unfair dismissal and direct age discrimination, providing it cannot be justified. Employers also need to ensure that dismissals on other grounds (such as capability) are not indirectly discriminatory on the grounds of age. For example, a policy of dismissing employees who are unable to work at a certain speed may particularly affect older workers who may be less able to work at a fast pace.

Automatically unfair reasons for dismissal

In the same way that the Employment Rights Act 1996 outlines potentially fair reasons for dismissal, it also specifies a number of reasons for dismissal that are automatically unfair. Below is a non-exhaustive list of such automatically unfair reasons for dismissal (note that a number of these reasons are outlined in legislation other than the ERA):

- dismissal for family reasons (e.g. pregnancy, taking of maternity leave or applying for flexible working) (ERA 1996, ss 99 and 104C);
- dismissal for a health and safety reason (e.g. acting as a health and safety representative, or refusing to work for health and safety reasons) (ERA 1996, s 100) (see Exhibit 8.3);
- dismissal of an employee for exercising rights under the Working Time Regulations 1998 (reg 32) or the National Minimum Wage Act 1998 (reg 25);
- dismissal of an employee for asserting statutory rights (i.e. for bringing a grievance or tribunal claim in connection with a statutory right) (ERA 1996, s 104);
- dismissal of employees for pursuing or attempting to enforce their rights under the **Part-time Workers** Regulations 2000 and the Fixed-Term Workers Regulations 2002;
- dismissal of shop workers and betting shop workers who refuse to work on Sunday (ERA 1996, s 101);
- dismissal for taking part in lawful, official **industrial action** within the statutory 12-week protected period (TULCRA 1992, ss 238A and 239) (see Exhibit 8.3);

Exhibit 8.3 Dismissal for taking industrial action and refusal to work in hazardous conditions

Common law. Since the nineteenth century, employees who strike or, in most circumstances, take part in 'industrial action short of a strike', breach their contracts of employment. Such action is a fundamental breach for which the employer may decide to summarily dismiss the employee. Effectively, there has been no legal 'right to strike'. However, since 2000, statute law has provided some limitations on the employer's ability to dismiss where there is 'lawful' industrial action. Essentially, to be 'lawful' there must have been an individual secret ballot to approve the industrial action; and the issues in dispute must relate to the employees' own workplace. Any picketing in support of industrial action must be peaceful (Trade Union and Labour Relations Consolidation Act 1992, Part V).

There are three sets of circumstances to be considered:

1 ***Dismissal for taking 'protected' industrial action***. It is unlawful for an employer to dismiss an employee for the reason that they are taking part in industrial action which has been approved by the trade union concerned following an individual secret ballot of its members (this is often known as 'official industrial action'). This protection lasts for 12 weeks. However, in circumstances where the employer fails to take 'reasonable procedural steps' to deal with the dispute (including seeking **conciliation**, mediation or **arbitration**; or restarting negotiations), the period of protection for employees can be extended. A dismissed employee can complain to an employment tribunal irrespective of length of service. Note that this protection only applies to industrial action which is officially sanctioned by a trade union following an individual, secret ballot of its members. If this does not take place the industrial action is therefore unofficial/unlawful and employers may lawfully dismiss the employees engaging in such action (see below).

2 ***Unlawful selective dismissal or re-engagement***. In addition to being unfair for employers to dismiss employees for taking 'protected' industrial action, it is unlawful for employers to *selectively dismiss* employees taking official industrial action. Employers may validly dismiss all employees taking such action (provided that the principal reason for this was not the fact they were taking industrial action, or if this was the reason, that the protected period has expired; and, in addition, provided the reason for dismissal was not one of the automatically unfair reasons for dismissal outlined above). If an employer attempts to dismiss selectively, then these dismissals will be automatically unfair. It will also constitute automatically unfair dismissal if an employer dismissed all employees taking part in official industrial action but then *selectively re-engages* only some of them. However, the latter protection only applies for three months following the dismissal.

3 ***Dismissal for taking unofficial industrial action***. As discussed above, there is no legal protection for employees dismissed while taking unofficial industrial action. However, here again, there are exceptions – where the reason for dismissal is an automatically unfair reason then an employee taking unofficial action is entitled to claim unfair dismissal.

'Taking part' in industrial action is not defined in statute law. For the overwhelming majority of participants, the issue will be clear-cut. However, there have been cases where uncertainty exists and the employee contends that, for whatever reason, they were not involved. The tribunal will decide the issue on the facts. Generally, participation concerns behaviour and not the motives of the individual worker. The **burden of proof** is on the employer. Case law has provided some examples:

- *Sick absence from work*. This may not, depending on the facts and circumstances, preclude a ruling of 'participation' (*Williams* v *Western Mail & Echo* [1980] IRLR 222, EAT; *Bolton Roadways Ltd* v *Edwards and Others* [1987] IRLR 392, EAT).
- *Threatened industrial action*. If the threat was specific that industrial action would take place on a particular date when the employees were due to work, this would be regarded as an 'anticipatory' breach of contract and the employer can regard 'participation' as beginning from the moment the employer was told of the intention to take the industrial action (*Winnet* v *Seamarks Brothers Ltd* [1978] IRLR 387, EAT; *Midland Plastics* v *Till and Others* [1983] IRLR 9, EAT).

Health and safety: protection from dismissal. An employee or group of employees is protected from dismissal when they stop work in relation to workplace hazards. This is where an employee 'in circumstances of danger which he reasonably believed to be serious and imminent and which he could not reasonably have been expected to avert, left or proposed to leave or (while the danger persisted) refused to return to his place of work or any dangerous part of his place of work' (ERA 1996, s 100(1)(d)).

- dismissal for trade union membership or participation in union activities (TULRCA 1992, ss 152 and 154);
- dismissal of an employee for acting as an employee representative in relation to redundancy and transfer of undertaking situations (ERA 1996, s 103) or as a trustee of an occupational pension scheme (ERA 1996, s 102);
- dismissal where the sole or main reason for the dismissal is a transfer of undertakings or a reason connected with a transfer that is not an 'economic, technical or organisational' reason (TUPE Regulations 2006, reg 7).

As noted earlier, where an employee has been dismissed for one of these reasons there is no requirement that they have one year's service in order to be eligible to apply to an employment tribunal for unfair dismissal. However, dismissals relating to a transfer of undertakings are an exception in this regard – in this instance employees are still required to have one year's service (see Chapter 3).

It is rather curious that discriminatory dismissals (e.g. dismissals on grounds of sex, race, disability, etc.) are not included in the Employment Rights Act as automatically unfair reasons for dismissal. In practice these generally *will* be automatically unfair reasons for dismissal, but given that, as outlined in Chapter 5, in certain circumstances it is possible for employers to defend or justify sex, race, age discrimination, it is therefore not possible for the Employment Rights Act to state that all dismissals on discriminatory grounds will be automatically unfair; it is necessary for tribunals to carefully examine the facts of each case to determine whether such dismissals are in fact fair or unfair.

The exclusion of discriminatory dismissals from the list of automatically unfair reasons has some important consequences. Most notably, while employees who have been dismissed in a discriminatory manner are entitled to claim unfair dismissal and indeed are likely to succeed in this, they will still be required to have one year's continuous service with their employer in order to be able to do so, as their claim will be dealt with under the 'normal' dismissal rules which require applicants to have one year's service. Of course, as outlined in Chapter 5, there is no service requirement for discrimination claims so they will be able to make one of those from day one (see further below on the possibility of bringing additional/alternative claims to unfair dismissal).

'Reasonableness' in the circumstances

If an employer has established a fair reason for dismissal, a tribunal will go on to consider the reasonableness of the decision to dismiss. The Employment Rights Act (s 98(4)) states that in these circumstances whether a dismissal is fair or unfair:

(a) depends on whether in the circumstances (including the size and administrative resources of the employer's undertaking) the employer acted reasonably or unreasonably in treating it as a sufficient reason for dismissing the employee, and
(b) shall be determined in accordance with equity and the substantial merits of the case.

The size and administrative resources at the disposal of the employer are specifically highlighted as factors to consider in determining fairness or unfairness. This means that what is expected of a small employer in terms of procedures and steps undertaken may be somewhat less than that expected of a larger, better resourced organisation.

Considered below are various other factors that should be taken into account by employers in addressing potential dismissal situations, namely: the employee's length of service and previous record; his/her position within the organisation; the nature of the business; possible mitigating circumstances; and consistency of treatment.

Length of service and previous record of the employee in question

Employers have generally been expected to give long-serving employees more time to learn new skills or ways of working than new or recently recruited employees, while in cases of misconduct the past records of individual employees involved may justify differences in treatment between them, notwithstanding the requirement for consistency in decision-making which is discussed below. The EAT has ruled on the relevance of an employee's disciplinary record (*Auguste Noel Ltd* v *Curtis* [1990] IRLR 326). Warnings for unconnected disciplinary offences (concerning conduct) could be taken into account. The nature and timing of such warnings could be considered by employers.

Employee's position

Employers may validly be more demanding and expect higher standards from employees in positions of authority or who hold senior posts involving substantial responsibility. For example, an employer would not be expected to give a chief executive or finance director who has been found to be incompetent, a lengthy period of time to improve their performance. These positions are of such responsibility that it is essential that the employees who hold them prove themselves to be competent soon after starting

Nature of the business

Employers' assessments of reasonableness may validly differ based on differences in the nature of the businesses they operate. For example, lighting up a cigarette in a chemical plant would be substantially more serious then doing it in a university classroom. The courts have also held that an employer may treat the theft of a perishable item (e.g. fresh produce from a supermarket) more seriously than theft of a non-perishable item (e.g. office stationery) (see Exhibit 8.4). The former may lawfully be treated as gross misconduct warranting dismissal (providing this is clearly outlined in the workplace disciplinary rules), whereas with regard to the latter an employer may be required to issue a final written warning prior to dismissal.

Mitigating circumstances

In addition to having a good disciplinary record and long service, as discussed above, whether a breach of discipline was provoked in any way may be regarded by an employer as 'mitigating circumstances' in considering what disciplinary action to take or by a tribunal in deciding whether a dismissal was fair or unfair.

Consistency

For a dismissal to be fair it is important that the employee in question was dealt with in a manner consistent with how other employees had been treated in similar circumstances. If an employee is dismissed while other employees are not or were not in similar situations in the past, then an employer is likely to find it difficult to show that the dismissal was reasonable. Employers, however, are permitted some flexibility in this regard. They may validly apply a different disciplinary sanction to individual employees depending on their disciplinary records (*London Borough of Harrow* v *Cunningham* [1996] IRLR 256, EAT). The essential requirement is that employers act reasonably.

Exhibit 8.4 Mr Howarth: a 'reasonable' decision?

British Bakeries Ltd v *Howarth* EAT/322/92

The facts and circumstances. Mr Howarth was employed by British Bakeries Ltd for 24 years. The bakery where he worked as a shift manager had introduced a system to reduce stock losses. Under this scheme staff who wished to buy the bakery's products had to make immediate payment and obtain a ticket recording the purchase. Mr Howarth was found leaving work with a loaf for which he had not paid. The company investigated the matter at a disciplinary inquiry carried out by the general manager, Mr Jenkins. Mr Howarth admitted that he had taken the bread but said that he had intended to pay for it the next day. Mr Jenkins' view was that there had been no such intention to pay. Mr Howarth was dismissed. There was an internal appeal to Mr Goodwin. He accepted that dismissal was the appropriate penalty.

Employment tribunal. Mr Howarth complained to an employment tribunal. This found that Mr Jenkins had carried out a reasonable investigation and had genuinely believed on reasonable grounds that Howarth was guilty of the alleged offence. It took the view that the company had acted reasonably in treating his conduct as a sufficient reason for dismissal.

However, the tribunal took the view that Mr Goodwin had acted unreasonably in not considering the particular circumstances of Mr Howarth's case and whether dismissal was the appropriate penalty. Mr Goodwin had told the tribunal that he 'could not conceive of any circumstances in which theft could result in any other penalty than dismissal'.

Employment Appeals Tribunal. The company appealed to the EAT, which declared the dismissal to be fair. It held that if a dismissal process was found to be intrinsically proper and that the employer's decision was proper, then, the fact that the penalty of dismissal was not considered at appeal did not necessarily mean that the dismissal was unfair overall. It stated that Mr Goodwin did not consider the penalty because he thought that dismissal was the only appropriate decision. He had satisfied himself that a fair disciplinary process had been undertaken.

The 'range of reasonable responses' test

The application of the reasonableness standard in s 98(4) of the ERA has attracted considerable interest and attention from both employment practitioners and academics. Importantly, the courts and tribunals have developed a test for determining whether dismissals for potentially fair reasons were in actual fact fair. This test is known as the 'range of reasonable responses' test, which was outlined by Lord Denning in the Court of Appeal in *British Leyland (UK) Ltd* v *Swift* [1981] IRLR 91, CA. Guidance for employment tribunals' determination of dismissal cases following this was set out in *Iceland Frozen Foods Ltd* v *Jones* [1982] IRLR 439 (see Exhibit 8.5).

Essentially, this means that in judging fairness or unfairness, tribunals and courts are not to judge the reasonableness of an employer's actions according to one general or absolute standard, and they also should not base a decision on their own personal views as to the reasonableness of the employer's conduct. Rather, they are required to ask themselves whether the decision to dismiss was within the range of actions that an employer could have been reasonably expected to take in the circumstances.

For example, while no reasonable employer would dismiss an employee for being a minute late for work on one occasion, one employer might decide to dismiss an employee for repeated absences following a written warning, while another might issue a final written warning. Both responses would arguably be valid and fall within the 'range of reasonable responses' which employers might bring to the situation.

Exhibit 8.5 The determination of 'reasonableness' by employment tribunals

EAT guidance for employment tribunals

Iceland Frozen Foods Ltd v *Jones* [1982] IRLR 439

- The starting point should be the legislation (see Employment Rights Act 1996, s 98(4), above).
- The tribunal members must consider the reasonableness of the employer's conduct, not simply whether they consider the dismissal fair.
- In judging the reasonableness of the employer's conduct, an employment tribunal must not substitute its decision as to what was the right course to adopt for that of the employer.
- In many (though not all) cases there is a range of reasonable responses to the employee's conduct within which one employer might reasonably take one view and another quite reasonably take another.
- The function of a tribunal is to determine whether in the particular circumstances of each case the decision to dismiss the employee fell within the range of reasonable responses which a reasonable employer might have adopted. If the dismissal falls within the range the dismissal is fair; if it falls outside the range it is unfair.

The 'range of reasonable responses' test is therefore designed to allow for the fact that individual employers may take a different view on a particular situation. In addition, a key feature of the test is that an employer's actions are judged against the standards of other employers of their type in the circumstances in question, as opposed to a tribunal chairman or judge. The case of Mr Howarth (Exhibit 8.4) is arguably a good example of the way in which the 'RORR' test is applied – the EAT ruled that the fact that the penalty of dismissal was not considered at the appeal did not make the dismissal unfair because the employer in question had followed a fair procedure and the decision made was in good faith.

Fair procedure

It is a long established principle of unfair dismissal law that unless a fair procedure has been followed a dismissal will not be found to have been fair. The guidelines as to disciplinary procedures contained in the ACAS code of practice are of central importance in this regard. It is important to note, as mentioned earlier, that prior to 2009, a statutory dismissal procedure had been in force since 2004. However, following a review of its operation (Gibbons 2007), this dispute resolution procedure was rescinded (by the Employment Act 2008) and greater emphasis is now placed, under a revised ACAS code of practice, on employers voluntarily ensuring compliance with the principles of **natural justice** (see Exhibit 8.1).

This section will discuss accepted standards and procedures:

- general procedural rules and principles;
- work performance and capability;
- medical capability;
- conduct;
- failure to follow a fair procedure and the '*Polkey* principle'.

General procedural rules and principles

The ACAS code of practice outlines that it is important for employers to follow certain principles of 'natural justice' in drawing up and implementing disciplinary procedures. Essentially, this means that:

- employees should be informed of the nature of the case against them;
- there should be a reasonable investigation; and
- employees should have an opportunity to defend themselves against an allegation and also to appeal any disciplinary sanction that is imposed.

One aspect confirmed in case law is that employees should be given the opportunity of a meeting with someone who has not been involved in the matter. In the case of *Byrne* v *BOC Ltd* [1992] IRLR 505, EAT, a dismissal was found to be unfair in circumstances where a manager who had instigated a disciplinary hearing also conducted the investigation and decided on the appropriate punishment. The manager in question had been too involved with the case to deal with it fairly. The principles of 'natural justice' had been breached. Hence there is a need to ensure that different people are involved in and responsible for the various stages. In addition, the code of practice states that wherever possible appeals should be dealt with by a manager who is more senior than the manager who conducted the first hearing. However ACAS's (draft) advisory handbook on discipline also notes that: 'In small firms, it may not be possible to find someone with higher authority than the person who took the original disciplinary decision. If this is the case, that person should act as impartially as possible when hearing the appeal, and should use the meeting as an opportunity to review the original decision' (para 98). Therefore, procedural requirements can be said to be somewhat more flexible in relation to small firms.

Capability or performance dismissals

For a dismissal on grounds of capability or poor performance to be fair, employers need to demonstrate that the employee in question received adequate training, was informed of the problems with his/her performance and given an opportunity to improve. In addition, it may be necessary to consider redeployment to another job. However, the ACAS code states that where an employee's first incidence of unsatisfactory performance is 'sufficiently serious' (e.g. a serious breach of health and safety), it may be appropriate to move directly to a final written warning.

Medical capability

In situations of ill health, it is essential for employers to consult with employees, base their decisions as far as possible on medical evidence, consider alternative employment and, if appropriate, consider the duty to make reasonable adjustments (under the Disability Discrimination Act 1995).

The importance of **consultation** in cases of medical incapability has been put this way: 'discussions and consultation will often bring to light facts and circumstances of which the employers were unaware, and which would throw new light on the problem . . . only one thing is certain and that is that if the employee is not consulted and given an opportunity to state his case, an injustice may be done' (Mr Justice Phillips in *East Lindsey District Council* v *Daubney* [1977] IRLR 181, EAT).

As far as medical evidence is concerned, this needs to be available. The decision of an employer to dismiss is determined in the light of this. The employer should seek it from the employee's general practitioner or occupational health doctor (or, as appropriate, a specialist). If the employee does not consent to the employer having access to medical evidence, then, the employer must act on the facts available. Important guidance on ill health and incapability is seen in *McAdie* v *Royal Bank of Scotland* [2007] IRLR 895, CA (see Exhibit 8.6). In relation to alternative employment, the employer should explore the possibility of this, but is not obliged to create a job.

Exhibit 8.6 Ill-health dismissal

McAdie v *Royal Bank of Scotland* [2007] IRLR 895, CA

The complaint. In this case the employer dismissed a long-serving employee who had been off work for over a year on grounds of incapacity. Her incapacity had been caused by workplace bullying and the employer's subsequent mishandling of the grievance she had raised in that regard. Mrs McAdie brought a claim for unfair dismissal which an employment tribunal upheld on the basis that her illness had been caused by her employer's unreasonable behaviour, i.e. the tribunal determined that it was unfair for the employer to dismiss the employee for an illness it had caused. The employer appealed to the EAT.

EAT ruling. It allowed the appeal, ruling that the fact that an employee's incapacity was caused by their employer did not mean that it would never be possible to dismiss on grounds of incapability. If this were the case, employers would be obliged to retain employees indefinitely even if they were incapable of any work.

Instead, the proper approach to adopt was to decide whether it was reasonable to dismiss the employee in all the circumstances, which included a consideration of the employer's responsibility for the employee's incapability. The EAT noted that where an employer is responsible for an employee's incapacity it should normally be expected to 'go the extra mile' in finding alternative employment or putting up with a longer period of sickness absence than would otherwise be reasonable.

Court of Appeal judgment. Mrs McAdie subsequently appealed to the Court of Appeal. This was reported as in 'complete agreement' with the EAT. It stated that the key question in unfair dismissal cases is whether or not the employer acted reasonably in the circumstances. The employer's responsibility for an employee's incapacity is relevant, but it is only one factor to consider when determining whether or not a dismissal is fair.

Conduct dismissals

Similar to situations of poor performance, employees guilty of misconduct should generally be provided with an opportunity to improve their behaviour. An issue arising in cases of misconduct is that an employer may not have absolute proof that a particular employee was guilty of the misconduct in question. However, in the case of *British Home Stores Ltd* v *Burchell* [1978] IRLR 379, the EAT set out a three-stage test for employers to satisfy in order to fairly dismiss on grounds of misconduct in these circumstances. The employer needs to:

1 demonstrate it held the *genuine belief* that the employee in question was guilty of misconduct;
2 show it had *reasonable grounds for that belief*; and
3 demonstrate that it had *conducted as much of an investigation into the matter as was reasonable in the circumstances.*

This means that although employers are required to undertake a reasonable investigation, they are not required to have irrefutable proof or evidence as to an employee's guilt in order to fairly dismiss. Clearly, this **standard of proof** is substantially below that in criminal proceedings where proof of guilt has to be 'beyond reasonable doubt'.

In the process of carrying out a misconduct investigation, evidence from an informant can be used. The EAT has provided guidance on how this might be approached and suggests that steps be taken to preserve anonymity where required:

- There should be a written statement setting out the information from the informer, noting any circumstantial evidence and confirming why the evidence might not be fabricated.
- Investigations should take place.

- If the informant refuses to attend a disciplinary hearing, he/she should be interviewed by an appropriate manager.
- The written statement should be provided to the employee who is alleged to have committed the offence.
- Full notes should be taken of the proceedings (*Linfood Cash and Carry Ltd* v *Thomson and Another* [1989] IRLR 235).

Failure to follow a fair procedure and the '*Polkey* principle'

A question that has historically caused great interest and debate in the area of dismissal is whether a dismissal decision that is fair in principle but procedurally flawed, should be regarded as fair or unfair for the purposes of the legislation. For example, if someone was dismissed for redundancy in circumstances where there was a genuine redundancy but the dismissal took place without prior notice or consultation, would this be fair or unfair? Historically, the case of *British Labour Pump* v *Byrne* [1979] ICR 347 established that where it could be shown that a procedural irregularity made 'no difference' to the actual dismissal decision, the dismissal should be regarded as fair. However, this rule was overturned by a judgment of the House of Lords in the case of *Polkey* v *A E Dayton Services* [1987] IRLR 503, which determined that where an employer failed to follow a fair procedure the dismissal would be regarded as unfair even though on the merits of the case the dismissal might be seen to be warranted or fair. However, as a counterbalance to this, the judgment also provided that where a dismissal was unfair on purely procedural grounds, the tribunal in question should reduce the compensation payable, with the exception of the basic award, to reflect the fact that the dismissal decision was fair in substance.

The *Polkey* case *did provide* for one narrow exception to the general principle that procedural failures make a dismissal unfair, namely that it would be permissible for an employer not to adhere to a particular procedural requirement when they decided, in the light of everything they knew at the time, that it would be completely futile to do so as this would not make any difference to the outcome; and that this decision was justified on the facts of the case.

Although there was a partial reversal of the '*Polkey* principle' from 2004 to 2009 following the implementation of the Employment Act 2002, it has recently been reaffirmed by the Employment Act 2008. From an employer's perspective, this is clearly onerous in that any breach or failure to follow a procedure may be likely to make a dismissal unfair. However, the potential severity of this principle is substantially mitigated by the fact that any compensation awarded to the employee in question may be reduced to reflect the substantive fairness of a dismissal decision.

Statement of reasons for dismissal

Dismissed employees with one year's continuous service with an employer are entitled to request from their employer a written statement of the reasons for their dismissal. Employees working on a fixed-term contract which expires without being renewed are also entitled to such a statement. Women who are dismissed while pregnant or on maternity leave are entitled to receive such a statement from their employer without requesting it and do not need to have one year's service. Once requested the statement must be provided within 14 days. The statement must outline what the employer believed to be the reason or reasons for the dismissal.

An employee may complain to an employment tribunal if an employer unreasonably fails to provide the statement or if the reasons given are inadequate or untrue, and a tribunal may award the employee two weeks' pay as a remedy if it finds in the employee's favour. Written statements provided by employers are admissible as evidence in unfair dismissal cases.

The statutory right to be accompanied

The Employment Relations Act 1999 (s 10) created a right for all workers (not just employees) to be accompanied during formal disciplinary and grievance meetings by a fellow worker or an employed official of a trade union or an accredited workplace union representative. A primary intention behind the introduction of this new right was to provide workers and employees with some support in what are frequently stressful and possibly complex circumstances (Saundry *et al.* 2006).

The right applies in relation to formal disciplinary hearings including meetings that could result in the issuing of a formal warning or the taking of some other disciplinary action (e.g. suspension without pay, demotion or dismissal). The right does not apply to informal discussions, counselling sessions or investigatory meetings. However, the ACAS code of practice (2009) recommends as good practice that an employee is allowed to be accompanied at disciplinary investigations.

In relation to grievances, the right applies to meetings concerning an alleged breach by an employer of either a statutory or common law duty – for example where it is alleged that the employer has broken a contractual term (for instance, in relation to remuneration or job role) or infringed a statutory requirement, such as the duty not to discriminate on grounds of gender or race.

Notably, there is no requirement that if the employer recognises a trade union for the purposes of **collective bargaining**, then workers/employees have to avail themselves of the right to be represented by a union official.

The fellow worker or trade union representative has a right to address the hearing on the worker's behalf, put across the worker's case, sum up the worker's case and respond on his or her behalf to any views expressed at the hearing. They can also confer with the worker during the hearing but are not entitled to answer questions on their behalf.

If the right to be accompanied is infringed by an employer in some way, he is liable to pay compensation of up to two weeks' pay following a complaint to an employment tribunal by the employee or worker affected.

If an employee asks to be accompanied by a solicitor at a disciplinary or grievance meeting, this is a matter at the discretion of the employer. Such requests are most likely to arise in gross misconduct cases. An important consideration as to whether such requests are made or accepted can be whether the employee may be subject to criminal proceedings as a result of the misconduct.

Obtaining redress for unfair dismissal at an employment tribunal

There are several aspects to this process of obtaining redress:

- Does the complainant qualify?
- When must a complaint be made?
- What is the role of ACAS in these tribunal complainants?
- What is a compromise agreement?

- What issues concern an employment tribunal in making its decision?
- What remedies are available to successful complainants?
- Dismissal complaints and other grounds/causes of action.
- Relationship with wrongful dismissal claims.

We will look at each of these in turn.

Does the complainant qualify?

A complainant must be an 'employee' (i.e. have a contract of employment) and have one year's continuous service with an employer. The exception to these qualifying provisions is where the dismissal is for an automatically unfair reason.

When must a complaint be made?

A complaint must be made to the employment tribunal office within three months of the incident complained of (see **www.employmenttribunals.gov.uk**).

What is the role of ACAS in these tribunal complaints?

ACAS is under a statutory duty to offer conciliation of all unfair dismissal claims as well as other claims lodged before an employment tribunal with a view to promoting a settlement. Essentially, this involves an ACAS conciliation officer communicating with both employer and employee and attempting to reach an agreement between them to settle their case. This process is voluntary. The parties are under no obligation to agree to conciliation. The conciliation officer explains tribunal procedures and relevant legal principles but does not decide on the merits of the case; rather any agreement reached is at the discretion of the parties. However if an agreement brokered by ACAS is reached, it will be legally binding.

Although conciliation is voluntary, a relatively high proportion of unfair dismissal claims are settled by means of ACAS conciliation. Most recent figures show that 43 per cent of unfair dismissal claims were settled in this way in 2007–08, while another 35 per cent were withdrawn before reaching the tribunal stage (ACAS Annual Report 2007–08 (**www.acas.org.uk**)). These figures reflect the important role that ACAS plays in the resolution of disputes through conciliation and the provision of advice.

ACAS also operates an arbitration scheme for the settlement of unfair dismissal disputes. In contrast to conciliation, this involves the parties agreeing to be bound by the decision of an independent arbitrator whose decision is final. In submitting a claim to arbitration, an employee also agrees to give up the right to subsequently apply to an employment tribunal. The ACAS arbitration scheme is intended to provide an informal and speedy mechanism for the resolution of disputes, with arbitrators' decisions made on the basis of general principles of fairness and good conduct in employee relations as opposed to legal tests or rules. However, the scheme has had very limited take-up, with only three unfair dismissal cases subject to arbitration in the year 2006–07 (ACAS Annual Report 2007–08).

What is a compromise agreement?

It is possible for the employer and the ex-employee to reach a compromise agreement. This would be a settlement of the unfair dismissal claim and an agreement by the ex-employee not to proceed with the tribunal complaint. Normally, such agreements to preclude the exercise of statutory rights would be void (ERA 1996, s 203(1)). However, special provision is made for 'compromise agreements' provided they meet certain conditions (ERA s 203(3)–(4)). These conditions are:

- the agreement must be in writing;
- it must relate to the particular complaint;
- the ex-employee must have received independent legal advice on 'the terms and effect of the proposed agreement' and 'in particular, its effect on his ability to pursue his rights before an employment tribunal';
- the adviser can be a qualified lawyer, a trade union officer, employee or member who has been certified in writing by the union as competent and authorised to give advice; or an advice-centre worker who is certified and authorised to give advice;
- the adviser must have in force indemnity insurance;
- the agreement must identify the legal adviser; and
- 'the agreement must state that the conditions regulating compromise agreements under this Act are satisfied'.

What issues concern an employment tribunal in making its decision?

There are a number of issues that an employment tribunal will consider when reaching its decisions. These are examined earlier in this chapter and are merely summarised here:

- whether the complainant qualifies;
- whether internal disciplinary procedures have been fully used;
- whether there is a dismissal in law;
- whether the dismissal was for a fair or automatically unfair reason;
- whether or not the employer has behaved reasonably in all the circumstances;
- whether fair procedures were used;
- if the dismissal was unfair, what remedies are appropriate.

What remedies are available to successful complainants?

There are three possible remedies available to employees who have been unfairly dismissed: reinstatement, re-engagement and compensation. Reinstatement and re-engagement are the first remedies considered by tribunals. Reinstatement means that an employee gets his or her old job back, as if they had never been dismissed. Re-engagement means that the employee is taken back by the employer but in a different position. However, these remedies are very rarely awarded, being ordered in only 0.3 per cent of unfair dismissal cases disposed of in 2006–07 (ACAS Annual Report 2006–07). An employment tribunal cannot force an employer to reinstate or re-engage an employee but where an order for reinstatement or re-engagement is not complied with, an employee is granted an 'additional award' of between 26 and 52 weeks' pay. (The amount of a 'week's pay' in this regard is, normally, determined annually. See **www.berr.gov.uk** for the current rate.)

The third remedy, compensation, is the most common. The compensation remedy is made up of a basic award and an additional award. The former is a non-discretionary, standard award that is calculated on the basis of a formula relating to the number of years' continuous service of the employee, as follows:

- $1^1/_2$ weeks' pay for every year of employment over the age of 41 years;
- 1 week's pay for every year of service between the ages of 22 and 41 years;
- Half a week's pay for every year of service completed before the age of 22.

The compensatory award is discretionary and designed to compensate an employee for current and future loss of earnings. It is awarded at a level that is 'just and equitable' in the circumstances, subject to a maximum limit (these are set in February each year – see **www.berr.gov.uk**). Importantly, compensation is for financial loss only and employees have a duty to mitigate their loss, for example by looking for another job.

Following the Employment Act 2008, employment tribunals may adjust compensation awards if they feel that the ACAS code of practice has not been followed without good reason. Where the employer has unreasonably failed to comply with the code the tribunal may increase any award to an employee by up to 25 per cent. Similarly, where the employee has unreasonably failed to comply with the code the award they receive may be reduced by up to 25 per cent.

In situations of constructive dismissal a tribunal may reduce an employee's compensation where they have not attempted to resolve the problem internally by raising a grievance with their employer before applying to a tribunal. This would be consistent with the law as it stood up until April 2009, which required employees to have first raised a grievance with their employer before they would be entitled to claim constructive dismissal at a tribunal.

Dismissal complaints and other grounds/causes of action

Depending on the circumstances, employees who have been dismissed may be in a position to bring a claim additional to their complaint of unfair dismissal. For example, an employee who was dismissed on grounds of age or sexual orientation would be entitled to bring a claim for discrimination in addition to dismissal, as would a woman dismissed on grounds of pregnancy or maternity leave. An employee dismissed for claiming his or her entitlement to the national minimum wage may be able to bring a claim for unlawful deduction of wages under the Employment Rights Act 1996 in addition to one for dismissal (there would be no requirement for one year's service here, as this situation comes within the category of automatically unfair reasons for dismissal).

Bringing an additional claim may be advantageous from the point of view of the remedies that are awarded. In particular, while compensation paid as a remedy in unfair dismissal claims is subject to a maximum limit and does not take into account possible injury to feelings, there is no upper limit on the compensation that may be payable for unlawful discrimination and there may be an award for injury to feelings (see Chapter 5). However, it should be noted that tribunals are not permitted to award compensation for both discrimination and unfair dismissal in respect of the same act, i.e. compensation may only be awarded on one of these grounds.

As well as making it possible for tribunal applicants to make more than one claim, it is, of course, also the case that they may be able to bring a claim instead of or as an alternative to one for unfair dismissal. This possibility is of particular importance to those employees who do not have the required one year's continuous service to claim unfair dismissal and also to casual workers who do not have employee status and therefore are unable to claim unfair dismissal at all.

Table 8.2 Redress for wrongful dismissal

Claim	*Time limit and qualifications*	*Comments*
***Damages over £25,000* for wages lost, or for breach of contract by the employer** Damages may be reduced because claimant has found new job; failed to mitigate his/her loss; or has received some payment from former employer Damages (which are unlimited) are for the loss experienced, but no compensation for the dismissal	• 6 years; 5 years in Scotland • no qualifying service necessary	Claims made in High Court in England and Wales, or, in the Court of Session in Scotland Legal representation needed; and, if employee loses, employer's costs could be awarded against him/her
Damages of less than £25,000* for breach of contract by the employer – associated with an unfair dismissal claim** (under Employment Rights Act 1996) Damages may be awarded for loss but ***no compensation for the wrongful dismissal itself. Limited compensation for unfair dismissal is possible only if claimant successful in that unfair dismissal claim	• Within 3 months of the dismissal • Claimant must qualify to bring unfair dismissal claim at employment tribunal • Claim must arise out of termination of employment.	Claims at employment tribunal introduced in 1994 Legal representation ***not*** necessary for complainant. Employer's costs only awarded against employee in very limited circumstances.
Damages of less than £25,000* for wages lost; or for breach of contract by the employer resulting in wrongful dismissal (not associated with an unfair dismissal claim)** Damages may be reduced because claimant has found new job; failed to mitigate his/her loss; or has received some payment from former employer Damages may be awarded; but ***no compensation for the wrongful dismissal itself	• 6 years; 5 years in Scotland • no qualifying service necessary	Claims made in county court in England and Wales, or in the sheriff's court in Scotland If both wrongful and unfair dismissal claims are made (in separate proceedings) the tribunal or court may 'stay' one action – probably the wrongful dismissal claim – until the other has been determined. Because, in terms of money, there can be no double recovery

Relationship with wrongful dismissal claims

The issue of wrongful dismissal was explained earlier in the chapter. Remedies for such dismissal can, depending on the circumstances, be sought in either the courts or at employment tribunal (see Table 8.2).

Grievances and disciplinary action

In this chapter various references have been made to the use of grievance procedures. Generally, grievances arise in the workplace in relation to terms of the contract of employment or in relation to the implementation of statutory employment rights and entitlements. However, there are two ways in which the grievance procedure can intertwine with disciplinary processes: in circumstances where an employee lodges a grievance during the process when disciplinary action is being considered against them; and in cases involving constructive dismissal. We will look at each of these circumstances in turn and also comment on general points of good practice relating to the lodging of grievances.

Grievance raised in the course of disciplinary action

Good practice advice in this regard was provided in the ACAS Code of Practice (2009, para 44):

> Where an employee raises a grievance during a disciplinary process the disciplinary process may be temporarily suspended in order to deal with the grievance. Where the grievance and disciplinary cases are related it may be appropriate to deal with both issues concurrently.

Constructive dismissal

As noted earlier, a claim alleging constructive dismissal is likely to have been preceded by a grievance about the unacceptable conduct of the employer. The grievance should have been raised through the formal workplace procedure. An employment tribunal will examine whether or not this internal step has been taken.

General guidance about grievances

The ACAS code (2009, paras 31–43 (**www.acas.org.uk**)) sets out the following key guidance in relation to employee grievances:

- *Informing the employer.* 'This should be done in writing.'
- *Meeting.* The employer should hold this 'without unreasonable delay'.
- *Statutory right to be accompanied.* This should be granted where the complaint is about an employer 'not honouring the worker's contract or is in breach of legislation'.
- *Employer's decision.* This should be communicated 'without unreasonable delay' and 'where appropriate should set out what action the employer intends to take to resolve the grievance'.
- *Appeal.* This should be provided and heard promptly; and 'the appeal should be dealt with impartially and wherever possible by a manager who has not previously been involved in the case'.

Although the statutory grievance procedure has now been repealed, case law relating to its operation is likely to have some continuing influence as a reference point for future tribunal rulings. Some of the important points to emerge from this are as follows:

- *Making a grievance.* The requirements regarding the taking of grievances were seen to be quite minimal. All an employee had to do was set out a grievance in writing, there was no need for comprehensive detail, with employees only required to set out the general nature or basis of claim (*Mark Warner* v *Aspland* [2006] IRLR 87, EAT).
- Although an employee's grievance needed to be set out in writing, it did not need to expressly state that it constituted a formal 'grievance' (*Canary Wharf Management Ltd* v *Edebi* [2006] IRLR 416, EAT).

- *Format.* A grievance could be contained in a letter of resignation (*Shergold* v *Fieldway Medical Centre* [2006] IRLR 76, EAT) and likewise a solicitor's letter (*Mark Warner* v *Aspland* [2006] IRLR 87, EAT).

Conclusion

There are various elements which employers need to take account of with regard to discipline and dismissal at work. However, for the most part the law in this area is relatively straightforward, with the adoption of a common sense approach generally enabling employers to satisfy the legal requirements. The categories of both fair and unfair reasons for dismissal are arguably both logical and encompassing, while the requirement for dismissal decisions to be reasonable is arguably also a suitable and appropriate provision. The ACAS code of practice and advisory handbook on discipline and grievance constitute very useful supplementary sources to the provisions in the Employment Rights Act, providing helpful guidance for employers and employees alike. In addition, the recent repeal of the demanding and rather confusing three-step statutory dispute resolution procedures has simplified the law in this area.

There are, therefore, strong reasons to conclude that dismissal law is beneficial for both employers and employees alike. For employers, it outlines clear rules and guidelines to be followed; while from an employee perspective it ensures not only that employers must have a valid reason for dismissal but that the dismissal decision and process followed are fair and reasonable. The emphasis in the ACAS code of practice on the use of disciplinary processes as a means of facilitating improved performance rather than simply punishing deviant behaviour is beneficial for employees, while the provisions relating to automatic unfair reasons for dismissal and constructive dismissal provide them with particular protection.

It is also very evident that the existence of the unfair dismissal legislation has had a direct impact on employers' actions and behaviour in this area. The introduction of dismissal legislation in the 1970s prompted many British employers to formalise their activities and approaches to discipline and dismissal. The extent to which this has now occurred is demonstrated by the WERS 2004 survey, which found that 91 per cent of workplaces in Britain had a formal disciplinary/dismissal procedure, and 88 per cent a formal grievance procedure (Kersley *et al.* 2006: 215).

The legislation, therefore, has undoubtedly enhanced the legal protection of employees. However, it has also been heavily criticised by academics writing from an employment rights perspective and is seen to have a number of serious weaknesses (Earnshaw *et al.* 2000; Collins 1992, 2003; Collins *et al.* 2005; Anderman 2001). The fact that protection against unfair dismissal applies only to employees with one year's continuous service is highlighted as a serious deficiency, while the minimal use of reinstatement and re-engagement as remedies also attracts great criticism. In addition, a number of the provisions of the ERA and the manner in which they have been interpreted and implemented by the courts have been highlighted as detrimental to the goal of providing employees with strong protection from being unfairly dismissed. In particular, academics such as Collins (1992, 2003) note how the 'range of reasonable responses' test, used to assess the reasonableness of a dismissal decision, arguably provides employers with too much leeway in making dismissal decisions. It is suggested that the fact that there is no one, fixed standard of reasonableness and that tribunals are not permitted to substitute their decision for that of the employer, means that the latter are largely prevented from developing strong general standards or principles regarding the reasonableness of dismissal decisions.

The courts' and tribunals' use of the 'some other substantial reason' provision provokes similar criticism – it is argued that this provision has been interpreted in such a way as to too easily enable employers to establish a fair reason for dismissal. Collins (2004) has recently undertaken a very detailed critique of the unfair dismissal legislation and outlines numerous suggestions for reform which address the weaknesses.

Exercises

8.1 **Jason**. Jason, 22, has worked as a customer service representative at Easywheels, a large car rental company, for two years. He is a full-time, permanent employee. Working in a team of four, his job involves taking customer bookings over the phone and processing them via the company's computer system. His hours are 8.30 to 5. He has always adopted a relaxed attitude to work but over the last four months his performance has been less than satisfactory. He has been between 20 and 40 minutes late for work on a number of occasions during this time. This is due to the fact that having recently split from his girlfriend, he is now living with his parents and so has a longer commute to work than before. He received an informal (oral) warning and a formal (written) warning from his line manager after the third and fourth times he was late. He has just been late for work for a fifth time.

In addition to the lateness, in each of the last two weeks Jason has failed to stay for an allocated evening shift (from 5.30 to 7.30), which all employees are required to do one day a week, explaining that he was 'stressed' and needed to go home to rest.

Jason's line manager asks you, Easywheels' HR manager, how his case should be handled in light of the continuing lateness and recent unexplained absences. In particular, she wants to know whether the company may be able to dismiss Jason for poor performance. What advice would you give the manager?

8.2 **Sarah**. Sarah has worked for five years as Product Designer at a small manufacturer of high quality pottery products employing 50 people. Her job involves physically drawing out designs and making trial runs of new product orders by hand before they are manufactured as full commercial runs. One weekend, while rock climbing, Sarah falls and badly breaks her right arm. She is taken to hospital and has an operation on the arm. While this successfully reinforces her bone structures she is left with permanent tissue and muscle damage meaning that she is no longer able to draw designs or operate a kiln (used to make the pottery products). While distraught at what has happened, Sarah is determined to return to work in some capacity. On hearing of the accident and seeing a copy of the medical diagnosis, the managing director of Sarah's company invites her, in writing, to a meeting to discuss her situation. In the letter he outlines the problematic nature of her position given the ongoing requirements of the business. At the meeting the MD tells Sarah that he will have to appoint a replacement for her immediately due to the need to keep up with customer orders. In addition, although a vacancy will shortly be coming available in the marketing department, as Sarah does not have the necessary qualifications for this job, he explains that she is not eligible to apply. Sarah is subsequently informed of her dismissal in writing. She is given an opportunity to appeal but her appeal is rejected.

Sarah asks for your advice about her rights and any action she might take against her employer.

8.3 **Jo**. Jo, with six years' service, works as a trader at GNC, one of the larger stockbroking firms in the City. Very few female traders are employed by GNC and she is the only woman in her department. Like many companies in the City, GNC is a fast-paced working environment with a somewhat 'macho' working **culture**. Jo has recently been dismayed to see that following a change in line management in her department, the 'macho' culture has become more noticeable over the last year or so. The new department manager has created an informal rule whereby all team members are expected to participate in 'team building' sessions in a pub or wine bar at least two evenings a week. Having two small children, Jo informally objected to this to the manager, but was told that 'it is important for all members of the department to attend' these events. Jo has suffered significant stress as a result of having to attend, in particular, due to her not being able to go home to her family but also as a consequence of the heavy drinking that takes place. She discusses the issue with her line manager's direct superior. However, he too treats the complaint as nothing serious, noting that 'this sort of thing is happening all across the City'. Most recently, after the announcement of the company's annual results, all the brokers were required to attend a social function that lasted from 6 p.m. to 2 a.m. where there was strong peer pressure to drink a large amount of alcohol in celebrating the company's success. As a result, Jo falls ill. Her doctor informs her that she is suffering from stress and will need to take three months off work.

She contacts a friend who studies employment law for advice about her situation, in particular, any relevant rights she has and also regarding the company's obligations towards her. What advice would the friend give her?

Feedback on these exercises is provided in the Appendix to this textbook.

References

Advisory, Conciliation and Arbitration Service. Annual Reports. London: ACAS (www.acas.org.uk).

Advisory, Conciliation and Arbitration Service (2004) *Code of Practice on Disciplinary and Grievance Procedures*. London: ACAS.

Advisory, Conciliation and Arbitration Service (2009) *Code of Practice on Disciplinary and Grievance Procedures*. London: ACAS.

Anderman, S. (1986) 'Unfair dismissals and redundancy', in Lewis, R. (ed.) *Labour Law in Britain*. Oxford: Blackwell.

Anderman, S. (2001) *The Law of Unfair Dismissal* (3rd edn). London: Butterworth.

Collins, H. (1992) *Justice in Dismissal: the Law on Termination of Employment*. Oxford: Clarendon.

Collins, H. (2003) *Employment Law*. Oxford: Oxford University Press.

Collins, H. (2004) *Nine Proposals for the Reform of the Law on Unfair Dismissal*. London: Institute of Employment Rights.

Collins, H., Ewing, K. and McColgan, A. (2005) *Labour Law: Text & Materials* (2nd edn). Oxford: Hart.

Earnshaw, J., Marchington, M. and Goodman, J. (2000) 'Unfair to whom? Discipline and dismissal in small establishments', *Industrial Relations Journal*, 31(1): 62–73.

Employment Tribunals Service. *Annual Reports*. London: The Stationery Office.

Gibbons, M. (2007) *A Review of Employment Dispute Resolution in Great Britain*. London: Department of Trade and Industry (www.berr.gov.uk/employment).

Kersley, B., Alpin, C., Forth, J., Bryson, A., Bewley, H., Dix, G. and Oxenbridge, S. (2006) *Inside the Workplace: Findings from the 2004 Workplace Employment Relations Survey*. London: Routledge.

Knight, K. and Latreille, P. (2000) 'Discipline, dismissals and complaints to employment tribunals', *British Journal of Industrial Relations*, 38(4): 533–55.

Saundry, R. *et al*. (2006) *Employee Representation in Grievance and Disciplinary Matters – making a difference*? Employment Relations Research Series, No. 69. London: Department of Trade and Industry.

9 Pay regulation

Learning objectives

To understand:

- The social policies that influence pay determination
- The legal regulation governing pay deduction
- The statutory framework governing the national minimum wage

Structure of the chapter

- *Introduction*: the growth of the legal regulation of pay
- *The context*: economic, social welfare and social and political policy issues in relation to pay; 'fair' pay and status differences, sex and race discrimination and minimum pay
- *Legal provisions*: definitions: wages and pay; common law of contract and pay; information about pay; methods of payment; overpayment; pay deduction; fines; disciplinary action; shortages and losses in retail employment; pay and sex discrimination, statutory national minimum wage
- *Employment policies and practices*: contracts of employment and collective agreements; information and records
- *Exercises*

Introduction

The legal regulation of pay, like working time, is an issue that goes to the heart of the employment relationship and as such has generated considerable controversy. Indeed, in the past 30 years, pay has been the subject of growing legal regulation by Parliament. The most notable examples are the enactment of equal pay legislation (Chapter 5), a statutory framework on lawful and unlawful pay deduction, and the introduction of a statutory national minimum wage.

Prior to the 1970s, although law regulated aspects of pay, it did so primarily through the **common law** of contract – particularly through the implied **duty** on the employer to pay wages and not to make unauthorised deductions. These duties remain important but affected by the expanding body of **statute law**. This statute law has concerned itself both with the *transaction* (the paying and receiving of wages that are due) and with the *level of pay*. The latter is reflected in the legal framework governing equal pay (between men and women) and, since 1998, in that relating to the statutory national minimum wage.

Statute law also regulates the transaction through the provisions of the Employment Rights Act 1996 (s 1), outlining contractual information to be disclosed, and is relevant in assisting **employees** to calculate whether they have received their correct pay. This is supplemented by the requirement for employers to provide an itemised pay statement (s 8) which must contain information on the gross amount of salary; the amount of any variable or fixed deductions (s 9) and the purposes for which they are made. The itemised pay statement must also provide details of the amount of wages or salary payable, and where different parts are paid in different ways, the amount and method of payment or part-payment.

The context

The context within which the law on remuneration has been developed has been characterised by two broad sets of factors:

1 the primacy, given by policy-makers, to the **economic determinants** of pay and the view that it should reflect the free play of market forces;
2 the view that pay levels should be influenced by **standards of social justice**, acknowledging there may be occasions when market forces either do not work or do not reflect concerns of equity and fairness.

Much legislation involves a blend of these economic and social justice issues. We will look at each in turn.

Economic issues

Much of the concern of legislation is with 'pay' or 'wages'. (These terms are defined below in the section on the legal framework, p. 283.) However, there are certain elements in the wider package of 'remuneration' that a person might acquire from employment, including private health insurance, a company car, non-contributory pension scheme and it is important in any individual case to be clear whether discussion is about 'pay' or broader issues of 'remuneration'.

The importance of pay to employees

Economists have traditionally worked with a model of human behaviour embodied in the concept of 'economic man', that individuals are rational, utility maximisers and will seek out opportunities to maximise their income. On this basis pay is the prime determinant of why people work and why they work where they do. Even relaxing this strict instrumental view slightly it is clear that pay is important as an *extrinsic reward* for work done. It provides purchasing power for goods and services, helps a person maintain or improve their standard of living, and is frequently important as an indication of social status (Phelps Brown 1979). However, as psychologists, sociologists and indeed many economists acknowledge, people may also derive *intrinsic reward* from work such as recognition, power and status and self-esteem. Individuals will differ in the significance they attach to these rewards or sources of satisfaction but it reminds us that people's motivations about work and employment are often complex and interlinked, and that they may not be solely motivated by a desire to maximise their income.

The importance of pay to employers

Pay is normally assumed to be important for employers in addressing three basic objectives. First, that of **recruitment**: here comparative salaries with competitor organisations are likely to influence an employer's ability to recruit staff. Organisations with an established reputation for paying salaries above those of their competitors may well secure the pick of available recruits in the labour market. Second, the issue of staff **retention**: pay may affect this through paying salaries above the market rate, lengthy salary scales where more experienced and competent employees receive higher rewards and through loyalty bonuses and share options. Third, pay may be important for employers in influencing **motivation**, in that cash inducements may be used to change attitudes and/or improve or modify performance.

In terms of meeting some or all of these objectives, organisations have a choice of payments systems available to them (see Exhibit 9.1).

Political policy: free markets and regulation

Under a pure 'free market' system employers would be free to set whatever pay level they choose and the payment system they felt most appropriate. Furthermore, they would be free to decide whether or not to pay 'wages' for work done, make deductions where they felt these to be appropriate, under the employment relationship and which (if any) benefits to provide. In practice, although employers do have considerable freedom in these areas there are constraints in their operation that affect employers' decision-making.

The main ways in which the free market is modified concern questions of equity and fairness and a perception that left to its own devices, the free market may operate against the interests of some of the weakest and most vulnerable groups in the labour market (Rubery and Edwards 2003). Historically, these concerns have been voiced by trade unions through the **collective bargaining** process, but more recently they are themes that have been asserted through legislation. Developments in the areas of equal pay, the national minimum wage, and constraints on employers' abilities to make lawful deductions from pay are illustrations of this shift and point to the recognition of social factors in the determination of pay that are dealt with below.

Contrasting positions on this issue of pay and the free market can be seen through a comparison of the policies of Conservative governments (1979–97), and those of the Labour

Exhibit 9.1 Payment systems

The payment systems available normally fit into one of three categories:

1. ***Time-based pay***. Pay is usually related to hours, weeks or months of work. Such systems focus on grade rates. They tend to be found in more bureaucratic organisations where the pattern of work is relatively stable and easy to define.
2. ***Output-based pay***. Pay is normally related to some measure of an employee's performance. It includes systems that link pay to some quantified measure such as the volume or value of output (such as piecework, profit-sharing), as well as those that are linked to more subjective assessments of performance through appraisal schemes (such as performance-related pay).
3. ***Skill-based pay***. Under this system, pay is related to the skill, experience and competence possessed by an employee. This is most commonly used for technical and 'knowledge' **workers**. It is intended to raise the quality and **flexibility** of the workforce. It is appropriate when the pace of change is rapid so that new ideas, methods and technology are being introduced regularly.

Payments under these systems may be fixed (e.g. basic weekly wages) with rates only changeable by agreement. Alternatively, payments may vary according to the amount of time an employee attends work or the time of day attended. So, for example, longer attendance can result in overtime pay, and night and shift working in special premium rates. Much output-based pay can be variable and as well as those examples identified above; those in sales-related work, who are often paid by commission (the volume of sales), may have a very large proportion of their pay determined in this way.

government since 1997. Much of the emphasis of Conservative labour market policy in the 1980s and 1990s was in removing what it saw as impediments to the efficient operation of a free market. Laws to curb the power and influence of trade unions and collective bargaining, and the abolition of Wages Councils were attempts to restore the primacy of economic factors in determining pay and other **terms** and conditions of employment (the specific details of this are contained in Exhibit 9.2). The gradual undermining of collective influence on pay throughout this period was part of a broader 'de-collectivisation' of employment relations and a simultaneous strengthening of individual performance factors in relation to pay.

The Labour governments after 1997 retained many of the free market approaches and initiatives of their Conservative predecessors. Labour market intervention has been limited, always ensuring that such intervention has not compromised competitiveness and flexibility and has focused mainly on individual rights, seeking to establish a legal minimum floor of rights below which individuals would not be permitted to fall (Davies and Freedland 2007). In

Exhibit 9.2 Conservative labour-market policy initiatives (1979–97)

- Abolition of Fair Wages resolution affecting public sector contracts.
- The abolition of Wages Councils (1993).
- Gradual reduction in use of 'comparability' as a basis for pay determination in the public sector.
- Introduction of competitive tendering and market testing in the public sector.
- Use of legislation to erode the power and influence of trade unions, in particular, in relation to the 'closed shop' and industrial action.
- Attempts in the public sector to encourage greater flexibility and remove many groups from collective bargaining coverage.
- Support for the de-recognition of trade unions.
- Promotion of performance related pay in public and private sectors.

the area of pay, the single most important development was the establishment of a Low Pay Commission and resulting legislation – the National Minimum Wage Act (NMWA 1998).

Social welfare factors

Although there have been elements of consistency in government policy between Conservative and Labour governments, the period since 1997 has marked a shift in policy concerns towards assisting the most vulnerable groups and individuals in the labour market. In addition to the NMW and other individual employment protection, there has also been a focus on the interlocking of pay and certain in-work social benefits. In the late 1990s there was increasing concern over the creation of a 'poverty trap' whereby an individual loses certain in-work benefits as pay increases. The effect of which is to make little change to disposable income and in many instances to discourage individuals from working more hours and to entrench not only 'in-work' poverty but also a dependency culture.

One of the areas highlighted by the first report of the Low Pay Commission (1998: 31) was the relationship between pay levels and social security benefits. The Commission pointed out that from the mid-1970s those on median earnings and those highest earners have experienced a significantly greater increase in earnings than the lowest paid (see Atkinson 2003; Machin 2003 on rising inequality). The Commission concluded that:

> The widening distribution of earnings has led to a substantial degree of in-work poverty, particularly among families with young children and a consequential increase in earnings than the lowest-paid workers.
> (Low Pay Commission 1998: 32)

The effects of this can be seen from the growth in Family Credit (and before this Family Income Supplement) from £200 million in 1987/88 to £2,000 million in 1996/97 with around three-quarters of a million families receiving Family Credit in the mid-1990s. In 1999, Family Credit was replaced by the Working Families Tax Credit and in 2003 two new schemes – the Working Tax Credit and the Child Tax Credit – replaced the Working Families Tax Credit. However, according to the Poverty Site (**www.poverty.org.uk**) these changes have not achieved the success that was anticipated. The generous eligibility criteria introduced as a result of the changes in 2003 has meant that in April 2008, 150,000 working-age households (approximately 17 per cent of all working-age households) were in receipt of tax credits, double the number in 2001 and treble that in 1998.

Social policy

It is against the background of economic determinism and the social-welfare poverty trap that new standards in relation to pay are being created by legislative action. Social policy in respect of remuneration has a number of aspects. Some of these relate directly to government policy and others have evolved in managerial policy approaches. The issues involved are:

- fair pay;
- status differences in remuneration between manual and non-manual workers;
- pay levels and sex and race discrimination;
- minimum pay;
- new social objectives.

We will look at each in turn.

Fair pay

The concept of fairness in pay is controversial. Free market economists would argue that fairness is determined by market forces, and if the market indicates a cleaner is worth £6.00 an hour and a professional footballer £60,000 a week then this is fair. However, others would point to the existence of monopsony power in parts of the labour market that mean that outcomes such as pay do not always reflect the free play of market forces (an example could be local employers facing limited competition for less skilled staff could take advantage of their market position and pay below the 'market rate'). It is argued further that these pressures are likely to impact particularly on the most vulnerable so that protection in the form of minimum pay legislation may be necessary to ensure some element of fairness for these groups.

Additionally, fairness can mean a fair reward for the work undertaken, something that extends to comparative pay. This notion of 'felt fair' (Jacques 1967) resonates with the work of psychologists such as Adams (1965) who developed the concept of equity theory – that individuals not only equate their effort to outcomes, but also equate it to that of others, and where a discrepancy exists individuals will experience some distress and seek to redress this. In terms of comparative pay, the law has played a role. In 1891, the House of Commons adopted the Fair Wages Resolution whereby employers engaged on government contracts should pay at least the wage level generally recognised for the sector or locality concerned. The Resolution was revised in 1946, and ultimately repealed in 1983 as part of the Conservative government's free-market economic policies. Although under pressure to re-introduce such a measure, Labour governments since 1997 have not revived it, presumably because they have felt that the national minimum wage has now created a more wide-ranging basis for equal pay.

Notions of fairness frequently impinge upon organisational decisions about pay through the operation of job evaluation schemes. Such schemes mediate the impact of market forces and provide a broader defence of pay differentials, something that has acquired particular importance in the area of equal pay (see discussion in Chapter 5).

Status-based pay

The status divide has long been a feature of employment in Britain and refers to the distinction between manual (or 'blue collar') and non-manual (or 'white collar') workers. Historically, there was a clear distinction between these broad groups reflected in very different terms and conditions of employment. Manual workers generally worked longer hours, had fewer holidays, no provision for sick pay nor of pensions, and had less job security. Frequently they were subject to one week's notice to terminate their **contracts** of employment, and pay was normally on a weekly basis and in manufacturing frequently fluctuated because of being output-based. In some cases pay was on a daily basis, depending on the availability of work, a phenomenon characteristic of industries such as port transport prior to de-casualisation in 1947. Inevitably hourly rates of pay for manual workers were frequently lower than the equivalent rates paid to 'white collar' staff.

Since the 1960s changes to these status distinctions have taken place although the extent of these has been the subject of debate (McGovern and Hill 2004). In any event the impact of legal and political initiatives in encouraging change in this area has been limited. Moves towards **single status** and harmonisation of conditions of employment have been initiated mainly by employers for reasons related to the management of their organisations.

Discrimination and pay

It is common to focus on discrimination-based pay under the provisions of the Equal Pay Act 1970, where direct comparisons are made in particular organisations between men's pay and women's pay. This aspect of pay has been discussed in Chapter 5. There reference was also made to discrimination in relation to general levels of pay, seen in particular in earnings distribution figures, giving rise to potential indirect discrimination. However, similar discriminatory treatment in relation to pay is also evident in respect of sex and ethnic origin.

As noted in Chapter 5, because of their over-representation in low paid jobs, women have been one of the main beneficiaries of the national minimum wage. In part this reflects the concentration of women in part-time work. In a recent report the Low Pay Commission has stated that almost two-thirds of minimum wage jobs are held by women and that over 60 per cent of all minimum wage jobs are part-time (LPC 2008: 8). Women also dominate in areas such as homeworking, with the Low Pay Commission stating that 'most homeworkers we met painted a vivid picture of low pay and in some instances outright exploitation' (LPC 1998: 42). Evidence also suggests that lone parents (who are predominantly women) 'tend to be more affected by low pay than female workers and workers in general' (LPC 1998: 41). According to the National Group on Homeworking, many homeworkers are still paid below the national minimum wage, and many are incorrectly classified as self-employed rendering them ineligible for employment rights such as sick pay, maternity pay, redundancy pay and rights against unfair **dismissal** (**www.ngh.org.uk** 'What we Do'). Indeed in its 2007 Report the LPC stated that 'in view of the difficulties faced by homeworkers we continue to believe this group warrants particular attention in terms of the enforcement of their minimum wage rights' (LPC 2007: xvii).

As far as **ethnic origin** is concerned, the evidence is mixed. It is the case that in general workers from ethnic minorities are more likely to be working in low paying sectors (LPC 2008: 75) but there are clear differences between ethnic groups with Pakistanis and Bangladeshis most likely to be affected (LPC 2008: 8). It is also probable that there is under-recording of work in sectors such as clothing and hosiery where homeworking is dominant and undertaken largely by groups from particular minority groups (LPC 1998: 38). As Heath and Cheung (2006) have argued, 'even after controlling for factors such as age, education and other personal characteristics there were still significant net disadvantages for Black Africans, Black Caribbeans, Pakistanis, and Bangladeshis with respect to unemployment, earnings and occupational attainment' (quoted in LPC 2008: 77).

Minimum pay

Policies to set minimum pay levels in Britain have focused on two sets of initiatives. The first, lasting from the early twentieth century until 1993 was the system of Wages Councils established to cover workers in particular industries and sectors. The second, and most recent has been the development of a statutory minimum wage applicable to all workers.

Wages Councils

Established under legislation in 1909, 'trade boards', as they were originally known, were devised as a means of addressing gaps in the coverage provided by **free collective bargaining** and the difficulties of developing trade union organisation in particular sectors of the economy. These 'trade boards' (the name was changed in 1945 to Wages Councils) comprised representatives of employers, trade unions and government and were charged with setting and implementing statutory minimum pay for specific sectors in the economy, the so-called 'sweated industries' with 'wages barely sufficient to sustain existence' (Select Committee on the Sweating System

5th Report 1890, in Collins *et al.* 2005: 388). At the outset it was always envisaged that Wages Councils would be a temporary measure, eventually replaced by full-blown collective bargaining. At their peak in 1953, there were 66 Wages Councils, covering some 3.5 million workers. The main sectors covered were retail distribution, catering and hotels, clothing, laundries, road haulage and agriculture, and at the time of abolition in 1993 there were 35 Wages Councils left in existence (26 in Britain, nine in Northern Ireland). Following abolition, one sector, agriculture, with institutions charged with establishing statutory minimum pay and conditions – the Agricultural Wages Boards – were permitted to continue, a reflection of the original concerns of the legislators in 1909 to protect workers in sectors where union organisation was weak and employers relatively powerful. It was also an acknowledgement that despite its history (the AWB had been established in 1948) low pay remained a problem in the sector and the hoped-for transition to free collective bargaining had not materialised.

In terms of their operation, Wages Councils made Wages Orders that were enforced through a Wages Inspectorate. In the 14 years prior to abolition, the annual average number of completed prosecutions via the Inspectorate was only seven but as the Low Pay Commission noted these figures understated their role as 'Inspectorate policy was to achieve compliance through advice and persuasion rather than legal action' (LPC 1998: 207).

As the earlier discussion indicated, the political climate of the 1980s and 1990s was not one favourable to institutions that were felt to be interfering with free market forces. Wages Councils were an obvious target, and the government's antipathy towards these institutions of wage determination was summed up by Nigel Lawson (then Chancellor of the Exchequer) when he stated that they were 'forcing employers to pay wages they cannot afford'. As well as adding to firm's costs, the other implication was that Wages Council rates could impact on jobs. The government's response was to reduce the remit of Wages Councils in 1986 and in 1993, with the exception of the Agricultural Wages Boards, to abolish them completely. At the time of abolition they covered 2.6 million workers.

Towards a national minimum wage

Although the concept of a national minimum wage is not new, and is a feature of employment legislation in a number of European states, political commitment to the idea in Britain is more recent. Historically, both the Labour Party and trade union movement preferred a minimum wage system that was limited to those areas where collective bargaining could not be achieved, in a context of a wider policy commitment to encourage and extend collective bargaining. However, the abolition of the Wages Council system, US evidence that minimum wage legislation brought benefits with limited negative effects (Card and Kreuger 1995) and New Labour's own deliberations on employment relations policies led to a reappraisal. During the 1990s, the Labour Party in opposition accepted a policy commitment to a national minimum wage as part of a package of labour market reforms designed to assist the low paid. Initially, the Party had considered determining the minimum wage on the basis of a formula – half the median male earnings – but after 1996, it developed the approach that became adopted by the Labour government. The essential elements of this were:

- the establishment of a low pay commission involving employers, unions and independent members;
- **consultation** with employers and employees;
- the responsibility of the commission to set the national minimum wage;
- consideration being given to economic circumstances.

In 1997, the Labour government appointed the Low Pay Commission, comprising employer, union and academic representatives. In making initial recommendations, the Commission undertook a comprehensive research and consultation programme including 'visits to over sixty cities, towns and villages throughout the UK, where we heard directly from small firms, rural businesses, local outlets of national companies, low-paid workers, the unemployed and some operating on the fringes of the formal economy' (LPC 1998: 1).

The Commission produces annual reports and is given terms of reference by the government which include making recommendations as to the rate of the NMW. In making these recommendations the Commission is instructed to have regard to the wider economic and social implications; the likely effect on the level of employment and inflation; the impact on the competitiveness of business, particularly the small firms sector; and the potential costs to industry and to the Exchequer. In general, government has tended to follow its recommendations as to appropriate minimum rates; and the bands to which these rates should apply (for example, the adult rate for those aged 22 and over, the youth development rate and the rate for 16–17 year olds).

The national minimum wage reflects a mix of economic and social justice considerations in its development and in its practice. As noted above, 'some groups of workers are more likely to be low paid than others' (LPC 1998: 35), with women, young workers, lone parents, homeworkers, **part-time workers** and those with disabilities particularly vulnerable. Indeed, women in low paid jobs are frequently seen as one of the main beneficiaries of the NMW (Bain 1999; Metcalf 1999b, 2007; Machin *et al.* 2002) with the NMW credited with having contributed to a narrowing of the gender pay gap since its introduction (see Chapter 5). Thus, legislation that provides a means of protecting the groups most 'at risk' in the labour market and who are most likely to find themselves in low paid jobs also has wider social objectives that link to concerns about equality, social inclusion and participation in the wider society. As we have seen, traditional neoclassical economics has tended to 'trump' this social justice argument or at least qualify it by emphasising the potential negative employment effects of a national minimum wage, and these have been recognised by the government in its remit to the Low Pay Commission that in considering its recommendations it 'shall have regard to the effect of this (NMW) Act on the economy of the United Kingdom as a whole and on competitiveness' (NMW Act 1998, s 7(5)(a)).

Before leaving this section we should note an increasingly influential branch of economics which provides a justification for minimum wage legislation. This is detailed in Exhibit 9.3.

Exhibit 9.3 New institutional economics and employment regulation

New institutional economics argues that the introduction of a minimum wage (and other forms of employment regulation) could have a positive impact on productivity and efficiency through a combination of 'shock effects' and 'efficiency wages' (Deakin and Wilkinson 1994; Sachdev and Wilkinson 1998). The 'shock' theory suggests that faced with rising costs firms will be 'shocked' into using resources more efficiently, so that rather than increasing costs, firms may find that they end up being more competitive as a result of the minimum wage. Similarly, the 'efficiency wage' theory suggests it may make sense to pay workers above the 'market rate', because such workers may be more motivated, work harder and more productively and value their jobs more highly if paid an efficiency wage' (Davies 2004: 140). Taken together these institutional economics perspectives provide a set of options to policy makers that support the use of legislation to close off or significantly deter firms from pursuing a low wage, low skill employment strategy. Although the empirical evidence in support of shock and efficiency wage effects (Card and Kreuger 1995; Machin *et al.* 2002) is mixed, they offer an important theoretical justification for minimum wage legislation and employment regulation generally and provide a counterpoint to traditional economic accounts of the operation of markets and the role of legal regulation.

The legal framework

In this section we will consider a number of legal issues under three broad areas:

1 the legal definition of 'wages' and 'pay';
2 the legal regulation of the pay transaction, covering the common law of contract and pay, information about pay, methods of payment, overpayment, pay deduction (including during **industrial action**), the use of fines as disciplinary action and the issue of shortages and losses in retail employment;
3 the principle of social justice influencing pay levels, particularly in respect of the national minimum wage.

Definitions

Wages

Under the statutory national minimum wage legislation, a 'wage' is defined narrowly as a 'single hourly rate (that) the Secretary of State may from time to time prescribe' (ERA 1996, s 27(2)(e)). However, the wage protection provisions governing unauthorised deductions under the Employment Rights Act (1996, s 13), define 'wages' more broadly as any sum payable to a worker in connection with their employment (s 27). The term includes:

- 'any fee, bonus, commission, holiday pay or other emolument referable to his employment, whether payable under their contract or otherwise';
- statutory sick pay;
- statutory maternity pay;
- statutory paternity pay;
- statutory adoption pay;
- a guarantee payment (under ERA 1996, s 28);
- any payment for time off (under ERA 1996, Part VI and TULRCA 1992, s 169);
- remuneration on suspension on medical grounds (ERA 1996, s 64) and on suspension on maternity grounds (ERA 1996, s 68);
- any sum payable under reinstatement or re-engagement order (ERA 1996, s 113);
- any sum payable in pursuance of an order for the continuation of a contract of employment (ERA 1996, s 130; TULRCA 1992, s 164);
- remuneration under a protective award (TULRCA 1992, s 189);
- non-contractual bonus (ERA 1996 s 27(3)).

The items excluded from this definition of wages are loans, an advance on wages, expenses, pension, allowance or gratuity in connection with retirement or loss of office, redundancy payment and 'any payment to the worker otherwise than in his capacity as a 'worker' (ERA 1996, s 27(2)(e)).

Pay

In contrast, 'pay' under the terms of the Equal Pay Act 1970, has been moulded by decisions of the ECJ interpreting Article 141 of the amended Treaty of Rome. These have defined pay as 'the ordinary basic or minimum wage or salary and any other consideration, whether in cash or in kind, which the worker receives directly or indirectly in respect of his employment from his employer'. As discussed in the section on equal pay, the relevant law encompasses not only basic pay but also redundancy pay, occupational pensions, incremental pay systems, sick pay and paid leave.

Regulating the 'wage–work bargain' under common law

At the core of the employment relationship and employment contract is 'the express legal promise to perform work in return for a promise to pay wages'. Like other contracts this provides '**consideration**' (something of value by which one party obtains the promise of the other party). The employee promises to work for the employer and this agreement is underpinned by the employer's commitment to pay wages. In the absence of consideration, there can be no legally enforceable contract. Furthermore, the promise to perform work in return for wages also provides the distinctive mutuality of obligation necessary for any contract of employment to exist (Collins *et al.* 2005: 75) (see Chapter 2).

Although wages are the most common, they are only one form of consideration. There can be a valid contract of employment even if no wages are set. The consideration may be entirely based on commission or the chance to earn tips from customers. Furthermore, the employee might be on a remuneration system which is entirely output based. In these instances, there can be an implied term of the contract of employment that the employer will provide the employee with a reasonable amount of work.

Under contract law, in situations where an employee performs work required by the employer but the employer fails to pay agreed wages, the employee can in principle bring a claim for the missing wages. Equally, if an employee fails to perform the specified work, the employer does not have to pay wages. Thus under contract law the legal principle of 'no work, no pay' applies, although in practice this is affected by particular disputes arising out of the course of employment (Collins *et al.* 2005: 76). The impact of industrial action on this principle is considered briefly in Exhibit 9.4.

As we noted earlier in this chapter, it is normal to make a distinction between time-service contracts, predicated on time-based payment systems and those based on pay linked to skill or performance. Time-service contracts offer remuneration on condition that an employee is available to perform work at the time prescribed by the employer and with pay calculated according to the amount of time labour power is made available. Performance-based contracts tend to make payment conditional on satisfactory completion of particular tasks or the achievement of specified targets (Collins *et al.* 2005: 77). In general, the systems apportion risks of defective or non-completed work in different ways, with employers tending to bear risks under time-service contracts, and employees under performance-based contracts. The general shift in the UK towards contracts that contain a performance-related element has been in part a reflection of employer desire to shift risks associated with contractual performance on to the employee (Collins *et al.* 2005).

The distinction between these contractual arrangements is important. Performance-based and piecework contracts normally require the employer to pay wages only when the tasks have been satisfactorily completed – each hour of work has to be completed in order for wages to be paid (Deakin and Morris: 2005: 293) – and although disputes may arise as to what constitutes satisfactory completion, the issues of when payment takes place and on what basis are clear-cut. The position under time-service contracts is potentially more complex. Here, the employee promises to be available and willing to work according to the employer's instructions for the hours laid down in the contract. In the case of time workers: 'No work means no pay; the consideration for work is wages and the consideration for wages is work' (*Browning* v *Crumlin Valley Collieries Ltd* [1926] 1 KB 522, 528, in Deakin and Morris 2005: 293).

If an employer can show that an employee has failed to work his or her prescribed hours, or performed the required tasks then the employer may withhold payment of wages. Where there has been a **breach of contract** by the employee then an employer may seek **damages** to compensate for losses that result from the contractual breach. Similarly, if an employee comes to work but not for all the hours laid down in the contract, the employer can refuse any or all of the work offered and avoid any payment or the employer could accept the work offered and pay on a ***pro rata*** basis (see Collins *et al.* 2005: 77–8).

Industrial action

These issues have assumed particular importance where employees engage in industrial action short of a strike. In *Miles* v *Wakefield Borough Council* [1987] AC 539, HL a government registrar of births, deaths and marriages was contracted to work 37 hours per week including three hours on Saturday mornings. He refused to work Saturday mornings and his employer deducted $\frac{3}{37}$ths of his salary to reflect this. Miles challenged the decision, and the case went to the House of Lords which held that the employer could deduct this proportion of his salary but added that the employer could have the option of not paying any salary to Miles on the grounds that partial performance of the contract was actually no performance. In effect, saying that individuals could not pick and choose which parts of the contract they wished to perform. This was essentially the judgement in *Wiluszynski* v *LB Tower Hamlets* [1989] IRLR 259, where a local government officer refused, as part of ongoing industrial action, to deal with queries arising from councillors, despite performing all other duties, and the Council concerned refused to pay any of his salary (see Exhibit 9.4 and *BT plc* v *Ticehurst* [1992] IRLR 219, CA). The judgment underlines the view that the contract of employment can be seen to be enforceable in its entirety, and although an employer could choose to opt for part payment for part performance, legally they are entitled to refuse payment altogether. One practical issue would be the extent to which an employer would wish to enforce such a legal entitlement given the wider repercussions that could result from such a decision in terms of the climate and conduct of future employment relations.

So, although contract law places an implied duty on employers to pay wages and not to make unauthorised deductions, there are exceptions to these principles. Industrial action is one such example (ERA 1996, s 14(5)); another is 'poor workmanship' (*Sagar* v *Ridehalgh & Son Ltd* [1931] Ch 310, CA). Overall, in the case of time-service contracts, the employer would appear to be in a relatively strong position to argue that an employee has broken the wage–work bargain in the case of unsatisfactory performance. The argument resting on the implied obligation placed on the employee to perform the contract 'in good faith'. However, 'in general, the power to refuse to pay full wages in response to the implied term to perform the contract in good faith will usually be subject to statutory controls over unlawful deductions' (Collins *et al.* 2005: 83) and it is to this that we now turn.

Statutory regulation of unauthorised deductions

The Employment Rights Act 1996, provides a right for the 'worker' (not just the employee) 'not to suffer unauthorised deductions' (1996, s 13). A deduction is defined in the following way:

Exhibit 9.4 Pay and industrial action

The ERA 1996 (s 14(5)) provides for appropriate deductions from wages in the case of industrial action. The key issues are:

- whether there has been a breach (fundamental or not) by the employee of the employment contract;
- whether the employee took part in the industrial action;
- in non-strike action, the extent of the 'partial performance' of the contract;
- whether or not the employer accepts or rejects this 'partial performance' of the contract;
- the appropriate amount of deduction for no work and for 'partial performance'.

In strike action, the principle of 'no work, no pay' usually prevails. In action short of a strike, the position is more complex. The Court of Appeal has set out several important principles about contractual obligations (*Wiluszynski* v *LB Tower Hamlets* [1989] IRLR 259):

- Employees are 'not entitled to pick and choose' what work they perform under the contract of employment.
- An employee cannot 'refuse to comply with his contract and demand payment'.
- An employer 'having told (an employee) that he was not required to attend for work (as a result of an employee's partial performance) and that if he did so it would be on a purely voluntary basis . . . could not, when he in fact attended, give him directions to work and at the same time not pay him'.
- An employer 'could not be expected to take action physically to prevent . . . staff who were refusing to comply with their contracts from entering (his) premises'.

Consideration of the character and volume of work is also an important factor. In the *Wiluszynski* case, although the refusal of local government officers to answer phone calls from councillors constituted a relatively small amount of their work in terms of time, it was work 'of considerable importance'.

See also *BT plc* v *Ticehurst* [1992] IRLR 219 where two managers who had participated in a short strike and withdrawn goodwill were sent home without pay because they refused to sign an undertaking to work in accordance with their contracts of employment. The court held that managers' contracts contained an implied term requiring them to further their employer's interests. In cases where partial performance has been accepted by an employer the issue has often been the appropriate calculation of remuneration for the part performance. See *Royle* v *Trafford Borough Council* [1984] IRLR 184, HC, where a teacher refused to accept another five pupils into a class of 31 but continued to perform his other duties. He was ruled to have 'part-performed' the contract and the employer was entitled to make a deduction of $\frac{5}{36}$ths of his salary over the relevant period of his refusal. The deduction made representing 'the notional value of the services rendered'.

> Where the total amount of wages paid on any occasion by an employer to a worker employed by him is less than the total amount of the wages properly paid by him to the worker on that occasion (after deductions), the amount of the deficiency shall be treated . . . as a deduction made by the employer from the worker's wage. (ERA 1996, s 13(3))

An employer may only be able to make deductions from an individual's wages if the deduction is authorised. Deductions are authorised in one of three ways:

1. **Act of Parliament.** As, for example, deduction of income tax and National Insurance contributions.
2. *Contract of employment.* A deduction may be authorised by a relevant provision of the contract of employment. Examples include the deduction of pension contributions, the possibility of a fine under relevant disciplinary procedures and the deduction of payments to meet cash shortfalls and stock deficiencies in retail import (see ERA 1996, ss 17–22, and discussion below).

3 *Individual consent.* A deduction may be authorised by the worker through his or her consent in writing to the deduction taking place. Common examples would include agreement for trade union contributions to be deducted from salary, and monthly repayment of loans for annual travel passes.

In practice the courts have required strict conformity with the ERA 1996 (s 13) (Collins *et al.* 2005: 84) demanding that deductions should be part of a worker's contract and that the worker should have been adequately notified of its content.

Cash shortages and deficiencies in retail employment

There is a statutory provision in respect of lawful deductions which is restricted to those engaged in 'retail employment'. This 'means employment (whether or not on a regular basis) involving the carrying out by the worker of retail transactions directly with members of the public or with fellow workers or other individuals in their personal capacities' or the collection by the worker of amounts payable in connection with retail transactions (ERA 1996, s 17(2)). A 'retail transaction' refers 'to the sale or supply of goods or the supply of services (including financial services)' (s 17(3)).

The origin of these specific provisions for retail employment lie in concerns relating to the operation of ss 1–2 of the Truck Act 1896 raised by studies (e.g. Goreily 1983), and latterly by **case law** (*Bristow* v *City Petroleum Ltd* [1988] ICR 165, HL). These pointed to the extent to which some retail workers worked under contracts of employment that permitted an employer to deduct the value of stock that went missing during a worker's shift. The issue was brought into sharp focus by the situation of attendants at self-service petrol stations who were having pay deducted when motorists who had filled up their cars with petrol then drove off without paying. Goreily (1983) cites two examples both involving attendants at self-service petrol stations. The first concerned an individual left 16 pence in their wage packet after their employer had made deductions for alleged till shortages; the second, an employee who had been deducted £250 in wages over a six month period because of 'unexplained till shortages'. The *Bristow* case brought the issue to a head and to a wider audience, but ironically was decided after the Truck Act 1896, which made such deductions possible, had already been repealed and replaced by the Wages Act 1986 (the provisions of which are now contained in ERA 1996 s 17(2) and (3)).

The Employment Rights Act 1996 permits authorised deductions for those in retail employment but lays down a range of specific requirements:

- The deduction must be for cash shortage or stock deficiency.
- The worker must be notified in writing of the total **liability** (ERA 1996, s 20(1)(a)).
- The demand for payment must be in writing (ERA 1996, s 20(2)).
- That the limit for deduction of pay is set at 10 per cent of gross wages due on any given day (ERA 1996, s 18(1)).
- That deductions of up to 10 per cent of pay can be made on successive pay days.
- That the 10 per cent rule does not apply to the final pay day when the employer can demand full reimbursement.
- The rule can be applied for up to 12 months following the shortage being established (ERA 1996, s 20(2)).

Overpayment

An employer is not prevented from making deductions in respect of overpayment of wages or an overpayment of expenses (ERA 1996, s 14). In practice, several issues can arise in this area:

- Does the employee dispute whether or not there has been overpayment? If so, a complaint can be made in the county court.
- Was the overpayment a consequence of an error in law? If so, it is generally recoverable. However, if the employee knew of the error and it would be inequitable to allow the money to be retained, then recovery is possible.
- Was the overpayment the result of a mistake by the employer? The general position is that the employer can recover the money provided that he can prove that the mistake was one of fact (see *Kleinwort Benson Ltd* v *Lincoln City Council* [1998] 4 ER 513). However, the Court of Appeal in *Avon County Council* v *Howlett* [1983] IRLR 171 outlined a number of issues that need to be considered. The *Avon* case involved an employee who was on leave of absence through illness, and paid at the full rate for the whole of his period of illness, although under the contract should have received only half his normal pay after six months. When the mistake was discovered the employers tried to recover the overpayment (£1,007) which the employee had already spent. The Court of Appeal in *Avon* held that an employer's ability to recover overpayments is subject to a number of conditions:
  - whether or not the employer led the employee to believe that s/he was entitled to the money that was overpaid;
  - whether the employee genuinely believed that they were entitled to the money and spent it;
  - whether the overpayment was not the fault of the employee.

In the *Avon* case, the employee claimed first of all that the employer had made a representation of fact leading them to believe the money was theirs; second, that they changed their position in good faith, in reliance on the representation; and third, that the overpayment was not caused by their own fault (Deakin and Morris 2005: 199). These conditions were held to be satisfied and the employee retained the entire amount by which he had been overpaid.

The National Minimum Wage Act 1998

The significance of the National Minimum Wage Act 1998 and the National Minimum Wage 1999 **Regulations** should not be underestimated. As one commentator argued at the time: 'It is arguable that the most radical and far-reaching reform of employment rights made by the 1997 Labour government will prove to be the introduction of the national minimum wage' (Simpson 1999a: 2).

However, Simpson went on to point out that discussions about a minimum wage have tended to be dominated by social and economic concerns, as mentioned above, with 'issues of legal policy either . . . completely ignored or relegated to the status of technical, and by implication, minor details' (1999a: 3). The Low Pay Commission was one element in turning a manifesto commitment into a workable policy. The other was to develop legislation that provided a comprehensive framework with maximum compliance, but which avoided any serious negative consequences for employment and the economy. The government attempted to do this through the National Minimum Wage Act 1998 which provides for minimum basic hourly rates of pay, with more detailed aspects of the regulation of the minimum wage left to the National Minimum Wage Regulations 1999. The extent to which the legislation adequately addresses the issue of low pay remains contentious (see Simpson 1999a, 1999b). Here we detail the main elements of the legislation and the implications for HR practitioners.

Coverage

The Act covers the whole of the United Kingdom, including Northern Ireland and relates specifically to those who work ordinarily in the UK and who are over the school leaving age. Unlike the common law terms regulating the contract of employment and therefore **employees**, the National Minimum Wage Act 1998 applies to **workers**, regardless of where they live or work, the sector they are employed in or the company in which they work. A worker is here defined as an individual who works under either a contract of employment or 'any other contract . . . whereby the individual undertakes to do or perform personally any work or services for another party to the contract whose status is not by virtue of the contract that of a client or customer of any profession or business undertaking carried on by the individual' (NMWA 1998, s 54). The Act explicitly ***includes***:

- part-time workers, temporary workers and agency workers (s 34);
- homeworkers (s 35);
- it also extends to Crown employees (s 36); and
- there is a reserve power (s 41) that enables the Secretary of State to propose additional regulations extending the Act to a specific category of workers.

Among those ***excluded*** are:

- the genuinely self-employed (independent contractors);
- office holders (such as police officers);
- company directors who are not also employees of the company;
- serving members of the armed forces;
- volunteers and voluntary workers with charitable organisations;
- offshore workers;
- schoolchildren;
- those on work experience who are not trainees under contracts of employment;
- prisoners in custody, including those on remand (s 45); and
- sharefishermen and women (s 43).

NMW rates

The Act provides for a facility for different rates to be determined for different age groups and according to whether a worker is a trainee (to address the concerns raised by some that paying younger workers adult rates may harm their employment prospects). The provisions of the Employment Equality (Age) Regulations 2006 specifically permit the age bands used in determining the national minimum wage. They are express exemptions from the provisions on age discrimination (reg 31). Increases in the NMW are not automatically linked to prices or earnings and the government considers uprating the rates periodically in light of advice from the Low Pay Commission and the economic circumstances at the time. Changes are brought into force by regulations laid before Parliament (see Table 9.1).

Table 9.1 Levels of the national minimum wage

Date	*National rate for 22 years and above*	*Rate for 18–21 year olds*	*Rate for 16–17 year olds (from October 2004)*
April 1999	£3.60	£3.00	
June 2000	£3.60	£3.20	
October 2000	£3.70	£3.20	
October 2001	£4.10	£3.50	
October 2002	£4.20	£3.60	
October 2003	£4.50	£3.80	
October 2004	£4.85	£4.10	£3.00
October 2005	£5.05	£4.25	£3.00
October 2006	£5.35	£4.45	£3.30
October 2007	£5.52	£4.60	£3.40
October 2008	£5.73	£4.77	£3.53

For October 2009 rates see www.berr.gov.uk/employment

The national minimum wage and employers

The Act places a clear obligation on employers to pay workers remuneration which is not less than the NMW in any pay reference period (see below). An employer is here defined in relation to an employee or worker (s 54(5)) as: 'The person by whom the employee or worker is (or where the employment has ceased, was) employed'. This definition is the same as that found in the ERA 1996, s 230(4).

The National Minimum Wage Act 1998 also covers the position of 'superior employers' (s 48), common in parts of the construction industry. These are defined as:

> Where (a) the immediate employer of a worker is himself in the employment of some other person and (b) the worker is employed on the premises of that other person, that other person shall be deemed for the purposes of the Act to be the employer of the worker jointly with the immediate employer. (NMWA, s 48)

In the case of a worker being employed by different employers on separate but parallel contracts, then each employer is responsible for ensuring compliance with the NMWA.

Calculating hourly rates

Once the rate for the NMW has been established the key issue becomes how the rate is then applied to different contractual arrangements governing pay and working time (Deakin and Morris 2005: 287–8). The main mechanism for this is via the provisions contained in the National Minimum Wage Regulations 1999 (implemented on 1 April 1999). These prescribe how to calculate a worker's hourly rate of remuneration for the purposes of determining compliance with the NMW. For some workers the calculation is relatively straightforward. However, difficulties arise where a person is paid by output or works on irregular patterns. The NMWA and the NMW Regulations address these issues through two core legal concepts (Simpson 1999a). These are;

- *Pay reference period* (s 1(4)). This is the time period for which the worker must be paid at least the national minimum wage. This is calculated by dividing the *total remuneration* by the total number of hours worked. The reference period is normally one month; or where a person has been employed for less time that this, that period.

- *The total remuneration*. This covers all 'payments that count towards the wage or remuneration of the worker, for the purposes of satisfying the employer's obligation to observe the minimum rate' (Deakin and Morris 2005: 288). Regulation 8 defines pay as payments paid to the worker in his capacity as a worker before any deductions are made; an amount that does not include 'any benefit in kind provided to the worker, whether or not a monetary value is attached to the benefit (reg 9), save an amount (in October 2008 this was set at £4.46 per day) that can be deducted for living accommodation'.

The starting point in calculating total remuneration is the gross wage or salary (i.e. pay before deductions of income tax and national insurance contributions). As the LPC stated in its first report,

> In whatever way workers' pay is defined or whatever hours they work, only their 'standard' pay shall count towards the National Minimum Wage. Here incentive payments, such as commission, tips and gratuities paid via the payroll and piece rate, should count. In contrast, allowances and premium payments which are provided for non-standard work or hours (e.g. overtime and shiftwork premia) as well as all benefits with the exception of accommodation, should not count towards compliance. A worker should be entitled to the National Minimum Wage for each hour of actual working time, averaged over the worker's normal pay reference period up to a maximum of one month.
>
> (LPC 1998: 51)

In essence, total remuneration is calculated by adding up:

- all payments made by the employer to the worker in the 'pay reference period';
- any payments made in the following or later reference periods relating to the 'earlier pay reference period';
- any amount permitted to be taken into account for the provision of living accommodation.

When all these are taken into account the law provides for various deductions (regs 31–37). These include money paid during absences from work; payments by the employer as tips and gratuities from customers but not paid through the payroll.

Tips distributed to workers via a troncmaster's bank account, which is used for that purpose, are not payments made by the employer to the worker because ownership of the money has passed to the troncmaster. Consequently, the payments cannot count towards the national minimum wage (***Commissioners for Her Majesty's Revenue and Customs*** v ***Annabel's (Berkley Square) Ltd and Others*** (2008) EAT/0562/07).

- *Working Time*. Under the regulations there are four different categories of employment types identified: time-work, salaried hours work, output work and unmeasured work.
  - *Time-work* relates to the specific number of hours that a person works to perform the work provided by the employer. See Exhibit 9.5 for cases in respect of hours that can be calculated as time working. The general position being that under time-work, time is included when a worker is required to be at the workplace, available for work, whether or not work is provided (Simpson 1999b).
  - *Salaried work* is where a worker is paid an annual salary for specific annual hours and paid in equal instalments (Deakin and Morris 2005: 290).
  - *Output work* relates to work in which payment is linked to the number of items or products produced and therefore an individual's performance. It can be calculated either by counting the number of hours spent on undertaking the work; and until recently by reaching a 'fair estimate' agreement of the hours to be worked (regs 24–26). However

Exhibit 9.5 The NMW and working time arrangements: cases relating to hourly rates

Wright v Scottbridge Construction Ltd [2001] IRLR 589

A nightwatchman: Mr Wright worked between 5 p.m. and 7 a.m. seven nights a week. He received wages of £210 per week. He was expected to respond if intruders set off an alarm. Otherwise, he was allowed to read or watch television or sleep when on the premises. Sleeping facilities were provided. He claimed entitlement to the NMW for each hour that he was on the premises. The EAT ruled that where a worker was required to be on the employer's premises to carry out his duties over a specific number of hours, then, *all* the hours were eligible for the NMW. It noted a distinction in the situation where the employer allowed a worker time off to sleep (reg 15(1)).

British Nursing Association v Inland Revenue (National Minimum Wage Compliance Team) [2002] IRLR 480

Nurse 'bank' administrator: The Court of Appeal, upholding decisions of the Employment Tribunal and EAT, ruled on the eligibility for the NMW of nurses who spent the night at home, answered phone calls requesting 'bank' nurses and allocated nurses. They were ruled to be working for the full shift and entitled to be paid the NMW for each hour of the shift. The Court of Appeal saw no difference between a worker in an office waiting for phone calls and a nurse in this case. To suggest that there were different rules for homeworkers was 'misconceived'.

since 2004 a system of 'fair piece rates' has operated whereby an employer must pay either the minimum rate for each hour actually worked, or put in place the 'mean hourly rate' for a particular rate or task (Deakin and Morris 2005: 290).

- *Unmeasured work* can be dealt with by paying at least the NMW for each hour worked; or by the employer and worker coming to a 'daily average' agreement to decide the number of hours the worker is likely to spend on work.

Collective agreements and contractual terms

The Act makes it clear that 'any provision in any agreement (whether a worker's contract or not) is void in so far as it purports (a) to exclude or limit the operation of any provision of the Act or (b) to preclude a person from bringing proceedings under this Act before an Employment Tribunal' (NMWA 998, s 49(1)). The exceptions to this are in relation to conciliated complaints (under the Employment Tribunals Act 1996, s 18) and in respect of compromise agreements (ETA 1996, s 18(1)(dd); NMWA 1998, ss 3–11).

Enforcement of the national minimum wage: civil proceedings

Significantly, the Act is enforceable through both civil action and criminal proceedings. It creates individual rights for workers and administrative enforcement via officers of Her Majesty's Revenue and Customs; with criminal sanctions underpinning the obligation to pay at the NMW rate, the administrative obligations (such as record keeping) and, the officers' powers to enforce them.

Since July 2005, the focus has been on 'targeted enforcement', focusing publicity and enforcement on key low paying sectors in turn to 'tackle the minority of bad employers' (quote from Gerry Sutcliffe in BERR: National Minimum Wage Annual Report 2005/06: 29; see Exhibit 9.6).

In this section we focus on the civil enforcement process which has three principal aspects: record-keeping, underpayment and the role of inspectors.

Record-keeping

There has been considerable emphasis placed in the Act on the need for an employer to keep records. Any employer of a worker who qualifies for the NMW has a duty to keep records, the purpose of which is to show that the worker is being remunerated at a rate at least equal to the NMW. Failure by an employer in these circumstances to maintain adequate records is a criminal offence.

A worker has the right to require their employer to produce 'relevant records' for establishing whether or not the worker has been paid at least the NMW; and to inspect and copy those records (s 10). There are three important provisions in the exercise of this right.

1 The worker must have reasonable grounds for believing that he/she is being paid less than the NMW.
2 The worker must give the employer a written 'production notice' requesting the production of any relevant records relating to a particular period. This notice should also indicate whether the worker wishes to be accompanied.
3 The employer can determine where the inspection takes place, having given the worker 'reasonable' notice of the place and time. Having received the 'production notice', the employer must produce the relevant records within 14 days, although a later time can be agreed during those 14 days between the employer and the worker in question.

The failure of an employer to produce 'relevant records' at a specified place and time or to allow inspection and copying of them by the worker entitles them to complain to an employment tribunal within three months of the production deadline (s 11). Such a case may be heard by a tribunal chairman sitting alone.

In the event that it is established that an employer prevented access to the 'relevant records' then, two remedies are available and must be granted:

1 a declaration;
2 an award to the worker of 80 times the national minimum wage in force when the award is made. This would be £484.40 with a NMW of £5.73. This award cannot be varied.

Underpayment

The second aspect to enforcement relates to underpayment. A worker, still in employment who has been underpaid has a right to claim the difference between what has been paid (if anything) and the prevailing NMW. The worker may complain to an employment tribunal (under ERA 1996, s 23(1)(a) alleging unauthorised deduction of wages). Alternatively, the worker may bring an action for breach of contract in the county court. A former worker can allege breach of contract at an employment tribunal in relation to the termination of his/her employment. Workers who successfully complain to an employment tribunal are entitled to recover the amount of underpayment but no interest. Those who go to the county court are entitled to interest also.

The normal **burden of proof** is reversed in cases concerning national minimum wage underpayment before both employment tribunals and the county court. The assumption is therefore that a person was paid below the NMW and qualifies for the NMW. In the event that the claim or status of the applicant is disputed, it is for the employer to show that the worker was paid the NMW or is not a worker covered by the protection of the Act.

Exhibit 9.6 National minimum wage enforcement: key statistics

- 61,000 queries dealt with by the helpline in 2005/06.
- Between 1 April 1999 and April 2006, the helpline dealt with over 500,000 enquiries and over 21,000 complaints.
- The majority of complaints are from adult workers between the ages of 22 and 59.
- In 2004/05 the number of complaints from women exceeded those from men for the first time, and this continued into 2005/06. In light of the high proportion of women in lower paid jobs, this is consistent with what would be expected.
- The sectors attracting complaints tend to remain consistent over time with the hospitality sector at the forefront of complaints followed by market services, hairdressing, retail and production/construction. The position of apprentices in hairdressing has been a particular focus of the attention of inspectors.
- The highest incidence of complaints now comes from the London area (with a significant rise since 2003/04), and the North West.
- In 2005/06, 32 per cent of employers were found not to be paying the NMW.
- Over 4,900 employers were subject to investigation in 2005/06 but this represents a fall since 2003/04 when over 5,500 employers were investigated.
- Around £3.3 millions in wage arrears was identified by compliance teams (cf. over £5 million in 2001/02).
- Workers for whom arrears had been identified rose in 2005/06 to 25,314 from 14,057 in 2004/05 although the average arrears per worker fell from £340 to £130 over this period.

Source: Department for Business Enterprise and Regulatory Reform (BERR) *National Minimum Wage Annual Report 2005/06*.

The Employment Act 2008 (s 8) changes the method by which arrears of the NMW are calculated for monies owed to a worker who has been paid less than the NMW. Arrears are to be calculated by reference to the current rate of NMW when the current rate is higher than that in force at the time of the underpayment. The worker will therefore be repaid any underpayment of NMW by their employer at a higher rate if NMW has increased since the time of underpayment.

The role of inspectors

The third element of the enforcement process is the role of inspectors (NMWA 1998 s 13). The enforcement body for the NMW, Her Majesty's Revenue and Customs (HMRC), have powers vested in them covering the following:

- *The serving of an enforcement notice on an employer* (NMWA 1998, s 19). This requires both the payment of the NMW to the worker or the worker concerned and any arrears. Such a notice is a warning to the employer. It is likely to have been preceded by informal discussions. The employer can appeal to an employment tribunal within four weeks of receiving the notice. Such an appeal can be heard by a tribunal chairman sitting alone. A tribunal may rescind or amend an enforcement notice. To succeed in a complaint, an employer needs to show that, for example, the workers concerned were genuinely self-employed, or that the workers had not been underpaid or that the amount of the alleged arrears was wrong.
- *Making a complaint to an employment tribunal* (NMWA, s 20). If an employer fails to comply with an enforcement notice, HMRC can take civil proceedings to recover the money. The enforcement officer may, on behalf of the workers concerned, also complain to a tribunal that the employer has made an unauthorised deduction. The officer must be satisfied that the employer has a case to answer. This will involve scrutiny of the evidence

and an interview with the employer, remembering that the burden of proof is on the employer to show wages were properly paid. Note though that a complaint by an enforcement officer does not take away the rights of individual workers to complain about non-compliance with an enforcement notice.

- *Taking other civil proceedings* (NMWA, s 20). This would be an alternative route through the county court.
- *The serving of a penalty notice* (NMWA, s 21). Where an employer fails to comply with an enforcement notice then a penalty notice may be served setting out the nature of the non-compliance and indicating a fine that must be paid within four weeks of receiving the penalty notice, the fine increasing the longer the employer takes to comply. The amount of the fine is twice the hourly rate of the NMW (currently in force) for each worker who is underpaid on each day of non-compliance. A penalty notice is not enforceable while the appeal process on an enforcement notice is still 'in train'. Furthermore, a penalty notice can itself be appealed against to an employment tribunal and so cannot be enforced until an employer's appeal has been decided upon. Again, a tribunal may rescind or amend such a notice.
- *Access to records* (NMWA, s 14). The NMWA (s 10) provides for employees to have access to records. In order to be effective in ensuring compliance the Act (ss 13–14) also provides for *administrative inspection* whereby inspectors are provided with certain powers in

Exhibit 9.7 Some successful cases

In Wales, a homeworker assembling crackers complained about non-payment of the NMW. Initially the employer thought that homeworkers were not 'workers' under the legislation. After the compliance officer explained the position, he accepted they were and contacted the National Group of Homeworkers to assist him in drawing up a fair estimate agreement. *Over £8,600 in wage arrears was identified for this worker* (BERR: *NMW Annual Report 2001/02*).

A bar worker complained that they were not being paid NMW – £36 arrears identified and repaid. During the course of the review it was found that the hotel was using student labour, mainly from Spain. They were paid a small training allowance making them far cheaper to employ than locals. Once NMW legislation came into play, *arrears identified as owing to overseas workers totalled £27,247* (BERR: *NMW Annual Report 2003/04*).

In the South-East of England, a compliance officer investigated a failure to pay the NMW to an 81-year-old worker who was employed as a car polisher. The company was unaware of its liability to pay pensioners the NMW. *It promptly paid arrears of £3,000* (BERR: *NMW Annual Report 2001/02*).

In Belfast, a case involved workers working for a housing association and the interpretation of the phrase being 'on call'. Following extensive work, an agreement was reached with the employer and payment of £47,248 was made, split between three employees (BERR: *NMW Annual Report 2003/04*).

Following an anonymous complaint to the helpline, a hairdressing company was visited. It was found that a young lady with special needs had been employed since July 1999. She worked 36 hours per week and had been paid a training wage of £78 per week. The company thought they were doing a favour by employing her. *Arrears of pay of £1,700 were paid and she was placed on the NMW rate* (BERR: *NMW Annual Report 2003/04*).

In a large company repairing and selling cars, a worker complained that he was an apprentice and not being paid the NMW after the appropriate exemptions ran out. HMRC investigated the employer who was found not to be operating the apprenticeship rules correctly. The result was a total of 13 apprentices who were due arrears under the Act. The total arrears due and paid were £10,676 (BERR: *NMW Annual Report: 2003/04*).

To these can be added the increasing concerns over alleged exploitation of migrant workers in parts of the UK (*BBC News*, 26/04/07).

respect of an employer's records. They can require production of these. They have a right to require additional information to be produced and can enter an employer's premises 'at all reasonable times' in order to exercise any of these powers. The Employment Act 2008 (s 10) provides for an extension of these powers to allow HMRC inspectors not only to obtain NMW information from employers but also to physically remove this from the employer's premises for the purpose of copying.

Exhibit 9.7 details some successful cases involving the intervention of inspectors.

Enforcement of the national minimum wage: criminal action

Under the NMWA (s 31) an employer commits a criminal offence who:

- 'Refuses or wilfully neglects to remunerate the worker for any pay reference period at a rate which is at least equal to the national minimum wage' (NMWA, s 31(1)).
- Fails to keep records in accordance with any regulations made under NMWA, s 9.
- 'Knowingly causes or allows to be made' in a record 'any entry which he knows to be false in a material particular' (NMWA, s 31(3)).
- 'Produces or furnishes or knowingly causes or allows to be produced, any records or information which he knows to be false in a material particular' (NMWA, s 31(4)).
- 'Intentionally delays or obstructs an officer' seeking to enforce the Act (NMWA, s 31(5)).
- 'Refuses or neglects to answer any question, furnish any information or produce any document when required to do so' (NMWA, s 31(6)).

An employer's defence in respect of the refusal or wilful neglect to pay the NMW or of keeping required records is 'to prove that he exercised all due diligence and took all reasonable precautions to secure that the provisions of this Act and of any relevant regulations made under it, were complied with by himself and by any person under his control' (NMWA, s 31(8)).

The prosecutor in these cases can be HMRC enforcement officers; and all offences are triable without a jury. They, therefore, can be heard in a magistrates' court or a court of summary jurisdiction in Northern Ireland. In Scotland, proceedings are initiated by the procurator fiscal. Conviction is determined against the criminal **standard of proof** – that the evidence shows beyond reasonable doubt that the offence was committed. The maximum fine is set at level 5, and the general view of government experts is that action in this area is likely to be rare. The Employment Act 2008 provides for additional criminal proceedings. Serious criminal offences relating to the NMW will be triable in the Crown Court.

Detriments and dismissal and the NMW

Under the NMWA (s 23), workers have the right not to be subject to any **detriment** because of the NMW or any reason related to its enforcement. The circumstances attracting such protection are where:

- A worker asserts in good faith his/her right to the NMW, right of access to records and right to recover the difference between what (if anything) the worker has been paid and the NMW.
- As a result of employees asserting their rights, the employer was prosecuted for an offence under the NMWA 1998.
- The individual worker qualifies, or will or might qualify for the NMW or for a particular, higher rate of the NMW.

Complaints about detrimental treatment should be made to an employment tribunal within three months of the alleged detriment being complained of. Note that employees have the right not to be unfairly dismissed if the reason or principal reason for their dismissal (including selection for redundancy) is related to their entitlement to the NMW or its enforcement (ERA 1996a, s 104A). The NMWA thereby extends unfair dismissal protection to employees but not to workers in general. In defending a tribunal claim the employer must show the reason for the act or omission.

If a tribunal finds that detrimental treatment has taken place, it must make a declaration and may award compensation. If the complainant was not an employee and the detriment was the termination of the employment relationship, the amount of compensation awarded must not exceed the amount that the worker would have received if he/she had been an employee who had been unfairly dismissed. However, in any other case the amount of compensation awarded is not limited; it is the amount that the tribunal considers just and equitable.

Employment policies and practices

From the perspective of HR practitioners and employers more generally, there are several practical issues that need to be considered in the application of the NMWA and accompanying regulations. These can be dealt with in terms of contracts of employment and collective agreements; special agreements; information and records.

Contracts of employment and collective agreements

The starting point for complaints about employment rights is inevitably the contract of employment. This will encompass any terms of a collective agreement with a trade union that is **incorporated** into the contract. Clearly, an employer needs to appreciate the importance of honouring contractual terms, particularly in respect of pay. Below we summarise the potential **repudiatory breaches of the contract** of employment that can arise and could result in **constructive dismissal** claims. These are:

- not paying wages due to a person for work undertaken;
- making deductions from pay without authorisation;
- varying pay without the consent of the individual employee (or where appropriate, the union);
- arbitrarily deducting overpayment of wages without consulting the employee concerned.

The contract of employment is therefore a source of entitlements to particular remuneration. Furthermore, it can be the source for authority for certain pay deductions (see the earlier discussion of the retail trade and disciplinary fines). See also Chapters 2 and 3.

Special agreements

There may be certain monies that an employer wishes to recover from an employee than might not be subject to contractual terms. A special agreement may be made. This should be in writing and should cover all relevant requirements and expectations. It should be made in advance of the expenditure being incurred. Examples of such special agreements could be:

- Where there is an undertaking to return company property on termination of employment. If that is not done, a special agreement may provide for permission to deduct the replacement value from the employee's final pay.

- An agreement by the employee to repay expenditure on expensive training courses if the employee leaves an organisation within a specified period of time.
- An agreement to repay a loan (for example for travel) during employment and on termination of employment.

Information and records

It should be remembered that there already exist well-established rights to the provision of information to employees. Such rights to information relate to:

- *Statement of Initial Employment Particulars* (ERA 1996, s 1). Employees are to be told the scale or rate of remuneration or the method of calculating it, and the intervals at which it is paid (weekly, monthly or otherwise). A linked information requirement concerns hours of work. Taking these together, it is possible for an employee to calculate their hourly rate of pay.
- *Written itemised pay statement and a statement of fixed deductions* (ERA 1996, ss 8–9): This must contain the following information:
  - the gross amount of wages and salary;
  - the amounts of any variable and fixed deductions from gross pay and the reasons for them;
  - the net amount of wages or salary payable; and
  - where different parts of the net amount are paid in different ways, the amount and method of payment of each part-payment.

New information requirements were introduced under the National Minimum Wage Act 1998. A critical part of its effectiveness in terms of enforcement is the availability of adequate records, and as we have noted earlier, failure to maintain these is a criminal offence (NMWA 1998, s 31).

Exercises

Read the following scenarios and decide whether or not the workers concerned are subject to any infringement of their statutory rights.

National minimum wage

9.1 A person is aged 17 years and works for six hours on a Saturday afternoon in a burger bar. His employer pays him £3.25 per hour.

Is he protected under the NMWA?

9.2 A person is aged 19 years and delivers a free newspaper for five hours a week at weekends. She is paid £4.50 per hour.

Is she protected under the NMWA?

9.3 A woman aged 26 years, works as a waitress on a permanent part-time contract; her basic pay is £4.50 per hour. Tips are paid through the till. Her hours and additional remuneration over a four-week period are as follows:

Week 1: 12 hours
Tips (through till) £12; tips (direct) £3

Week 2: 6 hours
Tips (through till) £6; tips (direct) £3

Week 3: 8 hours
Tips (through till) £10; tips (direct) £4

Week 4: 14 hours
Tips (through till) £22; tips (direct) £4

Is the woman receiving pay that is compliant with the national minimum wage?

9.4 A 30-year-old waiter has been supplied to the Gradgrind Hotel by an agency. He also works on a casual basis in the restaurant of a separate employer in between engagements at the hotel. His basic pay from the hotel is £4.60 per hour. Because he is a cousin of the owner, he is provided with free accommodation, although he has to pay for food and heating. His hours and additional remuneration for a four-week period of work for the hotel were as follows:

Week 1: 12 hours
Tips (through till) £7; tips (direct) £3

Week 2: 6 hours
Tips (through till) £6; tips (direct) £4

Week 3: 8 hours
Tips (through till) £6; tips (direct) £3

Week 4: 14 hours
Tips (through till) £11; tips (direct) £5

Is he being paid a rate compliant with the national minimum wage?

9.5 A cleaner has worked for one specific cleaning company for the past two years. She is 21 years old and has been paid £4.80 per hour. Just before her twenty-second birthday, her supervisor says that she is sacked, maintaining that they do not need her anymore.

Advise her on her legal rights and what action (if any) may be available to her?

9.6 A woman, aged 29 years, has just started work in a small 'open all hours' shop. It employs fewer than 20 staff – all of whom work on some form of part-time contract. She believes that she has been wrongly paid because her hourly wages over the past month average less than £5.50 per hour. She calculated that she should have received an hourly rate in line with the NMW. She has been given a handwritten piece of paper stating the hours she worked, her gross pay, the deductions made for tax and National Insurance and her net pay. She asks the owner of the shop if she can check his pay records to make sure that she has not been underpaid. He refuses.

Advise her on her legal position and what if anything she can request from her employer?

Pay deduction

9.7 A man had a loan agreement with his employer. It stipulated that when he left employment, payments would continue until the debt was paid off. His contract of employment was terminated and the employer did not pay his final wages of £273.50, saying it was to cover the outstanding loan payments.

Advise on the legal position in respect of pay deductions in this case.

9.8 A shiftworker worked under a contract, part of which incorporated terms of a collective agreement, and which provided for a shift allowance. During a temporary stoppage in production he was not required to work shifts and the allowance was not paid. He claimed that this was unlawful deduction.

Advise the shiftworker on his legal position.

9.9 A man has been overpaid by £250 in one month's pay cheque because of an administrative error. His normal gross pay is £1,200 per month. He had heard rumours that the union had negotiated a pay increase and so he decides to spend the money on a new tumble-drier. The company asks him to repay the overpayment immediately.

Advise the man on his legal rights in relation to repaying the overpayment.

9.10 A van driver was given a document with details of the vehicle insurance policy under which he would be liable for the excess for damage caused during personal use of the van. Private mileage was also limited. Further provisions covered charges for private phone calls made from the van. The amount of £305 was deducted from his final wages; £155 of this was for the cost of repairs for damage during private use, although he had agreed to repair the van himself; £150 was a provisional deduction for both private phone calls and excess private mileage. He claimed the deduction was unlawful.

Advise the van driver.

9.11 A woman works at a small café. As a result of a shortfall in the till, her boss deducted £15 from her weekly pay of £150. Her boyfriend tells her that her employer cannot do that.

Is her boyfriend correct? Advise the woman.

Feedback on these exercises is provided in the Appendix to this textbook.

References and useful websites

Adams, J.S. (1965) 'Inequity in social exchange', *Advanced Experiments in Social Psychology*, Vol. 62: 335–43.

Atkinson, A.B. (2003) 'Income inequality in OECD countries: data and explanations', *CESifo Economic Studies*, Vol. 49(4).

Bain, G.S. (1999) 'The national minimum wage: further reflections', *Employee Relations*, Vol. 21(1).

Card, D. and Krueger, A. (1995) *Myth and Measurement: The New Economics of the Minimum Wage*. Princeton: Princeton University Press.

Collins, H., Ewing, K. and McColgan, A. (2005) *Labour Law: Text and Materials* (2nd edn). Oxford: Hart.

Davies, A.C.L. (2004) *Perspectives on Labour Law*. Cambridge: Cambridge University Press.

Davies, P. and Freedland, M. (2007) *Towards a Flexible Labour Market: Labour Legislation and Regulation Since the 1990s*. Oxford: Oxford University Press.

Deakin, S. and Morris, G. (2005) *Labour Law*. Oxford: Hart.

Deakin, S. and Wilkinson, F. (1994) 'Rights v efficiency: the economic case for transnational labour standards', *Industrial Law Journal*, Vol. 23: 289.

Department for Business Enterprise and Regulatory Reform, *National Minimum Wage Annual Reports 2001/02, 2003/04, 2005/06*.

Goreily, T. (1983) 'Arbitrary deductions from pay and the proposed repeal of the Truck Acts', *Industrial Law Journal*, Vol. 12(4).

Heath, A. and Cheung, S. (2006) *Ethnic Penalties in the Labour Market: Employers and Discrimination*. London: DWP.

Jacques, E. (1967) *Equitable Payment*. Harmondsworth: Penguin.

Low Pay Commission (1998) *First Report*. London: LPC.

Low Pay Commission (2007) *National Minimum Wage: Low Pay Commission Report*. London: LPC.

Low Pay Commission (2008) *National Minimum Wage: Low Pay Commission Report*. London: LPC.

Machin, S. (2003) 'Wage inequality since 1979', in Dickens *et al.* (eds) *The Labour Market under New Labour*. Basingstoke: Palgrave.

Machin, S., Disney, R. and Rahman, L. (2002) *Where the Minimum Wage Bites Hard: The Introduction of the UK National Minimum Wage to a Low Pay Sector*. London: CEP, LSE.

McGovern, P. and Hill, S. (2004) 'The Status Divide Re-Visited', BUIRA Paper, July.

Metcalf, D. (1999a) 'The Low Pay Commission and the National Minimum Wage', *Economic Journal*, Vol. 109.

Metcalf, D. (1999b) *The British National Minimum Wage*. London: CEP, LSE.

Metcalf, D. (2007) *Why has the British National Minimum Wage had little or no impact on employment*, CEP Discussion Paper, No. 781. London: Centre for Economic Performance, LSE.

Phelps Brown, H. (1979) *The Inequality of Pay*. Oxford: Oxford University Press.

Rubery, J. and Edwards, P. (2003) 'Low pay and the National Minimum Wage', in Edwards, P. (ed.) *Industrial Relations: Theory and Practice* (2nd edn). Oxford: Blackwell.

Sachdev, S. and Wilkinson, F. (1998) *Low Pay, the Working of the Labour Market and the Role of a Minimum Wage*. London: Institute of Employment Rights.

Simpson, R. (1999a) 'A milestone in the legal regulation of pay: the National Minimum Wage Act 1998', *Industrial Law Journal*, Vol. 28(1).

Simpson, R. (1999b) 'Implementing the National Minimum Wage: the 1999 Regulations', *Industrial Law Journal*, Vol. 28: 171.

Useful websites

National Group on Homeworking **www.ngh.org.uk**

Poverty Site **www.poverty.org.uk**

Visit **www.mylawchamber.co.uk/willey** to access multiple choice questions, case flashcards and exercises to test yourself on this chapter.

mylawchamber

10 Regulation of working time

Learning objectives

This chapter considers the extent to which working time has been and continues to be regulated through both voluntary measures and legal regulation. Having read the chapter you should be able to:

- Understand the historic role of voluntary regulation of working time
- Understand the piecemeal growth of legal regulation of working time in Britain
- Understand the essential purposes and provisions of European law on working time regulation
- Advise your organisation on the implications of the Working Time Regulations 1998 and the relevant case law

Structure of the chapter

- *Introduction*: the scope of working time and its regulation
- *The context*: the role of voluntary regulation; the long hours culture; social policy objectives; economic considerations; individual choice and working hours and the impact of the Working Time Regulations 1998 and recent amendments to this
- *The legal framework*: the traditional, piecemeal approach to the regulation of working time; the 1998 Working Time Regulations – regulating the organisation and duration of working time
- *Employment policies and practices*: developing a strategic approach to implementation; a checklist of action to be taken; some problem scenarios
- *Exercises*

Introduction

As Arrowsmith and Sisson (2000: 287) have stated:

> Working time, along with pay, is the defining feature of the employment relationship . . . For employers, the arrangement of working time helps determine the way in which goods and services can be provided. For employees, these working time patterns shape the very experience of work . . . [it is] one of the most contested areas of workplace industrial relations.

This chapter focuses on how such working time is regulated and the issues raised for HR professionals. In doing so, we need to be clear as to what we mean by working time. Normally, it includes the following:

- the ***number of hours*** worked by an individual worker in a specified time period (e.g. the basic or standard working week);
- the arrangement of '***non-work*' *time*** (e.g. rest periods, rest days and holidays);
- the ***scheduling*** and availability of working time (e.g. night work, Sunday working and part-time working);
- the **flexibility** of working time (part-time, **job share**, casual, etc.);
- the ***quality of work*** (e.g. the adaptation of work to the worker).

In this chapter we will consider all of these issues.

Working time is measured and arranged in various ways, and so it is important to outline the commonly used definitions. The standard terms that occur in working time arrangements, collective agreements and the law are outlined in Exhibit 10.1.

Exhibit 10.1 Defining standard terms

Basic working week. The number of hours per week that an employee is expected to work. It will usually be an express term of the contract of employment and should be stated in the written statement of employment particulars (ERA 1996, s 1). For full-time workers this is usually specified as a number of hours above 30 per week. Historically, there was no general statutory provision on the length of the basic working week, in contrast to the position in some other countries, for example France. Although since 1998 there has been a statutory maximum working week (from which it is possible for workers to opt out), the length of this continues to depend on either management decision or the provision of a collective agreement.

Overtime. The number of hours per week performed in excess of the employing organisation's basic working week. Paid overtime has long been a significant feature of working time in Britain, particularly in manufacturing. In law, there is no specific ceiling on overtime. However, the regulations on the average maximum working week of 48 hours clearly have an impact on overtime arrangements (WTR 1998, reg 4).

Shift work. The Working Time Directive (2003) defines shift work as 'any method of organising work in shifts whereby workers succeed each other at the same work stations according to a certain pattern, including a rotating pattern and which may be continuous or discontinuous, entailing the need for workers to work at different times over a given period of days or weeks' (Article 2(5)).

The Health and Safety Executive estimate the number of shift workers in the UK at 3.6 million (which equates to around 14 per cent of the total working population (HSE 2006), of whom around 60 per cent are men). On the basis of past estimates, around 12 per cent of shift workers are on night shifts, with anything up to a quarter sometimes working nights and sometimes days; and well over a quarter on three-shift working.

Exhibit 10.1 continued

Annualised hours schemes. Under these schemes, the total number of hours worked each year are added together and then scheduled to be worked according to variations in customer demand for a product or service. This may result in variations in the length of working days at different times of the year. Bell and Hart (2005: 3) estimated that for 2002, between 3 and 4 per cent of full-time employees in the UK were covered by these arrangements. In general, annualised hours schemes appear to be more common in the private sector and among women in areas such as local government. The lowest incidence of such schemes, are found among managers and administrators.

Weekend working. This is normally regarded as any working on a Saturday and/or a Sunday. Weekend working has increased significantly in recent years with over half of men and over a third of women working at least one day at the weekend.

Part-time working. Normally defined as a situation where an employee works a number of hours less than the employing organisation's basic working week. This can include, therefore, those who work hours just short of the basic week as well as those who may work as little as two hours per week. In official statistics it is usually specified as working up to 30 hours per week. According to the Labour Force Survey (2008), over a quarter of the working population works part-time, although part-time working remains concentrated among certain groups and sectors, with around 85 per cent of part-time work undertaken by women.

Job share. This is a situation which 'involves dividing a single full-time job between two people who share the responsibilities, pay and benefits' (**www.acas.org.uk**). In principle the job could be split between more than two employees, but in any event those employees work on *pro-rata* terms and conditions of employment. Job sharing developed in the mid-1980s and is evident in a minority of organisations. ACAS reported that its introduction 'was greatest in industries which employ mainly white-collar staff such as public administration and banking' (ACAS 1988: 21). Despite a recent British Chambers of Commerce report of SMEs indicating that almost 17 per cent of organisations *offered* job shares to their employees (British Chambers of Commerce 2007), Labour Force Surveys (**www.statistics.gov.uk**) have consistently shown that only around one per cent of employees are actually job sharers.

Flexible hours. Those working flexible hours may well find their hours varying from day to day, week to week or month to month. Although driven in many cases by employer demands for flexibility to match hours of work with fluctuations in demand, there has also been a long history of this being instigated by employees, at least in some sectors of employment. In the latter, the employee may decide their arrival and departure time around a 'core time', in others these may reflect both employer and employee concerns, as with term-time working.

Zero-hours contracts. These are a development of flexible working, instigated by employers and which attracted considerable attention from the mid-1980s. There are three possible broad categories of such contracts:

1 Where an employee attends the employer's premises but is only regarded as 'working' when their services are required by a customer or client;
2 Where the employee is 'on call' (by telephone or at home) at specified times, should the employer require their services;
3 Where an employee is part of a 'bank' of potential workers and either the employer will contact the employee to see if the worker wants work or, alternatively, the employee might contact the employer to see if work is available.

Although these contracts attracted much adverse publicity in some quarters when they began to be used in areas like retail in the 1980s, it remains unclear how prevalent they remain. In the *Fairness at Work* White Paper (1998: para 3.14), the government estimated that around 200,000 people were on such contracts in the late 1990s.

The context

Introduction

Hours of work remain a core element in the employment relationship and in our working and non-working lives more generally. In general, the hours we spend at work have exhibited a long-term downward trend (see below). However, because of technological changes and the spatial re-configuration of work, such as teleworking, there may often be a considerable gap between formal contracted hours, and those actually worked which significantly understates the true scale of working time. It is largely because of this, and the nature of the Working Time Regulations 1998, that concern over the relatively long hours worked by certain groups in Britain remains. It is also the case that some features of long hours working and of flexible working, such as paid overtime and shift working, have long been established characteristics of particular sectors, such as manufacturing and the extractive industries (e.g. mining). What has changed, particularly in the last 30 years has been the growth in various forms of flexible working and within this the growth of temporal flexibility. In the earlier discussion this relates particularly to part-time working, weekend working, overtime working (that is now frequently unpaid for many groups), flexible hours and annualised hours working. Indeed, research conducted in the late 1990s indicates that over all industries 56 per cent of workers work variable hours – ranging from 70 per cent in oil and gas extraction to 42 per cent in textile manufacture (Casey *et al.* 1997).

Voluntary regulation

The volume, arrangement and regulation of working time in any economy are shaped by a range of factors that evolve over time. A defining characteristic of the regulation of working time in Britain has been the historical predominance of voluntary regulation – that is through collective agreements negotiated between employers and trade unions either on an industry-wide or single employer basis. These agreements, often covering very large numbers of employees, not only set the standard working week in the industries they covered but also influenced the regulation of working time in other industries. Frequently these agreements would also cover, if appropriate to working patterns in the sector, shift working arrangements and premium rates of pay for such shift working and for overtime working.

In view of the fact that in Britain, collective agreements have generally been presumed not to be legally enforceable, such voluntary regulation has normally been enforceable through their **incorporation** into contracts of employment of individual employees (see Chapter 2). Non-compliance by an employer therefore, would, constitute **breach of contract**.

Generally, this voluntary regulation of working time concerned the standard working week of manual workers in unionised industries and sectors. In practice, through concerted action, unions would often use a 'pace-setting' national deal to set a new maximum basic working week which would act as a basis for agreements in other industries. Historically, the engineering industry provided this lead through national agreements. By the 1970s this covered over three million workers; and it meant that pressure could then be placed on employers in other sectors to provide comparative treatment. Such action was often successful. Employers frequently did not require much persuasion when faced with the threat of possible action should they not comply and more pragmatically, the loss of staff to competitors that could follow non-compliance. The major changes to working time negotiated for manual workers through

Table 10.1 Standard nationally negotiated working week in engineering

1920s	48 hours
1947	44 hours
1960	42 hours
1965	40 hours
1979	39 hours

collective agreements in engineering are detailed in Table 10.1. These reflect the general reduction taking place throughout much of British industry at these times.

The 1979 agreement reflected an unsuccessful attempt to achieve a 35 hour week in the engineering industry, a campaign that continued throughout the 1980s. This campaign failed to secure a national agreement, although some individual companies in the industry negotiated local agreements at or close to this. By the late 1980s, national bargaining in engineering was terminated by the Engineering Employers' Federation (the employers' side of the national bargaining forum). This trend was repeated in many other industries, eroded national bargaining by the de-regulationist policies of the 1980s (Deakin and Morris 2005: 308). As a result, this co-ordinated voluntary approach to regulating hours of work, and other aspects of the employment relationship ceased to be a feature of British employment relations.

National or sector level agreements had some success, directly and indirectly in regulating the standard working week for the majority of workers in Britain for much of the last century. These agreements were also significant in establishing paid holidays, with a general four week entitlement becoming established in the early 1980s, and in some agreements this extended to five weeks (Deakin and Morris 2005: 309). Furthermore, these national agreements were frequently supported by local agreements on other aspects of working time such as overtime levels and shift-working arrangements.

However, voluntary regulation was rarely comprehensive and some groups remained outside the provision of collective agreements. An example of this is the question of paid holiday entitlement. Until the implementation of the Working Time Regulations, Britain was the only country in the EU where workers had no legal rights to paid annual leave. Consequently, in the mid-1990s there were 2.5 million workers who received no paid annual leave (most were **part-time workers** of whom 1.4 million were women); 4.1 million received fewer than three weeks of paid holiday; and 5.9 million, fewer than four weeks (Labour Force Survey, Autumn 1995 (**www.statistics.gov.uk**)).

It should also be noted that sector-level agreements, while important for establishing basic working hours and weeks, were less successful as a mechanism for regulating working time. For example, the Donovan Commission (1968) revealed the extent of practices such as overtime working in the engineering industry, whilst more recent research has shown actual hours worked in manufacturing have frequently exceeded the basic working week of 37–39 hours. As Deakin and Morris (2005) have argued, a consequence of the loose voluntary regulation in Britain has been that 'British employment patterns have displayed a wide variety of non-standard working-time arrangements' (Deakin and Morris 2005: 309).

In comparison with other countries, Britain's reliance on voluntary agreement was somewhat unusual. In many other countries, legal regulation featured more prominently, and the establishment of basic working hours and weeks through legislation was achieved in a number of countries in the first half of the twentieth century (Deakin and Morris 2005). This did not mean however that legal regulation was absent from British employment relations, but it was partial and limited to particular groups of workers seen as requiring some specific protection. These aspects of 'regulatory law' (Kahn-Freund 1983) can be traced to the Factories Acts of the mid-nineteenth century, providing for regulation of working hours for women, children and young persons; and in the twentieth century were reflected in protection for those working in retail by establishing the right for minimum meal breaks, Sunday working hours and weekly half-day holidays.

A long hours culture?

The voluntary regulation of working time (and specifically the standard working week) established what would become fundamental terms of the individual contract of employment. Although this specified the hours to be worked in a week, it did not provide a limit on working hours, merely a threshold beyond which any additional work would be paid at a higher hourly rate. This was so in the manufacturing industry in particular. For many workers, in this sector, where some overtime working was often a contractual requirement, it was not uncommon to work considerably in excess of standard contractual hours of 40 hours, so that a working week would often in practice extend to 48 hours and in some cases well beyond this. On average full-time employees in manufacturing in the 1970s and beyond, regularly worked between four and six hours' overtime per week, and for all industries this has ranged between three and four hours per week (Hart 2004).

Much of the debate surrounding the statutory regulation of working time focused on the scale and consequences of long hours working in the UK. Official statistics estimate that around 4.8 million people regularly work over 45 hours per week – 29 per cent of men employed and 9 per cent of women (Labour Force Survey 2008). The TUC has identified around 3.3 million people regularly working in excess of 48 hours (TUC 2008). Estimates have also suggested almost one in six workers commonly work more than 60 hours per week (Bunting 2005). The TUC (2008) has reported that after a slight decline between 1998 and 2006, long hours working is again increasing with the figure for those working more than 48 hours per week estimated at 3.3 millions (12.9 per cent). This increase has taken place against a background of a falling average standard working week for men and women. The fact that such working appears to be related to stress and mental ill health (White and Beswick 2003) is clearly a cause for concern and reflects the current focus on working time as a health and safety issue (see below and Chapter 12).

Drawing international comparisons can be difficult – particularly in light of the high incidence of part-time working in the UK – but if we look at *full-time male employees* the evidence suggests that in the UK average hours worked beyond the standard working week is roughly double that found on average in other EU countries, but somewhat less than that in the USA and Australia (CIPD 2003).

The evidence concerning long hours working in the UK suggests that it is undertaken predominantly by men – 85 per cent of those working long hours (TUC 2008). It was worked by those in their 30s and 40s with dependents, and is far more common in the private sector and within this, in manufacturing. A survey for the Department of Trade and Industry, reported the following factors most likely to be associated with long hours working (Kodz *et al.* 2003a, 2003b):

- Men were more likely to work long hours than women.
- Men with children slightly more likely than men without children.
- Women with children less likely than women without.
- People between the ages of 30 and 49.
- Managers, professionals and operative and assembly workers – with over two-thirds of managers and professional workers neither paid overtime nor given time off in lieu.

The reasons for this tendency to work long hours are complex. For employees, the freedom to work the hours they choose and to maximise earnings is clearly important, particularly when employees have dependency responsibilities; and to this can be added the relatively low basic hourly rates that have prevailed in Britain for manual work in the past, that made overtime working an attractive proposition.

For employers, overtime and shift working represent relatively easy and attractive (although not necessarily cost effective) forms of flexibility. The ability to extend or rearrange the hours of existing employees is often seen as preferable to hiring new staff to take on additional work that may only be required for a limited period of time. More recently, with the rise of service sector employment, where part-time working is far more established than in manufacturing and where overtime is frequently unpaid, working long hours appears to be linked to increasing workload (Kodz *et al.* 2003a, 2003b), organisational **cultures** where such working may be expected (cultures emphasising 'presenteeism' for example), and in some cases multiple job holding where the opportunities to increase earnings are available.

Research points to a number of factors associated with increasing volumes of work. These are: new organisational initiatives (e.g. de-layering, project-based working, and a greater emphasis on customer focus); staff shortages; IT and e-mail overload. The overall impression from the available research findings is that many people work long hours for a combination of reasons which can be difficult to disentangle, especially in an organisation or part of an organisation where a long hours culture is well-established (Kodz *et al.* 2003a, 2003b). This said, much of the available evidence points to long hours working among those having what under the Working Time Regulations 1998 is designated as 'unmeasured working time' (such as managers), and those who have 'opted-out' of the regulations.

Social issues

There are two broad social policy issues which relate to long hours and the regulation of working time: the health, safety and welfare of employees (see Chapter 12); and the impact on family life and work–life balance (see Chapter 11). Both issues are policy concerns for the EU and the present British government.

The originating Working Time Directive 1993 (now consolidated into the 2003 Directive) was significant primarily because it was conceived of as a ***health and safety*** measure, augmenting those related directives adopted under the 1989 Social Action Programme. A key feature of the directive is the expectation that 'work should be adapted to the worker' (Article 13). In the early 1990s the then Conservative Government was firmly opposed to the legal regulation of working time and to its construction as a health and safety measure, and challenged the legality of the directive at the ECJ. The challenge failed but delays in implementing the directive meant that the UK Working Time Regulations 1998 had to wait for the election of a Labour government sympathetic both to the broad thrust of the legislation and to its construction as a health and safety issue. The directive and the regulations have four elements that make up a health and safety dimension: maximum working time; patterns of breaks and leave from working time; health assessments; and job design.

The research undertaken for the Health and Safety Executive (Kodz *et al.* 2003a, 2003b; White and Beswick 2003) indicates 'clear grounds for concern' about the adverse effect of long hours working and the frequency of health and safety incidents. Kodz *et al.* (2003a, 2003b) note that much of the evidence on the impact of long hours working comes from a small number of occupations (e.g. long-distance road haulage, the medical professions) which makes it difficult to draw more general conclusions. Furthermore, the research indicates associations rather than causal links between long hours working and mental health and cardio-vascular problems. The evidence also suggests a relationship between employee health and specific work patterns, notably working unsociable hours and shift patterns.

The issue of ***work–life balance*** is explored in more detail in Chapter 11. Here it is sufficient to note both the political impetus to change and the social consequences of long hours. The government, in its consultation document (DTI 1997) on what was then proposed legislation, commented that the 'long hours' culture as well as giving rise to potential health issues for those working the hours had other negative effects on other groups. It noted that the culture had historically created barriers to work for women with caring responsibilities, and had prevented many men from taking an active role in their children's upbringing (DTI 1997: para 10). The consequences for family life were revealed in research which found that a quarter of all fathers were working over 50 hours per week, and that almost 10 per cent, were working more than 60 hours per week (Ferri and Smith 1996).

Economic considerations

Although the achievement of social objectives in the form of health and safety has been at the forefront of recent debates about working time, economic considerations have also shaped discussion about working time and the precise nature of statutory regulation. First, on the one hand, there are those who extend the concerns of psychologists, arguing that the long hours culture has an adverse economic effect on output and productivity. Secondly, on the other hand, there are those who see compliance with the legislation as costly – increasing unit labour costs and administration. An illustration of this is a British Chambers of Commerce report (2004) which estimated the cumulative cost of the Working Time Regulations at that time at £11.1 billions (Smith 2004). A third concern, influential in France's adoption of a 35-hour week, has been a wish to reduce unemployment (OECD 2004). The relative importance of these economic factors remains unclear but there is little doubt that the influence of economic considerations on policy makers has been considerable.

The effects on work performance

From an economist's perspective the issue of work performance tends to reduce to concerns around productivity and unit costs. Efficiency in the use of human resources is about how such resources are utilised, measured in terms of their output, and in terms of how much it costs to produce that output. In principle, working longer hours should produce more output (more customers served, more cars produced), but there are good reasons for believing that productivity need not increase and that beyond a certain point productivity (and indeed quality) may fall, and unit labour costs may rise. Indeed, although the research by Kodz *et al.* (2003a, 2003b) suggested that it was not possible to establish conclusively whether long hours working affected productivity, there is some evidence from France, following the Aubry Laws that introduced a 35-hour week, to suggest that shorter working hours may be associated with higher levels of productivity (Ashkenazy 2008; Hayden 2006; OECD 2004). That is, shorter working hours, particularly where pay is maintained may encourage more intensive and efficient working practices as firms have more of an incentive to use their resources more efficiently and effectively. (After being in force for over 10 years, this French law was repealed in 2008 as a result of employer campaigning in a sympathetic conservative political climate.)

Costs of compliance

This is a particularly difficult area to assess given the long-standing nature of working practices and the extent of embeddedness and institutionalisation that often comes with this. In view of the concern of the Working Time Directive of 'adapting work to the worker' and for a more general 'humanisation of work', there was considerable potential for a clash between the legislation and business cultures and practices. The government's efforts to address this through the decision to include an 'opt-out' in the Working Time Regulations, helped to allay the fears of many in the business community concerned about the costs of compliance, but angered others who saw this as undermining the aims and intent of the legislation and at worse, amounting to non-compliance with the directive (Bercusson 2003).

Research conducted on behalf of the DTI six months after the implementation of the Working Time Regulations, indicated considerable concern amongst employers about the costs and bureaucratic burden associated with new record-keeping requirements (Neathey and Arrowsmith 2001). However, the follow-up study conducted 12 months later (Neathey 2003) found that, once established, these systems were seen as less of a problem, and, in some cases, to have positive operational benefits.

Other DTI-sponsored work in 2001 (BMRB Social Research 2004) focusing on workers' experiences of the regulations pointed to considerable gaps in both the operation of the regulations 'on the ground' and in workers' awareness of the law on working time. This suggests a degree of ignorance or deliberate non-compliance with the legislation but also points to the potential for considerable transitional costs for both businesses and their staff as they adjust to the new arrangements.

Ultimately, as in any other area of law, the costs of compliance are closely linked to the enforcement mechanisms in place to monitor the operation of the law. In the case of working time, enforcement falls to the Health and Safety Executive in the case of issues relating to weekly working time and night-work limits; and to individuals on issues concerning rest periods, breaks and paid leave. However, in light of the resource constraints on the time of HSE inspectors, firms (particularly very small firms) may escape close scrutiny on practices for significant periods of time.

The legal framework

The current legal framework on working time regulation is considered under two headings:

- A brief review of piecemeal legal requirements that have developed in recent years in both statutory and **case law**, covering specific occupations or categories of workers.
- A detailed review of the Working Time Regulations 1998, amendments to these and relevant case law.

Piecemeal legal regulation

The piecemeal legislation covers the following: those working in certain specific occupations; those protected by sex discrimination law and by disability discrimination law; and those alleging overwork as a breach of contract.

Specific occupations

Working time is regulated for some specific occupations particularly in the transport sector, and includes drivers of public-service vehicles and certain commercial vehicles. Monitoring (where required) is undertaken through the use of the tachograph. Legislation was enacted in 1968 to protect the public against risks which arise in cases where the drivers of motor vehicles are suffering from fatigue. The working hours of those who work 'in and around shops' and betting shop workers has been affected by the choice as to whether to work on Sundays; and by protection from **victimisation** if the employer subjected them to a detriment in the exercise of this choice (Employment Rights Act 1996, Part IV).

Sex discrimination law

The relevant working time provisions of sex discrimination law relate to the repeal of the restrictions on night work undertaken by women (Sex Discrimination Act 1986); and the extent to which full-time work can be a condition of employment. The second area has arisen in case law and relates to women returning to work after maternity leave and concerns indirect sex discrimination (Sex Discrimination Act 1975, s (1)(b)), and the question as to whether or not an employer can 'justify' the requirements to work full-time in the individual case (see Chapters 5 and 11).

Disability discrimination

The Disability Discrimination Act 1995 places a **duty** on an employer to make reasonable adjustments to accommodate a disabled person (DDA 1995, s 4A). One possible adjustment is an alteration to a person's working hours. This could include allowing the disabled person to work flexible hours to enable additional breaks to overcome fatigue arising from the disability, or changing the disabled person's hours to fit with the availability of a carer (see former Disability Rights Commission Code of Practice on Employment and Occupation 2004).

Breach of contract

Under **common law**, breaches of two implied terms in the contract of employment – the duty to take reasonable care of an employee and the duty of mutual trust and confidence – can be invoked in circumstances where an employee is alleging physical or mental injury as a result of long working hours (Chapter 2). The duty of care issue in respect of working hours was brought into sharp focus by the case of *Johnstone* v *Bloomsbury Health Authority* [1991] IRLR 118, concerning a Senior House Officer at University College Hospital. Under the express terms of his contract, he was required to work 40 hours per week and to be 'on call', at the employer's discretion, for up to a further 48 hours. He claimed that he had been asked repeatedly to work long hours, at times in excess of 100 hours per week and that this had caused him both physical (sleep deprivation, physical sickness) and mental problems (stress, depression) and that this had put his patients at risk. He was successful in his claim with the Court of Appeal ruling that as a general principle, any additional hours requirement coming from the employer had to be exercised in ways that conformed with the overall duty of care. (For more on the issue of work-related stress see Chapter 12.)

The Working Time Regulations 1998

The key recent developments in the legal regulation of working time have come through the Working Time Regulations. These implement two directives:

- on the organisation of working time (now in the consolidated 2003 directive, repealing the original 1993 directive); and
- provisions of the Young Workers Directive 1994.

The regulations came into effect on 1 October 1998. They were amended in 1999 in respect of record-keeping and unmeasured working time; and in light of later amending directives covering specific occupational groups (non-mobile workers in various transport industries (2000), seafarers (2002), workers in civil aviation (2003), and mobile workers in road transport (2002) who were exempted from the original 1993 directive). The core rights provided by the regulations are detailed in Exhibit 10.2.

Who is covered?

The regulations apply to workers over the minimum school leaving age. They have wide-ranging coverage. They include 'employees' who work under a contract of employment and those who work under other forms of contract to work personally. The only people excluded are the genuinely self-employed and there are some special provisions that apply to 'young workers' (those over 16 but under 18).

In cases where there is some ambiguity about employment status, as in other areas of law, the facts and circumstances will be considered by the court and tribunal. In the case of *Byrne Brothers (Formwork) Ltd* v *Baird and Others* EAT 542/01, labour only contractors were held to be workers for the purposes of the regulations. On the facts of the case, the workers concerned had a contract of personal service – they undertook personally to provide work but

Exhibit 10.2 Working Time Regulations: core provisions for adults

- A limit of 48 hours' work per week.
- An ability to 'opt out' of this average working week.
- A basic entitlement of 28 days' paid annual leave each year (from 2009).
- Statutory rest periods – a minimum of 20 minutes' rest in any period of work of six hours or more.
- A minimum of 11 hours of rest in any one 24-hour period.
- A minimum of 24 hours of rest in any seven-day period.
- Specific regulations governing those on shift work.
- For night workers, a minimum of eight hours of work in any 24-hour period.
- Free health checks for night workers.
- Specific restrictions apply to the working time of those aged 16–18.

did not work as part of 'any profession or business undertaking' – and with limited powers to delegate work, were found not to be engaged in business on their own account, and that the necessary mutuality of obligations existed between them and others.

Although the breadth of coverage of the Regulations is wide, certain groups were excluded from the original 1993 directive. Subsequently, the EU has adopted amending directives that cover workers as follows:

- *Road transport.* Since August 2003, *non-mobile workers* have been covered by the full provisions of the Working Time Directive. This amends the situation where the ECJ ruled, in October 2001, that all workers in road transport, including office workers, were excluded from the 1993 Directive (*Bowden and Others* v *Tuffnells Parcels Express Ltd* ECJ C-133/00). Also, from August 2003, mobile workers have been entitled to paid annual leave, a 48-hour maximum working week and health checks for night workers. In addition, the Road Transport Directive sets out detailed working time for drivers covered by European drivers' legislation. This was implemented in 2005.
- *Rail transport.* In August 2003, the directive was extended in full to both mobile and non-mobile rail workers. It provides **derogations** from the entitlements to daily rest, rest breaks, weekly rest and the night work provisions for rail workers whose activities are intermittent, whose hours of work are spent on trains and whose activities are linked to rail transport timetables and ensuring the continuity and regularity of rail traffic.
- *Air transport.* In August 2003, the directive was extended in full to non-mobile workers, with mobile workers entitled to paid annual leave, a 48-hour maximum working week, health checks for night workers and adequate rest. A **Social Partners**' Aviation Directive, covering civil aviation was also implemented from December 2003. This limits the annual working time of airborne personnel to 2,000 hours, covers some elements of standby time and restricts flying time to 900 hours. It also requires 'appropriate' health and safety protection for all mobile personnel and contains provisions for a monthly and yearly number of rest days.
- *Sea transport.* In August 2003, the directive was extended in full to non-mobile workers, and together with the Seafarers' Directive implemented in 2002 and based on Convention 180 of the International Labour Organisation has extended protection to those working at sea. The Seafarers' Directive provides for a maximum working week of 72 hours and 14 hours of rest in any 24-hour period, or a minimum weekly rest requirement of 77 hours and 10 hours in any 24-hour period. It also provides for four weeks' paid annual leave and health assessments for night workers.
- *Junior doctors.* Arguably, this has been the most controversial area of application of the regulations. In principle, full implementation of the 48-hour week can be phased in over a possible 12-year period for this group. However, though the Working Time Regulations apply in full to junior doctors, following the Horizontal Amending Directive (2000/EC/34) the implementation of the 48-hour working week is being gradually phased in over a five-year period from 1 August 2004 until 1 August 2009. A limit of 58 hours applied between 1 August 2004 to 31 July 2007, one of 56 hours between 1 August 2007 and 31 July 2009, and 48 hours from 1 August 2009. Furthermore, specific rules have been introduced for calculating reference periods, based on a normal period of 26 weeks.
- *Other groups.* In addition to these amendments, there have been specific extensions of the 1993 Working Time Directive to workers engaged in inland waterway and lake transport, sea fishing and working offshore.

With these amendments and exclusions noted, the Working Time Regulations now apply to all workers, extend to Crown employees, House of Lords and House of Commons staff, the police, and members of the armed forces. However, they have been held not to apply to children below the minimum school leaving age (*Addison* v *Ashby* [2003] ICR 667) (see also Deakin and Morris 2005).

Definition of working time

The regulations, following the directive, identify only **two** periods associated with the employment relationship: *working time* and *rest periods*. The directive defines working time as 'any period during which the worker is working, at the employer's disposal and carrying out his activity or duties, in accordance with national laws and/or practice' (Article 2.1). The regulations, transposing the directive, define working time as:

- any period during which (a worker) is working, at his employer's disposal and carrying out his activity or duties;
- any period during which he is receiving relevant training, such as under a combined work/training scheme or an in-plant work-experience scheme (also defined in reg 2.1);
- any additional period which is to be treated as working time for the purpose of these Regulations under a relevant agreement (also defined in reg 2.1).

For most working people this definition is clear-cut. However, there will be uncertainties in respect of workers who are 'on-call' or who are on 'zero-hours contracts'. How much time is to be designated as 'working time'? To help resolve the issue of what is 'working time' and what is not, the regulations permit the negotiation of a '**relevant agreement**' between the employer and an individual employee. Such an agreement might be derived from a collective agreement with an **independent trade union** or by a '**workforce agreement**' (see below). A relevant agreement must be in writing and be legally binding.

In its guidance on working time the former Department of Trade and Industry included the following as working time (see **www.berr.gov.uk**):

- working lunches, such as business lunches;
- when a worker has to travel as part of his/her work – for example a 24-hour mobile repair worker or travelling salesperson;
- when a worker is undertaking training that is directly related to his/her job;
- time spent working abroad if the worker works for an employer who carries on business in Britain.

Case law has clarified a number of issues (see Exhibit 10.3) particularly in respect of those who are 'on duty' on the employer's premises – available for work and possibly sleeping – but not actually carrying out tasks. Also, this case law provides a framework within which it is possible to consider the situation of 'zero hours contract' workers.

Rest breaks and rest periods

A 'rest period' is defined in the directive as 'any period which is not working time' (art 2(2)). The regulations add 'other than a rest break or leave to which the worker is entitled under these Regulations' (reg 2(1)) (see issues raised in Exhibit 10.3). When considering the situation of an individual worker, the following specific provisions, relating to working time and rests/breaks, need to be considered ***all together***.

Exhibit 10.3 Defining 'working time'

The first two cases, one Spanish and one German, concern rulings by the European Court of Justice about doctors who were 'on call'.

SIMAP v *Conselleria de Sanidid y Consumo de la Generalidad Valenciana* [2000] IRLR 845

ECJ rulings:

- '. . . [T]o exclude duty "on call" from working time if physical presence is required would seriously undermine' the objective of securing breaks for health and safety reasons.
- The ECJ held that 'on-call' time is classified as 'working time' when a worker is physically required to be at their place of work. However, when a worker is away from the place of work when 'on-call' and free to take part in other activities so that even if they were at the disposal of their employer (in that it had to be possible to contact them) doctors could manage their time with fewer constraints and pursue their own interests, such on-call time should not be classified as 'working time'. In such circumstances, only time linked to the actual provision of primary care services can be regarded as *working time*.

Landeshauptstadt Kiel v *Jaeger* [2003] IRLR 804, ECJ

The ECJ held that 'on-call' duty, performed by doctors (who were required to be physically present in the hospital and who were permitted to rest or sleep in rooms provided for them there during periods when their services were not required) constituted, in its entirety, working time under the Working Time Directive. Periods of inactivity during on-call duty was not a 'rest period'. It reaffirmed and extended the principles set out in the *SIMAP* case.

The other cases are from British courts applying the principles of the European law.

MacCartney v *Oversley House Management* EAT/0500/05

The claimant, was a residential manager in a home for people over 60, she had contracted hours of 'four days per week of 24 hours on site cover' during which she had to be on or near the premises, 'on call', attending to the residents with whom she was in contact by mobile phone, answering emergency and non-emergency calls or doing administrative work in a small office in her flat in the home. The issue was whether duty 'on call' was working time.

EAT's finding:

- She was entitled to 20 minute ***rest break*** each day.
- She was 'working' for the purposes of the Working Time Regulations during the whole time that she was 'on call'. Because she was required to remain at a place determined by her employer (with a view to performing services if necessary as resident manager in a residential care home) the entire period of 'on-call' time constituted working time for the purposes of the regulations. She had not been granted the appropriate ***11-hour daily rest periods***.

Comment. An employer in this situation could ask employees to sign an 'opt-out'. However, if an individual refuses to do so, the employer will essentially be required to hire additional wardens (IRS *Industrial Relations Law Bulletin* 781.11, March 2006).

Gallagher and Others v *Alpha Catering Services Ltd* [2004] IRLR 102, CA

The claimants' job was to deliver meals to aircraft. It was a job that varies according to flight timetables and levels of business from day to day and as a result their shifts contained periods of downtime between loading and unloading aircraft, during which time they were in radio contact with their employers in case they were needed. They could take meals but were not allowed to sleep during 'down time'. Alpha Catering Services claimed that 'down time' constituted a rest break, but that it was entitled not to provide any formal breaks as the regulations

Exhibit 10.3 continued

provide for them to be excluded due to the need for continuous service at peak times. The issue was the status of 'downtime' under the Working Time Regulations.

The Court of Appeal ruled that periods of 'downtime' during which a worker is still at his employer's disposal do not count as rest periods under reg 12. A rest period is an uninterrupted period of at least 20 minutes in a work period of more than six hours that the worker can use as he or she pleases.

Comment. This case stresses that the directive (and the regulations which implement it in Britain) are intended to protect the health and safety of the worker. It should close off the temptation for an unscrupulous employer to call 'downtime' or waiting periods 'rest breaks' (IRS *Industrial Relations Law Bulletin* 753.8, January 2005).

Daily rest

For adult workers the regulations provide for 'a minimum daily rest period of 11 consecutive hours per 24-hour period' (adding) 'during which he works for his employer' (reg 10(1)). A young worker is entitled to a rest period of not less than 12 consecutive hours in each 24-hour period 'during which he works for his employer' (reg 10(2)).

There has been one case in this area which concerned bus drivers (*First Hampshire & Dorset Ltd* v *Feist & Others* EAT 0510/06). It was ruled that reg 10(1) did not apply to a worker where his/her activities involved the need for continuity of service or production. The regulations allow a worker to claim 'compensatory rest' where s/he is required to work during a period that would otherwise be a rest period or rest break (reg 24). However, mobile workers are specifically covered by an amendment enacted in 2003 that entitles them to 'adequate rest' that is sufficiently long and continuous to ensure that 'as a result of fatigue or other irregular work patterns' they do not cause injury to themselves, to fellow workers or to others; and that the worker 'does not damage his health either in the short term or in the longer term' (reg 24A). In the circumstances, the EAT said that the bus drivers were entitled to 'adequate rest' but not also to 'compensatory rest'.

Rest breaks

Where the working day is longer than six hours, every worker is entitled to a rest break. This break for ***adult workers*** is 'an uninterrupted period of not less than twenty minutes and the worker is entitled to spend it away from his workstation if he has one' (reg 12(3)). For ***young workers***, where the 'daily working time is more than four and a half hours', the entitlement is to a rest break of a least 30 minutes, 'which shall be consecutive if possible and he is entitled to spend it away from his workstation if he has one' (reg 12(4)). The aggregation of working time is required where a young worker works for more than one employer (reg 12(5)). This does not occur under any other provisions.

Weekly rest

For each seven-day period, every worker is entitled to a minimum uninterrupted rest period of 24 hours plus the 11 hour's daily rest. This shall 'in principle include Sunday'. The implication is a 35-hour period of rest. However, 'if objective, technical or work organisation conditions so justify, a minimum rest period of 24 hours may be applied'. For young workers this reduction may be not less than 36 hours (reg 11).

Shift work and night work

Shift work

This is work subject to minimum daily rest; maximum daily working hours; breaks during working hours; weekly rest periods; maximum weekly hours. Derogations are possible under the directive (Article 17(2) and (3)) in respect of daily rest and weekly rest. The regulations provide some flexibility in respect of shift working, subject to the provision of compensatory rest (reg 24).

Night work

An aim of the directive is to ensure that 'normal hours of work for night workers do not exceed an average of eight hours in any 24-hour period'. This is also provided for in the regulations (reg 6(1)). This is averaged over a 17-week reference period but can be extended by derogations (see below). Night-time is defined as a period of at least seven hours' duration between 11 p.m. and 6 a.m. (or midnight and 5 a.m. if there is a relevant agreement). A 'night worker' is, defined as 'a worker who, as a normal course, works at least three hours daily working time during night time' (reg 2 (1)) (see Exhibit 10.4). It is also possible for a collective or workforce agreement to modify or exclude the application of the provisions of the eight-hour maximum and the reference period (reg 23).

Although young workers should not work at night (reg 6A), there are certain permitted exceptions (regs 27 and 27A). In these circumstances they may work where there is no adult available and where it is necessary to maintain continuity of service or production or respond to a surge in demand for a service or product. They must be adequately supervised for their own protection. Furthermore, they may work when exceptional and unforeseen circumstances arise.

Health and safety issues

The directive aims to ensure that 'night workers whose work involves special hazards or heavy physical or mental strain do not work more than eight hours in any period of 24 hours during which they perform night work' (Article 8) (reg 6). This type of work can be defined in collective agreements and may be defined as such following a risk assessment made under the Management of Health and Safety at Work Regulations 1999. Adult night workers are also entitled to a health assessment (and a young worker to a health and capacities assessment)

Exhibit 10.4 Night work: case law

Case law in respect of night work is limited. However, in one early case defining 'night work', the Northern Ireland High Court ruled that under the directive (Article 2(4)), a worker is a 'night worker' if s/he works at least three hours during the designated hours of night *as a normal course* (*R* v *Attorney General for Northern Ireland* ex parte *Burns* [1999] IRLR 315, NIHC). The applicant in this case worked a rotating shift system at the relevant time under which she had to work night time hours one week in three.

The NIHC held that the words *normal course* entailed simply that night time working should be a regular feature of the applicant's employment. The court firmly rejected the argument that the definition of a night worker will only apply *to someone who does such work exclusively or predominantly*. The Working Time Regulations also use the phrase 'as a normal course' (reg 2(1)).

before being required to perform night work, and periodically thereafter (reg 7). If a registered medical professional advises that a night worker is suffering from health problems caused by or aggravated by working at night, s/he has a right to be transferred to suitable day work if possible (reg 7(6)).

Paid annual leave

For the first time the Working Time Directive and Regulations provide a right to paid holiday entitlement in British employment law. The directive provides for paid annual leave of at least four weeks (Article 7). Britain secured a transitional arrangement of three weeks (with effect from October 1998). The four-week statutory minimum entitlement has been in force since 23 November 1999 (reg 13). However, the regulations initially provided for a 13-week **qualifying period** before entitlement to the paid leave came into effect but this was challenged at the European Court of Justice, which ruled it to be unlawful (*R* v *Secretary of State for Trade and Industry* ex parte *BECTU* [2001] IRLR 559, ECJ). A worker's entitlement now accrues from the first day of employment. The EU Charter of Fundamental Rights was also relied upon and asserts the unqualified right of every worker to annual paid leave (Article 8). From October 2001, the British government amended the Working Time Regulations to give effect to this judgment.

The entitlement is for a worker to accrue one-twelfth of the annual leave entitlement each month from the first day of employment. Any week in which a worker has a contractual relationship with an employer – for all or part of the week – will count. Part-time workers are entitled to ***pro rata*** treatment. So, for example, a part-time worker who works for five hours each week, on completion of, for example, 13 weeks (i.e. 65 hours of work) will be entitled to paid leave. In this case, the worker will be entitled to be away from work for a minimum of four weeks, that is, 20 working hours (as one week equates to five hours). The worker is entitled to be paid for that number of hours.

Workers who work irregular hours are entitled to be away from work for the statutory minimum number of weeks. The number of hours for which they are entitled to receive payment might create problems. However, the law permits an averaging process with overtime hours not normally included as part of the calculations unless, contractually, a worker is bound to work some overtime hours.

It is important to note that the entitlement to paid annual leave does not prevent the employer, under the contract of employment, from specifying when that leave is to be taken. This has been confirmed by the EAT (*Sumsion* v *BBC* (*Scotland*) [2007] IRLR 678). In this case, a carpenter on a 24-week fixed-term contract was required to be available for work six days a week. The BBC said that where he was not required to work on Saturdays these days should be taken as annual leave. The EAT found that there was nothing restricting the employer nominating these days (when he might be required to work) as leave days. There was nothing special about weekends if it was a working day.

One controversial aspect of the initial paid annual leave entitlement in Britain was the provision which permitted an employer to include the eight statutory public holidays in the 20-day entitlement. Following campaigning, particularly by the Trades Union Congress, the law was amended (see Exhibit 10.5).

The issue of paid annual leave has given rise to much of the case law under the Working Time Regulations. In Exhibit 10.6 some of the more significant cases in this area are identified and described.

Exhibit 10.5 Increased holiday entitlement

- *Increase*: from 20 days (four weeks) to 28 days (5.6 weeks).
- *Phasing*: increase to 24 days (4.8 weeks) from 1 October 2007 then to 28 days (5.6 weeks) from 1 April 2009.
- Any time off for bank and public holidays can be included in the additional entitlement. So, a worker's holiday entitlement will not increase if s/he already received four weeks plus public holidays.
- *Pro rata* provision for part-timers as already established.
- Some or all of the holiday entitlement may be carried over to the following year with the agreement of the employer and the member of staff.
- Payment in lieu of the additional holiday ***not*** permitted from 1 April 2009 except on termination of employment.
- No qualifying period for the additional holiday.

Exhibit 10.6 Case law and paid annual leave

Robinson-Steele v *RD Retail Services Ltd and Other Cases* [2006] IRLR 386, ECJ

Issue: *the legality of 'rolled up holiday pay' under the Working Time Directive.*

The ECJ held that:

- It is unlawful for an employer to 'roll up' holiday pay so that, in effect, the minimum period of paid annual leave to which a worker is entitled is replaced by an allowance paid in instalments throughout the period of employment alongside the worker's normal pay. Holiday pay should be allocated to a period of leave and paid at the time the leave is taken.
- An employer will not act unlawfully if it offsets against a worker's entitlement to holiday pay for a specific period of leave *sums already paid* under a rolled-up holiday pay arrangement (provided that the rolled-up payments were made 'transparently and comprehensibly').

Comment. The British government has amended its guidance on the Working Time Regulations 1998 to state that employers with rolled-up holiday pay arrangements should renegotiate the relevant contracts as soon as possible so that payment for annual leave is made at the time that the leave is taken (IRS *Industrial Relations Law Bulletin* 783.14, April 2006).

Commissioners of Inland Revenue v *Ainsworth and Others* [2005] IRLR 465, CA

Issue 1: *entitlement to holiday pay by those on sick leave.*

Workers absent through long-term sick leave who have exhausted their entitlement to sick pay are not entitled to four weeks' holiday pay when they have done no work during the leave year. This would give them an unjustified windfall not intended by the Working Time Regulations 1998. Workers whose employment is terminated after 12-month periods of absence through sickness are not entitled to payment for holiday pay for 'leave' they have no taken while away from work on sick leave. (All cases in this appeal concerned sickness absence lasting longer than an entire holiday year.)

Issue 2: *claims to enforce the right to annual leave and holiday pay.*

Such claims must be made under the Working Time Regulations 1998 and not under the Employment Rights Act 1996 (as unauthorised deductions from wages).

(**Note**: This case was referred by the House of Lords to the European Court of Justice for guidance on interpretation. It is now called *HM Revenue and Customs* v *Stringer and Others*. The Advocate-General gave her legal opinion early in 2008. The ECJ's ruling is expected in 2009.)

Exhibit 10.6 continued

Federatie Nederlandse Vakbeweging v *Staat der Nederlanden* [2006] IRLR 561, ECJ

Issue. This was whether it was compatible with the directive for an EU member state to have a national law that allows for the possibility that an employee who has not fully taken minimum annual leave in a year might receive ***financial compensation*** for that leave in a subsequent year.

The ECJ ruled that, while it was not contrary to the directive to carry leave over, there was the possibility that financial compensation could create an incentive for annual leave to remain untaken. This was incompatible with the directive's health and safety objectives.

Enhanced leave under the contract

The statutory entitlement is to a *minimum* period of annual leave. It is possible that the employer might have an enhanced annual leave entitlement of more than 20 days. These additional days will be a contractual entitlement. Any dispute about them will be about the contract and not about the statutory entitlement. Furthermore, financial compensation for not taking this enhanced annual leave would be permissible if agreed by the employer and the employee.

Maximum working week

The directive (Article 6) states that the average working time for each seven-day period (including overtime) should not exceed 48 hours. Weekly working time can be averaged over a four-month period. Sick leave and 'periods of paid annual leave' 'shall not be included or shall be neutral in the calculation of the average' (Article 16).

Reference period

The Working Time Regulations specify a 48-hour maximum for a seven-day period over a 17-week reference period. There are provisions (in conformity with the directive) to extend the reference period to:

- 26 weeks in certain circumstances (reg 4(5)) (reg 21), for example in security and surveilliance work; or
- up to 52 weeks through a collective or workforce agreement (reg 23).

In calculating a person's average working time, certain periods are in effect 'neutral' for example when a person is sick, on maternity or other family leave or on holiday. Exhibit 10.7 provides an example of how average working hours are calculated under the regulations; the first example comes from government guidance (see **www.berr.gov.uk** on the making of these calculations).

A young worker should not work more than eight hours per day and 40 hours per week. There is no opt-out available. In certain circumstances they may work longer hours where there is no adult available and where it is necessary to maintain continuity of service or production; or respond to a surge in demand for a service or product. An employer 'shall take all reasonable steps, in keeping with the need to protect the health and safety of workers' to ensure that these limits are complied with (reg 5A).

Exhibit 10.7 Averaging examples

1 A worker has a standard working week of 40 hours and does overtime of 12 hours a week for the first 10 weeks of the 17-week reference period. No leave is taken during the reference period.

The total hours worked is:

17 weeks of 40 hours and 10 weeks of 12 hours of overtime

$(17 \times 40) + (10 \times 12) = 800$

Therefore, this average (total hours divided by number of weeks):

800 divided by 17 = 47.1 hours

The average limit of 48 hours has been complied with.

Where leave is taken within a referencing period the situation is as follows:

2 In the example above, let us assume that the worker takes three days' leave in the reference period.

The total hours worked is:

16 weeks of 40 hours and 2 days of 8 hours and 10 weeks of 12 hours of overtime.

$(16 \times 40) + (2 \times 8) + (10 \times 12) = 776$

To this has to be added the time taken on leave, which is three days of eight hours that should be added (3×8) taken from the next reference period:

$(3 \times 8) = 24$

His average, therefore, is (total hours divided by number of weeks):

$$\frac{776 + 24}{17} = 47.1 \text{ hours}$$

Again, the average limit of 48 hours has been complied with.

Source: BERR (2008) *Your Guide to the Working Time Regulations: Sections 1–4*, Example 1, Section 2.

The individual 'opt out'

One of the key concessions obtained by the British government in its implementation of the directive has been securing agreement that individual workers may opt to work in excess of 48 hours per week.

The worker should sign a simple opt-out agreement. The right for the individual worker to invoke the opt-out must comply with the following conditions (reg 5):

- the agreement must be in writing;
- it can be for a specific or indefinite period;
- notice to terminate agreement shall not exceed three months;
- if there is no notice period, then the agreement is terminable by seven days' notice;
- the only record required is that workers have signed the opt out;
- individuals have the right not to suffer detriment and are protected against unfair **dismissal** for failing to sign an opt-out if requested by the employer (ERA 1996, ss 45A and 101A). 'Detriment' can include pressure, harassment, disciplinary threats, overlooking for promotion, failure to provide pay and benefits to which the worker is entitled. For an example of a discriminatory dismissal, see ***Morris* v *Turista Travel Ltd*** ET case 2501197/99 (Exhibit 10.8).

The United Kingdom is the only EU member state to have used this provision although other countries have followed the UK at least in relation to specific sectors (cited in Collins *et al.* 2005), but it has been the subject of considerable controversy. The derogation relating to individual workers is subject to the general principles of the protection of the safety and health of workers as set out in the directive (Article 22). Effectively, the opt-out should not impose excessive working hours, sufficient to harm the health of the individual worker (*Hone* v *Six Continents Retail* [2006] IRLR 49 CA (Exhibit 10.8)). Furthermore, such agreements can be subject to scrutiny by the 'competent authorities'. In the UK this is the Health and Safety Executive. If there is no opt-out, then it is lawful for workers to refuse to exceed the 48-hour maximum as ruled in *Barber* v *RJB Mining (UK) Ltd* [1999] IRLR 308, HC (see Exhibit 10.8).

In view of the controversy surrounding it, this derogation has been subject to a prolonged examination by the Council of Ministers. The available research evidence shows that:

- Its use is widespread with an estimated 19 per cent of employees (3.8 million) having signed an opt-out. Its use is most common in the private sector (especially in manufacturing/construction) and in larger workplaces.
- There is substantial evidence that the opt-out is sought by employers as a precautionary measure. Around 81 per cent of establishments that had an opt-out reported no sustained long hours working.

In summary, as Barnard and her colleagues have argued, the individual opt-out is the principal means by which the potential impact of the directive has been diluted.

Exhibit 10.8 Case law relating to maximum working week

Morris v *Turista Travel Ltd* ET case 2501197/99

The issue was a discriminatory dismissal. The worker was given a draft contract which stated:

> You agree that the limit imposed by Regulation 4(1) and (2) of the Working Time Regulations 1998 . . . should not apply to your average weekly working hours. This part of your contract of employment . . . would have the effect that you may work longer hours than 48 hours average maximum working hours provided under the regulations. The opt out agreement which is effective from . . . may be terminated by either party giving the other party three months' notice in writing.

He refused to sign the opt-out and was sacked for his refusal. It was ruled as an unfair dismissal (under ERA 1996, s 101A).

Barber v *RJB Mining (UK) Ltd* [1999] IRLR 308, HC

The issue was the enforcement of the central provision in the directive/regulations – the 48-hour maximum working week (reg 4(1)).

The workers concerned had worked more than the maximum average hours permitted in an initial reference period. They worked under protest but sought a declaration of their rights and an **injunction** restraining the employer from requiring them to work additional hours beyond the maximum. It was ruled that this regulation is 'a mandatory requirement which must apply to all contracts of employment' (Mr Justice Gage). It was noted that this 'will have the effect of making it clear that (the employees) are entitled, if they so choose, to refuse to continue working until the average working hours come within the specified time limit'.

It has been commented that the reasoning in this case can be applied to the maximum length of night work (reg 6).

Hone v *Six Continents Retail* [2006] IRLR 49, CA

An employee's refusal to opt out of the 48-hour week, in combination with his very long hours, was held to be relevant in deciding that his subsequent stress-related mental health problems were reasonably foreseeable.

Exhibit 10.9 Proposed changes to the 'opt out'

In June 2008, the EU Social Affairs Council voted to allow the continuation of the 'opt out' provisions despite Members of the European Parliament voting in 2005 to end it. Among the key provisions of the agreement:

- those workers who have opted-out will be subject to a maximum working week of 60 hours (averaged over three months) unless the Social Partners agree otherwise;
- the individual 'opt out' will not be allowed to be signed before the contract of employment commences and not during the first four weeks of the contract;
- an individual 'opt out' cannot run for longer than a year without renewal;
- the 'opt out' provisions will be subject to further examination four years after implementation.

In December 2008, the European Parliament voted to end member states' ability to opt out of the maximum weekly working week of 48 hours. The unresolved issue now returns to the European Council for further negotiations.

> The opt-out provides employers with a low-cost mechanism to avoid the 48-hour limit, and the ease with which it can be deployed is one of the reasons for the limited use by employers of the collective derogations. They are complex to arrange, in particular for employers who, in the absence of a recognised trade union only have available the route of a workforce agreement.
>
> (Barnard *et al.* 2003: 252)

The deliberations surrounding the 'opt out' now appear to have been resolved, at least for the time being. Exhibit 10.9 details the proposed changes following a decision of the EU Social Affairs Council.

Unmeasured working time

Specific derogations from the regulations are permitted 'when, on account of the particular characteristics of the activity concerned, the duration of the working time is not measured and/or predetermined or can be determined by the workers themselves'. This 'unmeasured working time' applies particularly to 'managing executives and other persons with autonomous decision-making powers', 'family workers', and 'workers officiating at religious ceremonies in churches and religious communities' (Article 17(1)) (reg 20(1)).

Since 6 April 2006, the Working Time (Amendment) Regulations 2006 have been in force in respect of unmeasured working time and voluntary overtime by such workers as managing executives or others with 'autonomous decision-taking powers'. These replace the arrangements that have been in place since 1999.

The effect of the 2006 change is that a wide range of employers whose workers may choose to do additional work are required to take all reasonable steps to ensure that the total duration of their working time does not exceed an average of 48 hours a week. For many employers this is simply a case of asking affected workers to agree in writing that the limit on working time will not apply to them. If the 'opt out' (reg 4(1)) is duly signed, this will remove the problem.

> However, should a worker refuse to sign, the employer will need to take care to ensure that he or she is not victimised as a result. Particular care is required if the individual decides to assert his or her rights under the Regulations, declines to opt out and reduces the amount of additional work that he or she does. If doing less work leads to the worker being given unfavourable appraisals or performance ratings, this could amount to an unlawful detriment under s 45A of the Employment Rights Act 1996. (IRS *Industrial Relations Law Bulletin* 780.4, March 2006)

Derogations

The previous section has described some of the major **derogations** from the Working Time Regulations. The term 'derogation' is, to some extent a novelty in British employment relations. It means a specified 'waiver'. If a derogation exists, there is expected to be some equivalent compensation in return. Derogations, under the directive, are qualified by the need to have 'due regard for the general principles of the protection of the safety and health of workers' (Article 17(1)). The directive permits member states to make derogations in various broad areas (Article 17):

- those who have a degree of control over their own time (unmeasured working time);
- where the worker's activities are such that his place of work and place of residence are distant from one another or his different places of work are distant from one another;
- groups on whom rigid controls on working time may be inappropriate (e.g. security workers where a permanent presence on site is required);
- in the case of activities involving the need for continuity of service or production;
- where there is a foreseeable surge in activity (particularly in agriculture, tourism and postal services);
- certain shift workers;
- in cases of accident or imminent risk of accident.

Derogations may be achieved through:

- collective or workforce agreements;
- relevant agreements (by individuals);
- individual agreements to 'opt out' of the 48-hour maximum working week limit.

Collective and workforce agreements

These, as indicated above, constitute a means of implementing a derogation – which enables the Working Time Regulations to be implemented more flexibly. There are two forms of agreement:

- collective agreements negotiated with recognised independent trade unions;
- workforce agreements, in non-union workplaces, which are negotiated with elected workforce representatives or with the workforce as a whole.

Collective agreements

We have already noted the historic regulatory role of collective agreements in British employment relations, with these agreements subject to a statutory legal framework (Trade Union and Labour Relations Consolidation Act 1992, ss 178–179). Furthermore, the express or implied 'incorporation' of provisions of a collective agreement into the terms of individual contracts of employment is an accepted process under contract law (see Chapter 2).

Under the Working Time Regulations, a collective agreement may 'modify or exclude the application' of the following regulations for 'particular workers or groups of workers' (reg 23):

- The reference period of 17 weeks can be extended 'for objective or technical reasons or reasons concerning the organisation of work to a period not exceeding 52 weeks'. So, effectively, it ensures possible compliance of annual hours contracts with the regulations (reg 23(b)).

- The length of night work (regs 6(1) and 23b).
- Night work involving 'special hazards or heavy physical or mental strain' (reg 6(7)).
- Daily rest (reg 10).
- Weekly rest (reg 11).
- Rest breaks (reg 12).

Any modifications or exclusions negotiated to rest periods and night work are subject to the principle of 'compensatory rest' or other 'appropriate protection' (reg 24).

The use of collective agreements to modify or in some cases exclude the operation of a directive is well-established in European employment law. In the context of mainland Europe where **collective bargaining** remains a significant determinant of the terms and conditions of many workers this reflects an understandable wish to see the implementation of legislation remaining sensitive to the institutions and realities of employment relations. In many EU countries collective agreements cover between 65 and 90 per cent of workers, reflecting the continuing importance of sectoral and industry-wide bargaining in much of Europe. In contrast, the UK and the Irish Republic have seen a steady decline in collective bargaining coverage in recent years. In the UK, the numbers covered by collective agreements has fallen from around 72 per cent of the workforce in the late 1970s to below 40 per cent today, with the major decline taking place in the private sector. One important consequence of this change is that the facilities provided by Europe to aid implementation of legislation are potentially less able to give effect to such developments in the UK because of the decline in union organisation and with it collective bargaining. In the area of working time, an attempt to rectify this situation has been through the development of 'workforce agreements', which are discussed below.

Workforce agreements

These agreements are able, in non-union organisations, to achieve the same modifications and exclusions as collective agreements. However, a workforce agreement can only be made between an employer and a workforce (or part of a workforce) whose terms and conditions are **not** set by collective bargaining. To have the status of a 'workforce agreement' the following conditions and requirements must be satisfied (Working Time Regulations, Sch 1):

- It must be in writing.
- It must specify the date of application to the workers concerned.
- Before signature, 'all those workers to whom it is to apply must be provided by the employer with copies of the text of the agreement and with guidance'.
- It must be signed by either a majority of the relevant workforce or the representatives (or a majority of the representatives) of the relevant workforce.
- It should have an expiry date no later than five years after the commencement date, when it can be renewed or replaced.

It has not been clarified explicitly in law but it is presumed that the government wishes a workforce agreement to have an equivalent legal role to a collective agreement. That is, it is presumed not to be legally enforceable unless specified by the parties and capable of incorporation into individual contracts of employment.

Enforcement

There are two routes to enforcement of the regulations:

Individual entitlements

In common with other employment rights, these are enforceable through a complaint to an employment tribunal by a 'worker' irrespective of length of service, within three months of the act complained of, although the tribunal has the discretion to extend this period if it considers that 'it was not reasonably practicable' for the case to be presented (reg 30). As is usual with employment tribunal complaints, ACAS has a statutory duty to conciliate and attempt to achieve a settlement (reg 33; and Employment Tribunals Act 1996, s 18(1)).

These complaints can relate to the following:

- daily rest for adult workers and young workers;
- weekly rest for adult workers and young workers;
- in-work rest breaks for adult workers and young workers;
- paid annual leave.

Where an employment tribunal finds a complaint well founded, it 'shall make a declaration to that effect' and may make an award of compensation to be paid by the employer to the worker. The amount of compensation shall be such as the tribunal considers 'just and equitable in all the circumstances' having regard to 'the employer's default in refusing to permit the worker to exercise his right' and 'any loss sustained by the worker which is attributable to the matters complained of' (reg 30).

Limits

These (weekly working-time and night-work limits and health assessments for night workers) are enforced by the appropriate health and safety authorities (the Health and Safety Executive or local authority environmental health officers) (reg 28). The HSE is responsible for enforcing the working time limits where they apply in factories, building sites, mines, farms, fairgrounds, quarries, chemical plants, nuclear installations, schools and hospitals. Local authority environmental health officers have responsibility in the areas of retailing, offices, hotels and catering, sports, leisure and consumer services.

The powers of the inspectors provided in the Health and Safety at Work Act etc. 1974, apply to the enforcement of the Working Time Regulations 1998. A person guilty of an offence (HASWA 1974, s 33(1)) shall be liable to prosecution and on conviction in a magistrates court to a fine. If the conviction is on indictment, the fine is unlimited.

The number of working time cases can fluctuate significantly, depending on whether there are individual complaints or what are effectively groups of individual complaints. The number of claims made under the Working Time Regulations to the Employment Tribunal Service for the period since 2002/03 are detailed in Table 10.2. The figures for 2007–08 are from the ACAS Annual Report, recording cases received for conciliation.

Table 10.2 Claims made under the Working Time Regulations

Year	*Number of employment tribunal claims*
2007/08	17,407
2006/07	21,167
2005/06	35,474
2004/05	3,223
2003/04	16,869
2002/03	6,436

Are the Working Time Regulations working?

The research on the impact of the regulations suggests that it has been limited and uneven. Case study research (Neathey and Arrowsmith 2001; Neathey 2003; Barnard *et al.* 2003) has suggested a slow adjustment to the legislation and some significant costs in implementing the regulations. In general, the available evidence can be summarised as follows:

Impact of the regulations

Ten of the 20 organisations surveyed by Neathey and Arrowsmith (2001) indicated that the regulations had a 'marginal' impact or 'no impact' on the organisation of working time. This was confirmed in the follow-up study conducted by Neathey (2003) and by the research of Barnard and her colleagues (2003), which also argued that the implementation of the directive had not led to widespread changes in the way working time is organised: 'In particular it has not been a catalyst for organisational reforms aimed at using a reduction in the length of the working week to bring about productivity improvements . . . [adding that] . . . employers and employees . . . remain wedded to a long-hours culture' (Barnard *et al.* 2003: 251–2).

According to Neathey and Arrowsmith (2001), where there was an impact of the regulations, it included a review of working practices which could involve taking a more strategic approach to the organisation of working time.

Areas of uncertainty

In the research all but one of the case study organisations faced some difficulties interpreting provisions of the regulations (Neathey and Arrowsmith 2001). These included:

- *Defining Working Time.* In particular, this concerned travelling time and on-call time (see earlier section).
- *Unmeasured working time.* There were differences of opinion about whether the amendment (Working Time Regulations 1999) had clarified this area. A complaint by the trade union AMICUS (now UNITE) alleging that the 1993 Directive had not been fully implemented, was particularly concerned about the lack of obligation on employers to keep records of time worked voluntarily above normal working time, particularly for this group of workers.
- *Casual workers.* This was a particular problem for 'as and when' casuals in relation to their continuity of service and entitlements to paid annual leave.
- *Staff with more than one job.* The guide produced by the then DTI (2000: 26) suggested finding out this information from individuals and considering, if appropriate an opt-out to disapply the 48-hour maximum.

Neathey and Arrowsmith (2001) also found significant misrepresentation by employers, particularly in relation to the 48-hour week and the definition of workplace agreements.

The 48-hour maximum working week

The survey data in this area can appear conflicting. There are several issues involved:

- whether or not the employer has introduced the facility of the individual 'opt out' (to be operated as and when required);

- the proportion of the employer's workforce covered by individual 'opt outs';
- the actual use of the 'opt out' to exceed the 48-hour maximum; and
- the use of the alternative mechanism – varying the reference period through a collective or workplace agreement.

The evidence presented earlier in this chapter points to 'long hours working' remaining a feature of working life for many in the UK, indicating the extent to which such practices are embedded in the culture of many organisations and accepted by those who work in them (TUC 2008; Hart 2004). The TUC (2002 (**www.tuc.org.uk**)) quotes one survey which reported that 47 per cent of companies have used 'opt outs' for *some* of their workers, a figure that rose to 71 per cent in the case of companies employing between 500 and 5,000 employees. In 15 of the 20 companies surveyed by Neathey and Arrowsmith (2001), the proportion of the workforce regularly exceeding the limit was small. The principal method used was to encourage workers to sign forms opting out of the 48-hour limit. A third of employers had signed a collective or workforce agreement to vary the reference period and a similar proportion had changed working practices to reduce the hours worked by individual workers. These included revised shift arrangements and increases in staffing.

Holidays

This area seems to have presented the fewest problems of adjustment for many organisations. In the Neathey and Arrowsmith research, only two of the 20 organisations had leave entitlement of less than four weeks. The only significant change concerned the provision of leave for casual workers, where for four of the organisations the cost implications of the definition of 'holiday pay' were important.

Night work

The main implication of the regulations for most of the organisations with night workers concerned the health assessment requirements (Neathey and Arrowsmith 2001). However, once implemented these assessments did not lead to workers being moved away from night work.

Collective and workforce agreements

In their study, Neathey and Arrowsmith found that five organisations with recognised unions had used the flexibilities provided through collective agreements, and three non-union establishments had used workforce agreements. In the latter, the involvement of employee representatives had taken the form of **consultation** rather than negotiation.

Employment policies and practices

A strategic approach to implementation

In light of the traditional way of determining working time (through collective bargaining or unilateral employer decision), the regulations potentially have a disproportionate impact on British employee relations compared with these relations in other EU member states. Employers might be tempted to respond to the regulations in a piecemeal way. However, given their wide-ranging implications, there are good reasons for adopting a more strategic approach. There are six broad considerations for employers, which encompass corporate strategy, operational practice, the use of internal and/or external professional resources of advice and information, employee relations policy, and the contribution of personnel administration. These involve the following:

Identifying which members of their workforce are covered by the various provisions

This involves paying attention to specific grades of staff who might be covered by derogations, whether or not any are 'young workers', and those who work on particular working-time patterns (shift working and night work).

Using as appropriate, professional resources to diagnose workers' suitability for night work and shift work

This refers in particular to the issue of health and safety assessments, and the role of occupational health services within an organisation.

Identifying the impact of the regulations upon existing contractual terms and (where relevant) collective agreements

This involves considering whether or not the legislation, limits any existing contractual terms (for example on working hours) or whether it requires the introduction of new contractual rights (paid holiday entitlement) to comply with the law.

Considering the ways in which, for operational reasons, the organisation might wish to utilise the opportunities available within the regulations through derogations

As we have seen there are three main ways to introduce flexibilities provided by the regulations: 'collective agreements', 'workforce agreements', and an 'individual voluntary agreement'. Furthermore, the 'opt out' from the 48-hour week can be applied by all employers with the agreement of individual employees (reg 5).

For employers which recognise trade unions, the regulations provide for a collective agreement to modify or exclude the application of various of the regulations for 'particular workers or groups of workers'. The areas covered are the reference period for averaging working time (reg 4), the length of night work (reg 6(1)), night work involving special hazards of physical or mental strain (reg 6(7)), daily rest (reg 10), weekly rest (reg 11) and rest breaks (reg 12).

In the case of non-union workforces, workforce agreements are able to achieve these same modifications and exclusions. The agreements can only be made between an employer and a workforce (or part of a workforce) whose terms and conditions are **not** set by collective bargaining. The regulations stipulate requirements that must be satisfied in setting up representative machinery; these have been outlined in the earlier section on **workforce agreements**.

Deciding whether, procedurally, to use workforce or collective agreements, or agreements with individual workers to comply with the requirements

Individual employers need to weigh up the balances of advantages for their own organisations to determine which of the mechanisms to use.

Deciding on the likely use of individual voluntary agreements to disapply the 48-hour maximum working week

Individual employers need to consider the operational advantages of such agreements, to be aware of possible allegations of unlawful pressure to force employees to sign such agreements and to consider the operational implications that might arise if such an agreement is not secured or if it is not brought to an end by the employee.

Deciding on whether the staff (full-time, part-time, temporary, etc.) currently employed (as well as new staff) are already receiving the minimum annual paid leave entitlement

The regulations provide for a *minimum* period of paid leave.

Deciding on appropriate record systems

The records required cover the maximum working week, night-work patterns, and the assessment of night workers. The guidance on this by the Department for Business Enterprise and Regulatory Reform states that in terms of the ***maximum working week***, it is for the employer to determine the records to be kept, although the basis for such records may already be in existence.

In respect of ***night working and health assessments***, it is for the employer to decide on the records to be kept. The employer needs to be able to 'show who is a night worker, when they had an assessment and the result of the assessment' (DTI 2000: para 4.5).

Exploring the impact on organisations of the Working Time Regulations

In the final section we provide a suggested checklist that might help human resource practitioners consider, in a structured way, the impact of the regulations on their organisation. Finally, the scenarios in the Exercises, will help in understanding further the exploration of the practical application of the regulations.

A checklist for action

The following identifies the main questions and issues for HR practitioners to consider in securing compliance with the Working Time Regulations.

1 What is the profile of the workforce in terms of:
   - employment status (i.e. full-time, part-time, temporary, etc.)?
   - working patterns (shift and night working, annual hours arrangements)?
   - age (adult and young workers)?

2 Do existing arrangements comply with the standards set in the regulations?
   Where an independent trade union is recognised for the staff in question, would it be more constructive to undergo this diagnosis jointly?

3 Is any use to be made of 'individual voluntary agreements' to disapply the 48-hour working week average?

4 Is there any working time which cannot be 'measured, predetermined or fixed by the employer'? Is it therefore, appropriate to invoke the derogation?

5 If trade unions are not recognised for particular groups of staff, what use might be made of 'workforce agreements' to achieve some flexibility in the implementation of the regulations.

6 Is more detailed advice necessary on specific matters from, for example, the Department for Business and Regulatory Reform, the Advisory, Conciliation and Arbitration Service, the Health and Safety Executive or any relevant employers' association?

7 If necessary, does the organisation have its own (or access to) specialist health and safety/ occupational services to assist in the preparation of health and safety assessments?

8 What administrative arrangements need to be made to create (and maintain for two years) the necessary records; and can these records be integrated into existing computerised personnel records? Employers will need to hold records on the following to enable the competent authorities to monitor compliance (reg 8). These cover:

- a worker's average working time, including overtime (reg 4.1);
- the details of individual voluntary agreements to disapply the 48-hour working week maximum (reg 5);
- the operation of night work (reg 6);
- health and safety assessments (reg 7).

9 What are the likely implementation costs for the organisation – in respect of changed terms and conditions of employment, record keeping, and the provision/funding of health and safety assessments?

Exercises: Some scenarios

10.1 A small non-unionised print shop employing around 19 people occasionally has to deal with rush orders requiring 70-hour weeks.

How can the employer deal with the 48-hour maximum average working week?

10.2 A call centre has traditionally defined **'work'** as the period when the worker is dealing with a customer on the telephone. Sometimes staff have attended their place of work for eight hours but only received six hours' pay.

Can this now be challenged at an employment tribunal? How should working time be defined?

10.3 Maggie, a waitress, has been employed by a catering company on an 'as required' basis for some 15 months. Generally, this means that she works four or five evenings a week. A friend told her that she should be entitled to some paid holiday. When she spoke to her manager, she said she was entitled to nothing.

What is her situation?

10.4 A freezer engineer is based at home. He is 'on call' (through a mobile phone) to a supermarket chain in a specific region. He is only paid by the supermarket for specific tasks he carries out, as and when required.

Is he a worker as defined by the regulations and therefore protected by them?

10.5 A worker in a medium-sized company, tells her employer that she wants to terminate (in eight days' time) **an individual voluntary agreement** to disapply the 48-hour maximum working week limit. It has been in force for several months and no notice period is indicated for the termination of this agreement. The employer has indicated to her that it is not convenient to terminate the agreement and asks her for her reasons. She refuses to say and insists on ending the agreement. The employer does not say he will sack her immediately but implies that he might be looking for staff to replace her who will agree to disapply the limit.

Advise the worker on her legal rights under the regulations and the courses of action open to her.

10.6 A large non-unionised international hotel employs on **night work**, a night manager and a night team of eight staff in its front office between the hours of 11 p.m. and 8 a.m. Each member of staff works an average of 45 hours per week (over five days). The night team comprises the assistant night manager, a cashier, two receptionists and four porters.

The length of the shift is important. There needs to be a short overlap between the new day shift and the night shift to deal with any outstanding problems. In the morning, the concierge department shift does not begin until 8 a.m. This means that all the luggage of the guests arriving or departing in the morning before 8 a.m. is dealt with by the night staff. Furthermore, daytime staff start their shift at 7 a.m. The one hour overlap between the two shifts is used for hand-over.

Are these arrangements still permissible under the Working Time Regulations?

10.7 A shift worker visited his GP about periods of giddiness which he started to experience. These arose from sleepless nights or days (depending on his shifts). The GP's medical report stated that the varying shift pattern was probably the cause of the disrupted sleep patterns. The report was sent to the employer with the worker's permission when he requested to be placed on normal daytime work. The company refused his request on the ground that it needed to operate a night shift with a full complement of staff and because it could not change at short notice. It stated that it would take six months to rearrange the shift patterns to accommodate his request.

What protections and rights does he have in law?

Feedback on these exercises is provided in the Appendix to this textbook.

References and useful websites

Advisory, Conciliation and Arbitration Service (1988) 'Labour flexibility in Britain', Occasional Paper 41. London: ACAS.

Arrowsmith, J. and Sisson, K. (2000) 'Managing Working Time', in Bach, S. and Sisson, K. (eds) *Personnel Management: A Comprehensive Guide to Theory and Practice*. Oxford: Blackwells.

Ashkenazy, P. (2008) 'A primer on the 35-hour week in France 1997–2007', IZA Discussion Paper No. 3402.

Barnard, C., Deakin, S. and Hobbs, R. (2003) 'Opting out of the 48-hour week: employer necessity or individual choice? An empirical study of the operation of article 18(1)(b) of the Working Time Directive in the UK', *Industrial Law Journal*, Vol. 32, No. 4.

Bell, D. and Hart, R. (2005) *Annualised Hours Contracts*. London: ESRC.

Bercusson, B. (2003) 'Crunch Time for Working Time', *Thompson's Labour and European Law Review*, No. 83.

BMRB Social Research (2004) *A Survey of Workers' Experiences of the Working Time Regulations*, Employment Relations Research Series, No. 31. London: Department of Trade and Industry.

British Chambers of Commerce (2007) *Work and Life: How business Is Striking the Right Balance*. London: BCC.

Bunting, M. (2005) *Willing Slaves: How the Overwork Culture is Ruling our Lives*. London: Harper Perennial.

Casey, B. *et al.* (1997) *Employers' Use of Flexible Labour*. London: PSI.

Chartered Institute of Personnel and Development (2003) *Living to Work*. London: Chartered Institute of Personnel and Development.

Collins, H., Ewing, K. and McColgan, A. (2005) *Labour Law: Text and Materials*. Oxford: Hart.

Deakin, S. and Morris, G. (2005) *Labour Law*. Oxford: Hart.

Department of Trade and Industry (1997) *Measures to Implement Provisions of the EC Directive on the Organisation of Working: A Consultation Document*. London: Department of Trade and Industry.

Department of Trade and Industry (2000) *Your Guide to the Working Time Regulations*. London: DTI.

Disability Rights Commission (2004) *Code of Practice on Employment and Occupation*. (www.equalityhumanrights.com).

Donovan Commission (1968) The Royal Commission on Trade Unions and Employers' Organisations (1965–68). Cmnd 3623. London: HMSO.

Ferri, E. and Smith, K. (1996) *Parenting in the 1990s*. London: Joseph Rowntree Foundation and Family Policy Studies Centre.

Hart, R. (2004) *The Economics of Overtime Working*. Cambridge: Cambridge University Press.

Hayden, A. (2006) 'France's 35 hour week: attack on business? Win-win reform? Or betrayal of disadvantaged workers', *Politics and Society*, Vol. 34: 2.

Health and Safety Executive (2006) *A New Guide on Managing Shift Work*. London: HSE.

Kahn-Freund, O. (1983) *Labour and the Law*. Oxford: Oxford University Press.

Kodz, J., Davis, S., Lain, D., Strebler, M., Rick, J., Bates, P., Cummings, J., Meager, N. and Anxo, D. (2003a) *Working Long Hours: A Review of the Evidence, Volume 1 – The Main Report*, Employment Relations Research Series, No. 16. London: Department of Trade and Industry.

Kodz, J., Davis, S., Lain, D., Strebler, M., Rick, J., Bates, P., Cummings, J., Meager, N. and Anxo, D. (2003b) *Working Long Hours: Volume 2 – Case Studies and Appendices*, Employment Relations Research Series, No. 16. London: Department of Trade and Industry.

Labour Force Survey (2008) (www.statistics.gov.uk).

Neathey, F. (2003) *Implementation of the Working Time Regulations: Follow-up Study*, Employment Relations Research Series, No. 19. London: Department of Trade and Industry.

Neathey, F. and Arrowsmith, J. (2001) *Implementation of the Working Time Regulations*, Employment Relations Research Series, No. 11. London: Department of Trade and Industry.

Organisation for Economic Co-operation and Development (2004) *Observer*, Discussion Paper No. 244, September. Geneva: OECD.

Smith, D. (2004) 'Strangled', *Sunday Times*, 7 March.

Trades Union Congress (2008) *Return of the Long Hours Culture*. London: Trades Union Congress (www.tuc.org.uk).

White, J. and Beswick, D. (2003) *Working Long Hours*. Sheffield: Health and Safety Executive.

Useful websites

Advisory, Conciliation and Arbitration Service **www.acas.org.uk**

Department for Business Enterprise and Regulatory Reform **www.berr.gov.uk**

Equality and Human Rights Commission **www.equalityhumanrights.com**

UK Statistics Authority **www.statistics.gov.uk**

Trades Union Congress **www.tuc.org.uk**

Visit **www.mylawchamber.co.uk/willey** to access multiple choice questions, case flashcards and exercises to test yourself on this chapter.

mylawchamber

11 Family leave and work–life balance

Learning objectives

Having read this chapter you should be able to:

- Explain the reasons for the recent growth in interest in 'work–life balance' and appreciate the different approaches taken to defining this concept
- Summarise the primary pieces of legislation that apply in the area of family and dependency rights and outline their scope and main provisions
- Evaluate the grounds of action and remedies available to British workers in relation to the exercise of family and dependency rights

Structure of the chapter

- *Introduction*: a brief overview of the economic and social factors underpinning the recent growth of interest in work–life balance, and of attempts to define the concept
- *Legislation*: its scope and the relationship between legislative and contractual rights; rights and responsibilities in the areas of maternity, paternity, adoption, dependency and parental leave and the right to request flexible working; protection against dismissal or detriment for exercising family rights; the role of discrimination law in this area; enforcement procedures and remedies available for breach of the family rights outlined
- *Exercises*

Introduction

Work–life balance has arguably been the most high profile HR or employment related issue over recent years. It is one that HR practitioners are increasingly having to deal with, particularly in the context of the relatively tight labour market that has existed over the last number of years. Although the concept of 'work–life balance' is broad and rather nebulous, there has been notable recent legal intervention in this area with regard to rights to family leave. The goal of this chapter is to chart developments in this area and outline key rights and responsibilities of employers and **employees** alike.

Factors underpinning the growing interest in work–life balance

Workforce interest in striking a balance between home and work is not necessarily a new phenomenon. Indeed, it may be argued that employers and their workforces have always been in conflict over where the latter should expend their time and energy, and that both have had to show flexibility at times (Clutterbuck 2003). However, the drivers and underlying social dynamics of employment have changed dramatically in the last quarter of a century, and this has resulted in the notion of 'work–life balance' (WLB) gaining increased prominence in the contemporary employment vernacular.

Early industrialisation and the introduction of mass machinery created two distinct spheres of life – home and work (Felstead *et al.* 2005). These two spheres remained relatively distinct throughout much of the twentieth century, but the progressive development of information and communications technology (ICT) over the last two decades, whilst maximising work efficiency has extended the time and space of employment (e.g. via the use of e-mail and 'Blackberrys'). The resulting 'work intensification' has been compounded by increased global competition and the shift in many western economies from production to service-oriented industries, which increasingly operate on the basis of instant availability to customers (Suff 2002).

At the same time, major demographic and social shifts including an increasing number of women entering the workforce, declining birth rates and a rapidly ageing population, have changed the profile, attitudes and needs of the workforce (MacInnes 2002). More employees than ever have caring responsibilities, whilst simultaneously being subjected to longer working hours (TUC 2005). The result is described by Hoschild (1997) as a 'time-bind' and by Madeline Bunting (2004) as a 'crisis of human sustainability' that threatens the very fabric of family life and indeed the health and stability of society at large.

The tight nature of the UK labour market and the difficulty experienced by many organisations in recruiting and retaining staff has also been a significant recent 'push' factor, which has prompted the development and implementation of policies by employers on work–life balance and family friendly working (e.g. see CIPD 2007).

Legal and political developments have been important too. As with so many areas of employment regulation, the UK's membership of the European Union has had significant implications for the area of family rights and work–life balance. The Pregnant Workers Directive 1992 obliged the member states of the European Union to provide for a minimum 14-week maternity leave period, while also setting down standards for the protection of the health and safety of pregnant women. The Parental Leave Directive 1996 created a right to parental leave. In addition, the European Union's treaty articles and directives on gender equality have also been highly influential in this area.

Allied to these political/legal influences from Europe has been the commitment and legislative activism of the Labour government elected in 1997. One of its central, long-standing objectives has been to increase the female employment rate, while more recently government policy has reflected proactive and enthusiastic support for the wider promotion of work–life balance. This has resulted in the introduction of a range of new provisions.

Defining 'work–life balance'

This is a highly elastic concept that largely escapes precise definition. While previously it was seen to be centrally focused on the provision of assistance to workers with family and caring responsibilities, the contemporary notion of work–life balance represents a progression to practices that are intended to benefit all employees (Kodz *et al.* 2002). It is also now recognised that employee needs in relation to work–life balance change throughout life (Suff 2002), while the term 'balance' has acquired a dual meaning, referring both to the relationship between home and work and to the wider objective of meeting both employee and employer needs (Dex and Scheibl 1998). The notion of 'work–life balance', therefore, has evolved and become more inclusive (Suff 2002).

While conceptualisation of 'work–life balance' has therefore developed and expanded over time, this makes it difficult to identify precisely how this notion translates into policies and practices at workplace level. Indeed, work–life balance seems to be endowed with 'infinite elasticity' in the corporate context (IRS 2002: 6). Researchers have attempted to overcome this problem by grouping work–life balance practices into manageable categories, however these vary widely. For example, Dex and Smith (2002) categorise practices relating to 'hours of work' and 'location of work' separately, whereas IRS (2002) merges them into one group entitled 'flexible working (time and place)'. The definition of work–life balance in the Workplace Employee Relations Survey (WERS) series has focused on non-standard patterns of work and childcare assistance (Cully *et al.* 1999; Kersley *et al.* 2006). By contrast, Suff (2002) expands the definition to include previously unacknowledged practices such as 'employee development' and 'flexible careers'. Friedman and Greenhaus (2000) do the same, in defining Employee Assistance Programmes as a work–life balance practice.

It is therefore evident that a variety of approaches are taken to specifying what work–life balance means in practice. While some favour a narrow focus on perhaps the more obvious practices relating to the organisation of work, others are broader, encompassing a wider range of policies and practices. Although the validity of the latter approaches is recognised, the focus of this chapter is on more traditional practices relating to leave for family reasons and the organisation of work. This is because these are the areas regarding which legal **regulations** currently exist.

Legislation

As mentioned above, as in many other areas European Union law has been very important in establishing minimum rules and standards in relation to pregnancy, maternity and other family rights. The Equal Treatment Directive 2006 (which amends and consolidates previous equal treatment directives), prohibits less favourable treatment on grounds of pregnancy or maternity and provides women with the right to return to work after maternity leave. The Pregnant Workers Directive 1992 provides pregnant workers with a right to time off for ante-natal care and requires employers across Europe to take specific steps to protect the health and safety of pregnant women, and obliges them to provide a minimum of a 14-week, paid maternity leave period. The Parental Leave Directive 1996 provides rights to both parental and dependency leave.

The following Acts and Regulations give effect to this European legislation in a British context as well as the additional rights and responsibilities created independently by the British government. They contain the various rules and provisions that apply in the area of family and dependency rights and responsibilities:

- *Employment Rights Act 1996*: core provisions on maternity, adoption and dependency leave; also on right to request flexible working and not to suffer **detriment** or **dismissal** on family grounds; this act has been added to or amended on various occasions.
- *Maternity and Parental Leave Regulations 1999* (as amended in 2002 and 2006): additional rules and provisions on maternity and parental leave.
- *Paternity and Adoption Leave Regulations 2002* (as amended 2006): additional rules and provisions on paternity and adoption leave.
- *Flexible Working (Eligibility, Complaints and Remedies) Regulations 2002* and *Flexible Working (Procedural Requirements) Regulations 2002* (as amended 2006): two sets of regulations containing additional rules and provisions on flexible working.
- *Work and Families Act 2006*: introduced changes to provisions on statutory maternity and adoption pay and flexible working requiring amendments to above legislation; created power for government to legislate for additional paternity/adoption leave and pay.
- *Management of Health and Safety at Work Regulations 1999*: cover health and safety of pregnant women and right to ante-natal care.
- *Sex Discrimination Act 1975* (as amended by the Employment Equality (Sex Discrimination) Regulations 2005): specific provisions on pregnancy and maternity leave discrimination; provisions on direct and indirect sex discrimination also relevant.

Relationship with contract of employment

The rights and entitlements provided by legislation in the area of family leave constitute basic, minimum standards which can be supplemented by more generous contractual provisions. The latter may be enforceable within the context of employment tribunal cases relating to termination of employment or contractual claims in the civil courts.

Scope of statutory protection

This varies according to the employment status of individuals, as outlined in Table 11.1 below. Effectively, there are differences in respect to whether a worker is an 'employee' (i.e. on a **contract** of employment) or a 'worker on some other contract to work personally' (see Chapter 2).

As outlined in the table the majority of rights and entitlements in relation to pregnancy/ maternity and family leave apply to those with 'employee' status only. Only 'employees' are able to avail of entitlements to maternity, paternity, parental and adoption leave and the right to request flexible working. However, in relation to maternity pay, the definition of 'employee' adopted is relatively broad (the key issue is whether the organisation is liable to pay national insurance contributions in relation to the worker in question) and hence agency

Table 11.1 Family and dependency rights by employment status

Right or entitlement	*Application*
Ante-natal care	Employees only
Maternity leave	Employees only
Maternity pay	Employees only but definition used can encompass agency workers
Paternity leave	Employees only
Parental leave	Employees only
Adoption leave and pay	Employees only
Right to request flexible working	Employees only
Dependency leave	Employees only
Health and safety protection	All workers, i.e. employees, self-employed and casual workers
Protection from sex discrimination	Broad application: covers agency workers and self-employed may also be covered

workers may be entitled to this. Alternatively, they may be entitled to 'maternity allowance' (the Department for Work and Pensions provides detailed information on the rules governing statutory maternity pay – see **www.dwp.gov.uk/advisers/techguides**). Aside from this, the principal rights and entitlements of casual/atypical workers who lack employee status are in relation to health and safety and protection against discrimination.

The Management of Health and Safety at Work Regulations 1999 impose obligations on employers with regard to 'persons working' in their undertaking who may be pregnant or of childbearing age. The regulations therefore cover workers who do not have employee status. In addition, the Sex Discrimination Act 1975 applies to a broad notion of 'employment' including contracts to 'personally execute any work or labour', which means that self-employed workers may be protected provided that they personally undertake the work in question themselves. The Act also expressly covers 'contract workers', a category that includes temporary agency workers (see Chapter 5).

Note that in addition to requiring a particular employment status, the above legislation typically imposes additional qualifying conditions relating to length of service as well as other considerations. These additional conditions will be outlined in the various sections below, but, for example, to be entitled to request flexible working, employees must have 26 weeks of continuous service with their employer and also be the parent of a child aged under six years or under 18 years if the child is disabled; or partner to such a parent; or carer of an adult.

Health and safety protection

The Management of Health and Safety at Work Regulations 1999 oblige employers to protect the health and safety of pregnant women (see Chapter 12). Employers are required to carry out a risk assessment where there are women of childbearing age in the workplace, which involves considering the risks to the health of pregnant women arising from the physical nature of a job and also noise, vibration and radiation levels, among other factors. In addition to this general **duty**, employers are obliged to undertake a more specific risk assessment in relation to employees who inform them that they are pregnant.

The recent case of *Stevenson* v *J M Skinner & Co* (2008) EAT/0584/07/DA provided some guidance for employers about requirements in this area. The EAT noted that there is no definition of 'risk assessment' in the legislation and that there is no requirement for an assessment to be in writing. In addition, an employer is not obliged to physically give a risk assessment to an employee; rather they must record the findings of the assessment and provide information about those findings, which may be done orally. According to the EAT, 'a meeting with the employee where assessments are made and at which agreement is reached on the relevant risks, discharges the obligation on the employer'.

Where a risk to the health of a pregnant woman is identified, employers must take steps to eliminate or reduce the risk. This may involve an alteration to the woman's hours or working conditions. If this is not possible she should be offered suitable alternative work with similar **terms** and conditions. If this is also not possible, then the pregnant woman should be suspended from work with pay for as long as is necessary. The regulations also set out conditions regarding night working by pregnant women. In addition to giving rise to a case for breach of this legislation, an employer's failure to protect the employee's health and safety may lead to a claim for sex discrimination.

Time off for ante-natal care

The Employment Rights Act 1996 (s 55) sets out this right for pregnant employees. It is a right not to be unreasonably refused time off to attend ante-natal care (for example an appointment with a midwife or doctor or hospital appointment) and, in addition, the right to be paid for this period of absence. The pregnant woman is required to seek permission before she takes this leave and if the employer requests, must provide evidence of an appointment (note that this duty does not apply to the first such appointment). The right is to time off within working hours, so an employer is not permitted to rearrange the woman's working hours or insist that she make up the hours lost another time. The employer can only refuse such a request if it is reasonable to do so.

Maternity leave

From 1 April 2007, all pregnant employees have been entitled to take up to 52 weeks of maternity leave, regardless of their length of service with their employer. This entitlement is broken up into two periods: 26 weeks of 'ordinary' maternity leave (OML) followed by 26 weeks of 'additional' maternity leave (AML) (ERA 1996, ss 71–73).

A woman can choose when to start her maternity leave. This can be any date from the beginning of the eleventh week before the week the baby is due. However, there is a period of 'compulsory maternity leave' which is the two-week period following birth (this is four weeks for factory workers). Non-compliance by an employer with this provision may result in criminal **liability**. In order to be able to take up her right to maternity leave a woman must inform the employer of:

- the fact that she is pregnant;
- the expected week of childbirth;
- the date on which ordinary maternity leave is due to start.

This information must be provided fifteen weeks before the expected week of childbirth and employers are entitled to request a medical certificate stating the date of the expected week of childbirth. Once an employer has been informed of the pregnancy, he is obliged to notify the woman of the date on which she will return to work within 28 days.

Maternity pay

Pregnant employees with 26 weeks' continuous service by the fifteenth week before the expected week of childbirth are entitled to Statutory Maternity Pay (SMP) during the period of ordinary maternity leave. Since 1 April 2007 the maternity pay period now lasts for 39 weeks. The government intends to extend this further to 52 weeks. Under such an extension the whole of the maternity leave period would therefore then be paid. SMP is set at two levels. 'Higher rate' SMP is 90 per cent of a woman's average weekly earnings and is paid for the first six weeks. The amount a woman is due to be paid during this period is generally obtained by calculating her average earnings during the eight-week period up to and including the fifteenth week before the expected week of childbirth. Higher rate SMP is followed by 'lower rate' SMP, the level of which is reviewed annually (for current rates see **www.berr.gov.uk/employment/workandfamilies**) and was set at £117.18 a week as at April 2008. SMP is paid by the employer who then receives a rebate for the amount from the government.

The recent case of *Alabaster* v *Woolwich Building Society* [2004] IRLR 486, ECJ established that a woman on maternity leave is entitled to benefit from a pay rise awarded between the start of the reference period used to calculate average earnings for higher rate SMP, and the end of maternity leave. Where this situation applies an employer is obliged to recalculate the level of maternity pay to include the pay rise and pay her the difference between the two amounts. Women who are not entitled to SMP but meet certain qualifying conditions based on their employment and earnings record may claim up to 39 weeks' Maternity Allowance from a Job Centre Plus office.

The contract of employment during maternity leave

The contract of employment continues to exist during both ordinary and additional maternity leave. Previously, all the contractual terms, with the exception of those regarding remuneration, continued to apply during OML. During AML only a much smaller range of essential contractual terms applied. For example, while a woman on OML was legally entitled to continue benefiting from contractual terms relating to use of a company car or gym membership, a woman on AML was not, with only essential contractual terms such as those relating to duty of care or disciplinary procedures operational during AML. (Of course, a fuller range of terms could also be in force during AML if a woman's contract of employment expressly provided for this.)

However, recent decisions of the European Court of Justice (*Lewen* v *Denda* [2000] ICR 648; *Land Brandenburg* v *Sass* [2005] IRLR 147) and a judicial review of the revised Sex Discrimination Act brought by the Equal Opportunities Commission in early 2007, have challenged the legislation in this area. Consequently, it has been amended by the Sex Discrimination Act (Amendment) Regulations 2008, with effect from 5 October 2008. These new provisions (SDA 1975, s 6A) eliminate any legal distinction between the rights and treatment of women on OML and AML, and consequently in the types of claim they can bring in relation to these periods. This change will affect employers who have previously provided non-pay benefits to women on OML but not on AML (e.g. contractual leave above the statutory minimum, company cars, gym membership or mobile phones).

The change in the law also has implications for the treatment of maternity leave in calculating length of service for the purposes of both statutory and contractual rights. While both the OML and AML periods have historically counted as periods of employment for the purposes of calculating service with reference to statutory rights (e.g. protection against unfair dismissal), only the OML period has counted as such in the calculation of service for the purposes of contractual rights (e.g. pension entitlements). However, the amendment to the law in this area now means that the AML period must now also be included in calculating length of service for the purposes of both statutory and contractual rights. The change relating to compulsory maternity leave requires that in calculating a discretionary bonus any period on such leave must be included as if the employee had been at work and working normally.

Pension schemes during maternity leave

Employees on maternity leave continue to accrue pension rights during paid maternity leave only. They make their standard pension contribution, but this is based on the maternity pay received during the period. In contrast, the employer must continue to pay any earmarked contributions based on the pay the woman would have received had she been working normally. For periods of unpaid maternity leave, the minimum statutory requirement is that the periods before and after such leave be treated as continuous for the purposes of calculating pensionable service. The woman's contract or particular pension scheme may of course be more generous than this.

Bonus payments and maternity leave

The question of the entitlement of a woman on maternity leave to receive bonuses is rather complex. If a bonus is part of her contract then she is not entitled to it during maternity leave, as she is not entitled to contractual pay during this period. However, if a bonus to be paid either wholly or partly relates to a period when she was working then the bonus or a relevant ***pro rata*** amount should be paid; not to do so would constitute sex discrimination (*Lewen* v *Denda* [2000] ICR 648, ECJ; SDA 1975, s 6A(2)(b)).

If a bonus is a *discretionary*, retrospective bonus, any period during which a woman is on compulsory maternity leave must be included for the purpose of calculating it (*Lewen* v *Denda* [2000] ICR 648, ECJ; SDA 1975, s 6A(2)(c)). By implication, employers may exclude other periods. Finally, the position regarding *voluntary bonuses for future loyalty* is somewhat unclear, although the case of *Gus Home Shopping Ltd* v *Green and McLaughlin* [2001] IRLR 75 is authority for the view that not to pay such bonuses to women on maternity leave may be discriminatory.

Right to return to work

The Employment Rights Act (ss 71 and 73) provides women with the right to return to work after ordinary and additional maternity leave. A woman returning to work after OML has the right to return to the same job on the same terms and conditions as before, as if she had not been absent. Those returning after AML also have a right to return to the same job on the same terms and conditions as before. However, if it is 'not reasonably practicable' for the woman to return to the same job, she is entitled to a similar job that is 'suitable' and 'appropriate for her to do in the circumstances'; and 'on terms and conditions not less favourable than those which would have applied if she had not been absent' (Maternity and Parental Leave, etc. Regulations 1999, regs 18 and 18A). To date there has been only one EAT case to consider the meaning of the 'same job', in the case of *Blundell* v *St Andrew's Catholic Primary School* (2007) EAT 0329/06/RN (see Exhibit 11.1).

Exhibit 11.1 What is the 'same job'?

Blundell v *St Andrew's Catholic Primary School* (2007) EAT 0329/06/RN

Facts. This case involved a female primary school teacher who before her maternity leave was teaching the 'reception' class. However, after returning from leave, she was assigned to teach a year two class and she claimed that this was not a return to the same job.

EAT judgment. It held that she *had* in fact been returned to the same job. It set out how the relevant provisions in the Maternity and Parental Leave Regulations 1999 (reg 2) require three different factors to be taken into consideration:

- 'the nature of the work she is employed to do in accordance with the contract of employment';
- the 'capacity'; and
- the 'place' of the old and new jobs being undertaken.

In the case in question, the EAT outlined that Ms Blundell had been employed as a teacher in the school, not specifically as a teacher of the reception class. The nature of the work was therefore the same. The place of work (i.e. the school) was also the same, as was the capacity (i.e. of teacher). The employer had not therefore breached the legislation. An important observation made was that where the precise job a woman was doing before she went on maternity leave was variable, the key question to consider is whether the nature of the job she is given on her return was 'outside the boundary of what was permissible'; whether the new job was 'outside the normal range of variability which she could reasonably have expected'.

Where there is a redundancy situation a woman on maternity leave is entitled to a 'suitable alternative vacancy' where one is available. Employers are obliged to discriminate in favour of women on maternity leave, i.e. they should be offered an alternative position before others. If a woman wishes to return early from maternity leave she must inform her employer eight weeks in advance.

Contact during maternity leave

From April 2007, it has been possible for employees to undertake up to 10 days' work during maternity leave without breaking that period. These are known as 'keeping in touch days' and in addition to some pieces of work they are also envisaged to encompass training sessions or appraisals. These keeping in touch days can be paid, at a rate agreed between the employer and employee. There is no right for an employer to insist that an employee work such a day; nor for an employee to insist on working. This is seen to be a significant change as previously if a woman undertook paid work during maternity leave she would lose her entitlement to maternity pay for the week in question and her leave period would automatically come to an end.

Another change introduced by the Work and Families Act 2006 is that employers are now allowed to have 'reasonable contact' with employees during the maternity leave period. This is envisaged to enable an employer to provide an update regarding developments at the workplace and also allow communication regarding arrangements for the return to work.

Paternity leave

This leave is of two weeks and its purpose is 'caring for the child or supporting the mother' (Paternity and Adoption Leave Regulations 2002, reg 4). This right applies to employees only. In order to be eligible, an employee must be either the biological father of the child, or the mother's husband or partner (the partner may be of the same sex), or have or expect to have responsibility for the child's upbringing (they should have the main responsibility where they are not the biological father). Eligible employees should also have 26 weeks of continuous service with their employer by the fifteenth week before the expected week of childbirth. Adoptive parents or their partners are also entitled to take paternity leave.

Paternity leave must be taken as one week or two weeks together. It is not possible to take days here and there or one week now and another later on. The leave must also be taken within the eight weeks following birth. The leave is paid, with statutory paternity pay set at the same rate as lower rate SMP. To be eligible, an employee must also comply with certain notification requirements, namely to inform the employer at least 15 weeks before the expected week of childbirth, the date on which the paternity leave will begin and its duration.

One of the more high profile elements of the Work and Families Act 2006 was the inclusion by the government of powers for the creation of a right to up to six months' 'additional paternity leave' on top of the basic two week entitlement. Although legislation on this has not yet been implemented the intention is to do so by 2010. It is envisaged that where a mother returns to work after OML or before the end of AML, the father, husband or partner would be given the right to take the balance of the period remaining as 'additional paternity leave'. The intention is that this would be paid at the rate of statutory paternity pay, mirroring the proposed extension of paid maternity leave from six to twelve months referred to above. The Work and Families Act also provides for these rights to additional paternity leave to be granted in cases of adoption.

Parental leave

The Maternity and Parental Leave Regulations 1999 (regs 13 and 14) provide that employees with one year's continuous service who have or expect to have 'parental responsibility' for a child under the age of five have a right to parental leave for the purposes of 'caring for' that child. Adoptive parents are also entitled to take parental leave. This statutory leave is unpaid. However, the employer may agree to payment under the individual's contract of employment.

The intention of the government was to enable employers to provide contractual entitlements to parental leave, but where this does not take place the statutory 'default' scheme applies. The details of the latter are as follows:

- Employees are entitled to take 13 weeks of unpaid parental leave up to the fifth birthday of each child they have for the purposes of caring for that child. The entitlement in relation to disabled children is 18 weeks up until the eighteenth birthday.
- Leave must be taken in minimum periods of one week (this rule does not apply in relation to disabled children). A maximum of four weeks' leave can be taken in relation to an individual child in a particular year.
- Employees must give their employer 21 days' notice of leave and its duration.
- The employer may postpone leave for up to six months (although not at the time of birth and adoption) where their business would be 'unduly disrupted'.
- Written notice of postponement outlining the reasons for the same and providing a date when the postponed leave may be taken must be given to the employee within seven days of receiving their request.

Adoption leave

The Paternity and Adoption Leave Regulations 2002 (reg 15) provide that an employee who is the adoptive parent of a child newly placed for adoption may take adoption leave. To qualify an employee must have 26 weeks of continuous service by the week in which he or she is notified of being matched with a child for adoption. As with maternity leave, adoption leave is divided into two periods: 26 weeks' 'ordinary' adoption leave and 26 weeks' 'additional' leave. Only one adoptive parent is entitled to take adoption leave, although the other may be eligible to take two weeks of paternity leave if they meet the relevant criteria. Statutory Adoption Pay is also provided, which is the same as statutory maternity pay. The rules as to terms and conditions during leave and the right to return to work that apply in relation to maternity leave also apply with regard to adoption leave.

Dependency leave

A right to 'dependency leave' was introduced in 1999 (ERA 1996, s 57A). This is a right for employees to take a 'reasonable amount' of time off, to 'take action which is necessary' to deal with unexpected events concerning a dependant. Key aspects are as follows:

- There is no **qualifying period** for the right.
- The circumstances or activities regarding which the right to leave applies are as follows:
  - Provision of assistance to a dependant who falls ill, gives birth, or is injured or assaulted.
  - When a dependant dies or when arrangements need to be made for the care of a dependant who is ill or injured.
  - Where there is unexpected disruption to arrangements for the care of a dependant, including unexpected incidents arising from a child being at school. This provision was ruled on by the Employment Appeals Tribunal in a case where a parent had received two weeks' notification of the unavailability of a childminder (*RBS* v *Harrison* (2008) EAT/0093/08). The EAT ruled that the word 'unexpected' did not involve a time element and there was no warrant for the insertion of the words 'sudden' or 'in emergency' into the statutory provision.
- 'Dependant' is defined as a person's spouse or civil partner, child, parent or someone living with the employee other than a tenant or lodger. The legislation also provides that persons other than these (e.g. an elderly neighbour) who might reasonably rely on the employee for assistance come within the definition of a dependant.

Employees are obliged to inform their employer about the reason for their absence as soon as reasonably practicable and how long the absence is likely to last. The employer is obliged not to unreasonably refuse a request. There has been relatively little **case law** regarding these provisions but the case of *Qua* v *John Ford Morrison Solicitors* [2003] IRLR 184, EAT established the nature of the right (see Exhibit 11.2).

The EAT's decision in *Qua* has recently been followed by the EAT in another case on dependency leave, *Cortest Ltd* v *O'Toole* [2007] EAT/0470/07/LA. In this case a man, Mr O'Toole, requested up to two months' unpaid leave from his employer to care for his children in circumstances where his wife had to leave the house for several weeks and Mr O'Toole could not afford to employ a temporary carer. His employer told Mr O'Toole that he could take the time off provided that he resigned – as long as work was available he would be reinstated when his domestic situation improved. Mr O'Toole subsequently claimed unfair dismissal at a tribunal. The tribunal found that he had been dismissed and further that, as in its view, his request for time off satisfied the conditions imposed by s 57A of the Employment Rights Act, he had been dismissed for an automatically unfair reason (i.e. taking leave for family reasons, see further below).

Exhibit 11.2 The case of *Qua* v *John Ford Morrison Solicitors*

Qua v *John Ford Morrison Solicitors* [2003] IRLR 184, EAT

Facts. In this case a legal secretary working for a firm of solicitors was dismissed after taking 17 days off in a nine-month period in order to care for her sick son, who had a long term illness.

Judgments. The tribunal and subsequently the Employment Appeals Tribunal found that her dismissal had not been automatically unfair and that the employer was not in breach of the dependency leave provisions. They outlined that the dependency leave rights enable an employee to take time off to arrange for the care of a dependant, but that they do not allow an employee to take time off to provide the care him or herself on an ongoing basis. The statutory right applies to unforeseen and unexpected events as opposed to foreseeable or ongoing events. Leave to provide longer term care would come under the heading of parental leave. The right to dependency leave was a right to a 'reasonable amount' of time off 'to take action which is necessary'.

Comment. In the vast majority of cases a few hours, or at most one or two days, would be regarded as reasonable to deal with the particular problem.

The employer appealed to the EAT, which disagreed with the tribunal's decision. Following *Qua*, it ruled that the dependency leave provisions were intended to provide employees with a right to time off for a relatively short period of time so that they could make arrangements for the care of a dependant. A request to take one month or longer off would rarely, if ever, come within these provisions. As in the *Qua* case, the EAT noted that to allow a parent to become a childminder for such a period would create another form of time off not envisaged by s 57A, which was introduced to enable employees to deal with emergencies and give them a short period of breathing space. It ruled that Mr O'Toole, therefore, had not been unfairly dismissed on ground of exercising his right to dependency leave.

Although it follows the line of reasoning outlined in *Qua* and also the government's guidance on the legislation, on the facts this decision in *Cortest* v *O'Toole* appears to be rather harsh. It is difficult to see what else Mr O'Toole could have done in the circumstances, particularly as he could not afford to employ a temporary carer. Although he was eligible to apply for parental leave, the EAT recognised this is not possible in such emergency circumstances due to the requirements in that legislation for an application in writing to be made in advance of the intended leave date. It is evident, therefore, that the right to dependency leave has this far been interpreted quite narrowly in case law.

Right to request flexible working

This was introduced in 2003 (Employment Rights Act 1996, Part VIIIA; and the Flexible Working Regulations 2002). Employers are obliged to consider applications for flexible working from employees who have 26 weeks of continuous service who have children under the age of six (or disabled children under the age of 18). The purpose is to enable an employee to 'care for' his/her child. In addition to mothers, fathers, guardians, foster and adoptive parents, partners are entitled to apply if they have or expect to have responsibility for the upbringing of the child.

A notable change introduced by the Work and Families Act 2006 is that from April 2007 carers of adults are also eligible (provided they are employees with 26 weeks' service). Carers of adults encompass those caring for a spouse, partner, 'near relative' or another adult who is not within one of these categories but lives in the same house as the employee. The term 'near relative' covers parents, grandparents, adult children, siblings, uncles and aunts. In-laws, family members via adoptive relationships, step-relatives and half-blood relatives are also covered.

The government plans to further extend the flexible working legislation, to parents of older children. To this end, it commissioned the HR director of Sainsbury's, Imelda Walsh, to undertake a review of options in this area. This review was published in May 2008 (Walsh 2008) and recommended that the right to request be extended to employees with children aged 16 or under. The government has accepted this recommendation and intends to implement it. This is likely to happen in April 2009.

An employee can make an application to change terms and conditions relating to:

- hours of work;
- times required to work;
- place of work (specifically the choice is between working at home or at the employer's premises) (ERA 1996, s 80F).

Practices which come within these three categories include a change from full-time to part-time work; job-sharing; 'flexi-time'; compressed, annualised and staggered hours; and shift working. Importantly, the legislation does not provide an automatic right to flexible working but rather a right *to apply* for this and a duty on the employer *to consider* the application.

A specific decision-making process is specified. The employee must make the flexible working request in writing, outlining the proposed change, the effect it is likely to have on the employer and how this might be dealt with. The employer must then either agree or hold a meeting to discuss the request and inform the employee of the decision in writing. The employer must also provide an opportunity for the employee to appeal a decision where a request has been rejected. Particular deadlines are specified for each of these steps to take place. The employee has a statutory right to be accompanied by a fellow worker or union official at these meetings (Employment Relations Act 1999, s 10).

An employer may only refuse a request on eight 'business grounds' which are exhaustively outlined in the legislation (s 80G):

- burden of additional cost;
- detrimental impact on ability to meet customer demand;
- detrimental impact on performance of the business;
- detrimental impact on quality;
- inability to reorganise work among existing staff;
- inability to recruit additional staff;
- insufficiency of work during periods employee proposes to work;
- if the change is incompatible with planned structural changes.

Where an application is rejected, the written notice provided to the employee must specify the ground or grounds for refusal from this list and explain why they apply in the circumstances. Importantly, from an employee's perspective, any contract variation resulting from a flexible working request will be permanent unless otherwise agreed at the outset. In addition, employees may make only one variation application per year.

An employee is not permitted to apply to an employment tribunal claiming breach of the flexible working legislation until they have appealed their employer's decision regarding their application and received the outcome of the same. A tribunal can award a **remedy** where the stipulated procedure was not followed; the decision to reject was based on incorrect facts; or the ground for refusal was not one of those permitted. In terms of remedies, tribunals can make a declaration, ordering an employer to reconsider an application and/or award compensation. Tribunals have no power to order a request to be granted and in addition, they are not permitted to examine the reasonableness of a decision to reject a request, with their role largely limited to monitoring that the correct procedure was followed. However, the case of *Mehaffy* v *Dunnes Stores (UK) Limited* [2003] ET 1308076/03 does demonstrate that tribunals may ensure that requests have been given genuine, substantial consideration.

Here the employer, a retail chain, rejected a flexible working request by one of its managers on the basis that if approved this would negatively impact on quality and performance of the business and also impose additional costs. Although the company therefore provided reasons for refusal as required by the flexible working regulations, an employment tribunal found that the employer in fact had made no genuine consideration of the request. According to the tribunal, the employer had 'reluctantly paid lip-service to working through the flexible working provisions . . . without any genuine commitment to considering the claimant's proposals'. As a consequence, the tribunal found that the employer had breached the regulations.

A notable feature of the flexible working legislation is the possibility for disputes to be resolved under a dedicated **arbitration** scheme operated by ACAS, rather than by an employment tribunal. Claimants are free to choose whether to submit their claim to arbitration or to apply to a tribunal.

Protection from detriment and dismissal

Legislation provides that employees have a right not to be dismissed or subjected to detriment short of dismissal for exercising their entitlement to the various forms of family leave or for other reasons connected to pregnancy, maternity, family rights. Where the reason or principal reason for dismissing an employee is 'connected with' pregnancy, the taking of maternity leave or exercise of other family right(s), the dismissal will be automatically unfair. Importantly, this protection applies regardless of length of service (Employment Rights Act 1996, s 47C; Maternity and Parental Leave Regulations 1999, reg 19; Paternity and Adoptive Leave Regulations 2002, reg 28). An employee dismissed during pregnancy or maternity leave is entitled to a written statement of the reasons for dismissal (see Chapter 8). Examples of detriment short of dismissal would include a failure to promote or provide training on the grounds of a woman's pregnancy or a man's application for parental leave.

An interesting recent case regarding pregnancy-related dismissal was considered by the European Court of Justice (*Mayr* v *Bäckerei und Konditorei Gerhard Flöckner OHG* (2008) Case C-506/06, ECJ) (see Exhibit 11.3).

Family rights and sex discrimination

Less favourable treatment

It can be strongly argued that the less favourable treatment of women on grounds of pregnancy or maternity constitutes sex discrimination, as only women can become pregnant and pregnancy or maternity is intimately connected to the female sex. Although the need for a male comparator in discrimination law has historically been a substantial obstacle, the European Court of Justice ruled in the early 1990s that the EU Equal Treatment Directive 1976 encompassed protection against adverse treatment on the grounds of pregnancy and maternity. The latter was held to be a form of direct sex discrimination (*Dekker* v *Stichting*

Exhibit 11.3 When is a woman pregnant?

Mayr v Bäckerei und Konditorei Gerhard Flöckner OHG (2008) Case C-506/06, ECJ

Facts. This case concerned an Austrian waitress, Ms Mayr, who, having been undergoing in vitro fertilisation treatment (IVF treatment), was dismissed from her job. When dismissed, M's ova had been fertilised but had not yet been transplanted into her uterus. She brought a claim under the Austrian law on maternity protection, which prohibits dismissal during pregnancy. She argued that as her ova had been fertilised, she should be classed as pregnant for the purposes of the legislation.

Judgment. The case was referred to the European Court of Justice which ruled that, for the purposes of the EU's Pregnant Workers Directive, which prohibits dismissal of women on grounds of pregnancy, in cases of IVF the earliest a pregnancy could be said to begin is the date of implantation. The directive, therefore, was not applicable to her situation. This case is binding on UK courts. It means that in future it will be automatically unfair to dismiss a woman on the ground that she has undergone IVF treatment involving ova implantation, but not to dismiss a woman who has merely undergone fertilisation treatment.

Comment. This may seem quite harsh on a woman in this situation. However, this is alleviated somewhat because the ECJ also ruled that although a woman such as Ms Mayr may not be able to benefit from the law on pregnancy dismissal as she is not classed as being pregnant, dismissal or other detrimental treatment towards her *could be categorised as discrimination*, in breach of the Equal Treatment Directive (see further below).

Vormingscentrum Voor Jonge Volwassen Plus [1991] IRLR 27). In the *Dekker* case, a female candidate for a training instructor's position who, although regarded as the most suitable candidate, was not appointed because she was pregnant. The ECJ held that the fact that she had not been employed for a reason connected with pregnancy was contrary to the Equal Treatment Directive. Essentially, European judges have therefore supported the common sense view that adverse or less favourable treatment on grounds of pregnancy or maternity is sex discrimination and that no male comparator is necessary.

This position has recently been formalised by the revised Equal Treatment Directive 2002 (now consolidated into the Equal Treatment Directive 2006). British law was amended to this effect by the Employment Equality (Sex Discrimination) Regulations 2005. These regulations inserted a new provision into the Sex Discrimination Act 1975 (s 3A) expressly stating that less favourable treatment on grounds of pregnancy or maternity leave constitutes unlawful sex discrimination (this section has subsequently been subject to modification by the Sex Discrimination Act 1975 (Amendment) Regulations 2008).

This special protection against less favourable treatment, on the grounds of pregnancy or maternity, applies during a 'protected period' lasting from the beginning of pregnancy to the end of the maternity leave period or until the woman returns to work, if this is earlier. Any less favourable treatment on grounds of pregnancy during this protected period is automatically sex discrimination. Less favourable treatment *outside* this period may also be sex discrimination but it will be necessary for the woman to demonstrate less favourable treatment compared to a male comparator, whether real or hypothetical.

For example, treating a woman less favourably due to the fact that she has been off sick during her pregnancy with a pregnancy-related illness, would be automatic sex discrimination. However, to invoke a capability procedure against a woman who was off sick due to a pregnancy-related illness after the end of the maternity leave period, *would not* automatically constitute sex discrimination. It would only be so if the woman could demonstrate less favourable treatment compared to a man who had been off sick for a similar period.

Examples of the type of actions targeted by the provisions on less favourable treatment include a decision not to recruit, promote or train, or dismissal on grounds of pregnancy; not giving a woman on maternity leave an opportunity to undergo a performance appraisal (and thereby benefit from a pay rise) or not informing her of a vacancy in her area. In addition, failure to undertake a risk assessment or a decision not to recruit a pregnant woman on health and safety grounds may also constitute sex discrimination, providing that the woman can demonstrate she suffered a detriment.

In the case of *Mannell* v *Clinton Cards plc* (2006) ET 2304416/04, the employer failed to carry out a specific risk assessment in relation to Ms Mannell, a manager at one of its stores. Ms Mannell felt compelled to resign due to the fact that long hours and high levels of stress in the job were impacting negatively on her pregnancy. The tribunal found that the employer's failure to carry out the risk assessment led to Ms Mannell suffering a detriment (i.e. having to resign her job) and decided that the employer, therefore, was guilty of sex discrimination.

Discrimination against women undergoing IVF treatment

As indicated earlier, the case of *Mayr* v *Bäckerei und Konditorei Gerhard Flöckner OHG* (2008) (Case C-506/06, ECJ) (see Exhibit 11.3) has extended the protection offered by the law in this area to cover some women at an advanced stage of IVF treatment. Although as outlined above, in that case the European Court of Justice decided that for the purposes of protection against dismissal under the Pregnant Workers Directive 1992, a woman undergoing IVF would need to have undergone implantation of ova, it also decided that for the purposes of the Equal Treatment Directive it was sufficient for a woman just to have undergone fertilisation treatment. Less favourable treatment of such a woman on the basis that she has undergone IVF treatment would therefore constitute sex discrimination. The court ruled that it was appropriate to draw an analogy between women at such an advanced stage of IVF treatment and pregnant women. British employers will need to take note of this decision, given the increasing number of female employees having IVF treatment.

Discrimination on grounds of association

Another European Court of Justice decision (*Coleman* v *Attridge Law* (2008) Case C-303/06, ECJ) has potentially important consequences for those with caring responsibilities. Ms Coleman, who has a disabled son, brought a case to an employment tribunal claiming that she had been subject to less favourable treatment than parents of non-disabled children on ground of her association with her disabled son. The Employment Tribunal referred her case to the European Court of Justice to establish whether such 'disability discrimination by association' was unlawful. The ECJ ruled that it was, that the Equal Treatment in Employment Framework Directive 2000 prohibits discrimination by association on grounds of disability, age, sexual orientation, religion or belief etc. (see Chapter 5, Exhibit 5.13). This decision is of great significance because it means that employees with caring responsibilities, for example for disabled children or elderly parents, are protected from being discriminated against on that basis.

Indirect sex discrimination

The concept of indirect sex discrimination is also relevant in the area of pregnancy, maternity and family rights. For example, an employer's policy of refusing requests for part-time working may adversely affect women attempting to balance work with family commitments (e.g. women returning from maternity leave). Such a policy would be an example of a 'provision, criterion or practice' which puts women at a 'particular disadvantage'. These are two of the conditions that are required to establish a case of indirect discrimination (see Chapter 5). Unless the employer can show that such a rule or policy is a 'proportionate means of achieving a legitimate aim', a detriment or disadvantage suffered as a consequence will be classed as a case of indirect discrimination.

A notable trend here is the reliance by tribunal applicants on the law on indirect discrimination in cases relating to flexible working requests. Case law shows that even though an employer may satisfy the requirements of the flexible working legislation, a decision to reject a request for flexible working may still be held to be indirectly discriminatory.

An example is the case of ***Webster*** v ***Princes Soft Drinks*** (2005) ET 1803942/04 which involved a request by a senior accountant to transfer to part-time work following her return from maternity leave. The tribunal in this case found that although the employer had complied with the requirements of the flexible working regulations they had indirectly discriminated against Ms Webster. The employer had highlighted the large number of staff to be managed as a reason for refusing the request, yet Ms Webster had only three people reporting directly to her. The employer also argued that a job-share arrangement would be inefficient and that a full-time position was necessary in order to respond promptly to requests from head office for financial information. The tribunal was not persuaded by these arguments and concluded that no convincing reasons had been provided for the insistence on full-time work. The company had therefore indirectly discriminated against Ms Webster.

The recent high profile case, ***British Airways*** v ***Starmer*** [2005] IRLR 862, EAT 0306/05/SM is also relevant in this context (see Exhibit 11.4).

Although the bulk of decisions in this area relate to discrimination against women, in certain situations men may also be able to successfully bring a discrimination claim. While men are not usually in a position to claim indirect discrimination due to the fact that they are in general less likely than women to have family or caring commitments, a man may have a case for direct discrimination if a request to work flexibly is refused. For example, in ***Walkingshaw*** v ***The John Martin Group*** (2000) ET S/401126/00 a man requested a transfer to a two and a half day week in order to enable him to care for his baby son. His request was rejected but he succeeded in a claim for direct discrimination, as the tribunal found that his employer had always accommodated requests by women for flexible working. Mr Walkingshaw could

Exhibit 11.4 Reducing a pilot's hours of work

British Airways v *Starmer* [2005] IRLR 862, EAT

Facts. The employer refused a request from a female pilot to go to a 50 per cent fractional contract in order to be able to look after her new baby, and instead only permitted her to move to a 75 per cent contract.

Judgments. A tribunal and subsequently the Employment Appeals Tribunal held that the decision to only permit part-time working at 75 per cent of a full-time contract was a 'provision, criterion or practice' for the purposes of the Sex Discrimination Act. The EAT held that the tribunal had been correct in finding that British Airways had not provided sufficient justification for this decision and that there had therefore been indirect discrimination against Mrs Starmer. Resource constraints including the burden of additional costs and inability to reorganise work had been put forward by the employer, with the tribunal finding that the reasons outlined were not sufficient to justify the discriminatory effect of the decision made. In addition, a general policy of BA that inexperienced pilots should not be permitted to work below 75 per cent of a full-time contract was also rejected. The EAT ruled that the circumstances of individual workers needed to be considered.

also have compared himself with how a hypothetical female comparator in the same post would have been treated.

As outlined earlier, the role of sex discrimination law in the area of pregnancy, maternity and family rights is of particular importance to those workers who are not employees.

Enforcement and remedies

The issue of enforcement of family rights is rather complex. For some of the rights outlined in this chapter specific enforcement provisions and remedies apply, while the enforcement of others is via general provisions. It is also possible that employees can bring more than one claim, for example a claim for discrimination in addition to one for detriment or dismissal. Table 11.2 outlines the grounds on which employees may bring a case and the remedies available. This is based on various provisions of the Employment Rights Act 1996 and the Sex Discrimination Act 1975, both as amended.

Table 11.2 Grounds of action and remedies relating to family rights

Claim	*Summary*	*Possible remedies*
Leave • Unreasonable refusal of time off for ante-natal care or failure to pay for time off work • Unreasonable refusal of time off for dependency leave • Refusal or unreasonable postponement of parental leave request	Specific enforcement provisions relating to ante-natal care, dependency and parental leave	Declaration Compensation
Flexible working provisions • Failure to follow stipulated procedure for flexible working application • Decision based on incorrect facts • Grounds for refusal not one of those permitted • Detriment relating to flexible working application	Specific provisions relating to flexible working applications	Declaration Compensation (up to a maximum of eight weeks' pay – £2,640 as at February 2008) Order to reconsider flexible working request
Detriment for family and domestic reasons	Covers detriment in form of any act or failure to act on grounds of pregnancy, maternity leave, adoption leave, paternity leave, parental leave and dependency leave	Declaration Compensation
Unfair dismissal	Dismissal for a family related reason automatically unfair regardless of length of service	Re-engagement Reinstatement Compensation
Sex discrimination	Less favourable treatment on grounds of pregnancy/maternity is sex discrimination; indirect sex discrimination; discrimination on grounds of association (e.g. with a disabled child)	Declaration Recommendation Compensation (potentially unlimited and including compensation for injury to feelings in addition to financial loss)

A notable element of the legislation in this area is that a dismissal for a pregnancy, maternity or family related reason is automatically unfair and the employee will be entitled to claim unfair dismissal regardless of the employee's length of service. Applicants are normally required to have one year's service in order to claim unfair dismissal (see Chapter 8). In addition to a dismissal of an employee by an employer for one of these reasons, a woman or man subjected to detriment on grounds of pregnancy, maternity or other family rights may be entitled to resign and claim unfair **constructive dismissal**. As explained in Chapter 8, this will be the case where an employer's actions or conduct causes a fundamental or **repudiatory breach of contract**. Examples of this could be where a woman is not promoted on grounds of pregnancy or where an employer fails to undertake a health assessment in relation to a pregnant woman (e.g. *Mannell* v *Clinton Cards*). An employer's failure to inform a woman on maternity leave of vacancies arising in her department may also constitute grounds for constructive dismissal where the woman in question had a legitimate expectation that she would be so informed (*Visa International Service Association* v *Paul* [2004] IRLR 42, EAT).

As is evident from Table 11.2, the primary remedy available for breach of family rights is compensation. The legislation does not permit tribunals to order an employer to allow leave to be taken. At best tribunals are empowered to order an employer to reconsider a request, but this only applies to flexible working. Compensation awarded is generally that which is 'just and equitable' in the particular situation. In the case of breach of the flexible working regulations, the level of compensation a tribunal can order is capped at eight weeks' pay, with the level of a week's pay for this purpose set by legislation. At February 2008 a 'week's pay' was defined as £330, so this would mean a maximum compensation award of £2,640 (for current rates see **www.berr.gov.uk/employment/pay**). In discrimination cases, compensation levels are uncapped and may include compensation for injury to feelings.

Employees seeking to bring a claim on one or more of the above grounds must apply to an employment tribunal within three months of the act in question. However, following the ACAS *Code of Practice on Disciplinary and Grievance Procedures* (2009), before doing so they should firstly try to resolve the situation with their employer. Specifically, they should submit a written grievance about the issue in question, attend any meeting that is arranged and also appeal any decision if allowed to do so. If they do not take these steps any compensation subsequently awarded by a tribunal could be reduced by up to 25 per cent. Under the Employment Relations Act 1999, they would have a statutory right to be accompanied at such grievance or appeal meetings.

Employment policy and practice

There is a great deal of information available on the take-up and implementation of the various rights, entitlements and obligations outlined above. The government has sponsored comprehensive surveys on work–life balance and flexible working at regular intervals, while the Workplace Employee Relations Survey series (which is sponsored by BERR and ACAS, among other organisations) provides high quality, representative data on a range of relevant practices. Evidence is also available from a number of other sources such as reports of the former Equal Opportunities Commission and dedicated 'think tanks' or organisations such as Working Families. This section summarises some of the principal findings from these sources. It outlines trends and highlights what are perceived to be both positive aspects or 'success stories' and weaknesses or failures regarding the practice of flexible working and 'work–life balance' in the UK.

Maternity leave

A government-sponsored survey of new parents in 2005 (Smeaton and Marsh 2006) provided information on trends in maternity leave, which was comparable with a similar survey conducted in 2002. Some of the key findings were as follows:

- Nearly half of mothers' took six months' maternity leave in 2005 (compared with 9 per cent in 2002), while 14 per cent took 52 weeks (5 per cent in 2002).
- Eighty per cent of mothers returned to work after maternity leave and of these, 80 per cent returned to the same employer (59 per cent in 2002).
- The majority of returning mothers made a change to their employment pattern, with three-quarters returning on a part-time basis.
- Overall, the return to work was found to be easier for women in 2005 than 2002, due to greater employer flexibility and support.

Further information on trends in maternity leave is available from the Third Work–Life Balance Employer's Survey carried out in 2007 (Hayward *et al.* 2007). This found that 53 per cent of the workplaces surveyed in 2007 allowed all mothers 12 months of maternity leave despite the fact that the survey was conducted at a time when they were not obliged to do so. Fifteen per cent of workplaces, covering 41 per cent of employees, paid maternity pay at a rate higher than the statutory minimum.

These figures demonstrate that British employers have become more generous in the provision of maternity rights over the last number of years. The authors of these studies, although recognising the influence of a range of different factors, highlight the changes in the legislation on maternity leave and pay and flexible working as being important influences behind these trends.

Paternity leave

The 2005 survey (Smeaton and Marsh 2006) found that 93 per cent of fathers with employee status whose partners had given birth took time off work around the time of birth. The numbers of days off taken by fathers at this time had risen since 2002, with the proportion taking more than two weeks' leave increasing from 22 per cent to 36 per cent. Like those with regard to maternity leave, this trend was seen to be connected with the introduction of the statutory right to paternity leave in 2003. Seventy-one per cent of fathers made a change to their working arrangement following birth, for example 36 per cent worked more regular hours, while 27 per cent changed working hours to fit with their partner's job. The fathers surveyed also reported a substantial increase in the availability of flexible working patterns (e.g. part-time working or flexi-time) between 2002 and 2005.

Findings from the Workplace Employee Relations Survey (WERS) series similarly demonstrate an increase in paternity leave provision over time: while in 1998, 48 per cent of British workplaces provided paid paternity (or other discretionary) leave at the time of childbirth, by 2004, 92 per cent of workplaces were doing so (Whitehouse *et al.* 2007: 20).

Parental leave

The provision by employers of parental leave has increased notably since the introduction of legislation on this in 1999. In 1998, 38 per cent of workplaces in Britain allowed employees to take parental leave, but by 2004 this had increased to 73 per cent (ibid.). However it is evident that the actual *take-up* of parental leave remains very low. The Third Work–Life Balance Employer's Survey found that only 14 per cent of employers surveyed had at least one employee who had taken parental leave in the previous 12 months (Hooker *et al.* 2007: 7), while the Third Work–Life Balance *Employee* Survey, conducted in 2006, found that only one per cent of all employees and 6 per cent of employees who were parents of dependent children (up to the age of 18) had taken such leave (Hooker *et al.* 2007: 122).

Dependency leave

The survey evidence demonstrates that British employers are willing to give employees leave at short notice to deal with emergencies: 99 per cent of employers state that they almost always or sometimes grant time off for employees to care for a family member or to deal with a household emergency (Hayward *et al.* 2007: 17). For their part, 71 per cent of British employees surveyed in 2007 thought that their employer would 'almost always' give them time off at short notice to care for a dependant. Thirty-eight per cent reported that they had experienced an emergency at short notice during the working week. Of these, 90 per cent said they had taken time off to deal with such an emergency. This proportion was equivalent to 34 per cent of all employees surveyed. Over half (52 per cent) of the employees who had taken time off to deal with an emergency had taken fully paid leave (Hooker *et al.* 2007: 114, 229–30). These figures suggest that there has been strong adoption of the right to dependency leave across the British labour market.

Awareness and use of the right to request flexible working

The Third Work–Life Balance Employee survey (conducted in 2006) contained a number of questions about the right to request flexible working. Over half of all employees (56 per cent) said that they were aware of this right. This compared with 41 per cent in 2003, immediately before the right came into force. A higher proportion of parents with children under six (i.e. those legally entitled to the right to request) were aware of the right than were other employees (65 per cent compared with 53 per cent). Over the two years preceding the survey, 17 per cent of employees had made a request to their employer to change their working pattern (the 2003 survey produced an identical result). Twenty-two per cent of women had made such a request, compared with 14 per cent of men. In 60 per cent of cases requests were fully agreed to, while in 18 per cent they were partially agreed to. Seventeen per cent of requests were rejected, with the remaining 5 per cent still to be decided at the time of the survey (Hooker *et al.* 2007).

Interestingly, women were more likely to be successful than men in making a request – 66 per cent of female workers had their request fully agreed to compared with 53 per cent of men. Part-timers were also more likely than full-timers to have their request agreed to (74 per cent compared with 57 per cent).

Flexible working practices

The Workplace Employment Relations Surveys allow us to identify trends in flexible working over time. Table 11.3 provides figures on the availability of various flexible working practices in 1998 and 2004. Availability of each of the flexible working practices specified increased over

Table 11.3 British workplaces offering flexible working policies to non-managerial employees (%)

	1998	*2004*
Full-time to part-time	46	64
Job sharing	31	41
Home working	16	28
Flexi-time	19	26
Term-time only contracts	14	28
Annualised hours	8	13
Nine-day fortnight	3	7

Source: adapted from Whitehouse *et al.* (2007: 20).

the period, with some quite significant increases apparent. The possibility to switch from full-time to part-time work was the most common policy in place, with job sharing the second most popular. While these figures demonstrate that British employers are providing more opportunities to work flexibly, it should be noted that six of the seven practices listed were only available at a minority of workplaces.

The report on the Third Work–Life Balance Employee Survey (Hooker *et al.* 2007) provides more up-to-date information on flexible working in Britain. This report contains figures on the *availability* and *take-up* of flexible working practices in 2006 and also tables comparing the 2006 figures with those from the previous two work–life balance employee surveys conducted in 2000 and 2003.

Some of the information provided on trends in *availability* of flexible working practices over this period is reproduced in Table 11.4. It demonstrates an increase in the availability or provision of flexible working practices over the last number of years. The availability of part-time working, flexi-time, term-time working, a compressed working week and annualised hours, had all increased quite noticeably since 2000. In contrast, there was stability in the availability of reduced hours and job sharing. It is notable that working reduced hours, flexi-time or job sharing appears to be possible for around half of employees in Britain, while term-time working and a compressed working week are available to over a third. Homeworking and annualised hours appear to remain relatively uncommon, with only around a quarter of employees reporting that they were available to them.

Table 11.4 Trends in *availability* of flexible working arrangements 2000–06, percentage of employees reporting availability of practices

	2000	*2003*	*2006*
Part-time working	49	67	69
Reduced hours for a limited period	56	62	54
Flexi-time	32	48	53
Job share	46	41	47
Term-time working	22	32	37
Compressed working week	25	30	35
Annualised hours	17	20	24
Regular home working	n/a	20	23
One or more arrangements available	–	85	90
No arrangement available/don't know	–	15	10

Source: adapted from Hooker *et al.* (2007: 61).

Table 11.5 Trends in *take-up* of flexible working arrangements 2000–06, percentage of employees reporting use of practices

	2000	*2003*	*2006*
Part-time working	24	28	27
Reduced hours for a limited period	n/a	13	12
Flexi-time	24	26	27
Job share	4	6	6
Term-time working	14	15	13
Compressed working week	6	11	9
Annualised hours	2	6	8
Regular home working	n/a	11	10
Not worked flexibly in last 12 months	–	49	44
Currently working flexibly or has done so in the last 12 months	–	51	56

Source: adapted from Hooker *et al.* (2007: 62).

More pertinently, the report by Hooker *et al.* (2007) also contained figures on the actual *take-up* of these practices over time. These are outlined in Table 11.5. Although it is necessary to highlight that the authors advise that these figures are treated with caution, the table appears to demonstrate that while the availability of flexible working practices may be relatively high, their take-up in practice is in general very low, with a high degree of stability in this over time.

Although over half of the employees surveyed in 2006 stated that they were currently working flexibly or that they had done so in the previous 12 months, at most 27 per cent reported adopting the individual practices specified. Therefore, while over a quarter of employees were working part-time or flexi-time, only around one in ten were working reduced hours, a compressed week, term-time working, annualised hours or home working. Only 6 per cent of employees were job sharing. These figures, therefore, arguably illustrate that the adoption and implementation of flexible working practices in the British labour market continues to be very limited in many respects.

Degrees of success with flexible working and 'work–life balance'

The above evidence demonstrates that family leave and flexible working policies and practices are becoming more common in the British labour market. It is clear that the introduction and strengthening of the various pieces of legislation have partly underpinned this, prompting employers to reassess and amend their policies and practices. It is also evident that business considerations and general labour market pressures have been important push factors. Therefore, there is a substantial amount of positive evidence or 'good news' regarding flexible working and work–life balance in the UK. On the other hand, it is also clear that there continue to be many obstacles to the implementation of family friendly/flexible working policies and practices. This section explores the question of 'degrees of success' in this area in some detail.

Senior managers

In a report entitled *Hours to Suit: Working Flexibly at Senior and Managerial Levels*, Working Families (2007) presents the findings from semi-structured interviews conducted with 23 senior managers working reduced hours or flexibly, the large majority of whom were located in the private sector. Eight worked in City-based organisations and the majority had direct responsibility for managing a team of people. Eighteen of the 23 worked reduced hours, with eight job sharing and the other 10 working patterns such as a two-, three- or four-day week.

A key objective of the report was to address and challenge directly the common presumption that flexible working is not possible or feasible in senior, managerial positions, by drawing on examples of senior managers who are successfully working in this way.

The report is based on detailed case studies of each of the individual managers. Overall, these demonstrate how these were able to have successful careers while working on a flexible basis. The use of flexible/reduced hours was found to lead to advantages or improvements for the employing organisations in the areas of recruitment and retention. In addition, these practices improved the motivation, enthusiasm, effectiveness and loyalty of the managers in question. There was a strong view that flexible working was compatible with the roles and responsibilities of senior managers. The development of information and communication technologies greatly facilitated the flexible working patterns adopted (e.g. home working).

Despite these positive findings, there is a lot of other research which reports that family life and working flexibly are often not compatible with senior management positions. For example, the continuing dominance of long hours working and traditional work patterns in such positions was one of the key obstacles identified by the recent Women and Work Commission report (2006) as impeding the progress of women into higher level organisational positions. Relatedley, a more general problem is the persistence of the UK's long hours working **culture**.

In this regard, a June 2008 report by the Trades Union Congress (TUC 2008), which was based on official statistics – *The Return of the Long Hours Culture* – outlined that in 2008, 3.3 million workers in Britain were working more than 48 hours a week, with just under 13 per cent of employees doing so. Although there had been a substantial decrease in long hours working in the period 1998–2007, between 2007 and 2008 there was an increase of 180,000 in the number of people working more than 48 hours a week. The large majority of those working long hours were managers and senior officials and professionals. Of most relevance for our discussion here, the report notes that the TUC is 'concerned that so many senior positions disproportionately rely on long hours' and that in particular this will 'exclude women from these roles, since they still bear the greater part of caring responsibilities' (TUC 2008: 4).

Employee performance

A second recent report, based on a two-year research project undertaken by Cranfield School of Management (Working Families 2008), examines the impact of flexible working patterns on employee performance. The research for this report involved surveys, semi-structured interviews and focus groups at seven leading British companies. The majority of flexible workers and co-workers and managers of the same were of the view that flexible working had either a positive or neutral impact on the quantity and quality of work undertaken. The majority of employees reported that flexible working had a positive effect in reducing and managing stress levels, although for some individuals flexible working was itself a source of stress. Flexible workers had higher levels of organisational commitment than those not working flexibly; and in some cases they had a higher level of job satisfaction.

While the findings were therefore generally positive, some negative findings emerged from the report in addition to the observation about stress levels mentioned above. There was a general belief among respondents that adopting flexible working practices could harm their careers. In addition, the availability of flexible working was seen to be very much dependent on the culture of the organisation and views of line managers, with some of the latter not being supportive of it. In addition, the feasibility of flexible working was found to be contingent on the nature of work that individuals were doing – while some jobs were well suited to it others by their very nature were not (e.g. senior management roles).

Motherhood

Case study research by Gatrell (2007) provides sobering evidence about employers' policies and practice in relation to pregnancy and motherhood. Gatrell (2007) conducted interviews with 20 working mothers, seven of whom were working full-time and the remaining 13 reduced hours. The interviews highlighted how many organisations were effectively alien environments for pregnant women, with managers, colleagues and clients all being ill at ease with pregnant women, thereby creating very uncomfortable working environments for them.

While each of the women's organisations had policies promising equal opportunities to 'fractional' employees (i.e. those working reduced hours), the working mothers found that in practice fractional working was only available to those who were prepared to accept demotion or limited career opportunities. For example, Eleanor, a senior education manager in a public-sector organisation, was refused reduced hours on grounds of her seniority; she was told that if she wanted to work reduced hours she would have to accept a demotion. Another woman, Sarah-Jane, was obliged to give up her status as a hospital consultant when she returned to work on 80 per cent time.

Gatrell (2007: 472–3) concludes that the experience of the mothers she researched indicates that 'fractional working is not as conducive to "work life balance" as may be assumed, because it is accompanied by heavy penalties in terms of limited career prospects and blocked promotion'. She argues that 'business case' arguments in favour of flexible working for professional women are insufficient to counter employers' discriminatory behaviour regarding fractional working. Rather what is first required is an open discussion of the various 'taboos' that exist in organisations with regard to motherhood and paid work and a change in fundamental attitudes towards the same.

The extent to which British employers continue to be largely uncomfortable dealing with pregnancy and maternity is graphically illustrated by a report of the former Equal Opportunities Commission (EOC 2005). This presented the results of a 2005 survey of 1,000 pregnant or previously pregnant women which showed that 45 per cent of the women surveyed had experienced dismissal or disadvantageous treatment on grounds of pregnancy, which the authors calculated as being equivalent to 200,000 women per year across the labour market as a whole. Seven per cent of such women had been dismissed, made redundant or treated so badly they were forced to leave work (equivalent to 30,000 in total). Young, low income, ethnic minority women and those with short job tenure were particularly negatively affected, while discrimination was especially prominent in firms employing less than ten people.

Critical perspectives on the legislation

While the fact that it has substantially strengthened employee rights and had positive effects on employer policy and practice is recognised, the legislation on family rights and 'work–life balance' has attracted some strong criticism. For example, some authors (e.g. Smith and Thomas 2003: 421) have highlighted the fact that the maternity leave provisions do not provide women with the right to return to work on *different* terms and conditions, for example on a part-time basis. Requests for the latter would need to be made under the flexible working provisions, yet these have also been the subject of much criticism. In particular, it is noted that they do not give employees a right to flexible working but only a right *to apply* to work flexibly (Anderson 2003). In addition, it is argued that the legislation provides employers with a wide scope to justify refusal of an employee's application (i.e. the eight 'business grounds'). Further, it is suggested that the role and involvement of employment tribunals in this area is very weak. Their remit is seen to be largely procedural, with the fact that they are not permitted to examine the reasonableness or otherwise of an employer's decision highlighted (ibid.).

The legislation on parental leave has also been criticised along a number of dimensions, such as that the leave is unpaid, that employers can postpone the taking of it, and that the right to such leave is only provided to parents of children up to the age of five whereas the Parental Leave Directive envisaged application to children up to aged eight (McColgan 2000).

Conclusion

It is evident from the above evidence and discussion, that there is a need for balance and some healthy scepticism when evaluating the extent to which progress has been made in promoting family rights, work–life balance and flexible working in the UK labour market. While a range of legislative provisions have been introduced and subsequently enhanced and there is evidence of increasing adoption by employers of family leave and flexible working policies, the legislation also has a number of apparent weaknesses and there continue to be many problematic aspects regarding employers' policies and practices in these areas.

Exercises

11.1 **Pauline and Kate** work for a public relations (PR) agency employing 30 people, Pauline as an administrator and Kate as an account manager in the 'politics' section of the business (which offers PR advice to government departments and political parties). Both have recently completed a period of maternity leave, Pauline having taken OML and Kate AML, and, therefore, are planning to return to work.

In Pauline's case when she reports for work at the end of her leave she is informed by her manager that she cannot have her old job back, as the company wishes to keep on her temporary replacement, Elaine, who the manager says is more efficient. In addition, she is told that there is no other job she can do.

Similarly, Kate is not allowed to return to her old job. Her manager insists that Rob, who she trained up to cover for her during her maternity leave, keeps the job for the reason that 'this is better from the point of view of the customers'. Kate, therefore, is assigned to the position of account manager in the agency's other main department, 'corporate' (which advises private sector companies on how to improve their profiles in the press and media). Although at the same salary grade and location as her previous job, Kate wonders whether the company is allowed to do this.

Pauline and Kate ask you for advice as to any rights and remedies they may be entitled to arising from their employer's actions.

11.2 **Sarah and Lucy** work full-time for a food manufacturer that supplies ready-meals to the larger British retail chains. Sarah, who has been with the company for three years, works as a senior quality control manager, a position which involves overall responsibility for the quality and safety of products manufactured in the factory. She has a child aged four and has applied in writing to the HR manager to transfer to part-time work. Lucy has one year's service as a marketing manager, with responsibility for developing and overseeing marketing campaigns. She has recently returned from maternity leave and has also applied in writing to transfer to part-time work.

The HR manager holds meetings with both women to discuss their requests. Following this Sarah and Lucy's line managers (the operations and marketing directors respectively) are asked to provide a report on the likely operational and business consequences of a transfer by them to part-time working. The operations director provides a detailed report which outlines that the importance and responsibility of the role requires there to be a senior quality control manager on site on a full-time basis. In addition, it notes that creating a job share arrangement would also not be feasible due to the difficultly in recruiting someone to work part-time in such a senior, specialist position. In contrast, Lucy's manager provides only a very brief note stating that 'this position is not suitable for part-time work'. Both requests to work part-time are therefore rejected.

What entitlements or rights do Lucy and Sarah have in relation to their requests and what causes of action or remedies might their employer's refusal give rise to?

11.3 **Tom** has worked as a team leader for FirstCall Direct, an insurance company employing 3,000 people, for two years. His partner has recently given birth to twins. She has now returned to work and the twins have started at nursery. Tom wants to be able to take and collect the twins from the nursery and therefore makes an application for his hours to be reduced so that he can work from 10–4 instead of 9–5.30. Although similar requests by female teamleaders have been accepted, his line manager rejects his request, explaining that 'we can't have all our teamleaders working flexi-time, there needs to be enough teamleaders in place to supervise the staff'. He appeals this decision but his manager rejects his appeal, stating that he should 'just get on with doing the job you're employed to do'.

Tom asks for your advice regarding his position. What advice would you give regarding any rights or remedies he may be entitled to arising from his employer's actions?

11.4 **Paula** has worked as a tax solicitor at a large law firm for the last three years. Due to her extensive expertise in the tax field and recent success in winning a number of high-profile cases, she has been told by the managing director that she would make an 'ideal candidate' to become a partner at the firm, and that she should apply for the position in the next round of internal vacancies. Paula duly does so and is subsequently called for interview. The interview goes extremely well with strong indications that she will get the position. However, towards the end of the interview Paula informs the panel that as she is three months pregnant she will soon have to go on maternity leave. The chair of the interview panel expresses his shock at this, noting that he was under the impression that Paula was a 'career women', and that it would be difficult for the company to arrange cover during her maternity leave. Paula subsequently receives a letter informing her that she has not been successful in her application due to the 'outstanding calibre' of other applicants.

Advise Paula on any claim she may have against her employers.

Feedback on these exercises is provided in the Appendix to this textbook.

References and useful websites

Anderson, L. (2003) 'Sound bite legislation: the Employment Act 2002', *Industrial Law Journal*, March, Vol. 32(1): 37–42.

Bunting, M. (2004) *Willing Slaves – How the Overwork Culture is Ruling our Lives*. London: Harper Collins.

Chartered Institute of Personnel and Development (2007) *Work–life Balance Factsheet* (April 2007). London: Chartered Institute of Personnel and Development (available from www.cipd.org.uk).

Clutterbuck, D. (2003) *Managing Work–Life Balance: A Guide for HR in Achieving Organisational and Individual Change*. London: CIPD.

Cully, M., Woodland, S., O'Reilly, A. and Dix, G. (1999) *Britain at Work: as Depicted by the 1998 Workplace Employee Relations Survey*. London: Routledge.

Dex, S. and Scheibl, F. (1998) 'Should We Have More Family-Friendly Policies?', *European Management Journal*, 16(5): 586–99.

Dex, S. and Smith, C. (2002) *The Nature and Pattern of Family-Friendly Employment Policies in Britain*. London: for the Joseph Rowntree Foundation by the Policy Press.

Equal Opportunities Commission (2005) *Greater Expectations: EOC's Investigation into Pregnancy Discrimination*. London: EOC.

Felstead, A., Jewson, N. and Walters, S. (2005) *Changing Places of Work*. New York: Palgrave Macmillan.

Friedman, S. and Greenhaus, J. (2000) *Work and Family – Allies or Enemies? What Happens when Business Professionals Confront Life Choices*. New York: Oxford University Press.

Gatrell, C. (2007) 'A Fractional Commitment? Part-time work and the maternal body', *International Journal of Human Resource Management*, 18(3): 462–75.

Hayward, B., Fong, B. and Thornton, A. (2007) *The Third Work–Life Balance Employer Survey: Main Findings*, Employment Relations Research Series, No. 86. London: Department for Business, Enterprise and Regulatory Reform.

Hooker, H., Neathey, F., Casebourne, J. and Munro, M. (2007) *The Third Work–Life Balance Employee Survey: Main Findings*, Employment Relations Research Series, No. 58. London: Department of Trade and Industry.

Hoschild, A. (1997) *Time Bind*. New York: Metropolitan Books.

Industrial Relations Services (2002) 'Hanging in the balance', *IRS Employment Review*, 766: 6–11.

Kersley, B., Alpin, C., Forth, J., Bryson, A., Bewley, H., Dix, G. and Oxenbridge, S. (2006) *Inside the Workplace: Findings from the 2004 Workplace Employment Relations Survey*. London: Routledge.

Kodz, J., Harper, H. and Dench, S. (2002) *Work–Life Balance: Beyond the Rhetoric*, Report 384. Brighton: Institute for Employment Studies.

MacInnes, J. (2002) 'Work–Life Balance and the Demand for Reduction in Working Hours: Evidence from the British Social Attitudes Survey 2002', *British Journal of Industrial Relations*, 43(2): 273–95.

McColgan, A. (2000) 'Family friendly frolics? The Maternity and Parental Leave, etc. Regulations 1999', *Industrial Law Journal*, 29(2): 125–44.

Smeaton, D. and Marsh, A. (2006) *Maternity and Paternity Rights and Benefits: Survey of Parents 2005*, Employment Relations Research Series, No. 86. London: Department of Trade and Industry.

Smith, I.T. and Thomas, G. (2003) *Smith & Wood's Industrial Law* (8th edn). London: Lexis Nexis.

Suff, P. (2002) *Work–Life Balance*, Management Review No. 24. London: IRS.

Trades Union Congress (2005) *Future of Work: TUC Economics Department Briefing*. London: Trades Union Congress (available at www.tuc.org.uk/work_life/tuc-11016-f0.cfm).

TUC (2008) *The Return of the Long Hours Culture*. London: TUC (available at www.tuc.org.uk/extras/longhoursreturn).

Walsh, I. (2008) *Right to Request Flexible Working: A Review of How to Extend the Right to Request Flexible Working to Parents of Older Children*. London: Department for Business, Enterprise and Regulatory Reform.

Whitehouse, G., Haynes, M., MacDonald, F. and Arts, D. (2007) *Reassessing the 'Family-Friendly Workplace': Trends and influences in Britain, 1998–2004*, Employment Relations Research Series, No. 76. London: Department for Business, Enterprise and Regulatory Reform.

Women and Work Commission (2006) *Shaping a Fairer Future*. London: Women and Work Commission, London: Department of Trade and Industry.

Working Families (2007) *Hours to Suit: Working Flexibly at Senior and Managerial Levels*. London: Working Families.

Working Families (2008) *Flexible Working and Performance: Summary of Research*. London: Working Families and Cranfield University School of Management.

Useful websites

Department for Business Enterprise and Regulatory Reform **www.berr.gov.uk**

Chartered Institute of Personnel and Development **www.cipd.co.uk**

Department for Work and Pensions **www.dwp.gov.uk**

Trades Union Congress **www.tuc.org.uk**

Visit **www.mylawchamber.co.uk/willey** to access multiple choice questions, case flashcards and exercises to test yourself on this chapter.

mylawchamber

12 Health, safety and welfare at work

Learning objectives

To understand:

- The importance of contract and statute law in the regulation of health, safety and welfare at work
- The role of the workplace safety representative in ensuring compliance with safety standards
- The advisory and enforcement roles of the Health and Safety Executive
- Guidance from the courts about the handling of particular health and safety issues
- The role of management in the achievement of good health and safety practice

Structure of the chapter

Introduction

Health, safety and welfare are woven into operational management and the employment relationship in various important ways. Among the key factors that managers need to consider are the following:

- *The management of health and safety.* This involves dealing with a wide range of factors with health and safety implications: the nature of the technology used and related ergonomic considerations; the nature of the products and materials used; work organisation; the scheduling of working time; appropriate staffing levels; the nature of reward systems; and the relevance of training and development for staff.
- *Information.* Information necessary to consider the nature and extent of risk at work is likely to be drawn from various academic disciplines: physics, chemistry, biology, engineering, medicine, etc. Furthermore, financial considerations are also important: in respect of injuries and accidents and also the implementation of health and safety standards. This, in turn, requires knowledge of relevant details of the legal framework affecting work in the organisation. So, health and safety management is an integrative area involving the interlocking of many specialisms.
- *Employee relations context.* It is, also, important to remember that health and safety standards and good practice are implemented in an employee relations context. Standards and practice can control and influence how employees behave, how they are paid, staffing levels, their welfare and the conditions under which they work. So, the management of health and safety, then, needs to be linked with both strategic and day-to-day decision-making processes within organisations, as well as with specialist functions (finance, HRM and safety) and also with employee relations processes.

The concepts

'Health', 'safety' and 'welfare', are frequently used in ways which gloss over the differences between them. The terms are not defined in the Health and Safety at Work etc. Act 1974 nor in the European Framework **Directive** 1989.

Health

The International Labour Organisation defines 'health' in relation to work as 'not merely the absence of disease or infirmity; it also includes the physical and mental elements affecting health which are directly related to safety and hygiene at work' (Convention 155 concerning Occupational Safety and Health and the Working Environment). So, for example, workplace stress, exposure to toxic fumes and substances are likely to create hazards and harm to a person's health. The person might sustain some illness or medical condition from which s/he might recover. The prohibition of smoking in certain public places and in the workplace is regarded as a public health matter (see Exhibit 12.1).

Safety

This concerns protection from risk of injury, disease or death. It focuses on preventative steps that can be taken and possible protections (e.g. working practices, the scheduling of working

Exhibit 12.1 Smoking at work

Smoking in various public and work places was prohibited in Scotland (by the Scottish government) in 2006 and in England and Wales and in Northern Ireland in 2007 (by Parliament and the Welsh Assembly as appropriate).

There are limited exemptions to the bans. Employers and managers who control premises need to display non-smoking notices and take reasonable steps to ensure that staff, customers and visitors do not smoke in the premises. The Health and Safety Executive is ***not*** responsible for enforcement but supports local authorities in their responsibilities. Fines for breaches of the legislation may be imposed (see **www.hse.gov.uk**).

Relevant legislation:

- Health Act 2006;
- Prohibition of Smoking in Certain Premises (Scotland) Regulations 2006;
- Smoke-free Premises, etc. (Wales) Regulations 2007.

time, training, staffing levels, protective clothing and the physical guarding of machinery). There are substantial links with the concept of 'health' and, unsurprisingly, the two terms are invariably linked.

Welfare

This is a term rarely used in discussions. Yet it is explicitly part of the general duties placed on an employer (Health and Safety at Work etc. Act 1974, s 2(1)). The World Health Organisation speaks of 'a state of complete physical, mental and social well-being that does not consist only in the absence of illness or infirmity'. It interlocks with the other concepts. By adopting protective and preventative measures, it is anticipated that employees' welfare will be taken into account. Generally, it concerns minimising stress at work; helping employees reconcile the competing demands on their time (e.g. work and care for children or a disabled relative); evidence of concern for employees who are suffering personal problems (e.g. bereavement, financial or domestic difficulties); and support for employees who may have drug and alcohol problems.

Legal framework

This has a number of facets which are explored in detail below. In broad terms the structure is as follows:

Civil law

- **liability** of employer for breach of the contractual duty to take reasonable care;
- liability of employer for the **tort** of **negligence**;
- liability of employee for contributory negligence;
- **dismissal** of employee for breach of safety rules;
- **constructive dismissal** for employer's repudiatory (i.e. fundamental) breach of the contract of employment.

Criminal law

This involves the prosecution of an employer (usually by the Health and Safety Executive) for breaches of health and safety standards. If successful, this might result in a fine or, in exceptional cases, imprisonment. In addition, there is the possibility of prosecution by the Crown Prosecution Service for corporate homicide or manslaughter.

In varying ways the law covers employees as well as employers and individual managers. It also covers contractors and suppliers. It draws on the **common law** of contract, **statute law** and regulations approved by Parliament and, in part, provisions deriving from European Directives.

One way of illustrating the potential diversity of law involved in health and safety is to take a simple, yet serious, workplace accident and consider the legal consequences that might result (see Exhibit 12.2).

Exhibit 12.2 The unguarded machine

The incident: a machine operator loses a finger on an unguarded machine.

1 ***Tort of negligence***. Under civil law, the employer appears to have neglected to meet the common law **duty** to take reasonable care of the employee. So, it is possible for the employee to sue the employer (for damages) for this *negligence* in the county court. However, in his defence, the employer might be able to say that the employee contributed to the injury by deliberately removing the guard – in breach of workplace rules. The court would need to decide, on the facts, whether or not there was *contributory negligence*. If this is established, then any damages awarded could be reduced by up to 100 per cent – depending on the extent to which it was decided that the employee did contribute to his/her injury.

2 ***Disciplinary action***. The employer might feel that if the employee broke workplace rules, then disciplinary action should be taken against him/her. Obviously, the disciplinary procedure would need to be followed fully (in accordance with the ACAS *Code on Disciplinary and Grievance Procedures* 2009). The outcome of the disciplinary process could include *a warning or even dismissal*. If the employee was dismissed, depending on the circumstances, s/he might claim unfair dismissal before an employment tribunal. The employee's success would depend on the facts and circumstances of the case (see Chapter 8).

3 ***Constructive dismissal***. Under civil law, one further additional course of action is possible. The injury sustained by the employee might be entirely the fault of the employer. Furthermore, it might be the latest in a series of injuries that the employee has sustained in this employer's employment. Clearly, the employer is failing to comply with the implied contractual duty to take reasonable care of the employee. In these circumstances, the employee could view the employer's behaviour as a *fundamental breach of the contract of employment*. An employee can accept the employer's repudiation of the contract and resign. Depending on the circumstances, the employee could claim unfair constructive dismissal before an employment tribunal (see Chapter 8).

4 ***Prosecution***. Criminal law might also be used. This would involve the prosecution of the employer, *not* by the employee, but by the Health and Safety Executive. This prosecution would be brought under the Health and Safety at Work etc. Act 1974 in either the magistrates' court or the Crown Court (depending on the seriousness of the accident). Given that physical injury was sustained in an accident, criminal proceedings are probable. Evidence in such criminal proceedings would be the employer's failure to provide a safe system of work (including the way health and safety was managed) under the HASAWA 1974, and under regulations relating to the guarding of machinery that were not complied with. The most likely outcome would be a fine – although, in very serious cases, imprisonment is possible. A successful prosecution could help an individual's subsequent claim for compensation for the injury and also for proving a repudiatory breach of the contract of employment.

The range of legal action briefly outlined here is now discussed in more detail under the following headings: the common law, statute law, rights of employees, and **consultation** and representation.

Common law

There are two aspects of the common law relevant to health and safety at work: the tort (i.e. a civil wrong) of negligence, and the implied contractual duty of care owed by an employer to an employee.

Tort of negligence

An employer is under a duty to take reasonable care of the health and safety of each individual employee at work. Effectively, this comprises the provision of a safe place of work, safe plant and equipment, and competent and safe fellow employees. What is regarded as 'reasonable' will depend on such matters as the scale of the risk; whether risk of harm is, from the facts available to the employer, reasonably foreseeable; the seriousness of the consequences for the employee if the risk was not dealt with and the employee was injured; and the cost and practicality of preventing the risk.

An employer will, then, breach this duty if he fails to prevent reasonably foreseeable risks. A breach of this duty (i.e. the employer's neglect) usually provides the basis of personal injury claims. In this context both physical and/or mental health issues are relevant. So, if an employee suffers from a recognised psychiatric illness or condition and it can be proved on the balance of probabilities (the relevant **standard of proof** in civil matters) that the illness was caused by the respondent employer's breach of duty, then that employer is liable. One illustration of some of the issues relating to employer negligence and personal injury claims is seen in the *Walker* case (Exhibit 12.3).

Exhibit 12.3 The *Walker* case

Walker v *Northumberland County Council* [1995] IRLR 35, HC

This well-publicised early case relating to work-related stress involved a social services officer who alleged a failure by his employer to deal with excessive workload. Mr Walker said that his employer failed in a number of respects. First, the county council had not responded to his requests to restructure the department to provide more field officers to deal with increasing case work (particularly in respect of child abuse cases). Secondly, after he had suffered a nervous breakdown and subsequently returned to work, promises of assistance from a seconded member of staff and weekly visits by his boss were not delivered upon. Thirdly, during his four-month absence, a substantial volume of paperwork had built up. Fourthly, the number of pending childcare cases continued to grow at a considerable rate. Ultimately, within a few months he had a second nervous breakdown and was dismissed by the council on grounds of permanent ill health. He claimed damages against the council for breach of its common law duty of care in failing to take reasonable steps to avoid exposing him to a workload that endangered his health.

He was successful at the High Court (and the matter was *not* taken on appeal to the Court of Appeal). The duty of care owed to Mr Walker was ruled as encompassing the prevention of foreseeable psychiatric illness. An out-of-court settlement of £175,000 was agreed in 1996. (More detail on the current law on work-related stress is considered later in this chapter.)

Negligence claims are usually made in respect of one employer where there is strict liability. The personal injury arises from the negligence of that employer. However, it is important to note that, in certain cases, harm to health, arising from negligence, may not easily be attributed to one employer. The House of Lords ruled on this issue in the circumstances of **workers** suffering from mesothelioma. They had contracted this condition in the course of their employment with a number of employers as a result of exposure to asbestos dust. In 2002, the House of Lords made a **landmark judgment** in respect of tortious liability. It ruled on a test case (*Fairchild* v *Glenhaven Funeral Services Ltd and Others* [2002] IRLR 533) and several related cases which concerned liability for mesothelioma. Previously, the Court of Appeal had held that where a claimant suffered or might suffer mesothelioma as a result of exposure in the course of employment with more than one employer to asbestos dust, then s/he could *not* recover damages from any of the employers. This was because it could not be established, on the balance of probabilities, when the claimant inhaled the fibre which led to the development of mesothelioma. However, the House of Lords overturned this ruling. The defendant employers should be regarded as jointly and severally liable to the wrong.

Repudiatory breach of contract

A second aspect of common law relevant to health and safety issues concerns the implied contractual term: the employer's duty of care to the individual employee. Failure to meet this duty may be a **repudiatory breach of the contract**. If the employee accepts the breach, s/he can resign and claim unfair constructive dismissal at an employment tribunal. Alternatively, s/he might remain in employment but seek remedies in either the High Court or the county court. These remedies may include a declaration of contractual rights, damages, and an **injunction** which could prevent an anticipatory breach of contract.

Liability and vicarious liability

The issue of liability for breach of health and safety law covers both common law, and the duties under statute law (which are outlined in more detail below in Exhibit 12.6).

Common law

As we have seen, an employer is liable under this for breaches of duty (i.e. the tort of negligence) which are 'in the course of employment'. The issue of **vicarious liability** can also arise. This can occur, for example, where an employee injures a fellow worker or a customer or a contractor. The injured person may sue the employer for the injury because the employer is vicariously liable for the 'acts and omissions' of his employees. In practical terms, it is advantageous to the injured person because of the significantly better financial and insurance position of the employing organisation. It also acknowledges the employer's ultimate responsibility for the organisation of the work in question and for the deployment and training of staff.

A point of uncertainty that can arise in such cases is the meaning of 'in the course of employment'. Among the issues under health and safety law are:

- whether or not the employee is carrying out tasks wrongly;
- whether the work was performed by the employee negligently;
- whether the acts are outside working hours;

- whether the employee was travelling to or from work;
- whether the employee behaved violently (e,g. towards a customer or fellow worker).

Clearly, courts will need to consider the facts and circumstances of each case to establish liability.

An employer's defences

In such common law claims an employer might have defences available to him. There are two principal ones that may be possible: '*volenti not fit injuria*' and contributory negligence.

Volenti non fit injuria

Translated from Latin, this means 'no wrong is done to one who consents'. For this defence to be effective in health and safety matters, the employer would need to establish that the employee not only knew of the risk and continued working but also consented freely to work. This might be difficult for the employer to prove because the employee might have been ordered to work or, alternatively, the employee needed to work in such a way to carry out his duties. The view of academic lawyers is that *volenti* 'rarely succeeds' in industrial injury and employment cases (Smith and Thomas 2000: 734).

As to liability for breaches of statutory duty, 'the position is even clearer, for it has been held that *volenti* does not apply at all to an action for breach of a statutory duty laid upon the employer by the relevant legislation' (Smith and Thomas 2000: 735). The authors added: 'the principal reason being that it would be contrary to public policy to allow an employee by agreement or consent to "contract out" of his statutory protection'.

Contributory negligence

Contributory negligence can arise when an employee disobeys a safety instruction given by the employer or is reckless and, consequently, sustains an injury. This does apply to all cases involving breaches of both statutory duties as well as common law actions. (An employee's statutory duties are set out below.)

Statute law

In this section, the primary legislation (the Health and Safety at Work etc. Act 1974) and secondary legislation (principally, the Management of Health and Safety at Work Regulations 1999) are considered. Reference is also made to the relevance of other Regulations. In addition, the Corporate Manslaughter and Corporate Homicide Act 2007 is discussed.

Health and Safety at Work etc. Act 1974

Following the recommendations of the Robens Report (Robens 1972), a broad political consensus resulted in the enactment of the Health and Safety at Work etc. Act 1974. This had a number of purposes (both explicit and implicit):

- to extend the coverage of health and safety protection to a wider range of working people;
- to rationalise existing health and safety law;
- to impose general duties upon all employers;
- to permit some flexibility in implementation by qualifying the duties with the phrase 'as far as is reasonably practicable';

- to encourage self-regulation by employers and workforce representatives;
- to ensure that relevant information is available to employers and employees;
- to provide clear enforcement procedures and specific enforcement agencies (the Health and Safety Executive and, as appropriate, local authorities);
- to establish a tripartite body, the Health and Safety Commission, comprising employers, unions and certain independent people, to review and advise the Secretary of State on health and safety policy. (The HSC was abolished in 2008, making a reconstituted Health and Safety Executive the principal body for overseeing and enforcing health and safety legislation.)

The key provisions of this Act are outlined below.

Who is covered?

It covers all employers and every aspect of work. It brought into legal protection some seven million additional working people. The Act applies to the Crown (s 48). It covers an employer's responsibilities to contractors and to the general public. Domestic servants in a private household are exempt (s 51).

What is the nature of the Act?

It is described as enabling legislation. To promote health and safety standards in the workplace, regulations can be proposed to Parliament, under the authority of the Act. The Act sets general duties. Regulations, made under the Act, are more precise, setting detailed prescriptions. Examples of these regulations are the Control of Noise at Work Regulations 2005; Health and Safety (Display Screen Equipment) Regulations 1992; the Management of Health and Safety Regulations 1999. Regulations can cover the procedures to be adopted in the management of health and safety as well as the standards of safety practice in the workplace.

What are the general duties?

These are placed on employers, employees, self-employed persons and on designers, manufacturers, importers and suppliers.

Employers

The Act states that 'it shall be the duty of every employer to ensure, so far as is reasonably practicable, the health, safety and welfare at work of all his employees' (HASAWA 1974, s 2(1)). Several comments can be made about this basic duty.

- First, it is qualified by the phrase 'as far as is reasonably practicable'. Invariably, there can be a balance to be struck between risk reduction/minimisation and the cost, time and trouble involved.

- Secondly, it is important to remember that the duty relates to welfare, as well as health and safety. This is an all-encompassing duty and should result in appropriate employer policies.

- Thirdly, this duty is extended to other particular matters. These cover:
  - the provision and maintenance of plant and systems of work that are, so far as is reasonably practicable, safe and without risks to health;
  - arrangements for ensuring, so far as is reasonably practicable, safety and absence of risks to health in connection with the use, handling, storage and transport of articles and substances;

- the provision of such information, instruction, training and supervision as is necessary to ensure, so far as is reasonably practicable, the health and safety at work of his employees;
- so far as is reasonably practicable as regards any place of work under the employer's control, the maintenance of it in a condition that is safe and without risks to health and the provision and maintenance of means of access to and egress from it that are safe and without such risks;
- the provision and maintenance of a working environment for his employees that is, so far as is reasonably practicable, safe, without risks to health, and adequate as regards facilities and arrangements for their welfare at work (HASAWA 1974, s 2(2)).

An employer, in aiming to comply with health and safety duties, may not impose any levy upon an employee (s 9).

Employer's duties towards employees are, also, extended to cover responsibilities to non-employees. 'It shall be the duty of every employer to conduct his undertaking in such a way as to ensure, so far as is reasonably practicable, that persons not in his employment who may be affected thereby are not thereby exposed to risks to their health or safety' (s 3(1)). A parallel duty is imposed upon self-employed persons towards non-employees (s 3(2)). Furthermore, there are general duties placed upon 'persons concerned with premises to persons other than their employees' (s 4).

In interpreting this duty (s 3), the Court of Appeal (*R* v *Board of Trustees of the Science Museum* [1993] 3 All ER 853) adopted a **purposive** approach and emphasised the 'risk' of harm as opposed to evidence that actual harm had been sustained. This approach differs from the common law approach which requires evidence of actual harm for **damages** to be awarded.

Duty to promote self-regulation. These general duties on employers, outlined above, are supplemented by further ones, designed to promote self-regulation.

- First, '. . . it shall be the duty of every employer to prepare and as often as may be appropriate revise a written statement of his ***general policy*** with respect of the health and safety at work of his employees and the organisation and arrangements for the time being in force for carrying out that policy, and to bring the statement and any revision of it to the notice of all his employees' (s 2(3)). (Those employing fewer than five employees are exempt from this requirement.) (See Exhibit 12.9.)
- Secondly, there are provisions on ***safety representatives*** and on the establishment of a ***safety committee*** (s 2(4–7)). These roles and functions are discussed in more detail below. They are created within the context of the following general duty on an employer 'to consult any such representatives with a view to the making and maintenance of arrangements which will enable him and his employees to co-operate effectively in promoting and developing measures to ensure the health and safety at work of employees and in checking the effectiveness of such measures' (s 2(6)).
- Thirdly, as we shall see later in this chapter, there are supplementary duties arising from the Management of Health and Safety at Work Regulations 1999, particularly in respect of risk assessment, health surveillance of employees, and the protection of pregnant and young workers.

Employees and others

These general duties on employees do not absolve the employer from the primary responsibility for health and safety at work. The duty on employees states that 'it shall be the duty of every employee while at work (a) to take reasonable care for the health and safety of himself and other persons who may be affected by his acts or omissions at work; and (b) as regards any duty or requirement imposed on his employer or any other person by or under any of the relevant statutory provisions, to co-operate with him so far as is necessary to enable that duty or requirement to be performed or complied with' (s 7).

These duties on employees are supplemented by those in the Management of Health and Safety at Work Regulations 1999 (reg 14). An employee must 'use any machinery, equipment, dangerous substance, transport equipment, means of production or safety device provided to him by the employer in accordance both with any training . . . and instructions . . .' (reg 14). Additionally, an employee must inform the employer of situations which s/he reasonably believes 'represented a serious and immediate danger to health and safety', or of shortcomings in the employer's arrangements for health and safety protection.

An ancillary duty affects a wide range of people (including employees): 'No person shall intentionally or recklessly interfere with or misuse anything provided in the interests of health, safety, or welfare in pursuance of any of the relevant statutory provisions' (s 8).

Finally, in respect of general duties, designers, manufacturers, importers and suppliers of 'any article for use at work' must, as far as is reasonably practicable, ensure that the article is designed and constructed so as to be safe when properly used; must carry out testing and examination; must ensure that information is available about the article, its testing and its use; must carry out research to minimise any risks; and must ensure safe installation (s 6).

What is the role of regulations?

As stated earlier, the HASAWA 1974 was constructed as legislation to be supplemented by specific regulations (s 15). Regulations that have been prepared and approved over the past 35 years fall into two broad categories:

- *Hazards.* These set standards for dealing with specific hazards at work (e.g. noise, manual handling operations, eye protection).
- *Procedures.* These set procedural requirements for all employers (e.g. relating to the management of health and safety and information disclosure, and to the role and functions of safety representatives).

The range of regulations is considerable (see **www.hse.gov.uk**). The relevance of regulations to particular employers, obviously, varies. Some regulations can be industry-specific. However, others are more widespread in their application because the incidence of certain workplace hazards (e.g. the use of visual display units) extends across many industries and sectors. The regulations relating to procedures are, also, generally of broad application. The most fundamentally important of these is the Management of Health and Safety at Work Regulations 1999. Its provisions are considered below. Other key regulations are briefly outlined in Exhibit 12.4.

The Management of Health and Safety at Work Regulations 1999

These implement requirements of the European Health and Safety Directive 1989. They apply to all employers in respect of his own employees and 'persons not in his employment arising out of or in connection with the conduct by him of his undertaking' (reg 3). (See in Exhibit 12.6 reference to the issue of liability in *R* v *Associated Octel Ltd* [1994] IRLR 540.) They set out ways in which risk and health and safety can be managed systematically. There are several key provisions.

Exhibit 12.4 Some other key regulations

Control of Noise at Work Regulations 2005. These cover workers and the self-employed in all industry sectors. They set duties on employers to prevent damage to or loss of workers' hearing; or causing the suffering of tinnitus. There are parallel duties for designers, manufacturers, importers and suppliers. Daily personal noise exposure levels for workers are specified and must be assessed. Employers must reduce unacceptable noise exposure levels as far as is reasonably practicable.

Health and Safety (Display Screen Equipment) Regulations 1992. These cover the users of such equipment and are considered in detail in the final section of this chapter dealing with employment policies and practices.

Manual Handling Operations Regulations 1992. As far as reasonably practicable, employers are to avoid manual handling operations (e.g. lifting, pushing, pulling, carrying or moving) and consider whether such operations are necessary or could be achieved in a different way, or be automated or mechanised. A suitable assessment of the operations should be carried in consultation with employees. Risk should be reduced to the lowest level practicable. Attention should be paid to workers who have been pregnant and those with health problems. Weight limits are specified.

Workplace (Health, Safety and Welfare) Regulations 1992. These cover a wide range of workplaces (but excluding extractive industries, construction sites and outdoors agricultural and forestry workplaces). There are provisions on e.g. workplace temperatures, rest facilities, lighting, ventilation, cleanliness, space, and workstations.

Provision and Use of Work Equipment Regulations 1992. They cover all workers, including those working off-shore and the self-employed. Employers' duty is to ensure the suitability of work equipment for its purpose (by design, construction or adaptation). They must take account of likely risks (e.g. a wet or flammable atmosphere). Work equipment must be effectively maintained. All persons who use or supervise the use of work equipment must have received adequate information and health and safety training.

Personal Protective Equipment at Work Regulations. They cover workers and the self-employed. Employers must provide suitable, properly maintained personal protective equipment for workers who may be exposed to health and safety risks.

Control of Substances Hazardous to Health Regulations (COSHH) 2002. These cover, among other matters, employers' duties, prohibitions relating to certain substances, risk assessment, the prevention and control of exposure to substances hazardous to health, and monitoring exposure and health surveillance.

Reporting of Injuries, Diseases and Dangerous Occurrences Regulations (RIDDOR) 1995. They specify notification procedures (to the Health and Safety Executive or the local authority, as appropriate) for injuries, dangerous occurrences, work-related diseases (such as arsenic or lead poisoning) and for deaths of employees; and stipulate records to be kept by employers.

Risk assessment

General

The first step must be to make 'suitable and sufficient assessment' of risks in the workplace (reg 3). The assessment must look at the way work is actually done (which may sometimes be different from the way the employer expects it to be done). It must enable the employer to identify and prioritise significant risks and decide on appropriate action. Appropriate action can involve a number of considerations:

- whether the risk can be eliminated completely – for example, by not using a specific substance or by redesigning the way in which work is carried out;
- whether the hazard can be tackled at source – for example, isolating noisy machinery in an acoustic booth rather than providing ear protection;

- whether work should be adapted to the individual worker and not the other way – so avoiding monotonous work and work at a predetermined rate;
- making sure that all workers (including part-timers, temporary staff and trainees) are informed in 'comprehensible' form (reg 10) of safety standards and expectations about how work is to be carried out.

'Avoidance of risk' does not require the elimination of all possible risk to the employee but merely the reduction of risk to the lowest acceptable level (*New Southern Railway Ltd* v *Quinn* [2006] IRLR 266).

Pregnant and breast-feeding workers

Particular attention must be paid to the risks to which this group are exposed (regs 16 and 17). These can include physical hazards (such as noise, vibration, radiation, physical effort, etc.), and biological and chemical hazards. The employer should undertake a series of steps:

- An assessment of the risks and a consideration of any protective measures that would avoid it.
- If the risk cannot be avoided, then the employer should consider altering the woman's working conditions or hours of work.
- If such alteration is unreasonable or would not avoid the risk and there is no suitable work available, then the last resort is suspension on full pay for as long as necessary to protect the health and safety of both the employee and her child.

Young people

Furthermore, the employer must assess particular risks for young people, taking into account their inexperience, lack of awareness of potential risks and immaturity. Where the risks cannot be adequately controlled, young people should not be employed for that work (e.g. where the work is beyond their physical or psychological capacity, or work which involves exposure to harmful agents or radiation; or presents a risk to health from extreme cold or heat, noise or vibration). If children under the minimum school-leaving age are employed, then parents must be given details of the risk assessment and control measures (reg 19).

Health and safety arrangements

These follow from risk assessment and require effective planning, organisation, control of health and safety, review; and should also include health surveillance arrangements (reg 5).

Health surveillance

Where appropriate, the regulations require the employer to provide 'such health surveillance as is appropriate' of their workforce (reg 6). Central to this is monitoring. This can be carried out on various levels. For example, supervisors could be trained to check people's hands if they work with a substance which can cause skin rashes; whereas occupational health staff could undertake specific medical tests and examinations.

Competent persons

One or more such persons shall be appointed by an employer 'to assist him in undertaking the measures he needs to take to comply with the requirements and prohibitions imposed upon him by or under the relevant statutory provisions' (reg 7). Such a person must have sufficient training and experience or knowledge and other qualities to enable the function to be carried out. The person appointed must have:

- a good understanding of the principles of risk assessment and prevention;
- a knowledge of the employer's business and the work carried out by employees;
- awareness of the limitations of their own ability and when other expertise may be required.

Serious or imminent danger

Employers must plan in advance for foreseeable emergencies such as fire, a bomb scare, the release of toxic fumes, etc. Arrangements may involve a full evacuation of the work premises. In such an event, there should be sufficient trained designated people to supervise the evacuation. Staff who are required to enter a hazardous area (e.g. to close down a process) should be specially trained (reg 8).

Activity 12.1 Assessing risks

In small groups, discuss the working conditions of any number of the following and decide on the risks that you think that staff might encounter; and on the steps that the employer might and should take to deal with them:

- call-centre worker;
- bus driver;
- nurse in a hospital's accident and emergency department;
- social worker;
- school teacher;
- traffic warden;
- solicitor;
- prison officer;
- pharmacist in a retail chemist shop.

For guidance on risk assessment, see *Five Steps to Risk Assessment*, available from **www.hse.gov.uk**.

What is the machinery for enforcing health and safety?

Two levels are provided for in the legislation:

- *Workplace*: safety representatives and safety committees in combination with the relevant employer.
- *Public authority level*: the Health and Safety Executive, which manages Health and Safety Inspectors (HSIs).

Workplace level consultation and representation

Workforce representation (through the establishment of safety representatives and safety committees) was seen from the origin of the legislation as central to a 'self-regulation' model for implementing effective health and safety standards. However, in the period between the mid-1970s and 1996, Britain had a flawed system of representation. The 1977 Safety Representatives and Safety Committees Regulations were restricted to union-recognised health and safety representatives.

As unionisation diminished during the 1980s and 1990s, employees in the rapidly expanding non-union sector were without any legally enforceable rights of representation. This was clearly at variance with the 1989 Directive on Safety and Health. Article 11 outlined the responsibilities of 'workers' representatives' – with no distinction between unionised and non-unionised organisations. So, in 1996, the Health and Safety (Consultation with Employees) Regulations were approved by Parliament. These complement the 1977 regulations. Together they create a general framework of representation rights. There are several issues in this legal framework that we will consider:

- safety representation;
- the functions of safety representatives;
- information disclosure;
- protections against **detriments**;
- remedies and redress for detriments and dismissal.

Safety representation

Under the *1977 regulations*, a **recognised independent trade union** may appoint safety representatives from among the employees 'in all cases where one or more employees are employed by an employer by whom it is recognised' (reg 3.1). The person 'so far as is reasonably practicable' shall 'either have been employed by his employer throughout the preceding two years or have had at least two years' experience in similar employment' (reg 3.4). The *1996 regulations* merely describe 'representatives of employee safety'. Such a person will have been elected from a group of employees 'to represent that group – the purposes of . . . consultation' (reg 4.1b).

A safety committee should be established by an employer 'having the function of keeping under review the measures taken to ensure the health and safety at work of his employees and such other functions as may be prescribed' (HASAWA, s 2(7)). Under the accompanying *1977 regulations*, two union-recognised safety representatives are needed to request a committee (reg 9). The *1996 regulations* have no parallel provision. Under these, consultation can be directly with the workforce, with one representative or with more than one representative (reg 4). The creation of a safety committee is subject to management discretion.

The functions of union safety representatives

1977 regulations: in unionised workforces, the functions are:

- to represent employees in consultation with the employer (reg 4);
- to investigate potential hazards and dangerous occurrences at the workplace and examine the causes of accidents at the workplace;
- to investigate health and safety complaints made by any employee s/he represents;
- to make representations to the employer on general matters arising out of investigations;
- to make representations to the employer on general matters affecting the health, safety or welfare of the employees at the workplace;
- to carry out inspections in a number of circumstances (regs 5, 6 and 7) (e.g. where there has been no inspection for the past three months; where there has been 'a substantial change in the conditions of work'; where there has been 'a notifiable accident or dangerous occurrence in a workplace or a notifiable disease has been contracted'; where the employer has 'any document relevant to the workplace and to the employees');
- to represent the employees in consultation at the workplace with Health and Safety Inspectors and any other enforcing authority;
- to attend meetings of safety committees in connection with any of these functions.

1996 regulations: in non-union workforces, the functions are:

- to make representations to the employer on potential hazards and dangerous occurrences at the workplace which affect, or could affect, employees (reg 6);

- to make representations to the employer on general matters affecting the health and safety at work of the employees and, in particular, on such matters consulted about with the employer (see reg 3 below);
- to represent the employees in consultation at the workplace with inspectors.

These functions are exercised in the context of 'the duty of the employer to consult' provisions (reg 3). The employer 'shall consult in good time' (with either the workforce directly or with representatives) particularly regarding:

- the introduction of any measure at the workplace which may substantially affect the health and safety of those employees;
- arrangements for nominating 'competent persons' (under the MHSW Regulations, reg 7);
- any health and safety information he is required to provide to those employees by or under the relevant statutory provisions;
- the planning and organisation of any health and safety training he is required to provide to those employees by or under the relevant statutory provisions;
- the health and safety consequences for employees of the introduction (including planning) of new technologies into the workplace.

The *1996 regulations* are silent about inspections – though they could be implied from some of the above provisions.

Disclosure of information

Obviously, consultation and representation can only be effective if information is adequate. The *1977 regulations* for union safety representatives specify:

- ***Inspection.*** 'Safety representatives shall for the performance of their functions . . . if they have given the employer reasonable notice, be entitled to inspect and take copies of any document relevant to the workplace or the employees the safety representatives represent which the employer is required to keep . . . except a document consisting of or relating to any health record of an identifiable individual' (reg 7.1).
- ***Information.*** An employer shall make available to safety representatives the information, within the employer's knowledge, necessary to enable him to fulfil his functions except information which 'would be against the interests of national security'; the disclosure of which would infringe some statutory provision; information which relates to an individual (unless he has consented to disclosure); or information which would, if disclosed, cause 'substantial injury to the employer's undertaking'; or 'any information obtained by the employer for the purpose of bringing, prosecuting or defending any legal proceedings' (reg 7.2).

The *1996 regulations* provide a general duty to provide information (reg 5) to either employees directly or with their representatives 'as is necessary to enable them to participate fully and effectively in the consultation' and for representatives 'in the carrying out of their functions under these Regulations'. The exceptions set out in the 1977 regulations (reg 7.2) are restated.

This information disclosure is in the context of the general duty on the employer 'to provide such information . . . as is necessary to ensure, as far as is reasonably practicable, the health and safety at work of his employees' (HASAWA, s 2(2)(c)).

Protection against 'detriments' and unfair dismissal

Certain protections are enacted to help ensure the credibility and independence from undue employer influence on workforce safety representatives. These are outlined below in relation to the general protections for employees and specific postholders.

There are statutory protections 'from suffering detriments in employment' (Employment Rights Act 1996, s 44); and parallel protection against unfair dismissal (s 100). 'Detriment' is construed as putting a person at a disadvantage. It includes disciplinary warnings and dismissal, temporary transfers to other work and suspensions from work, refusals to grant a pay rise or allocate overtime to an employee, and overlooking an employee for promotion. In this context it is stated that 'an employee has the right not to be subjected to any detriment by any act, or any deliberate failure to act, by his employer done on the ground that' s/he exercised certain statutory rights (ERA 1996, s 44(1)) (see also Chapter 8).

There are five circumstances covered by protection:

1 ***'Competent persons'*** (appointed under MHSW Regulations 1999): who 'having been designated by the employer to carry out activities in connection with preventing or reducing risks to health and safety at work,' this employee 'carried out (or proposed to carry out) any such activities' (ERA 1996, s 44(1)(a)).

2 ***Safety representatives or safety committee members***: where an employee performed or proposed to perform the functions of this role.

3 ***Election of safety representatives***: where an employee took part or proposed to take part in consultation with the employer or in an election of safety representatives (Health and Safety (Consultation with Employees) Regulations 1996).

4 ***Informing the employer of hazards***: where 'being an employee at a place where (i) there was no such representative or safety committee, or (ii) there was such a representative or safety committee but it was not reasonably practicable for the employee to raise the matter by those means, he brought to his employer's attention, by reasonable means, circumstances connected with his work which he reasonably believed were harmful or potentially harmful to health or safety' (ERA 1996, s 44(1)(c)).

   It is expected that the employee would raise his/her complaint through the organisation's grievance procedure. This would be regarded as 'reasonable means' – whereas a direct complaint, in the first instance, to a director or an external body, like the HSE, would not be. Furthermore, the employee must show 'reasonable belief'. In an unfair dismissal case, the EAT provided the following guidance (*Kerr* v *Nathan's Wastesavers Ltd* EAT 91/95). An employee must show:

   - belief that, in fact, the circumstances were harmful, or potentially harmful, to health and safety;
   - that s/he had in mind reasonable grounds to sustain that belief;
   - that those grounds were based on all the relevant circumstances of the case.

5 ***Serious and imminent risk***: this relates to leaving the workplace where there is such a risk – which may be a one-off incident or an on-going situation. Protection against detriment relates to 'circumstances of danger which the employee reasonably believed to be serious and imminent and which he could not reasonably have been expected to avert, he left (or proposed to leave) or (while the danger persisted) refused to return to his place of work or any dangerous part of his place of work' (s 44(1)(d)). Such protection also concerns

Exhibit 12.5 The van driver

Rawlings v *Barraclough t/a Independent Delivery Services Ltd* 2.5.95, COIT, 15595/95

A van driver refused to drive what he said was a defective vehicle and was dismissed. His employer had assured him that the vehicle was in a safe condition. Although he had obtained no expert evidence, it was provided before the tribunal where it was stated that the vehicle would have failed its MOT test and would have been ruled as unroadworthy. The tribunal commented that the assurance about the vehicle's safety given by the company was 'so informal and so undetailed that [he] was still entitled to hold his belief notwithstanding the fact that others had driven the van in the meantime'. The dismissal was ruled to be unfair.

'circumstances of danger which the employee reasonably believed to be serious and imminent' where 'he took (or proposed to take) appropriate steps to protect himself or other persons from the danger' (s 44(1)(e)).

The issue of 'reasonable belief', arises. One aspect of this is the extent to which 'objective' evidence is required for the employee to sustain his 'subjective' belief that there is a 'serious and imminent danger'. It appears that there is no absolute obligation upon the employee to acquire such evidence – although, clearly, it can help (see Exhibit 12.5).

The question of whether the steps which the employee 'took or proposed to take were appropriate is to be judged by reference to all the circumstances including, in particular, his knowledge and the facilities and advice available to him at the time' (ERA 1996, s 44(2)). Furthermore, if an employer can show that what the employee did was 'so negligent' that 'a reasonable employer' would have taken action against such an employee, then 'an employee is not to be regarded as having been subjected to a detriment' (ERA 1996, s 44(3)). To this extent, an employer has a defence.

Remedies and redress for detriments and dismissal

- *Complaints to an employment tribunal.* An employee who believes that s/he has suffered such a detriment may complain to an employment tribunal. There are no qualifying conditions. The rights cover all 'employees' irrespective of age, hours of work or length of service. The complaint must be lodged within three months of the unfair dismissal or the detrimental treatment complained of. The tribunal has discretion to extend this three-month period both in respect of allegations of unfair dismissal and other detrimental treatment. Where a detrimental act continues over a period, the date of the act means the last day of that period.
- *Detriments short of dismissal.* If an employee successfully complains of this detrimental treatment, then the employment tribunal must make a declaration to that effect and may award the employee compensation (which is unlimited) which it regards as 'just and equitable' in all the circumstances. This will involve consideration of any loss sustained by the employee and any injury to feelings. The employee has a duty to mitigate his/her loss. The compensation might be reduced because of the behaviour of the employee in contributing to the circumstances.
- *Dismissal.* If the detrimental treatment is dismissal and the claim is successful, then, an ex-employee may be awarded compensation or an order for re-engagement or reinstatement can be made. The basic and compensatory awards are calculated in the normal way.

- *Dismissal of safety representatives.* If the person is dismissed for undertaking his/her duties as a safety representative, member of a safety committee or as a 'designated employee', then additional remedies are available. The first is interim relief (ERA 1996, s 128). A claim for this must be made to the employment tribunal within seven days immediately following the effective date of termination of employment. If it appears to the tribunal that the employee is 'likely' (ERA 1996, s 129(1)) to establish that the reason for the dismissal is one prohibited under s 100, and the employer is willing, then, it may order the reinstatement or re-engagement of the employee pending the final determination of the case at a hearing or settlement (e.g. through ACAS **conciliation**). Re-engagement means re-employment on terms that are 'not less favourable' than those that would have applied had the employee not been dismissed (ERA 1996, s 129(3)(b)). The employee may 'reasonably' refuse re-engagement (ERA 1996, s 128(8)(a)).

  If no agreement is reached on reinstatement or re-engagement, the tribunal must make an order for the continuation of the contract of employment from the date of termination until the date of determination or settlement of the complaint. Unreasonable refusal of re-engagement by an employee will result in the tribunal making no order to continue the contract of employment (ERA 1996, s 129(8)(b)). An order to continue the contract of employment is 'an order that the contract of employment continue in force . . . for the purposes of pay and any other benefit derived from employment, seniority, pension rights and other similar matters' and for the purposes of determining the employee's continuity of employment (ERA 1996, s 130(1)).

Health and Safety Executive and inspectors

What are the roles of the HSE?

In terms of the day-to-day management of health and safety at work, the statutory roles of health and safety inspectors are significant (HASAWA 1974, s 20). These are:

Entering premises

- at any reasonable time (or in a situation which in his opinion is or may be dangerous, at any time) to enter any premises which he has reason to believe it is necessary for him to enter . . . ;
- to take with him a constable if he has reasonable cause to apprehend any serious obstruction in the execution of his duty;
- . . . to take with him any person duly authorised by his [the inspector's] enforcing authority; and any equipment or materials required . . .

Investigation

- to make such examination and investigation as may in any circumstances be necessary . . . ;
- as regards any premises which he has power to enter, to direct that those premises or any part of them, or anything therein, shall be left undisturbed . . . for as long as is reasonably necessary for the purpose of any examination or investigation . . . ;
- to take such measurements and photographs and make such recordings as he considers necessary . . . ;
- to take samples of any articles or substances found in any premises which he has power to enter, and of the atmosphere in or in the vicinity of any such premises . . .

Action on substances or equipment

- . . . [if] an article or substance . . . appears to him to have caused or to be likely to cause danger to health and safety, to cause it to be dismantled or subjected to any process or test . . . or . . . unless [it] is in the circumstances necessary [destroyed] . . . ;
- in the case of any [such] article or substance . . . to take possession of it and detain it for so long as is necessary for all or any of the following purposes, namely
  - to examine it . . . ;
  - to ensure that it is not tampered with before his examination of it is completed;
  - to ensure that it is available for use as evidence in any proceedings for an offence.

Obtaining information

- to require any person whom he has reasonable cause to believe to be able to give any information relevant to any examination or investigation . . . to answer (in the absence of persons other than a person nominated by him to be present and any persons whom the inspector may allow to be present) such questions as the inspector thinks fit to ask and to sign a declaration of the truth of his answers;
- to require the production of, inspect, and take copies of, or of any entry in, any books or documents . . .

Requiring assistance

- to require any person to afford him such facilities and assistance with respect to any matters or things within that person's control or in relation to which that person has responsibilities as are necessary to enable the inspector to exercise any of the powers conferred on him by this section.

(HASAWA 1974, s 20(2))

What are the powers of the HSE?

- ***Improvement notice*** (HASAWA 1974, s 21). This may be issued by an Inspector and requires a person (usually an employer) to remedy a contravention of statutory provisions within a specified time period (normally 21 days). Appeal is possible to an employment tribunal within 21 days and this suspends the notice (HASAWA 1974, s 24). During 2006/07, the HSE issued 5,092 of these (see **www.hse.gov.uk** for the latest statistics).
- ***Prohibition notice*** (HASAWA 1974, s 22). This is issued to prevent a person from carrying on activities where there is or may be a 'risk of serious personal injury'. Such a notice can have immediate effect. Again, appeal is possible to an employment tribunal. However, appeal does not rescind the notice. This can only be done by the tribunal after the hearing (HASAWA 1974, s 24). During 2006/07, the HSE issued 50 deferred prohibition notices and 2,957 immediate prohibition notices (see **www.hse.gov.uk** for the latest statistics).
- ***Prosecutions.*** Criminal proceedings may be initiated in the courts for offences under the relevant statutory provisions. An Inspector is authorised (HASAWA 1974, s 39) to prosecute in magistrates' courts in England and Wales. In all other proceedings, the consent of the Director of Public Prosecutions is required. Contrary to the usual rules in criminal proceedings, it is for the defendant to prove what was reasonably practicable. Specific provision on the onus of proof is set out in the Act (HASAWA 1974, s 40). From January

2009, the Health and Safety (Offences) Act 2008 is in force, increasing the penalties available to the courts. During 2006/07, the HSE initiated 1,141 prosecutions which resulted in 848 convictions. The average fine was £15,370 (see **www.hse.gov.uk** for the latest statistics). An appeal, in 2008, against conviction illustrates some of the issues involved in the incidence of risk and an organisation's duty (HASAWA 1974, s 3) to non-employees (*R* v *Porter* [2008] EWCA Crim 1271, CA). The Court of Appeal's quashing of a headteacher's conviction for accidental injuries sustained by a three-year old pupil on school property is to be appealed to the House of Lords by the Health and Safety Executive. (See Exhibit 12.6.)

Exhibit 12.6 Who is liable for infringements of statutory health and safety standards?

An employer is liable for complying with the general duties 'as far as is reasonably practicable' and for compliance with relevant statutory provisions (HASAWA 1974, ss 2–4).

Directors and managers. It is possible for these to be personally liable for offences. 'Where an offence under any of the relevant statutory provisions committed by a body corporate is proved to have been committed with the consent or connivance of, or to have been attributable to any neglect on the part of, any director, manager, secretary or other similar officer of the body corporate or a person who is purporting to act in any such capacity, he as well as the body corporate shall be guilty of that offence and shall be liable to be proceeded against and punished accordingly' (HASAWA 1974, s 37(1)).

Non-employees employed by independent contractors. The issue of liability in circumstances where an organisation employs contractors was clarified by the Court of Appeal (*R* v *Associated Octel Ltd* [1994] IRLR 540). Interpreting the duty under HASAWA 1974, s 3(1), it established the liability of an employer for injuries caused to non-employees who were employed by independent contractors – whether or not the employer had actual control over how the work was carried out. Liability is subject to the defence of 'as far as is reasonably practicable'.

In this case a contractor's employee was badly burned in a flash fire that resulted from an explosion. This occurred when a lamp (which was not a safety lamp) broke and ignited acetone vapour within the tank he was cleaning. The court found that the cleaning and maintenance of the chlorine tank did form part of Octel's 'undertaking' and that it was reasonably practicable for Octel to give the contractor instructions on carrying out the work and on the safety measures to be adopted. Each case, of course, would be considered on its own facts.

An employee. He or she is liable for failing to take reasonable care of his/her health and safety and that of other people, and for failing to co-operate with the employer in the implementation of health and safety standards (HASAWA 1974, s 7). In practice, it is unlikely that an employee would have criminal proceeding taken against him/her unless the safety breach was so serious and, perhaps, involved recklessness or deliberate misuse of equipment, etc. (HASAWA 1974, s 8). Usually, a breach of safety rules by an employee would be dealt with through the internal disciplinary procedure.

Safety representatives. They are not legally liable for carrying out their function or for not carrying out their function. In the Safety Representatives and Safety Committees Regulations 1977 (reg 4.1) it is made clear that 'no function given to a safety representative by this paragraph shall be construed as imposing any duty on him'. In guidance to the regulations, the HSE states that 'a safety representative by accepting, agreeing with or not objecting to a course of action taken by the employer to deal with a health or safety hazard, does not take upon himself any legal responsibility for that course of action'. Furthermore, it is stated that the former Health and Safety Commission directed that the HSE 'shall not institute criminal proceedings against any safety representative for any act or omission by him in respect of the performance of functions assigned to him by the Regulations . . .' (Guidance Note 11).

The Corporate Manslaughter and Corporate Homicide Act 2007

This legislation was implemented in April 2008. It fills a significant gap in health and safety protection for working people. Historically, corporate manslaughter cases rarely came before the courts. Criminal liability of employers for unlawful killing has been very difficult to establish. Prosecutors have had to prove beyond reasonable doubt – the criminal standard of proof – that the individuals responsible for the death were 'the directing mind and will' and had the necessary 'guilty mind' (***mens rea***). These individuals had to be personally liable. The first successful prosecution did not occur until 1994, involving OLL Ltd which ran an activity centre. Four young people, on a canoeing trip organised by the company, drowned in Lyme Bay, Dorset. The conviction of OLL Ltd was possible because it was a small organisation. It was clear that its managing director was the embodiment of the company. He was gaoled for three years for the manslaughter. Other cases involving the death of working people were much more problematic (see Exhibit 12.7).

As a consequence of public concern about the limitations of the law and political campaigning, the Corporate Manslaughter and Corporate Homicide Act 2007 was eventually enacted. This does not hinge on personal liability but on the liability of the organisation. This legislation is applicable across the United Kingdom. It is not retrospective. So, it will only apply to fatalities caused by gross management failings that occur after the Act came into force on 6 April 2008. The new offence, under the CMCHA 2007, is 'intended to complement, not

Exhibit 12.7 The case of Simon Jones

(www.simonjones.org.uk)

Simon Jones, 24, a student on casual work, started a labouring job for Euromin, a Dutch-owned firm, at Shoreham Docks, on 24 April 1998. It was provided through a Brighton employment agency, Personnel Selection. His job involved unloading cobblestones from a ship. He was given no training and was provided with no safety equipment. He worked in the hold of the ship hooking bags of cobbles onto chains. The chains had been welded into the crane's open grab. Within two hours of starting work, he was dead. His head was crushed and partially severed by a two-tonne crane grab, which had been brought too low over the hold and accidentally closed on his head.

The question of prosecution for manslaughter was considered by the Crown Prosecution Service (CPS). It took the view that there was 'no realistic prospect of a conviction'. However, in March 2000, the High Court ordered the CPS to reconsider. This was the first successful judicial review of a decision not to prosecute for manslaughter over a workplace death. In November 2001, the prosecution of Euromin and of the general manager opened at the Old Bailey.

It was alleged that the system of work was not safe. The principal defects were:

- the welding to the hook attached to the grab was dangerous and done for reasons of speed and economy;
- instructions in the cab, which stated that no one should be in the grab's area when it is operating, were ignored;
- the 'hatchman' responsible for communication between the crane operator and the hold was not experienced and was a Polish speaker with little knowledge of English.

On a majority verdict, the jury cleared the general manager of manslaughter. However, the company was found guilty of two breaches of health and safety regulations and fined £50,000 and ordered to pay £20,000 costs.

replace, other forms of accountability such as prosecutions under health and safety legislation and is specifically linked to existing health and safety requirements' (Ministry of Justice guidance, 2007). In the Ministry's view, the legislation will be 'reserved for the very worst cases of corporate mismanagement leading to death'.

Key provisions of the 2007 Act

- *Organisations covered.* All companies and other corporate bodies, operating in the UK, in the private, public and third sectors. So, it includes, for example, private companies operating in the UK whether foreign-owned or not, local authorities, NHS trusts, police services, Crown bodies and incorporated charities and voluntary organisations. Subcontractors may be liable where they owe a duty of care to the victim. The jurisdiction relates to harm resulting in death within the UK; in the UK's territorial waters; on a British ship, aircraft or hovercraft; on an oil rig or other offshore installation already covered by UK **criminal law**.
- *The offence.* An organisation will commit the new offence if the way in which its activities are managed or organised causes a death and this amounts to a gross breach of a duty of care owed to the deceased (i.e. gross negligence). Juries will consider how the fatal activity was managed or organised throughout the organisation, including any systems and processes for managing safety and how these were operated in practice. A substantial part of the failure within the organisation must have been at a senior level (i.e. those who make significant decisions about organisational policy and procedure). It should be noted that directors, senior managers or other individuals cannot be prosecuted under this Act. It is the organisation that faces criminal proceedings. Nevertheless, failures by senior managers to manage health and safety adequately will leave organisations vulnerable to corporate manslaughter/homicide charges. It is, however, important to note that existing law (HASWA 1974) allowing individuals to be prosecuted for health and safety offences still remains in force.
- *Duty of care.* The Act does not create new duties. These are already owed in the civil law of negligence. A gross breach of the duty of care arises where the organisation's conduct falls far below what could have been reasonably expected. A judge will decide whether or not a duty of care is owed.
- *Exemptions.* These mean that the offence will not apply to deaths that are connected with the management of particular activities (e.g. military combat operations; police operations dealing with terrorism and violent disorder). The legislation also lists partial exemptions.
- *Decision to prosecute.* Investigations into workplace deaths will be carried out by the police, in partnership with the Health and Safety Executive, or local authority or other regulatory authorities (e.g. the Office of Rail Regulation or the Food Standards Agency). In England and Wales and in Northern Ireland, the consent of the relevant Director of Public Prosecutions is needed before corporate manslaughter proceedings can be initiated in the courts by the Crown Prosecution Service. In Scotland, all decisions to prosecute are taken by the Procurator Fiscal. It is also important to note that other health and safety charges may be brought at the same time as a prosecution under the CMCHA 2007.

It will not be necessary for the management failure to have been the *sole* cause of death. The prosecution will, however, need to show that 'but for' the management failure, including the substantial element attributable to senior management, the death would not have occurred. Whilst the injury and the death may, usually, occur at the same time, it is recognised that death may occur sometime after the injury. This will not preclude a prosecution. Neither will a person's death abroad – if the injury was sustained in the UK.

Penalties

An organisation guilty of the offence will be liable to *an unlimited fine*. The court may impose *a publicity order*, requiring the organisation to publicise details of its conviction and fine. Courts may also require an organisation, through *a remedial order*, to take steps to address the failures behind the death.

The Fatal Accidents Act 1976

Although not considered part of the normal range of health and safety legislation, a House of Lords ruling on employer liability has created an important legal **precedent** (see Exhibit 12.8).

Exhibit 12.8 Employer's liability for suicide

Corr (Administratix of Estate of Thomas Corr (Deceased)) v *IBC Vehicles Ltd* [2008] UKHL 13

Facts. Mr Corr worked as maintenance engineer on presses producing car panels. In 1996 while he was mending a fault, an automated arm moved unexpectedly striking his head and severing his right ear. He underwent reconstructive surgery and thereafter lived with some disfigurement as well as severe headaches, persistent unsteadiness and sleeping difficulties. He also developed post-traumatic stress disorder – suffering flashbacks and nightmares. He was diagnosed with depressive illness that required hospital treatment. In 2002, during a particularly severe depressive episode, his feeling of hopelessness worsened to such an extent that he jumped to his death from a multi-storey car park. Prior to the accident he had been happily married with an equable temperament and no psychiatric problems.

Claims. Mr Corr's widow brought proceedings against the employer on behalf of her husband's estate (which was awarded by the High Court). She also brought a claim for damages under the Fatal Accidents Act 1976, which enables the executor or administrator of a person whose death was caused by a wrongful act to claim damages on behalf of the deceased's dependants. The High Court, on the second claim, took the view that although the employer had breached its duty to protect her husband from personal injury (including psychiatric injury) his suicide was not a 'reasonably foreseeable' consequence of the accident. The matter went on appeal to the Court of Appeal (which found in Mrs Corr's favour) and, then, on further appeal (by the employer) to the House of Lords.

House of Lords judgment. Lord Bingham's judgment, which reflected the majority legal opinion:

- *Duty of care*: Mr Corr's employer owed him a duty to take reasonable care to avoid causing him personal injury (physical or psychological).
- It was common ground that the employer had breached that duty, causing injury of both kinds.
- Although Mr Corr was not insane (under the legal definition), he was not fully responsible for committing suicide.
- He would not have acted as he had but for the injury that he had suffered at work.
- So, the act could not be said to fall outside the scope of the employer's duty of care.
- **Foreseeability**. A person who commits a tort, who reasonably foresees the some damage occurring, need not, to become liable, foresee the precise form of that damage.
- Suicide is not outside the bounds of what is reasonably foreseeable for those with severe depression.
- *Causation*. Mr Corr's decision to take his life was not a voluntary, informed decision taken by him as an adult of sound mind. It was the response of a man suffering from a severe depressive illness, caused by his employer's negligence, which impaired his ability to make reasoned judgements.
- *Contributory negligence*. Mr Corr had no causal responsibility for his death. This was assessed at zero per cent. (This was not a unanimous view.)

Employment policies and practices

> The promotion of safety and health at work is first and foremost a matter of efficient management. But it is not a management prerogative. In this context more than most, real progress is impossible without the full co-operation and commitment of all employees. How can this be encouraged? We believe that work people must be able to participate fully in the making and monitoring of arrangements for safety and health in their place of work. (Robens 1972: 18)

The Chartered Institute of Personnel and Development (1996) has elaborated the business case in these terms: 'effective management of the health and welfare of people at work: contributes to performance improvement and increases competitive advantage; reduces unacceptable losses associated with ill-health and injuries; and lowers absenteeism, improves morale and reduces litigation costs'.

A structured approach to health and safety management involves consideration of procedures and institutions; and also how an employer might tackle particular health and safety issues. The discussion below considers some general issues relating to safety management and looks at how some of the key risks and hazards at work might be handled.

Managing health and safety:
- the creation of a safety culture;
- the formulation and implementation of safety policies;
- the contribution of an occupational health service;
- the availability of an employee assistance programme.

Handling particular workplace risks:
- use of display screen equipment;
- work-related stress.

Managing health and safety

Creating a safety culture

A 'safety culture' within an organisation needs to demonstrate a high degree of safety consciousness throughout the organisation. Safety would be perceived as a dimension of most, if not all, activities. Safety standards would be integrated into work operations, job design, working-time scheduling and reward systems. Appropriate training would be given to managers and employees. There would be regular and genuine consultation – backed by information disclosure. Standards would be enforced through inspections and other monitoring.

So, in certain industries, such as nuclear power, coal mining, chemicals, some sectors of engineering, air transport and the railways, health and safety is regarded as a central management issue – not just operationally but also in the employee relations system. Two factors encourage this: the nature of the hazards that exist and the serious consequences that might follow from an accident, and, in many instances, the presence of strong workplace trade unionism. Policies are developed which are concerned with not merely minimising risks but also setting and implementing standards on an integrated manner – i.e. linked to work organisation, payment systems and staffing levels, etc.

However, in industry at large, several factors, already mentioned, limit the achievement of such a culture: management and workforce perceptions about the seriousness of risks within their workplace; the balance between risk minimisation or elimination, on the one hand, and the associated economic costs, on the other; the conflicts of interests and expectations between employees and their employer; and the contribution of the workforce consultation to the achievement of safety standards.

A safety policy

Employers (except those with fewer than five employees) are under a statutory duty (HASAWA 1974, s 2(3)) to prepare and update a written safety policy. This should outline the organisation and arrangements in force for implementing health and safety standards (see Exhibit 12.9). Employees should be informed about the policy. Guidance on the details of such policies has been issued by the Health and Safety Executive. In any prosecutions for breaches of health and safety regulations, the issue of whether or not an employer has adopted a safety policy can be used in evidence.

Occupational health service

An occupational health service (OHS) resourced by an employer is likely to have access to a wide range of occupational health practitioners including physicians, hygienists, psychologists, ergonomic experts and occupational health nurses. These may be employees or used on a consultancy basis. Such a service will help an employer comply with the duties under health and safety law. It may, indeed, extend beyond the legal obligations to pioneer standards of good practice. Obviously, an OHS is more likely to be provided by larger organisations. It is, however,

Exhibit 12.9 Recommended provisions of a safety policy

- ***Statement*** of the organisation's commitment to good health and safety practice, phrased in terms which emphasise not merely management efficiency, but also the human resource management objectives of valuing staff. It might also draw attention to commitments to reduce accidents, injuries and work-related sick absence, and to promote employee welfare. It could be linked to the organisation's overall mission statement (if one exists).
- Explanation of ***possible risks*** and ***preventative measures*** (including for dealing with emergencies).
- ***Outline of procedures*** for implementing, monitoring and reviewing health and safety standards. This can cover consultation with safety representatives; and also periodic formal in-company inspections and 'spot-checks'.
- Commitment to the provision and funding of ***appropriate training***, and an indication of how statutory obligations will be complied with.
- Commitment to ***dissemination of relevant information*** to employees and other interested people (i.e. contractors, customers, the public).
- Commitment to maintain ***adequate recording*** of risk assessments, accidents, injuries and dangerous occurrences.
- ***Statement of ultimate responsibility*** of chief executive and board of directors (or equivalent people) for compliance with legal standards.
- ***Statement of the responsibilities of managers and supervisors*** for implementation and monitoring of safety standards.
- Outline of roles of ***specialist and advisory functions*** (e.g. safety officers, occupational health staff, medical advisers and nurses).
- Indication of those who are designated as '***competent persons***', and of their role and function in implementing safety policy.
- Statement of functions of ***trade union*** or ***employee safety representatives***.
- Outline of the ***consultation arrangements*** with trade union or employee safety representatives.
- Procedure for employees to raise ***health and safety grievances*** and issues.
- Statement of the ***rights and responsibilities of individual employees***.

possible for smaller ones to subscribe to a group service, covering a number of employers. It is estimated that about half of employees are covered by an OHS. An OHS will have four broad, related functions concerning both the physical and psychological health of staff:

1 ***Prevention*** will cover pre-employment assessment of an individual's suitability for particular tasks by means of a pre-employment questionnaire and/or a medical examination. Also, it will be achieved by regular surveillance of particular risks and hazards associated with the workplace. This would involve periodic reviews of materials, processes and procedures; periodic health reviews of staff, and monitoring the effectiveness of personal protection measures. Finally, the OHS would be responsible for the training and supervision of first aiders.
2 ***Treatment*** would cover the medical treatment by OHS staff of minor illnesses and accidents.
3 ***Monitoring*** would encompass the monitoring and support of sick employees and pregnant workers; the recording of accidents, sickness and absence; compliance with the organisation's notification duties under the 1995 RIDDOR (Reporting of Injuries, Diseases and Dangerous Occurences) Regulations; and monitoring of work-related stress.
4 ***Health promotion*** could include the provision of counselling and treatment (e.g. in relation to stress, harassment, drug and alcohol abuse), guidance for an employer on redesigning the work environment, general feedback to improve work practices, referral to specialists for treatment and professional advice, and the promotion of health education programmes.

Employee assistance programmes and counselling

These programmes are an important aspect of the promotion of employee welfare. Given the duties in law placed upon an employer, counselling and assistance is essential. The EAP may be resourced by professionally qualified specialists employed by the company (as well as specially trained employees). They may also rely on the use of appropriately qualified external consultants. Some companies in the United Kingdom have established such programmes. In other instances they may use ad hoc counselling.

The role of EAPs has expanded over the years. Many work-related and non-work factors can, and do, have an impact upon an employee's attendance at work and his/her performance whilst there. These factors cover, for example, personal traumas like death within the immediate family; divorce; the diagnosis of a serious, possibly incurable, illness; harassment at work or within the family; or having to deal with a traumatic situation in the course of employment. The consequences, in terms of employee behaviour, can, for example, be evidence of post-traumatic stress, other stress symptoms, a too heavy reliance on alcohol, or drug abuse.

Handling particular workplace risks

Use of display screen equipment

The Health and Safety (Display Screen Equipment) Regulations 1992 implement the European Display Screen Equipment Directive. They cover most types of display screen equipment. Excepted pieces of equipment are, for example, screens in drivers' cabs and on other means of transport, portable systems not in prolonged use, cash registers, calculators or other equipment with a small data display. The European Court of Justice ruled that the term 'graphic display screen' in the directive must be interpreted to include screens that display film recordings in analogue or digital form. So the employer of a film cutter had to plan into her daily work breaks and changes in activity (*Dietrich* v *Westdeutscher Rundfunk* (2000) case C-11/99) (see Exhibit 12.10 and Exercises).

Exhibit 12.10 Provisions of the Display Screen Equipment Regulations 1992

The whole workstation is covered:

- the display screen equipment and software, including keyboards and other inputting devices;
- optional accessories added to the DSE;
- equipment: disk drive, phone, modem, printer, document holder, work chart, desk or other equipment;
- the immediate work environment around the DSE.

Minimum requirements applicable to workstation use must be satisfied:

- *display screen*: well-defined characters of adequate size, stable image, easily adjustable brightness and contrast, easily tilting and swivelling screen, no reflective glare;
- *keyboard*: tiltable and separate from the screen, sufficient space in front of keyboard, matt surface, easy-to-use, adequately contrasted symbols on keys;
- *work surface*: sufficiently large and low-reflecting surface, allows a flexible arrangement of equipment, adequate space;
- *work chair*: stable, allows user easy movement and comfortable position, adjustable height (seat), adjustable height and tilt (seat back), footrests available on request;
- *space*: designed to allow operator to change positions;
- *lighting*: satisfactory lighting conditions, appropriate contrast between screen and background, prevention of glare through positioning of artificial lighting;
- *reflections*: positioning must prevent sources of light, such as windows, from causing distracting reflections on the screen;
- *noise*: must not distract attention or disturb speech;
- *heat*: must not produce excess heat causing discomfort;
- *radiation*: reduced to negligible levels in respect of user's safety, except for the visible part of the electromagnetic spectrum;
- *humidity*: establishment and maintenance of an adequate level;
- *software and systems*: software must be suitable for the task, easy to use and adaptable to the level of user's knowledge, no quantitive or qualitative checking facility may be used without user's knowledge, principles of software ergomonics must be applied.

Users. The regulations only apply to 'users' of display screen equipment – a person who 'habitually uses display screen equipment as a significant part of normal work'. Considerations in deciding whether a person is a user are: whether DSE work is an essential part of a job; how long a person spends on the machine, etc.

Under the Display Screen Equipment Regulations, there are four health and safety protection issues:

1. ***Daily work routine***. This could be achieved by periodic breaks or job rotation (i.e. carrying out tasks that do not involve the similar use of hands and arms). The HSE suggests that breaks should be taken before onset of fatigue and before productivity starts to fall. Breaks should be part of working time. Short and frequent breaks are better than occasional longer breaks. Where possible, 'users' should have discretion and individual control over how they do their jobs and when they take breaks.
2. ***Risk assessment***. This should be systematic and comprehensive. The likely risks: postural problems mainly caused by workstation design; visual problems such as sore eyes, headaches caused by glare, poor lighting; and stress and fatigue caused by workstation design, workload intensity. These risks can result in work-related upper-limb disorders (repetitive strain injury). Any risk must be reduced as quickly as possible. This could be fairly simple – repositioning or renewing equipment or providing the worker with some control over the tasks. The risk assessment should be reviewed where there is a significant change to the workstation, in the workforce or its capabilities or where new risks are established. As far as teleworkers are concerned, risks must be assessed regardless of whether the workstation is provided partly or wholly by the employer.
3. ***Eyesight***. Users entitled to a full eye and eyesight test by qualified optician or medical practitioner. The employer's liability for the cost of 'corrective appliances', usually spectacles, only applies to 'special' appliances required for DSE use or to special modifications to the user's normal spectacles.
4. ***Information and training***. Users must be provided with adequate health and safety training in the use of the workstation – tailored to the work the user does. Information must relate to all aspects of the workstation, daily work routine, and eyesight requirements.

Work-related stress

This has been regarded, by many observers and participants in the labour market, as both a consequence of working conditions (e.g. noise, dust, extremes of temperature); and a by-product of various managerial policies adopted since the 1980s:

- business process re-engineering, 'market testing' and competitive tendering;
- delayering, downsizing and fears of job insecurity;
- work intensification to increase labour productivity;
- greater surveillance and monitoring of staff;
- the expansion of the flexible labour market;
- tensions in the reconciliation of work and non-work (particularly family) life.

It has been identified as a feature of working life for professionals (e.g. teachers, junior hospital doctors and nurses); staff in the emergency services (i.e. the police, fire and ambulance services); manual workers; transport staff; and managers in public and private-sector employment.

The concept of stress

'Stress' is, however, a general term that can be misused. It is suggested in the scientific literature that a person can experience anxiety in two possible ways: through physical hazards at work (e.g. the danger of fire or explosion, the threat of violence, the danger of injury from equipment), or from psycho-social hazards. This latter set of hazards has been described by the International Labour Organisation as involving the interaction of job content, work organisation and management, together with environmental and organisational conditions together with an employee's competences. The psycho-social stressors have been categorised as shown in Exhibit 12.11.

Exhibit 12.11 Psycho-social stressors

The context of work

- *Organisation function and culture*: poor task environment and lack of definition of objectives; poor problem-solving environment; poor development environment; poor communications; non-supportive culture.
- *Role in organisation*: role ambiguity; role conflict; high responsibility.
- *Career development*: career uncertainty; career stagnation; poor status or status incongruity; poor pay; job security and redundancy; low social value to the work.
- *Interpersonal relationships at work*: social or physical isolation; poor relationships with superiors; interpersonal conflict and violence; lack of social support.
- *Home/work interface*: conflicting demands of work and home; low social or practical support at home; dual career problems.

The content of work

- *Task design*: ill-defined work; high uncertainty in work; lack of variety or short workcycles; fragmented or meaningless work; underutilisation of skill; continual exposure to client/customer groups.
- *Workload/work-pace* (quantitative and qualitative): lack of control over pacing; work overload or underload; high levels of pacing or time pressure.
- *Work schedule*: shiftworking; inflexible work schedule; unpredictable work hours; long or unsocial hours.
- *Decision latitude/control*: low participation in decision-making; lack of control over work; little decision-making in work.

Source: Cox (1993).

As a result of stress, a person may exhibit various reactions:

- ***adverse health conditions***: increased heart rate, heart disease, high blood pressure, thyroid disorders, ulcers, panic attacks, depression, headaches, blurred vision, aching neck and shoulders;
- ***behavioural consequences***: irritability, anxiety, insomnia, poor concentration, (increased) consumption of alcohol, tobacco and other drugs.

A person's response to the different types of pressure will, of course, vary. So widespread has been the public concern and discussion about stress that action on various levels has begun to be taken. Since 1995, the Health and Safety Executive has published guidance. In this, it clearly asserted the duty of employers:

> Ill health resulting from stress caused at work has to be treated the same as ill health due to other physical causes present in the workplace. This means that employers do have a legal duty to take reasonable care to ensure that health is not placed at risk through excessive and sustained levels of stress arising from the way people deal with each other at their work or from the day-to-day demands placed on their workforce. Employers should bear stress in mind when assessing possible health hazards in their workplaces, keeping an eye out for developing problems and being prepared to act if harm to health seems likely. In other words, stress should be treated like any other health hazard.
>
> (www.hse.gov.uk/stress)

Stress and the law

The law relating to an employer's liability for work-related stress needs to be considered under three headings:

- personal injury/negligence claim for damages in the High Court;
- constructive dismissal claim at an employment tribunal;
- disability discrimination claim at an employment tribunal.

The issues relating to the last two are considered elsewhere in this textbook (see Chapters 8 and 5 respectively). Recent **case law** in the Court of Appeal relating to personal injury claims have presented some detailed and valuable guidance which is considered here.

Personal injury claims

In these claims the following issues are relevant:

- Such a claim involves the tort of negligence – i.e. the employer's neglect to take reasonable care of the employee. The tort is not committed until an injury is actually suffered.
- It must be shown that the personal injury suffered was 'reasonably forseeable' and that the circumstances at work were a material cause of the injury. Such a claim will also involve consideration of the Court of Appeal's guidance (see Exhibit 12.12 and Exercises).
- The claimant must show that the stress caused a recognised disorder or recognised psychiatric illness. This raises the possibility of association with the Disability Discrimination Act 1995 if the person can show that s/he is disabled within the meaning of that Act.
- Consideration will be given as to whether or not there was a breach of the Health and Safety at Work etc. Act 1974 and any appropriate regulations.
- Consideration will be given as to whether the employer exercised the duty to be proactive and take initiatives in dealing with these matters (*Barber* v *Somerset County Council* [2004] IRLR 475).

Exhibit 12.12 Stress cases: Court of Appeal guidance on 'foreseeability'

Source: *Sutherland* v *Hatton* [2002] IRLR 263

It is important to remember that all cases should be judged on their own facts and circumstances.

- ***Employer liability***. The ordinary principles of employer liability apply. There are no special control mechanisms applying to claims for psychiatric or physical illness or injury arising from stress of doing the work the employee is required to do.
- ***The threshold question***. Whether this kind of harm to this particular employee was reasonably foreseeable. This has two components: (i) an injury to health as distinct from occupational stress which (ii) is attributable to stress at work (as distinct from other factors).
- ***Answering the threshold question***: The relevant factors include:
  - *The nature and extent of the work done by the employee*. Is the workload much more than is normal for the particular job? Is the work particularly intellectually or emotionally demanding for this employee? Are demands being made of this employee unreasonable when compared with the demands made of others in the same or comparable jobs? Or are there signs that others doing this job are suffering harmful levels of stress? Is there an abnormal level of sickness or absenteeism in the same job or the same department?
  - *Signs from the employee of impending harm to health*. Does s/he have a particular problem or vulnerability? Has s/he already suffered from illness attributable to stress at work? Have there recently been frequent or prolonged absences which are uncharacteristic of him or her? Is there reason to think that these are attributable to stress at work, for example, because of complaints or warnings from him or others?
- ***Foreseeability***. This depends upon what the employer knows or ought reasonably to know about the individual employee. Because of the nature of mental disorder, it is harder to foresee than physical injury. But it may be easier to foresee in a known individual than in the population at large. An employer is usually entitled to assume that the employee can withstand the normal pressures of the job, unless he knows of some particular problem or vulnerability.
- ***The test***. This is the same whatever the employment, there are no occupations which should be regarded as intrinsically dangerous to mental health.
- ***Taking at face value***. The employer is generally entitled to take at face value what he is told by his employee unless he has good reason to think to the contrary. He does not generally have to make searching enquiries of the employee or seek permission to make further enquiries of his medical advisers.
- ***Triggering the duty to take steps***. The indications of impending harm to health arising from stress at work must be plain enough for any reasonable employer to realise that he should do something about it.
- ***Breach of duty***. The employer is only in breach of the duty if he has 'failed to take the steps which are *reasonable* in the circumstances', bearing in mind (i) the magnitude of the risk of harm occurring; (ii) the gravity of the harm which may occur; (iii) the costs and practicality of preventing it; and (iv) the justifications for running the risk.
- ***What is reasonable?*** In deciding this, the following are relevant: the size and scope of the employer's operation and the demands it faces. These include the interests of other employees and the need to treat them fairly, for example, in the redistribution of duties.
- ***Reasonable expectation***. An employer can only reasonably be expected to take steps which are likely to do some good. The court is likely to need expert evidence on this.
- ***Confidential advice service***. An employer which offers this, with referral to appropriate counselling or treatment services, is unlikely to be found in breach of duty.
- ***Dismissal or demotion***. If the only reasonable and effective step would have been to dismiss or demote the employee, the employer will not be in breach of duty in allowing a willing employee to continue in the job.
- ***Identification of steps***. In all cases, therefore, it is necessary to identify the steps which the employer both could and should have taken before finding him in breach of his duty of care.
- ***Material contribution***. The claimant must show that the breach of duty has caused or materially contributed to the harm suffered. It is not enough to show that occupational stress has caused the harm.
- ***More than one cause***. Where the harm suffered has more than one cause, the employer should only pay for that proportion of the harm suffered which is attributable to his wrongdoing, unless the harm is truly indivisible. It is for the claimant to raise the question of apportionment.
- ***The assessment of damages***. This will take account of any pre-existing disorder or vulnerability and of the chance that the claimant would have succumbed to a stress-related disorder in any event.

- Was there a breach by the employer of the implied contractual term of mutual trust and confidence; and of the duty to take reasonable care of the employee? If so, there may be an associated constructive dismissal claim if the employee resigned alleging a repudiatory breach of the contract.
- If the court finds the employer to be negligent, it will set damages to be payable to the claimant.

Exercises

12.1 The VDU operators: a safety grievance. This case study encourages you to draw upon material in the regulations that have been outlined earlier – particularly the Management of Health and Safety at Work Regulations 1999 and the Health and Safety (Display Screen Equipment) Regulations 1992. Also, you will need to consider the 1977 and 1996 regulations on safety representation and consultation. The primary issue to be considered is how compliance by the employer can be ensured and how standards can be monitored, bearing in mind the employer's duty to ensure the health, safety and welfare of employees 'so far as reasonably practicable'.

The facts. Helen McDonald is one of eight VDU operators who work in the Central Administrative Services Department at the head office of a food processing company in Leeds. She has worked for six months in the department's open-plan office. She spends between 75 and 95 per cent of her working time at a VDU.

She has complained, on four occasions, to her supervisor about headaches arising from her work. The supervisor has been generally unsympathetic. Helen has just returned from two days' self-certified sick absence because of a severe migraine attack.

At lunchtime on her first day back she is chatting to Wendy who is the safety committee representative at the head office. Helen tells her that she is very unhappy about the working conditions for the VDU operators. She mentions her headaches and the pains that some other staff get. She feels that management should do something about it.

A two-stage task:

1. **In syndicates, carry out a diagnostic exercise by listing the issues that you think arise under the following categories:**
   - **operational issues for the company;**
   - **job design;**
   - **health and safety requirements;**
   - **employment relations.**
2. **Students are allocated to one of two syndicate groups: 'an employer group' and 'an employee group'. Consider the following questions:**
   - ***What are your objectives in resolving the grievance in terms of health and safety standards and in terms of employment relations?***
   - ***What would be your preferred outcome for resolving the grievance?***
   - ***What constraints might exist to limit your achievement of this preferred outcome?***

12.2 Matt: workplace violence. Matt works as a nurse in the accident and emergency department of a hospital. Late one Saturday evening, whilst he is attending a patient, he is headbutted by another patient who complains drunkenly that he has been 'waiting for hours' to be seen by a doctor. Matt has to go off duty for medical attention and, subsequently, he has a three-day sick leave.

His union representative complains to the management of the hospital trust that insufficient attention has been paid to the safety of A&E staff. He cites several incidents in the past 12 months of both verbal and physical abuse.

Consider the employer's liability for both Matt and other staff in the A&E department; and outline the steps that you think the hospital trust might reasonably take.

12.3 Christine Bonser: workplace stress. Christine Bonser was employed by RJB Coal Mining as its technical support and training manager from 1995. She had in fact worked in the coal industry for 20 years. She was said to be conscientious, extremely hard-working and skilled. However, unknown to her employer, she was also emotionally vulnerable, having suffered a period of depression (during her previous employment). She also had severe pre-menstrual stress which had required hormone therapy. Furthermore, her husband had given up work because of his emotional vulnerability which had added pressure upon her.

In the summer of 1996, Ms Bonser's line manager and his boss agreed to introduce a scheme to promote greater efficiency. All requests for project work and meetings were to be channelled through the line manager to ensure that the support resource (of which Ms Bonser formed a part) was being properly controlled and allocated. However, efficiency was not achieved. Teams suffered uneven workloads at a time when management were also paying close attention to the achievement of deadlines and were objectively assessing performance.

This change forced Ms Bonser to pack into an already long working week additional and often unexpected work. In August 1996, she had booked a much-needed holiday. But she was told shortly before she was due to go on leave that she would have to complete a project that would take an estimated 40 hours of extra work. She broke down in tears and told her line manager that she was exhausted and felt that her holiday was under threat.

Eventually, in February 1997, following continuing pressure at work, she suffered a psychiatric breakdown that led to a definable injury to her health and she gave up work in April 1997.

Consider whether you would find the employer liable in law for this psychiatric injury and for paying damages to Ms Bonser. What are your reasons for your decision?

12.4 Maggie: drinking at work. Maggie has worked as broker in a City of London financial institution. The work was very pressurised. Like many of the staff, she relaxed after work with colleagues at a pub near the office. Sometimes she went home on the train fairly drunk. Gradually, the situation became worse. On a couple of occasions she had come into work – once after lunch and once early in the morning – under the influence of alcohol. She was given an informal warning by her manager on the first occasion and a formal warning for the second incident.

Over the following weeks, there was no improvement. One afternoon, she was found slumped at her desk in a drunken state. After a disciplinary hearing, she was given a final written warning and was required to undertake counselling for alcohol abuse, under the supervision of Occupational Health.

Shortly after this incident, she was off work because of sickness. It transpired that she had a liver problem. She was signed off work by her general practitioner for six months. Her health did not improve significantly and she was eventually on sick leave for over 12 months. Her manager consulted the HR department with a view to dismissing her.

What advice would the HR director give the manager about the law and on the approach that the company should adopt?

Feedback on these exercises is provided in the Appendix to this textbook.

References

Advisory, Conciliation and Arbitration Service (2009) *Code of Practice on Disciplinary and Grievance Procedures.* London: ACAS.

Chartered Institute of Personnel and Development (1996) *Occupational Health and Organisational Effectiveness*, Key Facts, September. London: CIPD.

Cox, T. (1993) *Stress Research and Stress Management: Putting Theory to Work*, Contract Research Report 61. London: Health and Safety Executive.

Robens, Lord (1972) *Report of the Committee of Inquiry on Safety and Health at Work*. London: HMSO.

Smith, I. and Thomas, G. (2000) *Smith and Wood's Industrial Law*. London: Butterworth.

Other legal materials

International Labour Organisation: Convention 155 concerning Occupational Safety and Health and the Working Environment.

Useful website Health and Safety Executive **www.hse.gov.uk**

Visit **www.mylawchamber.co.uk/willey** to access multiple choice questions, case flashcards and exercises to test yourself on this chapter.

13 Conclusion

Employment law is continually developing through both statute law and judicial interpretations. In some periods the change is with great rapidity. Nevertheless, it is possible to discern certain continuing themes in both legislation and case law. These themes frequently reflect social and political attitudes and objectives. In this brief concluding chapter, we review several which are likely to be key in the development of employment law in the next few years. The principal ones considered are: ethical standards; minimum standards; 'juridification'; business interests; labour market flexibility; pregnancy and family and dependency issues; dispute resolution; and the enforcement of individual rights.

Ethical standards

One very important instrument for implementing ethical standards both in employment and in society, generally, is discrimination law. Since 2000, there has been a considerable extension of the grounds on which people are protected. Perhaps the most significant has been protection against discrimination on the grounds of age – any age. This covers employment and is being extended to the provision of goods, facilities and services. At the time of writing, this law is being gradually tested in courts and at employment tribunal (see Chapter 5). Given its legislative base in the EU Employment Equality Framework Directive 2000, it is certain that there will be further test cases referred to the European Court of Justice for its interpretation of the law.

Of overall significance in this area is the move to a single equality legislative structure embracing all strands of discrimination law. This is a gargantuan drafting task. Nevertheless, as indicated by government it should hopefully 'declutter and strengthen' the law (see Chapter 4, Exhibit 4.4).

Minimum standards

It is in the context of these ethical standards that a wider range of specific statutory minimum standards is being developed in employment relations. Standards of treatment in employment can, in fact, be enacted as *absolute* standards or as *minimum* standards. Examples of the former exist particularly in health and safety legislation. However, the tendency of most governments in the past 50 years has been to create minimum standards. The rationale is to provide a floor of rights (or, as far as remuneration is concerned, in the language of the Council of Europe, a 'decency' threshold) below which individuals will not fall. At the same time, employers are provided with flexibility to offer enhanced conditions above the minima. This approach is reflected in statutory provisions on, for example, contractual information, redundancy pay, maternity leave, notice to terminate employment, the minimum wage and paid annual leave. Effectively, as suggested in Chapter 2, we have moved decisively towards a minimum contract of employment.

'Juridification'

Standards for determining the treatment of working people have, over the past forty years or so, increasingly been determined in law. Employers, as we have seen, still have some discretion but this is narrowing. In most organisations, decisions relating to employment relations are now more likely to be reached by reference to these legal standards. Even where trade union recognition has been conceded by an employer, the standards set in collective agreements must reflect legal standards where they exist. It can be argued, of course, that this 'juridification' (Lewis 1986: 29–30) of human resource management is more likely to be found in larger organisations which have professional support and the advice of human resource practitioners. Certainly, evidence suggests that some managers, particularly in smaller organisations, are either ignorant of the legal standards or deliberately flout them. Clearly, if a minimum standards culture is promoted by government, then, steps to provide advice and guidance must be continually under review to aim at ensuring compliance.

Business interests

Legal standards, of course, are designed to mould the behaviour of employers and so promote degrees of social justice for working people. Inevitably, tensions exist. There are two negative business reactions to any legislation or new proposals: employers' concern about the cost of legal regulation; and their concern about the extent to which discrimination law and minimum standards can be implemented into organisations without too much disruption. Governments have responded, to some extent, to these concerns by claiming sensitivity to avoiding too much bureaucracy and unnecessary 'burdens on business'. Certainly, specific legislation does include opportunities for flexible responses to meet the operational and employment relations circumstances of businesses. Examples of this include the **derogations** in the Working Time Regulations 1998; the facility to 'justify objectively' certain forms of discrimination; the ability to provide enhancements above the minimum standards; the ability to defend certain treatment as 'reasonable' in the circumstances. Cost considerations can be factors in some of these situations.

Nevertheless, surveys undertaken, for example, for the Chartered Institute for Personnel and Development (see **www.cipd.co.uk**), show that some employers do see the standards of employment law and discrimination law as important underpinning for standards of good human resource management practice. This in turn is argued as contributing to business success.

Employers, of course, are not uniform in terms of size or the approaches and policies they adopt towards employment relations. There are marked differences in respect of knowledge of the law and espousal of good employment practice. The literature of employment relations provides various categorisations of management style (e.g. Fox 1966; Purcell and Sisson 1983). In summary, there are probably three broad theoretical 'types' of organisation:

- *'Sophisticated' organisations* which have a strategic perspective and develop policies which generally reflect professional standards of human resource management and comply with employment law. Faced with a complainant's success at employment tribunal, these employers may well revise corporate policy to try to ensure no repetition of any breaches of good practice.
- *'Pragmatic' or 'opportunistic' organisations* which react to situations as they arise and, generally, will only comply with good employment practice if there is a legislative 'stick' used against them.
- *'Exploitative' organisations* which are ignorant of the law or deliberately flout it.

Labour market flexibility

The 'flexible workforce' is likely to remain a significant feature of the British labour market. It has been central to government policy for the past 25 years or more. At the same time, whilst there is a concern about the economic imperative of labour flexibility, there is also public policy commitment to employment protection and social justice. Some progress at reconciling these concerns has been made through EU directives (which arose from EU-wide **framework agreements** by the **social partners**) covering the entitlements and protection for **part-time workers** and fixed-term workers. Nevertheless, there remain significant groups of working people who are liable to exploitation: casual workers; and temporary agency workers – and specifically, migrant workers recruited by gangmasters.

As far as temporary agency workers are concerned, some steps have been taken towards legislative action. But specific British legislation has not yet been published. The Temporary Agency Workers Directive was adopted in October 2008 by the European Parliament. Its purpose is to provide agency workers with equal treatment in their basic employment conditions in comparison with those of staff employed in the client company. Anticipating this, in May 2008, the British government brokered a deal between the Confederation of British Industry (CBI) and the Trades Union Congress (TUC) which granted agency workers equal treatment after 12 weeks of employment in the client organisation. It is anticipated that this British social partners' agreement will form the basis of domestic legislation to implement the Directive.

Pregnancy, family and dependency issues

The continuing feminisation of the labour market, the persistence of traditional caring responsibilities being undertaken by women, flexibility of working time and the 'long hours culture' continue to be factors in discussions about policies designed to accommodate work and non-work life. Indeed, there has been welcome progress in the political arena with family and dependency issues being acknowledged by both major political parties as important policy matters.

The range of leave entitlements and the facility to request flexible working are helpful as is discrimination law. Judicial decision-making and creativity show some signs of pushing the boundaries of discrimination law as evidenced in the *Coleman* case (see Chapter 5, Exhibit 5.13). However, the issue of compliance with statutory rights by organisations is still problematic – particularly in respect of pregnant workers who remain vulnerable to dismissal and other detrimental treatment. More fundamentally, the culture of organisations needs to be examined to ensure coherent policies in this area – possibly with enhancements. Furthermore, employer willingness to acknowledge that parenting is a male as well as female social responsibility and, therefore, flexibility and leave arrangements for fathers could be facilitated.

Dispute resolution

This remains a continuing concern for employers and government. However, it is also a concern for working people who wish to ensure effective resolution of workplace problems. The enactment in 2004 of the statutory dispute resolution procedures for grievances and dismissals proved a failure and they were rescinded. The emphasis on workplace resolution in accordance with standards of good procedural practice is the route now being adopted. The ACAS *Code of Practice on Disciplinary and Grievance Procedures* 2009 provides recommendations on practice. A respondent employer's compliance with this code continues to be used in evidence at an employment tribunal hearing. In addition, good employment practice suggests that employers, in their internal procedures, might consider the processes of mediation (strongly advocated by, among other bodies, ACAS and the Chartered Institute of Personnel and Development) and **conciliation**. Overall, it is to be hoped that workplace resolution develops more effectively in the immediate future – partly to limit complaints being made to an employment tribunal, but also to provide more immediate redress for complainant and to help improve the quality of employment relations.

Enforcement of individual rights

This issue involves a number of perennial problems – only a few of which are being tackled.

Access to statutory rights

This access can be restricted in two, often interlocking, ways:

1 by employment status: e.g. only '**employees**' are able to claim unfair dismissal;
2 by length of service with an employer: e.g. twelve months' continuous service for unfair dismissal complaints; 26 weeks for the right to request flexible working.

In recent years, the qualifications relating to the number of hours worked, age limits over 65 years, and the size of the employer's workforce have been removed. Nevertheless, although three key employment rights are available to the wide category of 'workers' irrespective of length of service (under Working Time Regulations 1998, National Minimum Wage Act 1998, and in respect of wage deduction), the restrictions on unfair dismissal claims and those for statutory redundancy pay exclude vulnerable groups from important remedies.

Individual complaints

Much survey evidence of the employment tribunal process (DTI 2002; Haywood *et al.* 2004; Aston *et al.* 2006; Armstrong and Coats 2007; Hammersley *et al.* 2007; Latreille 2007) shows that it can be stressful, consumptive of a great deal of time and may be costly to the individual in terms of the resources needed. There is also evidence of potential complainants not lodging a complaint because of these factors. There remains no financial assistance. Advice may be available from the Citizens' Advice Bureaux. Some 'no win no fee' lawyers may be willing to take cases. Otherwise, unless a person is a member of trade union or has their own resources, there can be disparate treatment in the way in which their complaint can be dealt with – particularly in comparison with the resources available to most employers. Using the language of the European Convention on Human Rights 1950, there is no 'equality of arms'.

This individual complaint process and the imbalance of resources is of particular significance in many discrimination cases. There can be complexities in the law; and in evidence where patterns of discrimination or harassment are alleged. One step under the proposed single equality legislation which could help is the opportunity to have 'representative actions' where patterns of discrimination (e.g. in respect of equal pay) cover a particular workgroup. Whether this would 'open up' consideration of similar representative actions in other areas (for example, transfers of undertakings or working time entitlements), where the treatment of work groups is relevant, is unknown.

Conclusion

It is dangerous to predict future developments and directions in employment law. Indeed, the field is littered with many unanticipated consequences. Those trends that are certain are the continued 'Europeanisation' of employment and discrimination law; further intricate legal arguments about the eligibility of 'workers' for employment protection in the flexible labour market; debates about the extension of effective rights for parents and carers; the continued 'juridification' of HRM and employment relations; and ever-present concerns about the extent to which working people have effective access to complaints procedures and remedies.

References and useful websites

Armstrong, K. and Coats, D. (2007) *The Costs and Benefits of Employment Tribunal Cases for Employers and Claimants*, Employment Relations Research Series No. 83. London: Department for Business Enterprise and Regulatory Reform (www.berr.gov.uk/employment).

Aston, J. *et al.* (2006) *The Experience of Claimants in Race Discrimination Employment Tribunal Cases*, Employment Relations Research Series, No. 55. London: Department of Trade and Industry (www.berr.gov.uk/employment).

Department of Trade and Industry (2002) *Findings from the 1998 Survey of Employment Tribunal Applications,* Employment Relations Research Series, No. 13. London: Department of Trade and Industry (www.berr.gov.uk/employment).

Fox, A. (1966) *Industrial Sociology and Industrial Relations*, Research Paper 3, Royal Commission on Trade Unions and Employers' Associations, Cmnd 3623. London: HMSO.

Hammersley, G. *et al.* (2007) *The Influence of Legal Representation at Employment Tribunals on Case Outcome,* Employment Relations Research Series, No. 84. London: Department for Business Enterprise and Regulatory Reform (www.berr.gov.uk/employment).

Haywood, B. *et al.* (2004) *Findings from the Survey of Employment Tribunal Applications 2003*, Employment Relations Research Series, No. 33. London: Department of Trade and Industry (www.berr.gov.uk/employment).

Latreille, P. (2007) *The Settlement of Employment Tribunal Cases: Evidence from SETA 2003*, Employment Relations Research Series, No. 61. London: Department for Business Enterprise and Regulatory Reform (www.berr.gov.uk/employment).

Lewis, R. (1986) 'The role of the law in employment relations', in Lewis, R. (ed.) *Labour Law in Britain*. Oxford: Blackwell.

Purcell, J. and Sisson, K. (1983) 'Strategies and practices in the management of industrial relations', in Bain, G. (ed.) *Industrial Relations in Britain*. Oxford: Blackwell.

Useful websites Chartered Institute for Personnel and Development **www.cipd.co.uk**

Department for Business Enterprise and Regulatory Reform **www.berr.gov.uk**

Appendix: Feedback on exercises

In considering these exercises, it is important to remember the necessity to comply, as appropriate with the ACAS *Code of Practice on Disciplinary and Grievance Procedures* (2009). Failure to follow the recommendations can be used in evidence at an employment tribunal (see Exhibit 8.1 in Chapter 8).

Chapter 3: Managing change in the employment relationship

Contract variation

3.1.1 Samantha. The issue is whether or not Samantha has a mobility clause in her contract of employment. If there is one, it could either be implied through custom and practice (although this would be relatively rare); or it could be an express term. This means that it would be in writing in the offer letter or in the contractual information she was given when she started employment. If there was such a mobility clause and the employer implemented it in a reasonable way, then she should comply with it. A distance of four miles might well be regarded as reasonable and it may well be an arrangement that she has complied with on previous occasions.

A related issue that could arise, even if the mobility clause is part of the contract, is the issue of indirect sex discrimination. For example, if Samantha has caring responsibilities, she might argue that the clause puts her at a 'disadvantage'. The employer would need to justify the clause objectively (see Chapter 5). Taken overall, it would be sensible and good practice for the employer to consult with Samantha about what was required and to consider any problems that she might have.

If there is no mobility clause, then, the employer should consult with her about varying the place of work under her contract of employment. The issues of sex discrimination and reasonable distance could be considered. If Samantha does not agree the variation, then the employer may terminate her contract of employment for 'some other substantial reason' (in this case 'business need') and offer a new one incorporating the changed place of work. She has the choice of accepting or refusing this new contract. She may, if she has one year's continuous service, claim unfair dismissal at an employment tribunal. However, if the employer has a good reason ('business need' can be such a reason); and has handled the matter in a procedurally correct way and in accordance with the ACAS Code of Practice, then the dismissal is likely to be fair.

3.1.2 Locksmith Engineering. The issue is the nature of the pay increase under the contract of employment. If it is *discretionary*, then, the employer may be able to refuse to award the increase. If it is *contractual*, then it would be a breach of contract not to make the payment and individual employees could sue for non-payment of wages due (Employment Rights Act 1996, Part II). It would, in fact, be a repudiatory breach of contract because pay is an essential term of the contract. So, it could result in resignation and claims of constructive dismissal. An employer could avoid the consequences of breach of contract by terminating with due notice the existing contracts of employment, consulting with staff and offering a new contract without any term relating to an automatic annual pay increase.

3.1.3 Beryl. The issue is whether Beryl can be instructed to carry out the tasks involved in the new and complex computerised system. An implied term in her contract of employment is the duty to obey the lawful and reasonable instructions of her employer. There is nothing unlawful in what the employer is requiring her to do. Whether it is reasonable is dependent on the answers to a number of questions. The principal ones are:

- Do the tasks that she is being required to undertake fall within her job description?
- Do they change substantially the work that she is normally required to do?
- Is she to be provided with training and support in order to undertake the new tasks?
- Has the employer consulted with her about the proposed changes? (See the *Cresswell* case.)

If she persists in refusing to attend the training, then, the employer might take disciplinary action. Alternatively, he might terminate her contract of employment for 'some other substantial reason' (on the grounds of 'business need') and offer her a new contract on condition that she participates in the training programme.

3.1.4 Jamila. The issue is whether she can be instructed to carry out the requirement of the employer. The task falls within the job description and the implied contractual duty of a retail assistant to promote her employer's business (see issues in Exercise 3.1.3, above). She is unlikely to be able to claim constructive dismissal because there is no evidence of a repudiation of her contract of employment by her employer.

Managing redundancies

3.2.1 Assuming the redundancies are genuine and there is a decline in the need for particular grades of staff, the employer will have to determine which print operators are to be made redundant (i.e. against which criteria); and to consult with them individually about the redundancy (see ACAS Code of Practice). Once the consultation process is completed, notice of the termination of there employment should be given to them. It should be due notice – i.e. what they are entitled to under their contracts of employment.

3.2.2 As in the previous case, assuming the redundancies are genuine and the business circumstances require a reduction in the number of employees, the employer should select staff according to specific objective criteria. Selection according to employment status is potentially discriminatory. It could be discriminatory on the grounds of sex if more women are on temporary contracts than men. It could also be potentially discriminatory under the Fixed Term Employees (Prevention of Less Favourable Treatment) Regulations 2002 – in terms of comparative treatment with permanent employees. Furthermore, it could also be that some workers on temporary contracts could have considerable service – up to four years before they become permanent. This might exceed the length of service of staff on permanent contracts if LIFO ('last in first out') was to be used as a criterion.

The approach to be adopted in terms of good practice (and possibly avoidance of claims under discrimination law) is to set out objective criteria for the selection of staff – whether they are permanent or temporary. Such criteria could include performance standards, disciplinary issues, absence record, etc.

3.2.3 Trisha. There are two principal issues here: the fact that Trisha's job is being made redundant under the reorganisation; and the question of whether her new post is suitable alternative employment. On this latter issue, she might argue that there has been a diminution of her status – in terms of direct responsibility to a course leader and in terms of autonomy. Having said that, the tasks remain generally the same and she could reasonably be expected to undertake the work required. The employer should provide a 'trial period'. If at the end of that she is dissatisfied with the post, then, the employment may be terminated. There may be another factor involved in the case. This is the potential for indirect sex discrimination. The 'provision, criterion or practice' which the employer needs to justify objectively is the requirement to work occasionally until 7 p.m. If she has dependency responsibilities, she may be disadvantaged by this provision. The employer, however, may be successful in defending it because of the operational needs of the college.

Managing transfers

3.3.1 The key issue here is whether or not the new employer (the 'transferee') is able to vary contracts of employment of the staff transferred. Essentially, the contracts of employees of the transferor are protected throughout the transfer situation. This period is not defined. It is unlawful to vary contracts if the variation is connected with the transfer. However, the law was amended in 2006, when it became permissible for a transferee to vary contracts for an economic, technical or organisational reason entailing a change in the workforce.

In this case, it is difficult to see the justification for the common pay structure being established. It could be argued that this is for reasons of harmonisation and is connected with the transfer. The deployment of staff might be an 'organisational' reason 'entailing changes in the workforce' if it is necessary to merge together two separate workforces. If such changes are to be proposed, they must be discussed and, if they are contractual, agreed with the staff.

3.3.2 There are two aspects to this transfer. First of all, the contracts of the staff transferred: these must be preserved through the transfer. If they incorporate terms of collective agreements, they will continue and 'live on' in the future – whether the transferee is union-free or not. Secondly, there is the issue of the transferee's attitude to trade union recognition. The transferee can derecognise the union after the transfer. This will not, however, affect the issue of incorporated terms deriving from collective agreements.

3.3.3 The transferee is liable for this employment tribunal claim. They should have been notified of it by the transferor as part of the 'employee liability information'. If the transferor failed to tell the transferee of a grievance or complaint that was known to it, then, the transferee can take legal proceedings against the transferor.

The transferee must respond to the employment tribunal complaint.

3.3.4 The Transfer of Undertakings (Protection of Employment) Regulations 2006 protect 'employees'. The self-employed workers would be excluded from protection during the transfer. They would have no rights under the Regulations. They may have certain rights under their contracts with the transferor and that organisation should ensure that they are complied with. The seasonal contract staff could be 'employees'. By considering their employment status and, in particular, the issue of mutuality of obligation, it might be possible to determine their entitlements under the Regulations.

Chapter 5: The strands of discrimination law

5.1 Taking the Ladele case by itself, there are several points that can be made. Clearly, any harassment and bullying against people who object to civil partnerships is not acceptable and is contrary to discrimination law. The central issue is whether it is indirectly discriminatory to require a member of staff to comply with specific key requirements of the job. The responsibilities of a registrar are to perform important public duties. The employer should make clear the nature of those responsibilities. Given the diverse nature of British society, the probability is that a registrar of civil marriage and partnership ceremonies is likely to encounter people with whose views s/he does not necessarily agree. The employer could inquire of the employee if there were any circumstances in which s/he would feel uncomfortable. In that situation, it might be possible, operationally, to arrange the allocation of work to avoid such a conflict of values. Whether the employer could require a registrar to perform ceremonies they disapproved of and could justify it in accordance with the Employment Equality (Religion or Belief) Regulations 2003 was ruled on by the EAT (see *London Borough of Islington* v *Ladele* UKEAT/0453/08). Also, failure to perform the required duties by the member of staff may be grounds for dismissal. The issue here which could arise is whether that would be direct discrimination on grounds of religious belief.

5.2 This is drawn from an actual case in 1999. The employment tribunal decided that Ninja could suffer discrimination on racial grounds by supporting his colleagues who where of different ethnic origins. He experienced a detriment, as they did, by being refused work.

5.3 This is an actual case from 2003. The tribunal found that the failure to invite Mrs Hill to the event and the subsequent comments were direct sex discrimination and that, because of the employer's unacceptable behaviour forcing her to resign, she was constructively dismissed because of the repudiation of her contract. The failure to invite her to an event designed to reward hard work was 'a refusal to afford her access to a benefit' and she was subjected to a detriment. The employer's failure to recognise the upset caused by effectively making a joke of it and then trying to dismiss her concerns enhanced the upset. She was awarded £3,000 for injury to feelings; and £22,219 for loss of earning and interest.

5.4 The reliance by some managers on 'commitment' might be a genuine attempt to appoint someone who will work to a high standard in the organisation. The problem with the term is that it can be used in a coded way to sift out people who may want some flexibility in employment arrangements and who may not be at ease with a 'long hours culture'. Such a view could well be indirectly discriminatory on the grounds of sex; it may also be discriminatory under disability law which requires the employer to consider some reasonable adjustment. If it appears to be potentially indirect sex discrimination, the manager must be prepared to justify objectively the provision, criterion or practice as a genuine business need. If adjustments are needed under disability legislation, then these must be reasonable and if they cannot be made, reasons should be given.

5.5 The size of the business is not relevant. She is likely to be a disabled person within the meaning of the Act and is protected as an applicant for employment. She clearly is suitable for the post but the withdrawal of the verbal offer is discriminatory. The employer should reinstate the offer formally and consult with her about any reasonable adjustments that she might need. It may be that careful management of her workload might help. If the offer is not reinstated, then, she may make a claim at employment tribunal for direct discrimination on the grounds of disability.

5.6 Lou is protected under the Disability Discrimination Act 1995 from the time of the diagnosis of multiple sclerosis even if the symptoms are not manifest. He has suffered a detriment because he was not considered as suitable for short-listing. This was not for any reason relating to his capability but to do with assumptions about his long-term health. He should be offered an interview and should be considered for the promotion. If he is refused the post, it must be for objective reasons. Otherwise he would be able to complain of direct discrimination. If he is offered the post, it may be that the nature of it is such that reasonable adjustments could be made more easily to accommodate him in the long-term. The employer would also need, as evidence of good practice to consult with him on any adjustments – which might be small scale initially.

5.7 The culture of this organisation is probably profit-driven and generally unsympathetic to good employment practice and to the requirements of discrimination law. The difficulty will be with the chief executive who no doubt is very influential in determining policy. One approach would be to identify the risks of the action he wishes to take and suggest ways of meeting his objectives lawfully. Age discrimination law is central. An advertisement which conveys the intention to discriminate is unlawful. A person specification setting out age group may be unlawful unless it can be objectively justified as a genuine business need. More critically for such a senior post the person specification should be identifying experience and qualifications. If flexible working is being ruled out, then, the rationale for this needs to be considered. Is it necessary for the business? If a structured, legally compliant approach is not adopted then the business may incur costs in terms of management time and possible compensation should there be an employment tribunal complaint. Much will depend on how the chief executive is likely to respond to the 'stick'.

5.8 This is a case of indirect discrimination on racial grounds. The specification of GCSE qualifications sets a standard of proficiency that the employer is looking for in applicants. However, it may be possible that such proficiency is evident in a range of other qualifications. The employer would need objectively to justify the indirect discrimination. It is unlikely that he would be able to demonstrate a genuine business need specifically for GCSE qualifications.

5.9 The issue here is whether or not there is a genuine occupational qualification on racial grounds. It is very much a borderline case. Clearly, there is to be liaison with the Chinese community. However, the nature of the job is fund-raising and administrative. It does not involve promoting culture identity or welfare directly but rather facilitating the work of other people through funding. One key issue might be the extent to which the postholder has to be proficient in a Chinese language to improve liaison. In this case, there may be a case for specifying this in the person specification. Even, then, a Chinese speaker may not have to be of Chinese ethnic origin.

5.10 This relates to the issue of genuine occupational requirement on grounds of religion or belief. There are two possible aspects to this. First, a GOR which is usually appropriate is that for a person who is promoting a particular faith or system of belief. This does not arise in this case. Secondly, the preservation or promotion of an 'ethos' in religious organisations. This appears to be the reason behind this specific GOR. Given the nature of the work he would be required to perform, it is difficult to see how such a GOR can be defended. If he suspected that he was being discriminated against because of his religion, then, he might be able to claim direct discrimination on grounds of religion or belief also at employment tribunal. He is protected as an applicant for employment and may make a complaint at an employment tribunal.

Chapter 7: Harassment and bullying at work

7.1 This scenario outlines some deeply-embedded cultural issues. To tackle these, a multi-level approach is necessary. The initial step must be the development of a strategy involving commitment from senior management to a detailed plan. The plan should consider several issues – ways of effectively gaining commitment from managers, the training necessary to achieve the proposed strategic outcomes, effective procedures for dealing with individual complaints, monitoring processes.

In evaluating the steps necessary for dealing with this cultural problem, draw on your own experience from any organisation in which you have worked. Think about the practicalities of implementing change and how any consequential further problems might be tackled. It might also be worth considering the relevant section of Chapter 6 concerning strategic approaches to eradicating discrimination.

7.2 Indira. The harassment that Indira experiences is, in part, 'personal' (in that it is directed to her) and also as a part of a general harassing culture within the organisation. Under the Sex Discrimination Act 1975 (as amended) an issue that has to be considered is whether the harassment is 'related to the sex of the recipient' or 'unwanted conduct of a sexual nature'. The e-mail message is likely to be the latter. The comments in the lift seem as if they are the former. Indira clearly finds both sets of behaviour upsetting. In the terms of the legislation they are 'unwanted'. She has rightly mentioned her concern to her supervisor who, wrongly, has suggested 'laughing off' the matter.

Angela in the HR department must, because of the employer's liability for discrimination and harassment, take the issue seriously as a formal grievance. First she should investigate what has happened. There may be some difficulty in establishing the facts of the unwitnessed incident in the lift. Nevertheless, if she forms a 'reasonable belief' that Jez behaved in the way that Indira claims (and this is probable given his reputation and his knowledge that she had complained about the e-mail message), then, Angela can accept, on the balance of probabilities, that Indira's version of events is true.

The issue for the employer, then, is whether to initiate disciplinary action against Jez. A view needs to be taken by the employer of the seriousness of Jez's conduct – is it gross misconduct or relatively minor? If he is guilty of misconduct, the appropriate penalty needs to be considered. If he is guilty of gross misconduct, then, the employer's starting point for a penalty could be dismissal. Depending on the circumstances (his record, length of service and any remorse he might show) then he could be given a warning – first formal or a final warning.

This response by the employer could be evidence of them taking 'such steps as were reasonably practicable' to deal with Indira's individual complaint. There are, of course, other more deep-seated problems about the culture of the organisation. The approaches suggested in the answer to Exercise 7.1 are worth considering.

If nothing effective is done to deal with Indira's complaint, then, she might be able to argue a breach of the implied contractual term of 'mutual trust and confidence'. There would be a repudiation of the contract and she could resign and complain to an employment tribunal of constructive dismissal – providing she has 12 month's continuous service. Alternatively, she might complain of harassment under the provisions in the Sex Discrimination Act. She would not need to resign in order to make such a complaint. Furthermore, any compensation awarded would be uncapped.

7.3 Ronke. The critical issue in this case is whether or not the remark of Joan Philips about 'you people' constitutes harassment on racial grounds or whether it refers to people like Ronke who have been long-serving members of staff. If it is the latter Joan's behaviour is more likely to be 'bullying' rather than harassment as outlawed under discrimination law. It may be difficult to prove that it is racial harassment unless there is some additional evidence of similar attitudes and behaviour. If it is accepted as bullying, then, it is still serious enough for senior management to deal with. Of particular concern is the power relationship between the two women; and in addition the need in a relatively small office environment for good working relationships to exist. So, in the circumstances, Ronke might be advised to raise the issue with Joan's boss as a grievance. She might indicate that she is prepared to participate in formal mediation. This could be a constructive way of helping resolve issues and achieving a satisfactory outcome for both parties. If the issue is not resolved, then, Ronke might resign and claim constructive dismissal at an employment tribunal.

7.4 Winston and Harry. Winston's behaviour is offensive and unwanted. He is entitled to have his religious beliefs about homosexuality. However, he does not have complete freedom of expression. Harry has made clear his objection to Winston's comments. He has also mentioned the situation to his manager. The manager, as a 'reasonable step', should have discussed the matter with Winston and Harry separately; and then, if appropriate, to try to mediate between the two of them. His failure to do this, probably, resulted in the continuing escalation of the interpersonal difficulties.

There are three principal sets of issues to be dealt with:

- *The fight.* This is gross misconduct. Establishing the facts of what happened and whether or not there was any provocation is critically important. Clearly, Harry had struck the first blow. However, in all the circumstances (including possible provocation), it may not be regarded by the employer as serious enough to dismiss him for gross misconduct.
- *Harry's grievance.* This should be dealt with prior to any disciplinary hearing. The facts that are established are material to the background of any disciplinary issues – i.e. management's failure to deal with Harry's earlier complaint about Winston's persistent and escalating offensive behaviour.
- *Winston's behaviour.* This also needs to be tackled. There is evidence of a breach of disciplinary rules by his harassing behaviour. Some disciplinary warning might be appropriate.

If Harry were to be dismissed, then he may have grounds to claim unfair dismissal at an employment tribunal. The employer could probably succeed in such a case if it proved that it was reasonable in all the circumstances – including the seriousness with which they viewed fighting – to dismiss Harry for gross misconduct. Perhaps a more certain complaint might be a claim by Harry under discrimination law (the Employment Equality (Sexual Orientation) Regulations 2003) that he had been harassed by association with his son's sexuality. He would claim that the employer was vicariously liable for this harassment.

Chapter 8: Discipline and dismissal

8.1 Jason. The HR manager should firstly explain to Jason's line manager that Jason is protected against unfair dismissal under the Employment Rights Act 1996 as he is an employee with more than one year's continuous service. The company, therefore, needs to be very careful in how they handle his case. For a dismissal to be fair under the ERA it needs to firstly come under one of the potentially fair reasons for dismissal. That this is the case in this scenario is very obvious – Jason's lateness and absence from work clearly relate to the 'conduct' ground. In addition to establishing a potentially fair reason for dismissal, employers are obliged to demonstrate that the actual decision to dismiss was reasonable in the circumstances.

In establishing whether a dismissal was reasonable or not, employment tribunals will refer to the principles and procedural guidance outlined in the ACAS Code of Practice. The ACAS Code outlines that before action is taken in response to a breach of disciplinary rules, organisations should inform the employee of the issue in question, undertake a comprehensive investigation, give the employee the opportunity to put their case forward, and also allow them to appeal any decision made. Jason would have a right to be accompanied at any formal disciplinary meeting. Easywheels may have taken such procedural steps before issuing Jason with a written warning. The company, therefore, may be justified in giving him a final written warning outlining that if he is late again he could be dismissed. This would arguably be within the 'range of reasonable responses' an employer might implement in such circumstances. Jason's recent absences from work could also be classed as misconduct, which could potentially support the issuing of a final written warning.

However, the circumstances of the case would perhaps suggest that the employer should look more closely into Jason's situation before issuing a final written warning and subsequently dismissing. Specifically, Jason's claim that his recent absences have been a result of stress should be carefully examined. The ACAS Code of Practice recommends that employers should check whether there are any special circumstances such as personal issues that may be affecting performance, in advance of disciplinary meetings. It would be good practice, therefore, for Easywheels to speak to Jason about this and possibly offer some form of counselling or other assistance if he is indeed found to be suffering from stress or depression, if they have not already done so. In addition, if not already considered an adjustment of working arrangements – for example a later starting time and/or temporary exemption from having to work in the evening – should also be discussed. Dismissing Jason without considering such issues and taking these additional steps could potentially be seen by a tribunal to be unfair.

If these additional steps were not undertaken and Jason was indeed found to have been unfairly dismissed, a tribunal could order him to be reinstated or re-engaged or alternatively award him compensation.

8.2 Sarah. As an employee (we can assume this from the facts of the case) with more than one year's continuous service, Sarah is protected against unfair dismissal under the ERA 1996. Sarah, therefore, could apply to an employment tribunal claiming that her dismissal was unfair. Her employer would have to demonstrate that she was dismissed for a fair reason and that the decision to dismiss was reasonable in the circumstances. The most obvious fair reason for dismissal here is capability, i.e. that Sarah is no longer physically capable of doing her job. In relation to the reasonableness of the decision, the company's status as a small business would be expressly taken into account by a tribunal. In particular, the small size of the company may mean that it does not have the financial resources to continue employing Sarah for a long period of time or to make potentially costly adjustments to her role (e.g. by modifying existing equipment); while there may also be limited opportunities to provide her with alternative work. The company's need to supply customer orders would also be seen to be of paramount importance.

By writing to her about the situation, holding a meeting to discuss it and providing for an appeal, Sarah's managing director has followed key procedural steps outlined in the ACAS

Code of Practice. However, it is well established that in capability cases tribunals generally require employers to take particular, additional procedural steps in order for dismissals to be fair. Employers should consult closely with the employee, consider carefully the medical evidence on the employee's condition and also whether it is possible to provide him or her with alternative employment or make an adjustment to the job so that they can continue working. In this case it is clear that the employer has examined the relevant medical evidence, consulted with Sarah and to a limited extent considered the issue of alternative employment. However, a tribunal could decide that the employer has given insufficient consideration to whether Sarah could take up the marketing vacancy. In addition, the managing director has not considered whether the making of adjustments to her role or the equipment used might enable Sarah to continue in her current position. This would suggest that the dismissal on grounds of capability might be found to be unfair, in which case Sarah could be reinstated, re-engaged or awarded compensation.

There is a second main aspect of this case, namely the possibility of a claim for disability discrimination, which Sarah could consider including in her application to a tribunal. Under the Disability Discrimination Act 1995, employers are obliged to make 'reasonable adjustments' for disabled employees to enable them to work or continue working effectively. To be classed as disabled under the Act, Sarah must have a 'physical or mental impairment' which has a substantial and long-term adverse effect on her ability to carry out 'normal day-to-day activities'. She does have a physical impairment that is long-term and which has a substantial adverse effect on her ability to carry out normal day-to-day activities (the effect on 'manual dexterity' is arguably key here).

The duty to make reasonable adjustments may include adjustment to equipment being used or the exact nature of the job undertaken. A tribunal, therefore, would closely consider, for example, whether if some piece of equipment were introduced Sarah could continue her design work. In addition, *Archibald* v *Fife Council* (2004) established that the duty to make reasonable adjustments may, depending on the circumstances, require companies to consider transferring employees who have become disabled into positions which they do not necessarily have the qualifications or experience for (see Chapter 5). It is therefore likely that a tribunal would hold that the employer in this case is in breach of the Disability Discrimination Act due to the fact that it has not properly addressed the duty to make reasonable adjustments. No consideration has been given to possible adjustments to her existing job that would enable Sarah to remain in employment, while the possibility of her transferring to do the job coming up in the marketing department has arguably not been considered sufficiently. A tribunal could also therefore make a declaration and recommendation and award compensation for disability discrimination.

8.3 Jo. As Jo has six years' service she is protected against unfair dismissal. The circumstances of her case suggest a possible claim for unfair constructive dismissal. Such a claim arises where, by reason of their conduct, an employer is responsible for a fundamental or 'repudiatory' breach of the contract of employment that entitles the employee to resign and treat the contract as having come to an end. By not taking Jo's complaint and concerns seriously it is arguable that the employer has failed in its duty to take reasonable care of her and is therefore guilty of a fundamental breach of contract, which could entitle her to resign and claim constructive dismissal.

However, following the ACAS Code of Practice, before resigning and making an application to a tribunal, Jo should try to resolve her situation with her employer. She should submit a written grievance about the company's policies and treatment of her, attend any meeting that is arranged and also appeal any decision if allowed to do so. If she does not take these steps any compensation subsequently awarded to her by a tribunal could be reduced by 25 per cent. If GNC did not respond satisfactorily to her grievance and she did take a case to a tribunal, it would be likely that she would be found to have been unfairly dismissed and therefore awarded compensation. (It would perhaps be unlikely that she would want to be either reinstated or re-engaged.)

Although there is no clear evidence of direct sex discrimination or sexual harassment, the facts also raise the possibility of a claim for indirect sex discrimination under the Sex Discrimination Act 1975. This may arise where an employer applies a provision, criterion or practice equally to male and female workers which puts a woman 'at a particular disadvantage' compared with men, and which cannot be shown to be a 'proportionate means of achieving a legitimate aim'. In this case, due to childcare commitments the requirement for all team members to attend evening social events twice a week is likely to put women at a particular disadvantage compared with men (and has put Jo at a disadvantage), and it would therefore be up to GNC to justify it. It would be very difficult for GNC to demonstrate that the social outings were justifiable and it may also therefore be liable for indirect sex discrimination. Remedies for this would be a declaration, recommendation and/or compensation (potentially unlimited and for injury to feelings in addition to financial loss).

Chapter 9: Pay regulation

9.1 He is a 'worker' protected under the National Minimum Wage Act 1998. He is entitled to receive the rate applicable to 16–17 year olds (set at £3.53 per hour in October 2008 and usually varied upwards each year). Advice can be given by Her Majesty's Revenue and Customs helpline. He has been underpaid and can complain to an employment tribunal for underpayment of his wages. He would be expected to lodge a grievance with his employer initially. The employer must not subject the employee to detrimental treatment nor dismiss them if the reason or principal reason is enforcing rights under the Act.

9.2 She is a 'worker' protected under the National Minimum Wage Act 1998. She is entitled to receive the rate applicable to 18–21 year olds (set at £4.77 per hour in October 2008 and usually varied upwards each year). Advice can be given by Her Majesty's Revenue and Customs helpline. She has been underpaid and can complain to an employment tribunal for underpayment of her wages. She would be expected to lodge a grievance with her employer initially. The employer must not subject the employee to detrimental treatment nor dismiss them if the reason or principal reason is enforcing rights under the Act.

9.3 She is a 'worker' protected under the National Minimum Wage Act 1998. The pay reference period is four weeks. Her relevant pay comprises basic pay (paid at £4.50 per hour – ***below*** the national minimum wage set at £5.73 per hour in October 2008); and tips paid through the till. Taking these two sets of figures together her relevant earnings for each of the four weeks was £66, £33, £46 and £85. The total was £230 for 40 hours' work. Her average hourly earnings in the pay reference period are £5.75 – two pence per hour ***above*** the relevant national minimum wage.

It is important to note that the system of paying tips through the till (known as the 'tronc' system) for them to be distributed by the 'troncmaster' has been considered by the Employment Appeals Tribunal. It ruled that gratuities distributed to workers by a troncmaster did

not amount to remuneration for the purposes of the national minimum wage legislation and so did not count towards the NMW. The tribunal explained that the tips were not 'money payments paid by the employer to the worker' because, although they were initially paid into the employer's bank account, the money was then transferred to the troncmaster's designated account for distribution according to the tronc system. Once the money was in the troncmaster's bank account, the employer had no control over it; and at the time of payment to the workers, it was the troncmaster, not the employer, who had ownership of the money (*Commissioners for Her Majesty's Revenue and Customs* v *Annabel's (Berkley Square) Ltd and Others* [2008] EAT/0562/07).

In this exercise, if the ruling of the EAT was followed, the worker would, then, be receiving a payment ***below*** the NMW and could take action at employment tribunal for payment of the appropriate remuneration.

9.4 He is a 'worker' protected under the National Minimum Wage Act 1998. The pay reference period is four weeks. His relevant pay from the hotel comprises basic pay and tips paid through the till. Accommodation provision counts towards pay (£4.46 per day; £31.22 per week as set in October 2008). In the four weeks in question his relevant earnings are: £62.20, £33.60, £42.80 and £75.40. The total was £214 for 40 hours worked. His average hourly earnings in the pay reference period was £5.35 per hour – ***below*** the national minimum wage. It is possible that the accommodation offset could bring his total remuneration up to the relevant NMW rate. However, the issues about the tronc system (mentioned in the preceding answer) are relevant. If the tips paid through the till are excluded, then, his hourly rate would clearly be ***below*** the NMW.

9.5 She has been paid at the appropriate rate for 18–21 year olds (set at £4.77 per hour in October 2008, but usually varied upwards each year). The key issue is the real reason for her dismissal. Is it her performance or conduct or redundancy, or is it that she is becoming eligible for the higher rate of the national minimum wage (set at £5.73 per hour in October 2008)? She would be able to claim unfair dismissal if the reason or principal reason was that she was being deliberately prevented from asserting her right to be paid the full rate.

9.6 She is entitled to see her pay records. She is also entitled to receive an appropriate itemised pay statement if she is an employee. She can report the employer to Her Majesty's Revenue and Customs. It can take action against the employer – even in the criminal courts if there is a deliberate refusal to pay the national minimum wage.

9.7 It is an unlawful deduction to withhold money in respect of a loan. An employee must agree to it. A complaint, irrespective of length of service can be made by a 'worker' to an employment tribunal.

9.8 It would depend on the terms of the collective agreement as it was 'incorporated' into the contract of employment. If the agreement says that the shift allowance should be paid, then, the employer is deducting it unlawfully. A complaint, irrespective of length of service can be made by a 'worker' to an employment tribunal.

9.9 In law, he is required to pay the money back to his employer. In requiring repayment, the employer should, according to case law, be reasonable. It was not a large sum of money, so, it is feasible that he might have thought that the money was legitimately his. Since he has already spent the money, the employer should consider an agreement that he pays it by instalments over, perhaps, six months. Any agreement should take account of his normal outgoings. The employer cannot deduct the money from his pay packet without consultation and his agreement.

9.10 The deduction of £155 seems to breach an agreement that the employee made to repair the van himself. The other deductions were provision and, so, based on little firm evidence. The employer may have good reason for wanting to withhold or deduct some money. But this should be done with the employee's agreement.

9.11 Her boyfriend is right! The maximum permissible deduction in retail employment (which a café is) is 10 per cent of a week's gross wages (i.e. £15) – unless it is the final week of employment.

Chapter 10: Regulation of working time

10.1 Presumably, only a proportion of the total workforce is likely to be required to work in excess of the maximum. These would be the 'relevant workforce'. Two possible routes are available to the employer under the Working Time Regulations 1998. First, the employer could ask each employee to make individual agreements to disapply the maximum 48-hour working week. From the employer's point of view this might not provide continuing operational certainty because employee's can give notice to terminate such agreements. (It is important to note the proposed change in European law advocated by the European Parliament.)

The second way would be to negotiate a 'workforce agreement'. This can be done in non-union workplaces. It would enable the averaging period of 17 weeks to be extended to 52 weeks. This would apply only to relevant members of the workforce. It would need to be signed by a majority, if not all, and would become a new condition of employment.

10.2 Under the Working Time Regulations 1998, 'working time' is defined as 'any period in relation to a worker during which he is working, at his employer's disposal and carrying out his activities or duties'. In this case, it is arguable that for the eight-hour shift the worker is at the employer's 'disposal' – dealing with in-coming calls; waiting for calls; and, depending on operational circumstances, available to cover colleagues at short notice; and to take over any other duties that the employer might allocate. The worker is unlikely to have any freedom of action in that eight-hour period. S/he will not be permitted to leave the workplace without permission.

The interpretation of the Directive's provision on 'working time' by the European Court of Justice in the *SIMAP* (2000) and *Jaeger* (2003) cases suggest strongly that these call-centre workers are entitled to regard the entire eight-hour shift as working time (aside from any rest breaks).

10.3 Maggie is what is usually called a 'casual worker'. Despite this employment status she has protection and entitlements under the Working Time Regulations 1998. These Regulations cover the wide category of 'workers'. She is entitled to paid annual leave. The statutory minimum under the regulations is 28 days (from April 2009). Because Maggie is not a full-time worker but only works occasional hours, she is entitled to *pro rata* paid annual leave, depending on how much work she has done (in comparison to a full-time worker). The European Court of Justice has ruled that the entitlement to paid annual leave means that the worker must have the time off work. The leave entitlement cannot be 'bought out' by means of an additional payment to wages (see the case of *Robinson-Steele* (2006)).

10.4 There are several factors in this case. The starting point is whether or not he is working solely for the supermarket chain. Assuming that he is, although he is working on an 'as and when required' basis, he is a protected worker under the Working Time Regulations 1998.

However, it could be that although he has an on-going commitment to the supermarket chain, he is also able, provided he gives the supermarket priority, to undertake other work (e.g. repairing and installing domestic fridges and freezers). So, some of his work is self-employment which he can 'pick and choose' to do. He is still a protected worker in relation to the work he does for the supermarket.

A final possibility is that if contacted to undertake work for the supermarket he is not personally required to undertake it and he can contract out the work to another engineer known to him. In this case, he is likely to be self-employed in relation to the work he does for the supermarket and not covered by the Working Time Regulations which explicitly exclude self-employed workers.

10.5 The worker is entitled to terminate the agreement; and in the absence of an agreed notice period, to do this with at least seven days' notice. It was short-sighted of the employer not to provide for a notice period in the written agreement which can be for any period up to (but no longer than) three months. The worker does not have to provide reasons for wanting to end the agreement. The implied threat of dismissal by the employer is unlawful. She was exercising her right – irrespective of the operational difficulties that might be caused to the employer. She has a right not to suffer any detriment, including dismissal, for asserting her right (Working Time Regulations, regs 29 and 30). Any detrimental action by the employer could result in a complaint to an employment tribunal.

10.6 Several issues arise in this case:

- the definition of night time;
- whether particular staff are 'night workers';
- the length of night work.

In this exercise, staff are normally working nine hours in a 24-hour period. Operationally, there are good reasons for this. However, in terms of their strict entitlements, it is not acceptable. If the hotel did not wish to change its shift-work arrangements, it could use the derogation provision and, as a non-union company, negotiate a workforce agreement.

10.7 The employer's duty under the Working Time Regulations 1998 is to have regard to the health and safety of night workers (reg 7). There should be a health assessment and further assessments at regular intervals. There needs to be consideration of whether patterns of working hours breach the regulations. As far as the circumstances of his ill-health are concerned, there is advice taken from a registered medical practitioner; and the employee has made a request to the employer. The employer is also under a duty to take reasonable care of the employee. Knowing about the ill-health, the employer may make himself liable for a personal injury claim if he does not respond to the request in a positive way. The employer may also be liable for a repudiation of the contract of employment (by breaching mutual trust and confidence) if he rejects or ignores the request out of hand. A constructive way might be to consult with the employee, consider the medical report in detail and any prognosis in it, and review whether suitable alternative employment is possible. If it is not possible, the employer may consider possible dismissal on the grounds of medical incapacity.

Chapter 11: Family leave and work–life balance

11.1 Pauline and Kate. Under the Employment Rights Act 1996 and the Maternity and Parental Leave Regulations 1999, after her period of OML, Pauline is entitled to return to the same job that she held previously on the same terms and conditions as before, as if she had not been absent. Not permitting an employee to return to work after maternity leave constitutes a dismissal. Further, any dismissal on grounds of pregnancy or maternity is automatically unfair regardless of an employee's length of service. Pauline, therefore, could claim unfair dismissal at an employment tribunal. (She would need to appeal her employer's decision under the organisation's disciplinary procedure.) Possible remedies for this would be reinstatement, re-engagement or compensation.

Because she has suffered less favourable treatment / detriment on grounds of her pregnancy and maternity leave, Pauline would also be entitled to bring a case for sex discrimination under the Sex Discrimination Act 1975 (as amended). Under this Act there is no upper limit on the compensation that might be awarded and an award for injury to feelings may also be covered.

After her period of AML, Kate is also entitled to return to the same job that she held previously on the same terms and conditions as before, as if she had not been absent. However, if it is not reasonably practicable for her to return to the same job, her employer can offer her a similar job which is 'suitable and appropriate' and no less favourable in terms of capacity, place and other terms and conditions.

In this instance, the employer may be justified in arguing that it was not reasonably practicable for Kate to return to her old job on the basis of the need for continuity in dealing with customers and in view of the small size of the company. In terms of the alternative job Kate has been offered, given that it is broadly similar in terms of content and also at the same seniority and pay levels and location as her previous job, a tribunal might arguably decide that the employer's actions met the conditions specified in the legislation and that it therefore did not infringe Kate's employment rights on her return.

11.2 Sarah and Lucy. This case is clearly related to the right to request flexible working contained in the Employment Rights Act 1996. Under this Act, employers are obliged to consider applications for flexible working from employees with children under six years (or 18 years if the child is disabled); or if the employee is a carer of a dependant adult. The employee must have 26 weeks of continuous service with the employer.

Both Lucy and Sarah meet the service requirement and therefore qualify for the right to apply for flexible working. Importantly, they do not have an automatic right to flexible working but rather only a right to apply for this. They have followed the correct procedure set out in the Act by applying in writing to the HR manager.

An employer may only refuse a request for flexible working on 'business grounds' which include such factors as detrimental impact on quality; or inability to recruit additional staff. Although tribunals are not permitted to consider the reasonableness or merits of an employer's decision, they will ensure that companies have genuinely considered the issue and provided arguments or evidence under the list of relevant grounds in the Act (see, for example, the case of *Mehaffy* v *Dunnes Stores* (2003)).

In this exercise, a tribunal would arguably be likely to hold that the company has met its obligations in relation to Sarah's request in that substantial, genuine business-related reasons for the refusal have been outlined. In contrast, it is questionable whether it has provided sufficient evidence in relation to Lucy's request. Lucy, therefore, needs to follow the procedure stipulated for the resolution of requests in this area: namely to appeal the decision to her employer. If her appeal is rejected, she may bring a claim to an employment tribunal. If the complaint is found in her favour, a tribunal could order the company to reconsider her request and/or award Lucy compensation.

There is an additional aspect to this case: the possibility that the employer's refusal to the requests to transfer to part-time working may constitute indirect discrimination under the Sex Discrimination Act 1975. To claim indirect discrimination, Sarah and Lucy would need to establish that their employer was applying a 'provision, criterion or practice' that put women 'at a particular disadvantage' compared with men and which cannot be shown to be a 'proportionate means of achieving a legitimate aim'. In this case, due to childcare commitments, the requirement to work full-time puts women at a particular disadvantage compared to men; and it will be up to the employer to show that this requirement is a proportional means of achieving a legitimate (a business) aim. In this regard, it is arguably again the case that the employer satisfies the necessary requirements in relation to Sarah. (However, see *Webster* v *Princes Soft Drinks* (2005) (*Equal Opportunities Review* 145) where refusing a job share to a senior manager was held to be discriminatory).

It is doubtful if this is so in relation to Lucy. If Lucy is successful in a claim for indirect sex discrimination, an employment tribunal could make a declaration, recommendation and award compensation and an award for injury to feelings.

11.3 Tom. This case is also related to the right to request flexible working (Employment Rights Act 1996). He meets the qualification requirements because he has more than 26 weeks' continuous service with his employer; and his children are under the age of six years.

The reason for the employer's refusal of the request – that it is not possible for all team leaders to be on flexi-time and there needs to be a sufficient number of team leaders in place to supervise staff – is potentially valid. It could come under one of the headings required in the Act such as detrimental impact on quality or performance of the business. However, an employment tribunal would require evidence from the company that granting Tom's request would have a detrimental impact, particularly in view of the fact that other requests have been accepted.

The fact that requests by female colleagues have been accepted could mean that the company might be found to be guilty of direct sex discrimination against Tom under the Sex Discrimination Act 1975. (Such direct sex discrimination against a male employee who had requested flexible working was found in *Walkingshaw* v *the John Martin Group* (2000) ET S/401126/00. Requests from women in the organisation had been accepted.)

To succeed in a sex discrimination claim, Tom needs to establish facts from which an 'inference' of discrimination can be drawn. It is then up to his employer to provide evidence that their actions were not in fact discriminatory in nature. Tom could argue that 'but for' his sex (i.e. the fact that he is a man), his request would have been accepted. His line manager's statement that he should just 'get on with' his job could also be highlighted as possibly discriminatory in nature, particularly if similar requests by female employees did not obtain the same reaction. His employer would then need to prove that no discrimination had in fact taken place.

An employment tribunal could order the company to reconsider Tom's flexible working request if it is found that it has not been genuinely considered and/or award him compensation. If he successfully claimed direct sex discrimination the possible remedies are a declaration, recommendation, compensation and an award for injury to feelings.

11.4 Paula. Under the Employment Rights Act 1996 and the Maternity and Parental Leave Regulations 1999, Paula is protected against a detriment or dismissal on grounds that she is pregnant or will take maternity leave. These rights apply regardless of length of service. The facts of the case strongly indicate that despite being well qualified, Paula has not been promoted to the partner position because she is pregnant and will go on maternity leave. She has therefore clearly suffered a detriment and would be entitled to a declaration and compensation for this at an employment tribunal. In addition, the nature of her treatment may entitle her to resign and claim constructive dismissal on the grounds that her employer has broken its duty of mutual trust and confidence. For this she would receive compensation. However, before applying to a tribunal (either for detrimental treatment or dismissal) she would need to use the company's grievance procedure.

It is also likely that Paula would be able to make a claim for sex discrimination. Any less favourable treatment on grounds of pregnancy or maternity is unlawful under the Sex Discrimination Act 1975 (as amended). Possible remedies would be unlimited compensation for sex discrimination and an award for injury to feelings.

Chapter 12: Health, safety and welfare at work

12.1 VDU operators: safety grievance

1 The issues that might arise:

- *Operational issues:*
  - the need to get work done;
  - the availability of substitute staff for job rotation.
- *Job design:*
  - the amount of time spent on the VDU;
  - the feasibility of job rotation.
- *Health and safety requirements:*
  - the work environment in the office (lighting, heating, ventilation, etc.);
  - the layout of the workstation;
  - compliance of the equipment with approved technical standards;
  - personal issues (e.g. the incidence of headaches and other physical pains).
- *Employee relations:*
  - the duty to consult;
  - the implications of establishing a consultation arrangement in a non-union organisation;
  - provision of training for representatives;
  - time off for representatives;
  - the relationship of the supervisor with the staff.

2 The differences and areas of possible consensus that might arise are:

- *Objectives:*
  - *Employer*
    - Get work done.
    - Improve quality of working relations.
    - Minimise cost of any action.

- *Employees*
  - Resolve grievance.
  - Improve working environment.
  - Ensure compliance with the regulations.
  - Establish some regular consultation on health and safety issues.
- ***Preferred outcomes***:
  - *Employer*
    - Discussion with Helen individually to try to resolve her grievance.
    - Some form of non-union consultation (as and when necessary) – possibly through team briefings.
  - *Employees*
    - Resolution of Helen's grievance.
    - More breaks from VDU work, and some job rotation.
    - Consultative committee to meet monthly, supported by a head office representative.
    - Possibly a claim for union recognition.
- ***Constraints***:
  - cost of any action;
  - commitment of management to follow through such action;
  - extent to which staff are committed to achieve their objectives.

12.2 Matt: workplace violence. The employer is liable under the contract to take reasonable care of Matt. It also has a statutory duty under the Health and Safety at Work Act 1974 to ensure the health, safety and welfare of staff and to provide a safe system of work. The employer needs to take steps which will demonstrate that it does take reasonable care of its staff; and also will demonstrate to the Health and Safety Executive that it is not criminally liable for failing to meet its statutory duties.

Among the steps the hospital could take are the following:

- The formulation, in agreement with the unions, of a policy on violence. This could provide a coherent basis for the following proposed action.
- A risk assessment of the probability of violence in the workplaces – in relation to the physical environment and also at particular times of day.
- Consideration of the suitability of various physical alterations to the working environment.
- Consideration of whether any protective equipment is necessary.
- Training for staff in conflict minimisation.
- Provision of additional and immediate support staff who could be 'on call' to assist in dealing with an serious incident.
- Provision of counselling for staff who are victims of violence.
- Preparedness to support the prosecution of the perpetrators of violence.

12.3 Christine Bonser: workplace stress. This is drawn from a real case. The issue, arising from the ruling of the Court of Appeal in the *Sutherland* v *Hatton* case, is the 'test' of whether a person claiming damages for psychiatric injury show not merely a risk of stress from overwork but also a 'reasonably foreseeable risk' of psychiatric breakdown. There are particular issues in the Court of Appeal guidance:

- An employer is normally entitled to assume that its employees are up to the normal pressures of the job.

- There is a distinction between signs of stress and signs of impending harm to health. Stress may, but not usually, lead to damage to health.

On the facts of the *Bonser* case, a single incident where the employee had broken down in tears showed that she may have been vulnerable to stress from overwork; but it was not sufficient to foretell the psychiatric breakdown she subsequently suffered. The Court of Appeal overturned a High Court decision to award Christine Bonser damages, saying that she did not meet the requirements of the test. It reached its decision with 'considerable misgivings', noting that the High Court judge had formed a very adverse view of the senior manager involved, whose conduct was 'justly condemned as cavalier'. However, in the light of the *Hatton* 'test', it found it could reach no other decision.

12.4 Maggie: drinking at work. Initially, there is clearly consideration of a disciplinary approach. Certainly, drunkenness at work is invariably regarded as gross misconduct and may lead to dismissal. However, it becomes apparent that there are welfare issues in this case. As a consequence, the employer rightly considers adopting a 'twin track' approach with a disciplinary dimension and a requirement to undertake counselling. In this way the employer is demonstrating that reasonable care is being taken of Maggie whilst at the same time reinforcing workplace standards of conduct.

The state of her health deteriorates and dismissal is considered. To defend a dismissal, the employer would need to show that there was a fair reason for the dismissal and that it was reasonable in the circumstances to dismiss the person for that reason. The fair reason would be 'medical incapability'. However, she has become a disabled person within the meaning of the Disability Discrimination Act 1995 (see Chapter 5). So, the issue to be considered is whether the employer is able to make reasonable adjustments for her continued employment. If the employer is unable to make such adjustments, then, termination of her employment is possible. The employer may be able to show that it behaved reasonably in all the circumstances by the provision of counselling and employee assistance when the alcohol problem first arose.

Glossary

Note: (q.v.) after a word means that it is defined in this Glossary.

Act of Parliament: see **statute law** below.

Arbitration: Dispute resolution process where the arbitrator (usually a single person but may be a panel) is invited by the parties in dispute to resolve the dispute by making an award (i.e. a decision). The arbitrator is an independent person and may be appointed under the auspices of ACAS. There are two possible types of arbitration: *collective* (relating to disputes between an employer and trade unions), and *individual* (relating to an employer and an employee who has made a complaint or grievance). An example of the latter is the scheme operated by ACAS for resolving unfair dismissal and flexible working claims as an alternative to an employment tribunal claim.

Breach of contract: Circumstances in which one party to a contract does not comply with the terms of the contract (q.v.). Many breaches are minor and may be resolved by an employee lodging grievance with the employer or, alternatively, by an employer taking disciplinary action against an employee. Some breaches are serious (e.g. non-payment of wages due; or allowing persistent bullying to continue). These would be fundamental (i.e. repudiatory) breaches – the equivalent of tearing up the contract. The employee may accept the repudiation and resign and possibly claim constructive dismissal (q.v.).

Burden of proof: Sometimes this is referred to as the 'onus of proof'. It is the responsibility of a party to tribunal or court proceedings to prove an allegation by reference to certain facts and circumstances that are presented in evidence.

Case law: Law set out in judicial decisions. This can help clarify and interpret the law – particularly statute law (q.v.) – and create precedents (q.v.).

Civil law: This is a mixture of statute law (q.v.) and common law (q.v.). It concerns disputes between private individuals (including organisations). In these cases someone is sued. There are two branches of civil law: the law of contract (q.v.) and the law of tort (q.v.). The bulk of employment and discrimination law is civil and so is subsumed under the law of contract or tort. The standard of proof (q.v.) under this branch of law is 'the balance of probabilities'.

Codes of practice: There are both voluntary and statutory codes. Voluntary codes have no legal significance but they can be important in setting standards of good employment practice. Statutory codes do have legal importance. They are used by courts and tribunals in considering the extent to which an employer is liable for a breach of particular statutory employment rights. They are particularly important in respect of discrimination law and dismissal (see Chapters 5, 6 and 8).

Collective bargaining: A process where an employer and a recognised trade union (q.v..) negotiate about differences of interest. These are likely to be about terms and conditions of employment (e.g. pay and working time). They may also be about the extent of workplace consultation (q.v..) and about the scope of collective bargaining itself. The successful outcome of negotiations is a collective agreement.

Common law: Part of English law based on rules developed by judges over many centuries.

Conciliation: Dispute resolution process where the conciliator (usually an officer from ACAS) aims to facilitate a settlement between the two parties in dispute. The settlement is one that the parties agree to themselves. It is not imposed by the conciliator. There are two possible types of conciliation: *collective* (relating to disputes between an employer and trade unions); *individual* (usually arising in relation to complaints made by working people to an employment tribunal). In relation to individual conciliation, ACAS has a statutory duty to promote a settlement where there is an employment tribunal claim.

Consensual variation: The situation where an employee and an employer agree to a change to the terms of a contract of employment (see Chapter 3).

Consideration: Something of value (usually wages) with which the employer buys the agreement of the employee to be ready willing and able to work under a contract of employment (see Chapter 2).

Constructive dismissal: An enforced resignation that is equivalent to dismissal from employment. It arises as a result of the employer's unacceptable behaviour showing that he does not intend to be bound by the contract's essential terms and so there is a repudiatory breach of contract (q.v.).

Consultation: A process where an employer and workforce representatives (and occasionally, the whole workforce itself) discuss employment relations-related issues. Theoretically, there are two types of consultation: pseudo consultation and genuine consultation. The former is where the employer is effectively giving information but is not influenced by the views of employees. The second is where there is a full dialogue and the employer responds to employees' opinions and may make changes to any proposed action. There are various statutory duties to consult (e.g. collective redundancies, transfers of undertakings, health and safety). In redundancies the individual employee is expected to be consulted.

Contract: A legally binding agreement, normally between two parties. With a contract of employment, it arises as a result of an offer of terms of employment and the acceptance by the employee of those terms. There must be consideration (q.v.) and an intention of the parties to create legal relations. The contract cannot agree to do something illegal. If it did, it would be void. Because it is an agreement, it is a basic principle that it can only be varied by consent.

Contributory negligence: see **negligence** below.

Criminal law: This is mainly in statutes (q.v.) and concerns wrongs against society (e.g. theft, actual bodily harm, public order). To convict a defendant the prosecution, usually the Crown Prosecution Service has to prove the case beyond reasonable doubt – the highest standard of proof (q.v.). Around 98 per cent of criminal cases are heard in the magistrates' courts. More serious matters are dealt with before a judge and jury at the Crown Court. Punishments can involve, for example, a fine, a community order or imprisonment. In the employment sphere, it is possible for prosecutions to be brought, for example, by the Health and Safety Executive (see Chapter 12); and by HM Revenue and Customs for infringements of the National Minimum Wage Act 1998 (see Chapter 9).

Culture: Organisational culture refers to the range of values, traditional practices and standards that apply. The culture of an organisation can be an important factor in facilitating or obstructing the effective implementation of, for example, discrimination law or health and safety standards.

Custom and practice: This may be a term of a contract of employment if it is well-known, reasonable and it is certain that the individual knows the effect of the custom on himself or herself.

Damages: Sum of money awarded by a court as compensation for a tort (q.v.) or breach of contract (q.v.).

Derogation: A waiver from the provisions of a statute that is permitted under that legislation (e.g. the Working Time Regulations 1998).

Detriment: Action by an employer which causes disadvantage, harm or damage to an employee (e.g. by victimisation or harassment, overlooking in promotion, depriving of benefits). It is a factor in discrimination law and in the statutory protection provided for employee representatives and workplace trade union officials.

'Direct effect': A doctrine developed by the European Court of Justice for the implementation of European law by member states. An article of the Treaty of Rome will have direct effect if it is clear and unambiguous, unconditional and needs no further action to come into force apart from legislative action by the member state (e.g. Article 141 on equal pay). It applies both horizontally (i.e. conferring rights on individuals against each other) and vertically (i.e. conferring rights that can be enforced against the state and emanations of the state (q.v.)). The provisions of directives (q.v.), on the other hand, only have vertical direct effect where they are clear, unambiguous and require no further action to be implemented.

Directives: The principal means by which European employment law is made. A directive is binding on member states and must, within a given timescale, be transposed fully into the law of each member state. Failure to do this can result in infraction proceedings (q.v.). In Britain, directives are enacted either through statute law (q.v.) or through regulations (q.v.).

Dismissal: The termination of an employee's employment – with or without notice. The law requires that a fair reason is given for the dismissal; that the disciplinary process leading to dismissal conforms with standards of fairness and natural justice (q.v.); and that the decision to dismiss is reasonable in all the circumstances. An employee may allege at an employment tribunal that the dismissal is *unfair* (against various statutory criteria and case law); or that the dismissal is *wrongful* (e.g. it has not been terminated in accordance with the terms of the contract).

Duty: Legal obligation on either an employer or an employee to carry out some action or to stop some particular act. Some duties are set out in statute law (q.v.) – e.g. the duty to consult about collective redundancies. Some are implied under the common law (q.v.) into the contract of employment – e.g. the duty to pay wages; or the duty on the employee to obey lawful and reasonable instructions.

Economic activity rate: This is used in labour market analysis to provide an indication of the percentage of people in a particular group (for example, women or disabled people) who are either in employment or, if unemployed, are actively seeking work.

Emanation of the state: A description of organisations that carry out public/state functions. They may not necessarily be part of central or local government. Examples would include the National Health Service or some privatised utilities (gas, water and electricity). This status is particularly relevant in relation to the application, or 'direct effect' (q.v.), of European Union law (see Chapter 1).

Employee: Defined in law as someone who works under a contract of employment. Case law has developed tests to establish employee status. Courts will look for the existence of mutuality of obligation (see Chapter 2).

ETO: An abbreviation for 'economic, technical and organisational'. It relates to the reasons that employers might give, under the Transfer of Undertakings (Protection of Employment) Regulations 2006, for either dismissing employees or for varying contracts of employment (see Chapters 3 and 8).

***Ex parte*:** (Latin) This expression, which means 'on behalf of', is used in the heading of some law reports with the name of a particular individual making an application to the court in question.

Flexibility: A term used in relation to a large number of management employment practices. The concept of the *flexible firm* was used in the 1980s to suggest a theoretical model which encompassed all forms of flexibility. *Numerical flexibility* describes the extent to which and ways in which an employer can vary the size of the workforce (e.g. through the use of casual and part-time workers). *Functional flexibility* concerns flexibility of task and arises when job demarcations are removed. *Temporal flexibility* is working-time flexibility. *Geographic flexibility* concerns the location of work and workers' mobility.

Foreseeability: The ability to foresee particular consequences arising from an event or set of circumstances. It has been used, for example, in relation to whether or not stress at work can result in some foreseeable or predictable harm to physical or mental health (see Chapter 12).

Framework agreement: These are reached, usually under European law, between the 'social partners' (q.v.). Such agreements usually set out particular objectives and general principles which can be embodied in directives of the European Union. Examples include those on Part-time Work 1997; Fixed-term Work 1999.

***Francovich* claims:** The possibility of such claims arose from an Italian case in the European Court of Justice (*Francovich and Bonifaci* v *the Republic of Italy* [1992] IRLR 84). The ECJ ruled that a citizen, not just an employee, can sue their government if it has failed to implement an EU directive. The individual would need to show that s/he has sustained loss and that there was a clear link between the government's failure and the damage suffered. In Britain, a claim can be made in the High Court.

Free collective bargaining: Bargaining whereby an employer and trade unions can negotiate terms of the agreement without any constraint imposed by legislation or government policy. Historically, the most significant interference with free collective bargaining has been the statutory imposition through incomes policies of the percentage increase in pay that can be awarded. Legislation does mould the terms of collective bargaining by requiring compliance for example, with standards set in discrimination law (see Chapter 5).

Immunities: The principal use of these legal protections in employment law arises in respect of industrial action (q.v.). Trade unions are protected from legal proceedings by employers claiming damages (q.v.) for economic torts (q.v.) if the industrial action they are organising is 'in contemplation of furtherance of a trade dispute' with that employer. Conditions are stipulated in statute law about the nature of the trade dispute and the holding of an approval ballot as a condition for attracting immunity.

Incorporation: Process whereby the terms of collective agreements are included, as appropriate, into individual contracts of employment. So, for example, the appropriate rates of pay (under a payment system); or the relevant standard working week will be applied to the individual. Through this process of incorporation the terms of the collective agreement relating to a particular individual become legally enforceable (see Chapters 2 and 3).

'Independent' trade union: A trade union which is not under the control or dominance of a particular employer through the provision of funds or facilities or not liable to employer interference in the running of its affairs. Legislation provides particular standards and a certificate of independence is conferred by the Certification Officer (Trade Union and Labour Relations Act 1992, ss 5 and 6). An 'independent' union has statutory rights in respect of, e.g. consultation in business transfers; and in collective redundancies.

Industrial action: Sanctions imposed by working people (usually organised by trade unions) against an employer. It arises because of a trade dispute (q.v.). Broadly, there are two categories of industrial action: a strike whereby work stops completely; and 'industrial action short of a strike' (e.g. working to rule, boycotting various tasks, overtime bans, etc.).

Infraction proceedings: Proceedings initiated in the European Court of Justice by the European Commission against an EU member state for not implementing particular European law – either in part or in its entirety.

Injunction: A court order requiring a person (including an employer or a trade union) to stop a certain course of action. Usually, a temporary or interlocutory injunction is granted initially, pending a full hearing of the claim before the court. A person who breaches an injunction is guilty of contempt of court and may be subject to a fine or imprisonment. (An **interdict** in Scotland.)

'Juridification': The extent to which decisions by employers in relation to terms and conditions of employment and the treatment of individual workers is made by reference to legal standards. The extent of employer discretion continues to narrow with the promotion of widespread minimum standards; the concept of less favourable treatment; and the conferring of entitlements on working people.

Job share: Circumstances where a full-time job is split between, usually, two employees who then receive *pro rata* (q.v.) conditions of employment.

Landmark case: Usually refers to a significant case which is the first interpretation by one of the higher courts of particular legislation. It is likely to be a precedent (q.v.).

Leading case: Any ruling by the higher courts which provide an authoritative interpretation of law and legal principles.

Liability: This arises in circumstances when wrongs have been committed. Examples include breach of contract, breach of discrimination law or of health and safety law. It concerns the issue of who is answerable in law for the wrong. Usually under employment law it is the employer. The employer may also be 'vicariously liable' for the behaviour (acts and omissions) in the course of employment of his workforce or of a contractor. A defence for the employer, depending on the legislation involved, may be that he took reasonable steps to prevent the wrong being committed. In employment, most issues of liability are civil. However, it is possible for an employer to be criminally liable if specified in particular legislation (e.g. relating to health and safety; national minimum wage) – in which case the employer would be prosecuted in the criminal courts by the relevant agency.

LIFO: It stands for 'last in first out'. A traditional selection method used in redundancies. Generally, it recognises the job rights of longer serving employees by making those with relatively short service the first to be made redundant. It is not recommended as good practice and may be discriminatory under both sex and age discrimination law.

Mens rea*:** (Latin) This means the 'guilty mind'. It is the state of mind that prosecutors have to prove that a defendant had at the time of committing a crime in order to secure a conviction. Common examples of *mens rea* are ***intention to do something; ***recklessness*** about the consequences of particular action; and ***negligence***. This can have particular relevance in the law on health and safety at work (see Chapter 12).

Natural justice: These rules, developed under common law (q.v.), are applicable in courts and tribunals. Under dismissal legislation, they influence the way in which disciplinary proceedings should be conducted. There are two principle rules: a person should have an opportunity to state his/her case and to answer the other side's case; and no one should be a judge in his own cause.

Negligence: Carelessness or neglect. The most common examples in employment arise in the area of health and safety where it is claimed an employer neglected to take reasonable care of the employee. An employer sued by an employee in a negligence claim may himself claim that the employee was also negligent (e.g. for failing to wear protective equipment). If this contributory negligence is proved, it could result in the employee's damages (q.v.) being reduced, depending on the circumstances, by up to 100 per cent.

'Non-standard' employment relationships: Employment relationships other than the full-time, permanent employment relationship. They involve flexible (q.v.) arrangements under which work is carried out – either in relation to working time, duration or place of work (e.g. whether it is on the employer's premises or at home). Such work is also described as 'atypical' work (see Chapter 2).

Part-time worker: Someone who works less than the normal working week set in a particular organisation. No specific hours are stipulated under law.

Precedent: A judgment or ruling of a court that is used as an authority for reaching a decision in subsequent cases. In English law, decisions of the Supreme Court (and formerly the House of Lords) are binding on the Court of Appeal and all lower courts. Likewise, decisions of the Court of Appeal and, below that, the High Court are binding on lower courts. Decisions of lower courts (and of employment tribunals) do not create any binding precedent.

***Prima facie*:** (Latin) It means 'from a first impression' or 'on the face of things'. Under discrimination law, a *prima facie* case made by a complainant whereby s/he presents an outline case of the facts known to him/her which are said to point to discriminatory treatment (see Chapter 5).

Procedural issues: In employment relations, these concern the operation of procedures used to structure the relationship between an employer and his workforce and, if relevant, recognised trade unions (q.v.). The procedures can concern grievances, discipline and dismissal, harassment, redundancies, consultation, health and safety matters, arrangements for negotiating terms and conditions, collective dispute resolution procedures.

***Pro rata* principle:** (Latin) In employment it refers to proportionality in the treatment of individuals under terms of the contract of employment. In particular, it relates to the comparative treatment of full-time employees and part-time employees. So, for example, if a part-timer works for half of a full-time employee's standard working week, then, the part-timer would be entitled to half the relevant holiday entitlement; and proportional treatment in relation to most other terms and conditions of employment.

Purposive interpretation: An approach adopted by the European Court of Justice for the interpretation of EU legislation. The judiciary consider the purposes of the legislation as set out by the legislators and this can mould their ruling on specific matters. As an approach it contrasts with the 'literal' approach (focusing on the precise meaning of words in the statute) adopted by the judiciary in Britain.

Qualified majority voting (QMV): It is used to approve certain EU legislation. It is a weighted voting system that requires more than a simple majority (i.e. over 50 per cent) to approve a measure. It has been used to approve health and safety directives and the Working Time Directive (which was ruled by the European Court of Justice to be health and safety law).

Qualifying period: The period of continuous employment with an employer that an employee (q.v.) or worker (q.v.) must have in order to claim certain statutory rights. For example, one year's qualifying service is required for most unfair dismissal claims at employment tribunal.

Recognition (of a trade union): The decision by an employer to negotiate with a trade union – i.e. engage in collective bargaining (q.v.) – about specified terms and conditions of employment and to reach collective agreements.

Regulations: see **statutory instruments** below.

Remedy: This is any method available at law for enforcing rights or for obtaining redress for their infringement. It can include an injunction (q.v.); damages (q.v.); or a declaration.

Repudiatory breach of contract: see **breach of contract** above.

Right to manage: Not a legal right. It is essentially management rhetoric to claim economic rights over the recruitment, deployment and remuneration of employees. It is freedom to manage – sometimes referred to as 'managerial prerogatives'. Common law (q.v.) and, in particular, statute law (q.v.) have limited this freedom by imposing standards of conduct, duties and minimum terms and conditions of employment.

Single status: Common treatment and terms and conditions of employment for employees whether they are manual workers or non-manual workers.

Social partners: Representative bodies of European trade unions and public and private-sector employers: ETUC (European Trade Union Confederation); CEEP (European Centre for Enterprises with Public Participation); UNICE (Union of Industrial and Employer's Confederation of Europe). Within the process of EU law-making, these bodies are consulted regularly on new European Commission proposals for social policy and employment legislation. They may negotiate framework agreements (q.v.) which can then form the basis of directives (q.v.) (e.g. that relating to Parental Leave 1996).

Socialisation: The process through which an individual's attitudes, values and standards of behaviour are inculcated and developed particularly within the family, within education, in religious organisations, in the workplace and within society at large.

'Standard' employment relationship: The most common form of employment relationship, characterised by being full-time and 'permanent' – i.e. the employee is on an 'open-ended' contract.

Standards of proof: There are two: beyond reasonable doubt; and the balance of probabilities. The first is used in criminal (q.v.) cases to establish conviction. The second arises in civil (q.v.) proceedings and is generally construed as follows: that it is more probable than not that something said to have happened did happen. This standard is used in employment tribunal cases.

Statute law: Law made by Parliament in the form of Acts of Parliament. It usually reflects the political policies of the government of the day; and also measures proposed by backbench MPs if approved by Parliament. It is interpreted by judges and new statute law can overturn judge-made law. Alongside statutory instruments (q.v.), it is a principal means for transposing EU Directives into domestic law.

Statutory instruments: They are delegated legislation and are presented as regulations to Parliament and come into force subject to its approval. Regulations are made under the authority of particular Act of Parliament. For example, the Working Time Regulations 1998 were made under the European Communities Act, s 2. Other examples include those made under the Health and Safety at Work Act 1974. Alongside statute law (q.v.), Regulations are a principal means of transposing EU directives into domestic law

'Subsidiarity': This concept relates to the political question of which is the most appropriate level for legal regulation and decision-making within the European Union. Proponents of 'subsidiarity' support the greatest possible devolution of regulation and decision-making to the level of the member states.

Substantive issues: In employment relations, this refers to the terms and conditions of employment under which an employee is employed.

Summary dismissal: Dismissal (q.v.) without notice.

Superior courts: The higher courts are the Supreme Court (formerly the House of Lords in its judicial capacity) and the Court of Appeal. Their decisions create precedents (q.v.).

Terms: These are the provisions of a contract of employment. They may be express (e.g. pay and hours) or implied from common law (q.v.) (e.g. the duty to take reasonable care).

Tight labour market: Economic circumstances where there are various forms of labour and skill shortage and it is difficult for employers to recruit particular staff.

Tort: A civil (q.v.) wrong other than a breach of contract (q.v.). In employment relations, examples include claims of personal injury (whether physical or psychological) through negligence. Claims are usually initiated in the High Court. Trade unions can commit 'economic' torts when they take industrial action against an employer because the industrial action damages the employer's business. The enactment of immunities (q.v.) provides some protection from trade unions being sued.

Trade dispute: A dispute between a workforce (usually unionised) and an employer about various terms and conditions of employment and employment related procedural issues.

Transferee: The employing organisation that receives a workgroup / workforce from a transferor (q.v.) in a business transfer.

Transferor: The employing organisation that transfers to a transferee (q.v.) a work group / workforce in a business transfer.

Vicarious liability: see **liability** above.

Victimisation: A form of detriment (q.v.). It involves singling out a person for unfair and usually unlawful treatment. Particular forms of victimisation to prevent claims being made to employment tribunals are specifically prohibited under all strands of discrimination law.

'Voluntarism': The situation where the state leaves employers and employees (probably through the medium of trade unions) relatively free to determine the nature of the employment relationship and terms and conditions of employment. Legislation plays a minimal role in regulating employment relations.

Unilateral variation: The circumstances where an employer imposes, without agreement with individual employees, changed terms and conditions of employment. It contrasts with consensual variation (q.v.) (see Chapter 3).

White Paper: A document published by government in which it sets out proposals for legislative action. Usually, they are open to limited consultation by interest groups.

Worker: A person who has an employment relationship with an organisation. It covers employees (q.v.) and others required to work personally. It does not cover the self-employed (see Chapter 2).

Index

Page numbers which are **emboldened** indicate entries which appear in the Glossary.

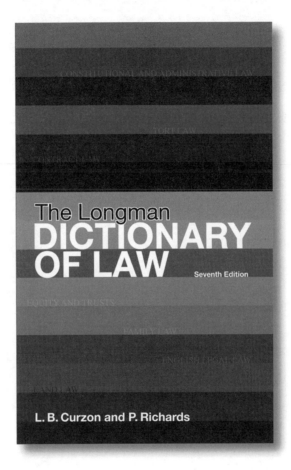